Advance in Control Theory and Optimization

Advance in Control Theory and Optimization

Guest Editors

Zhi Li

Sihai Guan

MDPI

Basel • Beijing • Wuhan • Barcelona • Belgrade • Novi Sad • Cluj • Manchester

Guest Editors
Zhi Li
School of Mechano-Electronic Engineering
Xidian University
Xi'an
China

Sihai Guan
College of Electronic and Information
Southwest Minzu University
Chengdu
China

Editorial Office
MDPI AG
Grosspeteranlage 5
4052 Basel, Switzerland

This is a reprint of the Special Issue, published open access by the journal *Mathematics* (ISSN 2227-7390), freely accessible at: https://www.mdpi.com/si/mathematics/6846MP2NSF.

For citation purposes, cite each article independently as indicated on the article page online and as indicated below:

Lastname, A.A.; Lastname, B.B. Article Title. *Journal Name* **Year**, *Volume Number*, Page Range.

ISBN 978-3-7258-5285-7 (Hbk)
ISBN 978-3-7258-5286-4 (PDF)
https://doi.org/10.3390/books978-3-7258-5286-4

Contents

mathematics

MDPI

Article

Research on Improved Differential Evolution Particle Swarm Hybrid Optimization Method and Its Application in Camera Calibration

Xinyu Sha [1], Fucai Qian [1,2,*] and Hongli He [3]

[1] School of Automation and Information Engineering, Xi'an University of Technology, Xi'an 710048, China; xinyusha@stu.xaut.edu.cn
[2] Autonomous Systems and Intelligent Control International Joint Research Center, Xi'an Technological University, Xi'an 710021, China
[3] Testing Technology Institute, China Flight Test Academy, Xi'an 710021, China; hhhl2003@163.com
* Correspondence: fcqian@xaut.edu.cn

Abstract: The calibration of cameras plays a critical role in close-range photogrammetry because the precision of calibration has a direct effect on the quality of results. When handling image capture using a camera, traditional swarm intelligence algorithms such as genetic algorithms and particle swarm optimization, in conjunction with Zhang's calibration method, frequently face difficulties regarding local optima and sluggish convergence. This study presents an enhanced hybrid optimization approach utilizing both the principles of differential evolution and particle swarm optimization, which is then employed in the context of camera calibration. Initially, we establish a measurement model specific to the camera in close-range photogrammetry and determine its interior orientation parameters. Subsequently, employing these parameters as initial values, we perform global optimization and iteration using the improved hybrid optimization algorithm. The effectiveness of the proposed approach is subsequently validated through simulation and comparative experiments. Compared to alternative approaches, the proposed algorithm enhances both the accuracy of camera calibration and the convergence speed. It effectively addresses the issue of other algorithms getting trapped in local optima due to image distortion. These research findings provide theoretical support for practical engineering applications in the field of control theory and optimization to a certain extent.

Keywords: camera calibration; hybrid optimization; particle swarm optimization; honey badger optimization algorithm; differential evolution

MSC: 9308; 37N40; 68W50

1. Introduction

Photogrammetric technology is an important measurement technique that can be applied to rotating machinery, to capture images of the objects inside the machinery using cameras. By analyzing the captured images, the displacement and structure of the targets can be measured.

Firstly, in the design and manufacturing of rotating machinery, photogrammetric technology can be employed to measure the position and shape of the internal components, as well as dynamic behavioral parameters during machinery operation. Secondly, in the maintenance and monitoring of rotating machinery, photogrammetric technology can be utilized to monitor the position, deformation, and vibration of rotating components. Through real-time monitoring, faults and defects can be promptly detected for repair and adjustment, thus enhancing their reliability and operational safety. Finally, the essential role of camera calibration in the context of photogrammetry is indispensable for the application of rotating machinery. The precision of camera calibration directly impacts the measurement results and reliability of photogrammetry, which in turn influences the effectiveness and benefits of the design, manufacturing, and maintenance aspects of rotating machinery.

Camera calibration, serving as the foundation of photogrammetry, is a technical process carried out to enable a camera to accurately capture objects in the real world and map them onto images. The implementation of camera calibration relies on the determination of specific camera parameters, encompassing focal length, principal point position, distortion, as well as external parameters like the camera's spatial position and orientation. This facilitates precise measurements of objects in the real world and their projection onto images through photogrammetry.

Camera calibration methods have their own characteristics in the selection of calibration techniques. Commonly used methods include the Direct Linear Transformation (DLT), Tsai's two-step calibration, and Zhang's calibration. The DLT method establishes a geometric imaging model for the camera and directly solves the model parameters using linear equations. However, it does not consider distortion and is not practical [1]. Tsai's two-step calibration combines the DLT method with nonlinear optimization, which improves the calibration accuracy compared to traditional methods. Nevertheless, it is complex and cannot meet industrial requirements [2]. Zhang's calibration method is based on planar chessboard patterns and overcomes the need for highly accurate calibration objects required in traditional methods by only requiring a printed chessboard pattern for experimentation [3]. However, Zhang's method exhibits drawbacks such as inaccurate calibration results and being too time-consuming when applied to practical engineering problems. Therefore, this paper proposed improvements to Zhang's method, aiming to achieve a faster and more accurate calibration approach.

To achieve better calibration results, previous studies have conducted research based on the traditional Zhang's calibration method. In 2020, Rui, Z. integrated feedforward artificial neural networks into the traditional calibration method to correct model errors, resulting in a twofold improvement in accuracy. However, the paper did not account for issues such as image blurring and lack of clarity [4]. In 2009, a simple and adaptable calibration method was proposed by Sarkka, S., utilizing neural networks to tackle the challenging calibration problem that arises when the object plane is nearly parallel to the image plane. However, the paper failed to consider the camera's nonlinear distortion and imposed stringent data prerequisites [5]. In 2020, Xu, H. introduced a neural network structure for binocular stereo vision camera calibration but did not specify the dataset or application methods [6]. In 2001, Liang, Y. introduced a new method for monocular camera calibration by combining the Harris corner detection algorithm with artificial neural networks, introducing camera-to-template angles into the calibration process. However, the paper did not detail specific application scenarios and usage restrictions [7]. In 2016, Jiang W et al. optimized the Zhang calibration method using a combination of genetic and particle swarm algorithms, ultimately discovering that combining these algorithms can improve calibration accuracy. However, the experiment did not explain the susceptibility of the algorithm to local optima [8]. In 2019, Liu, J.Y. utilized the Structure-from-Motion (SFM) principle to calibrate cameras internally and externally based on the paired relationships between cameras, but the impact of radial distortion on the algorithm remains to be verified in practice [9]. In 2010, Huang, D. applied Back-Propagation Neural Networks (BPNN) to calibrate Kinect depth cameras, using target corner information as training data and establishing an error compensation model based on error symmetry to reduce depth measurement errors. However, the selection of neural network parameters relied on empirical knowledge and could only be applied in specific circumstances [10]. In 2019, Wang, Z. implemented camera calibration using multiple directional images captured by a thermal infrared camera based on the multi-view theory [11]. However, this method suffers from slow calibration convergence and susceptibility to local optima, primarily due to the need to simultaneously solve many parameters and the involvement of high-dimensional, nonlinear, and sub-pixel-level precision requirements. Nonetheless, addressing these issues is crucial for the accuracy and efficiency of camera calibration. Improving calibration convergence speed and avoiding local optima can reduce calibration time, enhance calibration accuracy, and establish a foundation for subsequent applications. In response to this challenge, the paper introduced the concept of transforming differential evolution into optimization algorithms, put forward an enhanced particle swarm hybrid optimization algorithm derived from differential evolution, and applied it to improve the Zhang calibration method.

The organization of this document is structured as follows: Section 2 is dedicated to establishing the camera imaging and distortion models. Section 3 investigates methods for camera calibration. Section 4 integrates the concept of Differential Evolution with Particle Swarm Optimization algorithms, introducing an enhanced hybrid optimization algorithm derived from Differential Evolution. Section 5 conducts experiments, simulating various parameter optimization techniques and comparing the outcomes.

The primary novelty of this paper is the enhancement of the differential evolution algorithm, particularly in the parameter selection aspect, facilitating the algorithm's capability to explore the optimal population over the entire range. Consequently, when integrated with the particle swarm algorithm for searching the optimal individual within the optimum population, it enables the acquisition of superior calibration parameters and improves calibration accuracy.

2. Camera Imaging Model

The camera's imaging process operates on the principle of pinhole imaging, which delineates the projection correlation between the imaging plane and the target. Under ideal circumstances, the association between objects and images adheres to a linear model governed by the principles of triangulation. However, in practical measurement processes, the influence of various external factors can lead to nonlinear distortions in camera imaging. Therefore, to more accurately model the camera's imaging process, it is necessary to consider the distortions introduced by the camera and adopt a nonlinear camera imaging model.

2.1. Coordinate System and Its Transformation Relation

(1) Coordinate system

The coordinate systems involved in camera imaging are depicted in Figure 1.

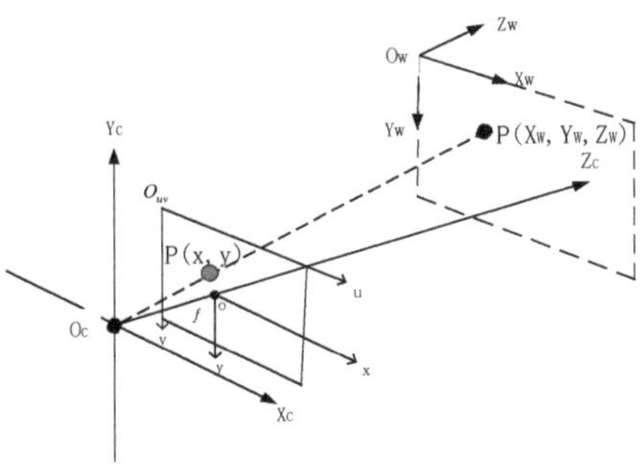

Figure 1. The coordinates of the camera imaging model.

1. The world coordinate system: $O_W - X_W Y_W Z_W$, it describes the position of the measured object in the three-dimensional world. The origin coordinates can be determined according to the specific requirements, and the unit is in meters (m).
2. Camera Coordinate System: $O_C - X_C Y_C Z_C$, the original coordinate system is positioned at the optical center, with the X_C-axis and Y_C-axis running parallel to the two edges of the image plane. The Z_C-axis coincides with the optical axis, and the unit of measurement is meters (m).

3. Pixel Coordinate System: $O_{uv} - uv$, the upper left corner is designated as the origin of the coordinate system for the image plane. The u-axis of the pixel coordinate system extends horizontally from left to right, while the v-axis extends vertically from top to bottom. The unit of measurement is pixels.
4. The coordinate system for the image, referred to as the Image Coordinate System, is defined by the central point of the image plane. The x-axis and y-axis are aligned in parallel with the u-axis and v-axis of the pixel coordinate system, respectively. The unit of measurement employed is millimeters.

(2) Coordinate system transformation relationship

The primary focus of the camera imaging model involves the mapping correlation between the pixel coordinates of an image point p and its corresponding coordinates within three-dimensional space. The camera imaging procedure operates on the principle of pinhole imaging, depicted in Figure 2.

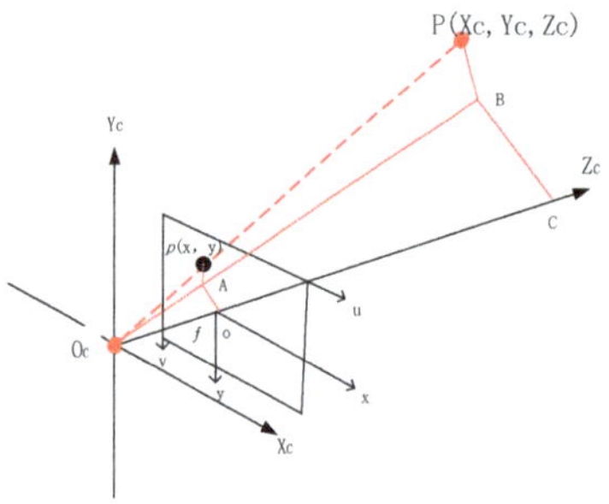

Figure 2. Relationship between camera coordinates and image coordinates.

The point P in the figure represents a point in the world coordinate system, with coordinates (X_W, Y_W, Z_W). In the camera coordinate system, the coordinates of point p are (X_C, Y_C, Z_C). The corresponding imaging point of point p in the image is located in the pixel coordinate system with coordinates (u, v), while the coordinates of point p in the image coordinate system are (x, y). The focal length of the camera, denoted as f, $f = \|o - O_C\|$, is the distance between o and O_C [12]. The projection transformation from camera coordinates to image coordinates follows specific transformations based on the principles of triangle similarity.

$$\frac{BC}{Ao} = \frac{CO_C}{oO_C} = \frac{PB}{pA} = \frac{X_C}{x} = \frac{Y_C}{y} = \frac{Z_C}{f} \tag{1}$$

According to Formula (1):

$$x = f\frac{X_C}{Z_C}, y = f\frac{Y_C}{Z_C} \tag{2}$$

According to Formula (2):

$$Z_C\begin{bmatrix} x \\ y \\ 1 \end{bmatrix} = \begin{bmatrix} f & 0 & 0 & 0 \\ 0 & f & 0 & 0 \\ 0 & 0 & 1 & 0 \end{bmatrix}\begin{bmatrix} X_C \\ Y_C \\ Z_C \\ 1 \end{bmatrix} \tag{3}$$

Figure 3 exhibits the process of converting camera coordinates into world coordinates.

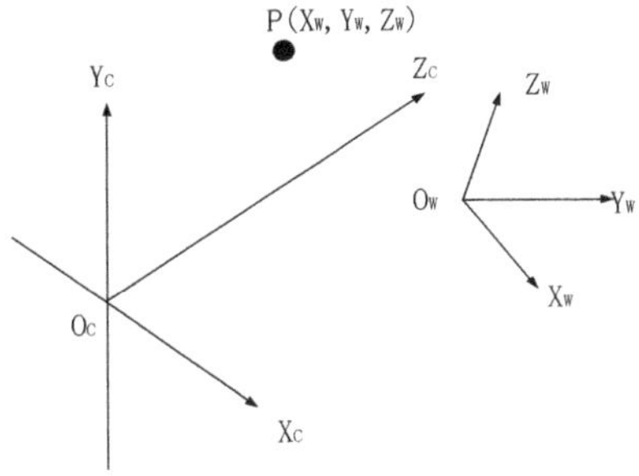

Figure 3. Schematic diagram of conversion between camera coordinate system and world coordinate system.

The conversion from world coordinates to camera coordinates involves only rotation and translation operations and is considered a rigid transformation. The equation for coordinate transformation is as follows:

$$\begin{bmatrix} X_C \\ Y_C \\ Z_C \\ 1 \end{bmatrix} = \begin{bmatrix} R & T \\ 0 & 1 \end{bmatrix} \begin{bmatrix} X_W \\ Y_W \\ Z_W \\ 1 \end{bmatrix} \quad (4)$$

The rotation matrix, denoted as R, is a 3×3 matrix, and the translation vector, denoted as T, is a 3×1 vector. The representation of the camera coordinate system's homogeneous coordinates is denoted as $O_C - X_C Y_C Z_C$, whereas the homogeneous coordinates of the world coordinate system are denoted as $O_W - X_W Y_W Z_W$. During the coordinate transformation process, rotation is performed by rotating around the z-axis with an angle of θ, and rotating around the x and y axes with angles α and β, respectively, resulting in the composite rotation matrix $R = R_1 R_2 R_3$.

$$R = \begin{bmatrix} \cos\theta & -\sin\theta & 0 \\ \sin\theta & \cos\theta & 0 \\ 0 & 0 & 1 \end{bmatrix} \begin{bmatrix} \cos\beta & 0 & \sin\beta \\ 0 & 1 & 0 \\ -\sin\beta & 0 & \cos\beta \end{bmatrix} \begin{bmatrix} 1 & 0 & 0 \\ 0 & \cos\alpha & -\sin\alpha \\ 0 & \sin\alpha & \cos\alpha \end{bmatrix} \quad (5)$$

$$\begin{bmatrix} X_C \\ Y_C \\ Z_C \end{bmatrix} = R \begin{bmatrix} X_W \\ Y_W \\ Z_W \end{bmatrix} + T \quad (6)$$

The camera captures two-dimensional images, and the output consists of pictures where pixels are arranged based on their pixel values. As a result, the pixel coordinate system is derived by discretizing the coordinate values and shifting the origin to the center [13].

Figure 4 illustrates the denotation of the pixel coordinate system as $O_{uv} - uv$ and the image coordinate system as $o - xy$. The representation of point p in the pixel coordinate system is indicated as (u, v), and the transformation relationship is expressed as follows:

$$\begin{cases} u = \frac{x}{dx} + u_0 \\ v = \frac{y}{dy} + v_0 \end{cases} \quad (7)$$

According to the above formula:

$$\begin{bmatrix} u \\ v \\ 1 \end{bmatrix} = \begin{bmatrix} \frac{1}{dx} & 0 & u_0 \\ 0 & \frac{1}{dy} & v_0 \\ 0 & 0 & 1 \end{bmatrix} \begin{bmatrix} x \\ y \\ 1 \end{bmatrix} \quad (8)$$

In the given equation, the physical dimensions along the x, y directions of the pixel are denoted as $1/dx$ and $1/dy$, respectively, whereas $o(u_0, v_0)$ signifies the displacement of the origin on the pixel plane.

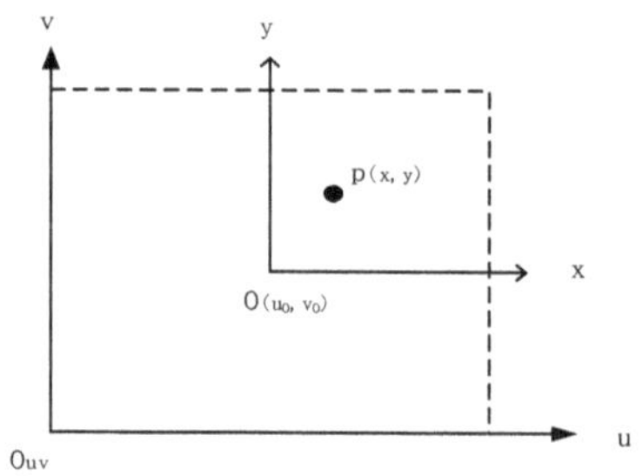

Figure 4. Schematic diagram of transformation between image coordinate system and pixel coordinate system.

2.2. Camera Imaging Model

(1) Linear camera model

In an ideal scenario where the distortion resulting from the camera imaging process is neglected, the rectification of a linear camera's distortion can be achieved by solving the intrinsic and extrinsic parameter matrices of the camera using only the image [14]. This is shown in the following equation:

$$Z_C \begin{bmatrix} u \\ v \\ 1 \end{bmatrix} = \begin{bmatrix} f_x & 0 & u & 0 \\ 0 & f_y & v & 0 \\ 0 & 0 & 1 & 0 \end{bmatrix} \begin{bmatrix} R & T \\ \vec{0} & 1 \end{bmatrix} \begin{bmatrix} X_W \\ Y_W \\ Z_W \\ 1 \end{bmatrix} \tag{9}$$

The internal parameter matrix is denoted as Equation (10), while the external parameter matrix is represented as Equation (11):

$$\begin{bmatrix} f_x & 0 & u & 0 \\ 0 & f_y & v & 0 \\ 0 & 0 & 1 & 0 \end{bmatrix} \tag{10}$$

$$\begin{bmatrix} R & T \\ \vec{0} & 1 \end{bmatrix} \tag{11}$$

(2) Nonlinear distortion model

Through analyzing the linear camera model, an ideal scenario would reveal a linear correlation, while practical measurement processes often encounter unattainable linearity and inevitable errors [15]. Due to manufacturing process variations, the camera lens generates distortions during the imaging process, leading to nonlinear distortions [16]. Nonlinear distortions can be further categorized into radial and tangential distortions, causing deviations between ideal projected points and actual projected points [17]. Let us assume a point P in the world coordinate system, represented as $P(X_W, Y_W, Z_W)$ in the $O_W - X_W Y_W Z_W$ coordinates. The corresponding theoretical image coordinate is denoted as $p(x, y)$. However, due to nonlinear distortions introduced by real-world imaging, the actual projected point of this point will deviate.

Expressed as follows is the deviation between the theoretical and actual points when $p(x,y)$ is shifted to point $p\prime(x',y')$:

$$\begin{cases} x' = x + \delta_x \\ y' = y + \delta_y \end{cases} \quad (12)$$

For the nonlinear distortion offset in the x direction, δ_x is used as a representation, while δ_y represents the nonlinear distortion offset in the y direction. In the case of nonlinear distortion offsets, the coefficients k_1, k_2, k_3 are employed to denote radial distortion. The expressions for the initial terms in the Taylor expansion are provided below:

$$\begin{cases} x' = x(1 + k_1r^2 + k_2r^4 + k_3r^6) \\ y' = y(1 + k_1r^2 + k_2r^4 + k_3r^6) \end{cases} \quad (13)$$

The radial distortion coefficients, denoted by k_1, k_2, k_3, $r^2 = x^2 + y^2$.

To ensure comprehensive distortion analysis, it is crucial to incorporate the consideration of tangential distortion. This type of distortion arises mainly from the disparity between the principal point of the optical system and the geometric center. The changes in tangential distortion are comparatively smaller in magnitude than that of radial distortion. The expression for tangential distortion is as follows:

$$\begin{cases} x' = x + [2p_1y + p_2(r^2 + 2x^2)] \\ y' = y + [p_1(r^2 + 2y^2) + 2p_2x] \end{cases} \quad (14)$$

The eccentric distortion coefficients, denoted by p_1, p_2, $r^2 = x^2 + y^2$.

2.3. Distortion Correction

Lens distortion is actually a collective term for inherent perspective distortions in optical lenses [18]. Generally, there are three types of camera distortions:

(1) Pincushion distortion: The magnification rate in the peripheral regions of the field of view is much larger than that near the optical axis center, commonly found in telephoto lenses [19].

(2) Barrel distortion: In contrast to pincushion distortion, the magnification rate near the optical axis center is much larger than that in the peripheral regions [20].

(3) Linear distortion: When the optical axis is not orthogonal to the vertical plane of objects being photographed, the convergence of the far side that should be parallel to the near side occurs at different angles, resulting in distortion. This distortion is essentially a form of perspective transformation, meaning that at certain angles, any lens will produce similar distortions [21].

The types of distortions in a camera are as follows (Figures 5–7):

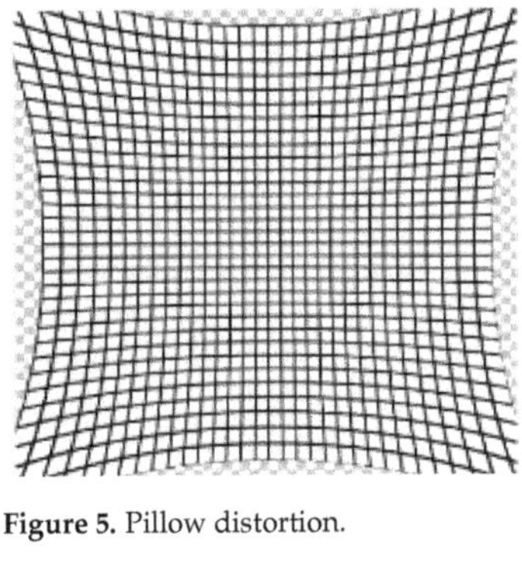

Figure 5. Pillow distortion.

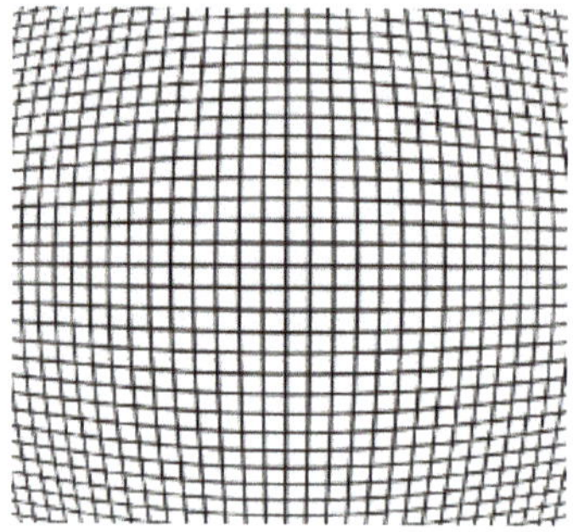

Figure 6. Barrel distortion.

Figure 7. Linear distortion.

The aforementioned distortions were taken into account during the calibration process [22]. Following the transformation Formulas (13) and (14), undistorted calibration results can be obtained using the following equation.

$$\begin{bmatrix} x_u \\ y_u \end{bmatrix} = [1 + k_1(x_d^2 + x_d^2) + k_2(x_d^2 + x_d^2) + k_3(x_d^2 + x_d^2)][x_d y_d] + \begin{bmatrix} 2p_1 x_d y_d + p_2(3x_d^2 + y_d^2) \\ p_2(3x_d^2 + y_d^2) + 2p_2 x_d y_d \end{bmatrix}$$

Here, a nonlinear model is introduced to account for distortion in camera calibration. In real-world scenarios, the calibration of distortion serves as an effective means to minimize the influence of distortion, thus safeguarding the precision of the calibration outcomes.

3. Camera Calibration

3.1. Camera Calibration Algorithm

After analyzing the coordinate transformation relationship in photogrammetric measurement and the previously delineated camera distortion model, the calibration of the camera is conducted [23].

First, construct the homograph matrix to establish the relationship between world coordinates and pixel coordinates. This matrix describes the homographs between the target point in the world coordinate system and the image point. Subsequently, solve the initial values for the camera's intrinsic and extrinsic parameters using orthogonal constraint conditions. Finally, an optimization algorithm is applied to obtain reliable matrices for the intrinsic and extrinsic parameters [24]. According to the camera imaging model and the transformation relationship between pixel coordinates and world coordinates, the expression for the camera imaging model is as follows:

$$s\overline{m} = A[R, T]\overline{M} \tag{15}$$

In Equation (15), the pixel coordinates of the image are denoted as $\overline{m}$, the world coordinates as $\overline{M}$, the intrinsic matrix as A, the extrinsic matrix as $[R, T]$, and the scale factor as s. The expression based on Equation (15) is presented in homogeneous coordinates as follows:

$$s\begin{bmatrix} u \\ v \\ 1 \end{bmatrix} = A[r_1 \quad r_2 \quad r_3 \quad t]\begin{bmatrix} X \\ Y \\ Z \\ 1 \end{bmatrix} \tag{16}$$

Then, the internal parameters of the camera can be expressed as:

$$A = \begin{bmatrix} f_u & \gamma & u_0 \\ 0 & f_v & v_0 \\ 0 & 0 & 1 \end{bmatrix} \tag{17}$$

Since the scale factor s does not alter the homogeneous coordinate values, in Zhang's calibration method, where pixel coordinates are in two dimensions, we can set $Z = 0$. Consequently, Equation (15) can be expressed as follows:

$$s\begin{bmatrix} u \\ v \\ 1 \end{bmatrix} = \lambda A[r_1 \quad r_2 \quad r_3 \quad t]\begin{bmatrix} X \\ Y \\ 0 \\ 1 \end{bmatrix} = \lambda A[r_1 \quad r_2 \quad t]\begin{bmatrix} X \\ Y \\ 1 \end{bmatrix} \tag{18}$$

Given that $\lambda = 1/s$, and the homographs matrix is denoted as H, we can set $H = \lambda A[r_1 \quad r_2 \quad t]$. Consequently, the camera model can be represented by Equation (19):

$$s\overline{m} = H\overline{M} \tag{19}$$

Let $H = [h_1 \quad h_2 \quad h_3] = \lambda A[r_1 \quad r_2 \quad t]$, the r vector is represented by the homologous matrix H as follows:

$$\begin{cases} r_1 = \frac{1}{\lambda}A^{-1}h_1 \\ r_2 = \frac{1}{\lambda}A^{-1}h_2 \end{cases} \tag{20}$$

According to orthogonality, the vector's own constraints are expressed as:

$$\begin{cases} r_1^2 = r_2^2 = r_3^2 = 1 \\ r_1r_2 = r_1r_3 = r_2r_3 = 0 \end{cases} \tag{21}$$

$$\begin{cases} r_1^T r_2 = 0 \\ \|r_1\| = \|r_2\| = 1 \end{cases} \tag{22}$$

By bringing Formula (21) into Formula (22), we can obtain:

$$\begin{cases} h_1^T A^{-T}A^{-1}h_2 = 0 \\ h_1^T A^{-T}A^{-1}h_1 = h_2^T A^{-T}A^{-1}h_2 \end{cases} \tag{23}$$

For each feature point in the target image, we can derive two equations. By selecting four points from the target image, as long as three of them are not collinear, the matrix H can be computed. Consequently, a matrix H can be derived, with the following expression:

$$s\begin{bmatrix} u \\ v \\ 1 \end{bmatrix} = \begin{bmatrix} h_{11} & h_{12} & h_{13} \\ h_{21} & h_{22} & h_{23} \\ h_{31} & h_{32} & h_{33} \end{bmatrix}\begin{bmatrix} X \\ Y \\ 1 \end{bmatrix} \tag{24}$$

The expression for Equation (24) can be transformed into a set of equations as follows:

$$\begin{cases} uXh_{31} + uYh_{32} + uh_{33} = h_{11}X + h_{12}Y + h_{13} \\ vXh_{31} + vYh_{32} + vh_{33} = h_{21}X + h_{22}Y + h_{23} \end{cases} \tag{25}$$

Expressing Equation (25) in matrix form, while setting $h' = [h_{11}\ h_{12}\ h_{13}\ h_{21}\ h_{22}\ h_{23}\ h_{31}\ h_{32}\ h_{33}]^T$, yields the following matrix expression:

$$\begin{bmatrix} X & Y & 1 & 0 & 0 & 0 & -uX & -uY & -u \\ 0 & 0 & 0 & X & Y & 1 & -vX & -vY & -v \end{bmatrix} h' = 0 \tag{26}$$

By applying the orthogonality condition stated in Equation (23), we can construct a matrix of homographs to determine the camera's intrinsic and extrinsic parameters. Since $A^{-T}A^{-1}$ is present within Equation (23), the following matrix is formed by setting $B = A^{-T}A^{-1}$. Its expression is as follows:

$$B = A^{-T}A^{-1} = \begin{bmatrix} B_{11} & B_{12} & B_{13} \\ B_{21} & B_{22} & B_{23} \\ B_{31} & B_{32} & B_{33} \end{bmatrix} \tag{27}$$

Bringing Equation (17) into Equation (27) yields the following expression:

$$B = A^{-T}A^{-1} = \begin{bmatrix} \frac{1}{f_u^2} & \frac{\gamma}{f_u^2 f_v} & \frac{v_0\gamma - u_0 f_v}{f_u^2 f_v} \\ -\frac{\gamma}{f_u^2 f_v} & \frac{\gamma^2}{f_u^2 f_v^2} + \frac{1}{f_v^2} & -\frac{\gamma(v_0\gamma - u_0 f_v)}{f_u^2 f_v^2} - \frac{v_0}{f_v^2} \\ \frac{v_0\gamma - u_0 f_v}{f_u^2 f_v} & -\frac{\gamma(v_0\gamma - u_0 f_v)}{f_u^2 f_v^2} - \frac{v_0}{f_v^2} & \frac{(v_0\gamma - u_0 f_v)^2}{f_u^2 f_v^2} + \frac{v_0}{f_v^2} + 1 \end{bmatrix}$$

The matrix B possesses a symmetric structure and can be represented by Equation (28):

$$b = \begin{bmatrix} B_{11} & B_{12} & B_{22} & B_{13} & B_{23} & B_{33} \end{bmatrix}^T \tag{28}$$

According to the orthogonal constraint: $h_i^T B h_j = v_{ij}^T b$, we can obtain:

$$v_{ij} = \begin{bmatrix} h_{i1}h_{j1} & h_{i1}h_{j2} + h_{i2}h_{j1} & h_{i2}h_{j2} & h_{i3}h_{j1} + h_{i1}h_{j3} & h_{i3}h_{j2} + h_{i2}h_{j3} & h_{i3}h_{j3} \end{bmatrix}^T$$

The equation's expression of orthogonality constraint results in $v_{12}^T b = 0$.

Similarly, based on another constraint, it can be represented as $(v_{11} - v_{22})^T b = 0$. These two constraints can be expressed in matrix form, and their expression is as follows:

$$\begin{bmatrix} v_{12}^T \\ (v_{11} - v_{22})^T \end{bmatrix} b = 0 \tag{29}$$

During the camera calibration process, for each image, we can obtain a homographs matrix H. Based on Equation (29), each of these matrices can be used to form the system of equations described in the equation. According to Equation (28), v_{ij} has six unknowns; thus, at least six sets of equations need to be established in order to solve them. In practical experiments, there are often redundant data available, allowing for the calculation of the B matrix. By solving the B matrix using the Cholesky (square root) method and taking its inverse, we can obtain the camera's intrinsic parameters. Its expression is given by Equation (30).

$$\begin{cases} v_0 = \frac{(B_{12}B_{13}-B_{11}B_{23})}{(B_{11}B_{22}-B_{12}^2)} \\ \lambda = \frac{B_{33}-\left[B_{13}^2+v_0(B_{12}B_{13}-B_{11}B_{23})\right]}{B_{11}} \\ f_u = \sqrt{\frac{\lambda}{B_{11}}} \\ f_v = \sqrt{\frac{\lambda B_{11}}{B_{11}B_{22}-B_{12}^2}} \\ \gamma = -\frac{B_{12}f_u^2 f_v}{\lambda} \\ u_0 = \frac{v_0\gamma}{f_v} - \frac{B_{13}f_u^2}{\lambda} \end{cases} \tag{30}$$

Then, according to $H = [h_1 \quad h_2 \quad h_3] = \lambda A[r_1 \quad r_2 \quad t]$, the external parameters are simplified, and the result is expressed as Equation (31):

$$\begin{cases} r_1 = \lambda A^{-1}h_1 \\ r_2 = \lambda A^{-1}h_2 \\ r_3 = r_1 r_2 \\ t = \lambda A^{-1}h_3 \\ \lambda = \frac{1}{\|A^{-1}h_1\|} = \frac{1}{\|A^{-1}h_2\|} \end{cases} \tag{31}$$

Solving Equations (30) and (31) allows for the determination of both the camera's internal and external parameters.

3.2. Binocular Stereo Calibration Method

Based on the camera imaging model, Equation (32) can be derived when considering the internal and external parameter matrices of the left and right cameras in a binocular vision system portrayed as R_1, T_1, R_2, and T_2, respectively. Furthermore, point P in world coordinates are P_W, while its coordinates on the imaging plane of the left camera and the right camera are p_1 and p_2, respectively.

$$\begin{cases} p_1 = R_1 P_W + T_1 \\ p_2 = R_2 P_W + T_2 \end{cases} \tag{32}$$

Equation (33) is obtained by eliminating P_W from the upper equations:

$$p_2 = R_2 R_1^{-1} p_1 + T_2 - R_2 R_1^{-1} T_1 = R p_1 + T \tag{33}$$

Equation (33) defines R as the rotation matrix relating the two cameras and T as the translation vector representing the spatial relationship between the cameras. Consequently, the positional correlation between the left and right cameras is articulated through Equation (34).

$$\begin{cases} R = R_2 R_1^{-1} \\ T = T_2 - R_2 R_1^{-1} T_1 \end{cases} \tag{34}$$

Based on Equation (34), the individual calibration of the internal and external parameters for the left and right cameras enables the definition of their positional relationship. This process completes the stereo calibration for the binocular vision system. Subsequently, intelligent optimization algorithms are utilized to enhance the obtained internal and external parameters, as they may not be optimal.

4. Camera Parameter Optimization Algorithm

The Zhang's calibration method yields unsatisfactory results when multiple images are used as input, with poor performance due to suboptimal initial values and noise-contaminated data. In order to tackle this issue, the linear model solution is utilized as the starting point for optimization, aiming to enhance the resilience of conventional optimization approaches [25]. However, these drawbacks require additional input constraints to obtain more accurate parameter results, making the traditional calibration process more complex and impractical. Hence, this section primarily utilizes intelligent optimization algorithms to optimize the method and address the aforementioned limitations.

Assuming there exist n template images depicting planar surfaces, with each image containing m calibration points within the identical environment, the formulation of the objective function is presented as follows:

$$f_{obj} = \min\sum_{i=1}^{n}\sum_{j=1}^{m}\left\|\hat{p}_{ij} - p(M_A, k_1, k_2, k_3, p_1, p_2, R_i, T_i, P_j)\right\| \tag{35}$$

The pixel coordinates of the j calibration point in the i image are represented by p_{ij} in the objective function, whereas k_1, k_2, k_3, p_1, p_2 represents the distortion parameters, and R_i, T_i denotes the rotation and translation matrix corresponding to the i image. By utilizing optimization algorithms to optimize the calibration objective function based on Equation (35), the optimal solution for the camera calibration parameters can be obtained.

4.1. Honey Badger Algorithm

The Honey Badger Algorithm (HBA) presents a pioneering heuristic optimization approach inspired by the foraging behavior of honey badgers, which has devised an efficient search strategy for addressing mathematical optimization problems. The key principle revolves around the honey badger's capacity to locate beehives through actions such as sniffing, digging, and following honeyguide birds, categorized as the excavation mode and the honey mode, respectively. During the excavation mode, the honey badger uses its keen sense of smell to estimate the beehive's location and chooses a suitable spot for excavation upon nearing the hive. Conversely, in the honey mode, the honey badger directly relies on the guidance of the honeyguide bird to find the beehive, ultimately yielding the optimal outcome.

The optimization of camera parameters based on the honey badger algorithm involves establishing an objective function using the residuals between the actual image coordinates (x, y) of calibration points and the projected coordinates (x', y') calculated from the camera model.

$$f(X) = \sum_{i}^{N}\left[(x - x')^2 + (y - y')^2\right] \tag{36}$$

By utilizing the excavation mode and honey mode to minimize the value of $f(X)$, an optimal set of parameters is obtained, achieving the optimization of camera parameters.

Here, X represents the parameter to be optimized, specifically $X = [f_x, f_y, C_x, C_y, k_1, k_2, k_3, p_1, p_2]$, with the parameter's search range set as $[X_{up}, X_{down}]$, as shown below:

$$X_{up} = [f_x + 3, f_y + 3, C_x + 2, C_y + 2, k_1 + 0.1, k_2 + 0.02, k3 + 0.002, p_1 + 2 \times 10^{-5}, p_2 + 0.02]$$

$$X_{down} = [f_x - 3, f_y - 3, C_x - 2, C_y - 2, k_1 - 0.1, k_2 - 0.02, k3 - 0.002, p_1 - 2 \times 10^{-5}, p_2 - 0.02]$$

The population of honey badgers, with a size of N, representing the optimization of D parameters, can be expressed as follows:

$$\begin{bmatrix} x_{11} & x_{12} & x_{13} & \cdots & x_{1D} \\ x_{21} & x_{22} & x_{23} & \cdots & x_{2D} \\ \vdots & \vdots & \vdots & & \vdots \\ x_{N1} & x_{N2} & x_{N3} & \cdots & x_{ND} \end{bmatrix} \tag{37}$$

The position of the i honey badger is:

$$\mathrm{x}_i = [x_{i1}, x_{i2}, x_{i3}, \cdots, x_{iD}] \tag{38}$$

The flowchart of the honey badger algorithm is as follows (Figure 8):

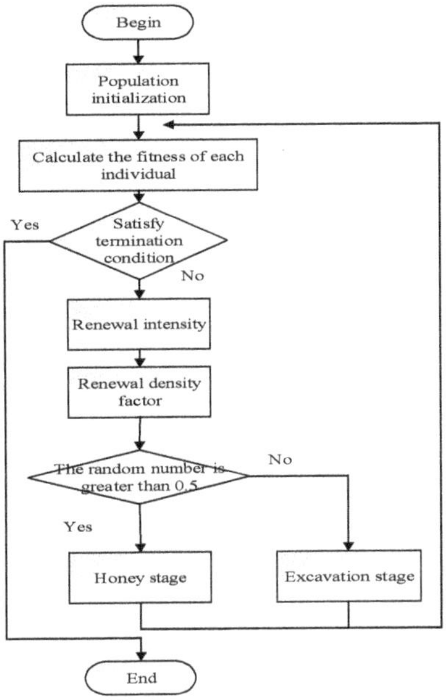

Figure 8. Honey badger optimization algorithm flowchart.

The algorithm steps are as follows:

Step 1: The initialization phase entails setting the population size N and determining the corresponding positions of the honey badgers.

$$x_i = lb_i + r_1 \times (ub_i - lb_i) \tag{39}$$

where r_1 denotes a random number within the range of 0 to 1, lb_i signifies the lower boundary of the search domain, and ub_i denotes the upper boundary of the search domain.

Determine the maximum number of iterations, denoted as T, as well as parameters C and β.

Step 2: Specifying the intensity I. The intensity is linked to the prey's concentration and the spatial separation between the prey and honey badgers. I_i denotes the olfactory potency of the prey, where a high olfactory strength results in fast movement, whereas a low olfactory strength leads to slow movement.

$$I_i = r_2 \times \frac{S}{4\pi d_i^2} \tag{40}$$

$$S = (x_i - x_{i+1})^2 \tag{41}$$

$$d_i = x_{prey} - x_i \tag{42}$$

In this section, the symbol r_2 represents a random number between 0 and 1, S denotes the source strength or concentration strength, and d_i represents the distance between the i-th honey badger and its prey.

Step 3: Enhancing the density factor. The density factor α controls the dynamic randomization process, facilitating a seamless transition from exploration to exploitation.

$$\alpha = C \times \exp\left(\frac{-t}{t_{\max}}\right) \tag{43}$$

Step 4: Escape from local optima. This step is aimed at escaping from local optima regions. The search algorithm employs a flag F to alter the search direction, facilitating an extensive exploration of the search space.

Step 5: Adjusting individual positions. The process of updating positions comprises two components: the "excavation phase" and the "honey collection phase".

Excavation phase:

$$x_{new} = x_{prey} + F \times \beta \times I \times x_{prey} + F \times r_3 \times \alpha \times d_i \times |\cos(2\pi r_4) \times [1 - \cos(2\pi r_5)]|$$

In this context, x_{new} signifies the revised location of the honey badger individual, while x_{prey} denotes the prey's position.

Meanwhile, β signifies the honey badger's capability to obtain physical items, where $\beta \geq 1$ with a default of 6, and d_i denotes the distance between the i-th honey badger and the prey. Additionally, r_3, r_4, r_5, r_6, r_7 are random numbers between 0 and 1.

$$F = \begin{cases} 1 \ if \ r_6 \leq 0.5 \\ -1 \ else \end{cases} \quad (44)$$

Honey gathering stage:

$$x_{new} = x_{prey} + F \times r_7 \times \alpha \times d_i \quad (45)$$

x_{new} represents the revised location of the honey badger individual, while x_{prey} indicates the position of the prey, which represents the globally optimal position. The variable d represents the distance between the i-th honey badger and the prey. The value of F can be calculated using Equation (44), and the value of α can be derived from Equation (43).

4.2. *Improved Differential Evolution Particle Swarm Algorithm*

Considering the limitations of the honey badger algorithm, including rapid convergence, low accuracy of convergence, tendency to diverge, and decreasing population diversity as iterations increase, the particle swarm optimization algorithm incorporates the differential evolution algorithm to overcome these limitations. In this enhanced algorithm, differential evolution mutation and crossover operations are integrated into the particle swarm algorithm at each iteration. This modification aims to preserve the diversity of the particle population and improve the selection of the optimal particle in each iteration, ultimately leading to enhanced performance.

4.2.1. Principle of Differential Evolution Algorithm

The main components of the differential evolution (DE) algorithm include mutation, crossover, and selection operations. Within this algorithm, a diverse subset of individuals is randomly chosen to form the variance vector. Subsequently, an additional individual is selected and incorporated into the variance vector to produce an experimental individual. The crossover operation is then executed between the original individual and the respective experimental individual, perturbing the existing population and extending the exploration range. Ultimately, a selection process takes place between the original and offspring individuals, retaining the individuals that satisfy the criteria for the subsequent generation population.

(1) The initialization of the population

The population of size (NP, D) is randomly generated in the solution space. Each individual, denoted by the i-th element, is given a random value within the predefined range.

$$X_i(G) = \{x_{i1}(G), x_{i2}(G), \cdots, x_{iD}(G)\},\ i = 1, 2, \cdots, NP \quad (46)$$

Within the context of this study, the value of NP corresponds to the population size, while D represents the number of decision variables. Each individual within the initial population is generated in the range $[x_{\min}, x_{\max}]$ according to Equation (46).

$$x_{iD}(0) = x_{\min} + rand(0,1) * (x_{\max} - x_{\min}) \tag{47}$$

In the above equation, the variable G indicates the G generation, and $[x_{\min}, x_{\max}]$ represents the search space domain of the decision variables.

(2) Variation operation

The mutation operation is employed in the process of G evolution to generate the mutation vector $V_i(G)$ for each individual $X_i(G)$ in the population of the current generation. The calculation of the mutation vector varies depending on the chosen mutation strategy, and the subsequent section outlines five frequently employed mutation strategies.

$$\begin{array}{l} DE/rand/1: \\ V_i(G) = X_{r1}(G) + F \cdot (X_{r2}(G) - X_{r3}(G)) \\ DE/best/1: \\ V_i(G) = X_{best}(G) + F \cdot (X_{r1}(G) - X_{r2}(G)) \\ DE/rand-to-best/1: \\ V_i(G) = X_i(G) + F \cdot (X_{best}(G) - X_i(G)) + F \cdot (X_{r1}(G) - X_{r2}(G)) \\ DE/best/2: \\ V_i(G) = X_{best}(G) + F \cdot (X_{r1}(G) - X_{r2}(G)) + F \cdot (X_{r3}(G) - X_{r4}(G)) \\ DE/rand/2: \\ V_i(G) = X_{r1}(G) + F \cdot (X_{r2}(G) - X_{r3}(G)) + F \cdot (X_{r4}(G) - X_{r5}(G)) \end{array} \tag{48}$$

In the above equation, r_1, r_2, r_3, r_4, r_5 is a mutually exclusive random integer within the range $[1, NP]$ and different from the index i. The scaling factor F is a positive controlling parameter of the differential vector. $X_{best}(G)$ represents the best individual vector in the G generation population with the optimal fitness value.

(3) Crossover Operation

For each pair of target vector $X_i(G)$ and mutation vector $V_i(G)$, a trial vector is generated through crossover. The differential evolution method employs a binomial crossover defined as follows in Equation (49): $U_i(G) = (u_i(G), u_i(G), \cdots, u_I(G))$.

$$u_i(G) = \begin{cases} v_i(G), \ (rand_j(0,1) \le CR) or (j = j_{rand}) \\ x_i(G), \ otherwise \end{cases} \quad j = 1, 2, \cdots, D \tag{49}$$

Among them, CR is a specified constant crossover probability between $(0,1)$, and j_{rand} is a randomly selected integer within the range $[1, D]$.

(4) Selection Operation

In the differential evolution method, a greedy selection rule is utilized to determine the offspring. This rule involves comparing the fitness values of the trial individuals with the target individuals and selecting the superior individuals to be inherited in the subsequent generation.

$$X_i(G+1) = \begin{cases} U_i(G), if(f(U_i(G)) \le f(X_i(G))) \\ X_i(G), otherwise \end{cases} \tag{50}$$

Among these, $f(\cdot)$ denotes the fitness value of the objective function for both the target individual and the trial individual in the G generation. The above operations are repeated in each generation until certain specific termination conditions are met.

4.2.2. Improved Differential Evolution Particle Swarm Hybrid Optimization Algorithm Design

The population size in the context of the differential evolution algorithm is denoted by N, with each individual possessing a multidimensional vector, which is expressed as the target vector and the trial vector: $X_i^t = (x_{i1}^t, x_{i2}^t, \ldots, x_{iD}^t)$, $V_i^t = (v_{i1}^t, v_{i2}^t, \ldots, v_{iD}^t)$. The population is initialized as $S = \{X_1, X_2, \ldots, X_D\}$, where T represents each target vector. Therefore, the mutation operation can be improved as follows.

$$V_i^T = x_{best}^t + f(x_{r2}^t - x_{r3}^t) \tag{51}$$

$$V_i^T = x_{r1}^t + f(x_{r2}^t - x_{r3}^t) \tag{52}$$

$$V_i^T = x_i^t + f_1(x_{best}^t - x_i^t) + f_2(x_{r1}^t - x_{r2}^t) \tag{53}$$

$$V_i^T = x_{\text{best}}^t + f(x_{r1}^t + x_{r2}^t - x_{r3}^t - x_{r4}^t) \tag{54}$$

$$V_i^T = x_{r1}^t + f(x_{r2}^t + x_{r3}^t - x_{r4}^t - x_{r5}^t) \tag{55}$$

The equation above introduces f as the mutation parameter, which serves to control the differential speed, while r_1, r_2, r_3, r_4, r_5 represents distinct random integers falling within the range of $[1, N]$. The population iteration algorithm incorporates a mutation method to enhance population diversity, ensuring that mutation takes place after each iteration. Moreover, it integrates crossover and selection operations to facilitate the selection of the optimal individual in each iteration.

The Figure 9 depicts the flowchart of the enhanced algorithm for differential evolution particle swarm optimization:

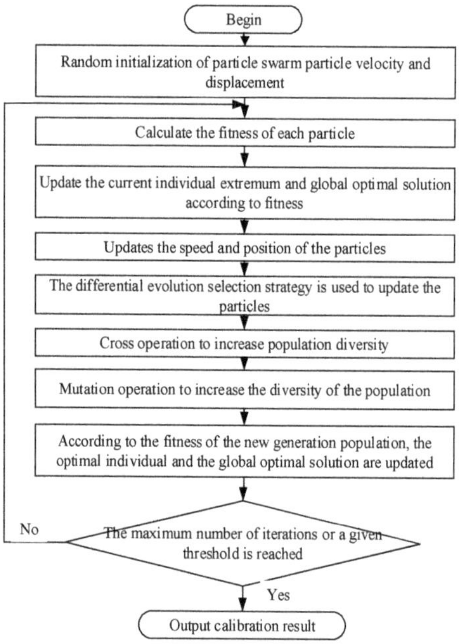

Figure 9. Flowchart based on improved differential evolution particle swarm hybrid optimization algorithm.

The algorithm implementation steps are as follows:

Step 1: Using calibration algorithm, obtain the coordinates (x', y') of calibration points and camera parameters $f_x, f_y, C_x, C_y, k_1, k_2, k_3, p_1, p_2$.

Step 2: A group of particles is initialized and distributed throughout the search space, with each particle possessing flight velocity denoted as V_i and position represented as X_i. Set the population size N, parameter search range, maximum flight velocity V_{up}, inertia weight coefficient ω, individual learning factor c_1, social learning factor c_2, and other parameters. Define the search range of the parameters as $[X_{up}, X_{down}]$.

Step 3: An enhanced dynamic adjustment strategy is introduced for the modification of the algorithm's weights w, mutation control parameter f, and crossover control parameter CR. The maximum number of iterations $\lambda_{\max}$ and the current iteration count λ are determined based on the upper and lower limits of the parameters specified in Step 2:

$$\delta(w, f, CR) = \delta_{\max} - \frac{\delta_{\max} - \delta_{\min}}{\lambda_{\max}}\lambda \tag{56}$$

Step 4: The fitness value of each particle is computed, and the fitness evaluation can be represented by Equation (57).

$$fitness = \min \sum_{i=1}^{m} \sqrt{(u_i - x_i)^2 + (v_i - y_i)^2} \tag{57}$$

Step 5: The current individual extreme value P_i^t for each particle is updated, and the best individual extreme value is recorded as the current global optimal solution P_g^t.

Step 6: Each particle updates its flight velocity and position information. The update equations for flight velocity and position information in the d-th dimension are as follows:

$$v_{id}^{t+1} = \omega v_{id}^t + c_1 r_1 (p_{id}^t - x_{id}^t) + c_2 r_2 (p_{gd}^t - x_{id}^t)$$

$$x_{id}^{t+1} = x_{id}^t + v_{id}^{t+1}$$

where $i = 1, 2, \ldots, N$ and $d = 1, 2, \ldots, D$, v_{id}^{t+1} and x_{id}^{t+1}, respectively represent the flight velocity and position information of the i particle in the $t+1$ generation.

Step 7: Executing the crossover operation enhances population diversity and promotes the adaptation of exceptional individuals.

Step 8: The mutation operation is performed to generate excellent individuals, with a higher probability of mutation for individuals with lower fitness.

Step 9: Updating the entire population is based on the new fitness values, which involves the update of individual best and global best.

Step 10: Checking if the termination condition is met to determine whether to output the results; if the condition is met, the results will be outputted. If not, the process will return to Step 2 for additional iterations.

5. Experimental Comparison and Result Analysis

Using Zhang's calibration method, the camera was calibrated to obtain the parameters necessary for rectifying the captured images. This process ensured the precise acquisition of pixel coordinates for the chessboard pattern captured by both the left and right cameras. A binocular stereo vision model was then employed to determine the world coordinates of the chessboard pattern. The obtained world coordinates were used as input, while the theoretical world coordinates were used as output. For data computation, a comparative analysis was conducted using different optimization algorithms, including genetic algorithm, particle swarm optimization algorithm, honey badger optimization algorithm, and an enhanced hybrid optimization algorithm that combines differential evolution and particle swarm optimization algorithm.

5.1. Procedure of Test

Step 1: Multiple calibration board images were captured using the experimental equipment. Subsequently, functions such as "findChessboardCorners", "calibrateCamera", and "stereoRectify" from the OpenCV library were invoked in C++ to solve for the camera's intrinsic and extrinsic parameters.

Step 2: Multiple sets of captured images were selected. Using OpenCV, pixel coordinates were first determined, followed by the calculation of world coordinates. Figure 10 depicts the calibration board employed in the experiment, which consists of a total of 40 corners. It was manufactured using photolithography techniques, with a fabrication error within 1 millimeter. Each chessboard square measures 80 mm × 80 mm, resulting in a total chessboard size of 800 × 600.

Step 3: The collected calibration images were input into the camera calibration data processing module, resulting in initial data after calibration, including initial values for various types of distortion coefficients.

Step 4: Different optimization techniques were applied to optimize the initial calibration parameters and obtain the global optimum solution.

5.2. Results and Analysis

A binocular camera is used to take multiple photos, which are shown in Figure 10:

Figure 10. Checkerboard for calibration.

In the camera calibration experiments, the calibration board underwent movement within the field of view of the camera, assuming different positions and angles. This allowed for the capture of multiple sets of detection images for the purpose of calibration. Due to the continuous movement of the calibration board, image blurring may occur during image acquisition, which in turn can affect the accuracy of subsequent corner detection. Therefore, high-quality, non-blurred images were selected from the collected calibration data for the calibration experiments. The process of binocular calibration and corner detection is illustrated in Figure 11.

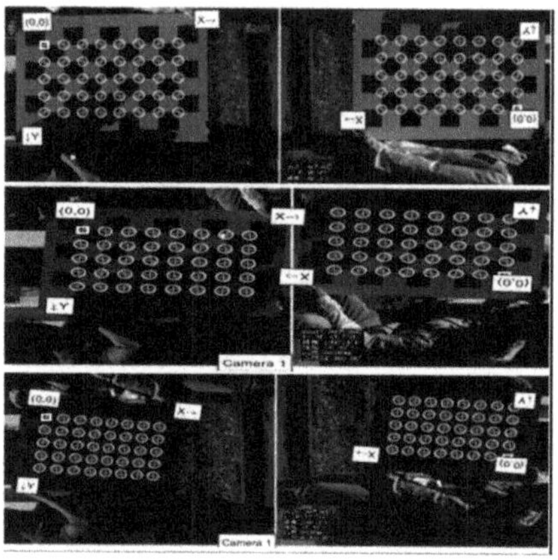

Figure 11. Camera calibration and corner detection results.

The method for camera calibration detailed earlier was applied to derive parameter matrices M_1 and M_2 for the left and right cameras. Correspondingly, matrices D_1 and D_2 representing the distortion parameters for the cameras were acquired. A summary of the findings can be found in Table 1, with all data rounded to five decimal places.

Table 1. The calibration parameter matrix for the left and right cameras.

Camera Parameter Matrix	Distortion Parameter Matrix
$M_1 = \begin{bmatrix} 5035.73040 & 0 & 533.22766 \\ 0 & 5036.77009 & 978.66847 \\ 0 & 0 & 1 \end{bmatrix}$	$D_1 = [-0.08209,\ 1.58242,\ -0.00166,\ -0.00032,\ 10.23747]$
$M_2 = \begin{bmatrix} 5018.27022 & 0 & 516.49581 \\ 0 & 5017.48057 & 905.64914 \\ 0 & 0 & 1 \end{bmatrix}$	$D_2 = [-0.05939,\ 0.48486,\ -0.00168,\ -0.00026,\ 38.70554]$

During this experiment, 15 sets of calibration board images were utilized. The intrinsic and extrinsic parameters of the camera, along with the distortion parameters obtained from the calibration process, were employed to project the corners of the calibration board onto the imaging plane. The calibration error was subsequently evaluated by comparing the pixel coordinates of these points with their actual coordinates on the calibration board. The tabulated results of the calibration errors are documented in Table 2.

Table 2. Calibration average error table.

Label	Average Error (Pixel)	Label	Average Error (Pixel)	Label	Average Error (Pixel)
1	0.172649	6	0.138521	11	0.189421
2	0.157981	7	0.137715	12	0.212029
3	0.081947	8	0.141941	13	0.118467
4	0.105237	9	0.166069	14	0.193648
5	0.160528	10	0.233748	15	0.189421

As shown in Table 2, the overall average calibration error falls within a range of 0.25 pixels.

Figure 12 illustrates the projection of the calibration board's corner coordinates onto the camera coordinate plane using the camera's intrinsic and extrinsic parameters derived from reverse projection. Discrepancies between these projected coordinates and the actual corner coordinates in the original image were computed in both the x and y directions. The deviations, quantified in pixels, are denoted by red "o" for the calibration disparities of the left camera and blue "+" for those of the right camera.

After the calibration of both the left and right cameras, the stereo vision calibration can be conducted. The calibration outcomes for the binocular vision system are displayed in Table 3.

Table 3. Binocular camera calibration results.

Rotation Matrix	Translation Vector
$R = \begin{bmatrix} -0.99993098 & 0.0004564127 & -0.011711541 \\ -0.00057125383 & -0.99995023 & 0.0098654972 \\ -0.011706779 & 0.0098716523 & 0.99988127 \end{bmatrix}$	$T = \begin{bmatrix} -15.728618 & 0.081634976 & -0.082594357 \end{bmatrix}$

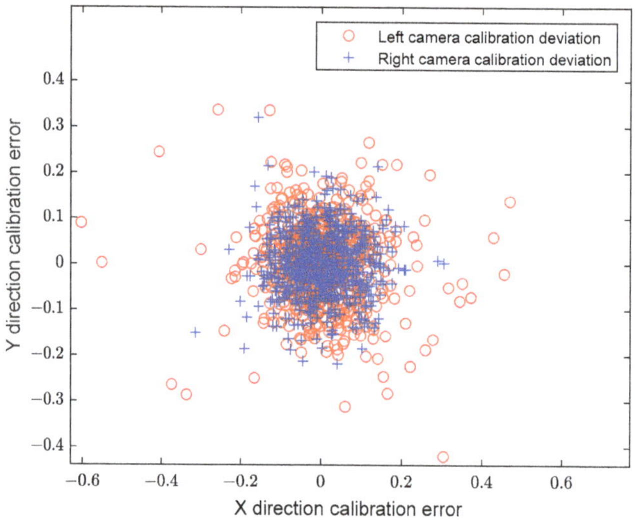

Figure 12. Calibration error analysis diagram.

The rotation matrix and translation matrix for stereo calibration, presented in Table 3, indicate that the rotation matrix bears a striking resemblance to the identity matrix. This similarity can be attributed to the meticulous efforts employed during the setup of the left and right cameras to achieve and maintain their equilibrium.

Following the procedure outlined in the preceding section, the MATLAB implementation of the optimization algorithm program utilized 10 sets of calibration images and experimented with maximum iteration numbers of 200, 400, 600, 800, and 1000. In order to evaluate the calibration performance of the algorithm proposed in this chapter, assessments were carried out employing the genetic algorithm, particle swarm algorithm, honey badger algorithm, and improved differential particle swarm algorithm. The evaluation criteria involved nine parameters, $f_x, f_y, c_x, c_y, k_1, k_2, k_3, p_1, p_2$, and their performance was compared, as presented in Table 4.

Table 4. Table of the optimization results of the four optimization algorithms for the nine calibration parameters.

Argument	GA	PSO	HBA	IDEPSO	DE
f_x	1156.7861	1154.4027	1156.4027	1157.8783	1157.4027
f_y	1154.2004	1155.0684	1155.0685	1153.6961	1152.0685
c_x	662.7546	660.9385	660.9385	663.02028	662.9385
c_y	387.9115	389.3181	389.1970	387.9177	387.8497
k_1	−0.2451	−0.26817	−0.26614	−0.245762	−0.245485
k_2	−0.044766	−0.06452	−0.06452	−0.044699	−0.044525
k_3	−0.00049006	−0.000713	−0.000313	−0.0004727	−0.0005139
p_1	5.6293×10^{-5}	4.1408×10^{-5}	8.1408×10^{-5}	4.5905×10^{-5}	6.1408×10^{-5}
p_2	0.045762	0.041302	0.045302	0.045686	0.0456797

Based on the findings displayed in Table 4, the camera parameter calibration performed in this investigation meticulously accounted for both radial and tangential distortions. As a result, the influence of distortion and lens aberrations on the measurement outcomes during the camera calibration process was significantly mitigated. To conduct a more comprehensive analysis of the optimization test results, the positional deviations were assessed using the error range and root-mean-square error (RMSE) as indicators of accuracy. The calculation formulas for these two evaluation criteria are provided below:

$$Er(k) = \sqrt{(\hat{X}(k) - X(k))^2} \quad k = 1, 2, \cdots, N \tag{58}$$

$$RMSE = \sqrt{\frac{1}{N}\sum_{i=1}^{N} (\hat{X}(k) - X(k))^2} \tag{59}$$

The root-mean-square errors for position in each direction calibrated by the four optimization algorithms are presented in Table 5.

Table 5. Comparison of the four optimization algorithms.

RMSE	X	Y	Z
GA	0.6189	0.5162	0.1124
PSO	0.4895	0.5137	0.0947
HBA	0.3201	0.5150	0.0657
IDEPSO	0.1690	0.3780	0.0638
DE	0.8758	0.5138	0.1151

Result 1: The fitness curve for the optimization using genetic algorithm is shown in Figure 13, with a maximum iteration number of 455. The fitness value decreases in a stepwise manner as the iteration number increases and finally reaches zero after 455 iterations. The solution stabilizes thereafter and remains consistent.

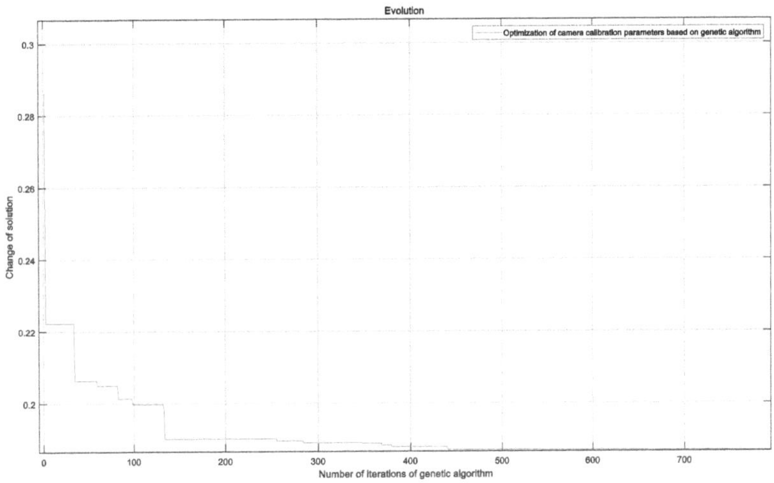

Figure 13. Fitness curve after genetic algorithm optimization.

Based on Figures 13 and 14, it can be observed that the optimization of calibration parameters using genetic algorithm resulted in significant improvement in the corresponding coordinate errors. The error in the x-coordinate was reduced from approximately 0.3 to within 0.05 after optimization, while the error in the y-coordinate improved from around -0.5 to within ± 0.07. The error in the z-coordinate was within 0.1 before parameter optimization.

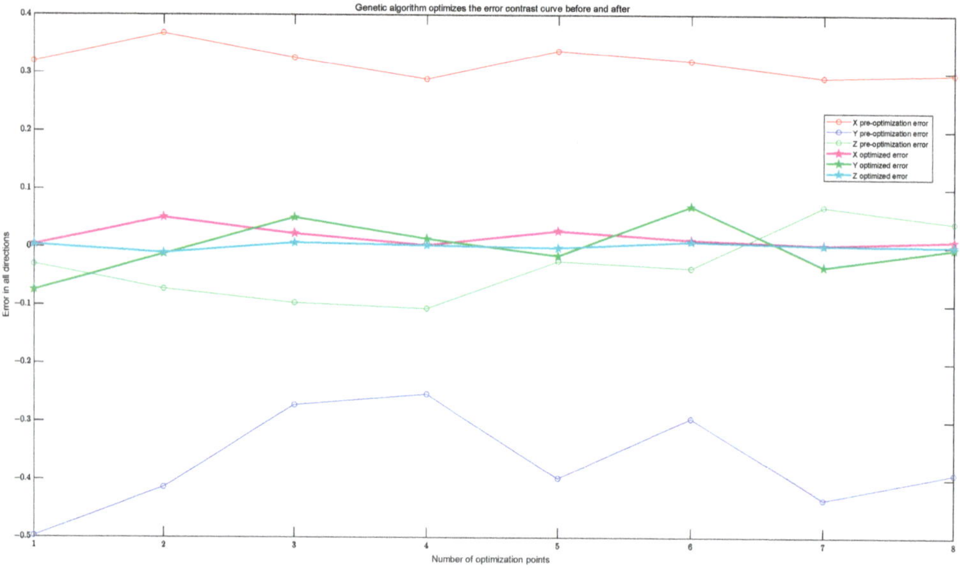

Figure 14. Genetic algorithm optimizes the coordinate error contrast curve.

Result 2: The fitness curve for the optimization using particle swarm algorithm is depicted in Figure 15. The algorithm terminated after 225 iterations, and the fitness value exhibited a stepwise decrease with the increase in iteration count. After 225 iterations, the solution approached zero and stabilized.

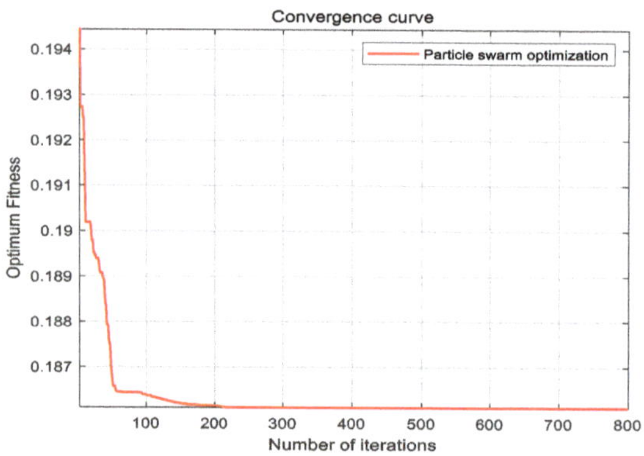

Figure 15. Fitness curve optimized by particle swarm optimization algorithm.

The error in the coordinates of the corresponding points before and after optimization can be obtained from Figure 16. Prior to optimizing the calibration parameters, the error in the x-direction of the corresponding points was approximately within 0.27, the y-direction error was within -0.65, and the z-direction error was within -0.12. After optimization using the particle swarm algorithm, the x-direction error was within 0.05, the y-direction error fluctuated within ± 0.07, and the z-direction error was within 0.07. It can be noted that the particle swarm optimization method demonstrated a relatively better improvement in the y-direction error.

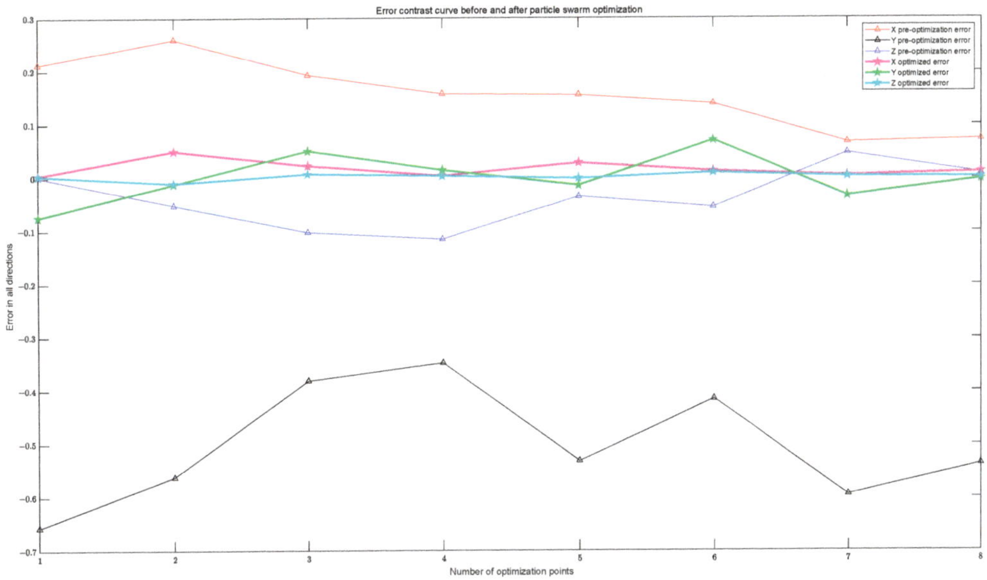

Figure 16. Particle swarm optimization before and after the coordinate error comparison curve.

Result 3: The fitness curve after optimizing using the honey badger algorithm is depicted in Figure 17. The algorithm terminated after 122 iterations, and the fitness value progressively decreased in a stepped manner with increasing iteration count. After 122 iterations, the solution approached zero and reached stability. Based on the convergence of the curve, it is evident that this algorithm exhibits noticeably faster convergence speed and requires fewer iterations compared to the previous two optimization algorithms.

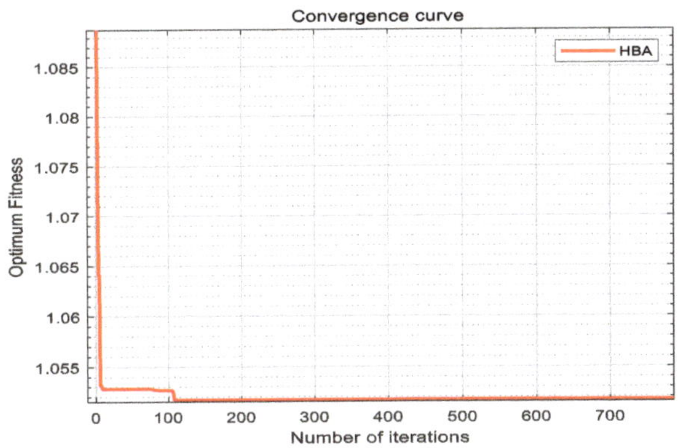

Figure 17. The fitness curve of honey badger optimization algorithm.

Figure 18 shows the coordinate error curve before and after optimizing the camera calibration parameters using the honey badger algorithm. Based on the error curve, it can be concluded that the honey badger optimization algorithm reduced the error in the x-direction from 0.56 before optimization to within 0.05 after optimization. Furthermore, the algorithm decreased the error in the y-direction from −0.66 to within 0.07 and in the z-direction from −0.14 to within ±0.06. These results indicate that the algorithm greatly improves the error.

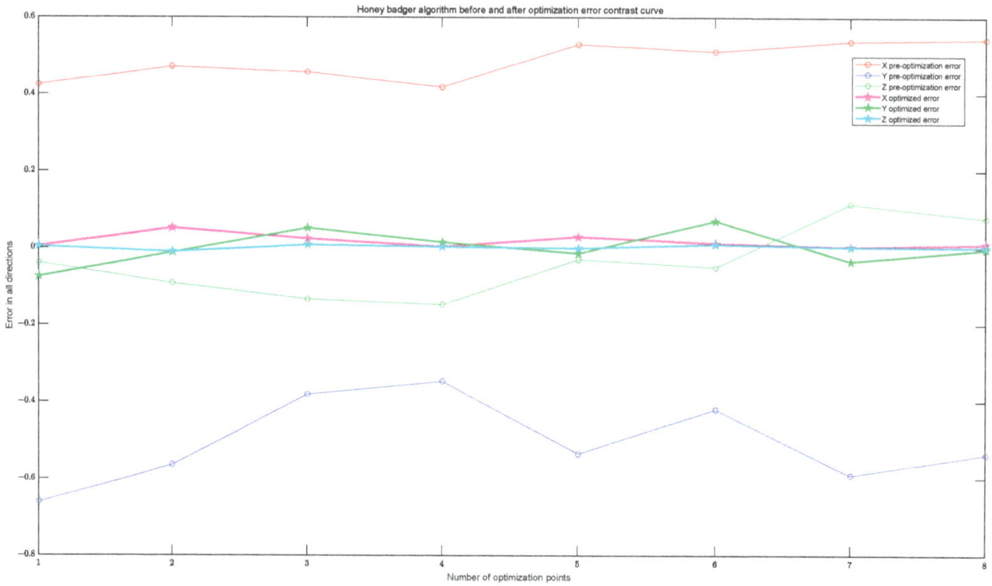

Figure 18. The honey badger optimization algorithm optimizes the coordinate error contrast curve.

Result 4: The fitness curve after optimizing using the improved differential evolution particle swarm algorithm is shown in the Figures 19 and 20. It can be observed that the curve depicted fluctuations throughout the first 150 iterations before stabilizing around iteration 400, at which point the calibration optimization results attain stability.

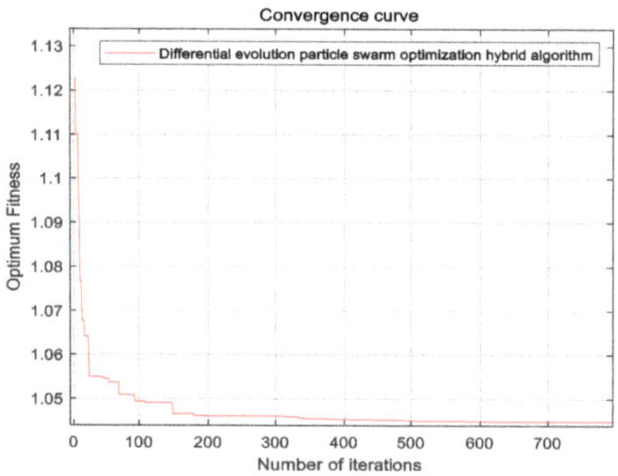

Figure 19. Improved differential evolution particle swarm hybrid optimization algorithm convergence curve.

As shown in the above figure, the error curve of the experimental data point coordinates before and after optimizing the camera calibration parameters using the mixed optimization algorithm based on improved differential evolution and particle swarm can be observed. It is apparent that prior to using the mixed optimization algorithm, the error in the x-direction was approximately 0.7, which was reduced to within 0.005 after optimization. Additionally, the error in the y-direction decreased from -0.66 to around -0.07, and the error in the z-direction decreased from -0.17 to near 0. These experimental results indicate that although the convergence speed and iteration count of this algorithm are not the fastest compared to several other optimization algorithms, the optimized parameter results are favorable. Therefore, the mixed optimization algorithm based on improved differential evolution and particle swarm demonstrates the best optimization effect with the lowest error.

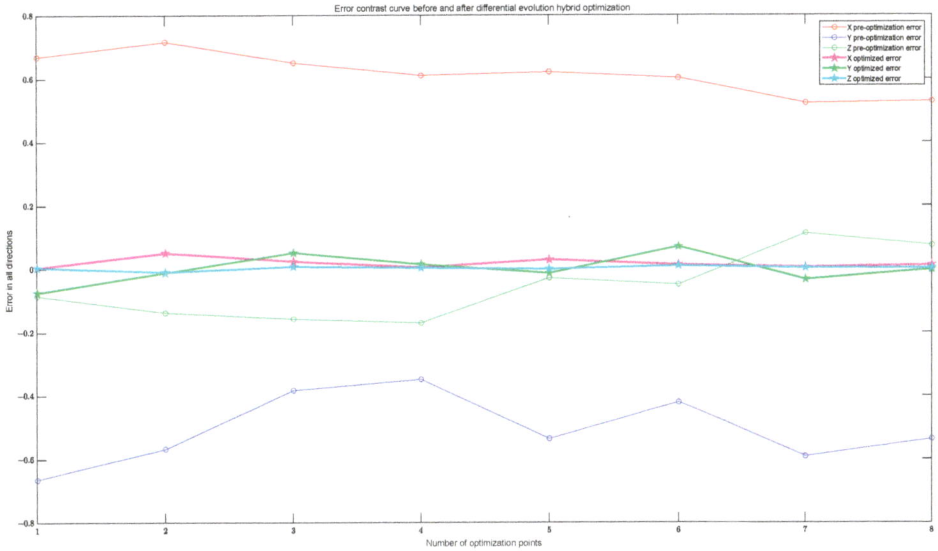

Figure 20. Improved differential evolution particle swarm hybrid optimization algorithm to optimize the coordinate error contrast curve.

Result 5: The fitness curve following DE optimization, as shown in Figure 21, concluded at iteration 335, demonstrating a stepwise decrease in fitness as the number of iterations increased.

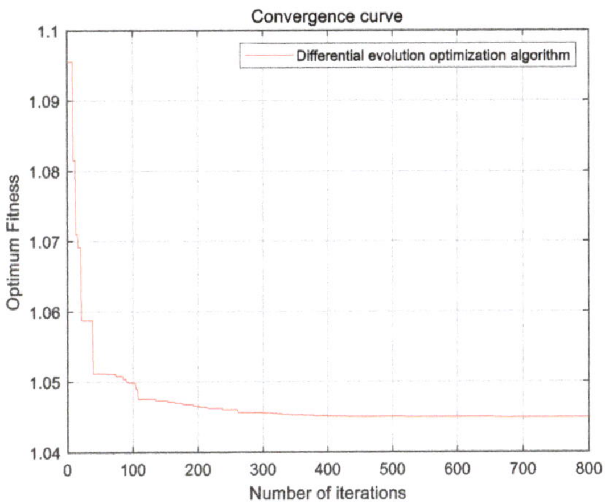

Figure 21. Fitness curve after optimization of DE algorithm.

As evidenced by Figures 21 and 22, notable changes in the corresponding coordinate errors are observed before and after optimization using the differential evolution algorithm. Specifically, errors in the corresponding x-coordinate parameters were approximately 1.5 before optimization and reduced to within 0.1 post-optimization. Errors in the corresponding y-coordinates were approximately 0.6 before optimization and reduced to within plus or minus 0.1 afterward. For z-coordinates, errors were within 0.2 before optimization and reduced to within 0.05 after optimization. It is evident that prior to optimization, error fluctuations were significant, whereas a substantial reduction in errors was observed following optimization.

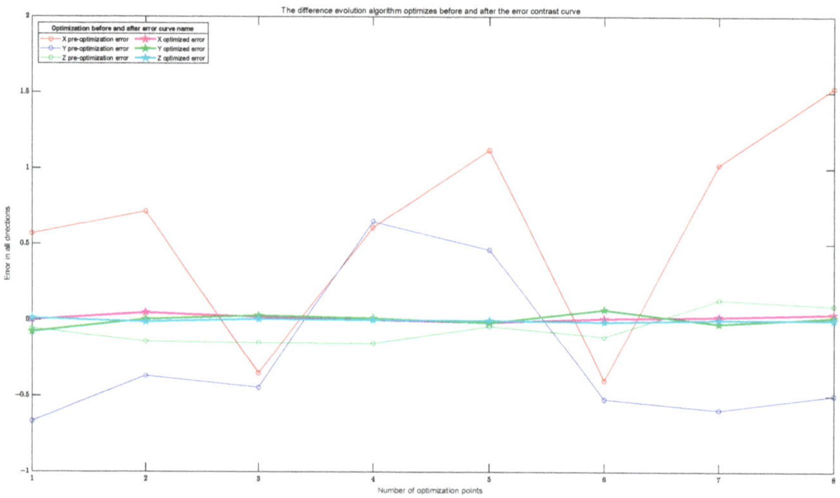

Figure 22. Comparison curve of coordinate error before and after optimization by differential evolution algorithm.

Upon comparison with the DE algorithm, it is noted that there is not a significant disparity in the fitness curves of the two algorithms. In light of this observation, additional experiments were conducted wherein the fitness curves of both algorithms were juxtaposed. The experiments were conducted over 200 iterations, yielding the following results (Figure 23):

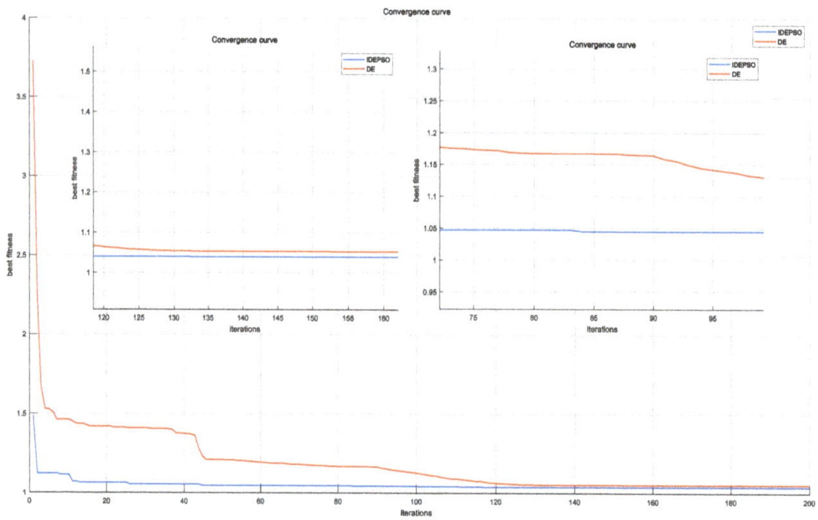

Figure 23. Comparison of convergence curves of the algorithm.

Specific indicators are shown in Table 6:

Table 6. Performance comparison of algorithm convergence curves.

	DE	IDEPSO
Fitness value	1.04488	1.04068
Number of iterations when stabilizing	128	84

The examination of the referenced charts reveals that the IDEPSO achieves a more rapid convergence compared to DE. It is observed that the proposed algorithm approaches stability after 84 iterations, exhibiting a stable fitness value of 1.04068, whereas the stability for the DE algorithm is reached after 128 iterations with a fitness value of 1.04488. In the context of mean-square errors (MSE) across various axes, it is evident that post-optimization, the algorithm we introduced demonstrates significantly reduced MSE values on all axes when juxtaposed with the DE algorithm. Furthermore, the enhanced Differential Evolution Particle Swarm Optimization (DEPSO) algorithm yields a mere 0.1690 root-mean-square error in the x-axis, 0.3780 in the y-axis, and 0.0638 in the z-axis. These calibration results undercut the calibration errors associated with the other three optimization calibration methods, substantiating the exemplary performance and high accuracy of our algorithm.

6. Conclusions

This paper first introduces the structure and coordinate system conversion of the photogrammetry system. It then provides a detailed description of commonly used camera calibration methods and investigates distortion models for camera calibration. Based on this research, an optimized method for calibrating cameras is proposed, which utilizes a new algorithm capable of accurately calibrating cameras. In this algorithm, iterations are incorporated into the mutation and crossover stages of the differential evolution process, and the dynamic adjustment strategy is refined. Introducing the concept of differential evolution ensures the preservation of particle population diversity, enabling the selection of the globally optimal particle at each iteration for the attainment of more precise results. Experimental comparisons among the calibration algorithm proposed in this paper and particle swarm optimization calibration, genetic algorithm optimization, and honey badger algorithm demonstrate its superior performance parameters, smaller calibration errors, and advantageous algorithm performance.

Author Contributions: Conceptualization, F.Q.; Validation, X.S.; Writing—original draft, X.S.; Writing—review & editing, F.Q.; Supervision, Guide experiment, Program making, H.H. All authors have read and agreed to the published version of the manuscript.

Funding: This work was supported by the National Natural Science Foundation of China under Grant 62073259; Key R&D projects in Shaanxi Province under Grant No. 2023-YBGY-380.

Data Availability Statement: The raw data supporting the conclusions of this article will be made available by the authors on request.

Conflicts of Interest: The authors declare no conflicts of interest.

References

1. Han, C.Z.; Zhu, H.Y. *Multi-Source Information Fusion*; Tsinghua University Press: Beijing, China, 2010; pp. 1–18.
2. Ma, T.L.; Wang, X.M. Variational Bayesian STCKF for systems with uncertain model errors. *Control Decis.* **2016**, *31*, 2255–2260.
3. Feng, X.X.; Chi, L.J.; Wang, Q. An improved generalized labeled multi-Bernoulli filter for maneuvering extended target tracking. *Control Decis.* **2019**, *43*, 2143–2149.
4. Rui, Z.; Yu, F.; Bin, D.; Jiang, Z. Multi-UAV cooperative target tracking with bounded noise for connectivity preservation. *Front. Inf. Technol. Electron. Eng.* **2020**, *21*, 1413–1534.
5. Sarkka, S. Recursive Noise Adaptive Kalman Filtering by Variational Bayesian Approximations. *IEEE Trans. Autom. Control* **2009**, *54*, 596–600. [CrossRef]
6. Xu, H.; Xie, W.C.; Yuan, H.D. Maneuvering Target Tracking Algorithm Based on the Adaptive Augmented State Interacting Multiple Model. *J. Electron. Inf. Technol.* **2020**, *42*, 2749–2757.

7. Liang, Y.; Jia, Y.G.; Pan, Q. Parameter Identification in Switching Multiple Model Estimation and Adaptive Interacting Multiple Model Estimator. *Control Theory Appl.* **2001**, *18*, 653–656.
8. Jiang, W.; Wang, Z. Calibration of visual model for space manipulator with a hybrid LM–GA algorithm. *Mech. Syst. Signal Process.* **2016**, *66–67*, 399–409. [CrossRef]
9. Liu, J.Y.; Wang, C.P.; Wang, W. SMC-CMeMBer filter based on pairwise Markov chains. *Syst. Eng. Electron.* **2019**, *41*, 1686–1691.
10. Huang, D.; Leung, H. Maximum Likelihood State Estimation of Semi-Markovian Switching System in Non-Gaussian Measurement Noise. *IEEE Trans. Aerosp. Electron. Syst.* **2010**, *46*, 133–146. [CrossRef]
11. Wang, Z.; Shen, X.; Zhu, Y. Ellipsoidal Fusion Estimation for Multisensor Dynamic Systems with Bounded Noises. *IEEE Trans. Autom. Control* **2019**, *64*, 4725–4732. [CrossRef]
12. Sun, W.; Zhao, X.Y. Maneuvering target tracking with the extended set-membership filter and information geometry. *J. Terahertz Sci. Electron. Inf. Technol.* **2018**, *16*, 786–790.
13. Mahler, R. General Bayes filtering of quantized measurements. In Proceedings of the 14th International Conference on Information Fusion, Chicago, IL, USA, 5–8 July 2011; pp. 1–6.
14. Ristic, B. Bayesian Estimation with Imprecise Likelihoods: Random Set Approach. *IEEE Signal Process. Lett.* **2011**, *18*, 395–398. [CrossRef]
15. Hanebeck, U.D.; Horn, J. Fusing information simultaneously corrupted by uncertainties with known bounds and random noise with known distribution. *Inf. Fusion* **2000**, *1*, 55–63. [CrossRef]
16. Duan, Z.; Jilkov, V.P.; Li, X.R. State estimation with quantized measurements: Approximate MMSE approach. In Proceedings of the 11th International Conference on Information Fusion, Cologne, Germany, 30 June–3 July 2008; pp. 1–6.
17. Miranda, E. A survey of the theory of coherent lower previsions. *Int. J. Approx. Reason.* **2008**, *48*, 628–658. [CrossRef]
18. Benavoli, A.; Zaffalon, M.; Miranda, E. Robust Filtering Through Coherent Lower Previsions. *IEEE Trans. Autom. Control* **2011**, *56*, 1567–1581. [CrossRef]
19. Peter, W. *Statistical Reasoning with Imprecise Probabilities*; Chapman and Hall: New York, NY, USA, 1991; pp. 1–35.
20. Noack, B.; Klumpp, V.; Hanebeck, U.D. State estimation with sets of densities considering stochastic and systematic errors. In Proceedings of the 12th International Conference on Information Fusion, Seattle, WA, USA, 6–9 July 2009; pp. 1–6.
21. Klumpp, V.; Noack, B.; Baum, M. Combined set-theoretic and stochastic estimation: A comparison of the SSI and the CS filter. In Proceedings of the 13th International Conference on Information Fusion, Edinburgh, UK, 26–29 July 2010; pp. 1–7.
22. Gning, A.; Mihaylova, L.; Abdallah, F. Mixture of uniform probability density functions for nonlinear state estimation using interval analysis. In Proceedings of the 13th International Conference on Information Fusion, Edinburgh, UK, 26–29 July 2010; pp. 1–6.
23. Henningsson, T. Recursive state estimation for linear systems with mixed stochastic and set-bounded disturbances. In Proceedings of the 47th IEEE Conference on Decision and Control, Cancun, Mexico, 9–11 December 2008; pp. 1–6.
24. Jiang, T.; Qian, F.C.; Yang, H.Z. A New Combined Filtering Algorithm for Systems with Dual Uncertainties. *Acta Autom. Sin.* **2016**, *42*, 535–544.
25. Matthew, J.B. *Variational Algorithms for Approximate Bayesian Inference*; University of Cambridge: London, UK, 1998; pp. 20–32.

mathematics

MDPI

Article

Multi-Objective Optimization of Cell Voltage Based on a Comprehensive Index Evaluation Model in the Aluminum Electrolysis Process

Chenhua Xu [1,*], Wenjie Zhang [1], Dan Liu [1], Jian Cen [1,2], Jianbin Xiong [1] and Guojuan Luo [1]

1 School of Automation, Guangdong Polytechnic Normal University, Guangzhou 510665, China
2 Guangzhou Intelligent Building Equipment Information Integration and Control Key Laboratory, Guangzhou 510665, China
* Correspondence: xchhelen@163.com

Abstract: In the abnormal situation of an aluminum electrolysis cell, the setting of cell voltage is mainly based on manual experience. To obtain a smaller cell voltage and optimize the operating parameters, a multi-objective optimization method for cell voltage based on a comprehensive index evaluation model is proposed. Firstly, a comprehensive judgment model of the cell state based on the energy balance, material balance, and stability of the aluminum electrolysis process is established. Secondly, a fuzzy neural network (FNN) based on the autoregressive moving average (ARMA) model is designed to establish the cell-state prediction model in order to finish the real-time monitoring of the process. Thirdly, the optimization goal of the process is summarized as having been met when the difference between the average cell voltage and the target value reaches the minimum, and the condition of the cell is excellent. And then, the optimization setting model of cell voltage is established under the constraints of the production and operation requirements. Finally, a multi-objective antlion optimization algorithm (MOALO) is used to solve the above model and find a group of optimized values of the electrolysis cell, which is used to realize the optimization control of the cell state. By using actual production data, the above method is validated to be effective. Moreover, optimized operating parameters are used to verify the prediction model of cell voltage, and the cell state is just excellent. The method is also applied to realize the optimization control of the process. It is of guiding significance for stabilizing the electrolytic aluminum production and achieving energy saving and consumption reduction.

Keywords: cell voltage; multiple targets; optimal control; electrolytic aluminum; aluminum electrolytic cell

MSC: 93C10

1. Introduction

The aluminum electrolytic production process mainly uses cryolite-alumina as a raw material, carbon as the anode and cathode of the electrolytic reaction, and is carried out by passing a strong direct current into the electrolytic cell to induce the electrochemical reaction in the cell, so as to complete the electrolytic aluminum production [1]. In actual production, costs play an important role to affect the development of capacity. And the cost of the largest proportion is the price of electricity, which varies and accounts for about 30% to 35% of the cost in different regions [2]. At present, with the decreasing resources of the Earth and the rising price of electricity, the cost of aluminum electrolysis production is getting higher and higher. Thus, it is important to achieve energy-saving and consumption reduction in the production of aluminum electrolysis. The method of energy saving in aluminum electrolysis is generally by improving current efficiency and reducing cell voltage [3]. Due to the complexity of improving current efficiency, most companies nowadays reduce the cell voltage to save energy and decrease consumption. However, the optimal cell voltage cannot be found by manually adjusting and changing a single parameter.

Cell voltage refers to the voltage through which the current passes in the electrolytic cell, and it is an important factor in the production process of aluminum electrolysis [4]. The parameters affecting cell voltage are the pole pitch, electrolyte level, molecular ratio, resistance, alumina concentration, aluminum output, electrolyte temperature, aluminum level, and electric current. All these parameters change in real time with cell state and cannot be measured online in real time [5]. DC power consumption is the most important part of production energy consumption, which is directly proportional to the size of the cell voltage, so appropriately reducing the cell voltage is one of the methods to achieve energy saving and consumption reduction in aluminum electrolysis [6]. At present, aluminum electrolysis production mainly relies on manual experience to control. However, due to the nonlinear and strong coupling relationship between aluminum electrolysis production parameters, to achieve the purpose of reducing consumption and increasing production, the manual adjustment of certain parameters may lead to the transformation of the state of the aluminum electrolysis cell to the evil cell. It is necessary to appropriately reduce the voltage of the electrolytic cell, and then use the corresponding method to optimally control the state of the electrolytic cell to produce electrolytic aluminum under the best conditions, conducive to energy-saving and consumption-reducing production.

Aluminum electrolysis data are characterized by strong coupling and nonlinearity, making it difficult to obtain to establish the relationship between sampled parameters and the cell state. To address this challenge of whether the cell state judgment is accurate or not. Researchers have predicted the aluminum electrolysis cell state by the methods of mechanism modeling, machine learning, and deep learning. Cui et al. proposed a method combined the multi-support vector machine with the cell condition classification based on fuzzy C-mean algorithm to predict aluminum electrolysis concentration, so as to judge the state of the cell [7]. He et al. proposed the use of deep learning to determine whether the aluminum electrolysis process would have an anodic effect, and thus whether the cell state would be in a normal or abnormal state [8]. Gao et al. used a neural network algorithm to predict the state of aluminum electrolysis cells [9]. Hou et al. proposed an LSTM-based prediction of aluminum electrolysis cell conditions [10]. Xu et al. proposed a multiple limit learning machine based on a genetic algorithm to realize the prediction of cell voltage [11]. However, due to the interference of external environment, the prediction effect often cannot reach the ideal state. Therefore, some other scholars have considered the use of different indicators such as current efficiency, temperature, anode effect, etc., to judge the state of aluminum electrolysis cell. Li et al. used the temperature as the main variable to determine whether the thermal equilibrium of the cell is in the normal state by thermocouple thermometry, infrared thermometry, and fiber grating thermometry [12]. Fan et al. achieved the optimization of reducing DC energy consumption by improving the current efficiency [13]. Some researchers have optimized cell voltage of aluminum electrolysis by using an intelligent algorithm to achieve energy-saving and consumption-reducing production [14,15]. Zhou et al. proposed an improved temporal convolutional network method to classify current sequences for the identification of cell states [16]. However, most of the above methods for optimizing and controlling aluminum electrolysis production are aimed at controlling a single parameter of the electrolytic cell, without judging the cell state from a global perspective. In order to obtain a more accurate cell state, more indicators need to be considered to reflect the production and operation state of the electrolytic cell.

In the actual production process, in order to reduce the industrial energy consumption, enterprises and researchers mostly adopt the strategy of reducing the cell voltage. However, the relationship between the cell voltage and the relevant technical conditions cannot be simply modeled using mathematical expressions [17]. Multi-index modeling can comprehensively consider multiple indicators or factors, making the model more comprehensive and closer to the actual situation. By considering multiple aspects, the complexity of the system can be better understood [18,19]. The relationship between the cell state and technical conditions can be well described by establishing a comprehensive evaluation index of groove state with multiple indexes. Compared with the traditional FCM algorithm, the adaptive FCM algorithm has stronger robustness, faster convergence speed, and wider applicability [20,21]. Therefore, the use of a multi-index comprehensive judgment model combined with an adaptive FCM algorithm can better judge the status of electrolytic cell. At present, the ARMA model is widely used in time-series data modeling and prediction for its advantages of wide applicability, simple use, and strong model interpretability. Gao et al. used the ARMA algorithm to analyze the historical data of abnormal population aggregation to predict the trend of abnormal human aggregation [22]. Sansa et al. established the ARMA model for small changes in solar radiation and predicted the changes in solar radiation more accurately [23]. The FNN algorithm has the advantages of strong adaptability, high parallel computing efficiency, strong generalization ability, flexible processing function approximation, and prediction problems [24]. Therefore, the ARMA-FNN prediction model is established to monitor the state of the prediction cell in real time. In addition, the establishment of relevant models according to the process itself can not only optimize the process parameters, but also optimize the model through continuous collection of analysis data [6]. In the aspect of cell voltage setting, the multi-objective optimization model of cell voltage can be established with the minimum difference between the average voltage and the target value and the good state of the cell as the goal, and the production operation requirement as the constraint condition, so as to obtain a set of better operating parameters, so as to achieve the purpose of energy saving and consumption reduction.

In this paper, when the cell condition is transformed into a wicked cell, a multi-objective optimization method of the cell voltage of the aluminum electrolysis process based on the comprehensive index judging model is proposed. First, a comprehensive index of cell states is established, and the cell states are categorized by the fuzzy C-means (FCM) clustering algorithm. Then, because of the severe hysteresis characteristics of the electrolysis cell, a cell-state model based on a fuzzy neural network is established to predict the trend of the cell state in the next 24 h. Finally, the important parameters of cell voltage are analyzed and simplified by using the PP algorithm. Aiming at the strong coupling characteristics between the parameters of aluminum electrolysis, the optimization setting model of the operating parameters is established to provide guidance for the energy-saving production of aluminum electrolysis.

2. Comprehensive Evaluation Model of Cell State

2.1. Mechanism Analysis

Aluminum electrolysis is a production process accompanied by many complex physical and chemical changes. There are many parameters to affect the cell state in the process, so that the cell state of aluminum electrolysis has complex and variable characteristics. A change in raw materials and operating parameters will probably transform a cell in good condition into a cold cell, hot cell, sick cell, or other bad cell.

The operating state of an electrolytic cell includes thermal balance state, material balance state, and stability state. The thermal equilibrium state of an electrolysis cell is defined as the state under the externally supplied electrical energy equaling the energy consumed by the decomposition of the alumina; that is, the heat income equals the heat expenditure. When the thermal equilibrium is disturbed, it will cause abnormal fluctuations in the electrolyte temperature. Material equilibrium is defined as a balanced relationship between the raw materials fed into the electrolysis cell and the raw materials consumed by the electrolysis process. The electrolyte height and the excess of aluminum fluoride can reflect the amount of material input, and the aluminum level and the amount of aluminum output reflect the amount of material consumption. If the amount of input is not equal to the amount of consumption, it will lead to fluctuations in the molecular ratio and the concentration of alumina in the electrolytic cell so as to cause the anode effect. Noise from the anode effect is a main parameter reflecting the stability of the electrolytic cell. In summary, aluminum fluoride excess (x_1), electrolyte temperature (x_2), aluminum level (x_3), aluminum output (x_4), alumina concentration (x_5), molecular ratio (x_6), noise (x_7), and electrolyte height (x_8) can be used as parameters to classify cell states.

DC power consumption is the most important part of production energy consumption. The relationship of cell voltage and current efficiency is defined as follows [25].

$$\text{DC power consumption} = \frac{2980 \times \text{average voltage}}{\text{Current efficiency}} \tag{1}$$

In the production process, the cell state is evaluated according to the experiences. The smaller the DC power consumption of the process is, the better the corresponding cell state is. That is, the average cell voltage is as small as possible, while the current efficiency is as large as possible. In addition, the anode effect reflects the stability of the electrolytic cell. The shorter the cumulative duration of the anode effect is, the better the cell condition is. Therefore, the degree of deviation of three parameters including the average cell voltage, current efficiency, and cumulative duration of anode effect from the ideal situation can be used as a comprehensive index for evaluating the state of an electrolytic cell.

2.2. Comprehensive Index of Cell State

After the state of an electrolytic cell is analyzed, the difference between its parameters in the equilibrium state and those in the ideal state is evaluated. These parameters contain cumulative effect time (T), average cell voltage (V), and current efficiency (W). The extent to the values of the three parameters deviating from the ideal conditions in the cell can be used as a basis for judging the cell state. In order to finish the optimization and control of the cell state, the cumulative incidence of anodic effects in a day is hoped to be less, the average cell voltage close to the optimized value, and the current efficiency achieving to 1. Therefore, the comprehensive cell state space is shown in Equation (2).

$$(u, v, w) = (\frac{T}{24}, \frac{V - V_{\text{sup}}}{V_{\text{sup}}}, 1 - W) \tag{2}$$

where V_{sup} is the optimized cell voltage. The u, v, and w represents the degree of deviation of the three quantities T, V, and W from the ideal state. A group of different (u, v, w) can represent a different cell state. The distance between (u, v, w) and the coordinate point of origin is used to measure the degree of superiority of the cell state.

Therefore, the composite index of cell state is defined as follows.

$$d = \sqrt{u^2 + v^2 + w^2} \tag{3}$$

where d is the distance between (u, v, w) and the point of origin. It means that the larger d is, the greater the corresponding cell state of the sample point deviates from the ideal state, and the worse the cell state is. On the contrary, the cell state is better.

2.3. Comprehensive Judgment Model Based on FCM Cell State

In the process of cell state assessment, it is necessary to cluster similar cell states together. It is called clustering analysis of electrolytic cell states. Fuzzy cluster analysis is a mathematical method of classification using fuzzy mathematical language. Aiming at the fuzzy characteristics of the cell state, the adaptive FCM algorithm is adopted to determine the affinity degree of the samples to realize the electrolytic cell state classification. The superiority of the proposed algorithm is that the number of clustering categories C of adaptive FCM takes values according to different experimental samples compared with traditional FCM. The affiliation matrix is defined as follows.

$$U = \{u_{ij} | i = 1 : n, j = 1 : C\} \tag{4}$$

where the samples of it are obtained for each experiment, and u_{ij} represents the affiliation of the i-th sample for the j-th class. The variable I explains the correlation of the i-th sample to the j-th class and is defined in the following equation.

$$I = \max(u_{ij}) \tag{5}$$

where the larger I is, the higher the correlation that the sample is assigned to that class. The samples set of cell state is set for $\{x(i,j)|i = 1 : n, j = 1 : p\}$.

The implementation steps of the adaptive FCM algorithm are as follows.

Step 1: Determine the number of cell state categories C, n is the number of samples, V_0 is the original clustering center, and set the initial iteration number t equal to 0.

Step 2: Calculate the cell state category classification matrix U of the sample according to Equation (6).

$$u_{ij} = [\sum_{k=1}^{C} (\frac{\|x_i - v_j\|^2}{\|x_i - v_k\|^2})^{\frac{1}{m-1}}]^{-1} \quad ,1 \le i \le n, 1 \le j \le C \tag{6}$$

where x_i is the i-th sample, v_j is the j-th center of clustering, v_k is the k-th center of clustering, and u_{ij} is the degree of affiliation of x_i to v_j. m is equal to 2.

Step 3: Calculate the clustering center for the next iteration $V(t+1)$ according to Equation (7).

$$v_j = \frac{\sum_{i=1}^{N} (u_{ij})^m x_i}{\sum_{i=1}^{N} (u_{ij})^m}, 1 \le j \le C \tag{7}$$

where v_j is the current clustering center.

Step 4: If

$$\|V(t) - V(t+1)\| \le \varepsilon \tag{8}$$

is true, then output the category partition matrix and the clustering center V. Otherwise, go to Step 1, where ε is the iteration stopping threshold.

Step 5: If $\bar{I}$ is maximal, stop. Otherwise, go to Step 1.

Step 6: The degree of deviation of the three quantities T, V, and W from the ideal state, that is (u, v, w), is derived from Equation (2).

Step 7: According to Equation (3), the composite index of cell state d is calculated for each category, with the larger d being assessed as a poor cell, and the smaller d being assessed as an excellent cell.

3. Cell-State Prediction Model Based on ARMA-FNN

When the electrolytic cell is disturbed and transited into a bad cell, the settings of controllable parameters can be adjusted in time according to the current state to prevent the electrolytic cell state from turning in a worse cell. To correctly predict the electrolytic cell state is the key to preventing the cell from transforming into a bad result. Therefore, a model for predicting the cell state is developed. As analyzed in Chapter 1, the variable d can reflect the production status of the electrolytic cell from a global perspective. Moreover, when the inputs of control system are unchanged, the variable d will evolve in a stable trend. When the inputs of control system are changed, the variable d will change with the original because a worker modifies the setting of controllable parameter in response to a change in cell state. Thus, the future cell state contains two parts. One is the historical continuation d_{k+1} of the current state d_k, and the other is the control effect of the current input of the system. To predict the future cell state, the composite index d is predicted by using a time-series method, and then a neural network is used to fuse d_{k+1} with the input parameters of the system.

3.1. Comprehensive Cell Condition Indicator Time-Series Prediction Model Based on ARMA

The time series of the comprehensive index d is similar to being stable. In a word, if the inputs to the system are constant, d will evolve in a relatively stable trend. The ARMA model is one of most widely used methods in time series. It firstly makes a difference operation to change the original series into a smooth time series. Then, an auto-correlation function (ACF) and partial auto-correlation function (PACF) are used to determine the initial order. Finally, the above function is estimated by the maximum likelihood method or weighted least squares method. The ARMA (m, n) model consists of an auto-regressive (AR) and moving average (MA). The general representation of the model is described in Equation (9) [26].

$$x_t = \varphi_1 x_{t-1} + \varphi_2 x_{t-2} + \cdots + \varphi_n x_{t-n} - \theta_1 a_{t-1} - \theta_2 a_{t-2} - \cdots - -\theta_m a_{t-m} + a_t \quad (9)$$

where x_t is the cell-state indicator d observed at moment t. $\varphi_i(1 \le i \le n)$ is the auto-regressive coefficient, $\theta_j(1 \le j \le n)$ is the moving average coefficient, and a_t is the white noise sequence.

The m and n in an ARMA model are generally determined by the Akaike information criterion (AIC) [27–29]. If the AIC of the ARMA (m, n) is minimized, then it means that the model is the most effective in forecasting the time series. The AIC criterion is shown in Equation (10).

$$AIC(l) = \widehat{\log \sigma_a^2} + \frac{2l}{N} \quad (10)$$

where $l = m + n$, σ_a^2 denotes the error variance of the model and N is the number of observations.

Because there is complex noise in the time series of the cell state, the AIC can easily fall into the local optimum. The ALO algorithm [30] is adopted to determine the order ARMA (m, n) of the model, and to predict the indicator d of the cell state in the time series. The steps of the algorithm are described. An individual $z = (z_1, z_2)$ represents a set of parameters of ARMA, and the fitness of the individual measures the performance of the algorithm for that set of parameters.

Step 1: Population random initialization. Randomly generate n ants and m antlions, set the upper and lower bounds of the search space U_d and L_d, set the population size N of antlions and ants, and set the maximum number T of iterations.

Step 2: Individual fitness values are calculated according to Equation (11).

$$f(i) = \min\left[\frac{\sum_{i=1}^{N} (d(i) - \hat{d}(i))^2}{\sum_{i=1}^{N} (d(i) - \overline{d})^2}\right] \quad (11)$$

where $f(i)$ represents the fitness value of the i-th individual, $\hat{d}(i)$ represents the predicted value of the i-th individual, and $\overline{d}$ represents the mean value of all samples.

Step 3: Update the location of ants, antlions, and elite antlions according to the ALO algorithm.

Step 4: Determine whether the termination condition is satisfied, if not then go to Step 3, if satisfied then obtain the optimization parameter (m, n) and execute the next step.

Step 5: The ARMA (m, n) model is applied to predict d_{k+1}.

3.2. A Prediction Model for Cell State Based on FNN

In the process of aluminum electrolytic production, the state of the electrolytic cell is affected by the workers adjusting the amount of aluminum discharged (x_4). The controllable parameters of electrolytic cell include alumina concentration (x_5), molecular ratio (x_6), and cell resistance (x_9). To obtain the future cell state, the method of fuzzy neural networks is modeled to predict and measure the cell state after controlled parameters happen to change. The inputs of the prediction model is the result of combining d_{k+1} with x_4, x_5, x_6, and x_9. The output of the prediction model is the future cell state (y). The y is defined in the following equation.

$$y = f(d_{k+1}, x_4, x_5, x_6, x_9) \tag{12}$$

The FNN method combines the excellent learning obtained using the computation ability of a neural network with the excellent fuzzy knowledge expression ability of fuzzy theory. Thus, this algorithm is often used in fault diagnosis of production and good diagnostic results are obtained [31]. FNN is used to model the future cell state, and its model structure is shown in Figure 1.

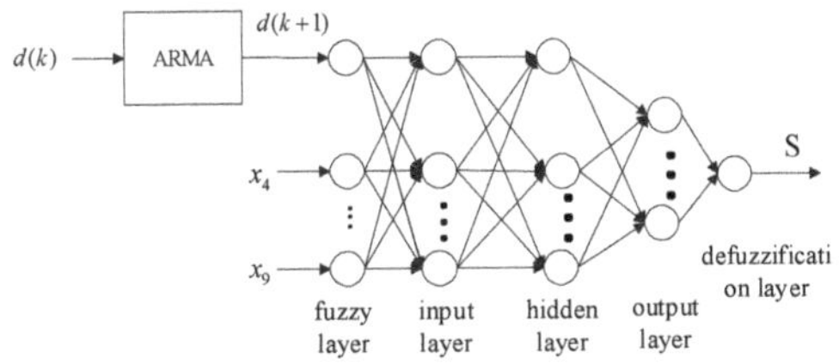

Figure 1. Structure of cell-state prediction model based on FNN.

Considering the single-peak characteristic of cell state, a Gaussian affiliation function is used in the fuzzification layer when modeling cell state. The Gaussian affiliation function is defined as follows.

$$U(x) = e^{-\frac{(x-c)^2}{2\sigma^2}} \tag{13}$$

where the parameter c represents the horizontal coordinate of the peak of the Gaussian affiliation function and the parameter σ represents the standard deviation.

The structure of the prediction model is based on a BP neural network. It has the advantage of setting the number of intermediate layers and the number of neurons in each layer according to the training effect of the model. The model has a good learning ability in dealing with nonlinear problems. The number of neurons in the fuzzification layer is the number of input parameters, equal to 5. The number of neurons in the defuzzification layer is 1. The number of neurons in the input layer is the result of the number of the output parameters multiplying the number of the fuzzification layer equal to 5. The number of neurons in the hidden layer is determined by the following empirical formula.

$$\rho = \sqrt{n+m} + d \tag{14}$$

where ρ is the number of neurons in the hidden layer, n is the number of input parameters, and m is the number of output parameters. $d \in [0, 10]$. Here, ρ is equal to 12.

4. Optimization Setting Model

For the excellent cell state, the operator can adjust the parameters to realize energy-saving production by reducing the cell voltage under the condition of ensuring a good cell state. When the electrolytic cell develops into an evil cell, the controllable parameter settings should be adjusted in time according to the current state to avoid the cell state from turning into a worse cell. For this reason, based on the above result of predicting the cell state in the Section 3.2, an optimized setting model is established according to the control target of adjusted parameters and the requirements of actual operation, and solved by the MOALO algorithm.

4.1. Influencing Cell Voltage Parameters

In electrolytic aluminum production, the electrolyte temperature, alumina concentration, and mole ratio are the main production parameters reflecting the equilibrium of the cell state. When the three parameters change, the conductivity of the electrolyte will be disturbed, so as to change the resistance of the electrolytic cell. If the production current remains constant, the cell voltage changes. The stability of alumina concentration is the key factor to ensure the stability of electrolytic production. When the alumina concentration is too low, anodic effects will happen; at the same time, the cell voltage will rise sharply. Pole pitch is defined as the distance from the bottom palm of the anode to the mirror surface of the aluminum liquid. When pole pitch transits, the resistance between the two poles will change, so as to affect the electrolyte pressure drop and ultimately lead to the change in the cell voltage. Changing the pole pitch is a more accurate and quicker way to change the cell voltage. Therefore, the main method used in the production process is to adjust the cell voltage by adjusting the pole pitch. Aluminum is a good heat conductor, so the height of the aluminum liquid affects the temperature and the heat balance of the electrolytic cell and the stability of the cell voltage.

The electrolyte level relates to the stability of the electrolytic cell. If the electrolyte level is too low, the anode effect occurs when the anode is not sufficiently wetted, which will lead to a high cell voltage. In summary, the main technical conditions affecting the cell voltage (y) were determined by electrolyte temperature (x_2), aluminum level (x_3), aluminum output (x_4), alumina concentration (x_5), molecular ratio (x_6), cell resistance (x_9), pole pitch (x_{10}), electrolyte level (x_{11}), and electric current (x_{12}).

4.2. Data Preprocessing Based on PP Algorithm

The actual production data contain a large amount of information, and there are numerous and only non-linear parameters affecting the cell voltage. In order to accurately analyze the parameters affecting the cell voltage to improve the accuracy of cell voltage prediction, the projection pursuit algorithm (PP) is used for data preprocessing [32]. The correlation of electrolyte temperature (x_2), aluminum level (x_3), aluminum output (x_4), alumina concentration (x_5), molecular ratio (x_6), cell resistance (x_9), pole pitch (x_{10}), electrolyte level (x_{11}), and electric current (x_{12}) to cell voltage are obtained by finding the optimal projection direction in the PP algorithm. The projection function in the PP algorithm is used to optimize the model, and the optimal projection direction can be found by a genetic algorithm to be (0.347, 0.089, 0.196, 0.550, 0.284, 0.628, 0.211, 0.083, 0.189). This is the value of the contribution of these parameters to the cell voltage. Since the contributions of x_3 and x_{11} are significantly smaller than those of x_2, x_4, x_5, x_6, x_9, x_{10}, and x_{12}, the input parameters of the model can be chosen as the electrolyte temperature x_2, the aluminum output x_4, the concentration of alumina x_5, the molecular ratio x_6, the cell resistance x_9, the pole pitch x_{10}, and the electric current x_{12}.

4.3. Model for Optimized Setting of Operating Parameters

In the process of electrolyte use, an electrolytic cell deviating from the optimal production state can be brought back to the optimal state through adjusting these operation parameters including temperature (x_2), aluminum output (x_4), alumina concentration (x_5), molecular ratio (x_6), cell resistance (x_9), pole pitch (x_{10}), and electric current (x_{12}). It is very important for energy saving to keep the fluctuation of cell voltage stable. Therefore, the cell state needs to be restored to the normal and cell fluctuation needs to be kept in stable range. Considering the production operation requirements as the constraints, the optimization setting model is established as follows.

$$fitness_1 = \min[f(\cdot) - V_{\text{sup}}] \tag{15}$$

$$fitness_2 = \min[S(\cdot) - 0] \tag{16}$$

$$\begin{cases} 172 \le x_2 \le 174 \\ 0 \le x_4 \le 40 \\ M_{base} - 1.3 \le x_5 \le M_{base} + 1.3 \\ O_{base} - 0.9 \le x_6 \le O_{base} + 0.9 \\ R_{base} - 0.002 \le x_9 \le R_{base} + 0.002 \\ 3.9 \le x_{10} \le 4.5 \\ 935 \le x_{12} \le 965 \end{cases} \tag{17}$$

where R_{base}, O_{base}, and M_{base} obtained by process analysis are the baseline cell resistance, baseline molecular ratio, and baseline alumina concentration, respectively. Here, R_{base} is equal to 0.0113, O_{base} is equal to 2.10, and M_{base} is equal to 3.32.

V_{sup} is obtained by Equation (2) and equal to 3.8446 in this paper [10]. $f(\cdot)$ is the average cell voltage from data collected at the factory, $S(\cdot)$ is the cell-state prediction model from Equation (12), and $\min[S(\cdot) - 0]$ represents the future cell state infinitely close to the optimal cell state. This optimization problem is that the value of the operating parameter needs to be adjusted to meet the requirements through effective intelligent optimization algorithm to restore the cell status to normal.

4.4. Optimization of Operating Parameters Based on MOALO

When solving multi-objective optimization problems, multiple objectives often conflict. As a multi-objective optimization set, Pareto optimal solutions [33,34] are often used to address the best trade-off between objectives.

The MOALO algorithm shows better convergence, accuracy, and robustness on solving multi-objective optimization problems. To search for a highly diverse set of Pareto-optimal solutions, the algorithm uses leader selection and archive maintenance to store Pareto-optimal solutions and roulette rules to select non-dominated solutions from them. The probability of choosing an antlion among them is as follows.

$$P_j = \frac{c}{N_j}, c > 1 \tag{18}$$

where N_j denotes the number of solutions in the neighborhood of the j-th solution and c denotes a constant. If the archive storing the optimal solution is full, the archived solution set will be deleted with the probability of $\frac{1}{P_j}$. Unlike ALO, the antlion position is updated in MOALO, and is described as follows.

$$Antlion_j^k = Ant_i^k, if\ f(Ant_i^k) < f(Antlion_j^k) \tag{19}$$

where $f(Ant_i^k)$ less than $f(Antlion_j^k)$ means that Ant_i^k prevails over $Antlion_j^k$.

The optimization setting model is solved using MOALO as follows.

Step 1: Population random initialization. Randomly generate n ants and m antlions, set the upper and lower bounds of the search space U_d and L_d, set the population size N of antlions and ants, and set the maximum number T of iterations.

Step 2: Calculate individual fitness values.

$$\begin{cases} fitness_1 = \min[f(\cdot) - V_{\text{sup}}] \\ fitness_2 = \min[S(\cdot) - 0] \end{cases} \tag{20}$$

Step 3: Update and archive locations of ants, antlions, and elite antlions according to the ALO algorithm. If the updated ant position is better than the selected antlion, the position of the antlion updates to the ant position.

Step 4: If the archive space is full, a portion of the solution is removed with the probability of $1/P_j$ using a roulette rule.

Step 5: Determine whether the stopping condition is reached. If it is reached, then the algorithm ends and the optimal operation parameter s^* is obtained. Otherwise, jump to Step 3.

To check whether the obtained operating parameters are optimal, the obtained values of the optimized setting are substituted into the cell-state prediction model to be verified. The optimization target is judged by analyzing the value composite index d. Furthermore, the derived optimization setpoints can be used to realize optimization control of the process.

5. Experimental Results and Analysis

All the experiments were carried out on MATLAB 2020a platform, and the experimental data were obtained from a factory site.

5.1. Results of Cell-State Evaluation Based on FCM

We took 150 samples for the experiment and set the parameters of the FCM cell state clustering model as follows. The fuzzy weighting index m is equal to 2, the maximum number of iterations is set to 20, and the iteration stopping threshold ε is equal to 10^{-6}. Experiments on FCM-based classification of cell state were carried out when C took different values, and the corresponding $\overline{I}$ values were calculated, and the results are shown in Table 1. From the table, it can be seen that $\overline{I}$ is at a maximum when C is equal to 3, so the parameter C being equal to 3 is used in the cell-state classification model. The results of the clustering experiments are shown in Table 2. The algorithm categorizes 150 sets of samples into 3 classes.

Table 1. The $\overline{I}$ of different C.

C	2	3	4	5	6	7	...
I	0.921	0.967	0.845	0.844	0.777	0.761	...

Table 2. Results of clustering.

Categories	Number of Samples/Size
Class1	9
Class 2	31
Class 3	110

The composite index d and its range were calculated individually for each type of sample as shown in Table 3. Since the d in Class 3 was the lowest, Class 3 was rated excellent and Class 2 was rated good. The d in Class 1 was the highest, so Class 1 was rated poor. In this paper, the 150 group samples were experimented on to cluster and evaluate the cell states. The results show that 110 groups remained excellent, 31 groups were good, and 9 groups were poor.

Table 3. Cell-state evaluation results based on adaptive FCM.

Categories	Index d	Result
Class 1	0.0758~0.6550	Poor
Class 2	0.0089~0.0545	Good
Class 3	0.0003~0.0086	Excellent

In the same way, current efficiency and apparent cell resistance were used as indicators to evaluate the cell state. Indicators and their ranges were calculated for each of the three categories of sample points and the results are shown in Table 4.

Table 4. Cell-state evaluation based on different indexes.

Categories	Range of Indexes			Result
	Index d	Current Efficiency/%	Cell Resistance/μΩ	
Class 1	0.0758~0.6550	72~85	14.0~16.1	Poor
Class 2	0.0089~0.0545	87~95	13.5~13.9	Good
Class 3	0.0003~0.0086	94~98	13.1~13.6	Excellent

Finally, the above model for judging cell state was validated using 31 additional data, and the results of the validation are shown in Table 4. It is worth noting that if the indicator value of sample is outside the known range in Table 4, it will be assessed as the closest category to it. It can be seen from Table 5 that the probability of correctly evaluating the cell state based on the comprehensive index model reaches 96.78%. It indicates that the proposed method can accurately be used to categorize and evaluate the current cell state. In addition, the experimental results of different assessment index in Table 5 shows that the composite metric d is more advantageous in improving the accuracy of the cell-state evaluation.

Table 5. Evaluation accuracy on different index.

Cell Status Index	Correct Rate/%
Current efficiency	77.42
Cell Resistance	93.55
d	96.78

5.2. Results of Cell-State Prediction Based on FNN

To illustrate the superiority of the ALO algorithm, experiments were conducted with the ALO and PSO and FWA algorithms, respectively, based on the same experimental samples. Firstly, the three algorithms are compared by using a public data set [35]. The population number was set to 30, the dimension was set to 30, and the three algorithms were iterated 1000 times, respectively. The average values and standard deviations of the three algorithms are shown in Table 6 (the bold font indicates the optimal). Secondly, optimization of cell voltage is carried out 10 times, the convergence speed of the three algorithms is shown in Figure 2, and the optimized cell voltage values are shown in Figure 3, respectively. The results of the 10-times optimization are statistically analyzed, and the standard deviation and mean comparison results are shown in Table 7.

Table 6. Comparison of baseline functions. (The bold font indicates the optimal).

Function	FWA		PSO		ALO	
	Mean	Std	Mean	Std	Mean	Std
F_1	1.19×10^{0}	8.15×10^{-1}	4.66×10^{-8}	1.19×10^{-7}	$\mathbf{3.16 \times 10^{-9}}$	$\mathbf{2.56 \times 10^{-9}}$
F_2	6.17×10^{1}	7.22×10^{1}	$\mathbf{9.73 \times 10^{-4}}$	$\mathbf{1.58 \times 10^{-3}}$	1.88×10^{0}	7.42×10^{-1}
F_3	1.18×10^{5}	2.49×10^{4}	1.49×10^{1}	6.75×10^{0}	$\mathbf{1.35 \times 10^{-6}}$	$\mathbf{1.20 \times 10^{-6}}$
F_4	7.88×10^{1}	8.30×10^{0}	6.29×10^{-1}	1.88×10^{-1}	$\mathbf{5.61 \times 10^{-5}}$	$\mathbf{7.89 \times 10^{-5}}$
F_5	4.98×10^{4}	4.45×10^{4}	4.69×10^{1}	2.77×10^{1}	$\mathbf{7.65 \times 10^{0}}$	$\mathbf{1.11 \times 10^{1}}$
F_6	1.04×10^{0}	4.80×10^{-1}	1.39×10^{-8}	3.73×10^{-8}	$\mathbf{2.15 \times 10^{-9}}$	$\mathbf{3.54 \times 10^{-9}}$
F_7	2.03×10^{-2}	7.17×10^{-2}	6.76×10^{-2}	$\mathbf{2.03 \times 10^{-2}}$	$\mathbf{1.32 \times 10^{-2}}$	$\mathbf{2.03 \times 10^{-2}}$
F_8	-6.02×10^{14}	1.84×10^{14}	-5.60×10^{3}	$\mathbf{1.17 \times 10^{2}}$	$\mathbf{-3.10 \times 10^{3}}$	1.34×10^{3}
F_9	2.53×10^{2}	4.58×10^{1}	4.58×10^{1}	$\mathbf{5.15 \times 10^{0}}$	$\mathbf{1.89 \times 10^{1}}$	5.42×10^{0}
F_{10}	6.85×10^{-1}	3.05×10^{-1}	4.38×10^{-5}	6.54×10^{-5}	$\mathbf{2.77 \times 10^{-5}}$	$\mathbf{3.66 \times 10^{-5}}$
F_{11}	9.36×10^{-1}	4.79×10^{-2}	$\mathbf{5.17 \times 10^{-3}}$	$\mathbf{7.38 \times 10^{-3}}$	1.82×10^{-1}	8.92×10^{-2}
F_{12}	2.77×10^{1}	2.91×10^{1}	$\mathbf{3.54 \times 10^{-9}}$	$\mathbf{1.09 \times 10^{-9}}$	9.60×10^{-5}	1.23×10^{-6}
F_{13}	3.57×10^{5}	9.25×10^{5}	2.20×10^{-3}	4.63×10^{-2}	$\mathbf{2.29 \times 10^{-10}}$	$\mathbf{4.21 \times 10^{-10}}$

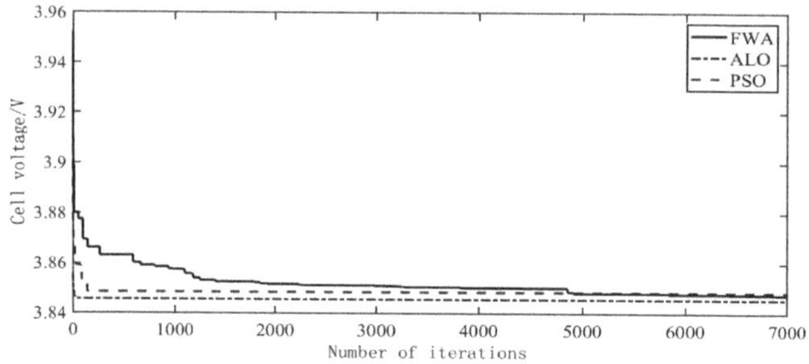

Figure 2. Convergence process curve.

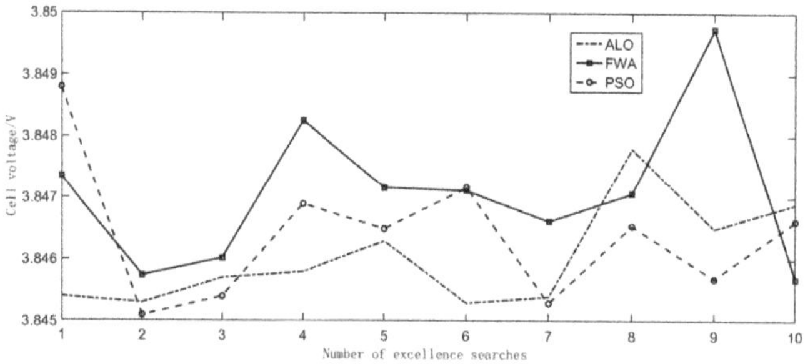

Figure 3. Cell voltage curve.

Table 7. Different algorithms standard deviation and mean.

	ALO	FWA	PSO
Average value	3.8454	3.8668	3.8464
Standard deviation	7.31×10^{-4}	10.83×10^{-4}	11.24×10^{-4}

It can be seen from Table 6 that the ALO algorithm is slightly worse than PSO in the three benchmark functions of F2, F11, and F12, but still better than FWA. Both the mean value and standard deviation of other benchmark functions are better than the other two algorithms, indicating that the ALO algorithm not only has a better optimization performance, but also has good robustness under the public data set. Compared with Figure 2, Figure 3, and Table 7, it can be seen that the convergence speed, convergence accuracy, and performance of the ALO algorithm in the actual data of aluminum electrolysis are superior to the other two algorithms, which is suitable for practical engineering problems of this topic.

A continuous time series of 300 sets of d_k cell-state metrics was selected as the experimental sample. Prior to the experiment, the samples must be differenced multiple times to smooth out the non-stationary time series. The AIC criterion was first used to determine the model order, and the ARMA (2,3) model was obtained in the experiments, and then this determined model was used to predict the time series of the composite index of cell state d. In addition, the ALO algorithm was also applied to order the model, and the resulting model order is (33,9), which is then used to predict d_{k+1}. The prediction results of the two models developed above are shown in Figure 4.

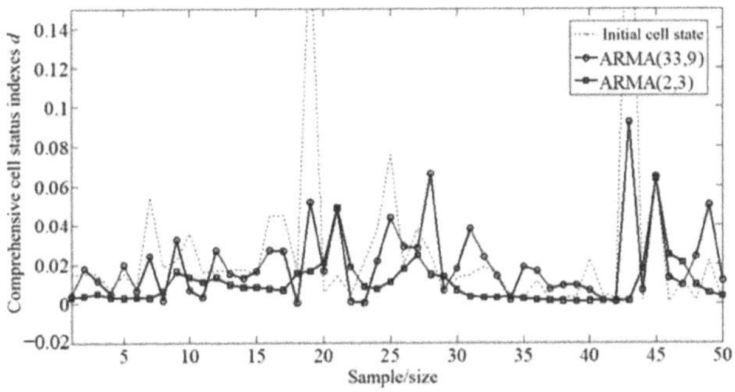

Figure 4. Time-series prediction of cell state index based on ALO-ARMA.

As shown in Figure 4, in general, both ARMA (2,3) and ARMA (33,9) can track the real time series, but the latter tracks better. To illustrate the tracking accuracy of the two models more accurately, the average prediction errors of the two models were calculated separately. As shown in Table 8, the tracking error of ARMA (2,3) is calculated to be 0.0139, while the tracking error of ARMA (33,9) is 0.0094, indicating that ARMA (33,9) has a higher tracking accuracy. The optimization of the order of ARMA using the ALO algorithm produces a set of optimal combinations of orders with the highest prediction accuracy, and the model has a higher accuracy than the model with the fixed order of the AIC criterion.

Table 8. Model prediction errors based on AIC and ALO.

Method of Ordering	Model	Prediction Error
AIC criterion	ARMA (2,3)	0.0139
ALO algorithm	ARMA (33,9)	0.0094

The composite indicators of cell state, d_{k+1} and x_4, x_5, x_6, and x_9 are used as inputs to the cell-state prediction model. After simply removing outliers, the processed 200 data sets were used as samples for the cell-state prediction experiments. Initially, 150 samples were selected as training data for the model and the remaining 50 data were used to test the trained model. The results of the cell-state prediction model are shown in Figure 5. As can be seen from the figure, 41 out of 50 samples are correctly predicted, with a prediction accuracy of 82%, indicating that the prediction model achieves a high level of accuracy and can be used as a reference for decision-makers in factories.

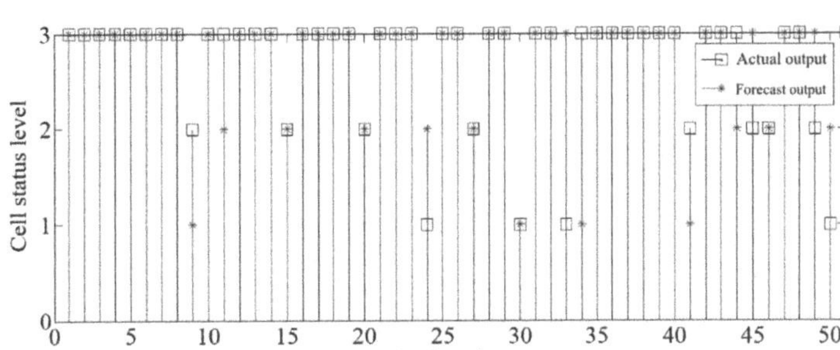

Figure 5. Training and testing results of cell-state prediction model based on FNN.

5.3. Optimization Setup Model Results

As described in Section 5.2 of this chapter, to obtain a set of optimized operating parameters, this experiment will solve the optimization setup model for 300 sets of historical data. A set of optimized operating parameters were found as follows. $x_4 = 32.0557$, $x_5 = 3.9611$, $x_6 = 2.2464$, and $x_9 = 0.0118$. Substituting this set of operating parameters into the cell-state prediction model, the prediction results show how the cell state changes when the electrolytic cell is set to this set of optimized parameters as shown in Figure 6. For example, at the ninth test point in Figure 6, when there is no output from the optimization setpoint, the state indicator d is 0.035, and the state of the electrolytic cell has deviated from the excellent state. This suggests that the optimization model can find an optimal set of operating parameters that will gradually bring a cell that has deviated from the optimum back to a good condition.

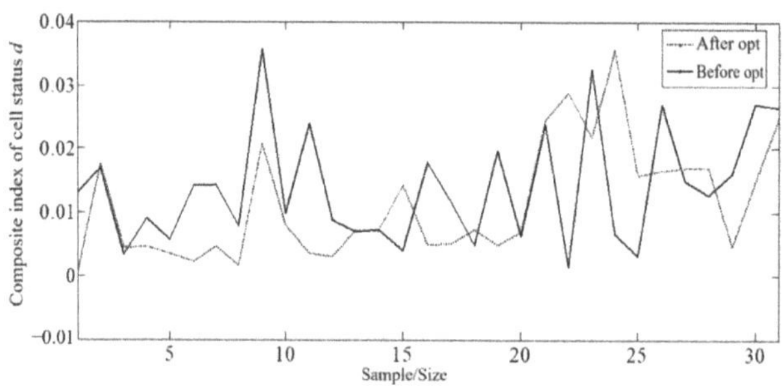

Figure 6. Cell state under optimal parameters.

Statistical information for the 31 state indicators d is shown in Table 9. The average value of the indicator d after optimization is 0.0026 lower than that before optimization, indicating that the cell condition is overall moving in the direction of excellence. The optimized variance is smaller, indicating that the cell state is gradually stabilized, and this set of optimized set values plays a role in stabilizing the cell state.

Table 9. Cell state index d before and after optimization.

d	Before Optimization	After Optimization
Average value	0.0140	0.0114
Variance	0.0092	0.0089

6. Conclusions

In this paper, a multi-objective optimization method for aluminum electrolysis process is proposed with the starting point of energy-saving and consumption-reducing production of aluminum electrolysis. To represent the three states of heat balance, material balance, and stability of the electrolytic cell, a comprehensive cell state index is defined, and the FCM is applied to judge the current cell state. In addition, a predictive model of the cell state was developed to predict the state after 24 h. Finally, the multi-objective optimal control of the aluminum electrolysis process is realized by establishing an optimization setting model. The method proposed in this paper focuses on the energy-saving and consumption-reducing production of aluminum electrolysis by setting operating parameters in case the cell condition develops into a bad cell. For the case of an excellent cell condition, the plant operator can realize energy-saving production of aluminum electrolysis by appropriately reducing the cell voltage without adjusting the electrolytic cell. When the cell condition develops into a vicious cell, the operating parameter optimization model can provide a set of reasonable operating parameter setting values. Then, the downstream control system can quickly stabilize the electrolytic cell and achieve energy saving and consumption reduction in the aluminum electrolysis production process through low-voltage production.

The above can provide a referable method for the aluminum electrolysis industry to achieve energy savings. However, since there may be more factors affecting the electrolytic cell with more uncertainties in an actual aluminum plant, the aluminum electrolysis production process should be analyzed from more perspectives in the future, such as such as cell condition diagnosis and superheat analysis of aluminum melting furnaces, in order to achieve a more energy-saving and higher energy-consumption reduction concept.

Author Contributions: Conceptualization, J.X.; Methodology, C.X.; Software, C.X.; Formal analysis, W.Z., D.L. and G.L.; Resources, J.C.; Data curation, W.Z.; Writing—original draft, C.X. and W.Z.; Writing—review & editing, C.X. and W.Z.; Funding acquisition, C.X. All authors have read and agreed to the published version of the manuscript.

Funding: This work was supported in part by the National Natural Science Foundation of China under Grant 62073090, and the Guangdong Polytechnic Normal University School Level Scientific Research Project No. 2021SDKYA118.

Data Availability Statement: The data presented in this study are not available due to privacy.

Conflicts of Interest: The authors declare no conflict of interest.

References

1. Liu, F.Q.; Qiu, D.S.; Gu, S.Q. Analysis on the Competitiveness and Development Trend of China's Aluminum Smelting Industry. *J. Eng. Sci.* **2022**, *44*, 561–572.
2. Yue, D.M.; Xu, W.; Wang, G.B.; Lin, H. Research on the current situation and development of Ningxia aluminum industry. *Light Metals* **2021**, 1–5. [CrossRef]
3. Zhou, Y.F.; Luo, L.F.; Wang, Y.F.; Li, C.L.; Zhang, F.F.; Zhang, F.P. Analysis and calculation of greenhouse gas emission reduction potential in aluminum electrolysis production process. *Light Metals* **2021**, 17–21. [CrossRef]
4. Zeng, Z.; Gui, W.; Chen, X.; Xie, Y.; Zhang, H.; Sun, Y. A cell condition-sensitive frequency segmentation method based on the sub-band instantaneous energy spectrum of aluminum electrolysis cell voltage. *Engineering* **2021**, *7*, 1282–1292. [CrossRef]
5. Xu, C.H.; Wu, G.H. Cell Voltage Optimization Method Based on STA-LSSVM. *Meas. Control Technol.* **2023**, *42*, 110–118.
6. Xu, C.H.; Tu, Z.C.; Zhang, W.J.; Cen, J.; Xiong, J.; Wang, N. A Method of Optimizing Cell Voltage Based on STA-LSSVM Model. *Mathematics* **2022**, *10*, 4710. [CrossRef]
7. Cui, G.M.; Yang, H.J.; Liu, P.L.; Yu, K. Prediction of Alumina Density in Aluminum Electrolysis Based on Data. *Comput. Simul.* **2018**, *35*, 305–309.
8. He, W. Research on prediction method of anode effect of aluminum electrolytic cell based on deep learning. *China Nonferrous Metall.* **2022**, *51*, 112–117.
9. Gao, T.; Zhang, K.; Shi, H.; Zhao, J.; Li, J. A two-stage classifier switchable aluminum electrolysis fault diagnosis method. *Trans. Inst. Meas. Control.* **2022**, *44*, 1708–1720. [CrossRef]
10. Hou, J.; Tian, X.F.; Kong, S.Q. Prediction of aluminum pot conditions based on LSTM. *Light Met.* **2021**, 33–37+62.
11. Xu, C.H.; Ping, J.M.; Lin, X.F.; Huang, Q.B.; Li, Z. Optimization Method of the Cell Voltage Based on The Improved Multiple Extreme Learning Machine. *Control. Eng. China* **2020**, *27*, 758–764.
12. Li, Z.Y.; Yang, S.; Zou, Z.; Li, J. Research progress of on-line detection for spatial distribution information in large-amperage aluminum reduction cells. *Light Met.* **2019**, *9*, 22–30.
13. Fan, Q.; Long, W.; Yao, L.Z.; Li, Y.Y. Multi-objective optimization of aluminum electrolysis based on functional evolution operator. *J. Sichuan Univ.* **2021**, *58*, 90–98.
14. Lin, M.; Ma, L. Research on Setting Voltage of Electrolyzer Based on LGBM-LSTM Algorithm. In Proceedings of the 2021 IEEE 4th International Conference on Computer and Communication Engineering Technology (CCET), Beijing, China, 13–15 August 2021; pp. 414–419.
15. Xu, C.; Zhang, J.; Cheng, R.; Chen, R.; Luo, Z.-G.; Li, H.-R. A ALO-LSSVM Model for the Cell Voltage Optimization in Aluminum Electrolysis Process. In Proceedings of the 2020 39th Chinese Control Conference (CCC), Shenyang, China, 27–29 July 2020; pp. 1431–1436.
16. Zhou, J.; Chen, X.; Xie, S.; Xie, Y. Anode Current for Aluminum Electrolysis Cell Condition Identification Based on Improved Temporal Convolutional Network. In Proceedings of the 2021 6th International Conference on Robotics and Automation Engineering (ICRAE), Guangzhou, China, 19–22 November 2021; pp. 35–39.
17. Lundby, E.T.B.; Rasheed, A.; Gravdahl, J.T.; Halvorsen, I.J. A novel hybrid analysis and modeling approach applied to aluminum electrolysis process. *J. Process Control.* **2021**, *105*, 62–77. [CrossRef]
18. Shuang, L.; Yong, B.L.; Zhong, Y.Z. Multi-index Evaluation Modeling Method Based on AHP and PCA and Its Application. *Inf. Control.* **2015**, *44*, 416–421.
19. Peng, H.; Zhang, S.; Li, L.; Qu, B.; Yue, X.; Wu, Z. Multi-strategy multi-modal multi-objective evolutionary algorithm using macro and micro archive sets. *Inf. Sci.* **2024**, *663*, 120301. [CrossRef]
20. Song, M. Visual Analysis of Project Investment Decision Information Platform based on FCM Algorithm. In Proceedings of the 2023 International Conference on Inventive Computation Technologies (ICICT), Lalitpur, Nepal, 26–28 April 2023.

21. Feng, Z.; Ding, W.; Cao, J.; Sun, C.; Shen, X.; Wang, H. Adaptive FCM Clustering Algorithm Based on Twin Multiple Population Genetic Evolution. In Proceedings of the 2021 IEEE 1st International Conference on Digital Twins and Parallel Intelligence (DTPI), Online, 15 July–15 August 2021.
22. Gao, Z.; Chen, Y.; Li, Z.; Li, T.; He, J.; Li, Y. An Improved Crowd Aggregation Prediction Algorithm Based on ARMA. In Proceedings of the 2022 6th International Conference on Innovation in Artificial Intelligence, Guangzhou, China, 4–6 March 2022.
23. Sansa, I.; Boussaada, Z.; Mrabet Bellaa, N. Solar radiation prediction using a novel hybrid model of ARMA and NARX. *Energies* **2021**, *14*, 6920. [CrossRef]
24. Wang, H.; Chen, Y.; Yu, H.; Xi, J. Social Cascade FNN: An Interpretable Learning-Based Decision-Making Framework for Autonomous Driving in Lane Changing Scenarios. In Proceedings of the 2023 IEEE 26th International Conference on Intelligent Transportation Systems (ITSC), Bizkaia, Spain, 24–28 September 2023.
25. Guo, J.; Gui, W.H.; Wen, X.H. Multi-objective optimization for aluminum electrolysis production process. *J. Cent. South Univ.* **2012**, *43*, 548–553.
26. Lotfan, S.; Fathi, R. Parametric modeling of carbon nanotubes and estimating nonlocal constant using simulated vibration signals-ARMA and ANN based approach. *J. Cent. South Univ.* **2018**, *25*, 461–472. [CrossRef]
27. Sharma, D.; Lie, T.T.; Nair, N.K.C.; Vallès, B. Wind speed forecasting using ANN, ARMA and AIC hybrid to ensure power grid reliability. In Proceedings of the 2015 IEEE Innovative Smart Grid Technologies-Asia (ISGT ASIA), Bangkok, Thailand, 3–6 November 2015; pp. 1–5.
28. Tang, W.H.; Röllin, A. Model identification for ARMA time series through convolutional neural networks. *Decis. Support Syst.* **2021**, *146*, 113544. [CrossRef]
29. Lv, W.; Zhu, X. Prediction of complaints at civil aviation airports based on ARMA model. In Proceedings of the Fourth International Conference on Computer Science and Communication Technology (ICCSCT 2023), Wuhan, China, 26–28 July 2023; Volume 12918, pp. 134–140.
30. Mirjalili, S. The ant lion optimizer. *Adv. Eng. Softw.* **2015**, *83*, 80–98. [CrossRef]
31. Nagabushanam, D.S.; Mathew, S.; Chowdhary, C.L. A study on the deviations in performance of FNNs and CNNs in the realm of grayscale adversarial images. *arXiv* **2022**, arXiv:2209.08262.
32. Zhu, J.; Hu, X.; Lou, Y. Ultra short term wind power forecasting method based on projection pursuit algorithm. In Proceedings of the 3rd International Conference on Applied Mathematics, Modelling, and Intelligent Computing (CAMMIC 2023), Tangshan, China, 24–26 March 2023; Volume 12756, pp. 559–563.
33. Koziel, S.; Pietrenko-Dabrowska, A. Constrained multi-objective optimization of compact microwave circuits by design triangulation and pareto front interpolation. *Eur. J. Oper. Res.* **2022**, *299*, 302–312. [CrossRef]
34. Gilani, V.N.M.; Hosseinian, S.M.; Behbahani, H.; Hamedi, G.H. Prediction and pareto-based multi-objective optimization of moisture and fatigue damages of asphalt mixtures modified with nano hydrated lime. *Constr. Build. Mater.* **2020**, *261*, 120509. [CrossRef]
35. Xu, C.; Zhang, W.; Tu, Z.; Liu, D.; Cen, J.; Song, H. Improved moth-flame algorithm based on cat chaotic and dynamic cosine factor. *Rev. Sci. Instrum.* **2024**, *95*, 024703. [CrossRef] [PubMed]

Σ mathematics

MDPI

Article

Neural Network-Based Distributed Consensus Tracking Control for Nonlinear Multi-Agent Systems with Mismatched and Matched Disturbances

Linxi Xu [1,2] and Kaiyu Qin [1,2,*]

1 School of Aeronautics and Astronautics, University of Electronic Science and Technology of China, Chengdu 611731, China; 201811100601@std.uestc.edu.cn
2 Aircraft Swarm Intelligent Sensing and Cooperative Control Key Laboratory of Sichuan Province, Chengdu 611731, China
* Corresponding: kyqin@uestc.edu.cn

Abstract: In practice, disturbances, including model uncertainties and unknown external disturbances, are always widely present and have a significant impact on the cooperative control performance of a networked multi-agent system. In this work, the distributed consensus tracking control problem for a class of multi-agent systems subject to matched and mismatched uncertainties is addressed. In particular, the dynamics of the leader agent are modeled with uncertain terms, i.e., the leader's higher-order information, such as velocity and acceleration, is unknown to all followers. To solve this problem, a robust consensus tracking control scheme that combines a neural network-based distributed observer, a barrier function-based disturbance observer, and a tracking controller based on the back-stepping method was developed in this study. Firstly, a neural network-based distributed observer is designed, which is able to achieve effective estimation of leader information by all followers. Secondly, a tracking controller was designed utilizing the back-stepping technique, and the boundedness of the closed-loop error system was proved using the Lyapunov-like theorem, which enables the followers to effectively track the leader's trajectory. Meanwhile, a barrier function-based disturbance observer is proposed, which achieves the effective estimation of matched and mismatched uncertainties of followers. Finally, the effectiveness of the robust consensus tracking control method designed in this study was verified through numerical simulations.

Keywords: consensus tracking; neural network; distributed observer; barrier function; multi-agent systems

MSC: 93C10; 93D50

1. Introduction

In recent years, there has been a significant increase in research attention toward the cooperative management of multi-agent systems, owing to its extensive applications in engineering, particularly in scenarios such as multi-UAV flights [1], multi-robot exploration [2], smart grids [3], and multi-sensor networks [4]. In summary, there are three typical architectures for the cooperative control of existing works in multi-agent systems, i.e., centralized, decentralized, and distributed [5,6]. Among them, distributed cooperative control architectures have been widely studied due to their advantages such as scalability and robustness. Existing studies on distributed cooperative control have concentrated on the following behaviors, i.e., consensus [7], formation [8], containment [9], and flocking [10] and distributed estimation [11]. Among them, consensus is the fundamental one, which refers to the eventual convergence of the states of all the agents in a multi-agent system. On the basis of the presence or absence of a leader agent, the issue of consensus for the multi-agent system can be further divided into two distinct categories: leaderless consensus and consensus tracking.

Consensus tracking refers to the capability of all followers in a multi-agent system to track the leader agent's trajectory. Recently, researchers have conducted thorough analyses on the constraints associated with multi-agent systems at the informational and physical layers and designed consensus tracking control schemes such as event-triggered control [12,13], finite-time control [14,15], bipartite consensus [16–18], security control [19], and fault-tolerant control schemes [20]. The issue of consensus tracking control for first-order multi-agent systems under a directed network topology was studied in [21]. On this basis, the authors in [22] focused on analyzing the problem of distributed consensus tracking for multi-agent systems that exhibit Lipschitz node dynamic models. They devised a consensus tracking protocol relying solely on the neighboring agents' relative states. They also demonstrated that with an appropriate selection of control parameters, achieving consensus tracking under a switching-directed topology is feasible. In addition, considering the bound of the control input, the authors in [23] put forward restrictions on the control input, and studies the tracking consensus under linear systems. Further, the authors in [24] used output feedback to design a distributed adaptive control input to implement output asymptotic tracking consensus. The adaptive protocol proposed was not reliant on system parameters and solely utilizes the relative outputs of adjacent agents. In addressing the convergence speed of consensus tracking control for multi-agent systems, the authors in [14] investigated the finite-time consensus tracking control issue formulated in the form of non-strict feedback. In utilizing the Lyapunov stability theory and the back-stepping method, an adaptive control input was developed to guarantee that the tracking error converges to a small neighborhood of zero in finite time. Furthermore, for high-order systems, a novel adaptive fixed-time consensus tracking control input was formulated through the utilization of fuzzy adaptive methods and fixed-time control theory in [25]. Considering the behavior expansion of consensus tracking, the authors in [26] studied the distributed bipartite tracking consensus problem of linear multi-agent systems under a single leader with a signed graph, in which the control input of the leader agent is permitted to be non-zero, while each follower's control input remains unknown. In addition, the authors in [27] considered a switched network topology and studied the distributed bipartite tracking consensus control problem under discrete systems. To address limited network communication resources, the sliding mode control approach with a dynamic event-triggered mechanism was employed in [28] to tackle the consensus tracking challenge in discrete-time multi-agent systems; meanwhile, the authors integrated a dynamic event-triggered mechanism into the sliding mode control system to reduce unnecessary data transmission. Furthermore, in [29], a novel approach was presented, involving the introduction of a fixed-time distributed observer with an event-triggered mechanism. Additionally, to effectively stabilize the tracking error system, an event-based fixed-time controller with an adaptive dynamic surface was developed.

It is noteworthy that the above literature focuses more on nominal multi-agent systems, i.e., there are no disturbances or uncertainties. However, due to the complexity of the environment and the inaccuracy of modeling, agents are inevitably subject to external disturbances and model uncertainties. Hence, there is a need to develop more robust control schemes for multi-agent consensus tracking. Overall, there are two main research ideas available for designing robust consensus tracking control schemes, i.e., feedback control [30–32] and feedforward control [33–36]. Feedback control mainly refers to further improving the performance of the system by suppressing disturbances or uncertainties. Typical control methods mainly include robust adaptive control [30], sliding model variable structure control [31], and H_∞ control [32]. In employing the fractional Lyapunov direct method, the robust consensus tracking problem in uncertain fractional-order multi-agent systems was investigated in [30]. An algorithm based on neural networks was designed to achieve distributed robust adaptation, ensuring exponential convergence of the consensus tracking error with fixed topology. Additionally, to tackle and alleviate the detrimental chattering effects associated with discontinuous controllers, a continuously distributed robust adaptive control scheme based on neural networks was introduced. In [31], the finite-time consensus tracking issue for multi-agent systems with disturbances was investigated through the application of integral sliding mode control (ISMC). Further, the adaptive mechanism and ISMC were integrated into the system to achieve disturbance suppression. Furthermore, in [32], the authors studied H_∞ consensus tracking control problem for linear multi-agent systems with directed and switching graphs while accounting for unknown disturbances. In this paper, the design criteria for consensus protocols are expressed in the form of linear matrix inequalities, leveraging the topologically dependent multiple Lyapunov function method and algebraic graph theory. It is demonstrated that ensuring the solvability of the consensus tracking issue for multi-agent systems under dynamic, directed topologies hinges on meeting specific switching conditions dictated by the average dwell time of the topology.

Different from feedback control, feedforward control mainly refers to estimating the disturbances or uncertainties through detection or a feedback channel, as well as further generating the feedforward term to achieve the compensation of disturbances and uncertainties through the control protocol. The key challenge of this method is to design an effective and easy estimation scheme to generate usable feedforward control terms. Typical robust consensus tracking control schemes based on disturbance and uncertainty estimation and compensation have been proposed in the literature, including active disturbance rejection control (ADRC) [33], an uncertainty and disturbance estimator UDE [34], a high-gain observer HGO [35], a disturbance observer (DOB) [36], and so on. The authors in [33] addressed the consensus tracking issue of multi-agent systems with second-order dynamics and unknown disturbances, employing the ADRC method. The tracking consensus protocol with random disturbance estimation was proposed to ensure system convergence. At the same time, real-time compensation was implemented for the random disturbance affecting each agent. By employing the UDE-based control method, ref. [34] delved into the robust consensus tracking control issue of switched multi-Lagrangian systems. Moreover, the UDE-based method was used to accurately adjust and asymptotically estimate the model uncertainty and disturbance. It is worth noting that several unbounded specified external disturbances can be handled with the help of applying diverse filters. Furthermore, the authors in [35] accomplished the design of a control protocol for multi-agent robust global consensus tracking. In employing a predetermined high-gain design technique, a control input based on the state feedback method was introduced to attain global consensus tracking and disturbance suppression within these systems, considering the dynamics of the agents and network topology. A distributed disturbance observer was developed in [36] to estimate the disturbances affecting followers. Subsequently, in leveraging this disturbance observer, a novel distributed control method was presented to address the consensus tracking issue with disturbance suppression within a fixed directed network topology, and its effectiveness was proved. It is worth noting that the above literature has not yet taken into account the uncertainty that the leader agent may have, and mostly focuses only on the robust control of the follower agents.

According to the above discussions, it is evident that few existing studies related to consensus tracking control have simultaneously considered the following constraints, i.e., external disturbances, mismatched uncertainties, and the leader agent being subject to uncertain dynamics. Therefore, this study focuses on the problem of robust multi-agent consensus tracking control with the above constraints. It should be noted that due to the unknown uncertainty of the leader's dynamics, only some of the followers are able to obtain the leader agent's position, while other higher-order information, such as velocity, acceleration, etc., is not available to all the followers. The main contributions of this paper are summarized as follows:

(1) A robust consensus tracking control scheme is proposed, which consists of three components: a neural network-based distributed observer, a barrier function-based disturbance observer, and a back-stepping-based tracking controller. Each of the three compo-

nents plays a different role, and in complementing each other's functions, it enables the follower to track the leader agent's trajectory. Moreover, the proposed control scheme is effective in achieving the convergence of the consensus tracking error and the uncertainty estimation error.

(2) A distributed observer based on neural networks was designed, and an adaptive update law of the parameters is provided, which can effectively realize the online estimation of leader information. The proposed distributed observer can estimate the leader's dynamic states (e.g., velocity, acceleration) for all follower agents despite the absence of direct higher-order information, enhancing the system's adaptability and responsiveness in uncertain environments.

(3) A barrier function-based disturbance observer was designed for a follower agent to estimate the unknown matched/mismatched uncertainties. In turn, the effective compensation of disturbances and uncertainties can be achieved using a simple feedforward control component design. Furthermore, the boundedness of the closed-loop error system was rigorously proved, while extra assumptions on the derivatives of the uncertainty terms were avoided.

The subsequent sections of this paper are structured as follows. Some theories that need to be used in this paper are introduced in Section 2, including graph theory, barrier function, etc. Section 3 then firstly establishes the dynamic model of the followers and leaders and describes the problem studied. The proposed robust coherent tracking control scheme is presented in Section 4. Firstly, a distributed observer based on neural networks is introduced, followed by the design of a perturbation observer based on the barrier function, and then the back-stepping method is introduced for the design of the robust tracking controller. Section 5 verifies the effectiveness of the control method designed through some simulation examples. Lastly, Section 6 summarizes the full work and discusses some of the future research directions.

2. Preliminaries

The relevant mathematical theories related to graphs (for network connections) and barrier functions will be covered in this part. Next, we shall provide the following definitions for several types of widely used notations.

Notation $\mathbf{col}_i^n[\delta_i] \triangleq [\delta_1^T, \delta_2^T, \ldots, \delta_n^T]^T$ or $\mathbf{col}^n[\delta] \triangleq [\delta^T, \delta^T, \ldots, \delta^T]_n^T$ generates a vector in the form of a column. The vector $\mathbf{1}_n$ is thus represented as $\mathbf{1}_n \triangleq \mathbf{col}^n[1]$. $\|\cdot\|$ represents the Euclidean norm. For a matrix $\mathcal{M} \in \mathbb{R}^{n\times n}$ with all the eigenvalues being real, $\mathcal{M}$'s maximum and minimum eigenvalues are represented as $\lambda_{\min}(\mathcal{M})$ and $\lambda_{\min}(\mathcal{M})$. Moreover, $\exp(\cdot)$ denotes an exponential function.

2.1. Graph Theories

A connected undirected graph with n agents is denoted as $G = (V, E)$, in which a node is represented as an agent and $V = \{1, 2, \ldots, n\}$ is the node set of the multi-agent system. The set of edges $E \subseteq V \times V$ defines the communication topology relationship between the agents, where the presence of an edge $(i, j) \in E$ signifies the existence of information exchange between agent i and agent j. The adjacency matrix $A = [a_{ij}] \in R^{n\times n}$ represents the connectivity relationship of the multi-agent system. $L = [l_{ij}] \in R^{n\times n}$ is a Laplacian matrix, which is defined as the difference between the degree matrix D and the adjacency matrix A. Specifically, the degree matrix D is represented by $D = \text{diag}[d_1, \ldots, d_n]$ with $d_i = \sum_{j=1, i\neq j}^{n} a_{ij}$.

This paper explores leader-tracking issues, with the leader being treated as an external entity in a multi-agent system. Specifically, the node set related to $\mathcal{G}$ excludes the leader agent node. To express the relationship between the leader and a follower, we define $B = \mathbf{diag}_i^n[b_i]$, where the ith agent can receive state information from the leader agent; we denote this using $b_i > 0$ to represent information weight, or else $b_i = 0$. Hence, it can be derived that $(L + B)$ forms a positive definite matrix.

2.2. Barrier Function

Definition 1 ([37]). *A barrier function is defined for some $\lambda > 0$ as follows:*

$$F_p(x) = \frac{|x|}{\lambda - |x|}. \tag{1}$$

It is a continuous even function with the following three properties:

- $F_p : x \in (-\lambda, \lambda) \to F_p(x) \in [0, \infty)$ *is strictly increasing in the interval* $[0, \lambda)$.
- $\lim_{|x| \to \lambda} F_p(x) = +\infty$.
- *The function* $F_p(x)$ *has a unique minimum as* $F_p(0) = 0$.

Lemma 1 ([37]). *Take into account the following system:*

$$\dot{\delta}(t) = u(t) + d(t), \tag{2}$$

in which $0 \leq |d(t)| \leq d_{\max}$, *and* $d_{\max}$ *is a positive constant that is unknown. Assume that the function* $u(t)$ *is represented as*

$$u(t) = -F(t, \delta(t))\mathrm{sgn}(\delta(t)), \tag{3}$$

and

$$F(t, \delta(t)) = \begin{cases} F_\delta(t), \dot{F}_\delta(t) = \bar{F}|\delta(t)|, \ if\ 0 < t \leq \bar{t}, \\ F_p(\delta(t)), \ if\ t > \bar{t}, \end{cases} \tag{4}$$

where $F_\delta(0)$ *and* $\bar{F}$ *hold the following conditions* $F_\delta(0) > 0$ *and* $\bar{F} > 0$, *respectively.* $\mathrm{sgn}(\cdot)$ *denotes a signum function. Then, we can obtain that the variable* $\delta(t)$ *can converge to the domain* $|\delta(t)| \leq \delta_1$ *within a finite amount of time* T_δ, *where* $\delta_1 = \lambda\left(\frac{d_{\max}}{d_{\max}+1}\right)$.

3. Problem Statement

In this paper, we consider the following second-order nonlinear multi-agent system with both unmatched and matched uncertainties:

$$\begin{cases} \dot{x}_{i1}(t) = x_{i2}(t) + d_{i1}(t), \\ \dot{x}_{i2}(t) = f_i(x_{i1}(t), x_{i2}(t)) + g_i(x_{i1}(t), x_{i2}(t))u_i(t) + d_{i2}(t), \\ y_i(t) = x_{i1}(t), \end{cases} \tag{5}$$

where $x_{i1} \in \mathcal{R}$ and $x_{i2} \in \mathcal{R}$ are the system states, $y_i \in \mathcal{R}$ is the system output, $f_i(x_{i1}, x_{i2}) \in \mathcal{R}$ is the known nonlinear function, $g_i(x_{i1}, x_{i2}) \in \mathcal{R}\backslash\{0\}$ is the non-zero control gain, and $d_{i1} \in \mathcal{R}$ and $d_{i2} \in \mathcal{R}$ represent the aggregated uncertainties across various channels, encompassing model and parameter uncertainties as well as external disturbances. The agents are indexed by $i \in \{1, 2, \ldots, n\} \triangleq \mathcal{I}$. The system described by Equation (5) is taken from [38], which describes the motion of objects in general, such as angular motion.

Assumption 1. *The mismatched uncertainties* d_{i1} *and external disturbances* d_{i2} *are bounded, i.e.,* $|d_{i1}| \leq D_1$ *and* $|d_{i2}| \leq D_2$ *hold, where* D_1 *and* D_2 *are unknown positive constants.*

Furthermore, the target agent with an index of 0 can be modeled as a differential equation:

$$\begin{cases} \dot{x}_0(t) = f_0(x_0, t), \\ y_0(t) = x_0(t), \end{cases} \tag{6}$$

where the smooth function $f_0(x_0, t)$ is unknown to all other agents. $x_0(t)$ represents the state variable. The agent designated as the leader is referred to as the target agent, while the other ith agents ($i \in \mathcal{I}$) are referred to as followers. The output $y_0(t)$ corresponds to the information that is accessible to at least one follower.

Definition 2 (Bounded Consensus Tracking Control). *The control protocol $u_i(t)$ in (5) is said to be a bounded consensus tracking control if the state variables $x_i(t)$ of all the followers end up boundedly tracking the leader's, i.e., for all $i \in \mathcal{I}$*

$$|x_{i1}(t) - x_0(t)| \leq b, \forall t \geq t_b, \tag{7}$$

where $b \geq 0$ is the ultimate bound of the tracking error, and $t_b \geq 0$ is the corresponding settling time.

In order to realize the bounded consensus tracking control problem proposed by the above definition, we need to design the corresponding control strategy for the followers.

4. Main Results

In this section, a two-module robust consensus tracking control scheme is proposed for the ith agent shown in Figure 1 to tackle the issue at hand. The scheme combines a neural network-based distributed observer and a back-stepping-based tracking controller. Firstly, the neural network-based distributed observer is able to efficiently estimate the information of the leader through all the followers. Then, the back-stepping-based tracking controller was designed to enable the followers to track the estimates of the trajectory of the leader, which is generated by a distributed observer. Eventually, the tracking of the leader's trajectory can be achieved.

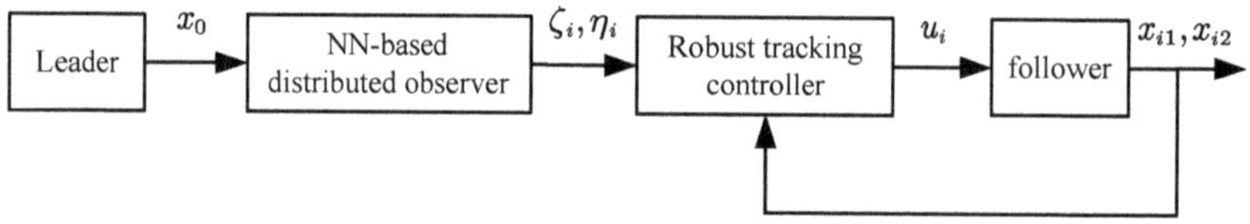

Figure 1. The proposed control scheme.

As discussed in the preceding section, there are two issues that need to be addressed in this process: (1) the leader dynamics involve an uncertainty term, thereby causing each follower agent to lack precise velocity and acceleration information about the leader agent; and (2) each follower agent is subject to matched and mismatched uncertainties. Thus, followers need not only a valid estimate of the leader's information, but also compensation for the unknown uncertainty terms.

4.1. Neural Network-Based Distributed Observer Design

The initial step in addressing the robust consensus tracking issues involves mitigating uncertainties within the leader agent model. In order to achieve this goal, we need to use neural networks to fit unknown function values. Therefore, we need the following assumption:

Assumption 2. *$\gamma(x,t) \triangleq f_0(x,t)$ can be expressed on a prescribed compact set $\Omega_{\gamma i} \subset \mathbb{R}^2$ using linearly parameterized neural networks as follows:*

$$\gamma(x,t) = \phi_\gamma^T(x,t)\theta_\gamma + e_\gamma, \tag{8}$$

where $\phi_\gamma^T(x,t) = \boldsymbol{col}_k^{h_{\gamma i}}[\phi_{\gamma i,k}(x,t)] \in \mathbb{R}^{h_{\gamma i}}$; the parameter $\theta_\gamma = \boldsymbol{col}_k^{h_{\gamma i}}[\theta_{\gamma i,k}] \in \mathbb{R}^{h_{\gamma i}}$ is an unknown constant vector; and e_γ is the NN approximation error.

Remark 1. *In traditional adaptive control theories, extensive research has focused on linearly parameterized models of unknown nonlinear dynamics [39,40]. Assumption 2 will be satisfied once the fundamental function ϕ_γ is suitably chosen, and the receptive fields cover the respective value ranges of the smooth functions $\gamma(x,t)$.*

Throughout the paper, $\hat{\alpha}$ is used to represent the estimate of a quantity α, and $\tilde{\alpha} \triangleq \hat{\alpha} - \alpha$, to denote its estimation error. Then, the estimate of the ith agent for $\gamma(x,t)$ is $\hat{\gamma}_i(x,t) \triangleq \phi_\gamma^T(x,t)\hat{\theta}_{\gamma i}$, and the corresponding estimate error is designated by $\tilde{\gamma}_i(x,t)$. The following formula shows that

$$\underline{\tilde{\gamma}_i}(x,t) \triangleq \phi_\gamma^T(x,t)\tilde{\theta}_{\gamma i} = \phi_\gamma^T(x,t)[\hat{\theta}_{\gamma i} - \theta_\gamma], \tag{9}$$

and the estimation errors can also be represented as

$$\tilde{\gamma}_i(x,t) = \underline{\tilde{\gamma}_i}(x,t) - e_\gamma. \tag{10}$$

Based on the NN's approximation theorems, we can make the following assumption.

Assumption 3. *The approximation error e_γ is bounded by unknown constants δ_γ in the corresponding compact set Ω_γ. That is, $|e_{\gamma i}| \leq \delta_{\gamma i}$.*

In order to obtain the estimated value of the leader's state, we can construct the following neural network-based distributed observer:

$$\begin{aligned}
\dot{\zeta}_i =& \eta_i, \\
\dot{\eta}_i =& -k_\epsilon \epsilon_{1i} - k_p p_{2i} + \phi_\gamma^T(\zeta_i,t)\dot{\hat{\theta}}_{\gamma i} + \frac{\partial}{\partial \zeta}\phi_\gamma^T(\zeta_i,t)\hat{\theta}_{\gamma i}\eta_i + \frac{\partial}{\partial t}\phi_\gamma^T(\zeta_i,t)\hat{\theta}_{\gamma i} \\
&- \mathrm{rec}(p_{2i})(|k_\epsilon \epsilon_{1i}| + |k_\epsilon \epsilon_{1i}|\hat{\delta}_{\gamma i}), \\
\epsilon_{1i} =& \sum_{j=1}^{n} l_{ij}(\zeta_i - \zeta_j) + b_i(\zeta_i - x_0),
\end{aligned} \tag{11}$$

where ζ_i and η_i are distributed observer states, and k_ϵ and k_p are distributed observer gains. Moreover, $\mathrm{rec}(\alpha)$ is the safe reciprocal function such that $\mathrm{rec}(\alpha) \cdot \alpha$ equals unity for non-zero α, or equals zero otherwise.

Through formulating the subsequent coordinate transformation,

$$\begin{aligned}
p_{1i} &= \zeta_i - x_0, \\
p_{2i} &= \eta_i - \hat{\gamma}_i(\zeta_i,t),
\end{aligned} \tag{12}$$

one obtains

$$\begin{aligned}
\dot{p}_{2i} =& \dot{\eta}_i - \phi_\gamma^T(\zeta_i,t)\dot{\hat{\theta}}_{\gamma i} - \frac{\partial}{\partial \zeta}\phi_\gamma^T(\zeta_i,t)\hat{\theta}_{\gamma i}\dot{\zeta}_i - \frac{\partial}{\partial t}\phi_\gamma^T(\zeta_i,t)\hat{\theta}_{\gamma i} \\
=& \dot{\eta}_i - \phi_\gamma^T(\zeta_i,t)\dot{\hat{\theta}}_{\gamma i} - \frac{\partial}{\partial \zeta}\phi_\gamma^T(\zeta_i,t)\hat{\theta}_{\gamma i}\eta_i - \frac{\partial}{\partial t}\phi_\gamma^T(\zeta_i,t)\hat{\theta}_{\gamma i}.
\end{aligned} \tag{13}$$

Accordingly,

$$\dot{p}_{2i} = -k_\epsilon \epsilon_{1i} - k_p p_{2i} - \mathrm{rec}(p_{2i})(|k_\epsilon \epsilon 1i| + |k_\epsilon \epsilon 1i|\hat{\delta}_{\gamma i}). \tag{14}$$

Let $X \triangleq \mathbf{col}_i^n[\zeta_i]$, $P_1 \triangleq \mathbf{col}_i^n[p_{1i}]$, $P_2 \triangleq \mathbf{col}_i^n[p_{2i}]$, $X_0 \triangleq x_0\mathbf{1}_n$, $\Delta = \mathbf{col}_i^n[\mathrm{rec}(p_{2i})(|k_\epsilon \epsilon_{1i} + |k_\epsilon \epsilon_{1i}|\hat{\delta}_{\gamma i})]$, $E_1 \triangleq \mathbf{col}_i^n[\epsilon_{1i}]$, $\hat{R} \triangleq \mathbf{col}_i^n[\hat{\gamma}_i(\zeta_i,t)]$, $\underline{\tilde{R}} \triangleq \mathbf{col}_i^n[\underline{\tilde{\gamma}}(\zeta_i,t)]$, and $E_\gamma = \mathbf{col}_i^n[e_{\gamma i}]$. Apparently, $E_1 = (L+B)P_1$.

The matrix forms of state variables p_{1i} and p_{2i} are as follows:

$$\begin{aligned}
P_1 &= X - X_0, \\
P_2 &= \dot{X} - \hat{R} = \dot{X} - R - \underline{\tilde{R}} + E_\gamma,
\end{aligned} \tag{15}$$

with the following compact models:

$$\begin{aligned} \dot{P}_1 &= \dot{X} - \dot{X}_0, \\ \dot{P}_2 &= -k_\epsilon (L+B)P_1 - k_p P_2 - \Delta. \end{aligned} \tag{16}$$

Their adaptive rules are

$$\begin{aligned} \dot{\hat{\theta}}_{\gamma i} &= -k_f k_\epsilon \epsilon_{1i} \phi_\gamma(\zeta_i, t), \\ \dot{\hat{\delta}}_{\gamma i} &= k_\delta |k_\epsilon \epsilon_{1i}|. \end{aligned} \tag{17}$$

Remark 2. *As shown in (17), the adaptive law of $\hat{\delta}_{\gamma i}$ contains an absolute value function $|k_\epsilon \epsilon_{1i}|$. This implies that $\hat{\delta}_{\gamma i}$ is an increasing function until the consensus tracking error ϵ_{1i} is 0. When this parameter $\hat{\delta}_{\gamma i}$ remains constant, it also indicates that the consensus tracking control objective of this paper is achieved. It should be noted that this absolute value function $|k_\epsilon \epsilon_{1i}|$ does not produce chattering. In fact, this estimation value $\hat{\delta}_{\gamma i}$ compensates for the neural network fitting error $e_{\gamma i}$. In the proof, how to ensure the convergence of the closed-loop error system will be further described later on.*

Theorem 1. *The distributed observer given by* (11) *with the adaptive algorithm established in* (17) *achieves the estimation of the leader's states, i.e.,* $\lim_{t\to\infty}(\zeta_i - x_0) = 0$ *for all* $i \in \mathcal{I}$, *under Assumptions 2 and 3, if*

$$\frac{\partial}{\partial x}\gamma(x,t) < 0. \tag{18}$$

Proof. The positive definite Lyapunov function is

$$V_1 = \frac{k_\epsilon}{2} P_1^T (L+B) P_1 + \frac{1}{2} P_2^T P_2 + \frac{1}{2k_f} \sum_{i=1}^{n} \tilde{\theta}_{\gamma i}^T \tilde{\theta}_{\gamma i} + \frac{1}{2k_\delta} \sum_{i=1}^{n} \tilde{\delta}_{\gamma i}^T \tilde{\delta}_{\gamma i}, \tag{19}$$

and its derivative is

$$\begin{aligned} \dot{V}_1 =& k_\epsilon P_1^T (L+B)(\dot{X} - \dot{X}_0) - k_\epsilon (\dot{X} - R - \underline{\tilde{R}} + E_\gamma)^T (L+B) P_1 - P_2^T \Delta \\ &+ \frac{1}{k_f} \sum_{i=1}^{n} \tilde{\theta}_{\gamma i}^T \dot{\hat{\theta}}_{\gamma i} + \frac{1}{k_\delta} \sum_{i=1}^{n} \tilde{\delta}_{\gamma i}^T \dot{\hat{\delta}}_{\gamma i} - k_p P_2^T P_2 \\ =& k_\epsilon (R - \dot{X}_0)^T (L+B) P_1 + k_\epsilon \underline{\tilde{R}}^T E_1 + \frac{1}{k_f} \sum_{i=1}^{n} \tilde{\theta}_{\gamma i}^T \dot{\hat{\theta}}_{\gamma i} \\ &- k_p P_2^T P_2 - k_\epsilon E_\gamma^T E_1 - P_2^T \Delta + \frac{1}{k_\delta} \sum_{i=1}^{n} \tilde{\delta}_{\gamma i}^T \dot{\hat{\delta}}_{\gamma i}. \end{aligned} \tag{20}$$

According to (17), we can obtain that

$$k_\epsilon \tilde{R}^T E_1 = \frac{1}{k_f} \sum_{i=1}^{n} \tilde{\theta}_{\gamma i}^T \dot{\hat{\theta}}_{\gamma i} \tag{21}$$

and

$$\begin{aligned} -k_\epsilon E_\gamma^T E_1 - P_2^T \Delta + \frac{1}{k_\delta} \sum_{i=1}^{n} \tilde{\delta}_{\gamma i}^T \dot{\hat{\delta}}_{\gamma i} &= \sum_{i=1}^{n} \Big[- k_\epsilon \epsilon_{1i} e_{\gamma i} - |k_\epsilon \epsilon_{1i}| (\hat{\delta}_{\gamma i} - \tilde{\delta}_{\gamma i}) \Big] \\ &\leq \sum_{i=1}^{n} \Big(|k_\epsilon \epsilon_{1i}| \cdot |e_{\gamma i}| - |k_\epsilon \epsilon_{1i}| \cdot \delta_{\gamma i} \Big) \\ &\leq 0, \end{aligned} \tag{22}$$

Moreover, the composition rule reveals that $\dot{x}_0 = \gamma(x_0, t)$; then,

$$\begin{aligned} R - \dot{X}_0 &= \mathbf{col}_i^n[\gamma(\zeta_i, t) - \dot{x}_0] \\ &= \mathbf{col}_i^n[\gamma(\zeta_i, t) - \gamma(x_0, t)] \\ &= \mathbf{col}_i^n[\frac{\partial}{\partial x}\{\gamma(\xi_i, t)\}(\zeta_i - x_0)] \\ &= -\mathbf{diag}_i^n[-\frac{\partial}{\partial x}\gamma(\xi_i, t)]P_1 \\ &\triangleq -\Xi P_1. \end{aligned} \tag{23}$$

where $\xi_i \in [\min(\zeta_i, x_0), \max(\zeta_i, x_0)]$. Ξ is positive definite; consequently,

$$\dot{V}_1 \leq -k_\epsilon P_1^T \Xi (L + B) P_1 - k_p P_2^T P_2 \leq 0. \tag{24}$$

Therefore, V_1 keeps decreasing until $P_1 \equiv P_2 \equiv 0$, which implies that $P_1(\infty) \to 0$, i.e., $\lim_{t\to\infty}(\zeta_i - x_0) = 0$ for all $i \in \mathcal{I}$. The theorem is proven. □

4.2. Robust Tracking Controller Design

In the following, the design for a robust tracking controller will be shown for each follower to track the corresponding estimates generated through a neural network-driven distributed observer (11). Ultimately, consensus tracking from the followers to the leader is achieved.

Based on the idea of the back-stepping method, the controller design process of the second-order system (5) can be divided into two steps.

4.2.1. Step 1

Introduce a virtual control input v_i and define the tracking errors as follows:

$$e_{i1} = x_{i1} - \zeta_i, \tag{25}$$

$$e_{i2} = x_{i2} - v_i. \tag{26}$$

When considering (5), (25), and (26), the dynamics of e_{i1} are

$$\dot{e}_{i1} = e_{i2} + v_i + d_{i1} - \eta_i. \tag{27}$$

Design the virtual control input v_i as follows:

$$v_i = -k_{1i} e_{i1} - \hat{d}_{i1} + \eta_i, \tag{28}$$

where k_{1i} is a positive constant, while $\hat{d}_{i1}$ stands for the estimate of d_{i1} produced by a disturbance observer, which is shown later.

Consider the following Lyapunov candidate function:

$$V_{B1} = \frac{1}{2} {e_{i1}}^2. \tag{29}$$

Taking the derivative of V_{B1} leads to

$$\begin{aligned} \dot{V}_{B1} &= -k_{1i} {e_{i1}}^2 - e_{i1}(\tilde{d}_{i1} - e_{i2}) \\ &\leq -k_{1i}|e_{i1}|^2 + |e_{i1}|(|\tilde{d}_{i1}| + |e_{i2}|) \\ &= -k_{1i}(1-\sigma)|e_{i1}|^2 - k_{1i}\sigma|e_{i1}|^2 + |e_{i1}|(|\tilde{d}_{i1}| + |e_{i2}|) \\ &= -k_{1i}(1-\sigma)|e_{i1}|^2 - |e_{i1}|(k_{1i}\sigma|e_{i1}| + |\tilde{d}_{i1}| + |e_{i2}|), \end{aligned} \tag{30}$$

where $0 < \sigma < 1$, and $\tilde{d}_{i1} \triangleq \hat{d}_{i1} - d_{i1}$ is the estimation error of d_{i1}.

From the above equation, it can be derived that

$$\dot{V}_{B1} \leq -k_{1i}(1-\sigma)|e_{i1}|^2, \forall |e_{i1}| \geq b_{B1}, \tag{31}$$

where $b_{B1} = \frac{|\tilde{d}_{i1}|+|e_{i2}|}{k_{1i}\sigma}$.

According to Theorem 4.18 in [41], there exists $t_{B1i} \geq 0$ such that

$$|e_{i1}(t)| \leq b_{B1i}, \forall t \geq t_{B1i}. \tag{32}$$

Thus, the tracking error e_{i1} is bounded if e_{i2} and $\tilde{d}_{i1}$ are bounded.

In the following, the disturbance observer is shown for estimating d_{i1} based on the barrier function to ensure that $\tilde{d}_{i1}$ is bounded.

An auxiliary system is formulated as follows:

$$s_{i1} = \varphi_{i1} - x_{i1}, \tag{33}$$

where the dynamic equation of φ_{i1} is

$$\dot{\varphi}_{i1} = x_{i2} + \hat{d}_{i1}. \tag{34}$$

Combining (5), (33), and (34) yields

$$\dot{s}_{i1} = \hat{d}_{i1} - d_{i1}. \tag{35}$$

Based on the barrier function, $\hat{d}_{i1}$ is given by

$$\hat{d}_{i1} = -K_1(s_{i1}(t))\text{sgn}(s_{i1}), \tag{36}$$

and

$$K_1(s_{i1}(t)) = \begin{cases} K_{a1}(t), \dot{K}_{a1}(t) = k_{a1}|s_{i1}|, 0 < t \leq t_1, \\ K_{p_1}(s_{i1}) = \frac{|s_{i1}|}{\lambda_1 - |s_{i1}|}, t > t_1, \end{cases} \tag{37}$$

where k_{a1} and λ_1 are positive constants, and t_1 is the time when $|s_{i1}(t)| \leq \lambda_1$ is satisfied for the first time.

Theorem 2. *When considering the system (35) under Assumption 1, if we adopt the disturbance observer as detailed in (36) and (37) based on the barrier function specified in Definition 1, it can be established that s_{i1} achieves convergence to the domain $|s_{i1}(t)| \leq \lambda_1\left(\frac{d_{\max}}{d_{\max}+1}\right)$ within finite time. Additionally, the estimation error for d_{i1} exhibits bounded convergence.*

Proof. From (35), it is obvious that

$$\dot{s}_{i1} = \tilde{d}_{i1}. \tag{38}$$

By Definition 1, when $s_{i1} \in [-\lambda_1, \lambda_1]$, $K_{p1}(s_{i1}) \in [0, \infty]$. According to Lemma 1, it can be inferred that when $t > t_1$, $|s_{i1}| < \lambda_1$, and thus, $|\hat{d}_{i1}|$ is bounded. Meanwhile, it follows from Lemma 1 that s_{i1} converges to $|s_{i1}(t)| \leq \lambda_1\left(\frac{d_{\max}}{d_{\max}+1}\right)$ in finite time. In combination with with Assumption 1, both $\hat{d}_{i1}$ and d_{i1} are bounded such that $\tilde{d}_{i1}$ is bounded, and the boundedness of the integral $|s_{i1}|$ further ensures that the fluctuations of $\tilde{d}_{i1}$ are limited. The proof is complete. □

Remark 3. *Barrier function-based disturbance observers* (36) *and* (37) *have only the requirement that the disturbance be integrable and bounded, i.e., that it is capable of estimating bounded non-smooth nonlinear disturbances.*

4.2.2. Step 2

Next, we will show the design of the control input u_i to ensure that e_{i2} is bounded.

Combining (26) with the second equation of (5) yields the dynamic equation of e_{i2}:

$$\dot{e}_{i2} = f_i(x_{i1}, x_{i2}) + g_i(x_{i1}, x_{i2})u_i + d_{i2} + k_{1i}(x_{i2} + d_{i1} - \eta_i) + \dot{\hat{d}}_{i1} - \dot{\eta}_i. \tag{39}$$

We designed u_i as follows:

$$u_i = \frac{1}{g_i(x_{i1}, x_{i2})}\left(-k_{2i}e_{i2} - f_i(x_{i1}, x_{i2}) - \hat{d}_{i2} - k_{1i}\left(x_{i2} + \hat{d}_{i1} - \eta_i\right) + \dot{\eta}_i\right), \tag{40}$$

where $k_{2i} > 0$, and $\hat{d}_{i2}$ is the estimate of d_{i2}.

Consider the following Lyapunov candidate function:

$$V_{B2} = \frac{1}{2}{e_{i2}}^2. \tag{41}$$

The derivative of V_{B2} is

$$\begin{aligned} \dot{V}_{B2} &= -k_{2i}{e_{i2}}^2 - e_{i2}\left(\tilde{d}_{i2} + k_{1i}\tilde{d}_{i1} - \dot{\hat{d}}_{i1}\right) \\ &\leq -k_{2i}|e_{i2}|^2 + |e_{i2}|\left(|\tilde{d}_{i2}| + k_{1i}|\tilde{d}_{i1}| + |\dot{\hat{d}}_{i1}|\right) \\ &= -k_{2i}(1-\sigma)|e_{2i}|^2 - |e_{i2}|\left(k_{2i}\sigma|e_{i2}| + |\tilde{d}_{i2}| + k_{1i}|\tilde{d}_{i1}| + |\dot{\hat{d}}_{i1}|\right) \end{aligned} \tag{42}$$

where $\tilde{d}_{i2} \triangleq \hat{d}_{i2} - d_{i2}$ is the estimation error of d_{i2}.

From (42), it can be derived that

$$\dot{V}_{B2} \leq -k_{2i}(1-\sigma)|e_{i2}|^2, \forall |e_{i2}| \geq b_{B2}, \tag{43}$$

where $b_{B2} = \frac{|\tilde{d}_{i2}| + k_{1i}|\tilde{d}_{i1}| + |\dot{\hat{d}}_{i1}|}{k_{2i}\sigma}$.

According to Theorem 4.18 in [41], there exists $t_{B2i} \geq 0$ such that

$$|e_{i2}(t)| \leq b_{B2i}, \forall t \geq t_{B2i}. \tag{44}$$

Theorem 2 and Equations (36) and (37) guarantee that $\tilde{d}_{i1}$ and $\dot{\hat{d}}_{i1}$ are bounded. Consequently, the tracking error e_{i2} is bounded as long as the disturbance estimation error $\tilde{d}_{i2}$ is bounded.

Similar to the previous step, the disturbance observer for estimating d_{i2} was designed based on the barrier function.

Likewise, the subsequent auxiliary system is formulated as

$$s_{i2} = \varphi_{i2} - x_{i2}, \tag{45}$$

where the dynamics of φ_{i2} are given by

$$\dot{\varphi}_{i2} = f(x_{i1}, x_{i2}) + g(x_{i1}, x_{i2})u_i + \hat{d}_{i2}. \tag{46}$$

In combining the second equations of (5), (45), and (46), it can be obtained that

$$\dot{s}_{i2} = \hat{d}_{i2} - d_{i2}. \tag{47}$$

Then, $\hat{d}_{i2}$ is given by

$$\hat{d}_{i2} = -K_2(s_{i2}(t))\mathrm{sgn}(s_{i2}) \tag{48}$$

and

$$K_2(s_{i2}(t)) = \begin{cases} K_{a2}(t), \dot{K}_{a2}(t) = \bar{k}_{a2}|s_{i2}|, 0 < t \leq t_2, \\ K_{p_2}(s_{i2}) = \frac{|s_{i2}|}{\lambda_2 - |s_{i2}|}, t > t_2, \end{cases} \tag{49}$$

where k_{a2} and λ_2 are positive constants, and t_2 equals the time when $|s_{i2}(t)| \leq \frac{\lambda_2}{2}$ is satisfied for the first time.

It is obvious that Equations (47)–(49) have the same structure as Equations (35)–(37). Therefore, it follows from Theorem 2 that $\tilde{d}_{i2}$ is bounded. As a consequence, e_{i2} and e_{i1} are bounded.

Up to now, with the design idea of the back-stepping technique and based on the barrier function disturbance observers (36), (37), (48) and (49), we obtained the robust tracking controller composed by Equations (28) and (40).

Theorem 3. *Under Assumptions 1–3, considering multi-agent systems (5) and (6) subject to both matched and mismatched disturbances in combination with neural network-based distributed observer (11), the control strategy u_i achieves the bounded consensus tracking from the follower state $x_{i1}(i \in \mathcal{I})$ to the leader state x_0.*

Proof. For all $i \in \mathcal{I}$, define the tracking error of the ith follower with respect to the leader as

$$e_i = x_{i1} - x_0, \tag{50}$$

which can be transformed into

$$e_i = x_{i1} - \zeta_i + \zeta_i - x_0 = e_{i1} + \zeta_i - x_0. \tag{51}$$

From the design process of the robust tracking controller, it is evident that for $b_c = \max\{b_{B1i}(i \in \mathcal{I})\}$, there is a corresponding settling time t_b such that for all $i \in \mathcal{I}$,

$$|e_{i1}(t)| \leq b_c, \forall t \geq t_b. \tag{52}$$

Disturbance observers (36), (37), (48) and (49) guarantee that b_c is bounded.
According to Theorem 1, it is obtained that

$$\lim_{t\to\infty}(\zeta_i - x_0) = 0. \tag{53}$$

Thus, for all $i \in \mathcal{I}$ and for t_b, there exists a boundary $b_d \geq 0$ such that $|\zeta_i - x_0| \leq b_d$.
Hence, it can be obtained that for all $i \in \mathcal{I}$,

$$e_i(t) \leq b, \forall t \geq t_b, \tag{54}$$

where $b = b_c + b_d$ is the ultimate bound of the tracking error.

Subsequently, according to Definition 2, it can be deduced that the control protocol u_i is a bounded consensus tracking control. The proof is complete. □

The robust tracking control scheme was shown in this section. Initially, a distributed observer based on neural networks was introduced to accurately estimate leader information for all follower nodes. Subsequently, a robust tracking controller based on back-stepping technique was developed, demonstrating the boundedness of the closed-loop error system through the application of the Lyapunov-like theorem. Meanwhile, a barrier function-based disturbance observer was designed to accurately estimate matched and mismatched uncertainties among followers. Ultimately, bounded consensus tracking from the followers to the leader trajectory is achieved.

Remark 4. *It can be observed from (36), (37), (48) and (49) that for $j = 1, 2$, the solution s_{ij} reaches $\frac{\lambda_j}{2}$ in finite time t_j. At this point, the adaptive gain K_j switches from K_{aj} to K_{pj} and remains as K_{pj} thereafter. It is evident that as $s_{ij} \to 0$, $K_{pj} \to 0$. Consequently, K_{pj} exhibits the same behavior as $\frac{|s_{ij}|}{\lambda_i}$ in the vicinity of zero, that is, $\frac{s_{ij}}{\lambda_j} \ll 1 \Rightarrow K_{pj}(s_{ij}) = \frac{|s_{ij}|}{\lambda_j - |s_{ij}|} \approx \frac{|s_{ij}|}{\lambda_j}$. This implies that if d_{ij} and s_{ij} monotonically approach zero, $K_p(s_{ij})$ will tend to zero as well. Hence, the discontinuity of* *the signal $\hat{d}_{ij}$ only occurs once at time t_j [37]. It is worth noting that $\hat{d}_{ij}$ becomes continuous from time t_j, and there is no chattering generated by (36), (37), (48) or (49).*

Remark 5. *In the simulation, to mitigate the chattering effect resulting from discontinuous control signals, the emulation of the signum function* $\text{sgn}(x)$ *is carried out utilizing function* $\tanh(ax) = \frac{e^{ax}-e^{-ax}}{e^{ax}+e^{-ax}}$. *Here, parameter a may be set as* $a = 10$, *allowing for a smoother control signal while closely approximating the characteristics of the signum function.*

5. Simulation Results

Several simulation examples are presented to validate the efficacy of the proposed distributed consensus tracking control scheme in this section. Here, we considered that there are four followers and one leader, and Figure 2 depicts the communication topology among the agents. Then, L and B were derived as follows:

$$L = \begin{bmatrix} 2 & -1 & 0 & -1 \\ -1 & 3 & -1 & -1 \\ 0 & -1 & 1 & 0 \\ -1 & -1 & 0 & 2 \end{bmatrix}, B = \begin{bmatrix} 1.4 & 0 & 0 & 0 \\ 0 & 1.2 & 0 & 0 \\ 0 & 0 & 0 & 0 \\ 0 & 0 & 0 & 0 \end{bmatrix}.$$

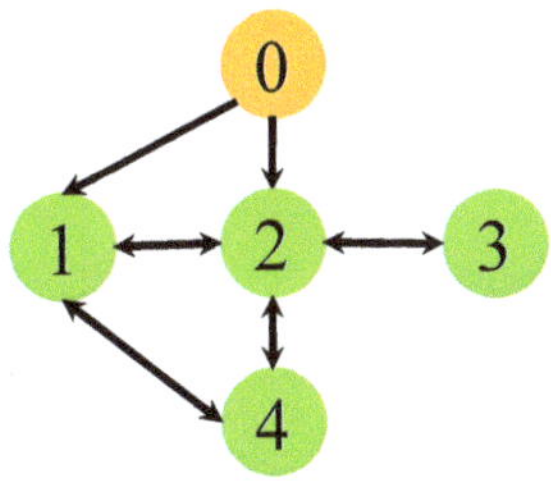

Figure 2. The communication topology among agents.

In addition, we consider that each follower agent's dynamics are characterized by the longitudinal height channel model of a four-rotor UAV system. According to the previous work in [42], the transnational dynamic model of the height channel of the four-rotor UAV system is

$$\begin{aligned} \dot{x}_{i1} &= x_{i2} + d_{i1}, \\ \dot{x}_{i2} &= \frac{\cos\phi_i \cos\theta_i u_i}{m} - g + d_{i2}, \end{aligned} \tag{55}$$

in which ϕ_i represents the rolling angle, and θ_i represents the pitch angle of a follower agent. The quadrotor's mass is denoted by m, while U_1 represents the total thrust force. The acceleration of gravity is expressed as g. Additionally, d_{i_1} and d_{i_2} correspond to the mismatched uncertainty and matched uncertainty, respectively.

The model parameters for the four-rotor UAV were chosen as $m = 3$ kg, $\phi_i = 0°$, $\theta_i = 0°$, and, in the simulation verification scenario of this paper, $g = 9.81$ m/s^2. Furthermore, d_{i1} and d_{i2} were regarded as follows: $d_{i1} = 0.2x_{i1} + \sin(0.2\pi t)$ and $d_{i2} = 0.2\text{sgn}(x_{i1}x_{i2})$.

Moreover, the dynamics of the leading agent were taken into account as follows:

$$\dot{x}_0 = -0.4x_0 + \cos(t^{0.8}) + 0.02t + 1. \tag{56}$$

A radial basis function (RBF) neural network was employed for the estimation of $\gamma(x,t)$ utilizing Gaussian basis functions:

$$\phi_\gamma^T(x,t) = e^{-\frac{(x-\mu_{\gamma ix,k})^2+(t-\mu_{\gamma it,k})^2}{\eta_{\gamma i,k}^2}}, k \in \{1,2,\ldots,h_{\gamma i}\}, \tag{57}$$

The widths of the Gaussian basis functions were $\eta_{\gamma i,k} = 6$, and the number of nodes was $h_{\gamma i} = 17 \times 17$. The centers $(\mu_{\gamma ix,k}, \mu_{\gamma it,k})$ were uniformly distributed within the range $[-25,25] \times [0,50]$. The initial conditions for the system were $x_0(0) = 3.5$, $\hat{\theta}_{\gamma i}(0) = 0$. The observer gain and adaptive law parameters were $k_f = 10$, $k_\epsilon = 5$, $k_p = 5$, and $k_\delta = 5$. Let $K_\theta(0) = 5$ and $K_p(0) = 10$. The step of sampling was chosen to be 0.01 s. Additionally, the control tracking parameters are presented in Table 1.

Table 1. The control parameters of each follower agent.

Parameter	Value	Parameter	Value	Parameter	Value
k_1	5	k_{a1}	100	λ_1	0.1
k_2	10	k_{a2}	100	λ_2	0.02

In [43], the authors addressed the consensus tracking control problem of second-order uncertain multi-agent systems with mismatched and matched disturbances. They designed a neural network-based consensus tracking control scheme and estimated the compound uncertainties utilizing a neural network approximator. In the simulation, we compared the differences between the controllers designed in this study and the controllers designed in the literature [43]. The simulation and comparison results of the numerical examples are illustrated in Figures 3–7. It is evident from Figure 3 that all follower agents successfully tracked the leader's trajectory, signifying the attainment of tracking control within the multi-agent system. Figure 4 demonstrates the trajectory of the consensus tracking error under the two control schemes. It can be seen that the control error judder is more obvious using the control scheme from the literature [43], while the error trajectory is relatively smooth using the control scheme designed in this study. In Figures 5 and 6, the disturbance estimation errors are shown under the two control schemes. It can be seen that the barrier function-based disturbance estimator designed in this study can effectively achieve compensation for unknown disturbances compared to the neural network-based estimation method in the literature [43]. Finally, the control input of each follower agent is shown in Figure 7.

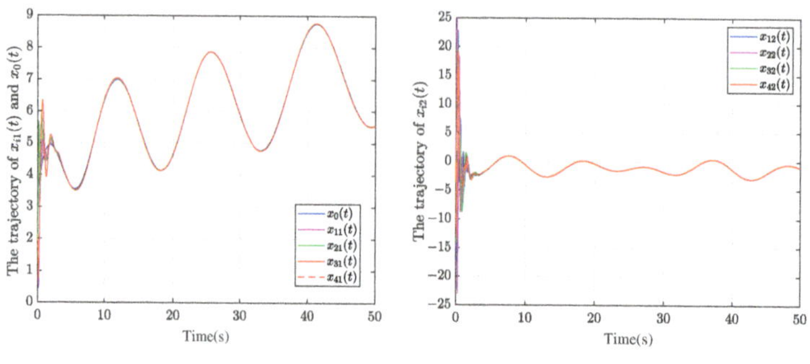

Figure 3. The position and velocity trajectories of agents, respectively.

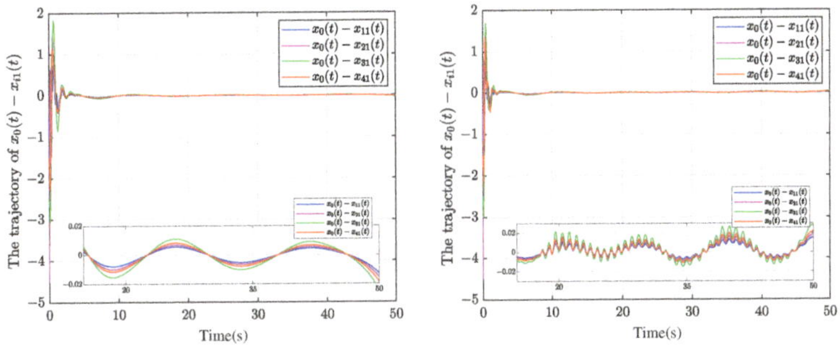

(a) (b)

Figure 4. The consensus tracking error trajectories of follower agents. (**a**) The proposed controller. (**b**) The NN-based controller in [43].

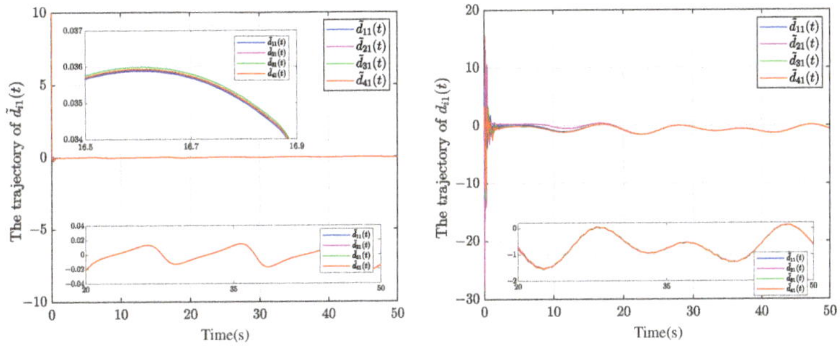

(a) (b)

Figure 5. The estimation error $\tilde{d}_{i1}$ trajectories of follower agents. (**a**) The proposed controller. (**b**) The NN-based controller in [43].

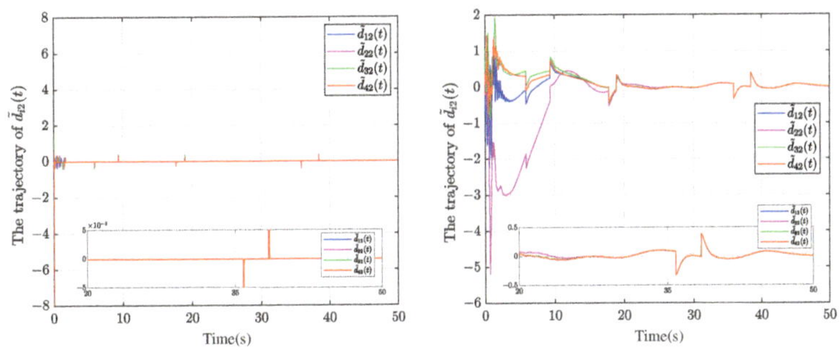

(a) (b)

Figure 6. The estimation error $\tilde{d}_{i2}$ trajectories of follower agents. (**a**) The proposed controller. (**b**) The NN-based controller in [43].

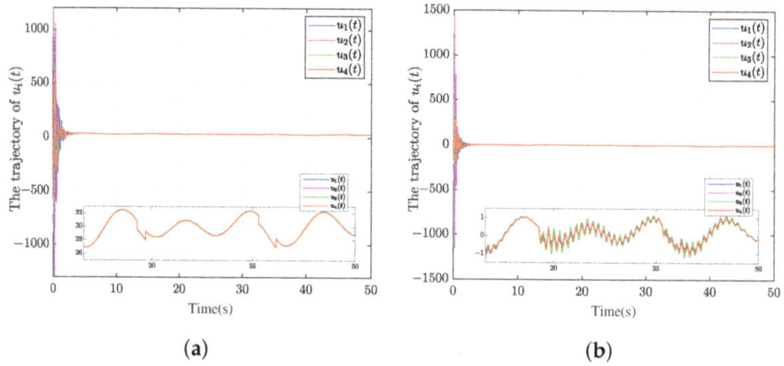

Figure 7. The control input trajectories of follower agents. (**a**) The proposed controller. (**b**) The NN-based controller in [43].

6. Conclusions

This research delved into the intricacies of addressing the consensus tracking control challenge in second-order multi-agent systems with both mismatched and matched uncertainties. By integrating a neural network-based distributed observer, a barrier function-based disturbance observer, and a back-stepping-based tracking controller, a robust tracking control method was developed. This scheme enables the distributed estimation of leader information, compensation for disturbances, and the effective tracking of the leader's trajectory by followers, despite the presence of uncertainties. Then, the stability of the error system was demonstrated and established using the Lyapunov theory. Additionally, simulation results are provided to validate the efficacy of the distributed consensus tracking scheme. It is important to point out that in this paper, we consider that followers can communicate with each other in both directions. In the future, there will be further exploration of the tracking control problem for uncertain multi-agent systems under a directed topology.

Author Contributions: L.X.: conceptualization, methodology, and writing—original draft. K.Q.: validation and writing—review and editing. All authors have read and agreed to the published version of the manuscript.

Funding: This work was supported by the Natural Science Foundation of Sichuan Province (2022NSFSC0037), Sichuan Science and Technology Programs (2022JDR0107, 2021YFG0130, MZGC20230069), Fundamental Research Funds for the Central Universities (ZYGX2020J020), and the Wuhu Science and Technology Plan Project (2022yf23).

Data Availability Statement: The data presented in this study are available on request from the corresponding author.

Conflicts of Interest: No conflict of interest exists in the submission of this manuscript, and all authors approve the manuscript for publication. I would like to declare on behalf of my co-author that the work described was original research that has not been published previously and is not under consideration for publication elsewhere, in whole or in part. All the authors listed have approved the manuscript that is enclosed. The authors declare that they have no known competing financial interests or personal relationships that could have appeared to influence the work reported in this paper.

References

1. Zhang, J.; Yan, J.; Zhang, P. Multi-UAV formation control based on a novel back-stepping approach. *IEEE Trans. Veh. Technol.* **2020**, *69*, 2437–2448. [CrossRef]
2. Madridano, A.; Al-Kaff, A.; Martín, D.; De La Escalera, A. Trajectory planning for multi-robot systems: Methods and applications. *Expert Syst. Appl.* **2021**, *173*, 114660. [CrossRef]

3. Wang, P.; Govindarasu, M. Multi-agent based attack-resilient system integrity protection for smart grid. *IEEE Trans. Smart Grid* **2020**, *11*, 3447–3456. [CrossRef]
4. Clark, D.E. Multi-sensor network information for linear-Gaussian multi-target tracking systems. *IEEE Trans. Signal Process.* **2021**, *69*, 4312–4325. [CrossRef]
5. Li, X.; Tang, Y.; Karimi, H.R. Consensus of multi-agent systems via fully distributed event-triggered control. *Automatica* **2020**, *116*, 108898. [CrossRef]
6. Chen, G. Global synchronization and asymptotic stability of complex dynamical networks. *IEEE Trans. Circuits Syst. II Express Briefs* **2006**, *53*, 28–33. [CrossRef]
7. Yang, H.; Li, Z. Finite-time consensus for multi-agent systems with directed dynamically changing topologies. *Int. J. Robust Nonlinear Control* **2023**, *33*, 8657–8669. [CrossRef]
8. Mehdifar, F.; Bechlioulis, C.P.; Hashemzadeh, F.; Baradarannia, M. Prescribed performance distance-based formation control of multi-agent systems. *Automatica* **2020**, *119*, 109086. [CrossRef]
9. Liu, Y.; Zhang, H.; Shi, Z.; Gao, Z. Neural-network-based finite-time bipartite containment control for fractional-order multi-agent systems. *IEEE Trans. Neural Netw. Learn. Syst.* **2022**, *34*, 7418–7429. [CrossRef]
10. Zou, Y.; An, Q.; Miao, S.; Chen, S.; Wang, X.; Su, H. Flocking of uncertain nonlinear multi-agent systems via distributed adaptive event-triggered control. *Neurocomputing* **2021**, *465*, 503–513. [CrossRef]
11. Li, Z.; Guan, S. Diffusion normalized Huber adaptive filtering algorithm. *J. Frankl. Inst.* **2018**, *355*, 3812–3825. [CrossRef]
12. Choi, Y.H.; Yoo, S.J. Neural-network-based distributed asynchronous event-triggered consensus tracking of a class of uncertain nonlinear multi-agent systems. *IEEE Trans. Neural Netw. Learn. Syst.* **2021**, *33*, 2965–2979. [CrossRef] [PubMed]
13. Cai, J.; Feng, J.; Wang, J.; Zhao, Y. Tracking consensus of multi-agent systems under switching topologies via novel SMC: An event-triggered approach. *IEEE Trans. Netw. Sci. Eng.* **2022**, *9*, 2150–2163. [CrossRef]
14. Dong, G.; Li, H.; Ma, H.; Lu, R. Finite-time consensus tracking neural network FTC of multi-agent systems. *IEEE Trans. Neural Netw. Learn. Syst.* **2020**, *32*, 653–662. [CrossRef] [PubMed]
15. Gong, P.; Han, Q.L.; Lan, W. Finite-time consensus tracking for incommensurate fractional-order nonlinear multiagent systems with directed switching topologies. *IEEE Trans. Cybern.* **2020**, *52*, 65–76. [CrossRef] [PubMed]
16. Wang, X.; Cao, Y.; Niu, B.; Song, Y. A novel bipartite consensus tracking control for multiagent systems under sensor deception attacks. *IEEE Trans. Cybern.* **2022**, *53*, 5984–5993. [CrossRef] [PubMed]
17. Ning, B.; Han, Q.L.; Zuo, Z. Bipartite consensus tracking for second-order multiagent systems: A time-varying function-based preset-time approach. *IEEE Trans. Autom. Control* **2020**, *66*, 2739–2745. [CrossRef]
18. Zhao, M.; Peng, C.; Tian, E. Finite-time and fixed-time bipartite consensus tracking of multi-agent systems with weighted antagonistic interactions. *IEEE Trans. Circuits Syst. I Regul. Pap.* **2020**, *68*, 426–433. [CrossRef]
19. Yang, H.; Ye, D. Observer-based fixed-time secure tracking consensus for networked high-order multiagent systems against DoS attacks. *IEEE Trans. Cybern.* **2020**, *52*, 2018–2031. [CrossRef]
20. Liu, C.; Jiang, B.; Zhang, K.; Patton, R.J. Distributed fault-tolerant consensus tracking control of multi-agent systems under fixed and switching topologies. *IEEE Trans. Circuits Syst. I Regul. Pap.* **2021**, *68*, 1646–1658. [CrossRef]
21. Ren, W. Multi-vehicle consensus with a time-varying reference state. *Syst. Control Lett.* **2007**, *56*, 474–483. [CrossRef]
22. Wen, G.; Duan, Z.; Chen, G.; Yu, W. Consensus tracking of multi-agent systems with Lipschitz-type node dynamics and switching topologies. *IEEE Trans. Circuits Syst. I Regul. Pap.* **2013**, *61*, 499–511. [CrossRef]
23. Li, Z.; Liu, X.; Ren, W.; Xie, L. Distributed tracking control for linear multiagent systems with a leader of bounded unknown input. *IEEE Trans. Autom. Control* **2012**, *58*, 518–523. [CrossRef]
24. Li, Z.; Ding, Z. Distributed adaptive consensus and output tracking of unknown linear systems on directed graphs. *Automatica* **2015**, *55*, 12–18. [CrossRef]
25. Zhang, L.; Chen, B.; Lin, C.; Shang, Y. Fuzzy adaptive fixed-time consensus tracking control of high-order multi-agent systems. *IEEE Trans. Fuzzy Syst.* **2020**, *30*, 567–578. [CrossRef]
26. Wen, G.; Wang, H.; Yu, X.; Yu, W. Bipartite tracking consensus of linear multi-agent systems with a dynamic leader. *IEEE Trans. Circuits Syst. II Express Briefs* **2017**, *65*, 1204–1208. [CrossRef]
27. Shao, J.; Zheng, W.X.; Shi, L.; Cheng, Y. Bipartite tracking consensus of generic linear agents with discrete-time dynamics over cooperation–competition networks. *IEEE Trans. Cybern.* **2020**, *51*, 5225–5235. [CrossRef]
28. Nie, R.; He, W.; Du, W.; Lang, Z.; He, S. Dynamic event-triggered SMC of multi-agent systems for consensus tracking. *IEEE Trans. Circuits Syst. II Express Briefs* **2021**, *69*, 1188–1192. [CrossRef]
29. Ni, J.; Shi, P.; Zhao, Y.; Pan, Q.; Wang, S. Fixed-time event-triggered output consensus tracking of high-order multiagent systems under directed interaction graphs. *IEEE Trans. Cybern.* **2020**, *52*, 6391–6405. [CrossRef]
30. Gong, P.; Lan, W. Adaptive robust tracking control for multiple unknown fractional-order nonlinear systems. *IEEE Trans. Cybern.* **2018**, *49*, 1365–1376. [CrossRef]
31. He, S.; Xu, Y.; Wu, Y.; Li, Y.; Zhong, W. Adaptive consensus tracking of multi-robotic systems via using integral sliding mode control. *Neurocomputing* **2021**, *455*, 154–162. [CrossRef]
32. Wang, X.; Yang, G.H. Distributed H-infty consensus tracking control for multi-agent networks with switching directed topologies. *Neurocomputing* **2016**, *207*, 693–699. [CrossRef]

33. Li, M.; Wu, Z.H.; Deng, F.; Guo, B.Z. Active Disturbance Rejection Control to Consensus of Second-Order Stochastic Multi-Agent Systems. *IEEE Trans. Control Netw. Syst.* **2022**, *10*, 993–1004. [CrossRef]
34. Sha, H.; Guo, R.; Zhou, J.; Zhu, X.; Li, N.; Miao, Z. Robust consensus tracking control for switched multiple Lagrangian systems by UDE-based control method. *J. Frankl. Inst.* **2023**, *360*, 14372–14387. [CrossRef]
35. Chu, H.; Chen, J.; Wei, Q.; Zhang, W. Robust global consensus tracking of linear multi-agent systems with input saturation via scheduled low-and-high gain feedback. *IET Control Theory Appl.* **2019**, *13*, 69–77. [CrossRef]
36. Ai, X.; Yu, J.; Jia, Z.; Yang, D.; Xu, X.; Shen, Y. Disturbance observer–based consensus tracking for nonlinear multiagent systems with switching topologies. *Int. J. Robust Nonlinear Control* **2018**, *28*, 2144–2160. [CrossRef]
37. Obeid, H.; Fridman, L.M.; Laghrouche, S.; Harmouche, M. Barrier function-based adaptive sliding mode control. *Automatica* **2018**, *93*, 540–544. [CrossRef]
38. Zhang, X.; Xu, L.; Zhu, Y.; Chen, L.; Li, G. Disturbance Observer-Based Finite-Time Tracking Control for a Class of Second-Order Nonlinear Systems with Mismatched and Matched Uncertainties. In Proceedings of the International Conference on Guidance, Navigation and Control, Tianjin, China, 5–7 August 2022; Springer: Berlin/Heidelberg, Germany, 2022; pp. 3981–3990.
39. Chen, W.; Hua, S.; Ge, S.S. Consensus-based distributed cooperative learning control for a group of discrete-time nonlinear multi-agent systems using neural networks. *Automatica* **2014**, *50*, 2254–2268. [CrossRef]
40. Liu, Z.; Lu, Z.; Zhao, Z.; Efe, M.Ö.; Hong, K.S. Single parameter adaptive neural network control for multi-agent deployment with prescribed tracking performance. *Automatica* **2023**, *156*, 111207. [CrossRef]
41. Khalil, H.K. *Nonlinear Systems*, 3rd ed.; Prentice Hall: New York, NY, USA, 2002; pp. 134–180.
42. Aboudonia, A.; Rashad, R.; El-Badawy, A. Composite hierarchical anti-disturbance control of a quadrotor UAV in the presence of matched and mismatched disturbances. *J. Intell. Robot. Syst.* **2018**, *90*, 201–216. [CrossRef]
43. Shi, M.; Qin, K.; Liang, J.; Liu, J. Distributed control of uncertain multiagent systems for tracking a leader with unknown fractional-order dynamics. *Int. J. Robust Nonlinear Control* **2019**, *29*, 2254–2271. [CrossRef]

mathematics MDPI

Article

Dynamic Analysis and FPGA Implementation of a New Linear Memristor-Based Hyperchaotic System with Strong Complexity

Lijuan Chen [1,2], Mingchu Yu [1], Jinnan Luo [3,*], Jinpeng Mi [2,4], Kaibo Shi [5] and Song Tang [2,4]

1 Kaiserslautern Intelligent Manufacturing School, Shanghai Dianji University, Shanghai 201306, China; tangchenlj@163.com (L.C.); yumingchu0520@gmail.com (M.Y.)
2 TAMS Group, Department of Informatics, Universität Hamburg, 20148 Hamburg, Germany; jp.mi@usst.edu.cn (J.M.); steventangsong@gmail.com (S.T.)
3 College of Electrical Engineering, Southwest Minzu University, Chengdu 610041, China
4 IMI Group, University of Shanghai for Science and Technology, Shanghai 200093, China
5 School of Information Science and Engineering, Chengdu University, Chengdu 610106, China; skbs111@163.com
* Correspondence: jinnanluo@outlook.com

Abstract: Chaotic or hyperchaotic systems have a significant role in engineering applications such as cryptography and secure communication, serving as primary signal generators. To ensure stronger complexity, memristors with sufficient nonlinearity are commonly incorporated into the system, suffering a limitation on the physical implementation. In this paper, we propose a new four-dimensional (4D) hyperchaotic system based on the linear memristor which is the most straightforward to implement physically. Through numerical studies, we initially demonstrate that the proposed system exhibits robust hyperchaotic behaviors under typical parameter conditions. Subsequently, we theoretically prove the existence of solid hyperchaos by combining the topological horseshoe theory with computer-assisted research. Finally, we present the realization of the proposed hyperchaotic system using an FPGA platform. This proposed system possesses two key properties. Firstly, this work suggests that the simplest memristor can also induce strong nonlinear behaviors, offering a new perspective for constructing memristive systems. Secondly, compared to existing systems, our system not only has the largest Kaplan-Yorke dimension, but also has clear advantages in areas related to engineering applications, such as the parameter range and signal bandwidth, indicating promising potential in engineering applications.

Keywords: hyperchaotic system; linear memristor; strong complexity; topological horseshoe; FPGA implementation

MSC: 93-08

1. Introduction

Hyperchaotic systems are a special kind of chaotic system with more than one positive Lyapunov Exponent (LE) number [1,2]. hyperchaotic systems with more directions have more complex dynamic behaviors than stretched ordinary hyperchaos with only a one-dimensional direction. Therefore, it is widely used in chaotic communication [3], chaotic encryption [4] and other fields [5].

In 1979, O. Rossler et al. [6] proposed the first hyperchaotic system. In the beginning, many researchers have conducted in-depth and extensive research in this field, and at the same time, many new Hyperchaotic systems have been proposed. For example, Wang et al. [7] constructed a Lorenz-like 4D Hyperchaotic system by introducing a nonlinear controller. Li et al. [8] proposed hyperchaotic memristive circuit by adding a quadratic ideal memristor. V.T.Pham et al. [9] proposed a Hyperchaotic system with no equilibrium point. Lai et al. [10] constructed a hyperchaotic system with no fixed points and an infinite number of coexisting attractors.

Among the aforementioned works, the primary focus lies in uncovering the intricate dynamical behaviors concealed within the proposed systems. These theoretical analyses and experimental observations are instrumental in comprehending the nonlinear operational mechanisms of these systems. However, while these discovered dynamic behaviors hold significance, they may not always be advantageous, and in certain cases, they can even prove detrimental to real-world applications. For instance, the transient nature of complex behaviors, such as hyperchaos, is evident in many systems. Following a period of evolution, hyperchaos tends to degrade into conventional chaos. In the context of encryption algorithms based on hyperchaos, this degradation can compromise confidentiality. For a secure communication process reliant on a chaotic system, quality communication without information errors can only be achieved when system parameters afford a wide range of chaotic behaviors. Unfortunately, system properties crucial for engineering applications, including complexity, parameter robustness, and signal bandwidth, are often overlooked.

Recently, researchers have shifted their focus to address the above-mentioned aspects related to engineering applications. For example, Mezatio et al. [11] developed a 6D hyperchaotic autonomous system by introducing a kind of two-order ideal memristor. Xiu et al. [12] adopted multimemristors to trigger the strong hyperchaotic state in a 6D system. Chen et al. [13] proposed a 4D hyperchaotic system characterized by high complexity. They further explored the system's engineering-related properties from the aforementioned perspectives. Thanks to its favorable engineering properties, this system has demonstrated promising applications in various fields, including public-key cryptography [14] and substitution-box construction [15]. Nevertheless, systems still possess certain shortcomings, primarily stemming from the intricate coupling of multiple complex nonlinear terms, which may pose challenges during specific physical implementations of memristors or circuits. At the same time, whether the simplest linear memristor can lead to strong complexity is an interesting and open problem.

Aiming at this limitation above, this paper proposes a new 4D hyperchaotic system based on the simplest linear memristor. In order to study the properties of the system, we first discuss the basic dynamic properties of the system through theoretical analysis and dynamic analysis. Then, the properties of the system related to engineering applications are analyzed. Moreover, based on topological horseshoe theory [16–18], the existence of strong hyperchaotic behaviors is proved strictly. Finally, Field Programmable Gate Array (FPGA) hardware platform successfully implements the proposed 4D hyperchaotic system. Our study indicates that the linear memristor can also lead to strong and robust complexity.

To be summarized, the main contribution of this work covers three folds:

(1) We introduce a new 4D hyperchaotic system by adding the simplest linear memristor to the Qi chaotic system, showing the potential of the linear memristor in constructing memristive systems with complex behaviors.
(2) We show that the developed system has a simpler structure and more intricate dynamic properties relevant to real-world applications compared to previous research.
(3) We perform in-depth dynamic analyses, including fundamental dynamic properties, computer-assisted proof for the existence of strong hyperchaos and hardware validation based on FPGA.

2. Related Work

The existing work for chaotic or hyperchaotic systems can be categorized into two groups. The first one focuses on constructing new chaotic or hyperchaotic systems. The representative works include: Wu et al. [19] proposed a hyperchaotic system with two large positive LEs and studied the Hopf bifurcation transient transition phenomenon in it. Qi et al. [20] proposed a system with strong hyperchaotic behaviors by introducing linear feedback. Kuate et al. [21] constructed a new three-dimensional chaotic system with up to eight coexisting attractors. The proposed system is multiplier-less, variable boost, and entirely based on Chua diode nonlinearity. Karawanich et al. [22] proposed a chaotic system based on the concept of third-order jerk. Zhang et al. [23] developed a simple non-equilibrium chaotic system with only one sign function. Besides, introducing memristors is a popular construction way. For example, by connecting two discrete memristors with sine and cosine memristors in parallel, Zhang et al. [24] constructed two novel dual-memristor hyperchaotic maps. Although many impressive research studies continue to make progress, the system construction mentioned above is focused on finding new dynamics. However, it does not adequately consider the challenges of physical implementation and the robustness of the system's behaviors, which limits its real-world applications.

The second group focuses on the complex dynamics in chaotic or hyperchaotic systems. These works are mainly in three lines. The first line focuses on the emergent mechanisms of complex behaviors. For example, in the paper by [25], the authors discussed the mechanism for generating hyperchaos from the micro-scale (intersection of homologous and heterogeneous orbits). Another paper by [26] discussed the evolutionary path from ordinary chaos to hyperchaos using the topological horse theory. The second line focuses on some interesting new dynamic phenomenons. For example, Tang et al. [27] found a new kind of topological horseshoe in the phase space of a hyperchaotic system constructed by introducing memory element. Yu et al. [28] addressed the transient behavior mechanism analysis of a new 4D chaotic system. The third line switches to systems with distinctive features. For instance, systems without equilibrium points [10,29] has attracted much attention. Within the context, the implicit dynamics, such as co-existence of multi-attractor [30,31] and hidden attractor [32,33], were found and analyzed further. From the work mentioned above, it is seen that these efforts have highlighted increasing system complexity, reported new physical phenomena and revealed the hidden working mechanism, losing focus on the system features closely attached to the real application.

In short, the study of new dynamic behaviors is an important topic in the field of nonlinear science, but it is not the only theme. The purpose of this paper is to introduce a new hyperchaotic system with excellent dynamic characteristics relevant to real engineering scenarios, such as system complexity, parameter robustness, and signal bandwidth. Therefore, the proposed system contributes to the nonlinear community by enhancing engineering applications. Additionally, to our knowledge, there are few works conducting research from this perspective, which is the main motivation behind our work.

3. The Proposed Hyperchaotic System

The mathematical model of the proposed novel 4D system is modified from the classical Qi system [34] by introducing the simplest linear memristor. According to [35], the adopted linear memristor can be defined as the following general form.

$$\dot{w}(t) = rx(t),\ \phi(t) = (v + kw(t))x(t) \tag{1}$$

In Equation (1), r, v and k are constants; $x(t)$ and $\phi(t)$ are two complementary constitutive variables standing for input and output of the memristor, respectively; $w(t)$ is the internal state variable. In practice, when $x(t)$ and $\phi(t)$ formulate the voltage and current of a two-terminal electronic element, respectively, Equation (1) essentially represents a flux-controlled memristor with linear memductance $v + kw(t)$.

Combining the linear memristor above with the Qi system, we describe the novel 4D system as Equation (2).

$$\begin{cases} \dot{x} = a(y - x) + eyz, \\ \dot{y} = cx - by - xz, \\ \dot{z} = xy - dz - \phi(w)x, \\ \dot{w} = rx, \end{cases} \tag{2}$$

where (x, y, z, w) are state variables, $\phi(w) = v + kw$ and (a, b, c, d, e, r, k, v) are system parameters. To present the complexity of the system (2), we perform a comprehensive numerical study from three aspects: (1) Basic dynamic behaviors, (2) engineering application-promising characteristics, and (3) computer-assisted proof of strong complexity. Furthermore, to verify the feasibility of the proposed system, a hardware platform based on FPGA is built to verify the numerical results experimentally. These details are elaborated in the following sections.

4. Basic Dynamic Behaviors

For the proposed system (2), when we take

$$(a,\ b,\ c,\ d,\ e,\ r,\ k,\ v) = (-39,\ 39,\ 15,\ 41,\ 123, -100, -35,\ 1), \tag{3}$$

the LEs are $LE_1 = 14.149$, $LE_2 = 8.421$, $LE_3 = 0$, $LE_4 = -63.475$, namely the system (2) is in a hyperchaotic state. In this paper, the LE computation uses the Jacobian method [36] with QR-decomposition. The code lec.c is available at https://drive.google.com/file/d/1sDXjSAjYKmmXSIiSN7zEvVuq58rKBmXg/view?usp=sharing. In the lec.c file, funtion 'odesolve' compute the trajectory of one step by local linearixed (i.e., the Jacobian method), while the QR-decomposition is achieved by the fuction 'qr'. Of note, the 'odesolve' is different from the ODE45 function in Matlab, which is used for discussing the engineering application-promising characteristics (Section 5). Specifically, 'odesolve' is a component of our LE computation based on the Jacobian method. In contrast, ODE45 is a built-in official Matlab function based on the Runge-Kutta method [37], computing the system's trajectory under a given time range containing multi-steps.

This specific parameter setting derives from a parallel random searching algorithm for parameter identification, which is based on the LE computation and the basic parameters of the Qi system. The corresponding hyperchaotic attractor in phase space is shown in Figure 1.

In order to verify whether the attractor has 2D stretching during large 1D stretching, we transformed the original continuous system (2) into Poincaré map by selecting an appropriate hyperplane and observed the distribution characteristics of the attractor. Specifically, the same as previous work [38,39], we choose Poincaré intersection:

$$P \triangleq \{(x,y,z,w)|x = 0, \dot{x} < 0\}, \tag{4}$$

then Poincaré map $H : P \to P$ can be defined as: for any point

$$X \triangleq (0,y,z,w) \in P, \tag{5}$$

$H(x)$ stands for the intersection when a trajectory of the system (2) first return the section P under initial condition of x.

The attractor of H is shown in Figure 2 where the attractor is distributed approximately on a 2D surface (Figure 2a). It shows that the system in one direction exists strong compression, namely $LE_4 < 0$. In addition, the distribution shape of the attractor has a certain area (Figure 2b), which indicates that the system trajectory has two directions of stretching, namely, $LE_1 > 0$, $LE_2 > 0$.

It is not hard to find out that the new system (2) is easy to the conclusion:

$$\begin{aligned} \nabla V &= \frac{\partial \dot{x}}{\partial x} + \frac{\partial \dot{y}}{\partial y} + \frac{\partial \dot{z}}{\partial z} + \frac{\partial \dot{w}}{\partial w} \\ &= -a - b - d = -41 < 0. \end{aligned} \tag{6}$$

where $(\dot{x}, \dot{y}, \dot{z}, \dot{w}) \neq -(\dot{x}, \dot{y}, \dot{z}, \dot{w})$, therefore, the new system (2) is not symmetrical and its dissipation.

The balance points of the hyperchaotic system (2) are found by solving the following algebraic system of equations:

$$
\begin{aligned}
a(y-x)+eyz &= 0 \\
cx-by-xz &= 0 \\
xy-dz+\phi(w)x &= 0 \\
rx &= 0
\end{aligned}
\tag{7}
$$

From the lastest sub-equation in Equation (7), we have $x = 0$. Substituting $x = 0$ into the second and third sub-equations, we get $y = 0$ and $z = 0$, respectively. Thus, w can be any real numbers, i.e., $w \in \mathbb{R}$. Namely, the system (2) has infinity equilibria as

$$s_0 = [0, 0, 0, w]. \tag{8}$$

To explore the nonlinear dynamics of the proposed system at a large range of parameters, we compute the spectrum of LE of the system (1) when parameter $40 \leq d \leq 56$ with a stepsize 0.25. The numerical results are shown in Figure 3a, from which it can be seen that two positive LEs exist in the range of $40 \leq d \leq 51.5$. The results show that our system can robustly operate in a hyperchaotic state over a wide range of parameters. At the same time, the bifurcation diagram with section hyperplane $\{x = 0, \dot{x} < 0\}$ is presented in Figure 3c. It seems that the bifurcation outcomes align with the Lyapunov spectrum, indicating accurate calculation of the LE. The initial condition for all computations above is $(0.5, 0, 0.5, 0.5)$.

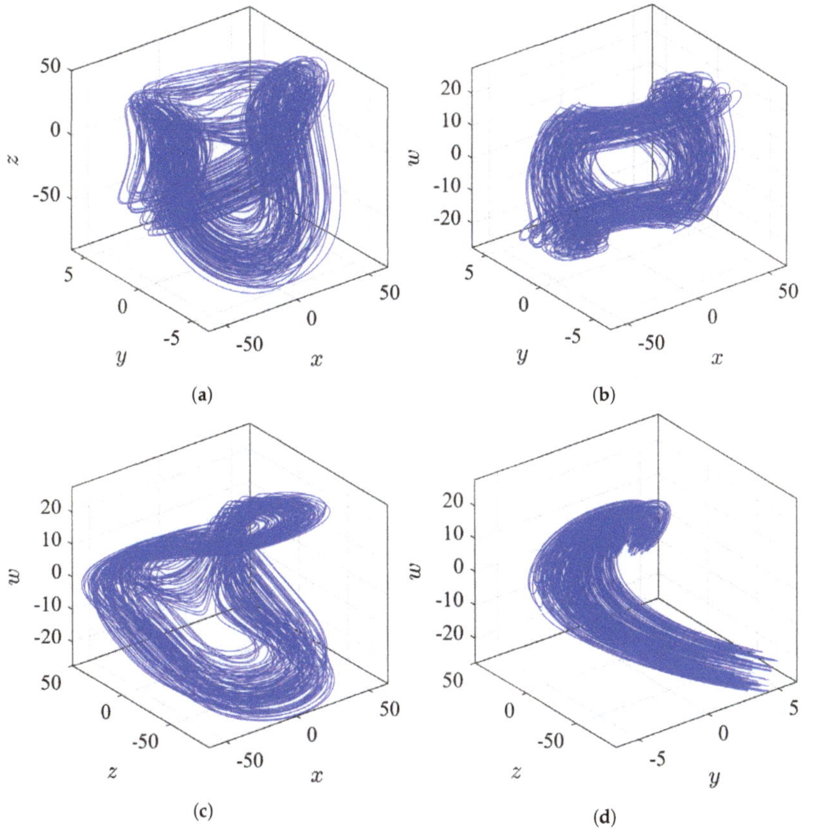

Figure 1. The hyperchaotic attractor in the phase space of the proposed system (2). (**a**) Projection in $x-y-z$. (**b**) Projection in $x-z-w$. (**c**) Projection in $x-z-w$. (**d**) Projection in $x-y-w$.

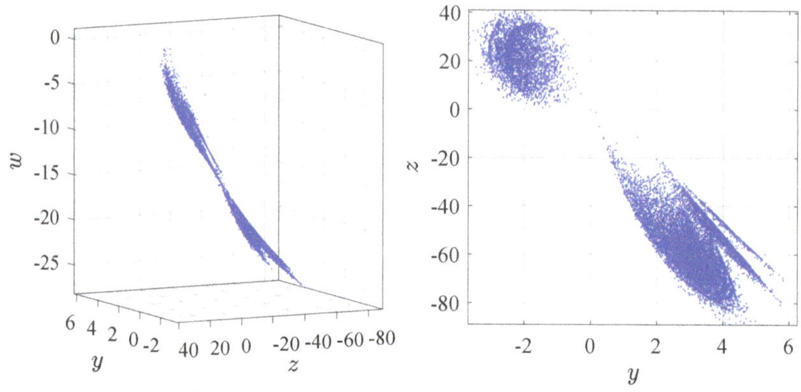

(a) (b)

Figure 2. Attractor in phase space of the Poincaré mapping H corresponding to the proposed system (2). (**a**) The side view. (**b**) Projection in $y - z$.

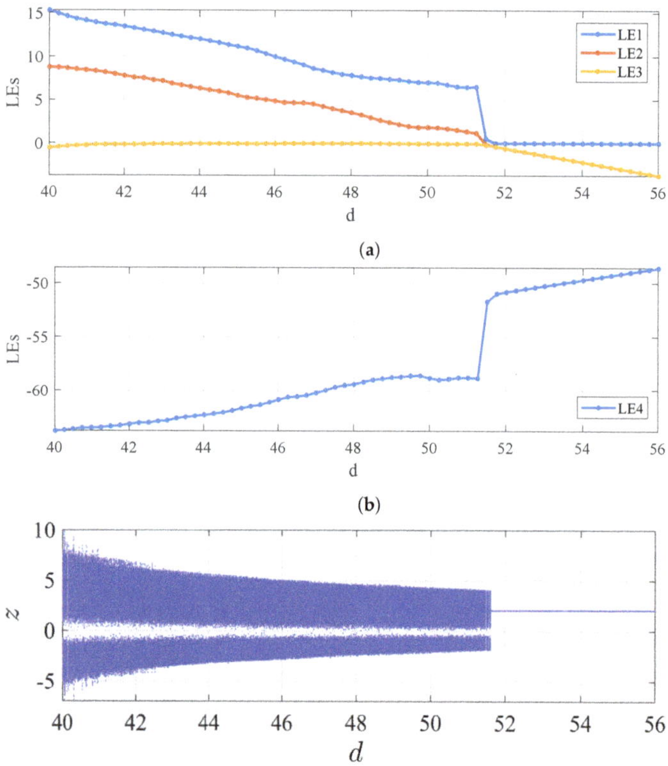

(a) (b) (c)

Figure 3. The LE spectrum of the proposed system (2). (**a**) The first three LEs corresponding to the expanding dimensions. (**b**) LE corresponding to the compression dimension. (**c**) The corresponding bifurcation diagram.

5. Engineering Application-Promising Characteristics

In this section, we discuss four dynamical features related to engineering applications, including (1) attractor complexity, (2) initial value sensitivity, (3) frequency spectrum and (4) robustness of system parameters.

5.1. Attractor Complexity

In chaos engineering applications, hyperchaos attractors generate random signals. The more complex the attractor means that it is more difficult to obtain all dynamic characteristics of the original system by signal analysis and signal reconstruction. Namely, the security properties of the generated signal are better. Generally, the Kaplan-Yorke dimension [40] is used to evaluate the complexity of attractors, and it is defined as follows.

$$D_{KY} = D + \sum_{i=1}^{D} \frac{LE_i}{|LE_D|} \tag{9}$$

where the constant D satisfies the following relation:

$$\sum_{i=1}^{D} LE_i \geq 0, \sum_{i=1}^{D+1} LE_i < 0 \tag{10}$$

Based on Equation (9), we can calculate the Kaplan–Yorke dimension of system (2) and compare it with six other typical systems. As shown in Table 1, system (2) outperforms all the comparison systems. This result suggests that the attractor of system (2) is more complex than those of the other systems. Notably, even when compared to the previously best-performing system [13] with multiple complex nonlinear terms, system (2) still outperforms it despite utilizing the simplest linear memristor.

Table 1. The Kaplan–Yorke dimension (D_{KY}) comparisons of typical hyperchaotic systems.

System	D_{KY}	LE_1	LE_2	LE_3	LE_4
System [41]	3.197	0.119	0.049	0	−0.852
System [42]	3.105	4.409	0.049	0	−0.852
System [18]	3.114	1.349	0.256	0	−14.095
System [19]	3.198	12.08	7.731	0	−97.229
System [20]	3.278	13.46	3.478	0	−61.231
System [13]	3.324	26.05	11.39	0	−115.518
System (2)	3.356	14.149	8.421	0	−63.475

5.2. Initial Value Sensitivity

For some applications, like image encryption, the initial value sensitivity of random signals is one of the key indicators. For dynamic systems, initial sensitivity can be measured the separating time, termed t_s, when two tracks clearly separated from each other. Meanwhile, at the beginning, the two tracks' initial values are very close. In the simulation, we select two different and sufficiently close points as initial values. They are respectively:

$$\begin{aligned} \mathbf{p}_1 &= [10, 10, 10, 10], \\ \mathbf{p}_2 &= \mathbf{p}_2 + [0, 0, 0, 0.01]. \end{aligned} \tag{11}$$

Also, we employ the ODE45 function in MATLAB to calculate the corresponding trajectory. The relative error and absolute errors were e^{-12} and e^{-9}, respectively. At the same time, another three typical hyperchaotic systems were selected as the comparison systems. Their orbits were calculated under the same initial value conditions.

The comparison results are presented in Figure 4. The two rails of system [19], system [20] and system [13] are separated obviously at $t_s = 0.9$, $t_s = 0.55$ and $t_s = 0.25$

respectively, whilst the separation time of the system (2) is $t_s = 0.15$. These results indicate that the system (2) is more sensitive to the initial conditions change.

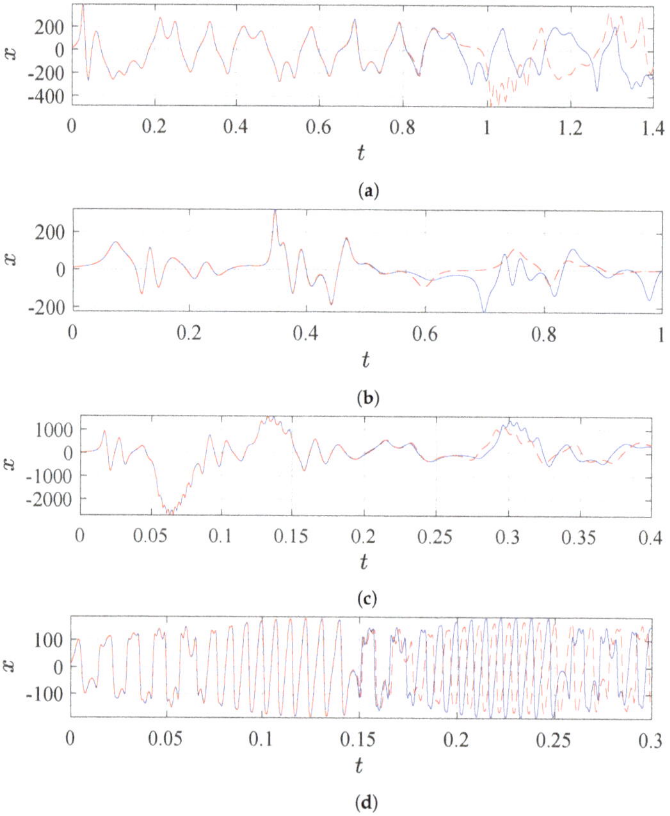

Figure 4. Initial value sensitivity comparison in terms of tracking the behaviours of two close initials. The results are in the x dimension. (**a**) System [19]. (**b**) System [20]. (**c**) System [13]. (**d**) The proposed system (2).

5.3. Frequency Spectrum

For secure communication, signal frequency bandwidth is a vital feature. According to signal theory, wider frequency bandwidth means signals comprise richer sine waves. The increase in high-frequency components makes the signal spectrum structure more complex, and the signals changes faster in the same time interval. Therefore, hyperchaotic signals with large bandwidths are more difficult to capture and extract, thus achieving secure communication purposes.

Here, we calculate the spectrum of the system [19], the system [20], the system [13], and the system (2) through simulation experiments Among them, the first three systems are used as comparison systems. In the calculation process, to eliminate the influence of variable step size in the Runge-Kutta method, the sampling time series with a sampling frequency of 400 is generated by interpolation, which was specifically realized by the DEVAL function in MATLAB.

In Figure 5, we present the one-side frequency spectra of three comparison systems and the system (2). The spectra values of y are normalized to be between 0 and 1. The same to the literature [13], the effective bandwidth is defined as spectrum frequency area of y is greater than 0.1. As shown in Figure 5d, the maximum effective frequency of system (2) is 120 Hz. Of note, There is also a 16 Hz gap width near 50 Hz (from 39 Hz to 55 Hz).

Therefore, the effective bandwidth of the system (2) is 104 Hz. Compared with the previous best 83 Hz [13], the bandwidth of this paper is increased by 21 Hz, relatively increased by 25%.

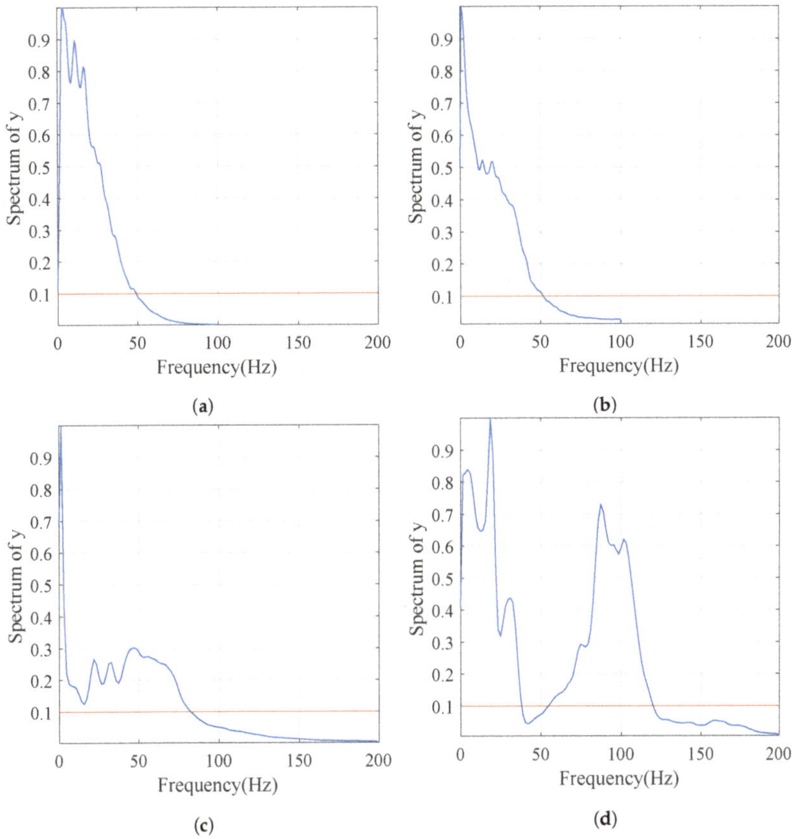

Figure 5. Frequency spectrum comparison based on the one-side normalized frequency spectra. The same to the literature [13], the effective bandwidth is defined as spectrum frequency area of y is greater than 0.1; the spectra computation is implemented by the DEVAL function in MATLAB. (**a**) System [19]. (**b**) System [20], (**c**) System [13], (**d**) The proposed system (2).

5.4. Robustness of System Parameters

In many practical applications, hyperchaotic systems are usually realized by employing physical circuits, and integrating them into the specific working system. However, the circuit is inevitably affected by factors such as thermal noise, thermal accumulation, electromagnetic interference, and so on, resulting in component parameter drift. Hyperchaotic systems with poor parameter robustness often degenerate into ordinary chaos or long-period orbits, negatively affecting communication systems' overall performance.

In this subsection, the parameter robustness of system (2) is discussed by the Lyapunov exponential spectrum method.

Specifically, for each system parameter, we select a real number range with a width of four, centring on a typical value of this parameter. Over this zone, we calculate the LEs of the system (2) and collectively present the values as a LE-varying curve. For example, for parameter $a = -39$, its corresponding changing range is $[-41, -37]$. Figure 6 shows the results of the LE-varying curve of all seven parameters.

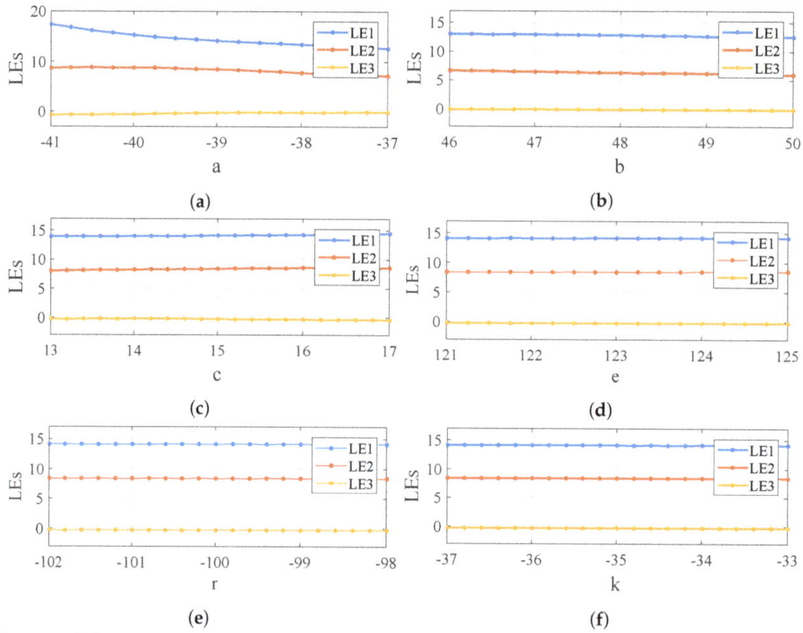

Figure 6. LE spectrum as parameters gradually vary. From (**a**–**f**), the results of (a, b, c, e, r, k) are presented, respectively (The result of d is presented in Figure 3).

From Figure 6, when all parameters of the system (2) have a drift of less than 2, the system still has two larger positive LEs with little value, and the system (2) continues to be hyperchaotic. Therefore, the system (2) can overcome hyperchaotic degradation caused by parameter drift to a certain extent.

6. Computer-Assisted Proof of Strong Complexity

As is known to all, LE is a numerical method, which inevitably has the computation error. Parameter selection significantly impacts the calculation results. It is not mathematically reliable to use it to judge system states. To fix this issue, in this section, we strictly prove the existence of chaos of system (2) with typical parameters utilizing computer-assisted proof.

Before proof, the symbolic dynamics and topological horseshoe are briefly introduced, which is essential for rigorous verification of chaos and estimation of topological entropy. If you want to know the detailed topological horseshoe and specific certification, you can refer to literature [16,17].

6.1. Result of Topological Horseshoes Theory

Let Σ_m is a sequence space that consists of all bi-infinite sequences with form as:

$$\begin{aligned} &s = \{\cdots, s_{-m}, \cdots, s_{-1}, s_0, s_1, \cdots, s_m, \cdots\}, \\ &s_m \in \{1, 2, \cdots, m-1\}. \end{aligned} \tag{12}$$

Definition 1. *Let $\sigma : \Sigma_m \to \Sigma_m$ to be m-shift map: for every element of s, it satisfies$\sigma(s_i) = s_{i+m}$. Mathematically, it is proved that Σ_m is Cantor set. It satisfies three properties [43]: (1) has a countable infinity of periodic orbits containing all periods; (2) has an uncountable infinity of periodic orbits; (3) has a dense orbit. From those properties above, we know that dynamics generated by the map σ is sensitive to initial conditions, which means σ is chaotic.*

Let X be a metric space, B be a compact subset of X and $f : D \to X$ be a map. Assume that there exists m mutually disjoint compact subsets $B_1, B_2, \cdots, B_m, 1 \le i \le m$. For each B_i, B_i^1 and B_i^2 indicate two disjoint compact subsets of B_i contained in the boundary ∂B_i.

Definition 2 ([18]). *Let Γ is B_i a compact subset, if for every subset $l \subset B_i$ and $\Gamma \cap l \neq \phi$, then Γ is said to completely separate B_i^1 and B_i^2, we denote it by $\Gamma \updownarrow (B_i^1, B_i^2)$.*

Definition 3 ([18]). *Let $\Gamma \subset B_i$ be a subset, we denote that $f(\Gamma)$ separates B_j with respect to B_j^1 and B_j^2, if Γ contains a compact subset Γ' such that $f(\Gamma') \updownarrow (B_j^1, B_j^2)$. In this case that $f(\Gamma) \mapsto B_j$ holds true for every subset $\Gamma \subset B_i$ with $\Gamma \updownarrow (B_i^1, B_i^2)$, we say that $f(B_i)$ separates B_j with respect to two pairs (B_i^1, B_i^2) and (B_j^1, B_j^2),or $f(B_i) \mapsto B_j$ in case of no confusion.*

Theorem 1 ([17]). *If the codimension-one crossing relation $f(B_i) \mapsto B_j$, hold for $1 \le i, j \le m$, then there exists a compact invariant set $K \subset B$, such that $f|K$ is semi-conjugate to the m-shift map, which is denoted by Σ_m and the entropy $ent(f) \ge \log m$. When $ent(f) > 0$, the map f is chaotic.*

6.2. Horseshoe and Topological Entropy Estimation in Dynamics of Poincaré-Map

In order to apply the above Definition and Theorem, we first convert the original continuous system (2) into the corresponding Poincaré-map. For the sake of simplicity, the subsequent proof is based on the Poincaré-map H defined in Section 3. Here, we find topological horseshoe geometry with 2D stretching, according to the algorithm for the 3D hyperchaotic topological horseshoes proposed in literature [44]. Firstly, through a series of attempts to find proper mapping zone containing periodic equilibrium points, the 2D topology horseshoe consisting of A and B is found on the attractor of map H, as shown in Figure 7. The four vertices of quadrilateral A in terms of $(y \times z \times w)$ are:

$$\begin{aligned} V_1^A &= [-1.8569, 25.3930, -5.8155], V_2^A = [-1.9594, 23.8266, -6.6488], \\ V_3^A &= [-1.9392, 23.7987, -6.6054], V_4^A = [-1.7935, 24.6516, -5.9051]. \end{aligned} \tag{13}$$

The four vertices of quadrilateral B in terms of $(y \times z \times w)$ are:

$$\begin{aligned} V_1^B &= [-1.8569, 25.3930, -5.5985], V_2^B = [-1.9594, 23.8266, -5.9157], \\ V_3^B &= [-1.9392, 23.7987, -5.9126], V_4^B = [-1.7935, 24.6516, -5.1736], \end{aligned} \tag{14}$$

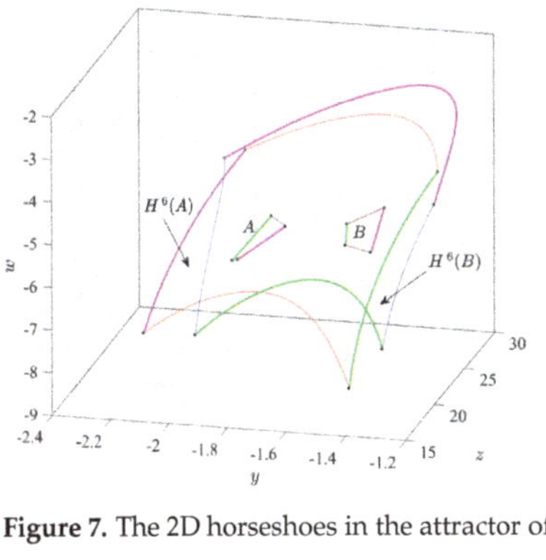

Figure 7. The 2D horseshoes in the attractor of map H.

Following that, based on the obtained quadrilateral A, hexahedron a is constructed through the following three steps:

(1) From the attractor of map H, the point near A is selected for surface fitting, and the surface equation is obtained.

(2) With the aid of this obtained equation, the normal direction of the centre of A is calculated.
(3) A is shifted along this normal line's positive and negative directions by 0.6, and two curved surfaces are obtained. Taking the surfaces as top and bottom surfaces, respectively, we can construct the hexahedron, namely the 3D subset a.

In the same way above, we can construct 3D subset b, which is corresponding to B in the 2D topological horseshoes.

Finally, the hexahedron a and b conduct six times Poincaré-map H respectively, a, b and their images $H^6(a)$, $H^6(b)$ form geometric relations as shown in Figure 8. It is easy to find that H_a^6 passes through both a and b clearly in the middle (Figure 8b), and there is no contact between a and b (Figure 8c). Therefore, H_a^6 satisfied $H^6(a) \mapsto a, b$. Similarly, by observing the geometry presented in Figure 8d, Figure 8e and Figure 8f, we can find that the $H^6(b) \mapsto a, b$ also hold.

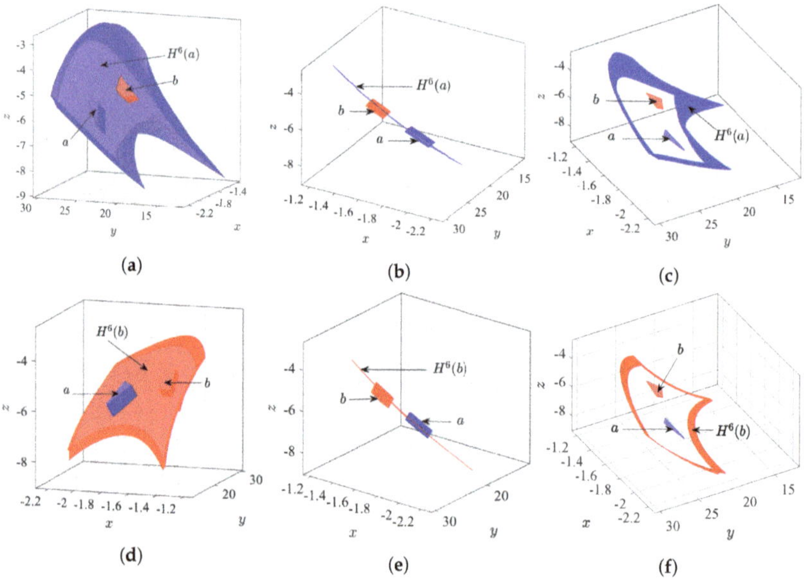

Figure 8. The 3D topoloical horseshoes. **Top** provides the case of $H^6(a)$ separates a, b where (**a–c**) show the details in 3D view, side view and top view, respectively. Similarly, **Bottom** provides the case of $H^6(b)$ separates a, b where (**d–f**) show the details.

Suppose that subsets a and b are considered as B_1 and B_2 in Theorem 1, respectively. Obviously, for any $1 \leq i, j \leq 2, H(B_i) \mapsto B_j$ is always is true. According to Theorem 1, we know that on the compact invariant set $\Lambda \subset a \cup b$, the map H is semi-conjugate to the 2-shift map and $ent(H) \geq \log 2$. Given that Σ_2 is chaotic. Therefore, H must be chaotic. Since that H^6(a) and H^6(b) expand in two directions, the expansions along each trajectory in Λ are also in two directions. So there must be exit two positive LEs. Therefore, the system (2) is hyperchaotic.

7. Fpga Implementation

Hardware implementation of the chaotic system contains two kinds of methods. One is to build chaos circuit with basic components of circuit [45], the other is to realize the chaos circuit with the platform of FPGA. Among them, the first method has many problems, because the phase diagram of the differential equation of the dynamical system built with circuit components are displayed by analogue filter [46], which is challenging to deal with a large amount of data in practical operation. The reason is that the circuit components will be affected by temperature, illumination, voltage, and other external factors, which increases the instability of the chaotic system. It is difficult to apply this hardware to achieve the method. Another method to realize the FPGA platform [47,48]. There are two aspects of advantages. On the one hand, FPGA is a digital signal processing device with high computational accuracy, widely used in multi-tasks [49]. It can strictly match the two chaotic parameters of its sending end and receiving end, which effectively improves the fidelity of the signal demodulated at the receiving end. On the other hand, the chaotic signal generated by FPGA has good portability and high confidentiality, which makes the circuit stable and not easily affected by external factors. It facilitates the further application of the chaotic system, e.g., typical image cryptosystem [50,51].

It is well known that FPGA is a semi-custom digital integrated circuits. Thus, the chaotic system's hardware implementation based on FPGA must first discretize the continuous system (2). Specifically, the sampling frequency ΔT must satisfy the chaotic signal cut-off frequency greater than at least twice. This makes the discrete chaotic system show dynamical characteristics closer to the system (2). The same to the other work [52,53], this paper adapts Euler's algorithm to discretize the system (2), which is described by:

$$\begin{cases} x_1(k+1) = \left[ax_2(k) - ax_1(k) + ex_2(k)x_3(k)\right]\Delta T + x_1(k) \\ x_2(k+1) = \left[cx_1(k) - bx_2(k) - x_1(k)x_3(k)\right]\Delta T + x_2(k) \\ x_3(k+1) = \left[x_1(k)x_2(k) - dx_3(k) - kx_4(k)x_1(k)\right]\Delta T + x_3(k) \\ x_4(k+1) = rx_1(k)\Delta T + x_4(k) \end{cases} \tag{15}$$

In Figure 9, we give the DSP-builder model of the system (2). Figure 10 shows the real FPGA hardware platform and the experimental results displayed by the digital oscilloscope. Clearly, as shown in Figure 11a–f, the chaotic attractor generated by the FPGA platform well matches the numerical simulation results of MATLAB displayed in Figure 1. These results confirm the feasibility of the proposed system.

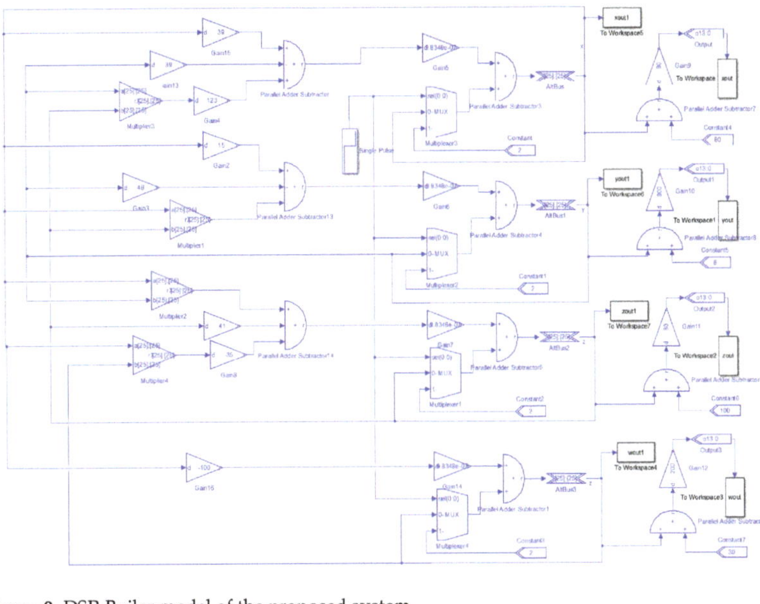

Figure 9. DSP-Builer model of the proposed system.

Figure 10. The implemented FPGA hardware.

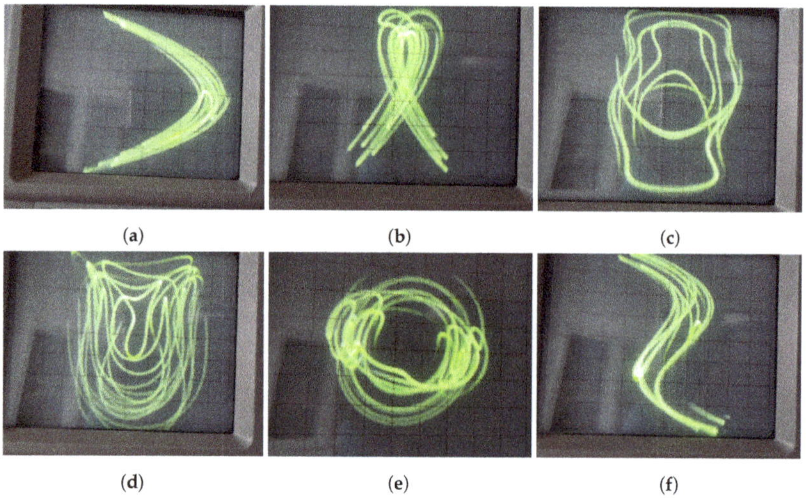

Figure 11. Tthe experimental results displayed by the digital oscilloscope.

8. Conclusions

Aiming at the core requirement of chaotic systems in engineering applications, a new 4D hyperchaotic system based on the linear memristor is proposed and analyzed comprehensively in this paper. Compared with existing systems, this new system exhibits improved properties such as strong complexity, initial value sensitivity, bandwidth, and parameter robustness. For instance, in terms of initial value sensitivity, our system relatively increased by 40% compared with the previous best system. In terms of theoretical analysis, we strictly prove the existence of the strong hyperchaos in given typical parameter condition. In addition, the new system with hyperchaotic was realized based on an FPGA digital development platform, which verifies the feasibility of the proposed system as a random number signal generator.

Our future work will focus on two main issues: First, we will explore the impact of the new dynamic characteristic of infinitely many equilibrium points. Second, we aim to expand this research to include systems with multi-linear memristors, which is significant for neuromorphic network research.

Author Contributions: Conceptualization, validation, writing—original draft preparation and review and editing and project administration, L.C.; investigation, validation and writing—review and editing, M.Y.; validation and formal analysis, J.L.; data curation and resources, J.M.; software and visualization, K.S.; Conceptualization, methodology and supervision, S.T. All authors have read and agreed to the published version of the manuscript.

Funding: This work is partly funded by National Natural Science Foundation of China (Grant No. 62206168, 62276048), Southwest Minzu University Research Startup Funds (Grant No. RQD2022024), Sichuan Science and Technology Program (Grant No. 2024NSFSC1404, 2023ZYD0006), Project of Qinghai-Tibetan Plateau Research in Southwest Minzu University (Grant 2024CXTD03), Shanghai SAST Funding (Grant SAST2023-084).

Data Availability Statement: The authors confirm that the data supporting the findings of this studyare available within the article.

Acknowledgments: Thanks to the editors and reviewers. All individuals included in this section have consented to the acknowledgement.

Conflicts of Interest: The authors declare no conflicts of interest.

Nomenclature

Abbreviation	Meaning
FPGA	Field programmable gate array
LE	Lyapunov Exponent
4/6D	4/6 dimensional
KY	Kaplan-York

References

1. Wolf, A.; Swift, J.B.; Swinney, H.L.; Vastano, J.A. Determining Lyapunov exponents from a time series. *Phys. Nonlinear Phenom.* **1985**, *16*, 285–317. [CrossRef]
2. Arnold, L.; Wihstutz, V. Lyapunov exponents: A survey. In Proceedings of the Lyapunov Exponents: Proceedings of a Workshop, Bremen, Germany, 12–15 November 1984; Springer: Berlin/Heidelberg, Germany, 2006; pp. 1–26.
3. Hua, Z.; Zhang, Y.; Zhou, Y. Two-dimensional modular chaotification system for improving chaos complexity. *IEEE Trans. Signal Process.* **2020**, *68*, 1937–1949. [CrossRef]
4. Bao, Y.; Zhao, D.; Sun, J.; Wen, G.; Yang, T. Resilient Synchronization of Neural Networks Under DoS Attacks and Communication Delays via Event-Triggered Impulsive Control. *IEEE Trans. Syst. Man, Cybern. Syst.* **2024**, *54*, 471–483. [CrossRef]
5. Deng, Y.; Fan, Z.F.; Zhao, B.B.; Wang, X.G.; Zhao, S.; Wu, J.; Grillot, F.; Wang, C. Mid-infrared hyperchaos of interband cascade lasers. *Light. Sci. Appl.* **2022**, *11*, 7–18. [CrossRef]
6. Rossler, O.E. An Equation for Hyperchaos. *Phys. Lett. A* **1979**, *71*, 155–157. [CrossRef]
7. Wang, X.; Wang, M. Hyperchaotic Lorenz system. *Acta Phys. Sin.* **2007**, *56*, 6–12.
8. Li, Q.; Hu, S.; Tang, S.; Zeng, G. Hyperchaos and horseshoe in a 4D memristive system with a line of equilibria and its implementation. *Int. J. Circuit Theory Appl.* **2014**, *42*, 1172–1188. [CrossRef]
9. Pham, V.T.; Volos, C.; Gambuzza, L.V. A memristive hyperchaotic system without equilibrium. *Sci. World J.* **2014**, *2014*, 368986. [CrossRef] [PubMed]
10. Lai, Q.; Yang, L.; Liu, Y. Design and realization of discrete memristive hyperchaotic map with application in image encryption. *Chaos Solitons Fractals* **2022**, *165*, 112781. [CrossRef]
11. Mezatio, B.A.; Motchongom Tingue, M.; Kengne, R.; Tchagna Kouanou, A.; Fozin Fonzin, T.; Tchitnga, R. Complex dynamics from a novel memristive 6D hyperchaotic autonomous system. *Int. J. Dyn. Control.* **2020**, *8*, 70–90. [CrossRef]
12. Xiu, C.; Fang, J.; Ma, X. Design and circuit implementations of multimemristive hyperchaotic system. *Chaos Solitons Fractals* **2022**, *161*, 112409. [CrossRef]
13. Chen, L.; Tang, S.; Li, Q.; Zhong, S. A new 4D hyperchaotic system with high complexity. *Math. Comput. Simul.* **2018**, *146*, 44–56. [CrossRef]
14. Liu, Y.; Jiang, Z.; Xu, X.; Zhang, F.; Xu, J. Optical image encryption algorithm based on hyper-chaos and public-key cryptography. *Opt. Laser Technol.* **2020**, *127*, 106171. [CrossRef]
15. Alzaidi, A.A.; Ahmad, M.; Ahmed, H.S.; Solami, E.A. Sine-cosine optimization-based bijective substitution-boxes construction using enhanced dynamics of chaotic map. *Complexity* **2018**, *2018*, 1–16. [CrossRef]
16. Gidea, M.; Zgliczyński, P. Covering relations for multidimensional dynamical systems. *J. Differ. Equ.* **2004**, *202*, 59–80. [CrossRef]
17. Yang, X.; Li, H.; Huang, Y. A planar topological horseshoe theory with applications to computer verifications of chaos. *J. Phys. Math. Gen.* **2005**, *38*, 4175. [CrossRef]
18. Ling, L.; Liu, C.; Zhang, Y. Theoretical analysis and circuit implementation of a novel complicated hyperchaotic system. *Nonlinear Dyn.* **2011**, *66*, 707–715.
19. Wu, W.; Chen, Z. Hopf bifurcation and intermittent transition to hyperchaos in a novel strong four-dimensional hyperchaotic system. *Nonlinear Dyn.* **2010**, *60*, 615–630. [CrossRef]
20. Qi, G.; Wyk, M.; Wyk, B.; Chen, G. On a new hyperchaotic system. *Phys. Lett. A* **2007**, *372*, 124–136. [CrossRef]
21. Kuate, P.D.K.; Tchendjeu, A.E.T.; Fotsin, H. A modified rössler prototype-4 system based on chua's diode nonlinearity: Dynamics, multistability, multiscroll generation and fpga implementation. *Chaos Solitons Fractals* **2020**, *140*, 110213. [CrossRef]

22. Karawanich, K.; Prommee, P. High-complex chaotic system based on new nonlinear function and OTA-based circuit realization. *Chaos Solitons Fractals* **2022**, *162*, 112536. [CrossRef]
23. Zhang, S.; Wang, X.; Zeng, Z. A simple no-equilibrium chaotic system with only one signum function for generating multidirectional variable hidden attractors and its hardware implementation. *Chaos Interdiscip. J. Nonlinear Sci.* **2020**, *30*, 053129. [CrossRef] [PubMed]
24. Zhang, S.; Zhang, H.; Wang, C. Memristor initial-boosted extreme multistability in the novel dual-memristor hyperchaotic maps. *Chaos Solitons Fractals* **2023**, *174*, 113885. [CrossRef]
25. Li, Q.; Tang, S.; Zeng, H.; Zhou, T. On hyperchaos in a small memristive neural network. *Nonlinear Dyn.* **2014**, *78*, 1087–1099. [CrossRef]
26. Bao, B.; Jiang, P.; Wu, H.; Hu, F. Complex transient dynamics in periodically forced memristive Chua's circuit. *Nonlinear Dyn.* **2015**, *79*, 2333–2343. [CrossRef]
27. Tang, S.; Chen, L.; Yang, F.; Li, Q. Simple hyperchaotic memory system with large topological entropy. *Nonlinear Anal. Model. Control.* **2017**, *22*, 230–247. [CrossRef]
28. Yu, H.; Du, S.; Dong, E.; Tong, J. Transient behaviors and equilibria-analysis-based boundary crisis analysis in a smooth 4D dynamical system. *Chaos Solitons Fractals* **2022**, *160*, 112220. [CrossRef]
29. Wang, Z.; Cang, S.; Ochola, E.O.; Sun, Y. A hyperchaotic system without equilibrium. *Nonlinear Dyn.* **2012**, *69*, 531–537. [CrossRef]
30. Rajagopal, K.; Khalaf, A.J.M.; Wei, Z.; Pham, V.T.; Alsaedi, A.; Hayat, T. Hyperchaos and coexisting attractors in a modified van der Pol–Duffing oscillator. *Int. J. Bifurc. Chaos* **2019**, *29*, 1950067. [CrossRef]
31. Chen, L.J.; Tang, S.; Yang, F.Y.; Zhong, S.M. Co-Existing of Multi-Attractor and Chaotic Transition in a Strong Hyperchaotic System. In Proceedings of the 2019 16th International Computer Conference on Wavelet Active Media Technology and Information Processing, Chengdu, China, 13–15 December 2019; pp. 49–54.
32. Ojoniyi, O.S.; Njah, A.N. A 5D hyperchaotic Sprott B system with coexisting hidden attractors. *Chaos Solitons Fractals Appl. Sci. Eng. Interdiscip. J. Nonlinear Sci.* **2016**, *87*, 172–181. [CrossRef]
33. Gong, L.H.; Luo, H.X.; Wu, R.Q.; Zhou, N.R. New 4D chaotic system with hidden attractors and self-excited attractors and its application in image encryption based on RNG. *Phys. A Stat. Mech. Appl.* **2022**, *591*, 126793. [CrossRef]
34. Qi, G.; Chen, G.; Du, S.; Chen, Z.; Yuan, Z. Analysis of a new chaotic system. *Phys. A Stat. Mech. Its Appl.* **2005**, *352*, 295–308. [CrossRef]
35. Bao, B.; Zou, X.; Liu, Z.; Hu, F. Generalized memory element and chaotic memory system. *Int. J. Bifurc. Chaos* **2013**, *23*, 1350135. [CrossRef]
36. Wu, G.C.; Baleanu, D. Jacobian matrix algorithm for Lyapunov exponents of the discrete fractional maps. *Commun. Nonlinear Sci. Numer. Simul.* **2015**, *22*, 95–100. [CrossRef]
37. Qin, X.; Jiang, Z.; Yu, J.; Huang, L.; Yan, C. Strong stability-preserving three-derivative Runge–Kutta methods. *Comput. Appl. Math.* **2023**, *42*, 171. [CrossRef]
38. Michalak, K. Optimization of Poincaré sections for discriminating between stochastic and deterministic behavior of dynamical systems. *Chaos Solitons Fractals* **2015**, *78*, 215–228. [CrossRef]
39. Lei, H. Dynamical Structures Associated with High-Order and Secondary Resonances in the Spin–Orbit Problem. *Astron. J.* **2024**, *167*, 121–137. [CrossRef]
40. Evans, D.J.; Cohen, E.; Searles, D.J.; Bonetto, F. Note on the Kaplan–Yorke dimension and linear transport coefficients. *J. Stat. Phys.* **2000**, *101*, 17–34. [CrossRef]
41. Zhou, P.; Wei, L.; Cheng, X. A hyperchaos system with only one nonlinear term. *Acta Phys. Sin.* **2009**, *58*, 5201–5208. [CrossRef]
42. Chen, Z.; Yang, Y.; Qi, G.; Yuan, Z. A novel hyperchaos system only with one equilibrium. *Phys. Lett. A* **2007**, *360*, 696–701. [CrossRef]
43. Wiggins, S. *Global Bifurcations and Chaos: Analytical Methods*; Springer Science & Business Media: Berlin/Heidelberg, Germany, 2013; Volume 73.
44. Li, Q.; Tang, S. Algorithm for finding horseshoes in three-dimensional hyperchaotic maps and its application. *Acta Phys. Sin.* **2013**, *62*, 8–15.
45. Fu, S.; Liu, Y. Complex dynamical behavior of modified MLC circuit. *Chaos Solitons Fractals* **2020**, *141*, 110407. [CrossRef]
46. Jiao, X.; Dong, E.; Wang, Z. Dynamic Analysis and FPGA Implementation of a Kolmogorov-Like Hyperchaotic System. *Int. J. Bifurc. Chaos* **2021**, *31*, 2150052. [CrossRef]
47. Sambas, A.; Vaidyanathan, S.; Tlelo-Cuautle, E.; Zhang, S.; Guillen-Fernandez, O.; Sukono; Hidayat, Y.; Gundara, G. A novel chaotic system with two circles of equilibrium points: Multistability, electronic circuit and FPGA realization. *Electronics* **2019**, *8*, 1211. [CrossRef]
48. Sambas, A.; Vaidyanathan, S.; Tlelo-Cuautle, E.; Abd-El-Atty, B.; El-Latif, A.A.A.; Guillen-Fernandez, O.; Sukono; Hidayat, Y.; Gundara, G. A 3-D multi-stable system with a peanut-shaped equilibrium curve: Circuit design, FPGA realization, and an application to image encryption. *IEEE Access* **2020**, *8*, 137116–137132. [CrossRef]
49. Humaidi, A.J.; Kadhim, T.M.; Hasan, S.; Kasim Ibraheem, I.; Taher Azar, A. A Generic Izhikevich-Modelled FPGA-Realized Architecture: A Case Study of Printed English Letter Recognition. In Proceedings of the 2020 24th International Conference on System Theory, Control and Computing (ICSTCC), Sinaia, Romania, 8–10 October 2020; pp. 825–830. [CrossRef]

50. Sambas, A.; Vaidyanathan, S.; Zhang, X.; Koyuncu, I.; Bonny, T.; Tuna, M.; Alcin, M.; Zhang, S.; Sulaiman, I.M.; Awwal, A.M.; et al. A novel 3D chaotic system with line equilibrium: Multistability, integral sliding mode control, electronic circuit, FPGA implementation and its image encryption. *IEEE Access* **2022**, *10*, 68057–68074. [CrossRef]
51. Vaidyanathan, S.; Sambas, A.; Tlelo-Cuautle, E.; El-Latif, A.A.A.; Abd-El-Atty, B.; Guillen-Fernandez, O.; Benkouider, K.; Mohamed, M.A.; Mamat, M.; Ibrahim, M.A.H. A new 4-D multi-stable hyperchaotic system with no balance point: Bifurcation analysis, circuit simulation, FPGA realization and image cryptosystem. *IEEE Access* **2021**, *9*, 144555–144573. [CrossRef]
52. Wang, Y.; Li, X.; Li, X.; Guang, Y.; Wu, Y.; Ding, Q. FPGA-Based implementation and synchronization design of a new five-dimensional hyperchaotic system. *Entropy* **2022**, *24*, 1179. [CrossRef] [PubMed]
53. Zhang, X.; Xu, J.; Moshayedi, A.J. Design and FPGA implementation of a hyperchaotic conservative circuit with initial offset-boosting and transient transition behavior based on memcapacitor. *Chaos Solitons Fractals* **2024**, *179*, 114460–114481. [CrossRef]

mathematics

Article

Robust Constrained Cooperative Control for Multiple Trains

Qijie Hu [1], Xinyu Fan [1,*] and Yue Wei [2]

[1] School of Automation, Central South University, Changsha 410081, China; huqijie_csu@163.com
[2] Guangdong Laboratory of Artificial Intelligence and Digital Economy (Shenzhen), Shenzhen 518000, China; weiyue@gml.ac.cn
* Correspondence: auxyfan@csu.edu.cn

Abstract: This paper investigates robust constrained cooperative control for multiple trains, taking into account disturbances, velocity and control input constraints, and nonlinear operation resistances. A robust constrained cooperative control algorithm is employed, utilizing position information from neighboring trains to ensure each train operates within the desired formation. The effects of external disturbances are examined through multiple transformations and the convexity of stochastic matrices, resulting in an error bound for the final relative positions. This error boundary is correlated with the parameters of the system matrix, initial state conditions, and disturbance amplitudes. The theoretical findings are substantiated with a numerical example.

Keywords: multiple trains systems; robust constrained cooperative control; velocity and control input constraints; disturbances

MSC: 93A16

1. Introduction

Railways play an important role in modern transportation [1]. Numerous research efforts have been dedicated to improving train control systems. Early works on train control primarily focused on cruise control for single trains. For instance, mixed control H_2/H_∞ [2], a robust adaptive control algorithm [3], adaptive iterative learning control [4], and velocity difference control [5] were derived for high-speed trains to study cruise control problems.

The control of multi-agent systems has been extensively studied. The multi-agent model was introduced to address the coordinated cruise control problem for multiple trains [6,7]. In [8], cooperative control was used in multiple train systems. In [9], the proposed event-triggered communication mechanism can reduce the effects of time delay on the coordinated control of multiple trains effectively. Under a moving block signaling mechanism, the adaptive control method was introduced to realize the coordinated control of multiple trains in [10]. Based on the model in [10], the braking distance and redundant safe distance were considered in [11]. Moreover, in [12], the robust constrained cooperative control problem for trains was transformed into an optimization problem that can be solved by the related optimization algorithms.

Additionally, addressing the cooperative control issue for multiple high-speed trains with constraints, [13] proposed a cooperative control strategy that considers constraints. In addition, there has been work focusing on energy-saving problems of coordinated control for multiple train systems in [14,15] and the discussion of cooperative time in [16].

However, most of the above results assumed that each train operates under ideal conditions without considering constraints and disturbances, which may lead to the poor performances of those algorithms under actual scenarios. In [4,17,18], constraints were addressed, but the results were given in the absence of external disturbances and uncertainties. As high-speed railways extend for hundreds of kilometers, the movement of high-speed trains is inevitably affected by complex environments [19]. Real-world factors, such as operational resistance, sensor measurement errors, and environmental disturbances like wind and rain, impact the control performance. In [19–23], external disturbances and uncertainties were studied, but it was assumed that the trains are not subjected to the constraints of states and inputs. There are few works that address the coexistence of constraints and external disturbances simultaneously. Motivated by these practical challenges, we investigate robust constrained cooperative control for multiple train systems considering disturbances, velocity and control input constraints, and nonlinear operation resistances.

Our work extends the approach in [17] by incorporating external disturbances. The robust constrained cooperative control algorithm using information from neighboring trains can guarantee that each train runs in the desired formation. The effects of external disturbances are studied by using multiple transformations and the convexity of stochastic matrices, based on which an error bound is given for the final relative positions, which are correlated with the parameters of the system matrix, initial state conditions, and disturbance maximums. The main contribution is the simultaneous consideration of four different kinds of nonlinearities and the provision of an explicit upper bound for the effects of external disturbances on robust constrained cooperative control of multiple train systems. This consideration enhances the robustness and reliability of train control systems in practical scenarios.

2. Problem Description

In this section, we present the problem description of a multi-train system, considering disturbances, resistance, and constraints on velocity and control inputs.

2.1. Graph Theory

Let $\mathcal{G}(\mathcal{I},\mathcal{E})$ be a directed graph composed of n nodes, where $\mathcal{I} = \{1,\ldots,n\}$ and $\mathcal{E} \in \mathcal{I} \times \mathcal{I}$ denotes the edge set. Edge $(j,i) \in \mathcal{E}$ if node i can obtain node j's information. Each edge weight satisfies that $a_{ij} \geq \xi_a$ for some constant $\xi_a > 0$ if $(j,i) \in \mathcal{E}$ and $a_{ij} = 0$ otherwise. The neighbor set of node i is denoted by $\mathcal{N}_i = \{j \in \mathcal{I} : (i,j) \in \mathcal{E}\}$.

The Laplacian matrix of $\mathcal{G}$ is defined as $[L]_{ij} = -a_{ij}$ and $[L]_{ii} = \sum_{j=1}^{n} a_{ij}$ for all $i \neq j$. A path is composed of a series of edges such as $(i_1,i_2),(i_2,i_3),\ldots$, where $i_j \in \mathcal{I}$. A strongly connected graph is one in which there is a directed path between every node [24]. The non-negative matrix $C \in \mathbb{R}^{n\times n}$ is stochastic if $C\mathbf{1} = \mathbf{1}$ [25].

2.2. Model

Suppose a multiple train system with n trains. Each train is considered as one node in graph $\mathcal{G}$ and is assumed to have the following dynamics

$$\begin{aligned} p_i((k+1)T) &= p_i(kT) + v_i(kT)T + \omega_{i1}(kT), \\ v_i((k+1)T) &= v_i(kT) + [u_i(kT) + \omega_{i3}(kT)]T - r_i(kT)T + \omega_{i2}(kT), \end{aligned} \tag{1}$$

where $p_i(kT), v_i(kT), u_i(kT) \in \mathbb{R}$ are the position, velocity and control input for train i, $\omega_{i1}(kT)$, $\omega_{i2}(kT)$, and $\omega_{i3}(kT)$ represent the different disturbances, such as uncertainty in the system parameters, sensor measurement errors, and uncertainty in air resistance, $r_i(kT)$ denotes the operation resistance, k is the time index, and T represents the sampling period. These disturbances affect the position, velocity, and control input of the trains, respectively. Usually, the operation resistance consists of aerodynamic drag, and mechanical resistance is assumed to have the following form, as in [26],

$$r_i(kT) = c_0 + c_v v_i(kT) + c_a v_i^2(kT), \tag{2}$$

where the coefficients are $c_0 > 0$, $c_v > 0$, and $c_a > 0$. The first two terms represent the mechanical resistance, and the third term is the aerodynamic drag. For simplicity, we use "(k)" instead of "(kT)" in the following when no confusion can arise.

In actual situations, the velocity and input for all trains usually satisfy some constraints due to the equipment restrictions. To this end, it is assumed that $v_i(k) \in V_i = [0, \bar{\theta}_{1i}] \subset \mathbb{R}$

and $u_i(k) \in U_i = [\underline{\theta}_{2i}, \bar{\theta}_{2i}] \subset \mathbb{R}$ for all trains, where $\bar{\theta}_{1i} > 0$ denotes the maximum velocity, $\underline{\theta}_{2i} < 0$ denotes the maximum braking acceleration, and $\bar{\theta}_{2i} > 0$ denotes the maximum forward acceleration, respectively.

Let $S_{X_i}[\cdot]$ represents the saturation operator for a set $X_i = [\underline{\zeta}_i, \bar{\zeta}_i]$, such that

$$S_{X_i}[x_i] = \begin{cases} x_i, & \underline{\zeta}_i \leq x_i \leq \bar{\zeta}_i \\ \bar{\zeta}_i, & x_i > \bar{\zeta}_i \\ \underline{\zeta}_i, & x_i < \underline{\zeta}_i. \end{cases} \tag{3}$$

The system (1) with constraints is expressed as

$$\begin{aligned} p_i(k+1) &= p_i(k) + v_i(k)T + \omega_{i1}(k), \\ v_i(k+1) &= S_{V_i}[v_i(k) + S_{U_i}[u_i(k) + \omega_{i3}(k)]T - r_i(k)T + \omega_{i2}(k)]. \end{aligned} \tag{4}$$

According to reference [26], the operation resistance is far less than the maximum braking acceleration and forward acceleration for trains. For simplicity of discussion, the following assumption is given.

Assumption 1. *Suppose that* $|\bar{\theta}_{2i}| > \kappa|r_i(k)|, |\underline{\theta}_{2i}| > \kappa|r_i(k)|$ *for some constant* $\kappa > 10$.

Our objective of this paper is to analyze the effects of the disturbances in an explicit manner when the trains move in the desired formation, i.e.,

$$\lim_{k\to\infty} |p_i(k) - p_j(k) - d_{ij}| = 0 \tag{5}$$

for all i and j. From reference [17], d_{ij} can be regarded as $d_{ij} = d_i - d_j$ for all $i, j \in \mathcal{I}$, where d_i and d_j are two constants.

3. Main Results

3.1. Robust Constrained Cooperative Control Algorithm

For all trains, the algorithm proposed in [17] is adopted as

$$\begin{aligned} u_i(k) &= u_{ri}(k) + u_{ci}(k) \\ u_{ri}(k) &= c_0 + c_v v_i(k) + c_a v_i^2(k) \\ u_{ci}(k) &= -h_i(v_i(k) - v_0) + \sum_{j\in\mathcal{N}_i} a_{ij}(p_j(k) - p_i(k) + d_{ij}), \end{aligned} \tag{6}$$

where $h_i > 0$ is a constant. It is assumed here that the desired velocity v_0 is known to all trains because of the high requirements of safety.

$u_{ri}(k)$ is used to counteract $r_i(k)$ for all trains, and $u_{ci}(k)$ is used to ensure all trains move in a desired formation by tracking the desired velocity v_0.

3.2. Model Transformations

In this subsection, we introduce transformations and scaling factors to handle constraints and resistance.

3.2.1. Constraint Set Transformations

In system (4), due to input constraints, $u_{ri}(k)$ cannot compensate the operation resistance directly. Here, we introduce the following equivalent transformations.

Let

$$\bar{V}_i = [-v_0, \bar{\theta}_{1i} - v_0]. \tag{7}$$

From reference [17,27], it follows that $S_{V_i}[v_i(k)] - v_0 = S_{\bar{V}_i}[v_i(k) - v_0]$.

From the definitions of v_0 and $\bar{V}_i$, we have $|S_{\bar{V}_i}[x]| \geq \underline{\beta}_{1i} \triangleq \min\{v_0, \bar{\theta}_{1i} - v_0\}$ and $|S_{\bar{V}_i}[x]| \leq \bar{\beta}_{1i} \triangleq \max\{v_0, \bar{\theta}_{1i} - v_0\}$ if $S_{\bar{V}_i}(x) \neq x$. Define

$$\bar{U}_i(k) = [\underline{\theta}_{2i} - r_i(k), \bar{\theta}_{2i} - r_i(k)]. \tag{8}$$

Then, we have $S_{U_i}[u_i(k)] - r_i(k) = S_{\bar{U}_i(k)}[u_i(k) - r_i(k)]$. From (2) and Assumption 1, we have $c_0 \leq r_i(k) \leq c_0 + c_v\bar{\theta}_{1i} + c_a\bar{\theta}_{1i}^2$.

Similarly, if $S_{\bar{U}_i(k)}[x] \neq x$, we have $|S_{\bar{U}_i(k)}[x]| \geq \underline{\beta}_{2i} \triangleq \min\{|\bar{\theta}_{2i} - c_0|, |\underline{\theta}_{2i} - (c_0 + c_v\bar{\theta}_{1i} + c_a\bar{\theta}_{1i}^2)|\}$ and $|S_{\bar{U}_i(k)}[x]| \leq \bar{\beta}_{2i} \triangleq \max\{|\bar{\theta}_{2i} - c_0|, |\underline{\theta}_{2i} - (c_0 + c_v\bar{\theta}_{1i} + c_a\bar{\theta}_{1i}^2)|\}$.

3.2.2. Model Transformations

Define $\hat{p}_i(k) = p_i(k) - v_0kT - d_i$, and $\bar{v}_i(k) = v_i(k) - v_0$.

It follows that

$$\begin{aligned}
\hat{p}_i(k+1) &= p_i(k+1) - v_0(k+1)T - d_i \\
&= p_i(k) + v_i(k)T + \omega_{i1}(k) - v_0(k+1)T - d_i \\
&= \hat{p}_i(k) + \bar{v}_i(k)T + \omega_{i1}(k) \\
\bar{v}_i(k+1) &= v_i(k+1) - v_0 \\
&= S_{V_i}[v_i(k) + S_{\bar{U}_i(k)}[u_{ri}(k) + u_{ci}(k) \\
&\quad + \omega_{i3}(k) - r_i(k)]T + \omega_{i2}(k)] - v_0 \\
&= S_{\bar{V}_i}[\bar{v}_i(k) + S_{\bar{U}_i(k)}[-h_i\bar{v}_i(k) + \omega_{i3}(k) \\
&\quad + \sum_{j\in\mathcal{N}_i} a_{ij}(\hat{p}_j(k) - \hat{p}_i(k))]T + \omega_{i2}(k)].
\end{aligned} \tag{9}$$

To remove the constraint operator $S_{F_i}[*]$, the following scaling factors $\rho_{1i}(k)$ and $\rho_{2i}(k)$ are introduced for all i and $k \geq 0$,

$$\rho_{1i}(k) = \begin{cases} \frac{S_{\bar{V}_i}[f_{1i}(k)]}{f_{1i}(k)} & , f_{1i}(k) \neq 0, \\ 1 & , f_{1i}(k) = 0, \end{cases} \tag{10}$$

and

$$\rho_{2i}(k) = \begin{cases} \frac{S_{\bar{U}_i(k)}[f_{2i}(k)]}{f_{2i}(k)} & , f_{2i}(k) \neq 0, \\ 1 & , f_{2i}(k) = 0, \end{cases} \tag{11}$$

where $f_{1i}(k) = \bar{v}_i(k) + S_{\bar{U}_i(k)}[u_{ci}(k) + \omega_{i3}(k)]T + \omega_{i2}(k)$, $f_{2i}(k) = u_{ci}(k) + \omega_{i3}(k)$. According to the definition of $\rho_{1i}(k)$, we have $\left\|S_{\bar{V}_i}[f_{1i}(k)]\right\| \leq \|f_{1i}(k)\|$. Note that $\left\|S_{\bar{V}_i}[f_{1i}(k)]\right\| > 0$ and $\|f_{1i}(k)\| > 0$. It follows that $0 < \rho_{1i}(k) \leq 1$. Analogously, we have $0 < \rho_{2i}(k) \leq 1$.

Applying algorithm (6), system (4) can be expressed as

$$\begin{aligned}
\hat{p}_i(k+1) &= \hat{p}_i(k) + \bar{v}_i(k)T + \omega_{i1}(k), \\
\bar{v}_i(k+1) &= \rho_{1i}(k)\bar{v}_i(k) - \rho_{1i}(k)\rho_{2i}(k)h_i\bar{v}_i(k)T \\
&\quad + \rho_{1i}(k)\rho_{2i}(k)\alpha_i(k)T + \rho_{1i}(k)\omega_{i2}(k) \\
&\quad + \rho_{1i}(k)\rho_{2i}(k)\omega_{i3}(k)T,
\end{aligned} \tag{12}$$

where $\alpha_i(k) = \sum_{j\in\mathcal{N}_i} a_{ij}(\hat{p}_j(k) - \hat{p}_i(k))$. In system (12), the constraints of the velocities and the inputs are removed by introducing $\rho_{1i}(k)$ and $\rho_{2i}(k)$. However, there still exists an integral relationship between the states $\hat{p}_i(k)$ and $\bar{v}_i(k)$, which makes the system analysis hard to be proceeded. To this end, a further model transformation needs to be made.

Let

$$\hat{v}_i(k) = \hat{p}_i(k) + c_i\bar{v}_i(k), \tag{13}$$

where c_i is a constant. It follows that

$$\begin{aligned}
\hat{p}_i(k+1) &= (1-\frac{T}{c_i})\hat{p}_i(k) + \frac{T}{c_i}\hat{v}_i(k) + \omega_{i1}(k), \\
\hat{v}_i(k+1) &= (1-\frac{T}{c_i} - \rho_{1i}(k)(1-\rho_{2i}(k)h_iT))\hat{p}_i(k) \\
&\quad + (\frac{T}{c_i} + \rho_{1i}(k)(1-\rho_{2i}(k)h_iT))\hat{v}_i(k) \\
&\quad + c_i\rho_{1i}(k)\rho_{2i}(k)\alpha_i(k)T + c_i\rho_{1i}(k)\omega_{i2}(k) \\
&\quad + c_i\rho_{1i}(k)\rho_{2i}(k)\omega_{i3}(k)T + \omega_{i1}(k).
\end{aligned} \tag{14}$$

Let $\psi(k) = [\hat{p}_1(k), \hat{v}_1(k), \ldots, \hat{p}_n(k), \hat{v}_n(k)]^T$, and $M(k) = \text{diag}\{M_1(k), \ldots, M_n(k)\}$ with

$$M_i(k) = \begin{bmatrix} 1-\frac{T}{c_i} & \frac{T}{c_i} \\ M_{1i}(k) & M_{2i}(k) \end{bmatrix}, \tag{15}$$

where $\text{diag}\{H_1, \ldots, H_m\}$ denotes a block diagonal matrix with H_i as the ith diagonal matrix block for all $i \in \{1,2,\ldots,m\}$. Let $M_{1i}(k) = 1-\frac{T}{c_i} - \rho_{1i}(k)(1-\rho_{2i}(k)h_iT)$, $M_{2i}(k) = \frac{T}{c_i} + \rho_{1i}(k)(1-\rho_{2i}(k)h_iT)$, $Q=\text{diag}\{Q_1,\ldots,Q_n\}$ with $Q_i=\begin{bmatrix} 0 & 0 \\ 0 & c_i \end{bmatrix}$, $P_1(k)=\text{diag}\{\rho_{11}(k),\ldots,\rho_{1n}(k)\}$, $P_2(k)=\text{diag}\{\rho_{21}(k),\ldots,\rho_{2n}(k)\}$ and $P(k)=P_1(k)P_2(k) = \text{diag}\{\rho_{11}(k)\rho_{21}(k),\ldots,\rho_{1n}(k)\rho_{2n}(k)\}$, $F = \begin{bmatrix} 0 & 0 \\ T & 0 \end{bmatrix}$, $\omega_1(k) = [\omega_{11}(k),\ldots,\omega_{n1}(k)]^T$, $\omega_2(k) = [\omega_{12}(k),\ldots,\omega_{n2}(k)]^T$, and $\omega_3(k) = [\omega_{13}(k),\ldots,\omega_{n3}(k)]^T$.

Write system (14) in a matrix form:

$$\psi(k+1) = \{M(k) - Q[P(k)L \otimes F]\}\psi(k) + \omega(k), \tag{16}$$

where $\omega(k)=\omega_1(k) \otimes [1,1]^T + Q\{[P_1\omega_2(k) + TP\omega_3(k)] \otimes [0,1]^T\}$, and $\otimes$ denotes the Kronecker product.

3.3. Convergence Analysis

In this subsection, we analyze the convergence of the robust constrained cooperative control algorithm for train systems.

Before the main analysis, some results are presented.

Assumption 2. *Suppose that* $\varpi_1 = \max_{i,k}\{|\omega_{i1}(k)|\}$, $\varpi_2 = \max_{i,k}\{|\omega_{i2}(k)|\}$, $\varpi_3 = \max_{i,k}\{|\omega_{i3}(k)|\}$, $0 < h_iT < 1$ *and* $q_i = max[L]_{ii} < \frac{\eta_{2i}^2 h_i^2}{4}$ *for all* i *and* $k \geq 0$, *where* $\eta_{2i} = min\{\underline{\beta}_{2i}/(\frac{\bar{\beta}_{1i}}{T} + nq_i(\max_{l,s}\{|\psi_l(0) - \psi_s(0)|\} + 4n(\varpi_1 + c_i\varpi_2 + c_i\varpi_3 T)) + \varpi_3), 1\}$. *Let* $c_i = \frac{2}{\eta_{2i}h_i}$; *it is clear that* $q_i < \frac{1}{c_i^2}$.

Lemma 1. *Under Assumptions 1 and 2,*

$$\eta_{1i} = \frac{\underline{\beta}_{1i}}{\bar{\beta}_{1i} + \bar{\beta}_{2i}T + \varpi_2} \leq \rho_{1i}(k) \leq 1, \tag{17}$$

and

$$\eta_{2i} \leq \rho_{2i}(0) \leq 1. \tag{18}$$

Proof. Since $S_{\bar{U}_i(k)}[-h_i\bar{v}_i(k) + \alpha_i(k) + \omega_{i3}(k)] \in \bar{U}_i(k)$ and $\bar{v}_i(k) \in \bar{V}_i$, it is clear that $\bar{v}_i(k) \leq \bar{\beta}_{1i}$, $S_{\bar{U}_i(k)}[-h_i\bar{v}_i(k) + \alpha_i(k) + \omega_{i3}(k)] \leq \bar{\beta}_{2i}$, and $\bar{v}_i(k) + S_{\bar{U}_i(k)}[-h_i\bar{v}_i(k) + \alpha_i(k) + \omega_{i3}(k)]T + \omega_{i2}(k) \leq \bar{\beta}_{1i} + \bar{\beta}_{2i}T + \varpi_2$. □

Therefore, we have

$$\frac{\underline{\beta}_{1i}}{\bar{\beta}_{1i} + \bar{\beta}_{2i}T + \varpi_2} \leq \rho_{1i}(k) \leq 1, \tag{19}$$

for all i and $k \geq 0$. Also, from the definition of $\rho_{2i}(k)$, $\rho_{2i}(k) = 1$ if $S_{\bar{U}_i(k)}[-h_i\bar{v}_i(k) + \alpha_i(k) + \omega_{i3}(k)] = -h_i\bar{v}_i(k) + \alpha_i(k) + \omega_{i3}(k)$, and $S_{\bar{U}_i(k)}[-h_i\bar{v}_i(k) + \alpha_i(k) + \omega_{i3}(k)] \geq \underline{\beta}_{2i}$ if $S_{\bar{U}_i(k)}[-h_i\bar{v}_i(k) + \alpha_i(k) + \omega_{i3}(k)] \neq -h_i\bar{v}_i(k) + \alpha_i(k) + \omega_{i3}(k)$. Note that $|S_{\bar{V}_i}(x)| \leq \bar{\beta}_{1i}$; therefore, we have $\rho_{2i}(0) \geq \min\{\underline{\beta}_{2i}/(\frac{\bar{\beta}_{1i}}{T} + nq_i\max_{l,s}\{|\psi_l(0) - \psi_s(0)|\} + 4n(\varpi_1 + c_i\varpi_2 + c_i\varpi_3 T) + \varpi_3), 1\}$.

Hence,

$$\rho_{2i}(0) \geq \eta_{2i}, \tag{20}$$

for all i.

Lemma 2. *Under Assumptions 1 and 2, the system matrix $\Psi(0,0)$ is a stochastic matrix with all nonzero elements larger than a positive constant.*

Proof. Under Assumptions 1 and 2, from Lemma 1, we have $c_i = \frac{2}{\eta_{2i}h_i} \geq \frac{2}{\rho_{2i}(0)h_i}$. It is found that $\frac{T}{c_i} \leq \frac{\rho_{2i}(0)h_iT}{2} \leq \frac{1}{2}$ and

$$\begin{aligned}
&1 - \frac{T}{c_i} - \rho_{1i}(0)(1 - \rho_{2i}(0)h_iT) \\
&\geq -\frac{T}{c_i} + \rho_{2i}(0)h_iT \\
&\geq \frac{\rho_{2i}(0)h_iT}{2} \\
&> 0.
\end{aligned} \tag{21}$$

Consider that $[L]_{ii} \leq q_i < \frac{1}{c_i^2}$. It is found that

$$\begin{aligned}
&1 - \frac{T}{c_i} - \rho_{1i}(0)(1 - \rho_{2i}(0)h_iT) - c_i\rho_{1i}(0)\rho_{2i}(0)T[L]_{ii} \\
&> \frac{\rho_{2i}(0)h_iT}{2} - c_iq_iT \\
&\geq \frac{T}{c_i} - \frac{T}{c_i} \\
&= 0.
\end{aligned} \tag{22}$$

Note that $a_{ij} \geq \xi_a$ if $a_{ij} \neq 0$. Thus, all elements of $\Psi(0,0)$ are non-negative. Also, note that the sum of each row in $M(k)$ is 1 and $L\mathbf{1} = \mathbf{0}$. It follows that $\Psi(0,0)\mathbf{1} = M(0)\mathbf{1} = \mathbf{1}$. Therefore, $\Psi(0,0)$ is a stochastic matrix with all nonzero elements larger than a positive constant. □

3.4. The Effects of External Disturbances

In this subsection, we discuss the system in the presence of external disturbances, i.e., $\varpi_1 \neq 0, \varpi_2 \neq 0$ and $\varpi_3 \neq 0$. By considering disturbance models, we assessed the algorithm's robustness and its ability to ensure that the trains reach a desired formation with bounded relative position errors despite external disturbances.

Let $\bar{\mu} = \min_i\{\frac{\eta_{2i}h_iT}{2} - \frac{2q_iT}{\eta_{2i}h_i}, \frac{2\eta_{1i}\xi_aT}{h_i}\}$, $\lambda_1 = \bar{\mu}^{2n}$ and $\lambda_2 = 2n(\varpi_1 + c_i\varpi_2 + c_i\varpi_3T)$. Let $\Psi(k,s) = \Pi_{l=s}^{k}\{M(l) - Q[P(l)L \otimes F]\}$. System (16) is equivalent to

$$\psi(k+1) = \Psi(k,s)\psi(s) + \sum_{l=s}^{k-1}(\Psi(k,l+1)w(l)) + w(k), \tag{23}$$

for all $k > s$.

Lemma 3. *Under Assumptions 1 and 2, $\rho_{2i}(k) \geq \eta_{2i}$ for all i and the system matrix $\Psi(k,k)$ is a stochastic matrix with all nonzero elements larger than a positive constant $\bar{\mu}$ for $0 \leq k < 2n$.*

Proof. Under Assumptions 1 and 2, according to Lemma 2, $\Psi(0,0)$ is a stochastic matrix. It follows that $\max_i \psi_i(1) - \min_i \psi_i(1) \leq \max_i \psi_i(0) - \min_i \psi_i(0) + 2(\varpi_1 + c_i\varpi_2 + c_i\varpi_3 T) \leq \max_{l,s}\{|\psi_l(0) - \psi_s(0)|\} + 4n(\varpi_1 + c_i\varpi_2 + c_i\varpi_3 T)$, and we have $\rho_{2i}(1) \geq \eta_{2i}$, similar to Lemmas 2, $\Psi(1,1)$ is a stochastic matrix with all nonzero elements larger than $\bar{\mu}$. By analogy, $\rho_{2i}(k) \geq \eta_{2i}$ for all i and $\Psi(k,k)$ is a stochastic matrix with all nonzero elements larger than $\bar{\mu}$ for $0 \leq k < 2n$. □

Theorem 1. *Consider that $\mathcal{G}$ is strongly connected and $\max_{l,s}\{|\psi_l(0) - \psi_s(0)|\} > \frac{\lambda_2}{\lambda_1} + 2\lambda_2$. Under Assumptions 1 and 2, applying control algorithm (6), all trains finally run in a desired formation with some certain relative position errors, i.e., $-\frac{\lambda_2}{\lambda_1} - 2\lambda_2 \leq \lim_{k\to\infty}[p_i(k) - p_j(k) - d_{ij}] \leq \frac{\lambda_2}{\lambda_1} + 2\lambda_2$.*

Proof. From Lemma 3, $\rho_{2i}(k) \geq \eta_{2i}$ for all i, and $\Psi(k,k)$ is a stochastic matrix with all nonzero elements larger than $\bar{\mu}$ for $0 \leq k < 2n$. It is proven that $\Psi(2n-1,0)$ is a stochastic matrix and from [reference [28], Lemma 2], we have

$$[\Psi(2n-1,0)]_{ij} \geq \lambda_1 = \bar{\mu}^{2n}, \tag{24}$$

for all $i,j \in \{1,2,\ldots,2n\}$. It follows that

$$\psi(2n) = \Psi(2n-1,0)\psi(0) + \sum_{l=0}^{2n-2}(\Psi(2n-1,l+1)w(l)) + w(2n-1). \tag{25}$$

Note that $\max_i(\sum_{l=0}^{2n-2}(\Psi(2n-1,l+1)w(l)) + w(2n-1)) \leq \lambda_2$.

Construct a Lyapunov function as

$$V(k) = \max_s\{\psi_l(k)\} - \min_s\{\psi_s(k)\}. \tag{26}$$

From (24), it follows that

$$\max_s\{\psi_s(2n)\} \leq (1-\lambda_1)\max_s\{\psi_s(0)\} + \lambda_1 \min_s\{\psi_s(0)\} + \lambda_2, \tag{27}$$

and

$$\min_s\{\psi_s(2n)\} \geq (1-\lambda_1)\min_s\{\psi_s(0)\} + \lambda_1 \max_s\{\psi_s(0)\} - \lambda_2. \tag{28}$$

As a consequence,

$$\begin{aligned} V(2n) &= \max_s\{\psi_s(2n)\} - \min_s\{\psi_s(2n)\} \\ &\leq (1-2\lambda_1)(\max_s\{\psi_s(0)\} - \min_s\{\psi_s(0)\}) + 2\lambda_2 \\ &= (1-2\lambda_1)V(0) + 2\lambda_2. \end{aligned} \tag{29}$$

Then,

$$V(2n) - V(0) \leq -2\lambda_1 V(0) + 2\lambda_2 = -2\lambda_1[V(0) - \lambda_2/\lambda_1]. \tag{30}$$

□

It follows that $V(2n) - V(0) < 0$, $\rho_{2i}(2n) \geq \eta_{2i}$ and $\Psi(2n,2n)$ is a stochastic matrix with all nonzero elements larger than $\bar{\mu}$. $\Psi(2n,1)$ is also a stochastic matrix with all elements larger than $\bar{\mu}^{2n}$. Similar to (27)–(29), it can be proven that $V(2n+1) - V(1) \leq -2\lambda_1[V(1) - \lambda_2/\lambda_1]$.

Note that when $V(1) > \lambda_2/\lambda_1$, $V(2n+1) - V(1) < 0$. When $V(1) \leq \lambda_2/\lambda_1$, from the stochasticity of $\Psi(2n,1)$, under Assumption 2, $\max_i \psi_i(2n+1) - \min_i \psi_i(2n+1) \leq \max_i \psi_i(1) - \min_i \psi_i(1) + 2(\varpi_1 + c_i\varpi_2 + c_i\varpi_3 T) < \lambda_2/\lambda_1 + 2\lambda_2 \leq \max_i \psi_i(0) - \min_i \psi_i(0) + 4n(\varpi_1 + c_i\varpi_2 + c_i\varpi_3 T)$ and $\rho_{2i}(2n+1) \geq \eta_{2i}$. $\Psi(2n+1, 2n+1)$ is a stochastic matrix with all nonzero elements larger than $\bar{\mu}$.

By analogy, $\rho_{2i}(k) \geq \eta_{2i}$, and $\Psi(k,k)$ is a stochastic matrix with all nonzero elements larger than $\bar{\mu}$ for all i and $k \geq 2n$. We have $\lim_{\bar{k}\to\infty} V(2\bar{k}n) \leq \frac{\lambda_2}{\lambda_1} + 2\lambda_2$ and $\lim_{\bar{k}\to\infty} V(2\bar{k}n + 1) \leq \frac{\lambda_2}{\lambda_1} + 2\lambda_2$. By analogy, it can be proven that $\lim_{\bar{k}\to\infty} V(2\bar{k}n + \tilde{k}) \leq \frac{\lambda_2}{\lambda_1} + 2\lambda_2$, where $0 \leq \tilde{k} \leq 2n-1$. Hence, $\lim_{k\to\infty} V(k) \leq \frac{\lambda_2}{\lambda_1} + 2\lambda_2$. Finally, from the relationship of $p_i(k)$, $\psi_i(k)$, and $V(k)$, it follows that $-\frac{\lambda_2}{\lambda_1} - 2\lambda_2 \leq \lim_{k\to\infty}[p_i(k) - p_j(k) - d_{ij}] \leq \frac{\lambda_2}{\lambda_1} + 2\lambda_2$ for all i, j.

4. Simulation

Consider a multiple train system with four trains. Suppose that the communication graph is as given in Figure 1, where the weight of each edge is 0.01. The maximum velocity of the trains, denoted as $\bar{\theta}_{1i}$, is 85 m/s. The control input parameters h_i and a_{ij} are set according to selection rule given by Assumption 2. The control input constraint set is $U_i = [-2\ \mathrm{m/s^2}, 2\ \mathrm{m/s^2}]$. The coefficients of $r_i(k)$ are $c_0 = 1.176 \times 10^{-2}$ N/kg, $c_v = 7.7616 \times 10^{-4}\ \mathrm{N \cdot s/(m \cdot kg)}$ and $c_a = 1.6 \times 10^{-5}\ \mathrm{N \cdot s^2/(m^2 \cdot kg)}$. The desired relative positions of all trains are set as $d_{12} = d_{23} = d_{34} = 8000$ m. The sampling time T is 0.8 s. The initial states of four trains are given by $p_1(0) = 27{,}000$ m, $p_2(0) = 18{,}500$ m, $p_3(0) = 7500$ m, $p_4(0) = 0$ m, and $v_1(0) = v_2(0) = v_3(0) = v_4(0) = 0$ m/s and $v_0 = 80$ m/s. The feedback gain is $h_i = 0.3$.

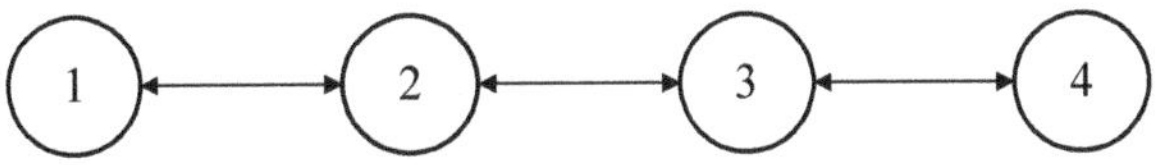

Figure 1. The directed communication graph.

Based on Theorem 1, when the controller coefficients are determined, the amplitude of disturbances needs to establish $\frac{\lambda_2}{\lambda_1} + 2\lambda_2 < d_{ij}$ for any $d_{ij} > 0$. Accordingly, suppose that the disturbances are $\omega_{11}(k) = 0.1$ m, $\omega_{12}(k) = 0.1$ m/s, $\omega_{13}(k) = 0.01\ \mathrm{m/s^2}$, $\omega_{21}(k) = -0.1$ m, $\omega_{22}(k) = 0.2$ m/s, $\omega_{23}(k) = -0.01\ \mathrm{m/s^2}$, $\omega_{31}(k) = 0.1$ m, $\omega_{32}(k) = -0.1$ m/s, $\omega_{33}(k) = 0.01\ \mathrm{m/s^2}$, $\omega_{41}(k) = -0.1$ m, $\omega_{42}(k) = -0.2$ m/s, and $\omega_{43}(k) = -0.01\ \mathrm{m/s^2}$.

Figures 2 and 3 show the states and control inputs of all trains. The distances between neighboring trains are shown in Figures 4 and 5. The results indicate that all trains will finally move in a desired formation with some certain relative position errors. By calculation, $\lim_{k\to\infty} |p_i(k) - p_j(k) - d_{ij}| \leq 7694$ m. The original relative position of 8000 m plus the maximum potential error of 7694 m, resulting in a total distance of 15,694 m, is acceptable because it meets the current safety requirements based on practical scheduling guidelines.

By taking disturbances into consideration, we assessed the algorithm's robustness and its ability to ensure that the trains reach a desired formation with bounded relative position errors despite external disturbances. The simulation results indicate that trains successfully keep the desired formation with bounded relative position errors despite external disturbances, demonstrating its effectiveness in disturbance scenarios.

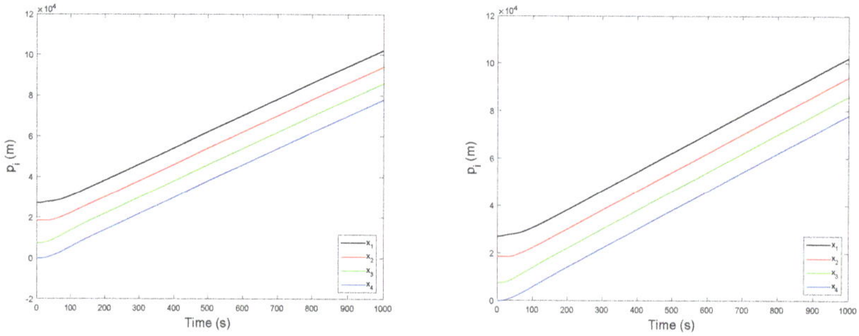

(**a**) (**b**)

Figure 2. The position trajectories of all trains (**a**) in the presence of disturbances and (**b**) in the absence of disturbances.

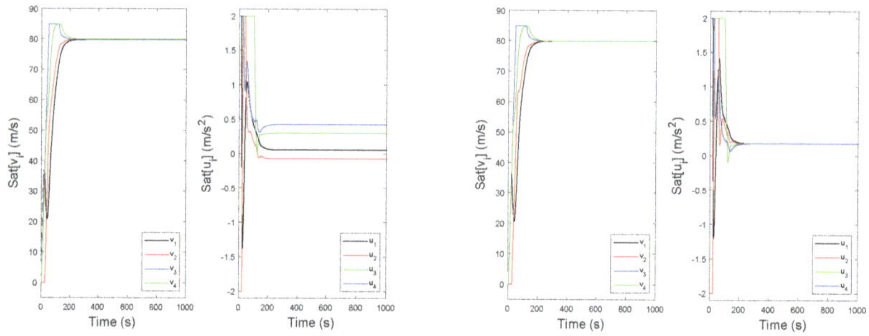

(**a**) (**b**)

Figure 3. The velocity and control input trajectories of all trains (**a**) in the presence of disturbances and (**b**) in the absence of disturbances.

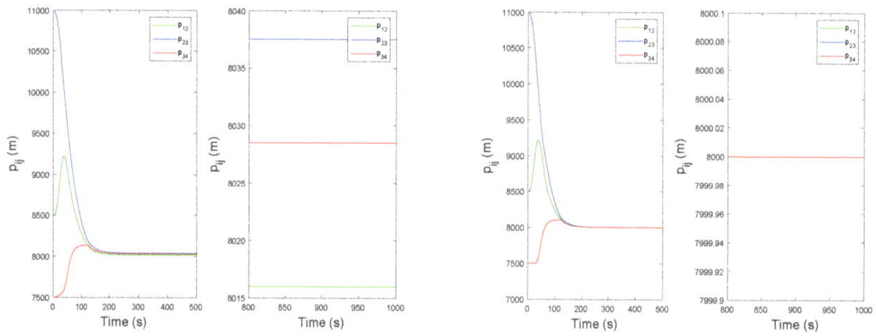

(**a**) (**b**)

Figure 4. Relative position trajectories between neighboring trains (**a**) in the presence of disturbances and (**b**) in the absence of disturbances.

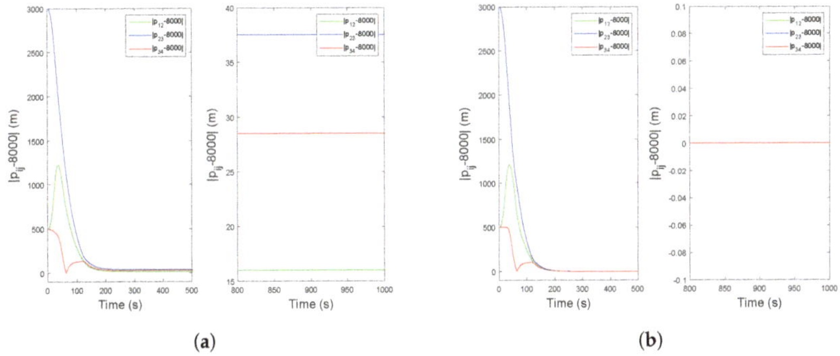

Figure 5. The error trajectories $|p_{ij} - d_{ij}|$ (**a**) in the presence of disturbances and (**b**) in the absence of disturbances.

5. Conclusions

This paper studied robust constrained cooperative control for multiple train systems with disturbances. A robust constrained cooperative control algorithm using position information of neighboring trains is employed to guarantee that all trains can run in a desired formation. The effects of disturbances on robust cooperative control, input constraints, and velocity constraints for multiple train systems were considered, based on which an explicit upper bound is given for the final relative positions, which are related to the initial state conditions and the disturbance maximums. This work might be the first effort to identify the specific impact boundaries for multiple train systems under the influence of external disturbances. This paper demonstrates that the robust constrained cooperative control method enables the safe operation of multiple trains systems under these nonlinearities, enhancing the robustness and reliability of train control systems in practical scenarios. Future work could be directed to consider communication delays and collision avoidance.

Author Contributions: Conceptualization, Q.H. and X.F.; methodology, Q.H. and X.F.; software, Q.H.; validation, Q.H.; formal analysis, Q.H. and X.F.; investigation, Q.H.; resources, Q.H., X.F., and Y.W.; data curation, Q.H.; writing—original draft preparation, Q.H.; writing—review and editing, X.F. and Y.W.; visualization, Q.H.; supervision, X.F.; project administration, X.F.; funding acquisition, X.F. All authors have read and agreed to the published version of the manuscript.

Funding: This research was funded in part by the National Natural Science Foundation of China under grant 62203475, and in part by the Natural Science Foundation of Hunan Province of China under grant 2023JJ40766.

Data Availability Statement: Dataset available on request from the authors.

Conflicts of Interest: The authors declare no conflicts of interest.

References

1. Lin, P.; Tian, Y.; Gui, G.; Yang, C. Cooperative control for multiple train systems: Self-adjusting zones, collision avoidance and constraints. *Automatica* **2022**, *144*, 110470. [CrossRef]
2. Yang, C.D.; Sun, Y.P. Mixed H_2/H_∞ cruise controller design for high speed train. *Int. J. Control* **2001**, *74*, 905–920. [CrossRef]
3. Song, Q.; Song, Y.D.; Tang, T.; Ning, B. Computationally inexpensive tracking control of high-speed trains with traction/braking saturation. *IEEE Trans. Intell. Transp. Syst.* **2011**, *12*, 1116–1125. [CrossRef]
4. Ji, H.; Hou, Z.; Zhang, R. Adaptive iterative learning control for high-speed trains with unknown speed delays and input saturations. *IEEE Trans. Autom. Sci. Eng.* **2016**, *13*, 260–273. [CrossRef]
5. Pan, D.; Zheng, Y.; Qiu, J.; Zhao, L. Synchronous control of vehicle following behavior and distance under the safe and efficient steady-following state: Two case studies of high-Speed train following control. *IEEE Trans. Intell. Transp. Syst.* **2018**, *19*, 1445–1456. [CrossRef]

6. Li, S.; Yang, L.; Gao, Z. Coordinated cruise control for high-speed train movements based on a multi-agent model. *Transp. Res. C Emerg. Technol.* **2015**, *56*, 281–292. [CrossRef]
7. Bai, W.; Lin, Z.; Dong, H.; Ning, B. Distributed cooperative cruise control of multiple high-Speed trains under a state-dependent information transmission topology. *IEEE Trans. Intell. Transp. Syst.* **2019**, *20*, 2750–2763. [CrossRef]
8. Zhao, Y.; Wang, T.; Karimi, H.R. Distributed cruise control of high-speed trains. *J. Frankl. Inst.* **2017**, *354*, 6044–6061. [CrossRef]
9. Bai, W.; Dong, H.; Lü, J.; Li, Y. Event-triggering communication based distributed coordinated control of multiple high-speed trains. *IEEE Trans. Veh. Technol.* **2021**, *70*, 8556–8566. [CrossRef]
10. Dong, H.; Gao, S.; Ning, B. Cooperative control synthesis and stability analysis of multiple trains under moving signaling systems. *IEEE Trans. Intell. Transp. Syst.* **2016**, *17*, 2730–2738. [CrossRef]
11. Gao, S.; Dong, H.; Ning, B.; Zhang, Q. Cooperative prescribed performance tracking control for multiple high-speed trains in moving block signaling system. *IEEE Trans. Intell. Transp. Syst.* **2019**, *20*, 2740–2749. [CrossRef]
12. Li, S.; Yang, L.; Gao, Z. Distributed optimal control for multiple high-speed train movement: An alternating direction method of multipliers. *Automatica* **2020**, *112*, 108646. [CrossRef]
13. Tian, Y.; Lin, P. Cooperative control for multiple high-speed trains with constraints and acceleration zone under moving block system. *Int. J. Robust Nonlinear Control* **2022**, *32*, 3662–3673. [CrossRef]
14. Yan, X.; Cai, B.; Ning, B.; ShangGuan, W. Online distributed cooperative model predictive control of energy-saving trajectory planning for multiple high-speed train movements. *Transp. Res. C Emerg. Technol.* **2016**, *69*, 60–78. [CrossRef]
15. Su, S.; Tang, T.; Roberts, C. A cooperative train control model for energy saving. *IEEE Trans. Intell. Transp. Syst.* **2015**, *16*, 622–631. [CrossRef]
16. Zhang, Z.; Song, H.; Wang, H.; Wang, X.; Dong, H. Cooperative multi-scenario departure control for virtual coupling trains: A fixed-time approach. *IEEE Trans. Veh. Technol.* **2021**, *70*, 8545–8555. [CrossRef]
17. Lin, P.; Huang, Y.; Zhang, Q.; Yuan, Z. Distributed velocity and input constrained tracking control of high-speed train systems. *IEEE Trans. Syst. Man Cybern. Syst.* **2021**, *51*, 7882–7888. [CrossRef]
18. Sun, X.; Zeng, M.; Lin, P. Distributed constrained control for multi-train systems with multiple cars. *Int. J. Robust. Nonlinear Control* **2024**, *34*, 2315–2332. [CrossRef]
19. Wang, X.; Zhu, L.; Wang, H.; Tang, T.; Li, K. Robust distributed cruise control of multiple high-speed trains based on disturbance observer. *IEEE Trans. Intell. Transp. Syst.* **2021**, *22*, 267–279. [CrossRef]
20. Yao, X.; Wu, L.; Guo, L. Disturbance-observer-based fault tolerant control of high-speed trains: A Markovian jump system model approach. *IEEE Trans. Syst. Man Cybern. Syst.* **2020**, *50*, 1476–1485. [CrossRef]
21. Tang, H.; Wang, Q.; Feng, X. Robust stochastic control for high-speed trains with nonlinearity, parametric uncertainty, and multiple time-varying delays. *IEEE Trans. Intell. Transp. Syst.* **2018**, *19*, 1027–1037. [CrossRef]
22. Xi, W.; Hu, M.; Wang, H.; Dong, H.; Ying, Z. Formation control for virtual coupling trains with parametric uncertainty and unknown disturbances. *IEEE Trans. Circuits Syst. II-Express Briefs* **2023**, *70*, 3429–3433. [CrossRef]
23. Wang, D.; Su, S.; Han, L.; Li, D. Finite-time distributed adaptive coordinated control for multiple traction units of high-speed trains. *IEEE Trans. Intell. Transp. Syst.* **2024**, 1–15. [CrossRef]
24. Godsil, C.; Royle, G.F. *Algebraic Graph Theory*; Springer: Berlin/Heidelberg, Germany, 2001; Volume 207.
25. Horn, R.A.; Johnson, C.R. *Matrix Analysis*; Cambridge University Press: Cambridge, UK, 2012.
26. Davis, W.J. The tractive resistance of electric locomotives and cars. *Gen. Electr. Rev.* **1926**, *29*, 685–707.
27. Lin, P.; Ren, W.; Yang, C.; Gui, W. Distributed consensus of second-order multiagent systems with nonconvex velocity and control input constraints. *IEEE Trans. Autom. Control* **2018**, *63*, 1171–1176. [CrossRef]
28. Lin, P.; Ren, W.; Gao, H. Distributed velocity-constrained consensus of discrete-time multi-agent systems with nonconvex constraints, switching topologies, and delays. *IEEE Trans. Autom. Control* **2017**, *62*, 5788–5794. [CrossRef]

mathematics

Article

Adaptive Iterative Learning Tracking Control for Nonlinear Teleoperators with Input Saturation

Bochun Wu [1], Xinhao Chen [1], Jinshan Huang [2], Jiawen Wen [2], Jiakun Liu [1], Fujie Wang [3] and Jianing Zhang [1,*]

[1] School of Mechanical and Electrical Engineering, Guangzhou University, Guangzhou 510006, China; 32107300017@e.gzhu.edu.cn (B.W.); 32107300013@e.gzhu.edu.cn (X.C.); 32207200002@e.gzhu.edu.cn (J.L.)
[2] School of Electronics and Communication Engineering, Guangzhou University, Guangzhou 510006, China; 32119500102@e.gzhu.edu.cn (J.H.); 32107400043@e.gzhu.edu.cn (J.W.)
[3] School of Engineering, Dongguan University of Technology, Dongguan 523808, China; fjwang@dgut.edu.cn
* Correspondence: zjn325@gzhu.edu.cn

Abstract: Addressing input saturation, external disturbances, and uncertain system parameters, this paper investigates the position tracking control problem for bilateral teleoperation systems with a time delay communication channel. Based on a composite energy function, we propose an adaptive iterative learning control (AILC) method to achieve the objective of position tracking under the alignment condition. This extends the existing research on the control of nonlinear teleoperation systems with time delay. The saturation constraint property of the Softsign function ensures that no state of the system exceeds its constraints. The controller learns to simultaneously deal with the uncertainty of system parameters online, reject external disturbances, and eliminate positional errors along the time and iteration axes. All signals in the system for any constant time delay are proved to be bounded. Ultimately, the performance of the proposed controller is further verified through numerical simulations.

Keywords: adaptive iterative learning control; position tracking; input saturation; nonlinear teleoperators; time delay

MSC: 93C10

1. Introduction

Known for the complexity of their nonlinear dynamics, bilateral teleoperation systems consist of a human operator, local manipulator, communication channel, remote manipulator, and environmental interaction. These systems are utilized in a wide range of real-life applications, such as space and deep-sea exploration [1,2], telerehabilitation training [3], nuclear waste disposal [4], and other challenging tasks in multiple fields [5–8]. Despite the complexity of the system and precision of the control objectives having improved, the development of teleoperation systems continues to face issues with input saturation, asymmetric time delays, limited input, and external disturbances [9–12].

In the past two decades, multiple methods have been proposed to deal with the above problems for robotic manipulators. A simple proportional–derivative (PD)-like controller was presented in [13] to allow positional tracking in nonlinear teleoperators under variable time delays. Other control stages have employed fuzzy system to estimate the system's uncertainties and eliminate nonlinear actuator faults [14]. Recently, an adaptive proportional damping control method was introduced in [15], where the authors added error-damping, operator force, and environmental force. The actuator saturation was addressed with an auxiliary compensation filter [16] and a proportional-plus-damping method [17,18].

Among the research investigating nonlinear teleoperator control, most methods achieve position tracking when the time converges to infinity. To achieve high-precision positional tracking within a fixed finite time interval, research on iterative learning control (ILC) has gradually developed, based on the assumption that robot manipulators are generally used in repetitive tasks [19–22]. As an intelligent control technology, ILC aims to improve the control performance from operation to operation [23,24].

Classical ILC of robotic manipulators based on classical contraction mapping theory imposes strict requirements with respect to knowledge of the robot dynamics [25,26]. Consequently, AILC has gradually become popular with researchers thanks to its feature of iteratively estimating uncertain parameters before generating the current control inputs. In general, projection or dead zone mechanisms are employed to construct an adaptive law in the iteration domain [27,28]. Scholars have focused on the fully distributed coordination of a time-varying global Lipschitz system with input saturation [29]. However, this imposes the stringent requirement that the initial state of the system be reset to the initial point of the desired trajectory. To relax this initialization condition, [30] proposed using an initial rectifying action to eliminate the undesired effects caused by impulsive action. Following this line, a new method was presented in [31,32] which simply required that the system start from where it stopped in the previous iteration. On the other hand, none of the above works addressed input saturation or time delay. Considering the state and input variables along the time and iteration axes, the stability of closed-loop teleoperation systems is worthy of further research.

Based on the above literature review and analysis, we consider the tracking capabilities of teleoperation systems from the perspective of ILC. The main contributions of this paper are summarized as follows:

(1) To relax the strict requirement for the application of ILC, we introduce a composite energy function as a tool for analyzing the stability under the alignment condition, which extends the results presented in [20,23,27,30]. Verification of the boundedness, non-increasing, and convergence properties is carried out successively.
(2) By expanding the preliminary work in [29–31], we propose a dual-loop AILC scheme for teleoperation systems. A D-type ILC loop is nested within a main loop constructed by the controller and system states. The proposed AILC accounts for parametric uncertainties, external disturbances, input saturation, and time delay.
(3) In comparison with [10,14,29], two adaptive laws are provided to deal with the uncertainties of the system parameters in an online manner while rejecting external disturbances. To compensate for the nonlinear input saturation, a Softsign activation function is designed with the saturation constraint property. Ultimately, the position errors simultaneously converge to 0 in both the time and iteration domains.

The rest of this paper is arranged as follows. Section 2 states the dynamic model of the teleoperation systems and some preliminaries. In Section 3, based on the composite energy function, a position tracking control scheme is developed through a dual-loop adaptive scheme. Section 4 provides analysis of the simulation and experimental results, followed by the conclusions in Section 5.

Throughout this paper, we employ the following notation: $\mathbb{R} := (-\infty, \infty)$, $\mathbb{R}_{>0} := (0, \infty)$, $\mathbb{R}_{\geq 0} := [0, \infty)$. For any function $\mathbf{g} : \mathbb{R}_{\geq 0} \rightarrow \mathbb{R}^n$, the square of the $\mathcal{L}_2$-norm is defined as $\|\mathbf{g}\|_2 := (\int_0^\infty |\mathbf{g}(t)|^2 dt)^{\frac{1}{2}}$ and the $\mathcal{L}_\infty$-norm as $\|\mathbf{g}\|_\infty : \sup_{t\geq 0} |\mathbf{g}(t)|$. The $\mathcal{L}_2$ and $\mathcal{L}_\infty$ spaces are represented as the sets $\{\mathbf{g} : \mathbb{R}_{\geq 0} \rightarrow \mathbb{R}^n : \|\mathbf{g}\|_2 < \infty\}$ and $\{\mathbf{g} : \mathbb{R}_{\geq 0} \rightarrow \mathbb{R}^n : \|\mathbf{g}\|_\infty < \infty\}$, respectively. Moreover, sgn$(*)$ is the signum function, $\mathbf{I}_n$ denotes an n-dimensional column vector with all elements equal to $\mathbf{I}$, and $\mathbf{I}_n$ represents an identity matrix of size n.

2. Preliminaries and Problem Description

2.1. Dynamics of Teleoperation Systems

It is assumed that the manipulators are modeled as a pair of serial links with identical degrees-of-freedom (DOFs), that they possess actuated revolute joints, and that friction can be neglected. We consider the teleoperation system illustrated in Figure 1, which has the following dynamic behavior [33,34]:

$$\begin{cases} D_m^j(q_m^j)\ddot{q}_m^j + C_m^j(q_m^j,\dot{q}_m^j)\dot{q}_m^j + G_m^j(q_m^j) = P_\tau \times sat\left(\frac{\tau_m^j}{\tau^*},1\right) + w_m^j + f_h \\ D_s^j(q_s^j)\ddot{q}_s^j + C_s^j(q_s^j,\dot{q}_s^j)\dot{q}_s^j + G_s^j(q_s^j) = P_\tau \times sat\left(\frac{\tau_s^j}{\tau^*},1\right) + w_s^j - f_e \end{cases} \tag{1}$$

where $i = \{m, s\}$ denotes local or remote robot manipulators, respectively; the superscript $j \in \mathbb{N}$ represents the iteration index; $\ddot{q}_i^j, \dot{q}_i^j, q_i^j \in \mathbb{R}^n$ are the accelerations, velocities, and joint positions; $D_i^j(q_i^j) \in \mathbb{R}^{n\times n}$ is the inertia matrix; $C_i^j(q_i^j,\dot{q}_i^j) \in \mathbb{R}^{n\times n}$ represents the Coriolis and centrifugal matrix; $G_i^j(q_i^j) \in \mathbb{R}^{n\times n}$ is the gravitational vector; $\tau_i^j \in \mathbb{R}^n$ is the vector of the control signal; w_i^j denotes the uncertain external disturbances; f_h and $f_e \in \mathbb{R}^n$ represent human operation; $\tau^* = [\tau_1^*, \tau_2^*, \ldots, \tau_n^*]^T$, with $\tau_p^*(p = 1, 2, \ldots, n)$ being a positive constant, denotes the upper bound on the magnitude of the control input; and the matrix $P_\tau \in \mathbb{R}^{n\times n}$ is defined as $P_\tau = diag(\tau_1^*, \tau_2^*, \ldots, \tau_n^*)$. The saturation function $sat(*)$ will be elaborated later.

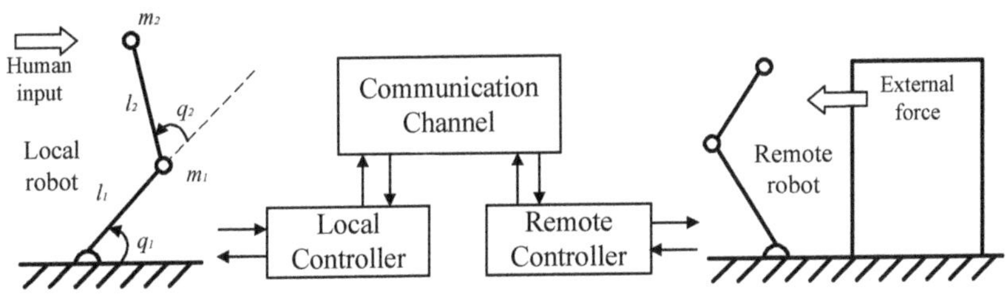

Figure 1. Teleoperation system based on 2-DOF mobile manipulators.

The robot dynamic models possess the following important properties [35,36]:

- **P1**. Positive definiteness: For any q_i^j, the inertia matrix $D_i^j(q_i^j)$ is uniformly positive definite, i.e., two positive constants α and β ensure that

$$0 < \alpha\mathbf{I} \le q_i^{jT} D_i^j(q_i^j) \le \beta\mathbf{I} < \infty. \tag{2}$$

- **P2**. Skew-symmetric property: The Coriolis and centrifugal matrix $C_i^j(q_i^j,\dot{q}_i^j)$ can be appropriately selected such that $\dot{D}_i^j(q_i^j) - 2C(q_i^j,\dot{q}_i^j)$ is skew-symmetric.
- **P3**. Linear in parameter: For any differentiable vector $\xi \in \mathbb{R}^n$, the dynamics can be linearly parameterized such that

$$D_i^j(q_i^j)\dot{\xi}_i^j + C_i^j(q_i^j,\dot{q}_i^j)\xi_i^j + G_i^j(q_i^j) = Y_i^j(q_i^j,\dot{q}_i^j,\xi_i^j,\dot{\xi}_i^j)\theta_i, \tag{3}$$

where $\theta_i \in \mathbb{R}^n$ represents an unknown constant vector of the manipulator physical parameters and the regressor $Y_i^j(q_i^j,\dot{q}_i^j,\xi_i^j,\dot{\xi}_i^j) \in \mathbb{R}^{n\times p}$ is the map of known functions.

- **P4**. Boundness of Coriolis forces: The Coriolis forces are bounded as $\forall q_i^j, \dot{q}_i^j \in \mathbb{R}^n\ \exists\ k_{c_i} \in \mathbb{R}_{>0}$ such that

$$|C_i^j(q_i^j,\dot{q}_i^j)| \le k_{c_i}|\dot{q}_i^j|^2. \tag{4}$$

Assumption 1 ([10,32])**.** *In teleoperation systems, the alignment condition is explained as the initial state of robot at the current iteration being the final state of the previous iteration, i.e.,* $q_i^j(0) = q_i^{j-1}(T_f)$, $\dot{q}_i^j(0) = \dot{q}_i^{j-1}(T_f)$.

Assumption 2 ([37]). *For an uncertain external disturbance w_i^j, let $w_i = [w_{i1}, w_{i2}, \ldots, w_{in}]^T$ bounded by $\overline{w}_i = [\overline{w}_{i,1}, \overline{w}_{i,2}, \ldots, \overline{w}_{i,n}]^T$, with all elements being positive $|w_i^j| < \overline{w}_i^j$ for $i \in \{m, s\}$.*

2.2. Description of the Softsign Activation Function

In this work, we propose a dual-loop AILC scheme based on the Softsign activation function. The mathematical expression takes the form below, as shown in [38]:

$$Softsign(x) = \frac{x}{|x| + 1} \tag{5}$$

$$Softsign'(x) = \frac{x}{(|x| + 1)^2} \tag{6}$$

where x serves as the independent variable of the aforesaid function and the value of $Softsign(x)$ shows asymptotic convergence to 1 as x approaches positive infinity or to -1 as x approaches negative infinity.

The Softsign function is a bidirectional soft saturation "S-type" activation function with smoothness, strict monotonicity, and saturation, which facilitates efficient learning and mitigates gradient vanishing. The input value of the Softsign function is small, and its output value exhibits nonlinear features in the vicinity of zero, which helps to alleviate or even eliminate the influence of jitter and in many cases to obtain a smooth control input without chattering phenomena.

We now introduce the learning gain parameter p and linear regulator ε to accommodate the control requirements:

$$f(p, x, \varepsilon) = p \times Softsign\left(\frac{x}{\varepsilon}\right). \tag{7}$$

Notably, the learning gain p alters the range of function values, while the linear regulator ε can adjust the magnitude of the function and the rate of change. As ε approaches infinity, the output of $f(p, x, \varepsilon)$ tends toward linearization, with a synchronous decrease in slope.

The sigmoid function, tanh function, Softsign function, and their derivatives are depicted in Figure 2. It can be seen that the sigmoid function and tanh function are more saturated than the Softsign function. By assigning a more slowly decreasing derivative, the sigmoid function shows a softer torque release strategy, indicating that it can reduce the possibility of oversaturation and the time to reach stability when the input torque is large for system. Therefore, the Softsign function learns more efficiently and solves the problem of gradient vanishing better than the sigmoid or tanh functions. Considering the above analysis, it is suitable for use in the design of an iterative learning controller.

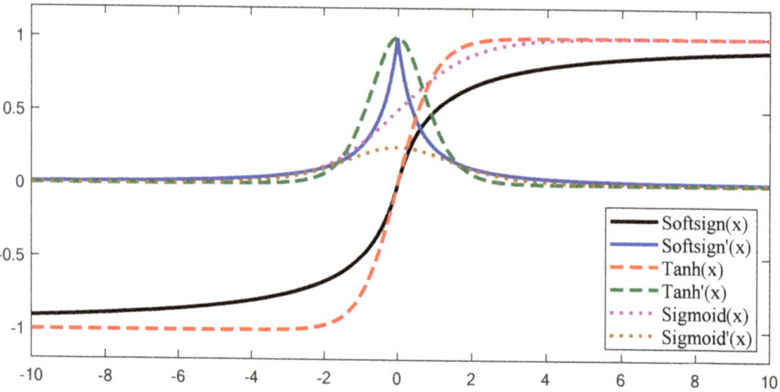

Figure 2. Saturation activation functions.

2.3. Input Constraint

For the vector $u_i^j(t) = P_\eta \times Softsign(\frac{z}{\eta}) - \chi^j(t)$ (where $u_i^j(t)$ is a continuous function, P_η is diagonal matrices with $P_\eta = diag(\eta_1, \eta_2, \ldots, \eta_n)$, and $\chi^j(t)$ indicates a continuous system condition signal), the vector-valued function Softsign($\frac{z}{\eta}$) is defined as

$$Softsign\left(\frac{z}{\eta}\right) = \left[Softsign\left(\frac{z_1}{\eta_1}\right), Softsign\left(\frac{z_2}{\eta_2}\right), \ldots, Softsign\left(\frac{z_n}{\eta_n}\right)\right]^T, \tag{8}$$

where $z_p, \eta_p (p = 1, 2, \ldots, n)$ denote the pth elements of vectors z and η, respectively.

To facilitate the subsequent control design, the saturation input function $sat(*)$ is designed as follows:

$$sat(\frac{u_i^j(t)}{u^*}, 1) = \mathrm{sgn}(u_i^j(t))\min\{\frac{|u_i^j(t)|}{u^*}, 1\} = \begin{cases} 1, & u_i^j(t) > 1 \\ \frac{|u_i^j(t)|}{u^*}, & |u_i^j(t)| \leq 1 \\ -1, & u_i^j(t) < -1 \end{cases} \tag{9}$$

where $u^* > 0$ stands for the upper bound in magnitude of the function u_i^j. Using the definition in (9), the vector-valued saturation function is presented as follows:

$$sat\left(\frac{\tau_i^j}{\tau^*}, 1\right) = \left[sat\left(\frac{\tau_{i_1}^j}{\tau_1^*}, 1\right), sat\left(\frac{\tau_{i_2}^j}{\tau_2^*}, 1\right), \ldots, sat\left(\frac{\tau_{i_n}^j}{\tau_n^*}, 1\right)\right]^T \tag{10}$$

where $\tau_{i_p}^j (p = 1, 2, \ldots, n)$ denotes the pth element of the vector τ_i^j. This can also be written as

$$P_\eta \times sat\left(\frac{u_i^j(t)}{\eta}, 1\right) = P_\eta \times \mathrm{sgn}(u_i^j(t))\min\left\{\frac{|u_i^j(t)|}{\eta}, 1\right\}. \tag{11}$$

- **P5** ([39]). Input saturation: For the vector $u_i^j(t) = P_\eta Softsign(\frac{z}{\eta}) - \chi^j(t)$, the saturation input function $sat(*)$ follows

$$\left\|P_\eta \times sat\left(\frac{u_i^j(t)}{\eta}, 1\right) - u_i^j(t)\right\| \leq \| \chi^j(t) \| . \tag{12}$$

3. Adaptive Iterative Learning Controller Design

The objective of this paper is to develop an adaptive iterative learning controller τ_i^j for a system of robot manipulators under the alignment condition. The states of local and remote robots synchronize when the derivatives of their velocities and position errors asymptotically approach zero; that is, we expect to ensure that $\dot{q}_i^j \to e_i^j \to 0$ as $j \to \infty, t \in [\Delta, T]$.

The actual positional errors for a constant time delay T between the local and remote robot are provided by

$$\begin{cases} e_m^j = q_s^j(t-T) - q_m^j \\ e_s^j = q_m^j(t-T) - q_s^j \end{cases}. \tag{13}$$

To facilitate the controller design, an auxiliary variable is defined as follows:

$$r_i^j = \dot{q}_i^j - v e_i^j \tag{14}$$

where v denotes a diagonal positive definite matrix. Differentiating the dynamic model of the auxiliary variable r_i^j, by virtue of (1), (14), and P3 leads to

$$\begin{cases} D_m^j(q_m^j)\dot{r}_m^j + C_m^j(q_m^j, \dot{q}_m^j)r_m^j = P_\tau \times sat\left(\frac{\tau_m^j}{\tau^*}, 1\right) + w_m^j + f_h - Y_m^j(q_m^j, \dot{q}_m^j, e_m^j, \dot{e}_m^j) \\ D_s^j(q_s^j)\dot{r}_s^j + C_s^j(q_s^j, \dot{q}_s^j)r_s^j = P_\tau \times sat\left(\frac{\tau_s^j}{\tau^*}, 1\right) + w_s^j - f_e - Y_s^j(q_s^j, \dot{q}_s^j, e_s^j, \dot{e}_s^j) \end{cases}. \tag{15}$$

By applying a dual-loop AILC scheme for the local and remote manipulators, the controller for the teleoperation system (15) is provided as follows:

$$\begin{cases} \phi_i^j(t) = P_\phi \times Softsign\left(\frac{\phi_i^{j-1}}{\phi^*}\right) - k_i r_i^j \\ \tau_i^j(t) = \phi_i^j(t) - \Gamma_i^j \hat{w}_i^j + Y_i^j(q_i^j, \dot{q}_I^j)\hat{\theta}_i^j - B\dot{e}_i^j \end{cases} \tag{16}$$

where controller gains k_i are positive definite matrices and B is a diagonal positive definite matrix $P_\phi = diag(\phi_1^*, \phi_2^*, \dots, \phi_n^*)^T$, with all entries being positive. In addition, it is assumed that the auxiliary term $\phi_i^j(t) = 0$ for $j < 0$ and that $\Gamma^j = diag(\text{sgn}(r_{i_1}^j), \text{sgn}(r_{i_2}^j), \dots, \text{sgn}(r_{i_n}^j))$, while $\hat{w}_i$ is used to estimate the uncertain bound of the disturbance w_i^j and $\hat{\theta}_i^j$ denotes the estimate of the dynamic parameter θ_i.

The time-varying estimates of the uncertain external disturbance $\hat{w}_i^j$ and unknown parameters $\dot{\hat{\theta}}_i^j$ evolve as follows:

$$\hat{w}_i^j = \hat{w}_i^{j-1} + \lambda \Gamma_i^j r_i^j, \tag{17}$$

$$\dot{\hat{\theta}}_i^j = \gamma_i Y_i^{jT} r_i^j, \tag{18}$$

where $\hat{w}_i^{-1} = \hat{\theta}_i^{-1} = 0$ and the positive constant λ and positive definite matrix γ_i represent the adaptation learning gain. The estimate errors are defined as

$$\widetilde{w}_i^j = \overline{w}_i - \hat{w}_i^j, \tag{19}$$

$$\widetilde{\theta}_i^j = \hat{\theta}_i^j - \theta_i, \tag{20}$$

where $\overline{w}_i$ is the bound of w_i defined in Assumption 2.

The controller in (16) is formed from three elements. The D-type terms $k_i r_i^j$ and $B\dot{e}_i^j$ are commonly featured in robotic controls; $Y_i^j \hat{\theta}_i^j$ aims to compensate for the uncertainties in the teleoperation system, while $\hat{w}_i^j$ is used to cope with the external disturbance.

Remark 1. *Let us define $T(x_i^j) = P_x \times sat(\frac{x_i^j}{x^*}, 1) - x_i^j$. According to P5 and the AILC law (16), we have $\|T(\phi_i^j)\| \leq \|k_i r_i^j\|$. By substituting τ_i^j into the function $T(\phi_i^j)$ and translating along the coordinate axis, we can obtain*

$$\left\| P_\tau \times sat(\frac{\tau_i^j}{\tau^*}, 1) - \tau_i^j \right\| \leq k_i \left\| P_b r_i^j \right\|, \tag{21}$$

where $P_b = diag(\frac{\tau_1^*}{\phi_1^*}, \frac{\tau_2^*}{\phi_2^*}, \dots, \frac{\tau_n^*}{\phi_n^*})$ and with τ_i^j provided by (16).

Remark 2. *It can be observed that the control scheme in (16) contains two loops (see Figure 3). The first equation in (16) constitutes the nested loop, while the second equation forms the main loop. Utilizing the signals in the previous iteration and incorporating the D-type feedback part in the current iteration, the auxiliary term* $\phi_i^j(t)$ *is constrained in the nested loop by applying the Softsign function term* $P_\phi \times Softsign(\frac{\phi_i^{j-1}(t)}{\phi^*})$. *Subsequently, additional nested loops are designed to tackle the estimation of uncertain system parameters online and attenuate external disturbances, as depicted in (17) and (18). Ultimately, the adaptive control scheme is executed in the main loop of the AILC (16) to achieve position tracking.*

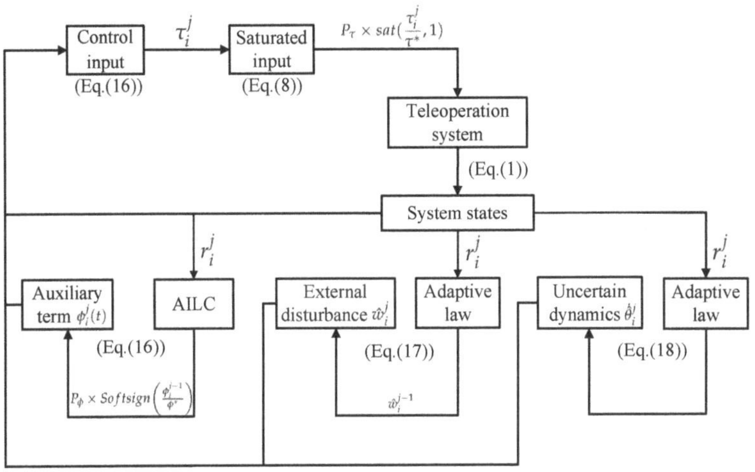

Figure 3. Block diagram of the proposed AILC scheme.

Theorem 1. *Under Assumption 1, the closed-loop system* ($f_h = f_e = 0$) *consisting of (1) and controllers (16)–(18) for any constant time delay T ensures that all signals in the system are bounded in the sense of the* $\mathcal{L}_2[0, T]$ *norm for* $i \in \{m, s\}, j \in \mathbb{N}_{\geq 0}$. *Moreover, the actual position error and velocities asymptotically converge to zero as the iteration number j approaches infinity, i.e.,* $|e_i^j(t)| \to |\dot{q}_i^j| \to 0$ *as* $j \to \infty$.

Proof. In this work, we discuss the iteration axis and time axis separately in the ILC. Considering the composite energy function $L_i^j(t)$, we can analyze the closed-loop stability of the system

$$L_i^j(t) = V_i^j(t) + E_i^j(t), \tag{22}$$

where $V_i^j(t)$ represents the energy term of the system, while $E_i^j(t)$ signifies the energy term which addresses the input saturation, external disturbances, and time delay, expressed as follows [40,41]:

$$V_i^j(t) = \sum_{i \in \{m,s\}} \frac{1}{2} r_i^{j^T} D_i^j(q_i^j) r_i^j, \tag{23}$$

$$E_i^j(t) = \sum_{i \in \{m,s\}} \left[\frac{1}{2k_i} \int_0^t \phi_i^{j^T} \phi_i^j ds + \frac{1}{2\lambda} \int_0^t \tilde{\varpi}_i^{j^T} \tilde{\varpi}_i^j ds + \frac{1}{2\gamma_i} \tilde{\theta}_i^{j^T} \tilde{\theta}_i^j + e_i^{j^T} v B e_i^j + \int_{t-T}^t \dot{q}_i^{j^T} B \dot{q}_i^j d\sigma \right]. \tag{24}$$

To ensure clarity, the proof is comprised of three parts. In Part A, the boundedness of the control input signals is shown. In Part B, the non-increasing quality of the composite energy function along the iteration axis is demonstrated. Finally, the asymptotic convergence of the position error is proven in Part C.

- *Part A: Boundedness Property.*

Along the trajectories of the closed-loop system (15), the time derivative of the function $V_i^j(t)$ is provided by

$$\dot{V}_i^j(t) = \sum_{i\in\{m,s\}} \left[r_i^{j^T} D_i^j(q_i^j)\dot{r}_i^j + \frac{1}{2} r_i^{j^T} \dot{D}_i^j(q_i^j) r_i^j \right]. \tag{25}$$

With the use of Assumption 2, P2 and P3, $\dot{V}_i^j(t)$ can be described as

$$\begin{aligned} \dot{V}_i^j(t) &= \sum_{i\in\{m,s\}} \frac{1}{2} r_i^{j^T} \dot{D}_i^j(q_i^j) r_i^j - r_i^{j^T} \left[C_i^j(q_s^j, \dot{q}_s^j) r_i^j + w_i^j + P_\tau \times sat(\frac{\tau_i^j}{\tau_i^*}, 1) - Y_i^j \theta_i^j \right] \\ &\leq \sum_{i\in\{m,s\}} \left[r_i^{j^T} \Gamma_i^j \varpi_i + r_i^{j^T} (P_\tau sat(\frac{\tau_i^j}{\tau_i^*}, 1) - \tau_i^j + \tau_i^j) - r_i^{j^T} Y_i^j \theta_i^j \right]. \end{aligned} \tag{26}$$

Remark 2 and P5 ensure $||P_\tau \times \text{sat}(\frac{\tau_i^j}{\tau_i^*}, 1) - \tau_i^j|| \leq k_i||P_b r_i^j||$ for $\forall t \in [\Delta, T]$ and $k_i \in \mathbb{N}$. Hence, $\dot{V}_i^j$ can be written as

$$\dot{V}_i^j(t) \leq \sum_{i\in\{m,s\}} \left[r_i^{j^T} \phi_i^j + r_i^{j^T} \Gamma_i^j \varpi_i^j + k_i||P_b|| r_i^{j^T} r_i^j + r_i^{j^T} Y_i^j \tilde{\theta}_i^j \right]. \tag{27}$$

Taking the time derivative of the function $E_i^j(t)$, we have

$$\dot{E}_i^j(t) = \sum_{i\in\{m,s\}} [\underbrace{\frac{1}{2k_i} \dot{\phi}_i^{j^T} \phi_i^j}_{\dot{E}_{1,i}^j} + \underbrace{\frac{1}{2\lambda} \dot{\varpi}_i^{j^T} \varpi_i^j}_{\dot{E}_{2,i}^j} + \underbrace{\frac{1}{\gamma_i} \dot{\tilde{\theta}}_i^{j^T} \tilde{\theta}_i^j}_{\dot{E}_{3,i}^j} + \underbrace{\dot{q}_i^j B \dot{e}_i^j - \frac{1}{2} \dot{q}_i^{j^T}(t-T) B \dot{q}_i^{j^T}(t-T) + \frac{1}{2} \dot{q}_i^{j^T} B \dot{q}_i^j}_{\dot{E}_{4,i}^j}]. \tag{28}$$

For $\dot{\tilde{\theta}}_i^j = \dot{\hat{\theta}}_i^j$ from (20), substituting the AILC law (16) and adaptive laws (17) and (18) into (28) and gathering the crossed terms yields

$$\begin{cases} \dot{E}_{1,i}^j(t) = \frac{1}{2k_i} \left[\left[softsign(\frac{\phi_i^{j-1}}{\phi^*}) \right]^T P_\phi \times P_\phi softsign(\frac{\phi_i^{j-1}}{\phi^*}) - k^2 r_i^{j^T} r_i^j - 2k \phi_i^{j^T} r_i^j \right] \\ \dot{E}_{2,i}^j(t) = \frac{1}{2\lambda} \left(\varpi_i^{j-1^T} \varpi_i^{j-1} - 2\lambda r_i^{j^T} \Gamma_i^{j^T} \varpi_i^j - \lambda^2 r_i^{j^T} r_i^j \right) \\ \dot{E}_{3,i}^j(t) = \tilde{\theta}_i^{j^T} Y_i^{j^T} r_i^j \\ \dot{E}_{4,i}^j(t) = -\frac{1}{2} \dot{e}_i^{j^T} B \dot{e}_i^j. \end{cases} \tag{29}$$

Combining (27), (29) and applying P1, we obtain

$$\dot{L}_i^j(t) \leq \zeta_i^j - \left(\frac{k_i + \lambda}{2} - k_i||P_b|| \right) r_i^{j^T} r_i^j - \frac{1}{2} \dot{e}_i^{j^T} B \dot{e}_i^j, \tag{30}$$

where

$$\zeta_i^j = \frac{1}{2k_i} \left[Softsign(\frac{\phi_i^{j-1}}{\phi^*}) \right]^T P_\phi \times P_\phi Softsign(\frac{\phi_i^{j-1}}{\phi^*}) + \frac{1}{2\lambda} \varpi_i^{j^T} \varpi_i^j. \tag{31}$$

Employing P1 and (22) and (23), it is implied that

$$\dot{L}_i^j(t) \leq \zeta_i^j - \mu V_i^j(t), \tag{32}$$

where the constant μ should satisfy the requirement that

$$\mu = \frac{k_i + \lambda - 2k_i||P_b||}{\beta} > 0. \tag{33}$$

Observing (33) and $\phi_i^{-1} = \tilde{w}_i^{-1} = \theta_i^{-1} = 0$, $\dot{L}_i^j(t)$ becomes

$$\dot{L}_i^0(t) \leq -(\frac{k_i + \lambda}{2} - k_i||P_b||)r_i^{0^T} r_i^0 - \frac{1}{2}\dot{e}_i^{0^T} B\dot{e}_i^0 \leq -\mu V_i^0(t). \tag{34}$$

Therefore, we can find the boundedness of $L_i^0(t)$ for $\forall t \in [\Delta, T]$. Considering (22) and (34) yields

$$\dot{V}_i^0(t) \leq \zeta_i^0 - \mu V_i^0(t). \tag{35}$$

Multiplying (35) by e^{ut} leads to

$$\frac{\partial}{\partial t}[V_i^0(t)e^{\mu t}] \leq \zeta_i^0 e^{\mu t}. \tag{36}$$

Integrating (36) from $[0, t]$, we derive

$$V_i^0(t) \leq [V_i^0(0) - \frac{\zeta_i^0}{\mu}]e^{-\mu t} + \frac{\zeta_i^0}{\mu} \leq V_i^0(0)e^{-\mu t} + \frac{\zeta_i^0}{\mu}. \tag{37}$$

Therefore, it can be concluded from (23) that

$$r_i^{0^T} r_i^0 \leq \frac{2}{\alpha}V_i^0(t)e^{-\mu t} + \frac{2\zeta_i^0}{\mu\alpha}. \tag{38}$$

Thus, it is evident that $r_i^0 \in \mathcal{L}_\infty, \phi_i^0,\ \hat{w}_i^0 \in \mathcal{L}_\infty$ from (16) and (17). Now, we present the boundedness of the signals in the closed-loop system in the iteration domain. When $j = 0, \phi_i^{-1} = \tilde{w}_i^{-1} = \tilde{\theta}_i^{-1} = 0$; thus, $\zeta_i^0 = 0$. Quoting the conclusions verified in Parts B and Part C in advance, we find that $e_i^0, \dot{q}_i^0, Y_i^0$ are bounded. Hence, $L_i^0(t)$ is also bounded, which leads to $\hat{\theta}_i^0$ being bounded. This additionally implies the boundedness of ζ_i^1 and $V_i^0(T_f)$. Under the alignment condition in Assumption 1, referring to $V_i^0(T_f) = V_i^1(0)$, it follows that $V_i^1(0)$ is bounded. Observing (38), we can infer that $r_i^1 \in \mathcal{L}_\infty$, leading to $\phi_i^1, \hat{w}_i^1 \in \mathcal{L}_\infty$. Repeatedly carrying out this deduction process, with the boundedness of $\tilde{w}_i^{j-1}$, a positive constant can be found to satisfy $||\tilde{w}_i^{j-1}|| \leq \mathcal{W}, \forall t \in [\Delta, T]$ and $j \in \mathbb{N}$. Therefore, we obtain

$$||\zeta_i^j|| \leq \bar{\zeta}_i^j = \frac{1}{2k_i}||P_\phi||^2 + \frac{1}{2\lambda}\mathcal{W}^2. \tag{39}$$

Considering the boundedness of $\bar{\zeta}_i^{j-1}$ and $V_i^{j-1}(T_f)$, we obtain $r_i^j \in \mathcal{L}_\infty$. Consequently, it can be proven that $\hat{w}_i^j, \tilde{\theta}_i^j, r_i^j$ are bounded in each iteration.

- *Part B: Non-increasing Property.*

The difference between $L_i^j(T_f)$ and $L_i^{j-1}(T_f)$ can be derived using integration by parts, as follows:

$$\Delta L_i^j(T_f) = L_i^j(T_f) - L_i^{j-1}(T_f). \tag{40}$$

In the case of Assumption 1, we have

$$\Delta L_i^j(T_f) = \Delta V_i^j(T_f) + \Delta E_i^j(T_f) = \int_0^{T_f} \dot{V}_i^j(r)dr + E_i^j(T_f) - E_i^{j-1}(T_f). \tag{41}$$

Considering (27), (29) and (41), it follows that

$$\Delta L_i^j(T_f) = -(\frac{k_i + \lambda}{2} - k_i||P_b||) \int_0^{T_f} r_i^{jT} r_i^j ds - \frac{1}{2}\dot{e}_i^{jT} B\dot{e}_i^j - e_i^{jT} vBe_i^j - \int_{t-T}^{t} \dot{q}_i^{jT} B\dot{q}_i^j d\sigma. \tag{42}$$

Because $\Delta L_i^j(T_f) < 0$, this implies that the composite energy function $L_i^j(T_f)$ is non-increasing along the iteration axis, that is, $L_i^j(t)$ is proved to be non-increasing.

- *Part C* ([42]): *Convergence Property*.

Repeatedly substituting (42) leads to

$$\begin{aligned} L_i^j(T_f) = &\; L_i^0(T_f) + \sum_{\kappa=1}^{j} \Delta L_i^j(T_f) \\ = &\; L_i^0(T_f) - (\frac{k_i + \lambda}{2} - k_i||P_b||) \sum_{\kappa=1}^{j} \int_0^{T_f} r_i^{\kappa T} r_i^\kappa ds - \sum_{\kappa=1}^{j} \left[\frac{1}{2}\dot{e}_i^{\kappa T} B\dot{e}_i^\kappa - e_i^{\kappa T} vBe_i^\kappa - \int_{t-T}^{t} \dot{q}_i^{\kappa T} B\dot{q}_i^\kappa d\sigma \right]. \end{aligned} \tag{43}$$

For bounded $L_i^0(T_f)$ and positive $L_i^j(T_f)$, this leads to $lim_{j\to\infty} \int_0^{T_f} r_i^{jT} r_i^j ds = 0$. Therefore, we can conclude that $||r_i^j||$ converges to zero as the iteration number approaches infinity.

According to the above conditions and $L_i^j(T_f) > 0, \Delta L_i^j(T_f) \leq 0$, we obtain $r_i^j, \tilde{\theta}_i^j, e_i^j \in \mathcal{L}_\infty, r_i^j, \dot{e}_i^j \in \mathcal{L}_2$, which leads to $\dot{q}_i^j, Y_i^j \in \mathcal{L}_\infty$. Furthermore, the boundedness of $\dot{e}_i^j$ it can be determined by differentiating (13). Because the known signals in (14) and (15) are bounded, we obtain $r_i^j \in \mathcal{L}_\infty, \tau_i^j \in \mathcal{L}_\infty$, respectively. Hence, the fact that $r_i^j \in \mathcal{L}_\infty \bigcap \mathcal{L}_2$ provides support for $|r_i^j| \to 0, \dot{e}_i^j, \ddot{q}_i^j \in \mathcal{L}_\infty$. Similarly, $\ddot{e}_i^j \in \mathcal{L}_\infty$ and $\dot{e}_i^j \in \mathcal{L}_\infty \bigcap \mathcal{L}_2$ prove that $|\dot{e}_i^j| \to 0$.

Now, $e_i^j, \dot{e}_i^j, \ddot{e}_i^j \in \mathcal{L}_\infty$ and $|\dot{e}_i^j| \to 0$ imply that $lim \int_0^t \dot{e}_i^j ds = e_i^j - e_i^j(0) = h_i < \infty$. Meanwhile, $lim|r_i^j| = lim\, |\dot{q}_i^j - ve_i^j| = lim\, |\dot{q}_i^j - v(h_i + e_i^j(0))| = 0$ imply that $\dot{q}_i^j \to v(h_i + e_i^j(0))$ is constant. Thus, we obtain $|\dot{q}_i^j| \to |\dot{q}_u^j|$ for $\dot{q}_u^j$ that is any constant vector and $q_m(t-T) - q_s \to q_m - q_s$. Thus, substituting (12) in the limit, $r_m^j = \dot{q}_u^j - ve_m^j = \dot{q}_u^j + ve_s^j$ and $r_s^j = \dot{q}_u^j - ve_s^j = \dot{q}_u^j - ve_s^j$ lead to $r_m^j + r_s^j = 2\dot{q}_u^j$. With the fact that $|r_i^j| \to 0$, this proves that $|\dot{q}_u^j| \to 0$. Hence, $|\dot{q}_i^j| \to |\dot{e}_i^j| \to 0$. □

4. Simulation Results

In order to examine the performance of proposed AILC scheme, we carried out numerical simulations employing local and remote manipulators modeled as a pair of 2-DOF serial links with revolute joints (see Figure 1).

Their corresponding nonlinear dynamics follow (1), where

$$D_i^j(q_i^j) = \begin{bmatrix} p_1 + 2p_2c_2 & p_3 + p_2c_2 \\ p_3 + p_2c_2 & p_3 \end{bmatrix}, \tag{44}$$

$$C_i^j(q_i^j, \dot{q}_i^j)\dot{q}_i^j = \begin{bmatrix} -2p_2s_2\dot{q}_{i_2}^j & -p_2s_2\dot{q}_{i_2}^j \\ p_2s_2\dot{q}_{i_1}^j & 0 \end{bmatrix}, \tag{45}$$

$$G_i^j(q_i^j) = \begin{bmatrix} \frac{g}{l_{i_2}} p_3 c_{12} + \frac{1}{l_{i_1}}(p_1 - p_3)c_1 \\ \frac{g}{l_{i_2}} p_3 c_{12} \end{bmatrix}, \tag{46}$$

$$Y_i^j(q_i^j, \dot{q}_i^j, e_i^j, \dot{e}_i^j) = \begin{bmatrix} \dot{e}_{i_1} & 2c_2\dot{e}_{i_1} + c_2\dot{e}_{i_2} - s_2\dot{q}_{i_2}^j e_{i_2} - 2s_2\dot{q}_{i_2}^j e_{i_1} & \dot{e}_{i_2} & gc_{12} & gc_1 \\ 0 & c_2\dot{e}_{i_1} + s_2\dot{q}_{i_1}^j e_{i_1} & \dot{e}_{i_1} + \dot{e}_{i_2} & gc_{12} & 0 \end{bmatrix}, \tag{47}$$

$$\theta_i^j = \begin{bmatrix} M_i l_{i_1}^2 + m_{i_2} l_{i_1}^2 & m_{i_2} l_{i_1} l_{i_2} & m_{i_2} l_{i_2}^2 & \frac{1}{l_2} m_{i_2} l_{i_2}^2 & \frac{1}{l_1}(M_i l_{i_1}^2 - m_{i_2} l_{i_2}^2 + m_{i_2} l_{i_2}^2) \end{bmatrix}^T, \tag{48}$$

in which l_i is the length and m_i the mass of the ith link of the planar robot and $q_i, \dot{q}_i$ denote the joint position and velocity of the ith link, respectively. Subsequently, $p_1 = (m_{i_1} + m_{i_2})l_{i_1}^2 + m_{i_2} l_{i_2}^2, p_2 = m_{i_2} l_{i_1} l_{i_2}, p_3 = m_{i_2} l_{i_2}^2$ and $M_i = m_{i_1} + m_{i_2}$. Furthermore, c_1, c_2, c_3 stands for $\cos(q_{i_1}^j)$, $\cos(q_{i_2}^j)$, $\cos(q_{i_1}^j + q_{i_2}^j)$, respectively, while s_2 abbreviates $\sin(q_{i_2}^j)$. In the presence of uncertain dynamics, θ_i^j is unknown to the controller and has to be estimated by the proposed adaptive laws in the system.

In the simulation, the physical parameters of the local and remote manipulators are set as follows: $m_{m_1} = 4.0$ kg, $m_{m_2} = 0.6$ kg, $m_{s_1} = 3.2$ kg, $m_{s_2} = 0.3$ kg, $l_{m_i} = l_{s_i} = 0.38$ m, and $g = 9.8\ \mathrm{m/s^2}$. There are four controller parameters in (16)–(18) that need to be tuned: k_i, λ, γ_i, and B, which are selected as $k_m = 80\mathbf{I}, k_s = 65\mathbf{I}, \lambda = 5, \gamma_m = 1.1\mathbf{I}, \gamma_s = 0.6\mathbf{I}, B = 5.8\mathbf{I}$ with the matrix $P_\tau = diag(300, 100), P_\phi = diag(100, 100)$.

The position and velocity of the manipulators are denoted as $q_i^j = [q_{i_1}^j, q_{i_2}^j]^T$ and $\dot{q}_i^j = [\dot{q}_{i_1}^j, \dot{q}_{i_2}^j]^T$. The initial conditions are $\ddot{q}_i^j(0) = 0, \dot{q}_m^j(0) = [0.02, -0.14]^T, \dot{q}_s^j(0) = [-0.12, 0.18]^T, q_m^j(0) = [-\frac{3\pi}{5}, -\frac{2\pi}{5}]^T, q_s^j(0) = [\frac{\pi}{5}, \frac{3\pi}{5}]^T$. The external disturbance and time delay are chosen as $w_i^j = \mathbf{I}\sin(j \times t), T = 0.4$ s, respectively.

The simulation results with the proposed controller under alignment condition are depicted in Figures 4–8. Figure 4 shows that the trajectory profiles of the remote robot at the first iteration have large deviations from the local robot. Contrary to Figure 4, the trajectory profiles of manipulator robot at the fifth iteration, illustrated in Figure 5, show that the remote robot's trajectory is distinguished with the developed controllers. At the fifth iteration, the position errors all decrease sharply, as shown in Figure 6. We define the root mean square (RMS) errors at the jth iteration as $e_i^j(RMS) = \sqrt{\frac{1}{N}\sum_{i=1}^{N} e_i^{j2}}$, where N is the number of data points. As shown in Figure 7, the RMS errors are reduced as the learning process evolves along the iteration domain. The control inputs τ_i^j and saturated inputs $P_\tau \times sat(\frac{\tau_i^j}{\tau_i^*}, 1)$ at the first iteration are portrayed in Figure 8, which shows that the latter are constrained with [−100N, 300N]. Consequently, the above simulation results confirm the validity of Theorem 1.

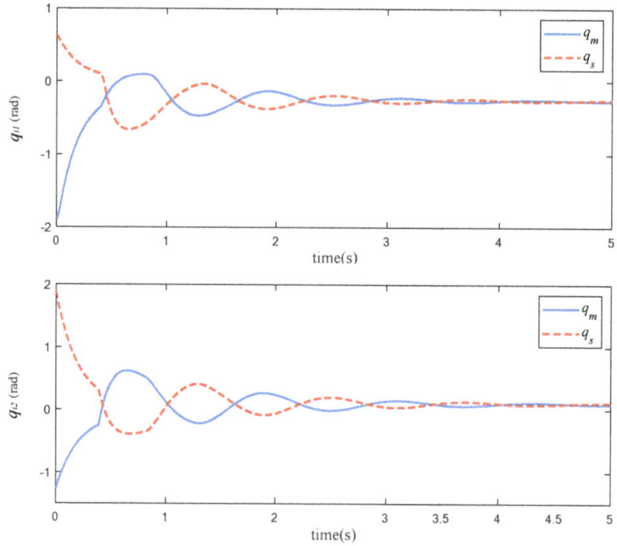

Figure 4. Trajectory profiles at the first iteration.

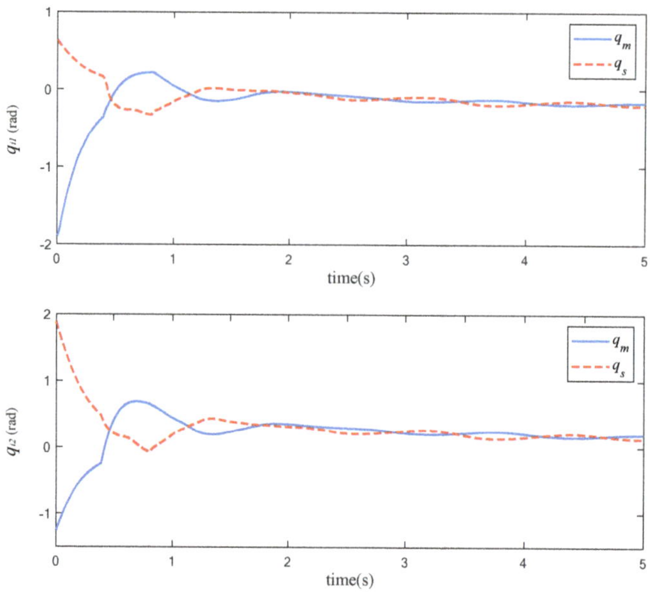

Figure 5. Trajectory profiles at the fifth iteration.

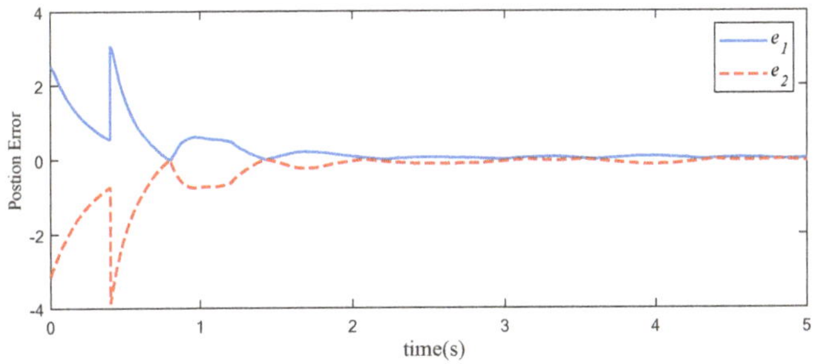

Figure 6. Position error profile.

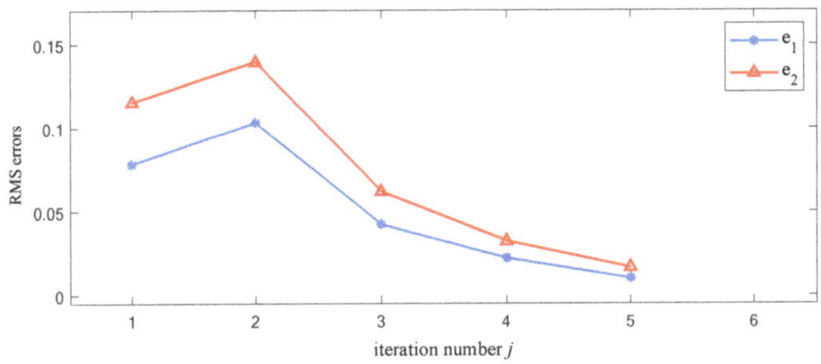

Figure 7. RMS error with iteration number j.

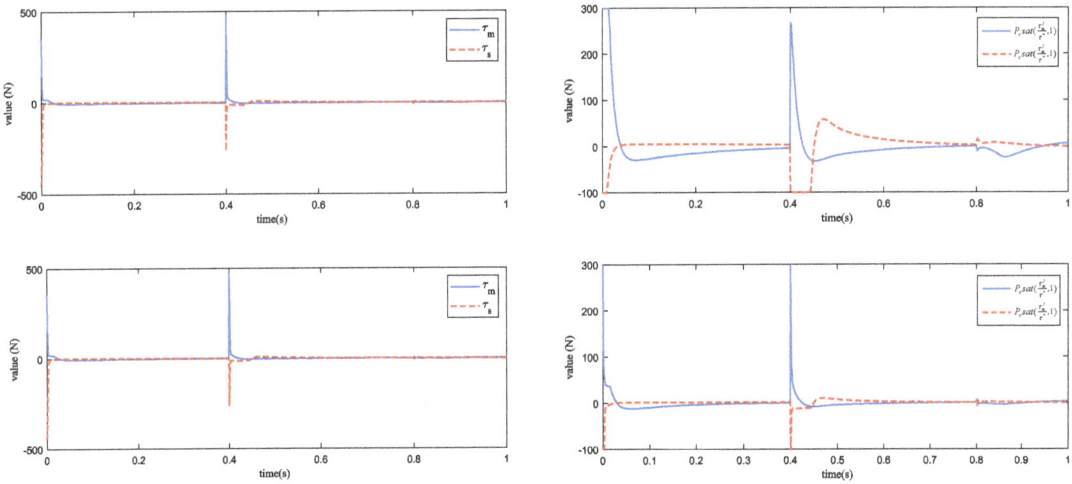

Figure 8. Control inputs τ_i^j and saturated inputs $P_\tau sat(\frac{\tau_i^j}{\tau_i^*}, 1)$.

In the real world, manipulators face electromagnetic interference, network transmission delay, uncertainties in the system parameters, and more. This is not a particularly intricate issue nowadays. Our simulation results validate that the proposed controller and AILC can guarantee the stability and tracking capabilities of the closed-loop saturated teleoperation system even in the presence of communication time delay, parametric uncertainties, and external disturbance.

5. Conclusions

With the aim of addressing input saturation, external disturbance, and uncertain system parameters in teleoperation systems, in this work we have proposed an AILC scheme for nonlinear teleoperators with a time delay communication channel. By utilizing two adaptive laws, the controller is able to tackle uncertainties in the system parameters and reject external disturbances. The stability and tracking performance were analyzed using the composite energy function. Under the alignment condition, the position errors and velocities asymptotically converged to zero and all signals in the system were bounded for any constant time delay. The above conclusions were verified by simulations.

It should be underscored that the design of the proposed controller requires the initial state to be known in advance under the alignment condition. This assumption is difficult to implement in practical applications and scenarios. Therefore, future work may be devoted to further relaxing this requirement of the AILC for extension to multi-agent systems.

Author Contributions: Conceptualization, F.W. and B.W.; data curation, B.W.; funding acquisition, J.Z.; investigation, B.W. and X.C.; methodology, J.Z., B.W. and J.H.; project administration, J.Z.; writing—original draft preparation, B.W.; resources, J.Z. and J.L.; software, X.C., J.L. and J.H.; visualization, J.W. and J.L.; supervision, X.C. and F.W.; validation, J.Z., B.W. and X.C.; writing—review and editing, B.W., X.C. and J.W.; formal analysis, J.W. and J.L. All authors have read and agreed to the published version of the manuscript.

Funding: The authors acknowledge the funding of the following science foundations: the College Students' Science and Technology Innovation Cultivation Project of Guangdong Province, China (pdjh2023a0404), the College Students' Innovation and Entrepreneurship Training Project of China (202211078115), the GuangDong Basic and Applied Basic Research Foundation(2024A1515010222), and the Tertiary Education Scientific Research Project of the Guangzhou Municipal Education Bureau (202235297).

Institutional Review Board Statement: Not applicable.

Informed Consent Statement: Not applicable.

Data Availability Statement: The data presented in this study are available by sending a request to 32107300017@e.gzhu.edu.cn.

Conflicts of Interest: The authors declare no conflicts of interest.

Abbreviations

The following abbreviations are used in this manuscript:

AILC	Adaptive Iterative Learning Control
PD	Proportional–Derivative
ILC	Iterative Learning Control
DOF	Degree of Freedom
RMS	Root Mean Square

References

1. Allard, P. *A Virtual Environment for Training Space Station Teleoperators;* McGill University: Montreal, QC, Canada, 1997.
2. Banerjee, P.; Muschter, E.; Singh, H.; Weber, B.; Hulin, T. Towards a VR Evaluation Suite for Tactile Displays in Telerobotic Space Missions. In Proceedings of the IEEE Aerospace Conference, Big Sky, MT, USA, 4–11 March 2023.
3. Wapler, M.; Urban, V.; Weisener, T.; Stallkamp, J.; Dürr, M.; Hiller, A. A Stewart platform for precision surgery. *Trans. Inst. Meas. Control.* **2003**, *25*, 329–334. [CrossRef]
4. Joaquin, C. *Digital Twin-Based Bilateral Teleautonomous System for Nuclear Remote Operation;* UKRI: Swindon, UK, 2019.
5. Urban, V.; Wapler, M.; Neugebauer, J.; Hiller, A.; Stallkamp, J.; Weisener, T. Robot-assisted surgery system with kinesthetic feedback. *Comput. Aided Surg. Off. J. Int. Soc. Comput. Aided Surg.* **1998**, *3*, 205–209. [CrossRef]
6. Lin, T.C.; Krishnan, A.U.; Li, Z.; Ieee. Physical Fatigue Analysis of Assistive Robot Teleoperation via Whole-body Motion Mapping. In Proceedings of the IEEE/RSJ International Conference on Intelligent Robots and Systems (IROS), Macau, China, 4–8 November 2019; pp. 2240–2245.

7. Liu, Y.C.; Chopra, N. Control of semi-autonomous teleoperation system with time delays. *Automatica* **2013**, *49*, 1553–1565. [CrossRef]
8. Paik, P.; Thudi, S.; Atashzar, S.F. Power-Based Velocity-Domain Variable Structure Passivity Signature Control for Physical Human-(Tele)Robot Interaction. *IEEE Trans. Robot.* **2023**, *39*, 386–398. [CrossRef]
9. Guajardo-Benavides, E.J.; Arteaga, M.A. On the finite time force estimation for bilateral teleoperation of robot manipulators with time varying delays. *Control. Eng. Pract.* **2023**, *138*, 105622. [CrossRef]
10. Bounemeur, A.; Chemachema, M. *Active Adaptive Fuzzy Fault-Tolerant Control for a Class of Nonlinear Systems with Actuator Faults*; Springer: Singapore, 2021; pp. 985–999.
11. Aldana, C.I.; Garcia-López, K.; Nuño, E.; Cruz-Zavala, E. Task-Space Teleoperation with Time-Delays and Without Velocity Measurements via a Bounded Controller. *IEEE Control. Syst. Lett.* **2023**, *7*, 1141–1146. [CrossRef]
12. Wang, Y.K.; Liu, Z.X.; Sun, M.W.; Wang, Z.H.; Chen, Z.Q. Adaptive Backstepping Attitude Control with Disturbance Rejection Subject to Amplitude and Rate Saturations of the Elevator. *J. Aerosp. Eng.* **2017**, *30*, 04016095. [CrossRef]
13. Nuño, E.; Basañez, L.; Ortega, R.; Spong, M.W. Position Tracking for Non-linear Teleoperators with Variable Time Delay. *Int. J. Robot. Res.* **2009**, *28*, 895–910. [CrossRef]
14. Bounemeur, A.; Chemachema, M. Optimal adaptive fuzzy fault-tolerant control applied on a quadrotor attitude stabilization based on particle swarm optimization. *Proc. Inst. Mech. Eng. Part I J. Syst. Control. Eng.* **2023**, *238*, 704–719. [CrossRef]
15. Bao, J.G.; Fu, L.Y.; Zhang, H.C.; Zhang, A.C.; Guo, W.H.; Chen, T.S. An Adaptive Proportional Plus Damping Control for Teleoperation Systems with Asymmetric Time-Varying Communication Delays. *Mathematics* **2022**, *10*, 4675. [CrossRef]
16. Zhang, H.C.; Song, A.G.; Li, H.J.; Shen, S.B. Novel Adaptive Finite-Time Control of Teleoperation System with Time-Varying Delays and Input Saturation. *IEEE Trans. Cybern.* **2021**, *51*, 3724–3737. [CrossRef]
17. Hashemzadeh, F.; Hassanzadeh, I.; Tavakoli, M. Teleoperation in the presence of varying time delays and sandwich linearity in actuators. *Automatica* **2013**, *49*, 2813–2821. [CrossRef]
18. Pourseifi, M.; Rezaei, S. Adaptive control for position and force tracking of uncertain teleoperation with actuators saturation and asymmetric varying time delays. *Int. J. Nonlinear Sci. Numer. Simul.* **2024**, *24*, 3113–3132. [CrossRef]
19. Yu, Q.X.; Hou, Z.S.; Xu, J.X. D-Type ILC Based Dynamic Modeling and Norm Optimal ILC for High-Speed Trains. *IEEE Trans. Control. Syst. Technol.* **2018**, *26*, 652–663. [CrossRef]
20. Tayebi, A. Adaptive iterative learning control for robot manipulators. In Proceedings of the Annual American Control Conference (ACC 2003), Denver, CO, USA, 4–6 June 2003; pp. 4518–4523.
21. Bristow, D.A.; Tharayil, M.; Alleyne, A.G. A survey of iterative learning control. *IEEE Control. Syst. Mag.* **2006**, *26*, 96–114. [CrossRef]
22. Ahn, H.S.; Chen, Y.; Moore, K.L. Iterative learning control: Brief survey and categorization. *IEEE Trans. Syst. Man Cybern. Part C Appl. Rev.* **2007**, *37*, 1099–1121. [CrossRef]
23. Xu, J.X. A survey on iterative learning control for nonlinear systems. *Int. J. Control.* **2011**, *84*, 1275–1294. 00207179.2011.574236. [CrossRef]
24. Shen, D.; Wang, Y.Q. Survey on stochastic iterative learning control. *J. Process. Control.* **2014**, *24*, 64–77. j.jprocont.2014.04.013. [CrossRef]
25. Norrlöf, M. An adaptive iterative learning control algorithm with experiments on an industrial robot. *IEEE Trans. Robot. Autom.* **2002**, *18*, 245–251. [CrossRef]
26. Wang, D.; Soh, Y.C.; Cheah, C.C. Robust motion and force control of constrained manipulators by learning. *Automatica* **1995**, *31*, 257–262. [CrossRef]
27. Yan, W.; Sun, M. Time-varying neural networks based indirect adaptive ILC for discrete-time varying nonlinear systems. In Proceedings of the 29th Chinese Control Conference, Beijing, China, 2010; pp. 2060–2065.
28. Xu, Q.Y.; Li, Y.; Cheng, J.; Xiao, T.F. Discrete-time Adaptive ILC for Uncertain Systems with Unknown Nonlinear Dead Zone Inputs and Control Directions. In Proceedings of the 9th IEEE Data Driven Control and Learning Systems Conference (DDCLS), Liuzhou, China, 20–22 November 2020; pp. 923–928.
29. Yang, N.; Li, J. Distributed iterative learning coordination control for leader–follower uncertain non-linear multi-agent systems with input saturation. *IET Control. Theory Appl.* **2019**, *13*, 2252–2260. [CrossRef]
30. Sun, M.X.; Wang, D.W. Iterative learning control with initial rectifying action. *Automatica* **2002**, *38*, 1177–1182. [CrossRef]
31. Sun, M.; Ge, S.S.; Mareels, I.M.Y. Adaptive repetitive learning control of robotic manipulators without the requirement for initial repositioning. *IEEE Trans. Robot.* **2006**, *22*, 563–568. [CrossRef]
32. Yang, S.; Xu, J.-X. Leader–follower synchronisation for networked Lagrangian systems with uncertainties: A learning approach. *Int. J. Syst. Sci.* **2016**, *47*, 956–965. [CrossRef]
33. Bounemeur, A.; chemachema, M.; Zahaf, A.; Bououden, S. *Adaptive Fuzzy Fault-Tolerant Control Using Nussbaum Gain for a Class of SISO Nonlinear Systems with Unknown Directions*; Springer: Singapore, 2021; pp. 493–510.
34. Spong, M.W.; Hutchinson, S. *Robot Modeling and Control*, 2nd ed.; John Wiley, Sons: New York, NY, USA, 2006. *IEEE Control. Syst. Mag.* **2006**, *26*, 113–115.
35. Slotine, J.-J.E.; Li, W. *Applied Nonlinear Control*; Pearson: London, UK, 1991.
36. Merat, F. Introduction to robotics: Mechanics and control. *IEEE J. Robot. Autom.* **1987**, *3*, 166. [CrossRef]

37. He, W.; Meng, T.; He, X.; Ge, S.S. Unified iterative learning control for flexible structures with input constraints. *Automatica* **2018**, *96*, 326–336. [CrossRef]
38. Li, J.; Zhuang, S.; Wang, H.; Deng, J.; Mao, Y. Design of Backstepping Control Based on a Softsign Linear–Nonlinear Tracking Differentiator for an Electro-Optical Tracking System. *Photonics* **2024**, *11*, 156. [CrossRef]
39. Xu, J.-X.; Tan, Y.; Lee, T.-H. Iterative learning control design based on composite energy function with input saturation. *Automatica* **2003**, *6*, 5129–5134. [CrossRef]
40. Mohammadi, H.; Rezapour, S.; Jajarmi, A. On the Fractional Sird Mathematical Model and Control for the Transmission of COVID-19: The First and the Second Waves of the Disease in Iran and Japan. *ISA Trans.* **2022**, *124*, 103–114. [CrossRef]
41. Baleanu, D.; Jajarmi, A.; Sajjadi, S.; Mozyrska, D. A New Fractional Model and Optimal Control of a Tumor-Immune Surveillance with Non-Singular Derivative Operator. *Chaos Interdiscip. J. Nonlinear Sci.* **2019**, *29*, 083127. [CrossRef] [PubMed]
42. Bounemeur, A.; Chemachema, M.; Essounbouli, N. Robust Indirect Adaptive Fuzzy Control Using Nussbaum Gain for a Class of Siso Nonlinear Systems with Unknown Directions. In Proceedings of the 2014 15th International Conference on Sciences and Techniques of Automatic Control and Computer Engineering (STA), Hammamet, Tunisia, 21–23 December 2014.

mathematics

MDPI

Article

Polynomial Iterative Learning Control (ILC) Tracking Control Design for Uncertain Repetitive Continuous-Time Linear Systems Applied to an Active Suspension of a Car Seat †

Selma Ben Attia [1], Sultan Alzahrani [2,*], Saad Alhuwaimel [2], Salah Salhi [1] and Houssem Eddine Ouerfelli [1]

[1] National Engineering School of Tunis, LR11ES20 Analysis, Conception and Control of Systems Laboratory, University Tunis El Manar, Tunis 1002, Tunisia; benattiaselma@gmail.com (S.B.A.); salah.salhi@isi.utm.tn (S.S.); houssemeddineouerfelli@gmail.com (H.E.O.)

[2] King Abdulaziz City for Sciences and Technology (KACST), Riyadh 11442, Saudi Arabia; huwaimel@kacst.gov.sa

* Correspondence: szahrani@kacst.edu.sa

† This paper is an extended version of our paper published in 2017 14th International Multi-Conference on Systems, Signals & Devices (SSD), Marrakech, Morocco, 28–31 March 2017; ISSN 2474-0446.

Abstract: This paper addresses the issue of polynomial iterative learning tracking control (Poly-ILC) for continuous-time linear systems (LTI) operating repetitively. It explores the design of an iterative learning control law by examining the stability along the pass theory of 2D repetitive systems. The obtained result is a generalization of the notion of stability along passages, taking into account transient performances. To strike a balance between stability along passages and transient performance, we extend our developed result in the discrete case, relying on some numerical tools. Specifically, in this work we investigate the convergence of tracking error with given learning controller gains. The key contribution of this structure of control lies in establishing an LMI (linear matrix inequality) condition that ensures both pole placement according to desired specifications and the convergence of output error between iterations. Furthermore, new sufficient conditions for stability regions along the pass addressing the tracking problem of differential linear repetitive processes are developed. Numerical results are provided to demonstrate the effectiveness of the proposed approaches.

Keywords: continuous-time linear repetitive system; iterative learning control (ILC); stability along the pass (SAP); D-stability regions; polynomial-type ILC; tracking control

MSC: 34H05; 34K35

1. Introduction

Iterative learning control (ILC) emerges as a potent tool for mitigating tracking errors in systems that operate repetitively. It has been heralded as a control strategy capable of enhancing the performance of systems engaged in batch repetitive servo tasks [1–3]. Over the past two decades, ILC has consistently drawn attention. The treatment of tracking problems within the ILC framework often necessitates consideration of certain 2D properties. Utilizing the delay operator in the time domain (via standard Laplace transformation), ref. [2] translates the dynamics of linear continuous-time systems into an iterative process, applicable to time-invariant parameters, input variables, output variables, and errors. This extension allows for the exploration of tracking and stabilization problems, a topic not extensively addressed in the literature despite its intrinsic connection to fundamental control issues like stability and stabilization. These core control problems can be readily extended to encompass robustness analysis and additional control performance specifications using norms [4–7]. Consequently, within the realm of robust analysis and control synthesis for uncertain linear systems, many results can be characterized by LMIs [2,8–10]. In the case of the studied LRP systems, the stability analysis of the system boils down to verifying the convergence of the tracking error to zero. Asymptotic stability of a repetitive system implies that the system's response approaches a stable behavior over time. Specifically, it means that as time goes to infinity, the system's output settles into a steady-state behavior where it remains bounded and does not exhibit any oscillatory behavior. Consequently, if a repetitive system is asymptotically stable, it suggests that any error between the desired output (reference signal) and the actual output of the system will tend to decrease and eventually converge to zero as time progresses [11,12]. This is because the system's dynamics, under asymptotic stability, ensure that any deviations from the desired behavior diminish over time until the system reaches a state of equilibrium where the error becomes negligible. In summary, the convergence of the tracking error to zero is a consequence of the asymptotic stability of a repetitive system, indicating that the system's response settles into a stable behavior over time, with the error between the desired and actual outputs approaching zero. In this context, the ILC tracking problem has been reformulated into a stability analysis concept along the pass of 2D repetitive systems [11,12]. A necessary and sufficient condition ensuring stability along the pass has been devised. This new formulation offers insight into the problem within the realm of 2D repetitive systems [13]. The primary contribution of this paper lies in providing the LMI characterization for stability along the pass and subsequently addressing the tracking error problem of continuous-time linear systems operating repetitively. Specifically, the theory of stability along the pass, employing the LMI condition to the processes, yields three conditions [14–17], as discussed earlier, which can be verified through direct application of the LMI condition. Two of these tests necessitate that the eigenvalues of the matrices describing the previous pass profile contribution to the current pass profile and the current pass state vector contribution to the along the pass dynamics lie within the open unit circle and the open left half of the complex plane, respectively [18]. Furthermore, this paper aims to provide a rigorous LMI characterization for stability along the pass to synthesize an ILC law guaranteeing asymptotic stability of the closed-loop repetitive system for any current pass state vector while ensuring three different performances simultaneously [19]. These performances include asymptotic stability with specified transient response and damping factor [20–22] determined by the pole locations of repetitive closed-loop linear systems. Polynomial iterative learning tracking (P-ILC) control is a method used to improve the tracking performance of repetitive systems over multiple iterations. It relies on the concept of learning from past errors to iteratively adjust the control input, aiming to reduce the tracking error between the desired and actual outputs. At its core, P-ILC is based on the notion of iterative learning, where the control input is updated at each iteration based on the error observed in the previous iterations. This iterative process allows the controller to gradually learn the system dynamics and improve its performance over time. The theoretical foundations of P-ILC involve several key concepts. First is the use of polynomial functions to model the desired trajectory of the system's output. These polynomial trajectories provide a flexible and adaptable framework for defining the desired behavior of the system over time [19,23]. Second is the incorporation of a learning mechanism that adjusts the control input based on the error between the actual and desired outputs. This learning mechanism typically involves updating the control input using a combination of past error measurements and a learning rate parameter, which governs the rate at which the controller adapts to changes in the system. In the context of repetitive continuous-time linear systems, P-ILC offers several advantages. By leveraging the repetitive nature of the system, P-ILC can exploit the similarities between successive iterations to improve tracking performance more efficiently. Additionally, the use of polynomial trajectories allows for smoother and more continuous tracking, which can be particularly beneficial for systems with continuous dynamics. Overall, the theoretical foundations of P-ILC provide a robust framework for improving the tracking performance of repetitive continuous-time linear systems. By combining the principles of iterative learning with polynomial trajectory modeling, P-ILC offers a flexible and effective approach to achieving accurate and reliable tracking in various applications [18]. The proposed idea in this work is, roughly, to evolve a nominal control law towards a more robust control law, thus elaborating the concept of stability along the iteration of LRP systems in this sense. This approach can be called D-stability along the iteration. Specifically, and in coherence with the objectives, it involves pole placement while satisfying the notion of stability along the iteration that is presented. Indeed, concerning the set objectives and satisfied requirements, they fall into two categories. On the one hand, there is stability and stabilization of LRP systems along the iteration while ensuring desired transient performance. On the other hand, there is the concept of D-stability along the iteration, which will be reformulated later as a tracking problem.Given the significance of ILC, this paper furnishes results necessary both for solving tracking problems and for ensuring diverse performances for proportional-type ILC and polynomial-type ILC. It demonstrates that robust stability and controller synthesis for continuous linear repetitive processes become feasible through efficient numerical techniques based on LMIs. Building upon these modeling and control methods, this paper establishes a polynomial-type ILC law and proposes a sufficient condition to achieve high-speed tracking control [24,25]. The remainder of this paper is structured as follows: Section 2 presents the problem formulation, introducing the concept of stability along the pass and providing LMI conditions to ensure this stability. In Section 3, the focus shifts to harnessing the ILC tracking problem, where the convergence of tracking error to zero and pole placement performance depend on the selection of suitable learning controller gains. The convergence condition for the tracking error problem is derived using 2D system theory and LMI formulation. Section 4 reveals that convergence and learning performance of this ILC scheme can be achieved through polynomial ILC controller design. Finally, numerical simulations are provided to demonstrate the efficacy of the proposed method.

Throughout this paper, for the designs and simulations, the software MATLAB 2019b was used. The null matrix and the identity matrix with appropriate dimensions are denoted by 0 and I, respectively. Moreover, the notation $X \geq Y$ (respectively, $X > Y$) means that the matrix $X - Y$ is positive semi-definite (respectively, positive definite). In large matrix expressions, the symbol $*$ replaces terms that are induced by symmetry. The expression $\rho()$ denotes the spectral radius of its matrix argument. Finally, the $\| \|$ denotes the induced operator norm, and the Laplace transform is an s-transform.

2. Problem Statement and Preliminaries

Stability along the Pass for 2D Repetitive Systems

The state-space model of a continuous linear repetitive process has the following form over $t \in [0, T]$ and $k \in IR_+$:

$$\begin{cases} \dot{x}_k(t) = Ax_k(t) + Bu_k(t) \\ y_k(t) = Cx_k(t) + Du_k(t) \end{cases} \qquad x(0) = 0, t \geq 0,\ k > 0 \tag{1}$$

where A, B, and C are a constant matrix; $x_{k+1}(t) \in IR^n$ is the state vector; $u_{k+1}(t) \in IR^m$ and $y_{k+1}(t) \in IR^p$ are the input and the output of the system, successively; and x_0 is the initial condition for each iteration. The stability challenge in linear repetitive processes arises from the potential presence of oscillations within the sequence of pass profiles, with oscillations increasing in amplitude from pass to pass (k variable). Stability theory for linear constant pass length examples is formulated using an abstract model of dynamics within a Banach space setting [3]. In this model, pass-to-pass updating takes the form $y_{k+1} = L_\alpha y_k$, where $y_k \in E_\alpha$ is a Banach space and L_α is a bounded linear operator mapping E_α into it. The property of stability along the pass necessitates the existence of finite real scalars $M_\infty > 0$ and $\lambda_\infty \in (0, 1)$ such that $\left\| L_\alpha^k \right\| \leq M_\infty \lambda_\infty^k$.

Figure 1 represents the dynamics of the repetitive process.

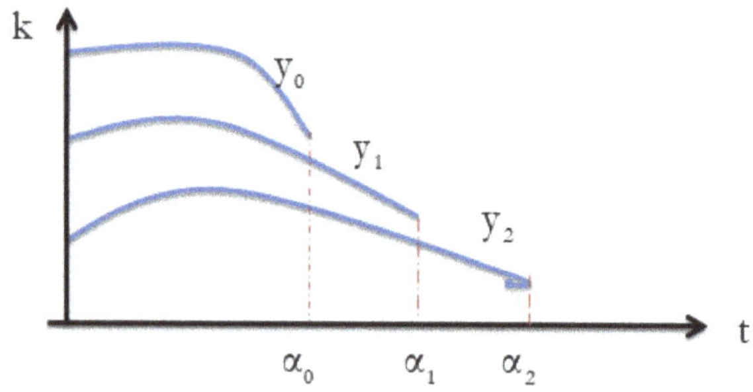

Figure 1. Graphical representation of a sequence of outputs.

For the autonomous case, where the only contribution to the current trial pass profile is the previous one, this condition ensures that the sequence of pass profiles produced will converge to zero. In the context of iterative learning control (ILC), the pass profile on any pass represents the error; thus, the direct application of repetitive process stability theory to ILC facilitates error convergence. In the sequel, a necessary and sufficient condition for stability along the pass for the 2D repetitive system (1) presented in [3] is given. The theory of stability along the pass to the processes produces three conditions, which are discussed in Theorem 1.

Theorem 1 ([3]). *A differential linear repetitive process of the form* (1) *is stable along the pass if and only if:*

(i) $\rho(D) < 1$,

(ii) $\rho(A) \in \mathbb{C}_{-}$,

(iii) *All eigenvalues of the transfer function* $G(s) = C(sI - A)^{-1}B + D$, *have a modulus strictly less than one* $\forall\,|s| = 1$.

Demonstrating stability along the pass easily confirms that the corresponding limit profile of the system (1) remains stable as a 1D linear system. When verifying the conditions outlined in Theorem 1, the first two conditions pose no significant challenge. Firstly, condition (i) represents the necessary and sufficient condition for asymptotic stability, ensuring stability over the finite pass length. This condition, proposed in [14,26], guarantees only trial-to-trial error convergence. The second condition of Theorem 1 entails the stability of the matrix, indicating a uniformly bounded first-pass profile. Lastly, the third test involves computing the eigenvalues of the transfer function, contributing to the dynamics of the previous pass profile to the current one, thereby ensuring error stability. Subsequently, a novel result concerning the stability analysis along the pass of 2D repetitive systems is presented. This robust condition holds significant importance in developing robust formulations and conducting design procedures within the context of ILC synthesis for continuous-time linear systems. The Objective of this part is to transform the algebraic conditions given by Theorem 1 into an LMI formulation. The original result proposed in the Theorem 2, considers a sufficient conditions that leads to the three stability conditions along the iterations given in the the Theorem 1 for continuous-time repetitive systems. They particularly access a unified framework for handling tracking problems and open up new perspectives for solving control problems. Below, we present a novel result developed within the framework of our previous research work for discrete case by concerning the stability analysis along the passage of 2D-repetitive systems. This robust condition holds significant importance in crafting resilient formulations and executing design procedures within the scope of ILC synthesis for continuous-time linear systems.

Theorem 2. *A differential linear repetitive process of the form (1) is stable along the pass if (if and only if in the MISO case) one of the following equivalent conditions holds:*

(i) *A is stable and*

$$\| G(s) \|_\infty < 1 \tag{2}$$

(ii) *There exists a positive symmetric matrix X such that the following LMI is feasible:*

$$\begin{bmatrix} A^T X + XA & * & * \\ B & -I & * \\ CX & D & -I \end{bmatrix} < 0 \tag{3}$$

Proof. Based on this configuration is the LMIs expression described by Figure 2.

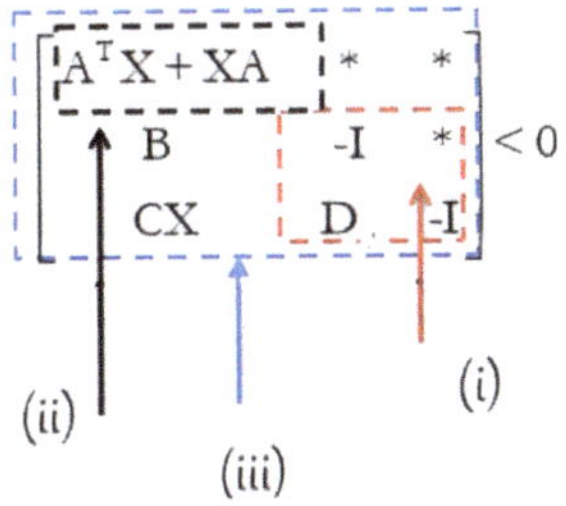

Figure 2. LMI conditions.

The condition (i) in Theorem 2 aims to ensure the asymptotic stability of the system over time and to minimize the ratio between the outputs of two successive iterations based on the H_∞ optimization problem. The combination leads us to a stability condition along passages described by the condition (ii) given in Theorem 2.

The equivalence between (i) and (ii) is a well-known result.

Note that the third condition of stability along the pass implies that $\rho(G(s)) < 1 \; \forall |s| = 1$, or if we consider $\sigma_{\max}$ as the maximum singular value and then the H_∞ norm of $G(s)$ ($\|G(s)\|_\infty = \sigma_{\max}(G(s))$), it is known that $\sigma_{\max}$ is an upper bound for the eigenvalues modulus of a matrix $\rho(G(s)) \leq \sigma_{\max}(G(s))$.

This equality occurs in the MISO case only when $G(s)$ is a scalar function. Then the LMI of Theorem 2 implies conditions (ii) and (iii) of Theorem 1.

The condition (i) of Theorem 1 is redundant since from the LMI of Theorem 2,we have $\begin{bmatrix} -I & D^T \\ * & -I \end{bmatrix} < 0$, which complete the proof. □

3. Main Results

3.1. Control Objective

The objective of this section is to transform the problem of stability along the pass of the continuous-time linear repetitive systems into a tracking problem [23].

Consider the following assumptions based on system (1):

- **(A1)** The desired output $y_d(t), t = 1, \ldots, T$ is given a prior over the same time duration; it is assumed that the initial resetting condition is satisfied, i.e., $y_k(0) = y_d(0)$.
- **(A2)** The initial state remains the same at each iteration, i.e., $x_k(0) = 0, \; \forall k = 1, 2, \ldots, N$. For any given assumption **A1** and **A2**, one desirable objective in ILC is that $y_k(t)$ converges monotonically to $y_d(t)$ when k tends to infinity for all t within the time interval $[0, T]$ since it can guarantee reasonable transients during the learning process [3]. In the sense of the, $\ell_{2,[0,T]}$ norm, this objective can be transformed by considering the index [8].

$$J(\gamma, k) = \sum_{t=1}^{N} \left[{e_{k+1}}^T(t) e_{k+1}(t) - \gamma^2 {e_k}^T(t) e_k(t) \right] \tag{4}$$

where $\gamma > 0$ is a prescribed scalar and $e_k(t)$ is the tracking error at the kth iteration, expressed as

$$e_k(t) = y_d(t) - y_k(t) \tag{5}$$

Obviously, the norm error $\|e_k(t)\|_{2[0,T]}$ can be guaranteed to converge monotonically along the iteration axis k if $J(\gamma) < 0$ holds for any $\gamma \in [0, 1]$.

3.2. ILC Tracking Control

In this section, the ILC scheme given by Figure 3 can focus perfectly to overcome the tracking problem when it tracks an iteration's desired trajectory as k tends to infinity. Following this idea, the concept of the stabilization along the pass can be shown as a tracking problem. The formulated problem is solved by using the iterative learning control described by the following updating ILC law [8]:

$$u_{k+1}(t) = \beta u_k(t) + K_1\dot{\eta}_{k+1}(t) + K_2\dot{e}_k(t) \tag{6}$$

$$\eta_{k+1}(t) = \int_0^t (x_{k+1}(t) - \beta x_k(t))d\tau \quad \eta_k(0) = 0 \tag{7}$$

where $\eta_{k+1}(t)$ denotes the state vector computed to the cycle direction, K_1, K_2 are switching learning gains with appropriately dimensioned matrices to be designed, and β is a positive scalar to be optimized.

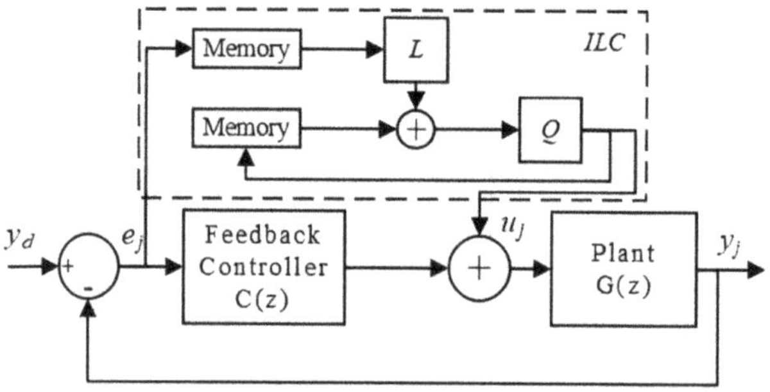

Figure 3. ILC controller.

Moreover, if it is assumed that the matrix $D = 0$, then clearly, (1) can be written as

$$\begin{cases} \dot{x}_k(t) = Ax_k(t) + Bu_k(t) \\ y_k(t) = Cx_k(t) \end{cases} \quad x(0) = 0, t \geq 0, \, k > 0 \tag{8}$$

(6)–(8) can be written as

$$\dot{\eta}_{k+1}(t) = \int_0^t (\dot{x}_{k+1}(t) - \beta\dot{x}_k(t))d\tau \tag{9}$$

$$\begin{aligned} \dot{\eta}_{k+1}(t) &= (A + BK_1)\eta_{k+1}(t) + BK_2e_k(t) \\ \beta e_k(t) - e_{k+1}(t) &= C\dot{\eta}_{k+1}(t) \\ e_{k+1}(t) &= -C(A_{k+1} + BK_1)\eta_{k+1}(t) + (\beta - CBK_2)e_k(t) \end{aligned}$$

Obviously (8) can be rewritten as

$$\begin{bmatrix} \dot{\eta}_{k+1}(t) \\ e_{k+1}(t) \end{bmatrix} = \begin{bmatrix} (A + BK_1) & BK_2 \\ -C(A_{k+1} + BK_1) & (\beta - CBK_2) \end{bmatrix} \begin{bmatrix} \eta_{k+1}(t) \\ e_k(t) \end{bmatrix} \tag{10}$$

The state-space model (10) is that of a continuous linear repetitive process of the form defined by the pass output and state vectors $e_{k+1}(t)$ and $\dot{\eta}_{k+1}(t)$, respectively.

Note that $T(s)$ is a transfer matrix between $E_k(s)$ and $E_{k+1}(s)$.

From (10) we can obtain

$$E_{k+1}(s) = T(s)E_k(s) \tag{11}$$

where

$$T(s) = \left[\begin{array}{c|c} A + BK_1 & BK_2 \\ \hline -C(A + BK_1) & (\beta - CBK_2) \end{array}\right] \tag{12}$$

Hence, it can be derived that if $\|T(z)\|_\infty < \gamma, \gamma \in [0,1)$ holds, then $\lim_{k\to\infty} \|e_k(t)\|_2 = 0$ (monotonic convergence in the sense of the norm l_2). This implies that although the tracking error over the finite time interval $[0, T]$ is considered in ILC, the monotonic convergence of the error $\|e_k(t)\|_2$ can also be guaranteed when $\|T(z)\|_\infty < \gamma$ is used to obtain the negative performance index $J(\gamma) < 0$.

Theorem 3 ([27])**.** *The output tracking error $e_k(t)$ converges monotonically to zero when k tends to infinity if and only if the 2D repetitive system (12) is stable along the pass.*

Starting from Theorem 3 and by applying the obtained Theorem 2 on the given system representation 12, we can state the following Theorem 4.

Theorem 4 ([23])**.** *The tracking error converges monotonically to zero when k tends to infinity if there exist matrices K_2, N_1 and a positive symmetric matrix X and the scalars $\beta, \gamma \in [0,1)$, such that the following LMI is feasible:*

$$\begin{bmatrix} (AX + BN_1) + sym(\ldots) & * & * \\ (BK_2)^T & -I & * \\ -C(AX + BN_1) & \beta - CBK_2 & -\gamma^2 \end{bmatrix} < 0 \tag{13}$$

then the gain matrices are given by: $K_2,\ K_1 = N_1X^{-1}$.

3.3. ILC Tracking Control Using D-Stability along the Pass

In this section, we address the issue of placing all poles of a system within a specified disk, which is commonly known as the D-pole placement problem for continuous-time linear repetitive systems. This method has been devised to control systems that exhibit favorable transient and steady-state responses. Several criteria have been put forth to guarantee that all the closed-loop eigenvalues of continuous-time linear repetitive systems reside within a designated disk $D(-(r+d), r)$ centered at $(-r+d, 0)$ with a radius of r, see Figure 4.

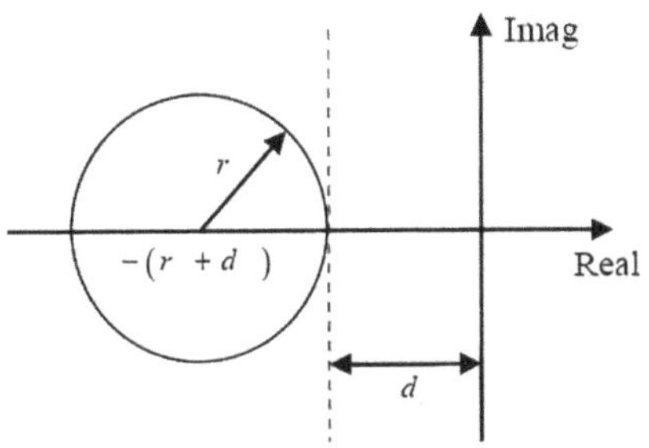

Figure 4. Pole placement for the closed-loop system.

Building upon this concept, the tracking control problem utilizing the notion of stabilization along the pass discussed earlier can be depicted as a pole placement problem.

Using the parameter d, it is possible to establish an upper bound for the settling time of the transient response given by $3\tau, 5\tau$ for a repetitive system undergoing the kth iteration, with $\tau = \frac{1}{d}$. This value r provides the upper bound on the natural frequency of oscillation for the transient response. Additionally, a lower bound on the damping factor ξ, which determines the overshoot, can be computed as follows:

$$\xi = \frac{\sqrt{(r+d) - r^2}}{r+d} \tag{14}$$

3.4. D-Stability along the Pass for Continuous Linear Repetitive Process

Consider the continuous linear repetitive process having this form over $t \in [0, T]$, $k \in IR_+$:

$$\dot{x}_k(t) = Ax_k(t), x(0) = 0, t \geq 0, k > 0 \tag{15}$$

The objective of this section is to establish criteria to ensure that all the eigenvalues of the repetitive system (1) reside within a designated disk $D(-(r+d), r)$ centered at $(-(r+d), 0)$ with a radius of r and a distance d from the imaginary axis, as illustrated previously in Figure 4. Initially, we introduce a computationally sufficient condition for ensuring D-stability in repetitive systems. This condition will serve as a fundamental component in deriving ILC tracking control results in the next section.

Theorem 5 ([22]). *All the poles of system (15) are located inside a specified disk D centered at $-(r+d)$ with radius r if the following condition is satisfied:*

$$(A+d)X + X(A+d)^T + \frac{1}{r}(A+d)X(A+d)^T < 0. \tag{16}$$

We use the well-known common quadratic Lyapunov function:

$$V_{k+1}(x) = {\eta_{k+1}}^T P \eta_{k+1}, P = P^T > 0 \tag{17}$$

A sufficient condition such that all the eigenvalues of $(A + BK1)$ of the repetitive system lie inside the circular region $\varsigma(d, r)$, as depicted in Figure 4, is given by the existence of a positive definite symmetric matrix $X = P^{-1}$ such that the following condition holds.

Theorem 6 ([23]). *The tracking error converges monotonically to zero when k tends to infinity if there exist matrices K_2, N_1, a positive symmetric matrix X, and the scalars $r > 0, d > 0, \gamma \in [0, 1), 0 < \beta < 1$ such that the following LMI is feasible:*

$$\begin{bmatrix} \{(AX + BN_1^T) + sym(\ldots)\} + 2dX & * & * & * \\ (XA + N_1^T B^T) + dX & -rX & 0 & 0 \\ (BK_2)^T & 0 & -I & * \\ -C(AX + BN_1) & 0 & (\beta - CBK_2) & -\gamma^2 \end{bmatrix} < 0 \tag{18}$$

In this case, the gain matrices are given by $K_2, K_1 = N_1 X^{-1}$.

Proof. Based on Figure 5, we consider the LMI condition of (13), then replace the bloc diagonal (1, 1) by (16) and apply the Schur complement we obtained (18).
□

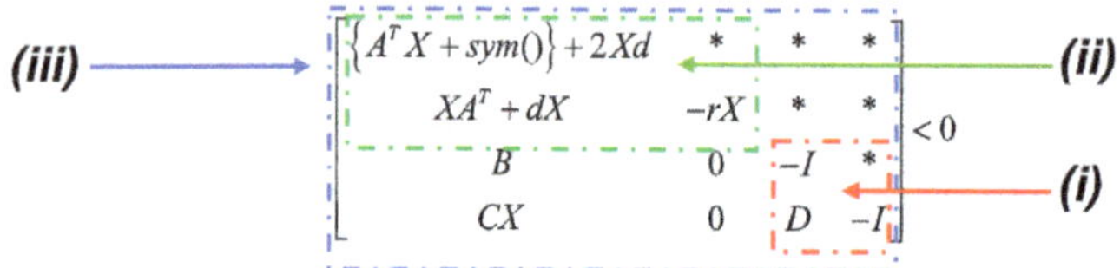

Figure 5. D-stability LMI.

The objective of the next section is to transform the condition for analyzing D-stability along the passages into a tracking problem using ILC control. This leads to a new interpretation of Theorem 6.

3.5. Polynomial ILC Control

This section builds upon the idea introduced in the previous section, where the concept of D-stabilization along the pass is framed as a tracking problem utilizing high-order iterative learning control.

The methodology for designing the iterative learning control (ILC) law, particularly in the context of polynomial-based approaches such as Poly-ILC, involves several key steps and considerations: modeling the system and defining the control law, learning mechanism, and iterative optimization. The rationale behind the choice of polynomial-based approaches like Poly-ILC lies in their flexibility and adaptability. Polynomial functions offer a versatile framework for representing complex trajectories and can capture a wide range of desired behaviors with relatively few parameters. Additionally, polynomial-based approaches provide smooth and continuous control signals, which can be advantageous for systems with continuous dynamics. Specific contributions of Poly-ILC include the following:

- Introducing a novel polynomial-based approach to iterative learning control, which offers a flexible and intuitive framework for defining desired trajectories.
- Advancing existing techniques by providing a systematic methodology for designing and optimizing polynomial-based control laws for repetitive systems.
- Demonstrating improved tracking performance and robustness compared to traditional ILC methods, particularly in applications with complex and time-varying dynamics. Overall, Poly-ILC represents a significant advancement in the field of iterative learning control, offering a powerful and versatile approach for achieving accurate and reliable tracking in repetitive systems.

We consider a control law in the following form over $t \in [0, T]$ and $k \in \mathbf{N}_+$:

$$u_{k+1}(t) = v_{k+1}(t) + L_1 x_{k+1}(t) \tag{19}$$

Applying the control law (19) to system (8), the following state space is then obtained:

$$\begin{cases} x_{k+1}(t+1) = (A + BL_1)x_{k+1}(t) + Bv_{k+1}(t) \\ y_{k+1}(t) = Cx_{k+1}(t) \end{cases} \tag{20}$$

where $t \in [0, T]$, $k = 0, 1, \ldots, N$.

Obviously, from (20), the transfer function matrix from $u_{k+1}(t)$ to $y_{k+1}(t)$ can be expressed as

$$Y_{k+1}(s) = G(s)U_{k+1}(s) \tag{21}$$

where

$$G(z) = C(sI - A + BL_1)^{-1}B \tag{22}$$

Now, we introduce the polynomial ILC law as follows:

$$V_{k+1}(s) = \beta V_k(s) + L_2(s)E_k(s) \tag{23}$$

$$L_2(s) = \sum_{q=0}^{r} L_{2,q} s^q \tag{24}$$

where the Laplace transform of the form $E_k(z) = Z[e_k(t)]$, $L_2(s)$ is a polynomial learning gain matrix to be designed, and r is the degree of the learning controller $L_2(s)$.

Given the system (20) with updating structure of control (23), and verifying assumptions **A1** and **A2**, we find appropriate learning controller $L_2(s)$ such that the robust monotonic convergence of e_k is achieved and the output error $e_k(t)$ for $t = 1, \ldots, T$ converges to zero as $k \to \infty$. Therefore, let us express the difference error as

$$e_{k+1}(t) - e_k(t) = -(y_{k+1}(t) - y_k(t)) \tag{25}$$

Consequently, the Laplace transform of the difference between errors at iterations takes the following form:

$$E_{k+1}(s) - E_k(s) = -(Y_{k+1}(s) - Y_k(s)) \tag{26}$$

$$E_{k+1}(s) - E_k(s) \ = -G(s)(U_{k+1}(s) - U_k(s)) \tag{27}$$

$$E_{k+1}(s) - E_k(s) \ = -G(s)L_2(s)E_k(s) \tag{28}$$

This leads to

$$E_{k+1}(s) = (I - G(s)L_2(s))E_k(s) \tag{29}$$

Based on the preceding developments, deriving a condition for the monotonic convergence of the ILC systems (20) and (21) is straightforward.

$$E_{k+1}(s) = \left[\beta - C(sI - (A + BL_1))^{-1}B\sum_{q=0}^{r} L_{2,q}s^q\right]E_k(s) \tag{30}$$

Let us use the transfer matrix defined by

$$T(s) = \beta - C(sI - (A + BL_1))^{-1}B\sum_{q=0}^{r} L_{2,q}s^q \tag{31}$$

Note that with the relative degree of the polynomial controller $r = 1$, building upon Equation (31), we arrive at this result:

$$T(s) = \beta - C(sI - (A + BL_1))^{-1}B[L_{21} + sL_{22}] \tag{32}$$

Considering the fact that

$$s(sI - A)^{-1} = I + A(sI - A)^{-1}$$

It results that

$$T(s) = \ -C(sI - (A + BL_1))^{-1}[(BL_{21} + (A + BL_1)BL_{22})] + (\beta - CBL_{22}) \tag{33}$$

If there exist matrices $\tilde{A}, \tilde{B}, \tilde{C}, \tilde{D}$, we can written $T(s)$ as

$$\begin{aligned} T(s) &= \tilde{C}(sI - \tilde{A})^{-1}\tilde{B} + \tilde{D} \\ &:= \left[\begin{array}{c|c} \tilde{A} & \tilde{B} \\ \hline \tilde{C} & \tilde{D} \end{array}\right] \end{aligned} \tag{34}$$

Referring to (34), $T(s)$ can be written as follows:

$$T(s) := \left[\begin{array}{c|c} (A + BL_1) & (BL_{21} + (A + BL_1)BL_{22}) \\ \hline -C & \beta - CBL_{22} \end{array}\right] \tag{35}$$

Now, we introduce LMI conditions aimed at ensuring the monotonic convergence of P-ILC. Considering the performance index $J(\gamma)$ and applying the BRL relative to robust H_∞ control theory [28,29], Theorem 7 is as follows.

Theorem 7. *The tracking error converges monotonically to zero when k tends to infinity if there exist matrices L_{21}, L_{22}, N, G, a positive symmetric matrix X, and the scalars $r > 0, d > 0, \gamma \in [0,1), 0 < \beta < 1, 0 < \alpha < 1$ such that the following LMI is feasible:*

$$\begin{bmatrix} 2(d-\alpha)X & * & * & * & * \\ (d-\alpha)X & -rX & 0 & 0 & * \\ (BL_{21})^T - \alpha BL_{22} & 0 & -I & * & * \\ -CX & 0 & (\beta - CBL_{22}) & -\gamma^2 & * \\ (GA^T + N^T B^T) + \alpha G^T + X^T & X^T & BL_{22} & 0 & -G - G^T \end{bmatrix} < 0 \quad (36)$$

Then $L_1 = NX^{-1}$.

Proof. Substitute the new model (35) in this LMI, guaranteeing the ILC tracking control using D-stability along the pass of theorem (6).

We obtain this LMI:

$$\begin{bmatrix} (A+BL_1)X + X(A+BL_1)^T + 2dX & * & * & * \\ X(A+BL_1)^T + dX & -rX & 0 & 0 \\ (BL_{21})^T + (BL_{22})^T (A+BL_1)^T & 0 & -I & * \\ -CX & 0 & (\beta - CBL_{22}) & -\gamma^2 \end{bmatrix} < 0 \quad (37)$$

We rewrite (37) as

$$\begin{bmatrix} 2dX - 2\alpha X & * & * & * \\ dX - \alpha X & -rX & 0 & 0 \\ (BL_{21})^T - \alpha BL_{22} & 0 & -I & * \\ -CX & 0 & (\beta - CBL_{22}) & -\gamma^2 \end{bmatrix} + \left\{ \begin{bmatrix} (A+BL_1) + \alpha I \\ 0 \\ 0 \\ 0 \end{bmatrix} \begin{bmatrix} X & X & BL_{22} & 0 \end{bmatrix} + sym\{\ldots\} \right\} < 0 \quad (38)$$

Furthermore, applying the projection lemma for inequality (38), the inequality (36) is obtained. This end the proof. □

4. Uncertain LRP Systems

4.1. Problem Formulation

In most synthesis problems, the desired objective is to achieve and maintain specific robust performance goals despite the often detrimental uncertainties of the system to be controlled. To demonstrate the robustness of the ILC (iterative learning control) used, we consider the LRP system (1) with polytopic modeling uncertainties.

$$\begin{cases} \dot{x}_k(t) = \hat{A}x_k(t) + \hat{B}u_k(t) \\ y_k(t) = \hat{C}x_k(t) + \hat{D}u_k(t) \end{cases} \quad x_k(0) = 0, t \geq 0, k > 0 \quad (39)$$

Such matrices as $\hat{A}$ and $\hat{B}, \hat{C}, \hat{D}$ are sets of matrices defined by

$$\left\{ \hat{A} = \sum_{i=1}^{N_A} \theta_i A_i, \ \sum_{i=1}^{N_A} \theta_i = 1, \ \theta_i \geq 0 \right\} \quad (40)$$

$$\left\{ \hat{B} = \sum_{i=1}^{N_B} \theta_i B_i, \ \sum_{i=1}^{N_B} \theta_i = 1, \ \theta_i \geq 0 \right\} \quad (41)$$

$$\left\{ \hat{C} = \sum_{i=1}^{N_C} \theta_i C_i, \ \sum_{i=1}^{N_C} \theta_i = 1, \ \theta_i \geq 0 \right\} \quad (42)$$

$$\left\{ \hat{D} = \sum_{i=1}^{N_D} \theta_i D_i, \ \sum_{i=1}^{N_D} \theta_i = 1, \ \theta_i \geq 0 \right\} \quad (43)$$

where N_A, N_B, N_C, and N_D are the number of vertices of the polytopes.

4.2. Poly-Quadratic Stability

The concept of a robust ILC synthesis method is based on the polyquadratic approach. This approach relies on the use of a Lyapunov function that depends on uncertain parameters. These functions enable the analysis of stability and stabilization of continuous-time LRP systems. We consider the LRP system described by Equation (39). The system modeling involves the use of Lyapunov functions that depend on uncertain parameters.

Let

$$V_i(k,t) = x^T \hat{P} x \tag{44}$$

$$V_i(k,t) = x^T \sum_{i=1}^{N_D} \theta_i P_i x \tag{45}$$

$$\hat{P} = \sum_{i=1}^{N_P} \theta_i P_i \tag{46}$$

where k describes the evolution of the Lyapunov function at the k^{eme} iteration and N_P is the number of vertices of the polytope.

Theorem 8. *Consider the uncertain repetitive LRPs system (39) in a closed loop. The system is D-stable along the pass and the tracking error $e_{k+1}(t)$ converges monotonically to zero as k tends to infinity if there exist scalars γ, α, r, d, matrices $K_{2,i}$,N_i, and positive symmetric matrices G_i such that the following optimization problem is feasible:*

$$\min_{0<\gamma,\alpha<1}(\gamma,\alpha)$$

$$\begin{bmatrix} \{A_i^T G_i + N_i^T B_i^T + sym(\ldots)\} + 2G_i d & * & * & * \\ A_i^T G_i + N_i^T B_i^T + dG_i & -rG_i & * & * \\ K_{2,i}^T B_i^T & 0 & -I & * \\ -C_i A_i G_i - C_i B_i N_i & 0 & \alpha - C_i B_i K_{2,i} & -\gamma^2 \end{bmatrix} < 0 \tag{47}$$

Then the learning gains are given by the following:
For $i = 1 \ldots N_A$,

$$K_{2,i}, K_{1,i} = N_i G_i^{-1}.$$

The construction of a robust ILC synthesis method is based on the polyquadratic approach. This approach requires the use of a Lyapunov function dependent on the uncertain parameters. The system with LRP described by Equation (39) is considered. The modeling of the system necessitates the use of Lyapunov functions that depend on the uncertain parameters. Theorem 8 is an extension of the results to the case of polytopic uncertainty, using polytopic Lyapunov functions.

5. Numerical Examples

5.1. Comparison between D-ILC Tracking Control and D-Poly-ILC Tracking Control

In this section, the effectiveness of the proposed design methods is demonstrated through simulation results utilizing MATLAB software. Consider the active suspension system of a car, as shown in Figure 6. All details regarding the system behavior and operation can be found in [20]. The matrices of the model (1) are presented as follows:

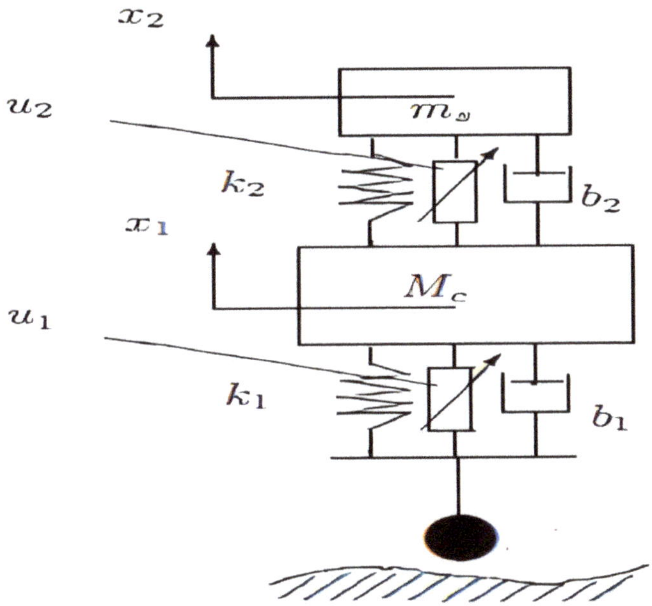

Figure 6. Active suspension of a car seat.

The model consists of a car mass M_c and a driver seat mass m_s. Vertical vibrations caused by a road can be partially attenuated by the stiffness k_1 and damping b_1 of the shock absorbers. The driver may still experience undesirable vibrations, which can be reduced by seat suspension elements of stiffness k_2 and damping b_2. Damping of the vibrations of M_c and m_s can be increased by changing the control inputs u_1 and u_2.

$$A = \begin{bmatrix} 0 & 1 & 0 & 0 \\ 0 & 0 & 0 & 1 \\ \frac{-k_1-k_2}{M_c} & \frac{k_2}{M_c} & \frac{-b_1-b_2}{M_c} & \frac{b_2}{M_c} \\ \frac{k_2}{m_s} & -\frac{k_2}{m_s} & \frac{b_2}{m_s} & -\frac{b_2}{m_s} \end{bmatrix}, B = \begin{bmatrix} 0 & 0 \\ 0 & 0 \\ \frac{1}{M_c} & -\frac{1}{M_c} \\ 0 & \frac{1}{m_s} \end{bmatrix}; C = \begin{bmatrix} 0 & 1 & 0 & 0 \end{bmatrix}.$$

with the following: $\mathrm{M_c} = 1500$ kg, $\mathrm{m_s} = 90$ kg, $\mathrm{k_1} = 4 \times 10^4$ N/m, $\mathrm{k_2} = 5 \times 10^3$ N/m, $\mathrm{b_1} = 4 \times 10^3$ Ns/m, $\mathrm{b_2} = 5 \times 10^2$ Ns/m.

5.1.1. ILC Controller for Desired Performances

The primary objective is to ensure certain step response performances such as settling time and overshoot. Based on Theorems 6 and 7, and by solving the set of LMIs (18) and (36), the system under consideration is monotonically stabilized by designing learning gains with the following desired performances:

1. Overshoot $\leq 5\%$.
2. Setting time at $2\% \leq 10\%$.

Therefore, it can be inferred that the proposed approach implements D-pole assignment, and the pole locations within the specified disk D are applied for $r = 1$ and $d = 0.685$. In this scenario, the computed learning gains are provided in Table 1:

Table 1. Proposed approaches.

Parameters	Approaches	Learning Gains
$\beta = 0.99$ $\gamma = 0.99$	Theorem 6	$K_1 = \begin{bmatrix} 2.25 & 0.25 & 0.041 & 0.753 \\ -0.52 & 0.451 & -0.050 & 0.013 \end{bmatrix} \times 10^4$ $K_2 = \begin{bmatrix} 23.02 \\ 0.072 \end{bmatrix}$
$\beta = 0.99$ $\gamma = 0.99$ $\alpha = 0.75$	Theorem 7	$L_1 = \begin{bmatrix} 4.007 & 0.01 & 0.15 & -0.029 \\ -0.53 & 0.44 & -0.55 & 0.008 \end{bmatrix} \times 10^4$ $L_{21} = \begin{bmatrix} 0.74 \\ 0.09 \end{bmatrix}$ $L_{22} = \begin{bmatrix} 0.83 \\ 0.12 \end{bmatrix}$

The closed-loop response achieved with the obtained controller as depicted in Figure 7 illustrates comparable desired specifications defined by the ILC Theorem 6 and the Polynomial-type ILC Theorem 7. Therefore, the resulting ILC process using the D-stability along the pass formulation can ensure a settling time of less than 10 s with no overshoot compared to the desired value previously listed. As is evident from Figure 8, when we opt for identical values of d and r for both LMIs given by Theorem 6 and Theorem 7, we can assess the effectiveness of polynomial ILC control in ensuring the desired system specifications. However, we will later demonstrate the impact of the slack parameter α on enhancing the desired system specifications while keeping d and r constant and varying α.

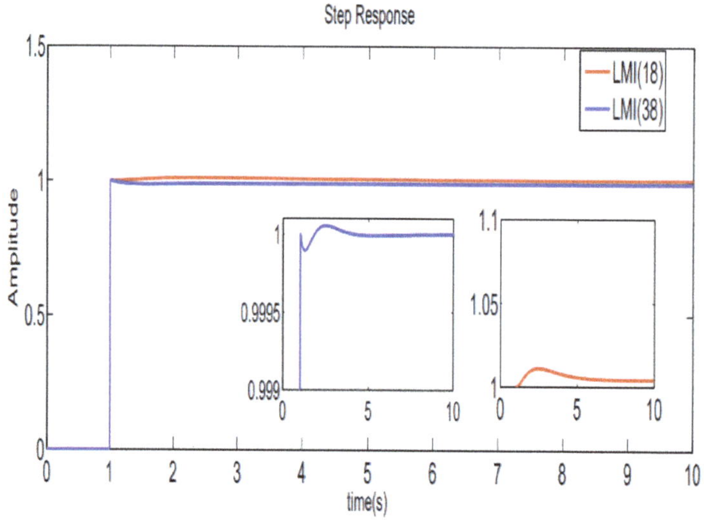

Figure 7. Step responses with D-stability along the pass.

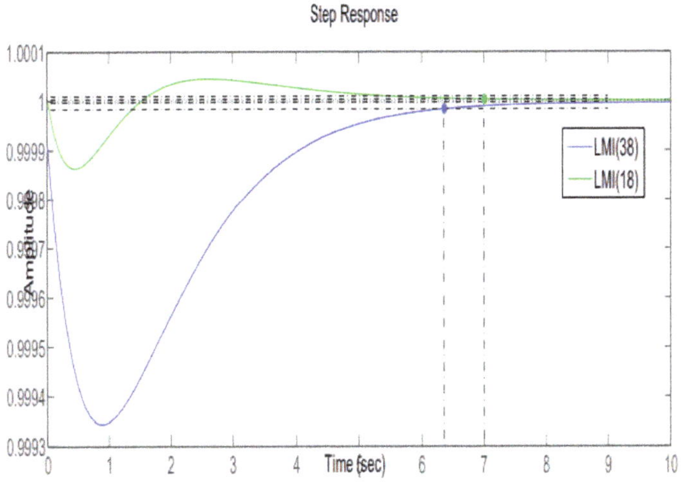

Figure 8. Zoom of settling time adjustment for Theorems 6 and 7.

In Figure 9, where $\alpha > 0.75$, the designed polynomial ILC proves to be highly effective in guaranteeing a critical system performance.

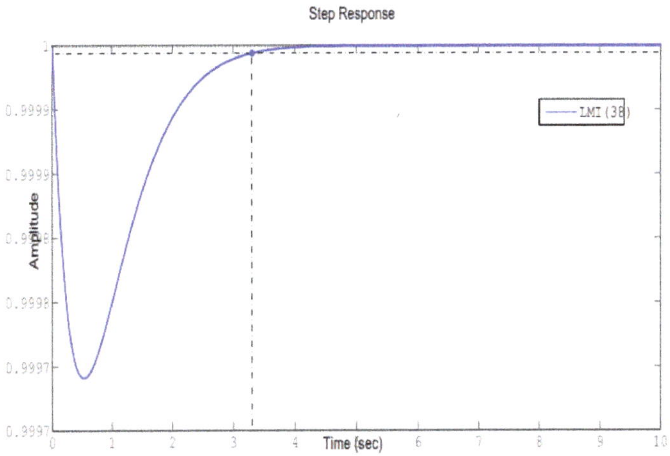

Figure 9. Settling time adjustment obtained with $\alpha > 0.75$: Theorem 7.

The achieved results are demonstrated in Table 2.

Table 2. Polynomial-ILC approach.

Parameters	Approach	Learning Gains
$\beta = 0.99$ $\gamma = 0.99$	Theorem 7	$L_1 = \begin{bmatrix} 2.25 & 0.27 & 0.16 & -0.02 \\ -0.52 & 0.43 & -0.55 & 0.008 \end{bmatrix} \times 10^4$ $L_{21} = \begin{bmatrix} 5.93 \\ 0.072 \end{bmatrix}$ $L_{22} = \begin{bmatrix} 6.2 \\ 0.1 \end{bmatrix}$

5.1.2. Tracking Error Convergence

In the sequel, consider the linear system (1). For this purpose, the desired trajectory is defined as follows:

$$y_d(t) = sin(t), t \in [0, 10] \tag{48}$$

Initially, Figure 10 illustrates the evolution of the tracking error in relation to the iteration number for $k = 14$ for the ILC schemes.

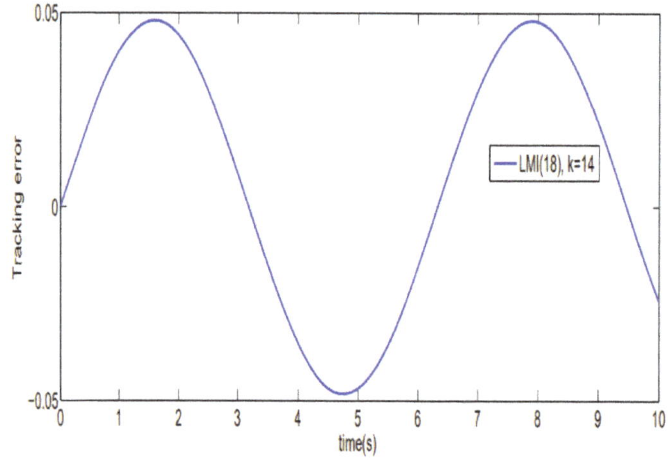

Figure 10. D-ILC tracking error given by Theorem 6 at 14th iteration.

Subsequently, Figure 11 depicts comparable tracking errors generated by the polynomial-type ILC (7) and ILC (6). Consequently, the resulting ILC process ensures that its tracking error converges to zero along the iteration axis. The root mean square error is defined by the following equation:

$$e_{RMS} = \sqrt{\frac{1}{\alpha}\sum_{p=0}^{\alpha-1} e_k^T(p)e_k(p)} \tag{49}$$

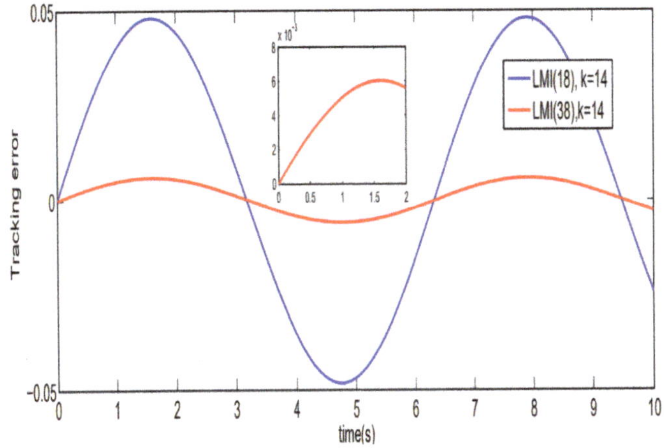

Figure 11. Polynomial D-ILC tracking error given by Theorem 7 at 14th iteration.

Additional quantitative information can be extracted from Figures 12, 13, 14, which display the root mean square (RMS) values of the tracking errors. The convergence of error from pass to pass is evaluated using the RMS error for both the polynomial-type ILC law and the proportional ILC.

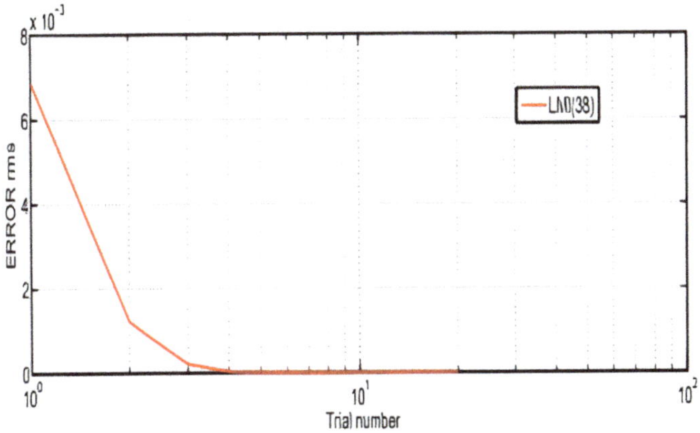

Figure 12. Polynomial ILC tracking error performance given by Theorem 7.

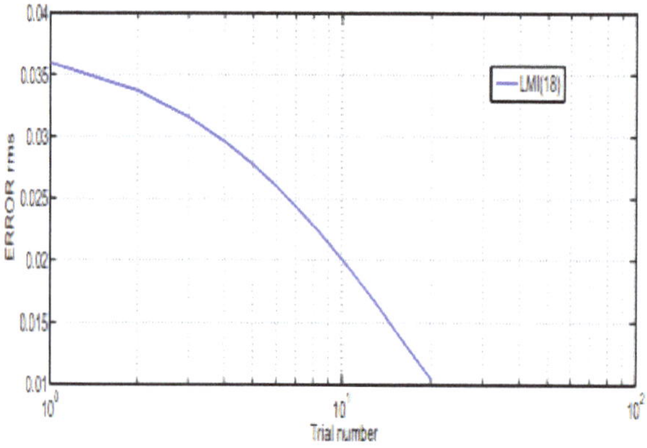

Figure 13. D-ILC root mean square error at 20th iteration.

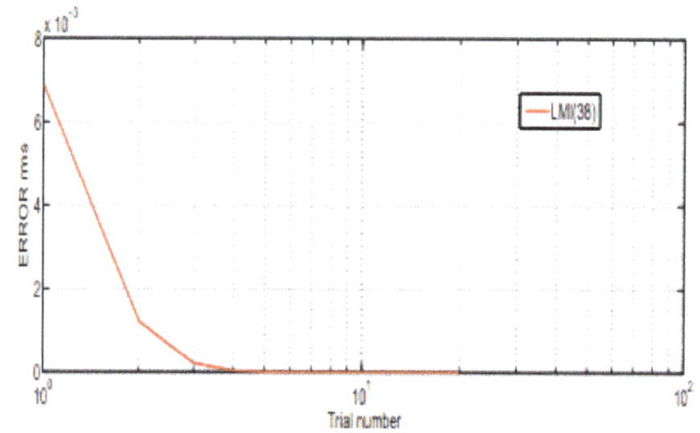

Figure 14. D-Poly-ILC root mean square error at 20th iteration.

5.1.3. Discussion

In theorem (7), the pass-to-pass updating error is represented by $e_{k+1}(t) = \varphi e_k(t)$, where φ is a bounded linear matrix operator. The property of convergence error between the different profiles along the iteration domain requires the existence of finite real scalars $\varphi \in [0,1)$ such that $\|e_{k+1}(t)\| \leq \varphi e_k(t)$. This prompts a discussion on the speed of convergence error after the iteration number as a function of φ such as

$$\varphi = \beta - CBL_{22} \tag{50}$$

The relaxed parameters β play a crucial role in ensuring the monotonic speed convergence of the system with the minimum number of iterations, illustrated by Table 3.

Table 3. The speed convergence error.

β	γ	α	φ
0.36	0.9	0.9	0.3503
0.25	0.9	0.9	0.232
0.15	0.9	0.9	0.148

On the contrary, Figure 15 illustrates the evolution of the tracking error for different values of β as listed in Table 3.

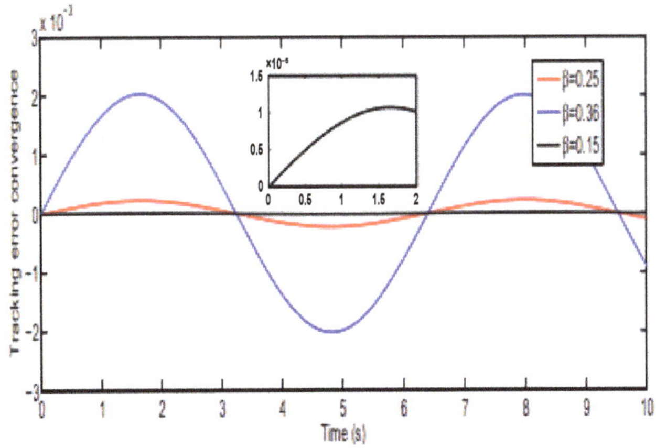

Figure 15. The tracking error for different values of β.

The main contribution consists of developing a new stability condition, which achieves the convergence of the error to zero, and solving the tracking error problem by applying a D-Poly-ILC control for continuous repetitive systems. The synthesis problem of the robust ILC produces 2D repetitive continuous systems. The derived conditions are expressed as a family of linear matrix inequalities (LMIs) parameterized by the scalar variables β_{opt} and γ_{opt}. These conditions reduce significantly the conservatism and the speed convergence of error and show the advantage of using the scalar variables in the case of ILC control.

5.2. Uncertain Case

For certain situations, we can consider the case where the stiffness of the spring adjustment mechanism and the hardness of the metal strip can degrade after some time. To account for this latter configuration, we consider uncertainties on both parameters λ_1, λ_2 with $\lambda_1 \in [\lambda_{1\,\min}, \lambda_{1\,\max}] = [550, 676]$ and $\lambda_2 \in [\lambda_{2\,\min}, \lambda_{2\,\max}] = [1924, 2178]$.

In this case, the state matrices (39) of Figure 6 transform into an uncertain polytopic model with four polytopes, with

$$A_1 = \begin{bmatrix} 0 & 1 \\ -0.427 & 0 \end{bmatrix}, B_1 = \begin{bmatrix} 0 \\ -0.002 \end{bmatrix}$$

$$A_2 = \begin{bmatrix} 0 & 1 \\ -0.5006 & 0 \end{bmatrix}, B_2 = \begin{bmatrix} 0 \\ -2.29 \times 10^{-4} \end{bmatrix}$$

$$A_3 = \begin{bmatrix} 0 & 1 \\ -0.439 & 0 \end{bmatrix}, B_3 = \begin{bmatrix} 0 \\ -2.015 \times 10^{-4} \end{bmatrix}$$

$$A_4 = \begin{bmatrix} 0 & 1 \\ -0.50024 & 0 \end{bmatrix}, B_4 = \begin{bmatrix} 0 \\ -2.6 \times 10^{-4} \end{bmatrix}$$

$$C = \begin{bmatrix} 1 & 0 \end{bmatrix}$$

The objective in this case is to determine the matrices $K_{1,i}$ such that the spectrum of $\hat{A}$ belongs to a region D for any $\theta_i \in N_A$. Furthermore, the varying gain matrices are given by

$$K_{1,1} = \begin{bmatrix} -3.5734 & -2.2572 \end{bmatrix}$$

$$K_{1,2} = \begin{bmatrix} 0.4056 & -0.2578 \end{bmatrix} 10^{-3}$$

$$K_{1,3} = \begin{bmatrix} 0.0273 & 0.0314 \end{bmatrix}$$

$$K_{1,4} = \begin{bmatrix} 0.4523 & -0.2858 \end{bmatrix} 10^{-3}$$

For

$$r = 1, d = 0.83$$

Figure 16 shows the step response of the uncertain closed-loop system for ($\alpha_{opt} = 0.94$, $\gamma_{opt} = 0.95$) with a response time of $t_r = 6.32$ s and an overshoot of ±5% equal to 0.00102.

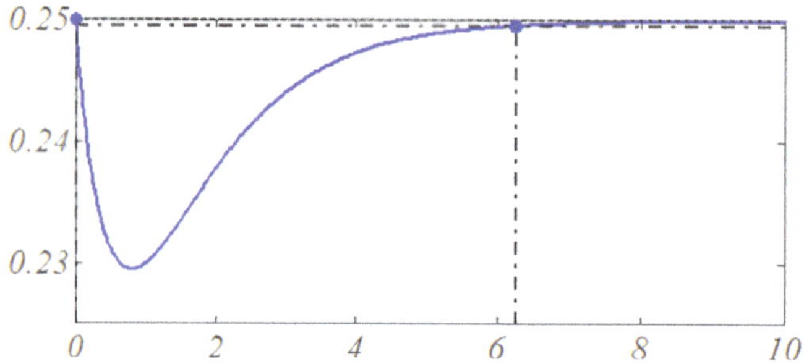

Figure 16. Step response of uncertain system in the closed loop.

Convergence of the tracking error: Based on the theoretical approach proposed in Theorem 8, it is evident from Figure 17 that the tracking error e_k converges to zero after a certain number of iterations. The tracking errors are obtained using varying tracking gains depending on the polytopes.

$$K_{2,1} = -2.4448, K_{2,2} = 0.1151, K_{2,3} = 0.1743, K_{2,4} = 0.0713$$

In this final part, an extension of the results to the case of polytopic uncertainties is considered, using polyquadratic Lyapunov functions as the theoretical foundation.

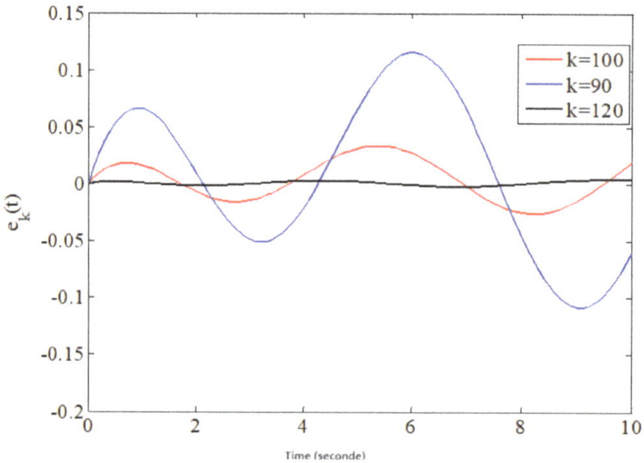

Figure 17. Tracking error after 120 iterations for $(\alpha_{opt} = 0.76, \gamma_{opt} = 0.99)$ with $0 \leq \theta_i \leq 1$.

6. Conclusions

This paper presents significant new findings regarding the ILC-tracking problem for 2D repetitive systems. Specifically, it demonstrates that the three conditions of stability along the iteration can potentially be replaced by a quadratic necessary and sufficient condition. This condition ensures the improvement of performance for repetitive systems and addresses the tracking error problem for this category of systems simultaneously. The primary contribution lies in proposing a new LMI condition that both achieves the convergence of the error to zero and ensures the desired specifications of the transient response of the repetitive system. By transforming the tracking problem with the real bounded lemma into an optimization problem using a variable-introducing control law, a degree of freedom is provided to ensure the feasibility of a stabilizing margin and guaranteeing the adjustment of the system's poles from one iteration to another using the concept of a stability disk known as "D-stability along the pass". The results demonstrate the usefulness of ILC in reducing the tracking error. Finally, the effectiveness of the proposed approach is validated through numerical examples.

Author Contributions: Conceptualization, Formal analysis, Methodology, Writing—review & editing S.B.A. and S.A. (Sultan Alzahrani); Conceptualization, Formal analysis, Methodology, Writing—review & editing, S.B.A. and S.A. (Saad Alhuwaimel); Validation, S.A. (Sultan Alzahrani); Formal analysis, S.B.A. and S.A. (Saad Alhuwaimel); Conceptualization, Investigation, Methodology, Writing—original draft, S.A. (Saad Alhuwaimel), S.S. and H.E.O.; Conceptualization, Formal analysis, Methodology, Writing—original draft, H.E.O.; Conceptualization, Investigation, Methodology, Writing—original draft, S.B.A. All authors have read and agreed to the published version of the manuscript.

Funding: This research received no external funding.

Data Availability Statement: The raw data supporting the conclusions of this article will be made available by the authors on request.

Conflicts of Interest: The authors declare no conflicts of interest. The funders had no role in the design of the study; in the collection, analyses, or interpretation of data; in the writing of the manuscript; or in the decision to publish the results.

References

1. Arimoto, S.; Kawamura, M. Bettering operations of robots by learning. *J. Robot. Syst.* **1984**, *2*, 123–140. [CrossRef]
2. Paszke, W.; Galkowski, K.; Rogers, E. Repetitive process based iterative learning control design using frequency domain analysis. In Proceedings of the IEEE Multi-Conference on Systems and Control, Dubrovnik, Croatia, 3–5 October 2012; pp. 3–6.
3. Rogers, E.; Galkowski, K.; Owens, D.H. *Control Systems Theory and Applications for Linear Repetitive Processes*; Springer Science & Business Media: Berlin/Heidelberg, Germany, 2007; pp. 96–140.
4. Hmamed, A.; Alfidi, M.; Benzaouia, A.; Tadeo, F. LMI conditions for robust stability of 2D linear discrete-time systems. *Math. Probl. Eng.* **2008**, *2008*, 356124. [CrossRef]
5. Mansouri, B.; Manamanni, N.; Guelton, K.; Kruszewski, A.; Guerra, T.M. Output feedback LMI tracking control conditions with H1 criterion for uncertain and disturbed T-S models. *Inf. Sci.* **2011**, *179*, 393–414.
6. Wu, L.; Su, X.; Shi, P. Mixed H_2/H_∞ approach to fault detection of discrete linear repetitive processes. *J. Frankl. Inst.* **2011**, *348*, 393–414. [CrossRef]
7. Paszke, W.; Bachelier, O. New Robust stability and stabilization conditions for linear repetitive processes. In Proceedings of the International Workshop on Multidimensional (nD) Systems, Thessaloniki, Greece, 29 June–1 July 2009, pp. 1–6.
8. Van De Wijdeven, J.J.M.; Donkers, M.C.F.; Bosgra, O.H. Iterative learning control for uncertain systems: Non causal finite time interval robust control design. *Int. J. Robust Nonlinear Control.* **2011**, *21*, 1645–1666. [CrossRef]
9. Paszke, W. Analysis and synthesis of multidimensional system classes using linear matrix inequality methods. In *Lecture Notes in Control and Computer Science* ; Springer: Berlin/Heidelberg, Germany, 2005; Volume 8, pp. 2298–2302.
10. Chen, Y.; Wen, C.; Sun, M. A robust high-order P-type iterative learning controller using current iteration tracking error. *Int. J. Control* **1997**, *68*, 331–342. [CrossRef]
11. Li, B.; Riaz, S.; Zhao, Y. Experimental Validation of Iterative Learning Control for DC/DC Power Converters. *Energies* **2023**, *16*, 6555. [CrossRef]
12. Jiang, Z.; Chu, B. Norm Optimal Iterative Learning Control: A Data-Driven Approach. *IFAC* **2022**, *55*, 482–487. [CrossRef]
13. Wei, Y.S.; Yang, X.; Shang, W.; Chen, Y.Y. Higher-Order Iterative Learning Control with Optimal Control Gains Based on Evolutionary Algorithm for Nonlinear System. *Complexity* **2021**, *2021*, 4281006. [CrossRef]
14. Paszke, W.; Rapisarda, P.; Rogers, E.; Steinbuch, M. Dissipative stability theory for linear repetitive processes with application in iterative learning control. In Proceedings of the Symposium on Learning Control (CDC), Shanghai, China, 16–18 December 2009; pp. 16–18.
15. Bristow, D.A.; Tharayil, M.; Alleyne, A.G. A survey of iterative learning control. *IEEE Control Syst. Mag.* **2006**, *26*, 96–114.
16. Ahn, H.S.; Chen, Y.; Moore, K.L. Iterative learning control: Brief survey and categorization. *IEEE Trans. Syst. Man Cybern. C Appl. Rev.* **2007**, *37*, 456–467. [CrossRef]
17. Hladowski, L.; Galkowski, K.; Cai, Z.; Rogers, E.; Freeman, C.T.; Lewin, P.L. Output information based iterative learning control law design with experimental verification. *ASME J. Dyn. Syst. Meas. Control* **2012**, *134*, 36–42. [CrossRef]

18. Xu, X.; Xie, H.; Shi, J. Iterative Learning Control (ILC) Guided Reinforcement Learning Control (RLC) Scheme for Batch Processes. In Proceedings of the IEEE 9th Data Driven Control and Learning Systems Conference, Liuzhou, China, 20–22 November 2020.
19. Spiegel, I.A.; Strijbosch, N.; Oomen, T.; Barton, K. Iterative learning control with discrete-time nonlinear nonminimum phase models via stable inversion. *Int. J. Robust Nonlinear Control* **2021**, *31*, 7985–8006. [CrossRef]
20. Faria, F.A.; Assunção, E.; Teixeira, M.C.M.; Cardim, R.; Da Silva, N.A.P. Robust state derivative pole placement Lmi-based designs for linear systems. *Int. J. Control* **2009**, *82*, 1–12. [CrossRef]
21. Haddad, W.M.; Bernstein, D.S. Controller design with regional pole constraints. *IEEE Trans. Automat. Control* **1992**, *37*, 54–69. [CrossRef]
22. Montagner, V.F.; Leite, V.J.S.; Oliveira, R.; Peres, P.L.D. State feedback control of switched linear systems: An LMI approach. *J. Comput. Appl. Math.* **2006**, *194*, 192–206. [CrossRef]
23. Attia, S.B.; Ouerfelli, H.E.; Salhi, S. ILC-tracking control design for repetitive continuous-time linear system using D-stability along the pass. In Proceedings of the 14th International Multi-Conference on Systems, Signals & Devices (SSD), Marrakech, Morocco, 28–31 March 2017.
24. Astolfi, D.; Marx, S.; van de Wouw, N. Repetitive control design based on forwarding for nonlinear minimum-phase systems. *Int. J. Control* **2021**, *129*, 109671. [CrossRef]
25. Li, L.; Meng, X.; Liao, Y. Preview Repetitive Control for Linear Continuous-time System. *Control Theory Appl.* **2023**, *129*, 508–518. [CrossRef]
26. Paszke, W.; Rogers, E.; Gałkowski, K. Design of robust iterative learning control schemes in a finite frequency range. In Proceedings of the International Workshop on Multidimensional (nD) Systems, Poitiers, France, 5–7 September 2011; pp. 1–6.
27. Leila, N.; Noueili, C.; Wassila, K. New Iterative Learning Control Algorithm Using Learning Gain Based on σ Inversion for Nonsquare Multi-InputMulti-Output Systems. *Model. Simul. Eng.* **2018**, *2018*, 4195938.
28. Dridi, J.; Attia, S.B.; Salhi, S. PD-ILC tracking control for discrete-time linear system. *Mediterr. J. Meas. Control* **2016**, *12*, 521–528.
29. Houssem, O.; Selma, B.A.; Salah, S. Robust monotonic Stabilizability for discrete time switched system using D type switching iterative learning control. *Mediterr. J. Meas. Control* **2016**, *12*, 598–605.

mathematics

MDPI

Article

The Impact of Digital Economy on TFP of Industries: Empirical Analysis Based on the Extension of Schumpeterian Model to Complex Economic Systems

Jiaqi Liu [1], Yiyang Cheng [2], Yamei Fu [2,3,*] and Fei Xue [2]

[1] School of Management, Xi'an University of Science and Technology, Xi'an 710054, China; vickyliu@xust.edu.cn

[2] School of Economics and Management, Northwest University, Xi'an 710127, China; chengyiyang@stumail.nwu.edu.cn (Y.C.); 20230094@nwu.edu.cn (F.X.)

[3] School of Statistics, Xi'an University of Finance and Economics, Xi'an 710100, China

* Correspondence: fuyamei@xaufe.edu.cn

Abstract: The digital economy (DE) is a new driver for enhancing total factor productivity (TFP). Using panel data from 30 provinces in China between 2011 and 2022, this study measures DE and TFP using the entropy-weighted TOPSIS method and the Global Malmquist–Luenberger method and further examines the impact of DE on the TFP of industries. The main findings are as follows: (1) DE can significantly improve TFP, though the extent of improvement varies. DE has the greatest impact on the TFP of the service industry, followed by the manufacturing industry, with the weakest effect on the agricultural industry. (2) The enhancement effect of DE on agriculture and the service industry is more pronounced in the central and western regions, while the improvement effect on manufacturing is more evident in the eastern region. (3) DE has facilitated the improvement of TFP in manufacturing industries such as textiles and special equipment manufacturing, as well as in service industries like wholesale and retail. However, it has not had a significant impact on the TFP of industries such as pharmaceutical manufacturing and real estate. This study has significant theoretical value and policy implications for China and other developing countries in exploring DE and achieving high-quality industrial development.

Keywords: digital economy; total factor productivity; agriculture industry; manufacturing industry; service industry

MSC: 91B44; 91B62

1. Introduction

In recent years, the digital economy (DE) has expanded into new dimensions of economic development on a global scale. The G20 Digital Economy Development and Cooperation Initiative highlights the significant role of DE in promoting inclusive growth and sustainable development worldwide. According to data released by the China Academy of Information and Communications Technology (Figure 1), during the period from 2005 to 2022, the value added of China's DE escalated from 2616.1 billion to 50,200 billion, representing an increase of approximately 14 times. The proportion of DE in GDP ascended from 14.2% to 41.5%, amounting to an increase of 27.3 percentage points.

High-quality industrial development is an important approach for China to establish the new "dual circulation" paradigm. Essentially, achieving high-quality industrial development implies enhancing the total factor productivity (TFP) of industries [1,2]. As the driving force of the new round of industrial transformation, DE demonstrates distinct features and patterns in infrastructure, production factors, and production and service methods compared to the eras of agricultural and industrial economies. Its economic development paradigm relies on the evolution of technological revolutions to create an economic and social network of ubiquitous connectivity, drive the explosive growth of data factors, and promote disruptive innovations in social production and lifestyle, thereby providing new impetus for improving the TFP of industries. At present, major economic entities such as the United States, Germany, and Japan all highly value the development of DE and seize the commanding heights of the new economic development era by concentrating on cutting-edge technological innovation and facilitating the digital transformation of industries. The Chinese government also considers DE as a new impetus for economic development and puts forward the proposal of realizing high-quality development of industries with the help of digital technology.

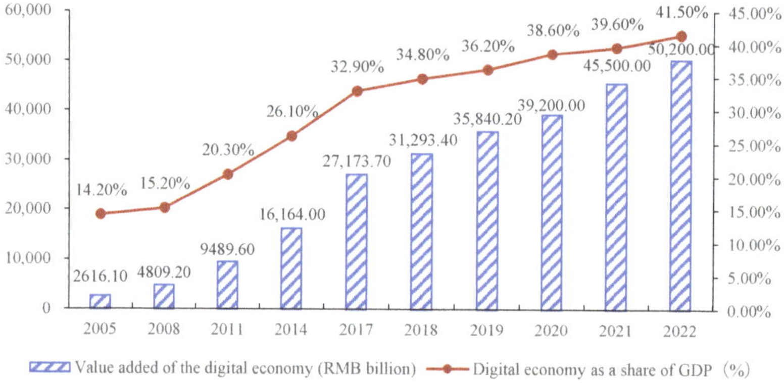

Figure 1. Value added of China's digital economy and its share of GDP, 2005–2022.

However, whether DE can indeed enhance the TFP of industries remains an unresolved research issue. In the late 1980s, the "Solow paradox" was proposed, depicting a paradoxical relationship between the vigorous expansion of investment in Information and Communication Technologies (ICT) in the United States and the low level of real productivity [3]. In the mid-1990s, the United States witnessed 118 months of high economic growth, high employment, and low inflation, co-existing with the phenomenon of the "new economy". Numerous studies have indicated that ICT was the driving force behind the emergence of the 'new economy' in the U.S. [4]. Nevertheless, some research has shown that the "Solow paradox" still exists and that the prosperity of the new economy stems from economic cycles and other factors [5]. With the extension of ICT technology to digital technology, the question of whether digital technology can enhance TFP and its mechanism of action has drawn continuous academic attention. Some scholars have discovered that DE can effectively enhance TFP [6–8]. Conversely, ref. [9], by combining the statistics of the United States, the United Kingdom, and Germany, pointed out that DE has not yet brought any improvement in the growth of TFP. Similarly, ref. [10] noted that DE has resulted in a much smaller increase in TFP than the electrification revolution.

Against this backdrop, this paper attempts to answer the following questions: Can DE break through the "productivity paradox" and promote the TFP of industries? Are there differences in the effects of DE on the TFP of agriculture, manufacturing, and service industries? Does the influence of DE on the TFP of industries exhibit regional heterogeneity and industrial heterogeneity? To address these questions, this paper first formulates a multi-sector Schumpeterian endogenous growth model to reveal the influence mechanism of DE on the TFP of industries within a complex economic system. Subsequently, it respectively computes the development level of the digital economy in Chinese provinces from 2011 to 2022, along with the TFP of agriculture, manufacturing, and service industries. Based on this, this paper establishes an econometric model, empirically examines the influence of DE on the TFP of industries, and elaborately dissects this influence from the perspectives of regional and industrial heterogeneity, providing policy support for the healthy and sustainable development of industries.

The contributions of this paper are as follows: First, considering the complexity of the economy, a multi-sector economic growth model is constructed from the perspective of efficiency-driven technological progress, providing a theoretical framework for analyzing the internal mechanism of DE's influence on the TFP of industries. Second, the provincial-industry TFP panel data for China's agriculture, manufacturing, and service industries are systematically calculated, revealing the effects, as well as regional and industrial heterogeneity, of DE on the TFP of different industries and providing empirical evidence for addressing the "Solow Paradox" of DE. Third, tools such as Python 3.11.4 and text analysis are utilized to measure the digital economy development index of each province in China by combining network and statistical data, which better reflects the overall impact of DE on the TFP of industries.

The rest of the paper is organized as follows: Section 2 provides a literature review. Section 3 establishes a theoretical model to define the relationship between DE and TFP in complex economic systems. Section 4 describes the measurement model configuration and data sources. Section 5 presents the empirical results and discussion. Section 6 summarizes the paper and offers policy recommendations and research limitations.

2. Literature Review

The empirical analysis of DE and the TFP of industries addresses three aspects: the connotation and measurement of DE, the connotation and measurement of TFP, and the influence of DE on the TFP of industries.

The concept of "digital economy" was first proposed by Don Tapscott in 1996. In the initial stage, when the concept was introduced, DE was essentially equivalent to the ICT industry [11]. With the advancement of digital technologies, the G20 Hangzhou Summit defined DE as "a series of economic activities that use digitalized knowledge and information as the key production factor, modern information networks as the important carrier, and the effective use of ICT as the crucial driving force for efficiency improvement and economic structure optimization" [12]. Based on this definition, scholars have conducted extensive discussions on statistical measurement, mainly including accessing the scale of DE [13] and measuring the development level of DE [14]. Among them, measuring the development level of DE provides a more comprehensive reflection of its connotation and is convenient for regional comparison [15].

The TFP of industries, as a crucial indicator for measuring the efficiency of industrial development, reflects the contribution of factors such as technological progress and improvements in organizational management, in addition to the input of elements like capital and labor, to the growth of output during the production process. Multiple studies have examined the measurement methods and influencing factors of the TFP of industries. Among them, the measurement methods include the Solow residual, Data Envelopment Analysis (DEA), and Stochastic Frontier Analysis (SFA) [16–18]. Among these methods, DEA, especially the Global Malmquist–Luenberger (GML) index method, can handle complex situations with multiple input and output factors and incorporate undesirable outputs, such as environmental pollution, into the analysis framework, thus reflecting the diversity and sustainability of the industrial production process more comprehensively [19]. Regarding the influencing factors, existing studies mostly focus on the effects of factors such as infrastructure investment, carbon emissions, and population aging [20–22]. In recent years, scholars have begun to pay attention to the impact of artificial intelligence (AI) and the Internet on the efficiency of different industries [23,24].

The study of the relationship between DE and the TFP of industries has a considerable history. Ever since the "Solow Paradox" was proposed, scholars have conducted extensive discussions on the impact of ICT on TFP and have formed two sharply contrasting viewpoints. One is the optimistic perspective. Some scholars have developed mathematical models from the perspective of task automation in their studies, suggesting that artificial intelligence will drive rapid growth in manufacturing productivity [25,26]. A study on TFP in different industries in Sweden found that although there was no significant correlation between ICT and TFP in the short term, there was a positive correlation after a lag of seven to eight years [27]. The other is the pessimistic perspective. Based on U.S. statistical data, ref. [28] argued that AI technology alone is insufficient to drive productivity growth. Ref. [29] proposed that excessive digitization leads to resource wastage and labor misallocation, which suppresses TFP growth.

In general, there are three aspects that require improvement in the existing studies. First, most studies rely on statistical data to reflect the development level of the DE. However, issues such as insufficient indicator coverage and poor data timeliness and availability make it difficult to objectively represent the overall impact of DE on the TFP of industries. Consequently, this paper constructs a multi-dimensional indicator system based on the connotation of DE and incorporates highly timely indicators, such as network indices, to more accurately depict the development level of China's DE, providing data support for researchers testing its impact on the TFP of industries. Second, previous research focuses on the impact of technical factors, such as ICT and AI, on the TFP of industries. However, as a new economic form, DE encompasses more than just technical characteristics. Currently, whether from a theoretical or empirical standpoint, research on the impact of DE on the TFP of industries remains relatively scarce. Therefore, this paper integrates DE and the TFP of industries into the same analytical framework for both theoretical analysis and empirical testing. Third, prior studies have analyzed the impact of DE on TFP within a single industry. Whether there are differences in the impact of DE on the TFP across different industries still needs validation. Therefore, this paper calculates the TFP of China's agriculture, manufacturing, and service industries, respectively, conducts comparisons using econometric regression, and performs extended analyses of regional and industry heterogeneity to enhance the understanding derived from existing studies.

3. Theoretical Model

To analyze the impact mechanism of DE on TFP, this paper incorporates DE into the firm's production activities based on the multi-sector Schumpeterian endogenous growth model constructed by [30]. Assume that an economy comprises three sectors: the general product sector, the industry product sector, and the research and development (R&D) sector. The role of the general products sector is to aggregate the final products produced by the n industry products sectors. The industry product sector operates under a perfect competition market. Each representative firm utilizes labor and intermediate goods as inputs for producing final products. The production of intermediate goods is carried out using optimal technological standards. Technological innovation in the economy originates from the R&D sector, which continuously generates new intermediate products for the economy through its R&D activities. This process facilitates technological progress within industries.

3.1. The Model

3.1.1. Firm Behavior in the General Product Sector

General products serve two functions: they are used for household consumption and firm investment. Assume that the production of general products is composed of final products from n sectors within the perfect competition market. The production function is specified as a Constant Elasticity of Substitution (CES) production function, which satisfies constant returns to scale, strict concavity, and the Inada conditions. The specific form is as follows:

$$Y_t = \left(\sum_{i=1}^{n} \varphi_i Y_{it}^{\frac{\varepsilon - 1}{\varepsilon}} \right)^{\frac{\varepsilon}{\varepsilon - 1}}, i = 1, 2, \cdots, n \tag{1}$$

where Y_t represents the quantity of general products, Y_{it} represents the quantity of final products from the i-th industry, and φ_i represents the importance of the i-th industry's final products in the general products. ε represents the elasticity of substitution between final product inputs across industries in production. When $0 < \varepsilon < 1$, there is complementarity between the final products of different industries, and when $\varepsilon > 1$, they are substitutable.

In a perfect competition market, producers of general products choose the optimal quantity Y_{it} of industry final products to maximize their profits, given the prices of industry final products P_{it} and the price of the general products P_t.

3.1.2. Firm Behavior in the Industry Product Sector

Assume that the economic system comprises n final product sectors, each characterized by perfect competition for both final products and factor markets, with each industry's final products produced by labor and specialized intermediate products distributed over the interval [0, 1]. The production function is specified as Equation (2):

$$Y_{it} = L_{it}^{1-\alpha} \int_0^1 A_{it}^{1-\alpha}(j) x_{it}^{\alpha}(j) dj \tag{2}$$

where L_{it} represents the labor input quantity used in producing final products of industry i, which ensures that the total labor across all industries equals the economy's endowment of labor. $x_{it}(j)$ represents the quantity of the j-th intermediate product used in the production process of final products in the industry i. $A_{it}(j)$ denotes the technological level of the j-th intermediate product in industry i; α represents the elasticity of specialized intermediate product output; $1 - \alpha$ represents the elasticity of labor output.

The production function of the industry's final products adheres to Harrod-neutral technological progress. In a perfect competitionmarket, firms producing final products in the industry i maximize profits by optimizing their inputs of intermediate product input $x_{it}(j)$ and labor input L_{it}, given predetermined prices for intermediate products $P_{it}(j)$ and wage rates W_{it}.

3.1.3. Firm Behavior in the R&D Sector

Assume that the R&D sector is composed of capitalists who produce a unique intermediate product. Their profit-driven behavior would incentivize them to enter industries with higher profitability. The production of intermediate products uses the industry's final products as inputs. Given the price P_{it} of the industry's final product, capitalists adjust the quantity and price of intermediate products to achieve profit maximization.

To sustain monopoly profits, capitalists rely on R&D activities to optimize production processes and enhance technological capabilities. Assume that the success probability of R&D activities is $\rho_{it}(j)$, and the technological level will increase from $A_{it}(j)$ to $\theta_i A_{it}(j)$, where $\theta_i > 1$. If R&D fails, the technological level of the intermediate product remains constant. Following the method proposed by [31], this paper expresses the probability of R&D success as a function of R&D input. The specific formulation is as follows:

$$\rho_{it}(j) = \lambda_i \left(\frac{R_{it}(j)}{L_{it} A_{it}^{*}(j)}\right)^{0.5} \tag{3}$$

where i represents industry, t represents time, j represents intermediate goods categories, $R_{it}(j)$ represents R&D inputs, $A_{it}^{*}(j)$ represents R&D objectives, and λ_i represents R&D efficiency.

According to the technological–economic paradigm characteristics of DE, innovation is the intrinsic force driving the development of digital economic paradigms. Digital technologies are universal and are capable of widespread application across multiple industries and domains, thereby empowering industry ecosystems and transforming enterprise business models and management practices, leading to disruptive innovation. Therefore, this paper incorporates digital technology into the innovation efficiency of the

R&D sector. Digital technologies contribute to the innovation efficiency of the R&D sector in two main aspects: First, by enhancing R&D efficiency through their pervasiveness and collaborative capabilities, thereby increasing the probability of R&D success. Second, by optimizing the combination of production factors through their use and thereby influencing the optimal innovation behavior of the R&D sector. This paper represents R&D efficiency as an increasing function of digital technology, which is denoted as digital, specifically as follows:

$$\lambda_i = \eta \times digital_{it}^{\beta} \tag{4}$$

where η represents the exogenous efficiency parameter, and β represents the efficiency parameter of digital technology.

3.2. *Optimal Behavior Derivation Process*

3.2.1. Optimal Behavior of Firms in the Industry Product Sector

The optimal behavior of firms in the industry's final product is defined as follows:

$$\max\left[P_{it}L_{it}^{1-\alpha}\int_0^1 A_{it}^{1-\alpha}(j)x_{it}^{a}(j)dj - W_{it}L_{it} - \int_0^1 P_{it}(j)x_{it}(j)dj\right] \tag{5}$$

Under conditions of perfect competition market in the labor and intermediate goods, the first-order partial derivatives of $x_{it}(j)$ in Equation (5) can be derived and set to zero yields. Then, $P_{it}(j)$ can be expressed as follows:

$$P_{it}(j) = \alpha P_{it}L_{it}^{1-\alpha}A_{it}^{1-\alpha}(j)x_{it}^{\alpha-1}(j) \tag{6}$$

Taking the first-order partial derivatives of L_{it} in Equation (5) and setting them to zero, we obtain Equation (7):

$$W_{it} = (1-\alpha)P_{it}L_{it}^{-\alpha}\int_0^1 A_{it}^{1-\alpha}(j)x_{it}^{\alpha}(j)dj \tag{7}$$

Given the demand for intermediate products, producers will determine the optimal price and quantity of intermediate products based on the principle of profit maximization. Assume that producing 1 unit of intermediate product requires consuming 1 unit of final product from the industry. The optimal behavior of intermediate product producers is represented by Equation (8):

$$\max[P_{it}(j)x_{it}(j) - P_{it}x_{it}(j)] \tag{8}$$

Combining Equations (6) and (8), the optimization behavior of intermediate product firms can be derived as follows:

$$\max\left[\alpha P_{it}A_{it}^{1-\alpha}(j)L_{it}^{1-\alpha}x_{it}^{\alpha}(j) - P_{it}x_{it}(j)\right] \tag{9}$$

By taking the first-order partial derivative of $x_{it}(j)$ in Equation (9) and setting it to zero, we obtain Equation (10):

$$x_{it}(j) = \alpha^{\frac{2}{1-\alpha}}A_{it}(j)L_{it} \tag{10}$$

According to Equations (6) and (10), $P_{it}(j)$ can be expressed as follows:

$$P_{it}(j) = \frac{P_{it}}{\alpha} \tag{11}$$

According to Equations (8), (10), and (11), a firm's profit from choosing to produce intermediate products is to be expressed as Equation (12).

$$\pi_{it}(j) = P_{it}(1-\alpha)\alpha^{\frac{1+\alpha}{1-\alpha}} A_{it}(j) L_{it} \tag{12}$$

This paper sets $\int_0^1 A_{it}(j)dj = A_{it}$ to achieve a simplified analysis. A_{it} represents the average level of technological progress in industry i. According to Equations (2) and (10), we obtain the optimal output of firms in industry i:

$$Y_{it} = \alpha^{\frac{2\alpha}{1-\alpha}} L_{it} \int_0^1 A_{it}(j)dj = \alpha^{\frac{2\alpha}{1-\alpha}} A_{it} L_{it} \tag{13}$$

Based on the preceding discussion, the success probability of intermediate product R&D activities depends solely on R&D efficiency. At equilibrium, the success probability of various types of intermediate product R&D activities in the industry is ρ_{it}. Therefore, the average level of technological progress A_{it} can be expressed as Equation (14):

$$A_{it} = \theta_i A_{i,t-1} \rho_{it} + A_{i,t-1}(1-\rho_{it}) \tag{14}$$

Based on Equation (14), the rate of technological progress growth for industry i is given by Equation (15).

$$g_{it} = \frac{A_{it} - A_{i,t-1}}{A_{i,t-1}} = \frac{\theta_i A_{i,t-1}\rho_{it} + A_{i,t-1}(1-\rho_{it}) - A_{i,t-1}}{A_{i,t-1}} = (\theta_i - 1)\rho_{it} \tag{15}$$

3.2.2. Optimal Innovation Behavior of the R&D Sector

The optimal behavior of the R&D sector is set as follows:

$$\max[\rho_{it}(j)\pi_{it}(j) - P_{it}R_{it}(j)] \tag{16}$$

From Equation (3), Equation (17) can be obtained as follows:

$$R_{it}(j) = L_{it} A_{it}^{*}(j) [\frac{\rho_{it}(j)}{\lambda_i}]^2 \tag{17}$$

From Equation (17), it can be observed that there is a positive correlation between $R_{it}(j)$ and $\rho_{it}(j)$. Therefore, the profit maximization of the R&D sector can be reformulated as the maximization of innovation probability. From Equations (12) and (17), Equation (16) can be expressed as follows:

$$max\left[\rho_{it}(j)P_{it}(1-\alpha)\alpha^{\frac{1+\alpha}{1-\alpha}} A_{it}^{*}(j) L_{it} - P_{it} L_{it} A_{it}^{*}(j) [\frac{\rho_{it}(j)}{\lambda_i}]^2\right] \tag{18}$$

Taking the first-order partial derivative of $\rho_{it}(j)$ in Equation (18) and setting it to zero yields:

$$\rho_{it}(j) = \frac{1}{2}(1-\alpha)\alpha^{\frac{1+\alpha}{1-\alpha}} \lambda_i^2 \tag{19}$$

From Equation (19), it can be seen that $\rho_{it}(j)$ depends only on α and R&D efficiency λ_i. Therefore, in industry i, the probabilities of success in innovating various types of intermediate products are equal, which means $\rho_{it}(j) = \rho_{it}$. From Equations (4) and (19), Equation (15) can be expressed as follows:

$$g_{it} = (\theta_i - 1)\frac{1}{2}(1-\alpha)\alpha^{\frac{1+\alpha}{1-\alpha}} \lambda_i^2 = \frac{1}{2}(\theta_i - 1)(1-\alpha)\alpha^{\frac{1+\alpha}{1-\alpha}} (\eta \times digital_{it}^{\beta})^2 \tag{20}$$

Equation (20) indicates that the rate of technological progress in industry i depends on parameters α, θ_i, η, β, and $digital_{it}$. It is evident that the development of DE can drive industry technological progress.

3.2.3. Optimal Behavior of the General Product Sector

According to Equation (1), the optimal behavior of the general product sector is as follows:

$$\max\left[P_t\left(\sum_{i=1}^{n}\phi_i Y_{it}^{\frac{1-\varepsilon}{\varepsilon}}\right)^{\frac{\varepsilon}{1-\varepsilon}} - \sum_{i=1}^{n}P_{it}Y_{it}\right] \tag{21}$$

Taking the first-order partial derivative of Y_{it} in Equation (21) and setting it to zero yields, we obtain the following:

$$Y_{it} = \left(\frac{P_t\phi_i}{P_{it}}\right)^{\varepsilon} Y_t \tag{22}$$

3.3. Efficiency-Enhancing Effects of the Digital Economy

Based on the optimal behavior of firms in the general product sector, the output structure between any two industries, i and k, can be represented by the following:

$$\frac{Y_{it}}{Y_{kt}} = \frac{(P_t\phi_i/P_{it})^{\varepsilon}Y_t}{(P_t\phi_k/P_{kt})^{\varepsilon}Y_t} = \left(\frac{\phi_i P_{kt}}{\phi_k P_{it}}\right)^{\varepsilon} \tag{23}$$

According to Equation (13), $\frac{Y_{it}}{Y_{kt}}$ can be expressed as follows:

$$\frac{Y_{it}}{Y_{kt}} = \frac{\alpha^{\frac{2\alpha}{1-\alpha}}A_{it}L_{it}}{\alpha^{\frac{2\alpha}{1-\alpha}}A_{kt}L_{kt}} = \frac{A_{it}L_{it}}{A_{kt}L_{kt}} \tag{24}$$

Assume that free mobility of labor across industry sectors, when the labor market reaches equilibrium, the wages in each industry sector are equal. According to Equation (7), we have the following:

$$1 = \frac{W_{it}}{W_{kt}} = \frac{(1-\alpha)P_{it}L_{it}^{-\alpha}\int_0^1 A_{it}^{1-\alpha}(j)x_{it}^{\alpha}(j)dj}{(1-\alpha)P_{kt}L_{kt}^{-\alpha}\int_0^1 A_{kt}^{1-\alpha}(j)x_{kt}^{\alpha}(j)dj} \tag{25}$$

According to Equations (10) and (25), $\frac{P_{it}}{P_{kt}}$ can be expressed as follows:

$$\frac{P_{it}}{P_{kt}} = \frac{A_{kt}}{A_{it}} \tag{26}$$

Taking the natural logarithm of Equation (26) on both sides and differentiating with respect to time, we obtain Equation (27):

$$\frac{\dot{P}_{it}}{P_{it}} - \frac{\dot{P}_{kt}}{P_{kt}} = \frac{\dot{A}_{kt}}{A_{kt}} - \frac{\dot{A}_{it}}{A_{it}} = g_{kt} - g_{it} \tag{27}$$

Equation (27) indicates that the relative price changes between industry sectors depend on the rates of technological progress across those sectors. Sectors experiencing faster technological progress have lower rates of product price change compared to sectors with slower technological progress.

According to Equations (23), (24), and (26), $\frac{L_{it}}{L_{kt}}$ can be expressed as follows:

$$\frac{L_{it}}{L_{kt}} = \left(\frac{\phi_i}{\phi_k}\right)^{\varepsilon}\left(\frac{A_{it}}{A_{kt}}\right)^{\varepsilon-1} \tag{28}$$

Taking the natural logarithm of Equation (28) on both sides and differentiating with respect to time, and further substituting Equation (27), we obtain the following:

$$\frac{\dot{L}_{it}}{L_{it}} - \frac{\dot{L}_{kt}}{L_{kt}} = (\varepsilon - 1)(\frac{\dot{A}_{it}}{A_{it}} - \frac{\dot{A}_{kt}}{A_{kt}}) = (\varepsilon - 1)(g_{it} - g_{kt}) \tag{29}$$

where ε represents the elasticity of substitution in general product manufacturing. When $0 < \varepsilon < 1$, labor will move from sectors with higher rates of technological advancement to those with lower rates. When $\varepsilon - 1 < 0$, labor will move from sectors with lower rates of technological advancement to those with higher rates. According to Equations (1) and (13), Y_t can be expressed as follows:

$$Y_t = \left[\sum_{i=1}^{n} \phi_i (\alpha^{\frac{2\alpha}{1-\alpha}} A_{it} L_{it})^{\frac{\varepsilon-1}{\varepsilon}} \right]^{\frac{\varepsilon}{\varepsilon-1}} \tag{30}$$

Let $L_t = \sum_{i=1}^{n} L_{it}$, where L_t represents the aggregate labor force across industries. According to Equation (28), L_{it} can be expressed as follows:

$$L_{it} = \frac{A_{it}^{\varepsilon-1} \phi_i^{\varepsilon}}{\sum_{i=1}^{n} A_{it}^{\varepsilon-1} \phi_i^{\varepsilon}} L_t \tag{31}$$

Let $d_{it} = \frac{L_{it}}{L_t}$, where d_{it} represents the share of labor force occupied by industry i, and then we obtain Equation (32):

$$d_{it} = \frac{L_{it}}{L_t} = \frac{A_{it}^{\varepsilon-1} \phi_i^{\varepsilon}}{\sum_{i=1}^{n} A_{it}^{\varepsilon-1} \phi_i^{\varepsilon}} \tag{32}$$

Equation (30) can be rewritten as follows:

$$Y_t = \left(\sum_{i=1}^{n} \phi_i^{\varepsilon} A_{it}^{\varepsilon-1} \right)^{\frac{1}{\varepsilon-1}} \alpha^{\frac{2\alpha}{1-\alpha}} L_t \tag{33}$$

For simplifying, let $A_t = \left(\sum_{i=1}^{n} \phi_i^{\varepsilon} A_{it}^{\varepsilon-1} \right)^{\frac{1}{\varepsilon-1}}$, where A_t represents the technological level of the general product sector. Then, per capita output can be expressed as Equation (34).

$$y_t = \frac{Y_t}{L_t} = \alpha^{\frac{2\alpha}{1-\alpha}} A_t \tag{34}$$

Taking the natural logarithm of $A_t = \left(\sum_{i=1}^{n} \phi_i^{\varepsilon} A_{it}^{\varepsilon-1} \right)^{\frac{1}{\varepsilon-1}}$ on both sides and differentiating with respect to time gives the following equation:

$$\frac{\dot{A}_t}{A_t} = \frac{\sum_{i=1}^{n} \phi_i^{\varepsilon} A_{it}^{\varepsilon-1} \frac{\dot{A}_{it}}{A_{it}}}{\sum_{i=1}^{n} \phi_i^{\varepsilon} A_{it}^{\varepsilon-1}} \tag{35}$$

Based on $\frac{\dot{A}_{it}}{A_{it}} = g_{it}$, Equation (35) can be transformed into Equation (36).

$$\frac{\dot{A}_t}{A_t} = \frac{\sum_{i=1}^{n} \phi_i^{\varepsilon} A_{it}^{\varepsilon-1} g_{it}}{\sum_{i=1}^{n} \phi_i^{\varepsilon} A_{it}^{\varepsilon-1}} = \sum_{i=1}^{n} d_{it} g_{it} = \frac{1}{2} \sum_{i=1}^{n} d_{it} (\theta_i - 1)(1-\alpha) \alpha^{\frac{1+\alpha}{1-\alpha}} \left(\eta \times digital_{it}^{\beta}\right)^2 \tag{36}$$

From Equation (36), it is evident that with the escalation of the digital economic development level, the rate of technological progress ascends concurrently. Generally speaking, the growth of technological progress is manifested as an augmentation in TFP. Consequently, the advancement of DE can propel the growth of TFP.

4. Materials and Methods

4.1. The Measurement of Digital Economy Development Index (DEDI)

The objective of this paper is to investigate the influence of DE on TFP. Hence, it is necessary to scientifically assess the development level of DE to uphold the reliability and accuracy of the empirical results. Scholars typically use statistical data to measure DEDI from the aspects of basic conditions, external environment, and integrated application of DE development. While this approach provides some reference value, it still faces issues such as inadequate coverage of DE indicators and limited timeliness and availability of data. This paper argues that DE signifies a novel economic form, with its main features displayed in three aspects: connectivity, data, and integration. Digital technology and infrastructure are fundamental in establishing interconnected networks. Data monetization underscores the economic value of data as a key component. Additionally, industrial digitalization and digital industrialization reflect the innovative application of digital technology in the real economy.

Based on existing research indicators, this paper develops a comprehensive DE measurement index system comprising five core indicators: digital technology, digital infrastructure, data monetization, digital industrialization, and industrial digitization, along with 21 underlying indicators, as illustrated in Table 1. In particular, network data such as the Baidu Index and the frequency of data-related words in government work reports are acquired using Python 3.11.4.

This paper evaluates China's DEDI using the entropy-weighted TOPSIS method. In contrast to the basic average method, the entropy-weighted TOPSIS method not only eliminates subjective biases, resulting in more objective and reliable weight calculations but also effectively demonstrates the significance of fundamental indicators in influencing DE metrics across various dimensions. The specific construction and measurement steps of DEDI are as follows:

1. Standardization Processing. To eliminate differences in dimensions and magnitudes among the various indicators, the range method is adopted to standardize each basic indicator in the measurement system. All the basic indicators selected in this paper are positive indicators, and the standardization formula is as follows:

$$Y_{ij} = \frac{X_{ij} - \min(X_{ij})}{\max X_{ij} - \min(X_{ij})} \tag{37}$$

where X_{ij} and Y_{ij} represent the original and standardized basic indicators for measuring DEDI, respectively.

2. Calculate the Information Entropy. Calculate the information entropy E_j of each basic indicator Y_{ij}.

$$E_j = \ln \frac{1}{n} \sum_{i=1}^{n} \left[\left(Y_{ij} / \sum_{i=1}^{n} Y_{ij} \right) \ln \left(Y_{ij} / \sum_{i=1}^{n} Y_{ij} \right) \right] \tag{38}$$

3. Calculate the Weights. Calculate the weights W_j of each basic indicator Y_{ij}.

$$W_j = (1 - E_j) / \sum_{j=1}^{m} (1 - E_j) \tag{39}$$

4. Construct the Weighted Matrix. Construct the weighted matrix R of the measurement indicators for the development level of the digital economy.

$$R = (r_{ij})_{n \times m} \tag{40}$$

where $r_{ij} = W_j \times Y_{ij}$.

5. Calculate the Euclidean Distance. Calculate the Euclidean distances d_i^+ and d_i^- between each measurement scheme and the optimal scheme Q_j^+ and the worst scheme Q_j^-:

$$\begin{aligned} d_i^+ &= \sqrt{\sum_{j=1}^{m} \left(Q_j^+ - r_{ij}\right)^2} \\ d_i^- &= \sqrt{\sum_{j=1}^{m} \left(Q_j^- - r_{ij}\right)^2} \end{aligned} \tag{41}$$

6. Calculate $DEDI_i$:

$$DEDI_i = \frac{d_i^-}{d_i^+ + d_i^-} \tag{42}$$

where the value of $DEDI_i$ ranges between 0 and 1.

Table 1. Evaluation index system of digital economy.

Primary Indicators	Secondary Indicators	Tertiary Indicators
Digital Economy	Digital Technology	Number of artificial intelligence patents (units) Number of industrial robot patents (units) Baidu index of digital technology
	Digital Infrastructure	Number of Internet broadband access ports (ten thousands) Number of web pages (ten thousands) Number of digital television users (ten thousands) Number of websites owned by every hundred enterprises (units) Fixed investment amount in the electronic information industry (billion CNY)
	Data Monetization	Number of data exchanges/data trading platforms (units) Number of enterprises ranking top 10 globally in cloud computing enterprises (units) The frequency of data-related words in government work reports
	Digital Industrialization	Output of mobile phones, integrated circuits, and microcomputer devices (ten thousands) Main business income of the manufacturing industry of communication equipment, computers, and other electronic equipment (billion CNY) Total volume of telecommunications services (billion CNY) Employees in the information transmission, software, and information technology service industry (ten thousand people) Software business revenue (billion CNY)
	Industrial Digitization	Number of rural broadband access users (ten thousand households) The proportion of villages with the Internet broadband service opened (%) Integration Development Index of Informatization and Industrialization Digital Finance Index E-commerce transaction volume (billion CNY)

4.2. The Measurement of Total Factor Productivity (TFP)

Referring to [32], this paper utilizes the GML index method to measure the TFP of agriculture (TFP_agri), the TFP of manufacturing (TFP_manu), and the TFP of services (TFP_serv) across 30 provinces in China. The calculation processes are shown in Appendix A. The input, desirable output, and undesirable output indicators used for calculating different industries are as follows:

1. Total Factor Productivity of Agriculture (TFP_agri). Input indicators include ① labor, quantified by the number of people employed in agriculture; ② land, measured by the sown area of crops; ③ machinery, measured by the total power of agricultural machinery; ④ fertilizer, measured by the amount of agricultural fertilizer applied; ⑤ pesticide, measured by the amount of pesticide utilized. Output indicators include ① desirable outputs, measured by agricultural value added and adjusted for inflation using 2011 constant prices; ② undesirable outputs, measured by the total amount of agricultural carbon emissions.
2. Total Factor Productivity of Manufacturing (TFP_manu). Input indicators include ① capital, measured by the capital stock; ② labor, represented by the average number of employees in manufacturing. Output indicators include ① desirable outputs, measured by the gross output value of manufacturing and its sub-sectors, adjusted using the producer price index of industrial products; ② undesirable outputs, measured by the weighted average of emissions from waste gas, wastewater, and solid waste.
3. Total Factor Productivity of Service (TFP_serv). Input indicators include ① labor, measured by the number of employed personnel at the end of the year in the service industry and its sub-sectors; ② capital, measured by the capital stock of the service industry. Output indicators include ① desirable output, measured by the value added of the service industry and its various sub-sectors; ② undesirable output, measured by pollution emissions.

4.3. The Estimation Model

In order to accurately identify the impact of DE on the TFP of industries, referring to [33], this paper constructs a panel regression model for analysis. The specific model setting is as follows:

$$TFP_{i,t} = \alpha_0 + \alpha_1 DEDI_{i,t} + \alpha_c CV_{i,t} + \mu_i + \delta_t + \varepsilon_{i,t} \tag{43}$$

where $TFP_{i,t}$ is the dependent variable, representing the TFP of industries in the i-th province and the t-th year. $DEDI_{i,t}$ is the independent variable, denoting the development level of DE. μ_i represents individual fixed effects, δ_t represents time fixed effects, and $\varepsilon_{i,t}$ represents random error terms that are independently and identically distributed.

This paper focuses on coefficient α_1 of the DEDI to determine whether it is significantly positive for testing the relationship between TFP and DE. To alleviate the estimation bias caused by omitted variables, this paper controls for other factors that may have an impact on the TFP of industries. These factors include the following: Per Capita Gross Domestic Product (Pgdp): The improvement in the level of economic development not only provides conditions for technological progress but also increases the demand for technological innovation, thereby promoting the enhancement of the TFP of industries. In this paper, the logarithm of Pgdp is selected to represent it. Fiscal Autonomy (FA): The influencing factors of the TFP of industries also comprise institutional factors. In regions with higher fiscal autonomy, the government has greater flexibility in adjusting fiscal expenditures, which benefits the flow of resources toward technological progress. In this paper, the ratio of general budgetary fiscal revenue to general budgetary fiscal expenditure is utilized to represent it. Foreign direct investment (FDI): Opening up to the outside world can drive the improvement of the TFP of industries by promoting employment growth in the industry, deepening material capital accumulation, and introducing advanced production technologies and management experiences. In this paper, the proportion of foreign direct investment in GDP is employed to measure it, and deflation and price conversion processing have been implemented.

4.4. Data Sources

The datasets utilized in this study are available from the China Statistical Yearbook, the China Fixed Assets Investment Statistical Yearbook, the China Rural Areas Statistical Yearbook, the China Industry Statistical Yearbook, the China Environment Statistical Yearbook, the DRCNET Database, and the Wind Database. The word frequency of the Baidu Index and government work reports is captured using Python 3.11.4. Missing data are imputed using the average growth rate. The study encompasses data from 30 provinces in China (excluding Hong Kong, Macao, Taiwan, and Tibet). The panel period is from 2011 to 2022, and 360 samples are obtained.

5. Results

5.1. The Baseline Regression Analysis

The specific regression results are presented in Table 2. The regression results of Models (1) to (6) demonstrate that, regardless of the inclusion of control variables, DE exerts a markedly positive influence on the TFP of agriculture, manufacturing, and service industries. Furthermore, by comparing Models (2), (4), and (6), it is evident that there are differences in the enhancing effect of DE on the TFP of different industries. The coefficients for TFP_agri, TFP_manu, and TFP_serv are 0.602, 0.942, and 1.865, respectively, all of which are significantly positive, at least at the 5% level. Evidently, DE is currently focusing its efforts primarily on the service industry. It has transcended the constraints of time and space, limited information, and precise dissemination. It is likely to disrupt the pattern that "the era of the service industry is an era of low growth." In traditional service industries, production and consumption must occur simultaneously in the same location and cannot be stored or transported. Nevertheless, DE has subverted these inherent features. Service commodities, such as artistic performances, education, and healthcare, can now be exchanged across time and space in the form of data via digital platforms, facilitating the trade of services and demands that were previously difficult to address. The advancement of digital technologies has also led to the emergence of business models like e-commerce and live streaming for selling goods. Economies of scale, economies of scope, and the long-tail effect in the service industry have progressively emerged and become prominent.

Table 2. The results of baseline regression.

	TFP_Agri		TFP_Manu		TFP_Serv	
	(1)	(2)	(3)	(4)	(5)	(6)
DEDI	0.612 **	0.602 **	1.865 ***	0.942 **	4.753 ***	1.865 ***
	(0.304)	(0.289)	(0.549)	(0.410)	(1.188)	(0.491)
Ln pGDP		0.174 *		0.189 **		0.258 **
		(0.095)		(0.090)		(0.104)
FD		−0.212 *		−0.245 *		−0.220 **
		(0.125)		*(0.124)		(0.094)
Finance		0.174 *		0.010		0.241 **
		(0.099)		(0.008)		(0.121)
FDI		−0.078 *		0.367 ***		0.246 **
		(0.046)		(0.073)		(0.103)
Constant	0.929 ***	0.839 ***	0.599 ***	0.245 **	−0.342 ***	−0.243
	(0.111)	(0.137)	(0.145)	(0.103)	(0.090)	(0.203)
Individual FE	Yes	Yes	Yes	Yes	Yes	Yes
Time FE	Yes	Yes	Yes	Yes	Yes	Yes
N	360	360	360	360	360	360
R^2	0.736	0.835	0.843	0.746	0.805	0.824

Note: ***/**/* indicate statistical significance at 1%, 5%, and 10% levels. Robust standard errors are reported in parentheses.

In conclusion, DE is capable of promoting the TFP of agriculture, manufacturing, and service industries in China, with variations in the enhancement effects across different industries. Specifically, the digital economy exerts the most substantial positive influence on the TFP of the service industry, followed by the manufacturing industry, while having the least impact on agriculture. This indicates that the effect of the digital economy on the TFP of the manufacturing and agricultural industries requires further enhancement. In the future, it is indispensable to accelerate the in-depth integration of DE with the manufacturing industry and facilitate the transformation from "Made in China" to "Intelligently Made in China". Additionally, it is of crucial significance to enhance the application of digital technologies in agriculture to achieve high-quality, efficient, and sustainable development in this sector.

5.2. The Endogenous Analysis

The baseline regression indicates a significant positive correlation between the development of DE and the enhancement of TFP in industries. Nevertheless, the baseline analysis merely utilized OLS regression. If there are latent endogenous issues in the model, the baseline estimation results might be inaccurate.

There are two main sources of potential endogeneity in this study. First, despite including control variables and accounting for both time-variant and invariant unobservable factors, some factors may still be difficult to capture, such as regional institutional differences and dynamic variations in industrial scale. Second, there is a two-way causality between DE and TFP. The technological level is a crucial driver of DE's development, and the TFP level, to some extent, reflects the strength of technological advancement. Therefore, the level of TFP may also influence the development of DE. To address this issue, this paper constructs a panel instrumental variable for DEDI (IV_DEDI) by multiplying the cross-sectional data of the number of fixed-line telephone subscribers at the end of 1998 in each province by the first-order lag of the Internet penetration rate [34].

As shown in Table 3, the Kleibergen–Paap rk LM statistic is significant at the 1% level, indicating that there are no issues with unidentifiable instrumental variables in the model. The Kleibergen–Paap rk Wald F statistic is also much larger than the critical value of 16.38 for the Stock–Yogo weak identification test at the 10% level, suggesting that the problem of weak instrumental variables can be excluded and that the selected instrumental variables are valid. The regression results from the first stage show a positive correlation between IV_DEDI and DEDI for agriculture, manufacturing, and service industries, at least at the 5% significance level. The second-stage regression results are 0.465, 0.646, and 1.746, respectively, and are significant at least at the 5% level. This implies that the positive effect of the digital economy on TFP across different industries remains robust even after accounting for endogeneity.

Table 3. The results of instrumental variable regression.

	TFP_Agri		TFP_Manu		TFP_Serv	
	First Stage	Second Stage	First Stage	Second Stage	First Stage	Second Stage
IV_DEDI	0.015 *** (0.004)		0.083 ** (0.038)		0.057 *** (0.011)	
DEDI		0.465 ** (0.194)		0.646 *** (0.092)		1.743 ** (0.814)
Controls	Yes	Yes	Yes	Yes	Yes	Yes
Individual FE	Yes	Yes	Yes	Yes	Yes	Yes
Time FE	Yes	Yes	Yes	Yes	Yes	Yes
N	360	360	360	360	360	360
R^2		0.952		0.913		0.945
F	77.53	2.67	74.24	18.35	76.35	44.82
Kleibergen–Paap rk LM	53.170 (0.0000)					
Cragg–Donald Wald F	1378.940					
Kleibergen–Paap rk Wald F	244.380					

Note: ***/** indicate statistical significance at 1%, 5% levels. Robust standard errors are reported in parentheses. p-values are reported in parentheses for Kleibergen–Paap rk LM.

5.3. The Robustness Test

To ensure the robustness of regression results, the following tests are conducted in this paper, as shown in Table 4:

1. Change the Empirical Model. In view of the temporal accumulation of TFP, the first-order lag term of the TFP, $TFP_{i,t-1}$ is added to Equation (37), and the first and second-order lag terms of DEDI are chosen as instrumental variables for the Generalized Method of Moments (GMM) estimation. Across different models, the results consistently show that the impact of DE on TFP remains positive;
2. Change the Independent Variable. In order to avoid the estimation bias caused by the estimation method, the vertical and horizontal scatter degree method is used to recalculate DEDI for robustness analysis, whose results robustly support the above conclusions;
3. Add the Control Variables. Additional control variables are incorporated, including levels of technological innovation, marketization, and infrastructure. The level of technological innovation typically contributes to the TFP of industries. A high degree of marketization confers a greater degree of innovation in industries, thereby facilitating the enhancement of the TFP. The upgrading of infrastructure levels, such as those of railways and highways, also expedites the flow of production factors and boosts industrial efficiency. The results reveal that the impact of DE on the TFP of industries is consistent with the baseline regression.

Table 4. The results of robustness test.

	TFP_Agri			TFP_Manu			TFP_Serv		
	Change the Independent Variable	**Change the Independent Variable**	**Add the Control Variables**	**Change the Independent Variable**	**Change the Independent Variable**	**Add the Control Variables**	**Change the Independent Variable**	**Change the Independent Variable**	**Add the Control Variables**
DEDI	0.465 ** (0.194)	0.576 *** (0.064)	0.432 *** (0.096)	0.886 ** (0.372)	0.986 * (0.557)	0.821 ** (0.345)	1.167 ** (0.558)	1.485 *** (0.160)	1.094 *** (0.168)
L.TFP_agri	1.197 *** (0.203)								
L.TFP_manu				0.985 *** (0.095)					
L.TFP_serv							0.814 *** (0.158)		
Controls	Yes	Yes	Yes	Yes	Yes	Yes	Yes	Yes	Yes
Individual FE	Yes	Yes	Yes	Yes	Yes	Yes	Yes	Yes	Yes
Time FE	Yes	Yes	Yes	Yes	Yes	Yes	Yes	Yes	Yes
AR(1)	0.017			0.026			0.015		
AR(2)	0.793			0.868			0.754		
Sargan	0.989			0.993			0.996		

Note: ***/**/* indicate statistical significance at 1%, 5%, and 10% levels. Robust standard errors are reported in parentheses. The *p*-values are in parentheses for AR(1), AR(2), and Sargan.

5.4. The Region Heterogeneity Analysis

Given the distinct spatial variance in the regional distribution of DEDI, this paper categorizes the samples into the eastern region, as well as central and western regions, for heterogeneity tests. Prior to conducting the sub-sample tests, this paper executed the between-group difference test. The outcomes demonstrated that the *p*-values of the SUR test all passed the significance test, suggesting that significant differences existed between the groups.

As shown in Table 5, DE exerts a significant facilitating effect on TFP_agri in the central and western regions, whereas its impact on TFP_agri in the eastern region is not notable. The possible reasons are as follows. The eastern region, driven by industrial construction and radiated by urban expansion, has manifested the feature of concentrated interests. The digital infrastructure in eastern cities is more advanced, and the level of human capital is higher as well. Thus, the marginal utility that the digital economy brings to industrial efficiency is relatively low. Under the traditional economic model, it has been difficult for agricultural development in the central and western regions to benefit from land value appreciation resulting from industrial agglomeration and infrastructure investment. Nevertheless, the strong diffusibility and high innovativeness of the digital economy have effectively broken the resource barriers between the eastern and the central and western regions and can optimize the allocation of resources such as capital and labor effectively. Especially, the implementation of the "E-commerce Assisting Farmers" program has offered a new channel for the sales of agricultural products in the central and western regions. Therefore, the digital economy is more conducive to promoting the enhancement of agricultural TFP in the central and western regions.

Table 5. The results of region heterogeneity analysis.

	TFP_Agri		TFP_Manu		TFP_Serv	
	East Region	Central and Western Region	East Region	Central and Western Region	East Region	Central and Western Region
DEDI	0.456	0.734 *	1.467 ***	0.835 ***	1.073 **	1.753 **
	(0.326)	(0.399)	(0.511)	(0.317)	(0.481)	(0.737)
Constant	0.942 **	0.991 *	−3.368 ***	−0.839	0.086	0.386 ***
	(0.410)	(0.583)	(0.812)	(0.742)	(0.261)	(0.102)
N	132	228	132	228	132	228
R^2	0.943	0.843	0.633	0.574	0.885	0.825
Chi^2	5.65 ***		6.35 **		5.38 ***	
p-value	0.005		0.014		0.001	

Note: ***/**/* indicate statistical significance at 1%, 5%, and 10% levels. Robust standard errors are reported in parentheses.

In the manufacturing sector, DE's promoting effect on TFP_manu is more pronounced in the eastern region than in the central and western regions. The possible reasons are as follows: From the perspective of the foundation of economic development and resource endowment, the eastern region has a first-mover advantage in the manufacturing sector. Its industrial structure is relatively mature and diversified, having accumulated substantial physical capital and human capital in the early stages. This creates favorable conditions for the in-depth integration of the digital economy and manufacturing, enabling it to employ digital technologies more effectively to enhance production efficiency. From the perspective of technological innovation, the eastern region possesses dense research institutions, high-level universities, and innovative enterprise clusters, which can generate numerous technological innovation achievements and promptly apply them to manufacturing. This robust innovation ecosystem promotes the research, development, and promotion of digital technologies, further boosting the TFP of manufacturing in the eastern region. In contrast, the dominant industries in the central and western regions remain predominantly traditional manufacturing, and the integration of digital technologies in the manufacturing field is relatively lagging. Nevertheless, with the continuous reinforcement and improvement of the central and western regions in infrastructure construction, talent cultivation, policy support, and other aspects, the digital economy is anticipated to play a more significant role in the development of manufacturing in the central and western regions in the future.

Regarding the service industry, the impact of DE on TFP_serv in the central and western regions is greater than that in the eastern region. The possible reasons are as follows: Firstly, from the perspective of the spatial layout of industrial development, DE has optimized the industrial spatial organization pattern, giving rise to a virtual agglomeration mode that integrates online and offline services. Under this virtual agglomeration mode, the development, production, and sales of services can be accomplished via virtual platforms. For example, Taobao has enabled the virtual agglomeration of the wholesale and retail industry; Ctrip and Meituan have facilitated the virtual agglomeration of the accommodation and catering industry; DiDi has brought about the virtual agglomeration of the transportation industry; and the MOOC has realized the virtual agglomeration of the education industry. The service industries in the central and western regions have benefited from the "spatial spillover" dividend of this virtual agglomeration, leading to a more substantial improvement in productivity. In addition, in terms of cost and market access, service enterprises in the central and western regions, aided by the virtual agglomeration mode of the digital economy, can build online service platforms at a lower cost, break through geographical restrictions, rapidly expand their market scope, and lower market access thresholds. In contrast, due to the relatively complete offline service system in the eastern region, the transformation costs and resistance are relatively large.

5.5. The Manufacturing Industry Heterogeneity Analysis

The baseline regression results have considered the overall influence of DE on the TFP of industries. Whether there are disparities in the impact of DE on each subdivided industry awaits further validation. Based on data availability, the effect of DE on 21 subdivided manufacturing industries was examined and categorized into three types: low-skill manufacturing, medium-skill manufacturing, and high-skill manufacturing, based on the average education level of the employed personnel.

As shown in Table 6, it is evident that within the low-skill manufacturing industries, DE exerts a notably positive influence on the TFP of the agricultural and sideline food processing industry, food manufacturing, textile industry, textile and apparel industry, paper and paper products industry, and non-metallic mineral products industry. These industries are predominantly labor-intensive. The progressive attenuation of the demographic dividend and the escalating labor costs, among other factors, have compelled manufacturers to increase the utilization of intelligent equipment. It is precisely due to the initiative of "Replacing Humans with Machines" that the TFP of these industries has been elevated.

In the medium-skill manufacturing industries, with the exception of chemical raw materials and chemical manufacturing, DE has a remarkable enhancing impact on the TFP of other manufacturing industries. These industries are typically capital-intensive and possess the financial strength to support the transformation toward automation, digitalization, and intelligence. Nevertheless, the chemical raw materials and chemical products manufacturing industry lacks the necessary incentive mechanisms and management models for digital transformation and is more inclined to focus on the research and development of new materials. Consequently, it has dispersed its investments in digital development, resulting in an insignificant improvement in efficiency due to DE.

In high-skill manufacturing industries, DE has significantly elevated the TFP of general equipment manufacturing, special equipment manufacturing, and transportation equipment manufacturing industries. These industries are capital-intensive and have undergone a relatively high degree of digital transformation within enterprises. Nevertheless, DE has not exerted a significant impact on pharmaceutical manufacturing, as well as computer, communications, and other electronic equipment manufacturing. The potential reasons could be as follows: these industries are technology-intensive and demand a large number of highly skilled labor. However, at present, the application of DE in China's manufacturing sector remains at the simplistic stage of "Replacing Humans with Machines", lacking mastery of core digital technologies.

In conclusion, the impact of DE on the TFP of different industries in the manufacturing sector is heterogeneous. DE can significantly enhance the TFP of industries such as food manufacturing, rubber and plastic products industry, and special equipment manufacturing. However, it has no significant effect on the TFP of industries such as wine, beverage, and refined tea manufacturing. The possible reason is that these industries have high profit margins, and their production technologies are usually passed down through traditional craftsmanship, lacking the motivation for intelligent transformation. Furthermore, the digital economy can suppress the TFP of the tobacco industry, which may be due to the management model and distribution mechanism of state-owned enterprises in China.

Therefore, differentiated digital economy development strategies should be formulated for different industries.

Table 6. The results of manufacturing industry heterogeneity analysis.

	Low-Skill Manufacturing Industry						
	Agricultural and Sideline Food Processing Industry	Food Manufacturing	Wine, Beverage, and Refined Tea Manufacturing	Textile Industry	Textile and Apparel Industry	Paper and Paper Products Industry	Non-metallic Mineral Products Industry
DEDI	0.765 *	0.746 **	0.142	1.375 **	1.243 ***	0.943 **	0.915 ***
	(0.447)	(0.336)	(0.129)	(0.598)	(0.249)	(0.393)	(0.083)
R^2	0.835	0.924	0.975	0.825	0.856	0.867	0.817
	Medium-skill Manufacturing Industry						
	Chemical raw materials and chemical manufacturing	Chemical Fiber Manufacturing	Rubber and plastic products industry	Ferrous Metal Smelting and Rolling Processing Industry	Non-ferrous Metal Smelting and Rolling Processing Industry	Metal Products Industry	Electrical Machinery and Equipment Manufacturing
DEDI	0.675	0.745 **	0.798 *	0.636 ***	0.717 **	0.623 *	0.613 ***
	(0.681)	(0.339)	(0.424)	(0.091)	(0.306)	(0.565)	(0.102)
R^2	0.884	0.726	0.758	0.683	0.902	0.868	0.826
	High-skill manufacturing industry						
	Tobacco Industry	Oil, Coal, and Other Fuel Processing Industries	Pharmaceutical Manufacturing	General Equipment Manufacturing	Special Equipment Manufacturing	Transportation Equipment Manufacturing Industry	Computer, Communications, and Other Electronic Equipment Manufacturing
DEDI	−0.445 **	−0.356	0.754	0.785 *	0.926 **	0.757 ***	0.835
	(0.223)	(0.297)	(0.580)	(0.444)	(0.389)	(0.076)	(0.596)
R^2	0.913	0.698	0.801	0.984	0.635	0.703	0.755
Constant	Yes	Yes	Yes	Yes	Yes	Yes	Yes
Controls	Yes	Yes	Yes	Yes	Yes	Yes	Yes
Individual FE	Yes	Yes	Yes	Yes	Yes	Yes	Yes
N	360	360	360	360	360	360	360

Note: ***/**/* indicate statistical significance at 1%, 5%, and 10% levels. Robust standard errors are reported in parentheses.

5.6. The Service Industry Heterogeneity Analysis

To investigate the heterogeneity of DE's impact on the service industry, this paper examines its influence of DE on five subdivided service industries, as shown in Table 7.

DE exerts a significantly positive influence on the TFP of service industries, with the exception of the real estate industry. In the aspect of the wholesale and retail industry, the connectivity of DE has heightened the precision and efficacy of supply–demand matching, giving rise to business models such as business-to-customer and manufacturers to consumer. In the domain of transportation, warehousing, and postal services, the innovation of DE business models has generated considerable logistics demands. Furthermore, digital technologies have empowered processes like logistics transportation and goods distribution, effectively connecting and optimizing the reorganization of scattered transportation resources in the market and facilitating the standardization, large-scale operation, and intensification of logistics. In the financial industry, digital technologies enhance traditional banking, investment, and insurance, facilitating the optimization of business processes, user credit ratings, and investment risk assessments and consequently improving the efficiency of financial transactions.

Table 7. The results of service industry heterogeneity analysis.

	Wholesale and Retail Industry	Transportation, Warehousing, and Postal Services	Accommodation and Catering Industry	Financial Industry	Real Estate Industry
DEDI	1.356 ** (0.565)	1.325 *** (0.189)	0.104 ** (0.043)	1.007 *** (0.168)	0.843 (0.766)
Constant	Yes	Yes	Yes	Yes	Yes
Control variable	Yes	Yes	Yes	Yes	Yes
Individual FE	Yes	Yes	Yes	Yes	Yes
N	360	360	360	360	360
R^2	0.3753	0.3435	0.3213	0.3865	0.3654

Note: ***/** indicate statistical significance at 1%, 5%levels. Robust standard errors are reported in parentheses.

In summary, the impact of DE on the TFP of different industries within the service sector also exhibits heterogeneity. At present, DE has a significantly positive effect on TFP in most industries, such as the wholesale and retail industries. However, it does not have a noticeable enhancing effect on the TFP of the real estate industry. The possible reasons are as follows: Currently, the real estate industry has a relatively low reliance on data elements, and the application of digital technologies in real estate development, construction, operation, and decoration is relatively weak. Although consumers can obtain property information through real estate trading platforms, actual transaction activities are significantly influenced by regional factors and market policies.

6. Conclusions

6.1. Conclusions and Policy Recommendations

In recent years, research on DE and TFP has witnessed a substantial increase. Nevertheless, empirical analysis at the industrial level remains relatively scarce in China. This paper utilizes panel data from 30 provinces in China, spanning from 2011 to 2022, to establish an econometric model examining the influence of DE on the total factor productivity of industries. In general, this paper provides empirical evidence at the industrial level for addressing the "Solow Paradox" and offers policy recommendations for the development of the digital economy in China. The main conclusions are as follows:

Firstly, DE can effectively promote the TFP of industries. The order of the enhancement effects in various industries is as follows: TFP of the service industry, TFP of the manufacturing industry, and TFP of agriculture. This conclusion remains valid after robustness tests and endogenous treatment. Secondly, compared with the central and western regions, DE has a stronger promoting effect on the TFP of manufacturing in the eastern region. However, DE has a more significant enhancing effect on the TFP of agriculture and services in the central and western regions than in the eastern region. Thirdly, the effect of DE on the TFP of industries presents industrial heterogeneity. In the manufacturing sector, DE can significantly enhance the TFP of traditional manufacturing industries such as agricultural and sideline food processing industry, but it has not yet shown a significant effect on the TFP of high-skill manufacturing industries such as computer, communications, and other electronic equipment manufacturing. In the service sector, the promoting effect of DE is more pronounced in industries such as wholesale and retail, while the real estate industry has not yet benefited from the dividends of DE.

Based on the above research and considering the current development status of DE, this paper presents the following suggestions:

Firstly, enhance the application of digital technologies in agriculture and fully leverage the role of technological progress in improving the TFP of agriculture. Strengthen the application of technologies such as the Internet of Things and artificial intelligence across all stages of agricultural production, processing, and sales. Accelerate the transformation and application of agricultural digital technology achievements, such as specialized sensors and agricultural robots, by holding exhibitions of these advancements and creating platforms for sharing, training, and promotion.

Secondly, formulate differentiated development strategies for manufacturing. For low-skill manufacturing, upgrading production equipment to be more intelligent, networked, and digital enables large-scale, customized, and flexible production. For medium-skill manufacturing, enhance connectivity among individuals, machines, objects, and systems. For high-skill manufacturing, focus not only on intelligent transformation, such as "replacing humans with machines", but also on emphasizing research, development, and the creation of advanced digital technologies.

Finally, there is a need to deepen the application of digital technology in productive service industries and leverage technological progress to enhance the TFP of these industries. The focus should be on facilitating the digital upgrading of productive service sectors. Technologies should be used to develop precise marketing and intelligent decision-making services. Additionally, focus on advancing scientific and technological innovation services, such as research and development and technological consultation, as well as services like green, inclusive, efficient, and secure digital finance. Avoid excessive allocation of resources, such as capital, talent, and R&D, to consumer service industries to prevent falling into the "dividend trap".

6.2. Limitations and Future Research

Given the constraints imposed by data availability and research methodologies, the article still has the following shortcomings: Firstly, although the paper provides empirical evidence of the digital economy's impact on improving the TFP of industries, the exploration of the underlying mechanism is insufficient. In the future, this issue should be addressed from a broader perspective to uncover the black box mechanism between the DE and TFP. Secondly, the paper focuses solely on the comprehensive indicator of TFP without examining the specific impacts of DE on individual production factors such as capital productivity and labor productivity. This lack of detail may obscure the differentiated effects of DE on various production factors. Therefore, subsequent research could delve into the independent impacts of DE on single-factor productivity, such as capital or labor, to construct a more comprehensive and detailed map of the influence pathways. Lastly, concerning research methodologies, the paper employs a traditional panel regression model for empirical analysis. With rapid advancements in big data and machine learning technologies, future research could incorporate these advanced techniques to validate and expand upon the conclusions. By leveraging modern data analysis tools, we can capture the intricate relationship between DE and TFP more precisely and provide policymakers with more scientific and reliable decision-making foundations, thus facilitating the sustainable and healthy development of DE.

Author Contributions: Conceptualization, J.L. and Y.F.; methodology, F.X. and Y.F.; software, J.L. and F.X.; validation, J.L., Y.F. and F.X.; formal analysis, Y.C.; investigation, Y.F.; resources, J.L.; data curation, J.L. and Y.C.; writing—original draft preparation, J.L.; writing—review and editing, Y.C.; visualization, J.L.; supervision, F.X.; project administration, Y.C.; funding acquisition, J.L. All authors have read and agreed to the published version of the manuscript.

Funding: This research was funded by the Social Science Foundation of Shaanxi Province, China (grant No. 2023D042), and the Soft Science Research General Project of Shaanxi Province, China (grant No. 2024ZC-YBXM-079).

Data Availability Statement: The data will be made available by the authors on request.

Acknowledgments: The authors gratefully acknowledge the editor and anonymous reviewers for their helpful comments and suggestions, which improved this paper.

Conflicts of Interest: The authors declare no conflicts of interest.

Appendix A. Process for Calculating Total Factor Productivity (TFP) of Industries

This paper employs the Global Malmquist–Luenberger (GML) index approach to measure the TFP of industries. This method not only resolves the multi-input and multi-output issues involving undesirable outputs but also overcomes the limitations of the Malmquist–Luenberger (ML) index model, and it possesses transitivity and cumulative multiplicability. The specific procedures are as follows:

1. Construct the Production Possibility Set. Suppose that there are K decision-making units (DMUs), each DMU having N inputs, $\mathbf{x} = (x_1, x_2, \cdots, x_N) \in R_+^N$, M desirable outputs, $\mathbf{y} = (y_1, y_2, \cdots y_M) \in R_+^M$, and J undesirable outputs, $\mathbf{b} = (b_1, b_2, \cdots, b_J) \in R_+^J$. The input, desirable output and undesirable output in each period t can be expressed as $x^{k,t}$, $y^{k,t}$, and $b^{k,t}$, respectively. On this basis, the current production possibility set $P^t(\mathbf{x}^t)$ is constructed.

$$P^t(\mathbf{x}^t) = \left\{ \begin{array}{l} \left(\mathbf{y}^t, \mathbf{b}^t\right) : \sum\limits_{k=1}^{K} z_k^t y_{km}^t \geq y_m^t, \quad m = 1, \cdots, M; \sum\limits_{k=1}^{K} z_k^t b_{kj}^t = b_j^t, \quad j = 1, \cdots, J; \\ \sum\limits_{k=1}^{K} z_k^t x_{kn}^t \leq x_n^t, \quad n = 1, \cdots, N; \sum\limits_{k=1}^{K} z_k^t = 1, z_k^t \geq 0, \quad k = 1, \cdots, K \end{array} \right\} \tag{A1}$$

where $P^t(\mathbf{x}^t)$ is a bounded closed convex set. The input and desirable output are highly disposable; that is, if $(\mathbf{x}^t, \mathbf{y}^t, \mathbf{b}^t) \in P^t(\mathbf{x}^t)$ and $\mathbf{x}'^t \geq \mathbf{x}^t$ or $\mathbf{y}'^t \leq \mathbf{y}^t$, then $(\mathbf{x}'^t, \mathbf{y}^t, \mathbf{b}^t) \in P^t(\mathbf{x}^t)$ or $(\mathbf{x}^t, \mathbf{y}'^t, \mathbf{b}^t) \in P^t(\mathbf{x}^t)$. In addition, two assumptions are required for dealing with undesirable outputs.

Axiom A1 (weak disposability axiom A1). *If* $(\mathbf{x}^t, \mathbf{y}^t, \mathbf{b}^t) \in P^t(\mathbf{x}^t)$ *and* $0 \leq \theta \leq 1$, *then* $(\mathbf{x}^t, \theta\mathbf{y}^t, \theta\mathbf{b}^t) \in P^t(\mathbf{x}^t)$. *This axiom means that if the undesirable output is to be reduced, the desirable output must be reduced at the same time, indicating that the improved environment and the pollution reduction are costly, so the idea of environmental regulation should be included in the analytical framework.*

Axiom A2 (zero combination axiom A2). *If* $(\mathbf{x}^t, \mathbf{y}^t, \mathbf{b}^t) \in P^t(\mathbf{x}^t)$ *and* $\mathbf{b}^t = 0$, *then* $\mathbf{y}^t = 0$. *This axiom means that if there is no undesirable output, then there is no desirable output. In other words, whenever a desirable output is produced, the undesirable output accompanies concurrently.*

In Equation (A1), z_k^t represents the weight of the cross-sectional data. If $z_k^t \geq 0$, then there are constant returns to scale; if $\sum\limits_{k=1}^{K} z_k^t = 1, z_k^t \geq 0$, then there are variable returns to scale. However, $P^t(\mathbf{x}^t)$ determines the current production frontier using current period data, which may lead to technological regress. For this reason, this paper constructs the global production possibility set, which enhances the comparability between the technical efficiencies of DMUs.

$$P^G(\mathbf{x}) = \left\{ \begin{array}{l} \left(\mathbf{y}^t, \mathbf{b}^t\right) : \sum\limits_{t=1}^{T} \sum\limits_{k=1}^{K} z_k^t y_{km}^t \geq y_m^t, \quad m = 1, \cdots, M; \sum\limits_{t=1}^{T} \sum\limits_{k=1}^{K} z_k^t b_{kj}^t = b_j^t, \quad j = 1, \cdots, J; \\ \sum\limits_{t=1}^{T} \sum\limits_{k=1}^{K} z_k^t x_{kn}^t \leq x_n^t, \quad n = 1, \cdots, N; \sum\limits_{t=1}^{T} \sum\limits_{k=1}^{K} z_k^t = 1, \ z_k^t \geq 0, \quad k = 1, \cdots, K \end{array} \right\} \tag{A2}$$

2. Calculate the Global Directional Distance Function. Taking period t as an example, the solution model of the DMU global directional distance function is shown in Equation (A3):

$$
\begin{aligned}
& D_0^G(\mathbf{x}^t,\mathbf{y}^t,\mathbf{b}^t;\mathbf{y}^t,-\mathbf{b}^t) = \max\beta \\
& s.t. \quad \sum_{t=1}^{T}\sum_{k=1}^{K} z_k^t y_m^{k,t} \geq (1+\beta)y_m^{r,t}, \quad m=1,\cdots,M \\
& \qquad \sum_{t=1}^{T}\sum_{k=1}^{K} z_k^t b_j^{k,t} = (1-\beta)b_j^{r,t}, \quad j=1,\cdots,J \\
& \qquad \sum_{t=1}^{T}\sum_{k=1}^{K} z_k^t x_n^{k,t} \leq (1-\beta)x_n^{r,t}, \quad n=1,\cdots,N \\
& \qquad z_k^t \geq 0, \qquad k=1,\cdots,K
\end{aligned}
\tag{A3}
$$

3. Construct the GML Index. The global directional distance function is $\overrightarrow{D}_o^G(x^\tau, y^\tau, b^\tau; g^\tau) = \max\{\beta : (y^\tau, b^\tau) + \beta g^\tau \in P^G(x^\tau)\}$, where $\tau = t, t+1$, $P^G(x^\tau)$ represents the global production possibility set and $g = (y, -b)$ is the directional vector. Under constant returns to scale, the GML can be expressed as follows:

$$
GML_t^{t+1} = \frac{1 + \overrightarrow{D}_o^G(x^t, y^t, b^t; y^t, -b^t)}{1 + \overrightarrow{D}_o^G(x^{t+1}, y^{t+1}, b^{t+1}; y^{t+1}, -b^{t+1})} \tag{A4}
$$

References

1. Yue, H.; Zhou, Z.; Liu, H. How does Green Finance Influence Industrial Green Total Factor Productivity? Empirical Research from China. *Energy Rep.* **2024**, *11*, 914–924. [CrossRef]
2. Li, Q.; Hou, J. Industrial Digitalization and High-Quality Development of Manufacturing Industry: Synchronizing Growth in the Yangtze River Economic Belt. *J. Knowl. Econ.* **2024**, *6*, 1–43. [CrossRef]
3. Solow, R.M. We'd Better Watch Out. *N. Y. Times Book Rev.* **1987**, *36*, 36.
4. Jorgenson, D.W.; Ho, M.S.; Stiroh, K.J. A Retrospective Look at the U.S. Productivity Growth Resurgence. *J. Econ. Perspect.* **2008**, *22*, 3–24. [CrossRef]
5. Mallick, S.K.; Ho, S.J. On Network Competition and the Solow Paradox: Evidence from US Banks. *Manch. Sch.* **2008**, *76*, 37–57. [CrossRef]
6. Lyu, Y.W.; Wang, W.Q.; Wu, Y.; Zhang, J.N. How does Digital Economy Affect Green Total Factor Productivity? Evidence from China. *Sci. Total Environ.* **2023**, *857*, 159428. [CrossRef]
7. Pan, W.R.; Xie, T.; Wang, Z.W.; Ma, L.S. Digital Economy: An Innovation Driver for Total Factor Productivity. *J. Bus. Res.* **2022**, *139*, 303–311. [CrossRef]
8. Lyu, Y.; Xiao, X.; Zhang, J. Does the Digital Economy Enhance Green Total Factor Productivity in China? The Evidence from a National Big Data Comprehensive Pilot Zone. *Struct. Change Econ. Dyn.* **2024**, *69*, 183–196. [CrossRef]
9. Van Ark, B. The Productivity Paradox of the New Digital Economy. *Int. Prod. Monit.* **2016**, *31*, 3–18.
10. Parteka, A.; Kordalska, A. Artificial intelligence and productivity: Global evidence from AI patent and bibliometric data. *Technovation* **2023**, *125*, 102764. [CrossRef]
11. Newlands, G.; Lutz, C. Mapping the Prestige and Social Value of Occupations in the Digital Economy. *J. Bus. Res.* **2024**, *180*, 114716. [CrossRef]
12. Teece, D.J. Profiting from Innovation in the Digital Economy: Enabling Technologies, Standards, and Licensing Models in the Wireless World. *Res. Policy* **2018**, *47*, 1367–1387. [CrossRef]
13. Zhao, Y.; Zhou, Y. Measurement Method and Application of a Deep Learning Digital Economy Scale Based on a Big Data Cloud Platform. *J. Organ. End User Comput.* **2022**, *34*, 1–17. [CrossRef]
14. Sidorov, A.; Senchenko, P. Regional Digital Economy: Assessment of Development Levels. *Mathematics* **2020**, *8*, 2143. [CrossRef]
15. Ma, D.; Zhu, Q. Innovation in Emerging Economies: Research on the Digital Economy Driving High-Quality Green Development. *J. Bus. Res.* **2022**, *145*, 801–813. [CrossRef]
16. Moghaddasi, R.; Pour, A.A. Energy Consumption and Total Factor Productivity Growth in Iranian Agriculture. *Energy Rep.* **2016**, *2*, 218–220. [CrossRef]
17. Chen, Y.; Miao, J.; Zhu, Z. Measuring Green Total Factor Productivity of China's Agricultural Sector: A Three-Stage SBM-DEA Model with Non-Point Source Pollution and CO_2 Emissions. *J. Clean. Prod.* **2021**, *318*, 128543. [CrossRef]
18. Du, K.; Lin, B. International Comparison of Total-Factor Energy Productivity Growth: A Parametric Malmquist Index Approach. *Energy* **2017**, *118*, 481–488. [CrossRef]
19. Ali, M.U.; Wang, Y. Is Participation in Global Value Chains a Blessing or a Curse for Green Total Factor Productivity in Belt and Road Initiative Countries? *J. Clean. Prod.* **2023**, *426*, 138963. [CrossRef]

20. Rehman, F.U.; Islam, M.M. Financial Infrastructure-Total Factor Productivity (TFP) Nexus within the Purview of FDI outflow, Trade Openness, Innovation, Human Capital and Institutional Quality: Evidence from Brics Economies. *Appl. Econ.* **2023**, *55*, 783–801. [CrossRef]
21. Hasanov, F.J.; Mukhtarov, S.; Suleymanov, E.; Shannak, S.D. The Role of Renewable Energy and Total Factor Productivity in Reducing Carbon Emissions: A Case of Top-Ranked Nations in the Renewable Energy Country Attractiveness Index. *J. Environ. Manag.* **2024**, *361*, 121220. [CrossRef] [PubMed]
22. Li, H.; Zhou, X.; Tang, M.; Guo, L. Impact of Population Aging and Renewable Energy Consumption on Agricultural Green Total Factor Productivity in Rural China: Evidence from Panel VAR Approach. *Agriculture* **2022**, *12*, 715. [CrossRef]
23. Chang, L.; Taghizadeh-Hesary, F.; Mohsin, M. Role of Artificial Intelligence on Green Economic Development: Joint Determinates of Natural Resources and Green Total Factor Productivity. *Resour. Policy* **2023**, *82*, 103508. [CrossRef]
24. Tian, Y.; Feng, C. How does Internet Development Drive the Sustainable Economic Growth of China? Evidence from Internal-Structural Perspective of Green Total-Factor Productivity. *Sci. Total Environ.* **2023**, *887*, 164125. [CrossRef] [PubMed]
25. Lu, C.-H. The Impact of Artificial Intelligence on Economic Growth and Welfare. *J. Macroecon.* **2021**, *69*, 103342. [CrossRef]
26. Yang, C.-H. How Artificial Intelligence Technology Affects Productivity and Employment: Firm-level Evidence from Taiwan. *Resour. Policy.* **2022**, *51*, 104536. [CrossRef]
27. Edquist, H.; Henrekson, M. Do R&D and ICT Affect Total Factor Productivity Growth Differently? *Telecommun. Policy.* **2017**, *41*, 106–119.
28. Gordon, R.J. Declining American Economic Growth Despite Ongoing Innovation. *Explor. Econ. Hist.* **2018**, *69*, 1–12. [CrossRef]
29. Acemoglu, D.; Restrepo, P. The Race between Man and Machine: Implications of Technology for Growth, Factor Shares, and Employment. *Am. Econ. Rev.* **2018**, *108*, 1488–1542. [CrossRef]
30. Aghion, P.; Howitt, P. Joseph Schumpeter Lecture Appropriate Growth Policy: A Unifying Framework. *J. Eur. Econ. Assoc.* **2006**, *4*, 269–314. [CrossRef]
31. Yi, X. Study on New Round of Scientific and Technological Revolution and the Impact of Industrial Change on Economic Growth: Quantitative Analysis Based on Multi-Sector Schumpeter Endogenous Growth Theory. *Macroeconomics* **2018**, *11*, 79–93.
32. Ru, S.; Liu, J.; Wang, T.; Wei, G. Provincial Quality of Economic Growth: Measurements and Influencing Factors for China. *Sustainability* **2020**, *12*, 1354. [CrossRef]
33. Kumar, H. Decision Making for Hotel Selection Using Rough Set Theory: A Case Study of Indian Hotels. *Int. J. Appl. Eng. Res.* **2018**, *13*, 3988–3998.
34. Nunn, N.; Qian, N. US Food Aid and Civil Conflict. *Am. Econ. Rev.* **2014**, *104*, 1630–1666. [CrossRef]

mathematics

MDPI

Article

A Fixed-Time Event-Triggered Consensus of a Class of Multi-Agent Systems with Disturbed and Non-Linear Dynamics

Yueqing Wang, Te Wang and Zhi Li *

School of Mechano-Engineering, Xidian University, Xi'an 710126, China
* Correspondence: zhli@xidian.edu.cn

Abstract: This paper investigates the problem of fixed-time event-triggered consensus control for a class of multi-agent systems with disturbed and non-linear dynamics. A fixed-time consensus protocol based on an event-triggered strategy is proposed, which can ensure a fixed-time event-triggered consensus, reduce energy consumption, and decrease the frequency of controller updates. The control protocol can also be applied to the case when the systems are free of disturbances; it solves the problem of high convergence time of the systems and reduces energy consumption of the systems. Sufficient conditions are proposed for the multi-agent systems with disturbed and non-linear dynamics to achieve the fixed-time event-triggered consensus by using algebraic graph theory, inequalities, fixed-time stability theory, and Lyapunov stability theory. Finally, simulation results show that the proposed control protocol has the advantages of both event-triggered and fixed-time convergence; compared to previous work, the convergence time of the new control protocol is greatly reduced (about 1.5 s) and the update times are also greatly reduced (less than 50 times), which is consistent with the theoretical results.

Keywords: consensus; multi-agent systems; non-linear; event-triggered control; fixed-time

MSC: 93A16

1. Introduction

Consensus is a relatively important issue in the collaborative control [1–4] of multi-agent systems. The convergence rate is an important performance metric for evaluating the proposed consensus protocols [5]. The convergence rate was shown to be influenced by the algebraic connectivity, which is the second smallest eigenvalue of the Laplacian matrix. In [6], researchers can improve the convergence rate to linear protocols, but only asymptotically. In practice, it is sometimes necessary for multi-agent systems to achieve consensus in finite time [7–9]. However, the finite-time consensus has a major drawback in that the convergence time of the systems still depends on the initial conditions of the multi-agent systems. Therefore, it is difficult to provide a strict estimate of the convergence time. Furthermore, the issue of how to decrease the loss of energy of the agents is also a noted research topic. Therefore, the aim of this paper is to research this problem; specifically, it will be based on fixed-time convergence and event-triggered mechanisms to propose a new strategy: a fixed-time event-triggered consensus control protocol.

Fixed-time stability [10] refers to a state where the convergence time of a closed-loop system is independent of the initial conditions. A fixed-time averaging consensus algorithm was discussed for multi-agent systems with integrator dynamics in an undirected topology [11]; then, conclusions on finite-time and fixed-time stability analysis of non-linear systems were presented by using an implicit Lyapunov function approach [12]. Then, the robust fixed-time consensus problem for multi-agent systems with non-linear dynamics and uncertain disturbances was studied [13]. Researchers investigated the fixed-time consensus problem for a class of heterogeneous non-linear multi-agent systems and proposed a new control protocol to achieve the fixed-time consensus problem for leaderless and leader-following systems by using fixed-time control theory and graph theory [14]. In [15], the fixed-time leader-following consensus problem for higher-order non-linear multi-agent systems was studied. Based on a fixed-time distributed observer and a dynamic gain control method, a dynamic controller was proposed to achieve fixed-time tracking consensus. In [16], a non-singular sliding-mode control law was designed based on fixed-time synchronization stability, thus solving the fixed-time synchronization consensus problem. Researchers studied the fixed-time consensus tracking problem of second-order multi-agent systems under a directed interaction topology, designed a sliding surface, and established a non-singular terminal sliding-mode consensus protocol to achieve fixed-time convergence of the tracking error to the origin [17]. In [18], an ideal fixed-time stable virtual control protocol was derived by adding power integrator techniques, radial basis function neural network approximation, and adaptive methods; it solved the problems of unknown control direction and external disturbances of the system. In [19], the fixed-time control of a second-order perturbed non-linear multi-agent system was studied. A new non-singular terminal sliding-mode control protocol was proposed to achieve the fixed-time convergence of the system, and an explicit estimation of the settling time was given. It is worth noting that the loss of energy of the agents is not considered in the above-mentioned studies on the fixed-time consensus of multi-agent systems. Additionally, the event-triggered control problem is closely related to the measurement feedback control problem. An event-triggered control system is a sampled-data system in which the sampling time instants are determined by events generated by the real-time system state. By taking advantage of the inter-sample behavior, event-triggered sampling may realize improved control performance over periodic sampling. It also has the advantages of saving communication bandwidth, improving system response speed, reducing control cost, improving system robustness, and applying to complex systems [9,20–24]. Therefore, it is important to combine the event-triggered mechanism with multi-agent systems with fixed-time consensus to reduce the energy consumption and the frequency of controller updates. Additionally, researchers studied the fixed-time event-triggered consensus problem of uncertain non-linear multi-agent systems [20], proposed two fixed-time event-triggered consensus controllers, and obtained sufficient conditions for the fixed-time convergence of the system. Ref. [21] studied the problem of achieving fixed-time average consensus for a class of multi-agent systems under switching topology and intermittent communication based on the event-based control strategy, and obtained sufficient conditions for the system to achieve fixed-time average consensus. Ref. [22] proposed a new fixed-time event-triggered control protocol based on a dynamic compensator approach to obtain a sufficient condition for the fixed-time consensus of linear multi-agent systems. An event-triggered consensus protocol was proposed in [23]; it obtained sufficient conditions for convergence of event-triggered attitude consensus for multi-agent systems. In [24], researchers studied the fixed-time event-triggered consensus of a class of non-linear multi-agent systems with switching topologies and gave an upper bound on the fixed-time convergence time of the system and sufficient conditions for the convergence of the system.

It should be noted that the previous works have made significant contributions to the field of multi-agent consensus control, but some issues have not been considered. In [13], a non-linear multi-agent system control protocol was proposed in first-order multi-agent systems with disturbed and non-linear dynamics, but when the agents are internally powered by their own power supply or battery, the bandwidth is easily limited and the loss of communication resources occurs, which have not been considered. In addition, researchers studied the fixed-time event-triggered consensus problem for a class of non-linear multi-agent systems. Ref. [24] proposed a control algorithm that considers its influence by uncertain non-linear terms, but the disturbance of the systems was not considered; the algorithm provided a high prediction of the upper bound on the convergence time. Motivated by the previous works, in this paper, a fixed-time event-triggered consensus control protocol is proposed, which can achieve fixed-time event-triggered consensus for multi-agent systems with disturbed and non-linear dynamics. The control protocol is also suitable for the case when the systems are free of disturbances. Compared with the previous works, the results shown in this paper have the following features: Firstly, this protocol reduces power consumption. Secondly, compared to [24], this paper can provide a more accurate upper bound estimation of convergence time and save more resources. Finally, the multi-agent systems with external disturbances are considered. Results about the fixed-time event-triggered consensus for multi-agent systems with disturbed and non-linear dynamics are available.

This paper is organized as follows: Preparation and problem formulation are presented in Section 2. In Section 3, a fixed-time event-triggered consensus control protocol is proposed and consensus analyses are reviewed. In Section 4, some simulation examples are provided to illustrate the effectiveness of the fixed-time event-triggered consensus protocol. Conclusions are drawn in Section 5.

2. Preparation and Problem Description

In this section, firstly, the knowledge of the graph theory will be introduced. Secondly, some lemmas used in this paper will be introduced. Finally, the problem formulation will be presented.

A. the basic graph theory

Let $G(V,E,A)$ be an undirected graph G of order N. The $V = \{1,2,\cdots,N\}$ indicates that the graph has N nodes and $E \subseteq V \times V$ is the set of edges. An edge $(i,j) \in E$ indicates that note j can exchange information state from note i and note i can also exchange information from note j. In this paper, agents are considered nodes. Agent i and j can communicate with each other. $A = [a_{ij}] \in R^{n\times n}$ is an N order matrix when edge $(i,j) \in E$, $a_{ij} > 0$; otherwise, $a_{ij} = 0$, A is known as an adjacency matrix. The degree matrix is defined as $D = diag\{d_1,\cdots,d_N\}$, $d_i = \sum_{j=1,j\neq i}^{N} a_{ij}$. The Laplacian matrix of graph G is defined by $L = D - A$.

B. Some lemmas

Lemma 1 ([13]). *The graph G is undirected and connected, and the following three conclusions hold:*

(1) *0 is an eigenvalue of the matrix L and the corresponding eigenvector is 1_n, $L1_n = 0$.*

(2) *The Laplace matrix is positive semidefinite, and all the eigenvalues of the matrix satisfy the following relation:*

$$0 \leq \lambda_2 \leq \cdots \leq \lambda_n, 1^T x = 0 \text{ then } x^T L x \geq \lambda_2 x^T x.$$

Algebraic connectivity of the graph G; the second smallest eigenvalue of the Laplace matrix is λ_2.

(3) *For any $x = (x_1, x_2, \cdots, x_N)^T \in R^N$, $x^T L x = \frac{1}{2}\sum_{i=1}^{N}\sum_{j=1}^{N} a_{ij}(x_j - x_i)^2$.*

Lemma 2 ([11]). *If there is a continuous radial unbounded function $V(x(t))$: $R_n \to R^+ \cup \{0\}$ such that $x = 0 \Leftrightarrow V(x) = 0$*

x satisfies the inequality

$$\dot{V}(t) \leq -aV^p(x(t)) - bV^q(x(t)) \tag{1}$$

for $a,b > 0, p \in (0,1), q > 1$. $p = 1 - \frac{1}{2\gamma}, q = 1 + \frac{1}{2\gamma}, \gamma > 1$. then, the fixed-time stable can be achieved and the settling time T satisfies the following conditions: where, γ

$$T(x) \leq T_{\max} = \frac{\pi\gamma}{\sqrt{ab}}, \forall x_0 \in R^n \tag{2}$$

Lemma 3 ([13]). *Let $x_1, x_2, \cdots, x_N \geq 0, 0 < p \leq 1$ and $q > 1$. Then*

$$\sum_{i=1}^{N} x_i^p \geq (\sum_{i=1}^{N} x_i)^p,\ \sum_{i=1}^{N} x_i^q \geq N^{1-q}(\sum_{i=1}^{N} x_i)^q \tag{3}$$

C. the problem formulation

The multi-agent systems consist of N agents and the dynamics model of the agents can be described by the following differential equation:

$$\dot{x}_i(t) = u_i(t) + f(x_i(t), t) + d_i(x_i(t), t) \tag{4}$$

where $i = 1, 2, \cdots, N, u_i(t) \in R^N$ is the control input of the multi-agent systems, $x_i(t) \in R^N$ is the state of agent, $f(x_i(t), t)$ is a non-linear function, and $d_i(x_i(t), t)$ are disturbances. In this paper, before moving on, the following assumptions are made:

Assumption 1. *$f(x_i(t), t)$ is a non-linear function; there exists a positive constant k, $0 < p < 1$ and $q > 1$, $p < \eta < q$, p, q and q are the ratios of positive odd numbers, such that*

$$|f(x_i(t), t) - f(x_j(t), t)| \leq k|x_i(t) - x_j(t)|^\eta \tag{5}$$

For example, a non-linear function $f(x(t)) = \frac{1}{2}|x(t) + 1| + sin(t)$, and $x_i(t)$ is the state of agent i, $x_j(t)$ is the state of agent j, so $|f(x_i(t)) - f(x_j(t))| = \left|\frac{1}{2}|x_i(t) + 1| - \frac{1}{2}|x_j(t) + 1|\right| \leq \frac{1}{2}|x_i(t) - x_j(t)|$, $k = \frac{1}{2}$, $\eta = 1$.

Assumption 2. *The disturbances $d_i(x_i(t), t)$ are bounded by*

$$|d_i(x_i(t), t)| \leq d \tag{6}$$

where the number d is assumed to be given, and $i = 1, 2, \cdots, N$.
For example, a disturbances function $d(x(t), t) = sin(x(t)cos(x(t)))$, then for the state of agent i, $d(x_i(t), t) = sin(x_i(t)cos(x_i(t))) \leq 1$ as well as $d = 1$.

Definition 1. *With a given control protocol, the fixed-time consensus of the multi-agent systems (4) is that there exists a fixed-time T such that $\lim_{t\to T}|x_i(t) - x_j(t)| = 0$ and when $t \geq T$, $x_i(t) = x_j(t)(i, j = 1, 2, \cdots, N)$, if for any initial value $x_i(0)$, there is a positive constant T_{max}, such that $T \leq T_{max}$, multi-agent systems will be said to achieve fixed-time consensus.*

3. Fixed-Time Event-Triggered Consensus Protocol

In this section, the main results of the fixed-time event-triggered consensus of the system (4) are investigated.

Consider the following control protocol:

$$\begin{aligned} u_i(t) = &-k_1\textstyle\sum_{j=1}^{N} a_{ij}(x_i(t_k^i) - x_j(t_k^i))^p \\ &-k_2\textstyle\sum_{j=1}^{N} a_{ij}(x_i(t_k^i) - x_j(t_k^i))^q \\ &-k_3\textstyle\sum_{j=1}^{N} a_{ij}(x_i(t_k^i) - x_j(t_k^i))^\eta \\ &-k_4\textstyle\sum_{j=1}^{N} a_{ij}sign(x_i(t_k^i) - x_j(t_k^i)) \end{aligned} \tag{7}$$

where $k_1, k_2, k_3, k_4 > 0, 0 < p < 1, q > 1, p < \eta < q$. p, η and q are the ratios of positive odd numbers. t_k^i is the kth event-triggered instants of the agent i. Additionally, parameters k1, k2, k3, and k4 affect the consistency of different orders, respectively, and the interaction reaches the consistency of fixed time.

Define a measurement error; the event-triggered function is related to this measurement error.

$$\begin{array}{c} e_i(t) = k_1\Sigma_{j=1}^{N} a_{ij}(x_i(t_k^i) - x_j(t_k^i))^p + k_2\Sigma_{j=1}^{N} a_{ij}(x_i(t_k^i) - x_j(t_k^i))^q \\ +k_3\Sigma_{j=1}^{N} a_{ij}(x_i(t_k^i) - x_j(t_k^i))^\eta + k_4\Sigma_{j=1}^{N} a_{ij}sign(x_i(t_k^i) - x_j(t_k^i)) \\ -k_1\Sigma_{j=1}^{N} a_{ij}(x_i(t) - x_j(t))^p - k_2\Sigma_{j=1}^{N} a_{ij}(x_i(t) - x_j(t))^q \\ -k_3\Sigma_{j=1}^{N} a_{ij}(x_i(t) - x_j(t))^\eta - k_4\Sigma_{j=1}^{N} a_{ij}sign(x_i(t) - x_j(t)) \end{array} \tag{8}$$

The following event-triggered function is constructed based on the measurement error:

$$\begin{array}{c} \varphi(t) = |e_i(t)| - mk_1\Sigma_{j=1}^{N} a_{ij}|x_i(t) - x_j(t)|^p - mk_2\Sigma_{j=1}^{N} a_{ij}|x_i(t) - x_j(t)|^q \\ -mk_3\Sigma_{j=1}^{N} a_{ij}|x_i(t) - x_j(t)|^\eta - mk_4N \end{array} \tag{9}$$

where $0 < m < 1, k_1, k_2, k_3, k_4 > 0, 0 < p < 1, q > 1$.

The event-triggered conditions are as follows:

$$t_{k+1}^i = \inf\left\{t > t_k^i | \varphi(t) \geq 0\right\} \tag{10}$$

Based on trigger conditions, at the next trigger moment, each agent will be updated within its trigger period and will send the updated state information to its neighbors.

Theorem 1. *Under all assumptions above, the multi-agent systems, composed of the controlled plant (4) and the control protocol (7), satisfy the event-triggered condition (10); the multi-agent systems can achieve fixed-time consensus, if the following inequalities hold:*

$$\sqrt{2}mN\lambda_N(L_{2/p})^{\frac{p}{2}} \leq N^{1-p}\lambda_N(L_{2/p+1})^{\frac{p+1}{2}} \tag{11}$$

$$\sqrt{2}mN\lambda_N(L_{2/q})^{\frac{q}{2}} \leq \lambda_N(L_{2/q+1})^{\frac{q+1}{2}} \tag{12}$$

$$k2^{\frac{\eta+1}{2}} \leq 2^\eta k_3\lambda_2(L_{2/\eta+1})^{\frac{\eta+1}{2}} \tag{13}$$

$$\sqrt{2}N^{\frac{1}{2}}(mk_4N + d) \leq k_4\lambda_2(L_2)^{\frac{1}{2}} \tag{14}$$

where $L_{2/p}$ denotes the Laplacian matrix of a graph, where the value of each element is $a_{ij}^{2/p}$; $L_{\frac{2}{p+1}}$ denotes the Laplacian matrix of a graph, where the value of each element is $a_{ij}^{\frac{2}{p+1}}$; $L_{\frac{2}{q+1}}$ denotes the Laplacian matrix of a graph, where the value of each element is $a_{ij}^{\frac{2}{q+1}}$; and $L_{\frac{2}{\eta+1}}$ denotes the Laplacian matrix of a graph, where the value of each element is $a_{ij}^{\frac{2}{\eta+1}}$.

The systems (4) can achieve fixed-time consensus under the control protocol (7), and the system convergence time satisfies:

$$T \leq T_{\max} = \frac{\pi\gamma}{\sqrt{\overline{\alpha}\overline{\beta}}} \tag{15}$$

where the parameters $\overline{\alpha}, \overline{\beta}$ are as follows:

$$\overline{\alpha} = k_1 2^p N^{1-p}\lambda_N(L_{2/p+1})^{\frac{p+1}{2}} - k_1 2^p\sqrt{2}mN\lambda_N(L_{2/p})^{\frac{p}{2}} \tag{16}$$

$$\overline{\beta} = 2^q k_2\lambda_N(L_{2/q+1})^{\frac{q+1}{2}} - \sqrt{2}2^q k_2 mN\lambda_N(L_{2/q})^{\frac{q}{2}}. \tag{17}$$

Proof. Introducing $\overline{x}(t)$, let $\overline{x}(t) = \frac{1}{N}\Sigma_{j=1}^{N} x_j(t)$ define the state error as follows:

$$\varepsilon_i(t) = x_i(t) - \overline{x}(t) \tag{18}$$

Consider the Lyapunov function as

$$V(t) = \frac{1}{2}\sum_{i=1}^{N} \varepsilon_i^2(t) \tag{19}$$

Differentiating,

$$\begin{aligned} \dot{V}(t) &= \textstyle\sum_{i=1}^{N} \varepsilon_i(t)(u_i(t) + f(x_i(t),t) + d_i(x_i(t),t) - \dot{\overline{x}}(t)) \\ &= \textstyle\sum_{j=1}^{N} \varepsilon_i(t)(-e_i(t) - k_1\sum_{j=1}^{N} a_{ij}(x_i(t) - x_j(t))^p - k_2\sum_{j=1}^{N} a_{ij}(x_i(t) - x_j(t))^q \\ &\quad -k_3\textstyle\sum_{j=1}^{N} a_{ij}(x_i(t) - x_j(t))^\eta - k_4\sum_{j=1}^{N} a_{ij} sign(x_i(t) - x_j(t)) + d_i(x_i(t),t)) \\ &\quad +\textstyle\sum_{i=1}^{N} \varepsilon_i(t)(f(x_i(t),t) - \dot{\overline{x}}(t)) \end{aligned} \tag{20}$$

According to the state error and the inequalities, one obtains

$$\begin{aligned} \dot{V}(t) &\leq \textstyle\sum_{i=1}^{N} \varepsilon_i(t)(f(x_i(t),t) - f(\overline{x}(t),t) + f(\overline{x}(t),t) \\ &\quad -\frac{1}{N}\textstyle\sum_{j=1}^{N} f(x_j(t),t) - \frac{1}{N}\sum_{j=1}^{N} d_j(x_j(t),t)) \\ &\quad +\textstyle\sum_{i=1}^{N} |\varepsilon_i(t)|(|e_i(t)| + d) \\ &\quad -k_1\textstyle\sum_{i=1}^{N} \varepsilon_i(t)(\sum_{j=1}^{N} a_{ij}(\varepsilon_i(t)-\varepsilon_j(t))^p) \\ &\quad -k_2\textstyle\sum_{i=1}^{N} \varepsilon_i(t)(\sum_{j=1}^{N} a_{ij}(\varepsilon_i(t)-\varepsilon_j(t))^q) \\ &\quad -k_3\textstyle\sum_{i=1}^{N} \varepsilon_i(t)(\sum_{j=1}^{N} a_{ij}(\varepsilon_i(t)-\varepsilon_j(t))^\eta) - k_4\sum_{i=1}^{N} \varepsilon_i(t)(\sum_{j=1}^{N} a_{ij} sign(\varepsilon_i(t)-\varepsilon_j(t))) \\ &\leq \textstyle\sum_{i=1}^{N} \varepsilon_i(t)(f(x_i(t),t) - f(\overline{x}(t),t) + f(\overline{x}(t),t) \\ &\quad -\frac{1}{N}\textstyle\sum_{j=1}^{N} f(x_j(t),t) - \frac{1}{N}\sum_{j=1}^{N} d_j(x_j(t),t)) + \sum_{i=1}^{N} |\varepsilon_i(t)|(|e_i(t)| + d) \\ &\quad -\frac{k_1}{2}\textstyle\sum_{i=1}^{N}\sum_{j=1}^{N} a_{ij}(\varepsilon_i(t) - \varepsilon_j(t))(\varepsilon_i(t) - \varepsilon_j(t))^p \\ &\quad -\frac{k_2}{2}\textstyle\sum_{i=1}^{N}\sum_{j=1}^{N} a_{ij}(\varepsilon_i(t) - \varepsilon_j(t))(\varepsilon_i(t) - \varepsilon_j(t))^q \\ &\quad -\frac{k_3}{2}\textstyle\sum_{i=1}^{N}\sum_{j=1}^{N} a_{ij}(\varepsilon_i(t) - \varepsilon_j(t))(\varepsilon_i(t) - \varepsilon_j(t))^\eta \\ &\quad -\frac{k_4}{2}\textstyle\sum_{i=1}^{N}\sum_{j=1}^{N} a_{ij}(\varepsilon_i(t) - \varepsilon_j(t)) sign(\varepsilon_i(t) - \varepsilon_j(t)) \end{aligned} \tag{21}$$

Since $\sum_{i=1}^{N} \varepsilon_i(t) = 0$, one has $(\sum_{i=1}^{N} \varepsilon_i(t))(f(\overline{x}(t),t) - \frac{1}{N}\sum_{j=1}^{N} f(x_j(t),t)) = 0$ and $(\sum_{i=1}^{N} \varepsilon_i(t))(\frac{1}{N}\sum_{j=1}^{N} d_j(x_j(t),t)) = 0$ and

$$\sum_{i=1}^{N}\sum_{j=1}^{N} a_{ij}(\epsilon_i(t) - \epsilon_j(t)) sign(\epsilon_i(t) - \epsilon_j(t)) = \sum_{i=1}^{N}\sum_{j=1}^{N} a_{ij}|\epsilon_i(t) - \epsilon_j(t)| \tag{22}$$

Substituting Assumption 1 with Assumption 2, and substituting the event-triggered conditions, one has

$$\begin{aligned}
&\dot{V}(t) \leq k\textstyle\sum_{i=1}^{N}|\varepsilon_i(t)|^2 + (mk_4N+d)N^{\frac{1}{2}}\left(\textstyle\sum_{i=1}^{N}|\varepsilon_i(t)|^2\right)^{\frac{1}{2}} \\
&+mk_1N\left(\textstyle\sum_{i=1}^{N}|\varepsilon_i(t)|^2\right)^{\frac{1}{2}}\left(\textstyle\sum_{i=1}^{N}\sum_{j=1}^{N}a_{ij}^{\frac{2}{p}}|\varepsilon_i(t)-\varepsilon_j(t)|^2\right)^{\frac{p}{2}} \\
&+mk_2N\left(\textstyle\sum_{i=1}^{N}|\varepsilon_i(t)|^2\right)^{\frac{1}{2}}\left(\textstyle\sum_{i=1}^{N}\sum_{j=1}^{N}a_{ij}^{\frac{2}{q}}|\varepsilon_i(t)-\varepsilon_j(t)|^2\right)^{\frac{q}{2}} \\
&+mk_3N\left(\textstyle\sum_{i=1}^{N}|\varepsilon_i(t)|^2\right)^{\frac{1}{2}}\left(\textstyle\sum_{i=1}^{N}\sum_{j=1}^{N}a_{ij}^{\frac{2}{\eta}}|\varepsilon_i(t)-\varepsilon_j(t)|^2\right)^{\frac{\eta}{2}} \\
&-\frac{k_1}{2}N^{1-p}\left(\textstyle\sum_{i=1}^{N}\sum_{j=1}^{N}a_{ij}^{\frac{2}{p+1}}|\varepsilon_i(t)-\varepsilon_j(t)|^2\right)^{\frac{p+1}{2}} -\frac{k_2}{2}\left(\textstyle\sum_{i=1}^{N}\sum_{j=1}^{N}a_{ij}^{\frac{2}{q+1}}|\varepsilon_i(t)-\varepsilon_j(t)|^2\right)^{\frac{q+1}{2}} \\
&-\frac{k_3}{2}\left(\textstyle\sum_{i=1}^{N}\sum_{j=1}^{N}a_{ij}^{\frac{2}{\eta+1}}|\varepsilon_i(t)-\varepsilon_j(t)|^2\right)^{\frac{\eta+1}{2}} -\frac{k_4}{2}\left(\textstyle\sum_{i=1}^{N}\sum_{j=1}^{N}a_{ij}^{2}|\varepsilon_i(t)-\varepsilon_j(t)|^2\right)^{\frac{1}{2}}
\end{aligned} \tag{23}$$

Invoking Lemma 1, the following inequalities can be obtained:

$$\sum_{i=1}^{N}\sum_{j=1}^{N}a_{ij}^{\frac{2}{p}}|\varepsilon_i(t)-\varepsilon_j(t)|^2 = 2\varepsilon^T L_{2/p}\varepsilon \geq 4\lambda_2(L_{2/p})V(t)$$

$$\sum_{i=1}^{N}\sum_{j=1}^{N}a_{ij}^{\frac{2}{p}}|\varepsilon_i(t)-\varepsilon_j(t)|^2 = 2\varepsilon^T L_{2/q}\varepsilon \geq 4\lambda_2(L_{2/q})V(t)$$

$$\sum_{i=1}^{N}\sum_{j=1}^{N}a_{ij}^{\frac{2}{\eta}}|\varepsilon_i(t)-\varepsilon_j(t)|^2 = 2\varepsilon^T L_{2/\eta}\varepsilon \geq 4\lambda_2(L_{2/\eta})V(t)$$

$$\sum_{i=1}^{N}\sum_{j=1}^{N}a_{ij}^{\frac{2}{p+1}}|\varepsilon_i(t)-\varepsilon_j(t)|^2 = 2\varepsilon^T L_{2/p+1}\varepsilon \geq 4\lambda_2(L_{2/p+1})V(t)$$

$$\sum_{i=1}^{N}\sum_{j=1}^{N}a_{ij}^{\frac{2}{q+1}}|\varepsilon_i(t)-\varepsilon_j(t)|^2 = 2\varepsilon^T L_{2/q+1}\varepsilon \geq 4\lambda_2(L_{2/q+1})V(t)$$

where $L_{2/p}$, $L_{2/q}$, $L_{2/\eta}$, $L_{2/p+1}$, and $L_{2/q+1}$ are the Laplacian matrices of the weighted graphs $G(A^{[2/p]})$, $G(A^{[2/q]})$, $G(A^{[2/\eta]})$, $G(A^{[2/p+1]})$, and $G(A^{[2/q+1]})$, respectively.

By Lemma 2, the following inequality can be obtained:

$$\begin{aligned}
\dot{V}(t) \leq &-(k_1N^{1-p}\lambda_N(L_{2/p+1})^{\frac{p+1}{2}} - k_1\sqrt{2}mN\lambda_N(L_{2/p})^{\frac{p}{2}})2^pV^{\frac{p+1}{2}}(t) \\
&-(k_2\lambda_N(L_{2/q+1})^{\frac{q+1}{2}} - \sqrt{2}k_2mN\lambda_N(L_{2/q})^{\frac{q}{2}})2^qV^{\frac{q+1}{2}}(t) \\
&+(k2^{\frac{\eta+1}{2}} - 2^{\eta}k_3\lambda_2(L_{2/\eta+1})^{\frac{\eta+1}{2}})V^{\frac{\eta+1}{2}}(t) \\
&+(\sqrt{2}N^{\frac{1}{2}}(mk_4N+d) - k_4\lambda_2(L_2)^{\frac{1}{2}})V^{\frac{1}{2}}(t)
\end{aligned} \tag{24}$$

By Inequalities (13) and (14)

$$\dot{V}(t) \leq -\overline{\alpha}V^{\frac{p+1}{2}}(t) - \overline{\beta}V^{\frac{q+1}{2}}(t) \tag{25}$$

When $p = 1+\frac{1}{\gamma}, q = 1-\frac{1}{\gamma}, \gamma > 1$, one has

$$\dot{V}(t) \leq -\overline{\alpha}V^{1-\frac{1}{2\gamma}}(t) - \overline{\beta}V^{1+\frac{1}{2\gamma}}(t) \tag{26}$$

According to Lemma 2, the systems' convergence time satisfies:

$$T \leq T_{\max} = \frac{\pi\gamma}{\sqrt{\overline{\alpha}\overline{\beta}}} \tag{27}$$

Here are the parameters $\overline{\alpha}$, $\overline{\beta}$ as follows:

$$\overline{\alpha} = k_1 N^{1-p} 2^p \lambda_N(L_{2/p+1})^{\frac{p+1}{2}} - k_1\sqrt{2}2^p mN\lambda_N(L_{2/p})^{\frac{p}{2}}$$

$$\overline{\beta} = k_2 2^q \lambda_N(L_{2/q+1})^{\frac{q+1}{2}} - \sqrt{2}2^q k_2 mN\lambda_N(L_{2/q})^{\frac{q}{2}}$$

where $\lambda_N(L_{2/p+1})$, $\lambda_N(L_{2/p})$, $\lambda_N(L_{2/q+1})$, and $\lambda_N(L_{2/q})$ are the biggest eigenvalues of the Laplacian matrices $L_{2/p+1}$, $L_{2/p}$, $L_{2/q+1}$, and $L_{2/q}$ in the connected undirected graphs $G(A^{[2/p+1]})$, $G(A^{[2/p]})$, $G(A^{[2/q+1]})$, and $G(A^{[2/p]})$. The multi-agent systems can achieve fixed-time consensus.

Under the control protocol (7), the inter-event interval is lower bounded; this can be proven in the following theorem: □

Theorem 2. *Considering the multi-agent systems (4) with disturbed and non-linear dynamics, for any initial condition, the inter-event interval is lower bounded by the strictly positive.*

Proof. The presence of a functional term in the measurement error is non-differentiable, and the next proof process involves the derivation of the measurement error, which is now generally treated in two ways in the literature—either by approximating the symbolic function with a saturation function, which requires a segmented discussion, or by replacing the symbolic function with a hyperbolic tangent function. The second approach will be used in this part of the proof. The measurement error can be written as

$$\begin{aligned} e_i(t) = k_1\textstyle\sum_{j=1}^N a_{ij}(x_i(t_k^i) - x_j(t_k^i))^p + k_2\sum_{j=1}^N a_{ij}(x_i(t_k^i) - x_j(t_k^i))^q \\ + k_3\textstyle\sum_{j=1}^N a_{ij}(x_i(t_k^i) - x_j(t_k^i))^\eta + k_4\sum_{j=1}^N a_{ij}\tanh(n(x_i(t_k^i) - x_j(t_k^i))) \\ - k_1\textstyle\sum_{j=1}^N a_{ij}(x_i(t) - x_j(t))^p - k_2\sum_{j=1}^N a_{ij}(x_i(t) - x_j(t))^q \\ - k_3\textstyle\sum_{j=1}^N a_{ij}(x_i(t) - x_j(t))^\eta - k_4\sum_{j=1}^N a_{ij}\tanh(n(x_i(t) - x_j(t))) \end{aligned} \tag{28}$$

For $\tanh(n(x_i(t) - x_j(t))$, $n \gg 1$, one has

$$\begin{aligned} |\dot{e}_i(t)| \leq |\textstyle\sum_{j=1}^N a_{ij}(k_1 p(x_i(t) - x_j(t)))^{p-1} + k_2 q(x_i(t) - x_j(t))^{q-1} + k_3\eta(x_i(t) - x_j(t))^{\eta-1} + k_4 n(1 - \tanh^2(n(x_i(t) - x_j(t)))) \\ *(u_i(t) + f(x_i(t), t) + d_i(x_i(t), t) - u_j(t) + f(x_j(t), t) + d_j(x_j(t), t))| \end{aligned} \tag{29}$$

Substitute Assumptions 1 and 2

$$\begin{aligned} |\dot{e}_i(t)| \leq |\textstyle\sum_{j=1}^N a_{ij}(k_1 p(x_i(t) - x_j(t)))^{p-1} + k_2 q(x_i(t) - x_j(t))^{q-1} \\ + k_3\eta(x_i(t) - x_j(t))^{\eta-1} + k_4 n) * (|u_i(t) - u_j(t)| + k|x_i(t) - x_j(t)|^\eta + 2d) \end{aligned} \tag{30}$$

Substituting the state error and deflating:

$$\begin{aligned} |\dot{e}_i(t)| \leq k_1 pk\textstyle\sum_{j=1}^N a_{ij}|\varepsilon_i(t) - \varepsilon_j(t)|^{p+\eta-1} + k_2 qk\sum_{j=1}^N a_{ij}|\varepsilon_i(t) - \varepsilon_j(t)|^{q+\eta-1} \\ + k_3\eta k\textstyle\sum_{j=1}^N a_{ij}|\varepsilon_i(t) - \varepsilon_j(t)|^{2\eta-1} + k_4 nk\sum_{j=1}^N a_{ij}|\varepsilon_i(t) - \varepsilon_j(t)|^\eta \\ + \textstyle\sum_{j=1}^N a_{ij}(k_1 p|\varepsilon_i(t) - \varepsilon_j(t)|^{p-1} + k_2 q|\varepsilon_i(t) - \varepsilon_j(t)|^{q-1} \\ + k_3\eta|\varepsilon_i(t) - \varepsilon_j(t)|^{\eta-1}) * (|u_i(t) - u_j(t)| + 2d) \end{aligned} \tag{31}$$

According to Lemma 1,

$$
\begin{aligned}
|\dot{e}_i(t)| \leq\ & k_1pk(4\lambda_N(L_{2/p+\eta-1})V(0))^{\frac{p+\eta-1}{2}} + k_2qk(4\lambda_N(L_{2/q+\eta-1})V(0))^{\frac{q+\eta-1}{2}} \\
& + k_3\eta k(4\lambda_N(L_{2/2\eta-1})V(0))^{\frac{2\eta-1}{2}} + kk_4n(4\lambda_N(L_{2/\eta})V(0))^{\frac{\eta}{2}} \\
& + [k_1p(4\lambda_N(L_{2/p-1})V(0))^{\frac{p-1}{2}} + k_2q(4\lambda_N(L_{2/p-1})V(0))^{\frac{q-1}{2}} \\
& + k_3\eta k(4\lambda_N(L_{2/\eta-1})V(0))^{\frac{\eta-1}{2}}] * (N|u_i(t_k^i)| + |\textstyle\sum_{j=1}^{N} u_j(t_{\bar{k}}^j) + 2d)
\end{aligned} \tag{32}
$$

The Equation (32) can be written as the sum of two functions on t_k^i, $t_{\bar{k}}^j$.

$$
|\dot{e}_i(t)| \leq l_1(t_k^i) + l_2(t_{\bar{k}}^j) \tag{33}
$$

It is also clear from the event-triggering mechanism that the following equation holds:

$$
e_i(t_k^i) = 0 \tag{34}
$$

By the integral inequalities, one has

$$
\begin{aligned}
|e_i(t)| &\leq \int_{t_k^i}^{t} |\dot{e}_i(t)| du \leq \int_{t_k^i}^{t} (l_1(t_k^i) + l_2(t_{\bar{k}}^j)) du \\
|e_i(t_{k+1}^i)| &\leq \int_{t_k^i}^{t_{k+1}^i} (l_1(t_k^i) + l_2(t_{\bar{k}}^j)) du \leq \int_{t_k^i}^{t_{k+1}^i} (l_1^* + l_2^*) du
\end{aligned} \tag{35}
$$

where $l_1^* = \max\{l_1(t_0^i), l_2(t_1^i), \cdots\}, l_2^* = \max\left\{l_1(t_0^j), l_2(t_1^j), \cdots\right\}$.

The inter-event interval is

$$
t_{k+1}^i - t_k^i \geq \frac{mk_4}{l_1^* + l_2^*} > 0 \tag{36}
$$

The multi-agent systems under the control protocol (7) have a positive lower bound on the event-triggered interval. □

4. Numerical Examples

In this section, numerical simulation examples and comparative experiments are used to verify the effectiveness of the proposed solution. It is assumed that the multi-agent systems consist of five agents with the following dynamics models described by

$$
\dot{x}_i(t) = u_i(t) + f(x_i(t), t) + d_i(x_i(t), t) \tag{37}
$$

The control input for the multi-agent systems is (7).

$$
\begin{aligned}
u_i(t) = & -k_1\textstyle\sum_{j=1}^{N} a_{ij}(x_i(t_k^i) - x_j(t_k^i))^p - k_2\sum_{j=1}^{N} a_{ij}(x_i(t_k^i) - x_j(t_k^i))^q \\
& -k_3\textstyle\sum_{j=1}^{N} a_{ij}(x_i(t_k^i) - x_j(t_k^i))^\eta - k_4\sum_{j=1}^{N} a_{ij} sign(x_i(t_k^i) - x_j(t_k^i))
\end{aligned}
$$

The interaction topology is represented by the following undirected graph shown in Figure 1. Furthermore, suppose the five agents in Figure 1 represent five smart car robots or aircraft. The collaboration between them is shown in the figure.

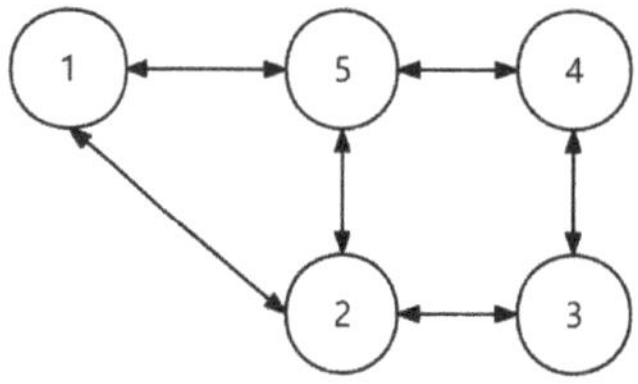

Figure 1. Communication topology.

From the graph, we can obtain the adjacency matrix and the Laplacian matrix:

$$A = \begin{bmatrix} 0 & 1 & 0 & 0 & 1 \\ 1 & 0 & 1 & 0 & 1 \\ 0 & 1 & 0 & 1 & 0 \\ 0 & 0 & 1 & 0 & 1 \\ 1 & 1 & 0 & 1 & 0 \end{bmatrix}$$

$$L = D - A = \begin{bmatrix} 2 & -1 & 0 & 0 & -1 \\ -1 & 3 & -1 & 0 & -1 \\ 0 & -1 & 2 & -1 & 0 \\ 0 & 0 & -1 & 2 & -1 \\ -1 & -1 & 0 & -1 & 3 \end{bmatrix}$$

Let $f(x_i(t),t) = 0.3x_i(t) + 0.5\cos(t)$, $d_i(x_i(t),t) = 0.5\cos(x_i(t))$, choose the initial conditions of the multi-agent systems. Additionally, the goal of setting two different initial states is to verify that the control protocol presented in this article is not affected by the initial state.

$$x_1(0) = [-4, -1, 0, 1, 3]^T$$

$$x_2(0) = [-400, -100, 0, 100, 300]^T$$

The Laplacian matrix L satisfy Lemma 1 and the second smallest eigenvalue $\lambda_2 = 2$. When the system is in a small initial condition, the values of the parameters of the fixed-time control protocol are $\eta = 1$, $p = 0.6$, $q = 1.4$, $k_1 = 0.5$, $k_2 = 0.6$, $k_3 = 1.5$, $k_4 = 1.5$. $m = 0.3$, $\gamma = 2.5$ which satisfy the conditions. The simulation results for the proposed non-linear control protocol are shown in Figure 2.

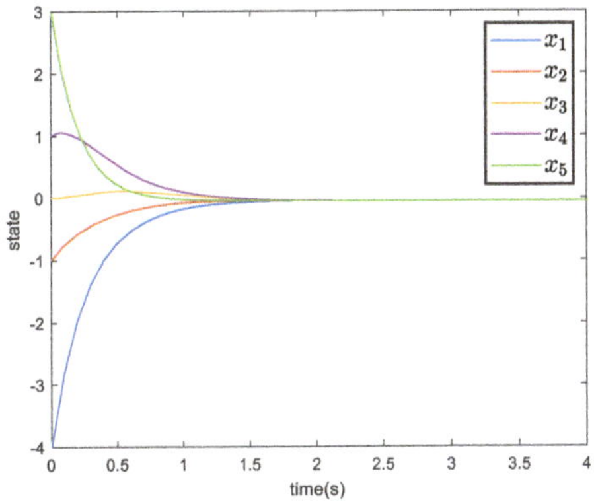

Figure 2. The states of the agents of a small initial condition.

The parameters are substituted into the expression for estimating the upper bound on the convergence time of the system; the time to converge T satisfies that $T \leq T_{\max} = 2.12\,s$ when the system is in a big initial condition The simulation results for the proposed non-linear control protocol are shown in Figure 3.

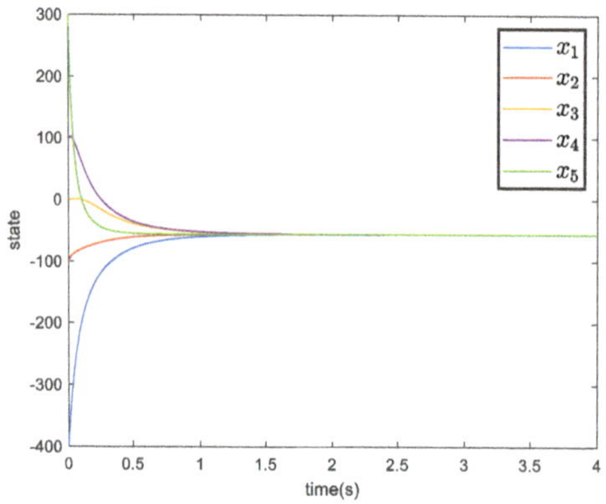

Figure 3. The states of the agents of a big initial condition.

A comparison of Figure 2 with Figure 3 shows that the convergence time of the system is not affected by the initial state of the intelligence in the system under the action of the control protocol proposed in this paper.

It is assumed that the multi-agent systems consist of five agents with the following dynamics models described by

$$\dot{x}_i(t) = u_i(t) + f(x_i(t), t) \tag{38}$$

where $i = 1, 2, \cdots, N, d_i(x_i(t), t) = 0$; the interaction topology is represented by the following undirected graph shown in Figure 1. In [24], consider the following control protocol:

$$\begin{aligned} u_i(t) = -k_1(\textstyle\sum_{j=1}^{N} a_{ij}(x_i(t_k^i) - x_j(t_k^i)))^p - k_2(\sum_{j=1}^{N} a_{ij}(x_i(t_k^i) - x_j(t_k^i)))^q \\ -k_3(\textstyle\sum_{j=1}^{N} a_{ij}(x_i(t_k^i) - x_j(t_k^i))) \end{aligned} \tag{39}$$

Let $f(x_i(t), t) = 0.3x_i(t) + 0.5\cos(t)$, and the values of the parameters of the fixed-time control protocol be $p = 0.5,\ q = 1.5, k_1 = 0.5, k_2 = 0.6,\ k_3 = 1.5$,

$$T \leq T_{1\max} = \frac{1}{k_1 2^{\frac{p-1}{2}} \lambda_2^{\frac{p+1}{2}} (1-p)} + \frac{1}{k_3 2^{\frac{q-1}{2}} \lambda_2^{\frac{q+1}{2}} N^{\frac{1-q}{2}} (q-1)} \tag{40}$$

The theoretical estimates $T \leq T_{1\max} = 7.04$ *s* and the simulation results for the proposed non-linear control protocol are shown in Figure 4. Control inputs of the agents are shown in Figure 5.

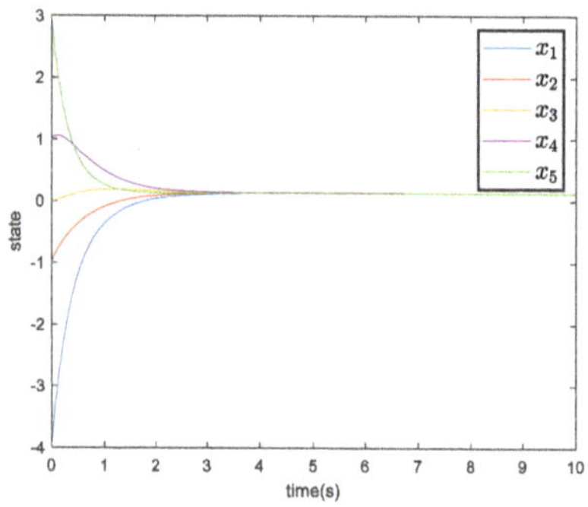

Figure 4. The states of the agents under the control protocol (39).

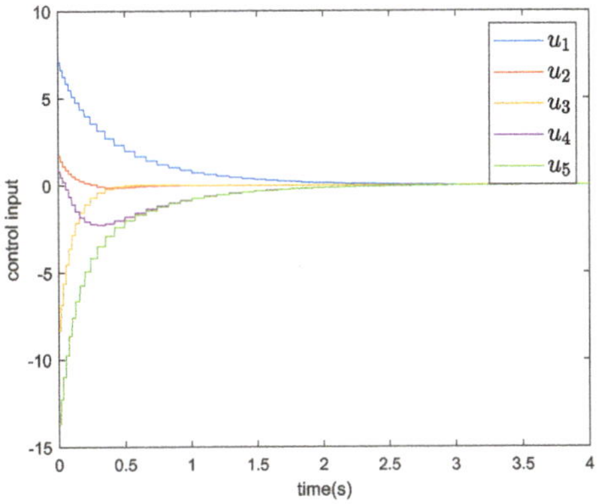

Figure 5. The control inputs of the agents under the control protocol (39).

The simulation results for the proposed non-linear control protocol (7) are presented in Figure 5. The values of the parameters of the fixed-time control protocol are $p = 0.5$, $q = 1.5$, $k_1 = 0.5$, $k_2 = 0.6$, and $k_3 = 1.5$; from the analysis of Theorem 1, the time to converge T satisfies that

$$T \leq T_{\max} = \frac{\pi\gamma}{\sqrt{\overline{\alpha}\overline{\beta}}} \tag{41}$$

The theoretical estimates $T \leq T_{1\max} = 1.52\ s$ and the simulation results for the proposed non-linear control protocol are shown in Figure 6. Control inputs of the agents are shown in Figure 7.

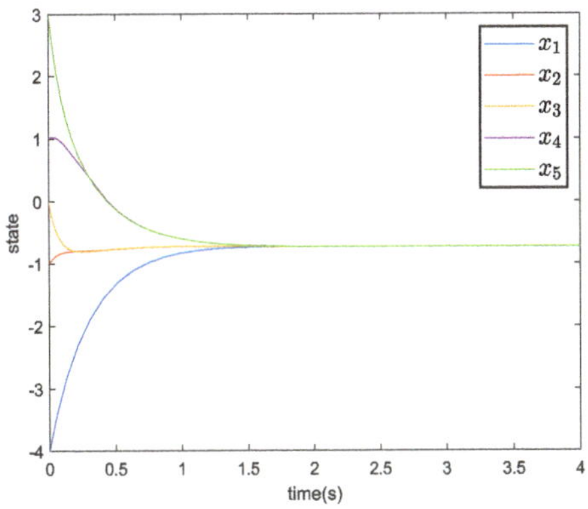

Figure 6. The states of the agents under the control protocol (7).

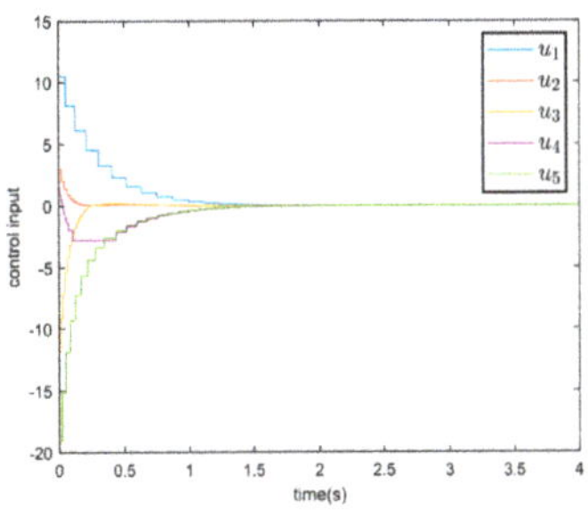

Figure 7. The control inputs of the agents under the control protocol (7).

A comparison of Figure 5 with Figure 7 shows that the event-triggered fixed-time consensus protocol (7), where the controller updates only at its event time, updates in Figure 7. Figure 5, where the controller achieves synchronous updates, has a higher number of controller updates compared to Figure 7. Figure 8 shows the event-triggered interval of the five agents in the systems under the control protocol proposed in this paper. The agents are triggered at their respective event times to update the control inputs under this scheme to reduce the resource consumption of the system and the number of updates to the system controller. The event-trigger interval under protocol (37) is shown in Figure 9.

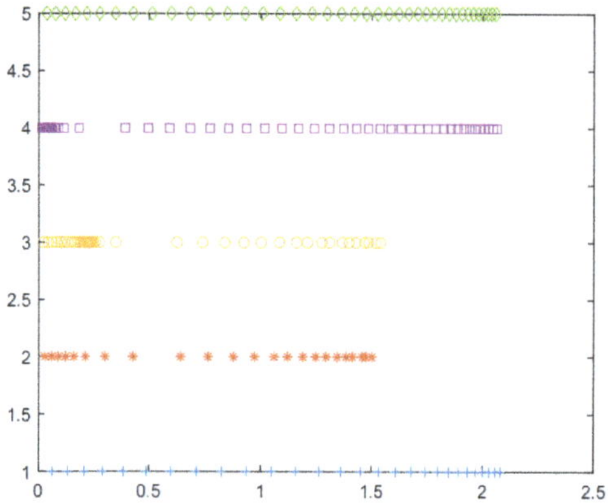

Figure 8. The event-triggered interval under the control protocol (7).

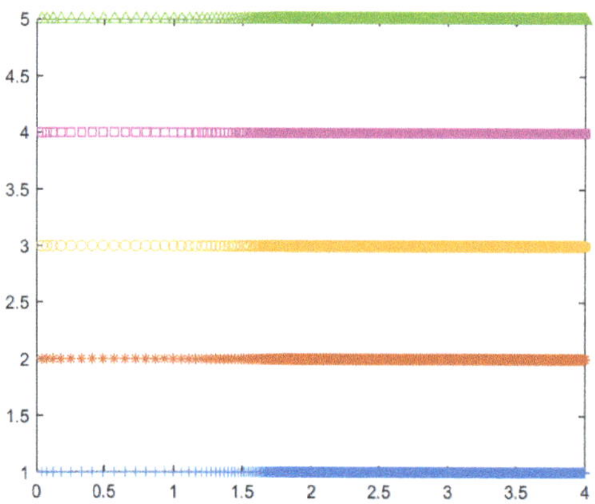

Figure 9. The event-triggered interval under the control protocol (39).

Comparing Figure 8 with Figure 9 shows that the event-triggered fixed-time consensus control protocol (7) can reduce the frequency of system controller updates and save the system's energy.

Figures 5 and 7–9 show that the event-triggered protocol reduces updates, and a numerical analysis of how significant this reduction is shown in Table 1. In short, from the results outlined above, we can determine that the simulation results show that the proposed control protocol has the advantages of both event-triggered and fixed-time convergence, the convergence time of the new control protocol is greatly reduced (about 1.5 s), and the update times are also greatly reduced (less than 50 times), which is consistent with the theoretical results.

Table 1. A summary table comparing the number of updates.

	Theoretical Convergence Time	Simulation Convergence Time
Figure 5—under control protocol (39)	$\leq$7.04 s	$\approx$3.30 s
Figure 7—under control protocol (7)	$\leq$1.52 s	$\approx$1.53 s
	Agent	the number of updates
Figure 8—under control protocol (7)	Agent 1	28
	Agent 2	23
	Agent 3	34
	Agent 4	51
	Agent 5	39
Figure 9—under control protocol (39)	Agent 1	number of iterations $\gg$ 51
	Agent 2	number of iterations $\gg$ 51
	Agent 3	number of iterations $\gg$ 51
	Agent 4	number of iterations $\gg$ 51
	Agent 5	number of iterations $\gg$ 51

5. Conclusions

For disturbed and non-linear dynamics, in this paper, the main contribution is the proposal of a fixed-time event-triggered consensus method protocol that can shorten the time to reach conformance and reduce the update times of the control protocol. Compared with the consensus protocol in Equation (39), the proposed protocol in this paper can reduce the frequency of system controller updates and obtain a more accurate estimate of the upper bound of the convergence time. Finally, examples are presented to show the effectiveness of the control protocol. It has a fast convergence time and does not need to control updates frequently. Therefore, this has potential applications in UAV formation, smart car collaboration, and factory smart robot collaboration. Furthermore, many existing AI models adopt progressive convergence and non-event triggering, so if the consistency control strategy of fixed-time event triggering can be applied to existing AI models, replacing the progressive convergence and non-event-triggering strategies would greatly improve AI performance.

However, this paper does not consider the problem of transmission delay between sensor nodes, the network attacks on nodes, or the problem of limited transmission. The transmission delay will cause the information interaction between each node and the neighbor node to be inappropriately timed. Failure to interact with real-time information can result in poor consistency performance. These questions are also the focus of follow-up research.

Author Contributions: Conceptualization, methodology, software, and writing—original draft preparation, Y.W. and T.W.; conceptualization, validation, formal analysis, investigation, writing—review and editing, supervision, project administration, and funding acquisition, Z.L. All authors have read and agreed to the published version of the manuscript.

Funding: This research was funded by the National Natural Science Foundation of China, Grant/Award Number: 61673310.

Data Availability Statement: All data generated or analyzed during this study are included in this article.

Conflicts of Interest: The authors declare no conflicts of interest.

References

1. Zhi, H.; Chen, L.; Li, C.; Guo, Y. Leader–Follower Affine Formation Control of Second-Order Nonlinear Uncertain Multi-Agent Systems. *IEEE Trans. Circuits Syst. II Express Briefs* **2021**, *68*, 3547–3551. [CrossRef]
2. Yu, J.; Dong, X.; Li, Q.; Lü, J.; Ren, Z. Adaptive Practical Optimal Time-Varying Formation Tracking Control for Disturbed High-Order Multi-Agent Systems. *IEEE Trans. Circuits Syst. I Regul. Pap.* **2022**, *69*, 2567–2578. [CrossRef]
3. Qin, J.; Ma, Q.; Yi, P.; Wang, L. Multi-Agent Interval Consensus with Flocking Dynamics. *IEEE Trans. Autom. Control* **2021**, *6*, 3965–3980.
4. Yazdani, S.; Su, H. A Fully Distributed Protocol for Flocking of Time-Varying Linear Systems With Dynamic Leader and External Disturbance. *IEEE Trans. Syst. Man Cybern. Syst.* **2022**, *52*, 1234–1242. [CrossRef]
5. Wang, L.; Xiao, F. Finite-time consensus problems for networks of dynamic agents. *IEEE Trans. Autom. Control* **2010**, *55*, 950–955. [CrossRef]
6. Zhou, J.; Wang, Q. Convergence speed in distributed consensus over dynamically switching random networks. *Automatica* **2009**, *45*, 1455–1461. [CrossRef]
7. Wang, Q.; Dong, X.; Yu, J.; Lu, J.; Ren, Z. Predefined Finite-Time Output Containment of Nonlinear Multi-Agent Systems With Leaders of Unknown Inputs. *IEEE Trans. Circuits Syst. I Regul. Pap.* **2021**, *68*, 3436–3448. [CrossRef]
8. Bu, X.; Zhu, P.; Hou, Z.; Liang, J. Finite-Time Consensus for Linear Multi-Agent Systems Using Data-Driven Terminal ILC. *IEEE Trans. Circuits Syst. II Express Briefs* **2020**, *67*, 2029–2033. [CrossRef]
9. Luo, Y.; Zhu, W.; Cao, J.; Rutkowski, L. Event-Triggered Finite-Time Guaranteed Cost H-Infinity Consensus for Nonlinear Uncertain Multi-Agent Systems. *IEEE Trans. Netw. Sci. Eng.* **2022**, *3*, 1527–1539. [CrossRef]
10. Polyakov, A. Nonlinear feedback design for fixed-time stabilization of Linear Control Systems. *IEEE Trans. Autom. Control* **2012**, *57*, 2106–2110. [CrossRef]
11. Parsegov, S.E.; Polyakov, A.E.; Scherbakov, P.S. Fixed-time consensus algorithm for multi-agent systems with integrator dynamics. *IFAC Proc.* **2013**, *27*, 110–115. [CrossRef]
12. Polyakov, A.; Efifimov, D.; Perruquetti, W. Finite-time and fixed-time stabilization: Implicit Lyapunov function approach. *Automatica* **2015**, *6*, 332–340. [CrossRef]
13. Hong, H.; Yu, W.; Wen, G.; Yu, X. Distributed Robust Fixed-Time Consensus for Nonlinear and Disturbed Multiagent Systems. *IEEE Trans. Syst. Man Cybern. Syst.* **2017**, *47*, 1464–1473. [CrossRef]
14. Zou, W.; Qian, K.; Xiang, Z. Fixed-Time Consensus for a Class of Heterogeneous Nonlinear Multiagent Systems. *IEEE Trans. Circuits Syst. II Express Briefs* **2019**, *67*, 1279–12838. [CrossRef]
15. You, X.; Hua, C.-C.; Li, K.; Jia, X. Fixed-Time Leader-Following Consensus for High-Order Time-Varying Nonlinear Multiagent Systems. *IEEE Trans. Autom. Control* **2020**, *65*, 5510–5516. [CrossRef]
16. Li, D.; Ge, S.S.; Lee, T.H. Fixed-Time-Synchronized Consensus Control of Multiagent Systems. *IEEE Trans. Control Netw. Syst.* **2021**, *8*, 89–98. [CrossRef]
17. Ni, J.; Tang, Y.; Shi, P. A New Fixed-Time Consensus Tracking Approach for Second-Order Multiagent Systems Under Directed Communication Topology. *IEEE Trans. Syst. Man Cybern. Syst.* **2021**, *51*, 2488–2500. [CrossRef]
18. Ni, J.; Shi, P. Adaptive Neural Network Fixed-Time Leader–Follower Consensus for Multiagent Systems with Constraints and Disturbances. *IEEE Trans. Cybern.* **2021**, *51*, 1835–1848. [CrossRef]
19. Wang, L.; Liu, X.; Cao, J.; Hu, X. Fixed-Time Containment Control for Nonlinear Multi-Agent Systems with External Disturbances. *IEEE Trans. Circuits Syst. II Express Briefs* **2022**, *69*, 459–463. [CrossRef]
20. Liu, J.; Zhang, Y.; Yu, Y.; Sun, C. Fixed-Time Event-Triggered Consensus for Nonlinear Multiagent Systems without Continuous Communications. *IEEE Trans. Syst. Man Cybern. Syst.* **2019**, *49*, 2221–2229. [CrossRef]
21. Liu, J.; Yu, Y.; Xu, Y.; Zhang, Y.; Sun, C. Fixed-Time Average Consensus of Nonlinear Delayed MASs Under Switching Topologies: An Event-Based Triggering Approach. *IEEE Trans. Syst. Man Cybern. Syst.* **2022**, *52*, 2721–2733. [CrossRef]
22. Zhang, Z.; Chen, S.; Zheng, Y. Cooperative Output Regulation for Linear Multiagent Systems via Distributed Fixed-Time Event-Triggered Control. *IEEE Trans. Neural Netw. Learn. Syst.* **2022**, *19*, 338–347. [CrossRef] [PubMed]
23. Jin, X.; Shi, Y.; Tang, Y.; Werner, H.; Kurths, J. Event-triggered Fixed-time Attitude Consensus with Fixed and Switching Topologies. *IEEE Trans. Autom. Control* **2021**, *67*, 4138–4145. [CrossRef]
24. Liu, J.; Yu, Y.; Wang, Q.; Sun, C. Fixed-time event-triggered consensus control for multi-agent systems with nonlinear uncertainties. *Neurocomputing* **2017**, *260*, 497–504. [CrossRef]

mathematics

MDPI

Article

Reinforcement Learning with Value Function Decomposition for Hierarchical Multi-Agent Consensus Control

Xiaoxia Zhu [1,2]

[1] School of Intelligent Manufacturing, Shanghai Zhongqiao Vocational and Technical University, Shanghai 201514, China; xiaoxiazhu@seu.edu.cn or xiaoxiazhu92@163.com
[2] School of Automation, Southeast University, Nanjing 210096, China

Abstract: A hierarchical consensus control algorithm based on value function decomposition is proposed for hierarchical multi-agent systems. To implement the consensus control algorithm, the reward function of the multi-agent systems can be decomposed, and two value functions can be obtained by analyzing the communication content and the corresponding control objective of each layer in the hierarchical multi-agent systems. Therefore, for each agent in the systems, a dual-critic network and a single-actor network structure are applied to realize the objective of each layer. In addition, the target network is introduced to prevent overfitting in the critic network and improve the stability of the online learning process. During the updating of network parameters, a soft updating mechanism and experience replay buffer are introduced to slow down the update rate of the network and improve the utilization rate of training data. The convergence and stability of the consensus control algorithm with the soft updating mechanism are analyzed theoretically. Finally, the correctness of the theoretical analysis and the effectiveness of the algorithm were verified by two experiments.

Keywords: reinforcement learning; value function decomposition; multi-agent; consensus

MSC: 93A16

1. Introduction

In recent years, due to the intense development of technology and the rapid improvement of data processing capabilities, many practical systems in the field of engineering have become increasingly complex. Therefore, the study of large and intricate systems has emerged as a prominent research focus. At present, the main research trend is to model complex network systems and divide them into multiple simple and identical subsystems [1]. The hierarchical multi-agent system is an architecture for organizing and managing multiple agents [2]. The agents of the systems can be divided into different layers, each of them having different responsibilities and control objectives. Typically, higher-layer agents are responsible for global policy making, while lower layer agents perform more specific tasks or operations. Therefore, the model of hierarchical multi-agent systems can be described by multiple subsystems. This holds significant practical relevance; that is, we can combine many of the same simple agents to form a large and complex system, or we can realize the complex tasks that cannot be completed by a single agent. In the control process of robotic swarms [3], hierarchical multi-agent systems can be employed to coordinate multiple robots to accomplish complex tasks. For example, in search-and-rescue missions [4], higher-layer agents can plan the search area, while lower layer agents carry out specific search actions. In intelligent traffic management [5], higher-layer agents can be responsible for overall traffic flow management, whereas lower layer agents control specific traffic signals or vehicles. In complex supply chain systems [6], higher-layer agents can perform global supply chain optimization, while lower layer agents handle specific tasks such as production, transportation, or inventory management. By decomposing complex tasks and allocating them to different layers of agents, hierarchical multi-agent systems can enhance the efficiency and flexibility of the system. Over the past decade, the analysis of hierarchical multi-agent systems and the development of distributed control schemes have become focal issues in the field of control and obtained numerous research outcomes [7].

For large-scale multi-agent systems, the model is usually described by a hierarchical structure because large-scale systems can usually be divided into some groups, and the number of agents in different groups and the communication topology may be different. The research on the consensus control of hierarchical multi-agent systems is the basis of all the problems mentioned above. Consensus control is critical for ensuring the stability and performance of the entire system. Williams et al. [8] outlined the concept of the hierarchy, which is used to describe relationships between subeformations, for example, "formations of formations". This concept could be valuable in fields like robotics, swarm intelligence, and military applications. The authors provide a strong theoretical foundation by discussing the dynamics of stability within hierarchical formations. This is important for ensuring that the structures they propose are robust and applicable in real-world scenarios. However, it may pose challenges in large-scale systems with unpredictable environmental factors. Smith et al. [9] studied the application of the hierarchical structure to the circular tracking of vehicle networks, and better results can be obtained compared with the traditional circular tracking algorithm; the convergence rate of vehicle groups to the center of mass is significantly increased. Hara et al. [10] proposed a general hierarchical multi-agent model with a fractal structure and studied the stability, global convergence, and low rank of the interconnection structure between different layers. Consensus in hierarchical systems with low-rank interconnections has practical implications in various fields, such as decentralized control systems and distributed optimization. However, like many theoretical papers, it may rely on certain simplifying assumptions that might not hold in real-world scenarios, potentially limiting the generalizability of the findings. Tsubakino and Hara et al. [11] propose a hierarchical characterization method based on eigenvectors for low-rank, interconnected, multi-agent, dynamical systems. This eigenvector-based approach could have practical implications in areas such as robotic coordination, decentralized decision-making, and networked systems, where efficient and stable intergroup communication is crucial. However, while low-rank interconnections aim to reduce complexity, eigenvector computations in large, dynamic systems may still be computationally expensive, especially in real-time applications where swift decisions are needed. Sang et al. [12] studied the group consensus problem based on hierarchical containment control in linear multi-agent systems. The influence of time delay in dynamic environments and systems on consensus is considered in this paper. A robust control strategy is designed to ensure that the system can achieve stable containment control and consensus in the presence of dynamic changes and communication delays. Wang et al. [13] proposed a new hierarchical control framework for distributed control of multi-agent systems. The framework divides the system into multiple levels, each responsible for a different control task. The framework is designed to improve the scalability and robustness of the system and simplify the control design of complex systems.

Hierarchical reinforcement learning is one of the effective methods of solving large-scale and multi-task reinforcement learning problems [14]. Through task decomposition, strategies are learned according to the goals of each subtask, and the learned strategies are combined to obtain a global strategy, which can effectively solve the dimensional disaster problem in large-scale systems. Makar et al. [15] propose a hierarchical reinforcement learning algorithm based on value function decomposition to solve the multi-agent discrete control problem. The combination of hierarchical structures with multi-agent reinforcement learning represents a novel framework. Hierarchical approaches allow for the decomposition of complex tasks into subtasks, making it easier to handle environments with multiple agents and large state-action spaces. However, implementing a hierarchical algorithm is often more challenging. Designing the appropriate hierarchy of tasks and subtasks and determining how agents should transition between them can require significant domain knowledge and expertise. To solve large-scale and complex continuous control problems, Yang et al. proposed the hierarchical Deep Deterministic Policy Gradient (DDPG) algorithm [16], which is a dual-critic network and multi-actor network structure. The critic network is divided into two layers. In the first layer, a Multi-DDPG algorithm structure is used to solve simple task problems, and the second layer focuses on solving complex combined tasks. At the same time, hierarchical reinforcement learning can also solve the problem of switching topology in the multi-agent systems. For example, Wang et al. [17] proposed a two-layer reinforcement learning framework to solve the output consensus problem of multi-agent systems under switching topology conditions. The first layer uses the Q-learning algorithm, wherein each agent selects the optimal action according to the current state, and the second layer selects the appropriate action strategy according to the current topology to ensure the output consensus of the entire system. This two-layer structure gives the control strategy strong adaptability and robustness and can be adjusted quickly when the topology changes.

The research concerning hierarchical consensus control mentioned above is largely based on the specific sequence of the tasks, which means that the performance of the algorithm convergence may be insufficient. However, in this paper, a hierarchical consensus control algorithm based on value function decomposition is proposed for hierarchical multi-agent systems. According to the communication content of each layer of the multi-agent systems and the corresponding control objectives, the reward function is decomposed, and two value functions are obtained. Specifically, for each agent in the system, the dual-critic network and single-actor network structure are designed. The updating of the dual-critic network is based on the decomposition of value functions in different tasks, and the two decomposed value functions have no logical order. It is also unnecessary to consider the training order of the double evaluation network during the training process. In addition, this paper introduces the target network to avoid overfitting in the critic network and improve the stability of the online learning process. In the updating of network parameters, a soft updating mechanism and experience replay buffer are introduced to slow down the update rate of the network and improve the utilization rate of training samples. The main contributions of this paper are as follows:

(1) For hierarchical multi-agent systems, a hierarchical consensus control algorithm based on value function decomposition is proposed. Firstly, the structure of the algorithm is that of a distributed actor–critic network, which ensures that the distributed characteristics of multi-agent systems are fully utilized. In addition, a value function decomposition algorithm is introduced to ensure the simultaneous optimization of the control objectives of agents at different levels, which gives the training process a certain robustness.
(2) The convergence and stability analysis of the consensus control algorithm with a soft update mechanism are proposed. It is proved that for each agent, the action value function estimated by the critic network can converge to the optimal value, the policy output from the actor network can converge to the corresponding optimal value, and the multi-agent system can be asymptotically stable.

In this paper, the implementation of the hierarchical consensus control algorithm based on value function decomposition is presented, and the convergence and stability of the algorithm are analyzed. Finally, the correctness of the theoretical analysis and the effectiveness of the algorithm were verified by two experiments. Multi-agent systems with and without leaders are both considered in the Section 5.

2. Preliminaries

2.1. Graph Theory

The communication of the leader–follower multi-agent system can be represented by a weighted directed graph $G(\mathcal{A}) = (V, E, \mathcal{A})$, which is composed of a set of N agents $V = \{v_1, v_2, \ldots, v_N\}$, a set of edges $E = \{e_{ij} = (v_i, v_j)\} \subset V \times V$, and a non-negative adjacency matrix $\mathcal{A} = [a_{ij}]$. $a_{ij} > 0$ if and only if $(v_i, v_j) \in E$, which means agent i and j can communicate with each other; otherwise, $a_{ij} = 0$. For $\forall i = 1, 2, \ldots, N$, $a_{ii} = 0$. The in-degree matrix $D = [d_{ij}]_{N \times N}$ is a diagonal matrix with $d_{ii} = \sum_{j \in \mathcal{N}_i} a_{ij}$, and the Laplacian matrix is defined as $L = D - \mathcal{A}$. The communication between the leader and followers is modeled by the diagonal matrix $\mathcal{B} = [b_{ii}]_{N \times N}$, and $b_{ii} > 0$ means there is a directed path between the leader and the ith follower; otherwise, $b_{ii} = 0$. If a digraph contains a directed spanning tree, it means there exists a directed path from the leader to any other follower.

2.2. Problem Formulation

Consider the hierarchical(two-layer) discrete multi-agent system [18]. The structure is shown in Figure 1. The system contains $N = p \times q$ agents:

$$x_i(k+1) = Ax_i(k) + Bu_i(k) \quad i = 1, 2, \ldots, N, \tag{1}$$

where $x_i(k) \in \mathbb{R}^n$ is the system state, and $u_i(k) \in \mathbb{R}^m$ is the control signal values. The system matrix parameters are $A \in \mathbb{R}^{n \times n}$ and $B \in \mathbb{R}^{n \times m}$. The number of agents is N, which is divided into q groups, and each group has p agents. Based on the graph theory mentioned above, the communication of p agents in the bottom $H2$ groups can be represented by the adjacency matrix $\mathcal{A}_1$ of dimensions $p \times p$. The communication between the q groups of the top layer $H1$ can be represented by the adjacency matrix $\mathcal{A}_2$ of dimensions $q \times q$. The Laplace matrices are $L_1 \in R^{p \times p}$ and $L_2 \in R^{q \times q}$, corresponding to the adjacent matrices $\mathcal{A}_1$and $\mathcal{A}_2$, respectively. The communication mode between groups and whether the agents in each group can receive inter-group information are crucial to the consensus of hierarchical multi-agent systems. In this paper, it is assumed that the agents in each group can receive information outside the group in the way of the topological structure $\mathcal{A}_2$. And the communication information between groups is fixed as the average value of all agents in each group, g_j [19]; that is, for each group of agents in the bottom layer, $g_j = \frac{1}{p} x_i(k), i \in p, j \in q$.

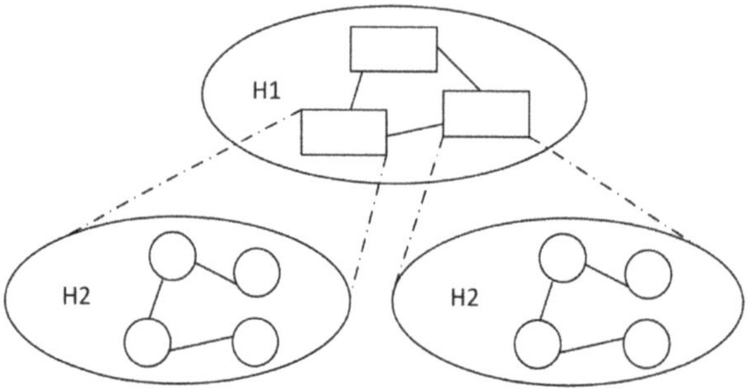

Figure 1. Hierarchical multi-agent systems. $H1$ is the top layer, and $H2$ is the bottom layer.

Assumption 1. *There is no time delay in intra-group communication and inter-group communication in hierarchical multi-agent systems. The number and topology of agents in each group are the same.*

In the two-layer discrete multi-agent systems, the agents in the same group are relatively concentrated. For example, the communication distance between robots or vehicles composed of communication nodes in the group is close, so the communication delay is small and can be ignored. The communication distance between groups is often very far because the communication line is long, the signal transmission capacity is limited, and the communication time delay of each group of agents can not be ignored. In order to reduce the difficulty of the algorithm, the problem of communication time delay is not considered in this paper.

In hierarchical multi-agent systems, the number and topology of agents within each group can indeed be the same, but this is not always necessary. If each group has the same number of agents, it simplifies the system design and interaction protocols. This uniformity makes coordination easier since each group can follow a similar communication and decision-making process. If each group shares the same topology, it typically means that the connections and interactions between agents are similar across groups. The specific number and topology of agents depend on the problem's requirements.

Definition 1. *The two-layer discrete multi-agent system (1) reaches hierarchical consensus, meaning that for any initial state, there is* $\forall i, j, \lim_{k\to\infty} \|x_i(k) - x_j(k)\| = 0$.

If the hierarchical multi-agent systems has a leader agent, it can be defined as follows:

$$x_0(k+1) = Ax_0(k), \tag{2}$$

where $x_0(k) \in \mathbb{R}^n$ is the reference signal value of multi-agent systems.

Definition 2. *The two-layer discrete multi-agent systems (1) and (2) can reach hierarchical consensus, meaning that for any initial state, there is* $\forall i, \lim_{k\to\infty} \|x_i(k) - x_0(k)\| = 0$.

Considering the communication characteristics of hierarchical multi-agent systems, each agent can obtain intra-group and inter-group information, so the local tracking error for agent i in each group is as follows:

$$e_i(k) = \sum_{j\in q}[a_{1,ij}(x_i(k) - x_j(k)) + b_{ii}(x_i(k) - x_0(k))] + \sum_{j\in p} a_{2,ij}(g_i(k) - g_j(k)). \tag{3}$$

According to the equation above, the global tracking errors are defined below; that is, $e(k) = [e_1^T(k), e_2^T(k), \ldots, e_N^T(k)] \in \mathbb{R}^{Nn}$:

$$e(k) = (I_q \otimes (L_1 + \mathcal{B}) \otimes I_n)(X(k) - X_0(k)) + \frac{1}{p}(L_2 \otimes \Delta_1 \otimes I_n)X(k), \tag{4}$$

where $\otimes$ is the Kronecker product, I_n is the n-dimensional unit matrix, I_q is the q-dimensional unit matrix, the state of the h group agent is $X_h(k) = [x^T_{(h-1)p+1}(k), x^T_{(h-1)p+2}(k), \ldots, x^T_{hm}(k)]^T$, the state vector for all agents is defined as $X(k) = [x_1^T(k), x_2^T(k), \ldots, x_N^T(k)]^T \in \mathbb{R}^{Nn}$, the state vector of the leader agent is $X_0(k) = [x_0^T(k), x_0^T(k), \ldots, x_0^T(k)]^T \in \mathbb{R}^{Nn}$, $\frac{1}{p}(L_2 \otimes \Delta_1 \otimes I_n)X(k)$ is the value of inter-group state error, and $\Delta_1 = [1, \ldots, 1]^T[1, \ldots, 1] \in \mathbb{R}^{p\times p}$ is the information interaction between each group structure. If the multi-agent systems has no leader, then both b_{ii} and $\mathcal{B}$ are zero.

According to (4), the global tracking errors can be defined as follows:

$$e(k) = e_1(k) + e_2(k), \tag{5}$$

where $e_1(k) = (I_q \otimes (L_1 + \mathcal{B}) \otimes I_n)(X(k) - X_0(k))$, $e_2(k) = \frac{1}{p}(L_2 \otimes \Delta_1 \otimes I_n)X(k)$.

For hierarchical multi-agent systems with a leader agent, in order to reach consensus, the global consensus error of the whole system is defined as follows:

$$\epsilon(k) = X(k) - X_0(k) + \frac{1}{p}(L_2 \otimes \Delta_1 \otimes I_n)X(k), \tag{6}$$

where $\epsilon_1(k) = X(k) - X_0(k)$, $\epsilon_2(k) = \frac{1}{p}(L_2 \otimes \Delta_1 \otimes I_n)X(k)$.

Lemma 1 ([20]). *If the matrix* $(L_1 + \mathcal{B})$ *is singular, then* $\|\epsilon_1(k)\| \le \|e_1(k)\|/\lambda_{min}(L_1 + \mathcal{B})$, *where* $\lambda_{min}(L_1 + \mathcal{B})$ *is the minimum singular value of matrix* $(L_1 + \mathcal{B})$.

Lemma 1 shows that if the global tracking error is small enough, then the global consensus error can be arbitrarily small. To ensure that the inequality in Lemma 1 holds, the following hypothesis is given:

Assumption 2. *The communication graphs $G(\mathcal{A}_1)$ and $G(\mathcal{A}_2)$ of the multi-agent systems are connected.*

2.3. Optimal Consensus Control Based on Value Function Decomposition

Considering the two-layer multi-agent systems, the performance index function of agent i in any group can be defined as follows:

$$\begin{aligned} J_i(e_i(k), \underline{u}_i(k)) = &\sum_{t=k}^{\infty} \gamma^{t-k} r_i(e_i(k), u_i(k)) \\ =& r_i(e_i(k), u_i(k)) + \gamma J_i(e_i(k+1), u_i(k+1)), \end{aligned} \tag{7}$$

where $\underline{u}_i(k) = (u_i(k), u_i(k+1), \ldots, u_i(\infty))$ is the control sequence composed of all the control quantities of agent i from the current moment, and $0 < \gamma < 1$ is the discount factor. The reward value of environment is $r_i(e_i(k), u_i(k))$.

The objective of the optimal consensus control is to minimize the performance index function (7). Therefore, according to Bellman's principle, the optimal value of the state value function $J_i^*(e_i(k))$ satisfies the following equation:

$$J_i^*(e_i(k)) = \min_{u_i(k)} \{r_i(e_i(k), u_i(k)) + \gamma J_i^*(e_i(k+1))\}. \tag{8}$$

The DTHJB equation for agent i can be expressed as follows:

$$J_i^*(e_i(k)) = r_i(e_i(k), u_i^*(k)) + \gamma J_i^*(e_i(k+1)). \tag{9}$$

Therefore, the DTHJB equation for hierarchical multi-agent systems can be expressed as follows:

$$J^*(e(k)) = R(e(k), u^*(k)) + \gamma J^*(e(k+1)). \tag{10}$$

The action value function Q and the optimal action value function Q^* are introduced. Then, the optimal action value function of agent i is as follows:

$$Q_i^*(e_i(k), u_i(k)) = r_i(e_i(k), u_i(k)) + \min_{u_i(k+1)} \gamma Q_i^*(e_i(k+1), u_i(k+1)). \tag{11}$$

By minimizing the action value function, the optimal control value u^* can be obtained directly as follows:

$$u_i^*(e_i(k)) = \arg\min_{u_i(k)} Q_i^*(e_i(k), u_i(k)). \tag{12}$$

For two-layer discrete multi-agent systems, a hierarchical reinforcement learning algorithm can be introduced to decompose the performance index function and action value function according to the control objectives of different layers. The following content gives the conditions that need to be satisfied by the decomposition of the action value function, so as to provide the basis for the implementation of the algorithm in the next section.

Theorem 1 ([21]). *Suppose the reward function r can be decomposed into M reward functions, namely, $r(e,u) = \sum_{k=1}^{M} r_k(e,u)$. Then, the performance index function and action value function can be decomposed into $J(e) = \sum_{k=1}^{M} J_k(e)$ and $Q(e,u) = \sum_{k=1}^{M} Q_k(e,u)$.*

Proof of Theorem 1. The performance index function $J(e)$ is expressed as follows:

$$J(e) = \sum_{l=0}^{\infty} \gamma^l r_{t+l+1}(e,u). \tag{13}$$

According to the decomposed form of the reward function in Theorem 1, the performance index function can be decomposed into the following:

$$\begin{aligned} J(e) &= \sum_{l=0}^{\infty} \gamma^l \sum_{k=1}^{M} r_{t+l+1,k}(e,u) \\ &= \sum_{k=1}^{M} \gamma^l \sum_{l=0}^{\infty} r_{t+l+1,k}(e,u) \\ &= \sum_{k=1}^{M} J_k(e). \end{aligned} \tag{14}$$

Similarly, the decomposition form of the action value function can be obtained:

$$Q(e,u) = \sum_{k=1}^{M} Q_k(e,u). \tag{15}$$

□

From Theorem 1, we can know that the action value function can be decomposed into several sub-functions for different objectives, and there is no sequential relationship between the objectives. How to optimize these sub-functions separately is also a problem to be studied below.

3. Proposed Algorithm

3.1. Consensus Algorithm Based on Action Value Function Decomposition

For hierarchical multi-agent systems which contain N agents, the overall consensus algorithm structure based on action value function decomposition in order to obtain the optimal control value (12) for each agent is shown in Figure 2. The reward function of agent i is decomposed into two rewards corresponding to the consensus control objective with the intra-group $r_{i,1}(e_i(k),u_i(k))$ and the inter-group $r_{i,2}(e_i(k),u_i(k))$. That is, the reward function is expressed as follows:

$$r_i(e_i(k),u_i(k)) = r_{i,1}(e_i(k),u_i(k)) + r_{i,2}(e_i(k),u_i(k)), \tag{16}$$

where $r_{i,1}(e_i(k),u_i(k)) = e_{i,1}^T(k)Q_i e_{i,1}(k) + u_i^T(k)P_i u_i(k)$, $r_{i,2}(e_i(k),u_i(k)) = e_{i,2}^T(k)Q_i e_{i,2}(k) + u_i^T(k)P_i u_i(k)$, $Q_i(k) > 0$, and $P_i(k) > 0$ are positive definite matrices. According to Theorem 1, the action value function of agent i can be decomposed into the following:

$$Q_i(e_i(k),u_i(k)) = Q_{i,1}(e_i(k),u_i(k)) + Q_{i,2}(e_i(k),u_i(k)). \tag{17}$$

Therefore, for agent i, the initial value of the action value function is defined as $Q_{i,1}^0(e_i(k),u_i(k))$ and $Q_{i,2}^0(e_i(k),u_i(k))$, and the corresponding control value is as follows:

$$u_i^0(e_i(k)) = \arg\min_{u_i(k)} Q_i^0(e_i(k),u_i(k)). \tag{18}$$

The objective of the hierarchical consensus control is to achieve consensus states of all agents; that is, for each agent i, the intra-group error $e_{i,1}$ and the inter-group error $e_{i,2}$ tend toward zero. Therefore, the action value function is decomposed and updated according to the reward function decomposition. Based on Formula (18), each sub-function of the action value function can be calculated as follows:

$$Q_{i,1}^1(e_i(k), u_i(k)) = r_{i,1}(e_i(k), u_i(k)) + \min_{u_i(k+1)} \gamma Q_{i,1}^0(e_i(k+1), u_i(k+1)),$$
$$Q_{i,2}^1(e_i(k), u_i(k)) = r_{i,2}(e_i(k), u_i(k)) + \min_{u_i(k+1)} \gamma Q_{i,2}^0(e_i(k+1), u_i(k+1)). \quad (19)$$

Similarly, the control value of the m-th iteration is as follows:

$$u_i^m(e_i(k)) = \arg\min_{u_i(k)} Q_i^m(e_i(k), u_i(k)). \quad (20)$$

The corresponding decomposed action value function is as follows:

$$Q_{i,1}^{m+1}(e_i(k), u_i(k)) = r_{i,1}(e_i(k), u_i(k)) + \min_{u_i(k+1)} \gamma Q_{i,1}^m(e_i(k+1), u_i(k+1)),$$
$$Q_{i,2}^{m+1}(e_i(k), u_i(k)) = r_{i,2}(e_i(k), u_i(k)) + \min_{u_i(k+1)} \gamma Q_{i,2}^m(e_i(k+1), u_i(k+1)), \quad (21)$$

where $m = 1, 2, \ldots$ indicates the number of iterations. The algorithm is based on Bellman's principle of optimality and adopts the iterative method to solve the problem. For each agent i, the optimal Q function and corresponding control value can be obtained by iteratively updating Formulas (20) and (21). The iterative algorithm presented in this paper can deal with the consensus control problem of hierarchical multi-agent systems with and without leaders. However, how to obtain optimal control and minimize the Q function is a problem that needs to be solved below.

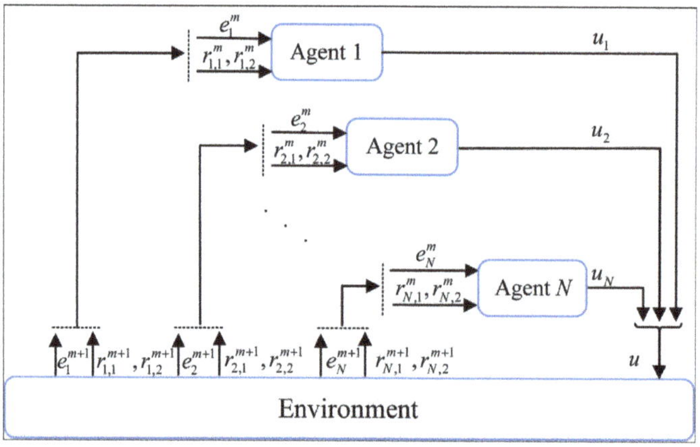

Figure 2. Schematic diagram of the reward function decomposition framework for two-layer multi-agent systems.

3.2. Algorithm Implementation

For each agent i, the hierarchical multi-agent consensus algorithm based on action value function decomposition is implemented by the dual-critic network and single-actor network. The corresponding offline training process is shown in Figure 3. The structure is similar to the hierarchical DDPG, but the difference is that the training of the dual-critic network has no primary and secondary order. The dual-critic network learns the control objectives of each layer and aggregates the learned knowledge into the same actor network to obtain the corresponding control value. For the actor network of each agent, the input is the local tracking error $e_i(k)$, and the output is the control policy $u_i(k)$, which can be obtained by minimizing the action value function $Q_i(e_i(k), u_i(k)) = Q_{i,1}(e_i(k), u_i(k)) + Q_{i,2}(e_i(k), u_i(k))$. According to Theorem 1, each agent has a dual-critic network θ^{C_1} and θ^{C_2}, output $\hat{Q}_{i,1}(e_i(k), u_i(k))$, and $\hat{Q}_{i,2}(e_i(k), u_i(k))$, which are used to evaluate the control effect of current control values on the intra-group consensus and inter-group consensus of hierarchical multi-agent systems. For the updating of the critic network, according to the Bellman equation, the temporal difference error is defined as follows:

$$\begin{aligned} E_{td,1} &= r_{i,1}(e_i(k), u_i(k)) + \gamma \min \hat{Q}_{i,1}(e_i(k+1), u_i(k)) - \hat{Q}_{i,1}(e_i(k), u_i(k)), \\ E_{td,2} &= r_{i,2}(e_i(k), u_i(k)) + \gamma \min \hat{Q}_{i,2}(e_i(k+1), u_i(k)) - \hat{Q}_{i,2}(e_i(k), u_i(k)), \end{aligned} \tag{22}$$

where $y_1(k) = r_{i,1}(e_i(k), u_i(k)) + \gamma \min \hat{Q}_{i,1}(e_i(k+1), u_i(k))$ and $y_2(k) = r_{i,2}(e_i(k), u_i(k)) + \gamma \min \hat{Q}_{i,2}(e_i(k+1), u_i(k))$ are the target value of the dual-critic network. The parameters of the critic network are updated according to the criterion of gradient descent by minimizing the square value of the temporal difference error.

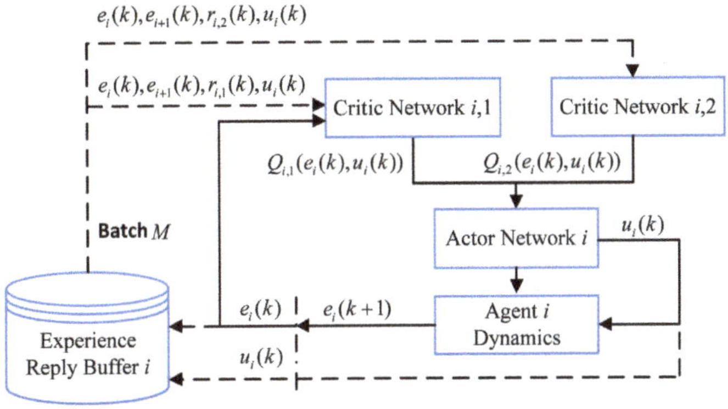

Figure 3. Training process and schematic diagram of the single agent. The solid black line indicates the signal flow, and the dashed line indicates the parameter adjustment path.

The traditional learning process of the critic network often tends to be unstable or even divergent. One reason is that the learning process of the critic network is based on the traditional Q-learning algorithm, which approximates the Q value by taking the maximum operation, which may suffer great performance loss. Meanwhile, the observation data used for the critic network training is limited and cannot fully reflect the dynamic characteristics of the system; therefore, the neural network may overfit, which leads to unstable training. Therefore, the target networks θ^{T_1} and θ^{T_2} and soft update mechanism are introduced into the training process of the critic network. The main idea is to slow down the parameter updating of the neural network to avoid overfitting of incomplete observation data so that the parameters of the target network gradually approximate the critic network. Thus, the accuracy of the output of the critic network is ensured. The setting of the initial weight of the target network is generally consistent with that of the critic network. The updating of the target networks θ^{T_1} and θ^{T_2} is as follows:

$$\begin{aligned} \hat{Q}_{i,1}(e_i(k), u_i(k)|\theta^{T_1}_{k+1}) &= (1-\tau)\hat{Q}_{i,1}(e_i(k), u_i(k)|\theta^{T_1}_{k}) + \tau\hat{Q}_{i,1}(e_i(k), u_i(k)|\theta^{C_1}_{k+1}), \\ \hat{Q}_{i,2}(e_i(k), u_i(k)|\theta^{T_2}_{k+1}) &= (1-\tau)\hat{Q}_{i,2}(e_i(k), u_i(k)|\theta^{T_2}_{k}) + \tau\hat{Q}_{i,2}(e_i(k), u_i(k)|\theta^{C_2}_{k+1}), \end{aligned} \tag{23}$$

where $\tau \in (0, 1]$ indicates the soft update rate, and when $\tau = 1$, the update process is the same as that of the traditional actor–critic network. The value of τ is generally small, which slows down the parameter updating of the target network. Accordingly, the temporal difference errors used to critic network updates are as follows:

$$\begin{aligned} E_{td,1} &= r_{i,1}(e_i(k), u_i(k)) + \gamma \min \hat{Q}_{i,1}(e_i(k+1), u_i|\theta_k^{T_1}) - \hat{Q}_{i,1}(e_i(k), u_i(k)|\theta_{k+1}^{C_1}), \\ E_{td,2} &= r_{i,2}(e_i(k), u_i(k)) + \gamma \min \hat{Q}_{i,2}(e_i(k+1), u_i|\theta_k^{T_1}) - \hat{Q}_{i,2}(e_i(k), u_i(k)|\theta_{k+1}^{C_2}). \end{aligned} \tag{24}$$

The hierarchical multi-agent consensus algorithm proposed in this paper based on action value function decomposition adopts an experience replay buffer and batch processing technology in the training process, which fully improves the utilization rate of historical data. Figure 3 shows the use of the experience replay buffer in the training process. The implementation of the hierarchical multi-agent consensus algorithm based on action value function decomposition is shown in Algorithm 1. For each agent i at the time step k, the data tuples $(e_i(k), u_i(k), r_{i,1}(k), r_{i,2}(k), e_i(k+1))$ are put into the experience replay buffer. Tuples $(e_i(k),\ u_i(k))$ are used as the input of the critic network by training the weights of the critic network which can output $Q_{i,1}(e_i(k), u_i(k))$ and $Q_{i,2}(e_i(k), u_i(k))$, and the objective of the critic network is to minimize a batch of temporal difference error, based on Formula (24). It is defined as follows:

$$\begin{aligned} TD_{i,1} &= \frac{1}{\mathcal{M}} \sum_n (E_{td,1}(n))^2, \\ TD_{i,2} &= \frac{1}{\mathcal{M}} \sum_n (E_{td,2}(n))^2, \end{aligned} \tag{25}$$

where $n = 1, \ldots, \mathcal{M}$. $\mathcal{M}$ is the number of tuples taken from the experience replay buffer.

Algorithm 1 Hierarchical consensus algorithm based on action value function decomposition

Initialization:
Randomly initialize the weights $\theta^{C_1}, \theta^{C_2}$ of the critic network $\hat{Q}_{i,1}, \hat{Q}_{i,2}$
Randomly initialize the weights $\theta^{T_1}, \theta^{T_2}$ of the target network
Randomly initialize the weights θ^{u_i} of theaction network u_i
Initialize the experience replay buffer $\mathcal{R}$ with the space $\mathcal{M}$
Learning process:
for Current training Episode $= 1, M$ **do**
  Initialize the exploration noise sequence
  Randomly initialize the system state
  Local tracking error $e_i(1)$ is obtained
  for Timestep k $= 1, T$ **do**
    Calculate control input $u_i(k)$ based on the noise
    Execute the control input $u_i(k)$ and observe the new state $r_{i,1}(k), r_{i,2}(k)$ and $e_i(k+1)$
    Store the data tuples $(e_i(k), u_i(k), r_{i,1}(k), r_{i,2}(k), e_i(k+1))$ into the experience replay buffer $\mathcal{R}$
    Sample the $\mathcal{M}$ training data from the experience replay buffer $\mathcal{R}$
    The weight parameters $\theta^{C_1}, \theta^{C_2}$ of the critic network are updated according to Formula (25)
    Update the weight parameters $\theta^{T_1}, \theta^{T_2}$ of the target network according to Formula (23)
    Update the weight parameters θ^{u_i} of the actor network according to (20)
  end for
end for

4. Theoretical Analysis

4.1. Convergence Analysis of the Proposed Algorithm

For agent i, the update mechanism (24) and (23) are simplified as follows:

$$\begin{aligned}\hat{Q}_i^C(e_i(k),u_i(k)) &= r_i(e_i(k),u_i(k)) + \gamma \min \hat{Q}_i^T(e_i(k+1),u_i),\\ \hat{Q}_i^T(e_i(k),u_i(k)) &= (1-\tau)\hat{Q}_i^T(e_i(k),u_i(k)) + \tau \hat{Q}_i^C(e_i(k),u_i(k)),\end{aligned} \tag{26}$$

where the critic network of agent i is $\hat{Q}_i^C(e_i(k),u_i(k)) = \hat{Q}_{i,1}^{C_1}(e_i(k),u_i(k)) + \hat{Q}_{i,2}^{C_1}(e_i(k),u_i(k))$, and the target network is $\hat{Q}_i^T(e_i(k),u_i(k)) = \hat{Q}_{i,1}^{T_1}(e_i(k),u_i(k)) + \hat{Q}_{i,2}^{T_1}(e_i(k),u_i(k))$. Considering the whole hierarchical multi-agent systems, and the control value is defined as $u(k) = [u_1(k),u_2(k),\ldots,u_N(k)]^T$, the overall optimization objective function is $Q(e(k),u(k)) = [Q_1(e_1(k),u_1(k))\ldots Q_N(e_N(k),u_N(k))]^T$. For simplicity of expression, we use u to represent $u(k)$, and Q represents $Q(e(k),u(k))$. When the layered multi-agent systems reach consensus, the optimal performance index is Q^* and the optimal control signal is u^*.

Theorem 2. *Let Q_1^0 and Q_2^0 represent the randomly initialized 2N critic networks, and each function is a bounded continuous function. Then, according to the action value function sequence Q_m generated by Formula (26) and the control sequence u_m generated by Formula (20), if the discount factor satisfies $\gamma \in (0,1)$, when the iteration number $m \to \infty$, there is $Q_m \to Q^*$ and $u_m \to u^*$.*

Proof of Theorem 2. For the layered multi-agent systems, the global tracking error is $e(k) = [e_1^T(k),e_2^T(k),\ldots,e_N^T(k)]^T$, and according to Formula (26), we introduce two operators S_q and T_q:

$$\begin{aligned}T_qQ(e,u) &= R(e,u) + \gamma \min_u Q(e',u'),\\ S_qQ(e,u) &= (1-\tau)Q(x,u) + \tau T_qQ(e,u),\end{aligned} \tag{27}$$

where $R(e,u) = [r_1(k),r_2(k),\ldots,r_N(k)]^T$. Based on the two mappings above, Formula (26) can be expressed as follows:

$$\begin{aligned}\hat{Q}_{k+1}^C(e,u) &= T_q\hat{Q}_k^T(e,u),\\ \hat{Q}_{k+1}^T(e,u) &= S_q\hat{Q}_k^T(e,u).\end{aligned} \tag{28}$$

First, the monotonicity of the operator T_q is proved; that is, let $f(e,u),g(e,u)$ be the estimates of two action-valued functions. For all (e,u), when $f(e,u) \ge g(e,u)$, then $T_qf(e,u) \ge T_qg(e,u)$. Let $u^* = \arg\min f(e,u)$, then

$$\begin{aligned}T_qf(e,u) &= R(e,u) + \gamma f(e,u^*)\\ &\ge R(e,u) + \gamma g(e,u^*)\\ &\ge R(e,u) + \gamma \min g(e,u)\\ &= T_qg(e,u),\end{aligned} \tag{29}$$

Therefore, it can be proved that the operator T_q is monotonic.

If the hierarchical multi-agent systems can reach consensus, the optimal value of Q^* must be the fixed point of mapping S_q; that is, $Q^* = S_qQ^*$. In order to prove that the mapping S_q has a unique fixed point, $\| \,.\, \|$ is simplified to represent $\| \,.\, \|_{sup}$, and two bounded continuous functions f and g are defined. Let $\boldsymbol{I}_N = [1,1,\ldots,1]^T$, then we can obtain $f \le g + \| f-g \|$:

$$\begin{aligned}S_qf &= (1-\tau)f + \tau T_qf\\ &\le (1-\tau)(g + \boldsymbol{I}_N \| f-g \|) + \tau T_q(g + \boldsymbol{I}_N \| f-g \|)\\ &= S_qg + (1-\tau+\tau\gamma)(\boldsymbol{I}_N \| f-g \|).\end{aligned} \tag{30}$$

Similarly, we can obtain the following formula:

$$S_q g - S_q f \leq (1 - \tau + \tau\gamma) \boldsymbol{I}_N \parallel g - f \parallel . \tag{31}$$

According to the Pareto optimality [22], we can obtain:

$$\parallel S_q f - S_q g \parallel \leq (1 - \tau + \tau\gamma) \parallel g - f \parallel . \tag{32}$$

Therefore, the above formula satisfies Banach's fixed point theorem [23], and the mapping S_q is a strictly compressed mapping with a unique fixed point. It is easy to verify that the optimal action value function Q^* is the fixed point of S_q, and therefore it must be unique.

Based on the above analysis, the following proves that when $m \to \infty$, there is $Q^m \to Q^*$:

$$\begin{aligned} \parallel Q_{m+1}^T - Q^* \parallel &= \parallel S_q Q_m^T - S_q Q^* \parallel \\ &\leq (1 - \tau + \tau\gamma) \parallel Q_m^T - Q^* \parallel \\ &= (1 - \tau + \tau\gamma) \parallel Q_m^T - Q_{m+1}^T + Q_{m+1}^T - Q^* \parallel \\ &\leq (1 - \tau + \tau\gamma) \parallel Q_m^T - Q_{m+1}^T \parallel \\ &+ (1 - \tau + \tau\gamma) \parallel Q_{m+1}^T - Q^* \parallel, \end{aligned} \tag{33}$$

Then, let $\delta = 1 - \tau + \tau\gamma$; the above formula can be written as follows:

$$\begin{aligned} \parallel Q_{m+1}^T - Q^* \parallel &\leq \frac{\delta}{1-\delta} \parallel Q_m^T - Q_{m+1}^T \parallel \\ &\leq \frac{\delta^{m+1}}{1-\delta} \parallel Q_1^T - Q_0^T \parallel, \end{aligned} \tag{34}$$

According to the analysis above, when $m \to \infty$, then $Q_m^T \to Q^*$. When the discount factor $\gamma \in (0,1)$, the performance index function Q_m and the control policy u_m can reach the optimal value. That is, $Q_m^C \to Q^*$, $Q_m^T \to Q^*$ and $u_m \to u^*$. □

4.2. Stability Analysis

Theorem 3. *Assuming that the Assumption 2 is true, the hierarchical multi-agent consensus algorithm based on action value function decomposition can make the global tracking error $e(k)$ of the multi-agent system (1) and (2) asymptotically stable, and the states of all agents can reach consensus.*

Proof of Theorem 3. The hierarchical multi-agent consensus algorithm is based on action value function decomposition, which considers the DTHJB equation of the multi-agent systems below:

$$J^*(e(k)) = R(e(k), u^*(k)) + \gamma J^*(e(k+1)), \tag{35}$$

Then, multiplying both sides by $\gamma^k \boldsymbol{I}_N^T$ gives the following:

$$\gamma^k \boldsymbol{I}_N^T J^*(e(k)) - \gamma^{k+1} \boldsymbol{I}_N^T J^*(e(k+1)) = \gamma^k \boldsymbol{I}_N^T R(e(k), u^*(k)). \tag{36}$$

In order to prove the stability of the system, the first difference of the Lyapunov function is defined as follows:

$$\Delta(\gamma^k \boldsymbol{I}_N^T J^*(e(k))) = \gamma^{k+1} \boldsymbol{I}_N^T J^*(e(k+1)) - \gamma^k \boldsymbol{I}_N^T J^*(e(k)). \tag{37}$$

Based on Formula (36), we can obtain the following:

$$\Delta(\gamma^k \boldsymbol{I}_N^T J^*(e(k))) = -\gamma^k \boldsymbol{I}_N^T R(e(k), u^*(k)) \leq 0. \tag{38}$$

Since the reward function R is the quadratic or absolute form of the global tracking error, there is $\Delta(\gamma^k \boldsymbol{I}_N^T J^*(e(k)) = 0$ if and only if $e(k) = 0$. Therefore, the global tracking error $e(k)$ of the multi-agent systems is asymptotically stable. The state of the entire multi-agent systems can reach consensus. □

5. Simulation

In this section, two simulation examples are used to verify the effectiveness of the proposed algorithm. For each agent, the dual-critic network, the actor network, and the target network all adopt the backpropagation three-layer neural network. The hidden layer of each agent contains 30 linear rectification units and is fully connected to the input layer. The output layer of each agent is a fully connected linear layer, and the weights of all networks are updated according to Algorithm 1. The Adaptive Moment Estimations (Adam) optimization method was used to update the weights. In order to ensure the implementation of the algorithm and the consensus control effect, hyperparameters of the neural network were employed and are given in Table 1. The capacity of the experience replay buffer was set to 50,000.

Table 1. Parameter settings in the experiment.

Parameter Name	Mumber
learning rate of critic network (l_c)	0.001
learning rate of action network (l_a)	0.001
discount factor (γ)	0.995
soft update rate (τ)	0.001
experience reply buffer ($\mathcal{R}$)	50,000
batch number ($\mathcal{M}$)	128
hidden layer nodes of ciric network (N_{ch})	30
hidden layer nodes of action network (N_{ah})	30

5.1. Multi-Agent Systems without Leader

Considering the topology structure of the multi-agent systems as Figure 4, the system contains 12 agents, which are divided into 3 groups, and each group has 4 agents. It can be seen from the figure that the topology structure of the agents in each group is a connected graph, and the dynamic performance of a single agent is defined as follows:

$$x_i(k+1) = Ax_i(k) + Bu_i(k), \tag{39}$$

where the system matrix is $A = \begin{bmatrix} 0.995 & 0.09983 \\ -0.09983 & 0.995 \end{bmatrix}$ and $B = \begin{bmatrix} 0.2 \\ 0.1 \end{bmatrix}$. The initial value of the system is randomly selected as $[-1, 1]$, and the safe value of the system state is set to ± 2.0. The reward function is decomposed according to the intra-group error and inter-group error, and Q is taken as the unit matrix, $R = 0.1$. To verify Theorem 2, we set $\gamma = 0.995$, and the offline training method was used, that is, the offline implementation of Algorithm 1. We set the soft update rate of the target network to $\tau = 0.001$ and used the experience replay buffer to maximize the use of historical data. The number of iterative steps in each episode during the training process was 500, and the total number of performed episodes was 300.

Figure 5 shows the control effect of the algorithm. In a randomly given initial state, the state of all agents can reach consensus after 200 time steps. Figure 6a,b show the convergence process of the intra-group error, and Figure 6c,d show the convergence process of the inter-group error. From all the simulation results, it can be seen that all the agents can reach the same state in 150 time steps.

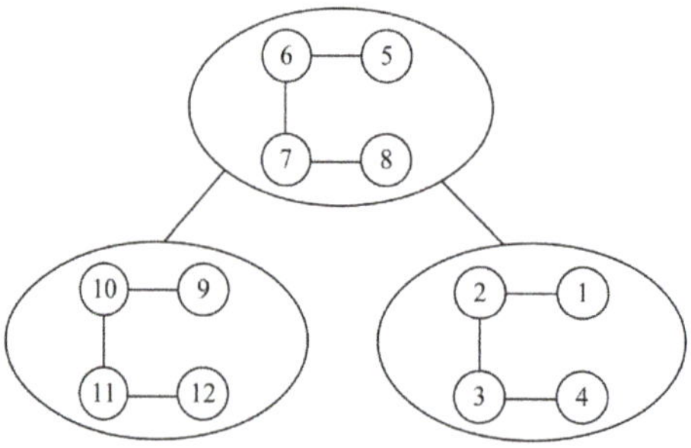

Figure 4. Hierarchical multi-agent system topology without leader.

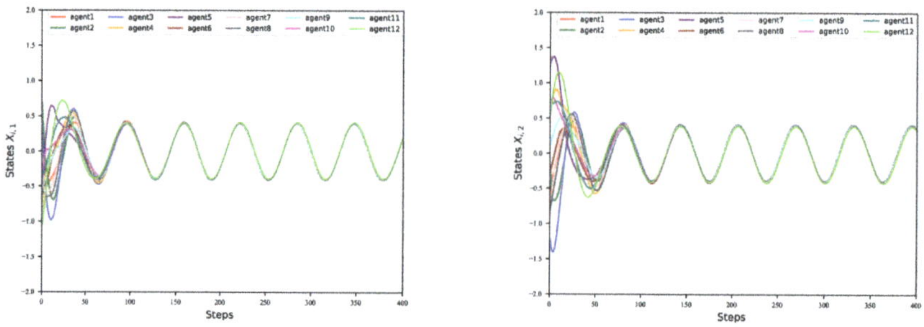

(a) (b)

Figure 5. State trajectories of the layered multi-agent systems in Experiment 1. For (**a**,**b**), the horizontal axis represents the simulation time steps, and the vertical axis represents the state of the system.

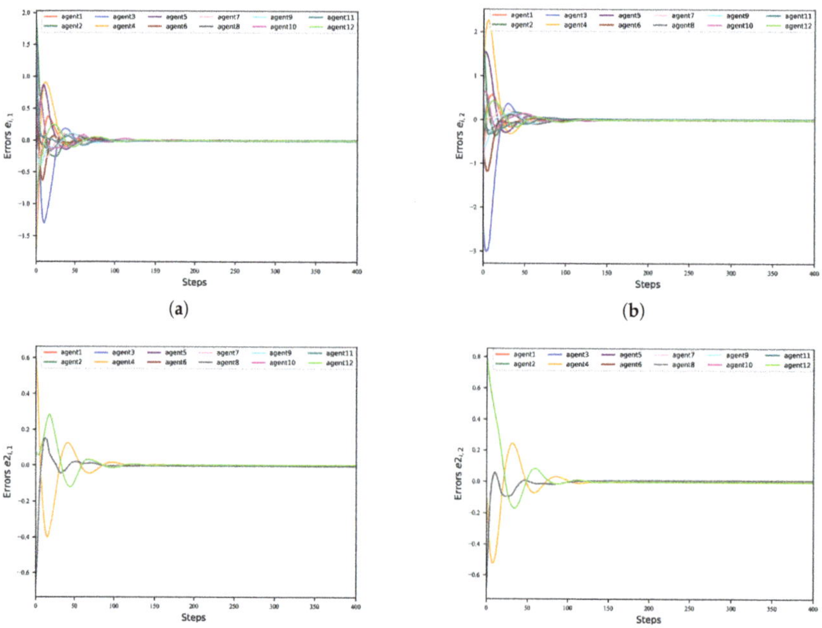

(a) (b)

(c) (d)

Figure 6. Local tracking error of the layered multi-agent systems in Experiment 1. The horizontal axis represents the simulation time steps, and the vertical axis represents the local tracking error value of the system.

5.2. Multi-Agent Systems with Leader

Consider the topology structure of multi-agent systems as Figure 7; the system contains 1 virtual leader agent and 12 follower agents. The 12 follower agents are divided into 3 groups, and each group has 4 agents. It can be seen from the figure that the topology graph of the agents in each group is connected. The multi-agent systems are defined as follows:

$$x_0(k+1) = Ax_0(k), \quad x_i(k+1) = Ax_i(k) + Bu_i(k), \tag{40}$$

where the system matrix is$A = \begin{bmatrix} 0.995 & 0.09983 \\ -0.09983 & 0.995 \end{bmatrix}$ and $B = \begin{bmatrix} 0.2 \\ 0.1 \end{bmatrix}$. The initial value of the system is randomly selected as $[-1, 1]$, and the safe value of the system state is set as ± 2.0. The reward function is decomposed according to intra-group error and inter-group error, and Q is taken as the unit matrix, $R = 0.1$. To verify Theorem 2, we set $\gamma = 1$ and used the offline training method, that is, the offline implementation of Algorithm 1, and set the soft update rate of the target network to $\tau = 0.001$. The number of iterative steps in each episode during the training process was 3000, and the total number of performed episodes was 100.

Figure 8 shows the control effect of the algorithm. In a random given initial state, all agents can follow the leader agent in 400 time steps. Figure 9a,b show the convergence process of the intra-group error, and Figure 9c,d show the convergence process of the inter-group error. It can be seen from all the simulation graphs that the consensus control algorithm based on action value function decomposition proposed in this paper can make all the agent states reach consensus.

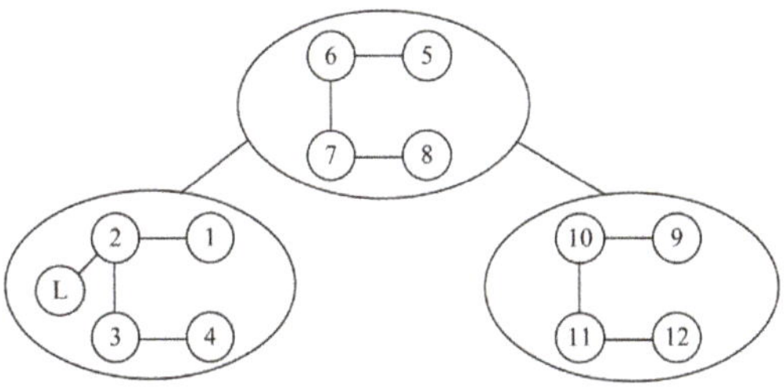

Figure 7. Hierarchical multi-agent system topology with leader.

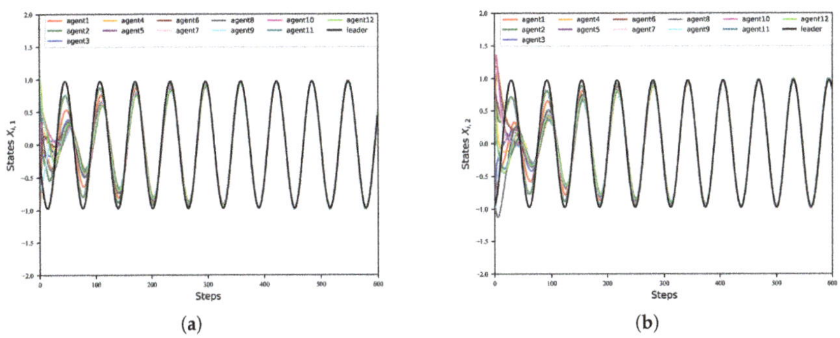

Figure 8. State trajectories of the layered multi-agent systems in Experiment 2. For (**a**,**b**), the horizontal axis represents the simulation time steps, and the vertical axis represents the state of the system.

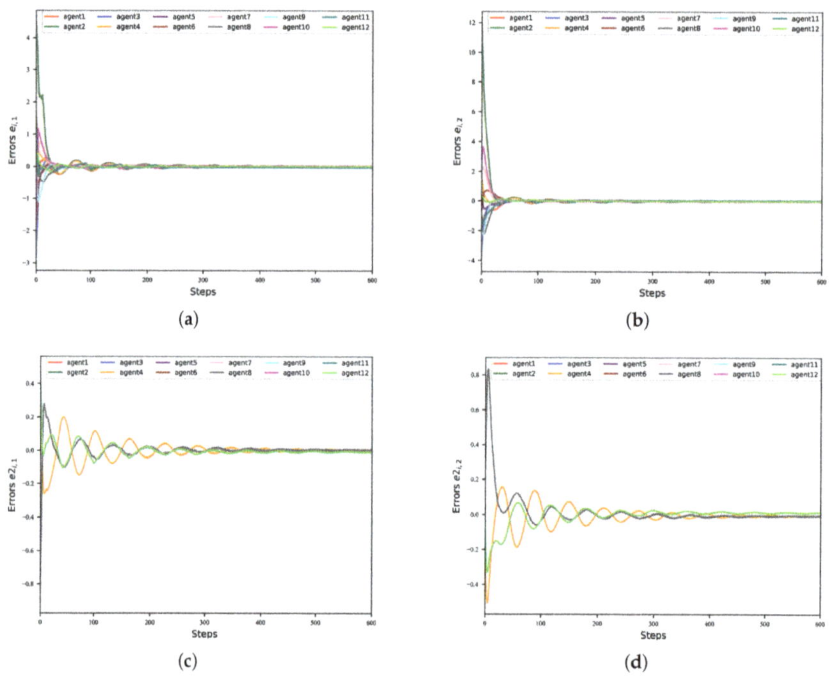

Figure 9. Local tracking error of the layered multi-agent systems in Experiment 2. The horizontal axis represents the simulation time steps, and the vertical axis represents the local tracking error value of the system.

6. Conclusions

In this paper, a hierarchical consensus control algorithm based on value function decomposition is proposed for hierarchical multi-agent systems. According to the communication content of each layer and the corresponding control objective of the multi-agent systems, the value function is decomposed according to the reward function of each layer. For each agent in the system, a dual-critic network and single-actor network are adopted. The target network is introduced to avoid overfitting in the critic network and improve the stability of the online learning process. The soft update mechanism and experience reply buffer are introduced in the network parameter update process to improve the utilization rate of training samples. In this paper, the convergence and stability of consensus control algorithm with a soft update mechanism are analyzed theoretically. Finally, the correctness of the theoretical analysis and the effectiveness of the algorithm were verified by two experiments. The value function decomposition method in this paper is used for hierarchical consensus control, but the multi-agent systems studied are homogeneous, and for heterogeneous multi-agent systems, achieving consensus control with this undifferentiated value decomposition method is of great research value. At the same time, in this paper, it is assumed that there is no time delay during the information interaction between the groups of agents, and communication delay often exists in actual systems. Therefore, the design of an effective hierarchical algorithm for multi-agent systems with communication delay must also be urgently studied.

Funding: This research was funded by Research on Intelligent Manufacturing Process Control Method based on Reinforcement Learning of Shanghai Zhongqiao Vocational and Technical University grant number ZQZR202419.

Data Availability Statement: All data generated or analyzed during this study are included in this article.

Conflicts of Interest: The author declares no conflicts of interest.

Abbreviations

The following abbreviations are used in this manuscript:

DDPG	Deep Deterministic Policy Gradient
Adam	Adaptive Moment Estimations

References

1. Hou, J.; Zheng, R. Hierarchical consensus problem via group information exchange. *IEEE Trans. Cybern.* **2018**, *49*, 2355–2361. [CrossRef]
2. Cheng, C.; Yang, B.; Xiao, Q. Hierarchical Coordinated Predictive Control of Multiagent Systems for Process Industries. *Appl. Sci.* **2024**, *14*, 6025. [CrossRef]
3. Albani, D.; Hönig, W.; Nardi, D.; Ayanian, N.; Trianni, V. Hierarchical task assignment and path finding with limited communication for robot swarms. *Appl. Sci.* **2021**, *11*, 3115. [CrossRef]
4. Yang, T.; Jiang, Z.; Dong, J.; Feng, H.; Yang, C. Multi agents to search and rescue based on group intelligent algorithm and edge computing. In Proceedings of the 2018 IEEE International Conference on Internet of Things (iThings) and IEEE Green Computing and Communications (GreenCom) and IEEE Cyber, Physical and Social Computing (CPSCom) and IEEE Smart Data (SmartData), Halifax, NS, Canada, 30 July–3 August 2018, pp. 389–394.
5. Li, Z.; Al Hassan, R.; Shahidehpour, M.; Bahramirad, S.; Khodaei, A. A hierarchical framework for intelligent traffic management in smart cities. *IEEE Trans. Smart Grid* **2017**, *10*, 691–701. [CrossRef]
6. Long, Q.; Zhang, W. An integrated framework for agent based inventory–production–transportation modeling and distributed simulation of supply chains. *Inf. Sci.* **2014**, *277*, 567–581. [CrossRef]
7. Zhou, H.; Li, W.; Shi, J. Hierarchically Distributed Charge Control of Plug-In Hybrid Electric Vehicles in a Future Smart Grid. *Energies* **2024**, *17*, 2412. [CrossRef]
8. Williams, A.; Glavaski, S.; Samad, T. Formations of formations: Hierarchy and stability. In Proceedings of the 2004 American Control Conference, Boston, MA, USA, 30 June–2 July 2004; Volum 4, pp. 2992–2997.
9. Smith, S.L.; Broucke, M.E.; Francis, B.A. A hierarchical cyclic pursuit scheme for vehicle networks. *Automatica* **2005**, *41*, 1045–1053. [CrossRef]
10. Hara, S.; Shimizu, H.; Kim, T.H. Consensus in hierarchical multi-agent dynamical systems with low-rank interconnections: Analysis of stability and convergence rates. In Proceedings of the 2009 American Control Conference, St. Louis, MO, USA, 10–12 June 2009; pp. 5192–5197.
11. Tsubakino, D.; Hara, S. Eigenvector-based intergroup connection of low rank for hierarchical multi-agent dynamical systems. *Syst. Control Lett.* **2012**, *61*, 354–361. [CrossRef]
12. Sang, J.; Ma, D.; Zhou, Y. Group-consensus of hierarchical containment control for linear multi-agent systems. *IEEE/CAA J. Autom. Sin.* **2023**, *10*, 1462–1474. [CrossRef]
13. Wang, X.; Xu, Y.; Cao, Y.; Li, S. A hierarchical design framework for distributed control of multi-agent systems. *Automatica* **2024**, *160*, 111402. [CrossRef]
14. Pateria, S.; Subagdja, B.; Tan, A.h.; Quek, C. Hierarchical reinforcement learning: A comprehensive survey. *ACM Comput. Surv. (CSUR)* **2021**, *54*, 1–35. [CrossRef]
15. Makar, R.; Mahadevan, S.; Ghavamzadeh, M. Hierarchical multi-agent reinforcement learning. In Proceedings of the Fifth International Conference on Autonomous Agents, Montreal, QC, Canada, 28 May–1 June 2001; pp. 246–253.
16. Yang, Z.; Merrick, K.; Jin, L.; Abbass, H.A. Hierarchical deep reinforcement learning for continuous action control. *IEEE Trans. Neural Netw. Learn. Syst.* **2018**, *29*, 5174–5184. [CrossRef] [PubMed]
17. Wang, Z.; Liu, Y.; Zhang, H. Two-Layer Reinforcement Learning for Output Consensus of Multiagent Systems Under Switching Topology. *IEEE Trans. Cybern.* **2024**, *54*, 5463–5472. [CrossRef] [PubMed]
18. Duan, Z.; Zhai, G.; Xiang, Z. State consensus for hierarchical multi-agent dynamical systems with inter-layer communication time delay. *J. Frankl. Inst.* **2015**, *352*, 1235–1249. [CrossRef]
19. Lin, Z.; Hou, J.; Yan, G.; Yu, C.B. Reach almost sure consensus with only group information. *Automatica* **2015**, *52*, 283–289. [CrossRef]
20. Abouheaf, M.I.; Lewis, F.L.; Vamvoudakis, K.G.; Haesaert, S.; Babuska, R. Multi-agent discrete-time graphical games and reinforcement learning solutions. *Automatica* **2014**, *50*, 3038–3053. [CrossRef]

21. Van Seijen, H.; Fatemi, M.; Romoff, J.; Laroche, R.; Barnes, T.; Tsang, J. Hybrid reward architecture for reinforcement learning. In Proceedings of the Advances in Neural Information Processing Systems, Long Beach, CA, USA, 4–9 December 2017.
22. Lopez Mejia, V.G.; Lewis, F.L. Dynamic Multiobjective Control for Continuous-time Systems using Reinforcement Learning. *IEEE Trans. Autom. Control* **2019**, *64*, 2869–2874. [CrossRef]
23. Ciarlet, P.G. *Linear and Nonlinear Functional Analysis with Applications*; Society for Industrial and Applied Mathematics: Philadelphia, PA, USA, 2013.

mathematics

Article

Adaptive Constraint Relaxation-Based Evolutionary Algorithm for Constrained Multi-Objective Optimization

Junming Chen [1,2,†], Kai Zhang [2,†], Hui Zeng [3], Jin Yan [4], Jin Dai [5,*] and Zhidong Dai [1,*]

1 School of Art and Design, Guangzhou University, Guangzhou 510006, China
2 Faculty of Humanities and Arts, Macau University of Science and Technology, Macau 999078, China
3 School of Design, Jiangnan University, Wuxi 214122, China
4 School of Computer Science and Engineering, Macau University of Science and Technology, Macau 999078, China
5 Graduate School of International Studies, Yonsei University, Seoul 03722, Republic of Korea
* Correspondence: 18010415@muc.edu.cn (J.D.); daizhidong@gzhu.edu.cn (Z.D.)
† These authors contributed equally to this work.

Abstract: The key problem to solving constrained multi-objective optimization problems (CMOPs) is how to achieve a balance between objectives and constraints. Unfortunately, most existing methods for CMOPs still cannot achieve the above balance. To this end, this paper proposes an adaptive constraint relaxation-based evolutionary algorithm (ACREA) for CMOPs. ACREA adaptively relaxes the constraints according to the iteration information of population, whose purpose is to induce infeasible solutions to transform into feasible ones and thus improve the ability to explore the unknown regions. Completely ignoring constraints can cause the population to waste significant resources searching for infeasible solutions, while excessively satisfying constraints can trap the population in local optima. Therefore, balancing constraints and objectives is a crucial approach to improving algorithm performance. By appropriately relaxing the constraints, it induces infeasible solutions to be transformed into feasible ones, thus obtaining more information from infeasible solutions. At the same time, it also establishes an archive for the storage and update of solutions. In the archive update process, a diversity-based ranking is proposed to improve the convergence speed of the algorithm. In the selection process of the mating pool, common density selection metrics are incorporated to enable the algorithm to obtain higher-quality solutions. The experimental results show that the proposed ACREA algorithm not only achieved the best Inverse Generation Distance (IGD) value in 54.6% of the 44 benchmark test problems and the best Hyper Volume (HV) value in 50% of them, but also obtained the best results in seven out of nine real-world problems. Clearly, CP-TSEA outperforms its competitors.

Keywords: adaptive relaxation; archive; mating pool; diversity-based ranking; constrained multi-objective optimization

MSC: 90C29; 68W50; 90C56

1. Introduction

Constrained multi-objective optimization problems (CMOPs) [1,2] refer to the optimization of multiple conflicting objective functions under constraints. In real life, constrained multi-objective optimization problems (CMOPs) manifest in many aspects, for example, as water resource management [3], robot manufacturing [4], and ICMES operation optimization [5]. The mathematical definition of a CMOP is as follows:

$$\begin{aligned}&\text{Minimize } F(x) = (f_1(x), \cdots, f_m(x))\\&\text{Subject to } g_i(x) \le 0, i = 1, \cdots, p\\&\qquad h_j(x) = 0, j = p+1, \cdots, q\\&\qquad x \in \Omega\end{aligned} \tag{1}$$

where $F(x)$ denotes a objective vector including m conflicting objective functions, $g_i(x)$ represents the ith inequality constraint, and $h_j(x)$ represents the j-th equality constraints. p represents the number of inequality constraints, and $q - p$ represents the number of equality constraints. For a CMOP, the constraint violation degree on the jth constrinat of solution x is caluculated by

$$CV_j(x) = \begin{cases} \max(0, g_j(x)), & j = 1, \cdots, p \\ \max(0, |h_j(x)| - \delta), & j = p+1, \cdots, q \end{cases} \tag{2}$$

where δ is a small positive tolerance parameter set as 10^{-6}. Based on (2), the total constraint violation degree of solution x is caluculated as follows:

$$CV(x) = \sum_{j=1}^{q} CV_j(x) \tag{3}$$

when $CV(x) = 0$, it indicates that solution x is feasible. On the contrary, solution x is a infeasible solution.

At present, most researchers are focused on constrained multi-objective optimization problems, aiming to balance the constraints and objectives.

The unconstrained Pareto idea is to approximate the constrained Pareto front (CPF) [6] as the unconstrained Pareto front (UPF) [7]. This approach makes it difficult to obtain highly feasible solutions and indirectly reduces the convergence of the algorithm. Therefore, it is essential not to consider constraints in isolation but to maintain a balance between objectives and constraints. Due to the population-based search characteristics of constrained multi-objective evolutionary algorithms (CMOEAs) [8], they have significant advantages in solving constrained multi-objective optimization (CMOP). However, CMOEAs often do not achieve the desired results when dealing with discrete and large infeasible regions. When addressing these issues, most researchers lack the utilization of information from infeasible solutions, causing the algorithms to become trapped in local optima. Therefore, strengthening the mining of infeasible solution information is the most urgent means at the current stage.

To further expand the algorithm's exploratory capabilities, researchers are dedicated to developing constraint-handling techniques (CHTs) [9]. At present, the methods for handling constraints mainly include constraint domination principle (CDP) [10], penalty functions, random ordering, and hybrid methods. The aforementioned methods have significant advantages in handling constrained single-objective optimization problems [11]. However, they often do not achieve the expected results when facing complex constrained multi-objective optimization problems (CMOPs). To address this issue and make full use of infeasible information, researchers have proposed dual-population-based methods [12–15]. The framework of dual population [13] aims to utilize information from infeasible solutions. To be specific, one population operating under unconstrained or relaxed constraints incorporates infeasible solutions into the candidate solution set, thus enhancing the population's exploratory capabilities. On the contrary, the other population considers constraints to increase the algorithm's convergence speed, prompting the population to obtain the complete Pareto front (PF). Although dual-population [16] algorithms have achieved promising results, most CMOEAs fail to promptly share information, the stagnation in population migration information. Wang et al. [17]. proposed an interaction method based on transfer information, which enhances the algorithm library and increases the feasibility of algorithms by solving the transfer probability of similar problems. However, it lacks the identification of transfer information.

For such issues, some researchers have proposed an archive mechanism [15] that updates throughout the algorithm's evolution, preserving the highest-quality solutions to drive the population towards convergence on the CPF. However, updating the archive involves identifying a large number of solutions, which consumes a lot of algorithm resources and greatly deteriorates the algorithm performance.

Faced with the aforementioned issues, this paper proposes an adaptive constraint relaxation based evolutionary algorithm (ACREA) for CMOPs. The main contributions of this paper are as follows:

(1) A novel archiving mechanism is designed, utilizing the constraint dominance principle (CDP) to filter and mine information on promising solutions, encouraging the population to explore more unknown areas. Additionally, as the algorithm evolves, the archive is updated based on diversity ranking.
(2) An adaptive relaxation mechanism is designed to fully utilize information from infeasible solutions, facilitating the population's ability to cross large and narrow infeasible regions in order to obtain a complete feasible area and prevent it from becoming trapped in local optima. This mechanism adaptively adjusts based on feedback from the proportion of feasible solutions, optimizing the search strategy to acquire more potentially valuable feasible solutions.
(3) When selecting parents, a strict domination principle is proposed to ensure the feasibility of the algorithm, prompting the population to obtain higher-quality solutions, enhancing the diversity and convergence of the population.
(4) In order to verify the effectiveness of the proposed ACREA algorithm, we compare the proposed ACREA algorithm with seven state-of-the-art algorithms on 44 test problems and 9 real-world problems. The experimental results show that the proposed algorithm (ACREA) significantly outperforms the competitors.

The remaining work in this paper is organized as follows: Section 2 introduces related work and motivations, Section 3 elaborates on the algorithm's principles, Section 4 conducts experimental research, and Section 5 provides a summary and outlook.

2. Related Work and Motivation

2.1. Related Work

In current CMOEAs, most researchers maintain a balance between objectives and constraints by improving various constraint handling techniques. These can generally be divided into the following four categories.

2.1.1. Penalty Function-Based CMOEA

These algorithms primarily use penalty factors to control the balance between objectives and constraints. Penalty factors can generally be classified into static [18] and dynamic [19] categories. Static penalty factors remain constant throughout the algorithm's evolution process. However, determining an appropriate penalty factor throughout the algorithm's entire process is extremely challenging because the penalty factor is not only influenced by the designed algorithm but also heavily dependent on different test problems. In contrast, dynamic penalty factors avoid this drawback. Researchers set up adaptive adjustment of penalty factors based on different penalty criteria. However, when setting up adaptive adjustment of penalty factors [20], the defined change rules greatly restrict the algorithm's performance. It is precisely because of these limitations that the emergence of self-adaptive penalty (SP) functions [21] occurred, where penalty factors adaptively change based on feedback information during the evolutionary process.

2.1.2. CHT-Based CMOEA

Deb et al. [22] proposed a method called constraint dominance principle (CDP) to handle complex CMOPs. The core idea of CDP is the preferential selection, where feasible solutions always dominate infeasible solutions. Fan et al. [23] proposed an angle-based CDP, which incorporates angle information between population solutions into CDP to adjust the dominance relationship of solutions. For example, when two infeasible solutions exceed a specified threshold, they are non-dominated. Ma et al. [24] proposed a novel fitness function that weights the constraint dominance principle (CDP) and Pareto dominance ranking. Takahama et al. [25] proposed a concept of ε constraint relaxation, where the ε constraint values change adaptively based on their own specified rules. Fan et al. [26] dynamically adjusted the ε level based on changes in the population's feasibility ratio, integrating the proposed ε constraint handling mechanism with MOEA/D to solve CMOPs. Peng et al. [27] set corresponding weights in the feasible and infeasible regions, respectively, prompting the algorithm to explore more of the objective space. Adel Younis et al. [28] explored promising regions using adaptive surrogate models to uncover more feasible domains, prompting the population to find a set of optimal solutions. Li et al. [14] proposed a dual-archive evolutionary algorithm called C-TAEA. One archive enhances the convergence of the population to obtain a complete PF, while the other archive only considers objectives, prompting the algorithm to obtain more information about solutions.

2.1.3. Multi-Stage Based CMOEA

Liu et al. [29] designed a novel two-stage framework. In the first stage, they transformed the constrained multi-objective problem into a constrained single-objective problem using weight vectors. In the second stage, they adopted the CMOEA/D [30] strategy to obtain a high-quality solution set. He et al. [31] proposed a parent crossover selection strategy to generate excellent offspring and improve the convergence speed of the population. Liu et al. [15] proposed a bi-directional cooperative evolution algorithm called BiCo, which utilizes feasible edges and infeasible edges to bound the boundaries of the feasible region. Ming et al. [13] proposed a multi-population multi-stage framework concept called CMOEMT. Zhou et al. [32] proposed a three-indicator evolutionary framework to balance convergence, diversity, and feasibility.

2.1.4. Based on Archive

Ming et al. [33] proposed a single-population archiving mechanism called C-TSEA. This algorithm stores the solutions of the Pareto front (PF) in an archive, which is continuously updated to encourage the population to obtain a set of evenly distributed high-quality solutions. Li et al. [34] proposed a dual-archived weakly cooperative evolutionary algorithm named CMOEA-TWC. This algorithm uses two archives: the driving archive and the ordinary archive. The driving archive only considers objectives, enhancing the algorithm's exploration ability and prompting the population to obtain a complete PF, while the ordinary archive considers both objectives and constraints to ensure the feasibility of the algorithm. The archive plays an irreplaceable role in the evolutionary process of the algorithm, not only identifying regional solutions but also continuously updating and preserving them to enhance the population's search capability. Therefore, selecting the archive to assist in population evolution is the most evident choice.

Based on the above discussion, we summarize the existing advantages and disadvantages of representative algorithms in Table 1. It is clear from the table that simultaneously improving both the diversity and convergence of algorithms is quite challenging. For example, CMOEA/D and CTAEA tend to favor diversity, which results in slower convergence, while the non-dominance principle of NSGA-II and the dynamic adaptive strategy of POCEA favor convergence, leading to poorer diversity. Therefore, to improve the overall performance of the algorithm, it is essential to overcome the challenges of balancing convergence and diversity.

Table 1. Summary of existing CMOEA techniques.

Algorithm	Key Feature	Strengths	Weaknesses
CMOEA/D [30]	Decomposition strategy	Good diversity	Slow convergence speed
NSGA-II [22]	Fast non-dominated sorting	Good convergence	Poor diversity in high-dimensional problems
ToP [29]	DE operator operation	High adaptability	Large computational workload
C-TAEA [14]	Two-archive evolutionary approach	Better diversity maintenance	Slower convergence in complex problems
TiGE2 [15]	Diversity maintenance mechanism	Strong in local search	Weak convergence ability
POCEA [31]	Dynamic adjustment of evolutionary strategies	Strong convergence ability	Multiple features make CMOP challenging
MSCMO [35]	Multi-stage constraint handling	Efficient constraint handling	Complexity in implementation
BiCo [15]	Bi-population cooperative co-evolution	Improved exploration	May require large population size

2.2. Motivation

At the current stage of research, researchers often struggle to achieve optimal results when dealing with complex CMOPs. Therefore, there is still considerable room for improvement in algorithms that handle CMOPs. Some algorithms, even with the help of existing techniques, still struggle to converge to the approximate CPF, as shown in Figure 1a,d. For instance, in POCEA, part of the solution set found on the general PF fails to converge to the CPF. The fundamental reason is the lack of solution quality filtering, which prevents some inferior solutions from converging to the Pareto front. To enhance the convergence ability of solutions, researchers design various metrics to serve as selection criteria for candidate solutions. However, excessive convergence may cause the algorithm to fail to traverse larger infeasible regions, resulting in it becoming trapped in a local search loop. As shown in Figure 1b,e, certain feasible regions in CMOEAMT and BiCO were not explored. To address this limitation, researchers aim to enhance the exploration capabilities of the solutions while maintaining convergence, ensuring that the population fully covers the objective space. To further improve algorithm performance, the dimensionality of the objectives is increased to test the algorithm's ability to handle complex CMOPs. For instance, Figure 1c shows the Pareto front of POCEA on the three-objective ZXH_CF15 test problem. POCEA successfully found the complete Pareto front, demonstrating its strong search performance. However, with increased search performance, the quality of solutions was overlooked, leading to some poor-quality solutions failing to converge to the Pareto front. Moreover, when exploring the objective space, the solution set often encounters many narrow and large infeasible regions. Many solutions are unable to traverse these narrow infeasible regions, causing the algorithm to become trapped in local optima, which severely affects its performance. As shown in Figure 1f, although the CMOEA/D algorithm has most of its solutions converging to the CPF, the population struggles to fully converge to the CPF when faced with narrow infeasible regions. To address this challenge, it is crucial not only to utilize the information from infeasible solutions to maintain diversity but also to rigorously design selection criteria for the solutions.

In summary, there is still significant room for expansion in current-stage algorithms. Faced with the aforementioned issues, we designed an adaptive constraint relaxation mechanim to encourage the algorithm to explore more of the objective space, thereby enhancing its diversity and convergence. To further maintain a balance between objectives and constraints, we adopted an archiving mechanism. Throughout the algorithm evolution, the archive is continuously updated, preserving high-quality solutions and encouraging population convergence to the PF, thereby obtaining the complete CPF. To maintain population diversity, it is crucial to strengthen the interaction between the archive and the population during the evolutionary process as well as to share information about infeasible solutions. Only when the population receives migration information from the archive can it further explore unknown regions, thus avoiding the algorithm becoming trapped in local optima. Therefore, this algorithm employs strict constraint dominance principles when selecting parents, further acquiring information about infeasible solutions, enhancing the population's external search capability, and enabling the population to traverse narrow and extensive infeasible regions.

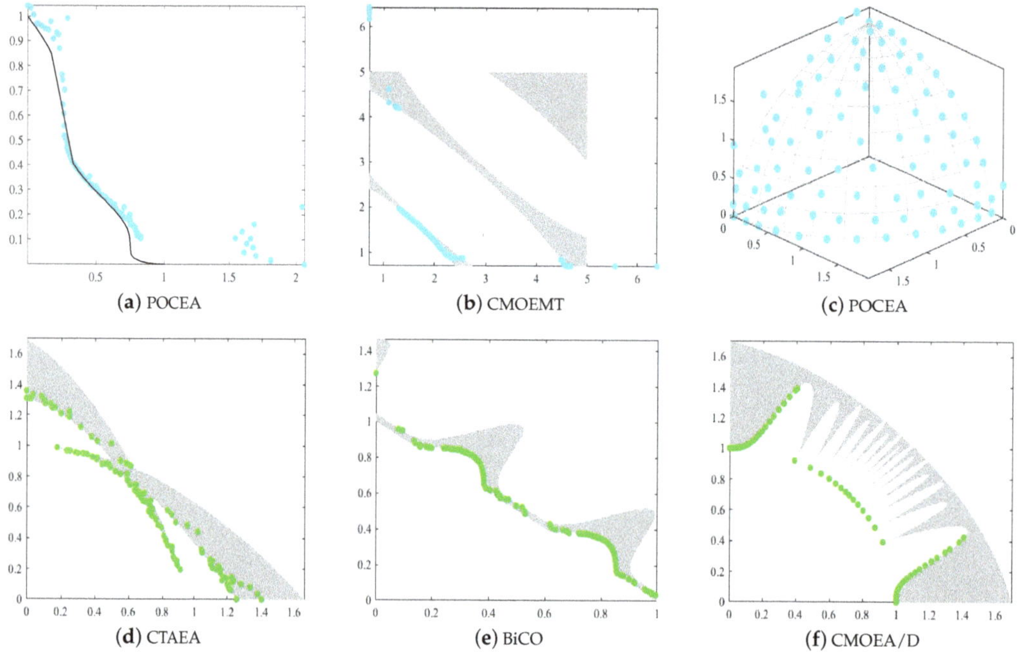

Figure 1. The obtained feasible and non-dominated solutions of (**a**) POCEA on ZXH_CF15, (**b**) CMOEMT on LIRCMOP8, (**c**) POCEA on LIRCMOP14, (**d**) CTAEA on MW9, (**e**) BiCO on MW3, (**f**) CMOEA/D on MW5.

3. Framework of ACREA

This section provides an overview of the framework of ACREA and describes the steps involved in ACREA, with detailed explanations of important components.

3.1. Framework of ACREA

Algorithm 1 offers the framework of ACREA. As shown in Algorithm 1, a population P_M is first initialized in the decision space. In Lines 2–3, the ω^t value is adaptively adjusted based on the proportion of feasible solutions, and solutions in population P_M that satisfy $(|CV| <= \omega^t)$ are stored in the archive. The calculation of ω^t is shown in Equation (5). ω^t controls the scaling of the boundaries and serves as a criterion for determining the entry of infeasible solutions into the population, thereby utilizing the information from high-quality infeasible solutions to enhance the diversity of the population. In the fifth line, the iteration of the algorithm is determined based on the maximum iteration count ($T = 20$). In Line 6, the Pareto front of P_F is obtained, and in Line 7, P_F and P_M are combined to generate P_1.

The main purpose is to increase the probability of selecting high-quality solutions, thereby enhancing the algorithm's convergence capability and driving the population to converge to the forefront CPF. In Line 8, an elitist selection is performed on P_1 and the archive to generate parent M_2. In Line 9, genetic operators are applied to M_2 to generate offspring Q_2. In Line 10, the *Archive* is sorted and updated. In Line 11, we adopted the NRC's IA [36] elite selection approach with the goal of finding as many high-quality solutions as possible to generate the final population P_M. To better understand ARCEA, we also created a flowchart, as shown in Figure 2. The entire flowchart process of ARCEA corresponds to the description of Algorithm 1. Additionally, the total execution time for one invocation of ACREA is 0.02 s.

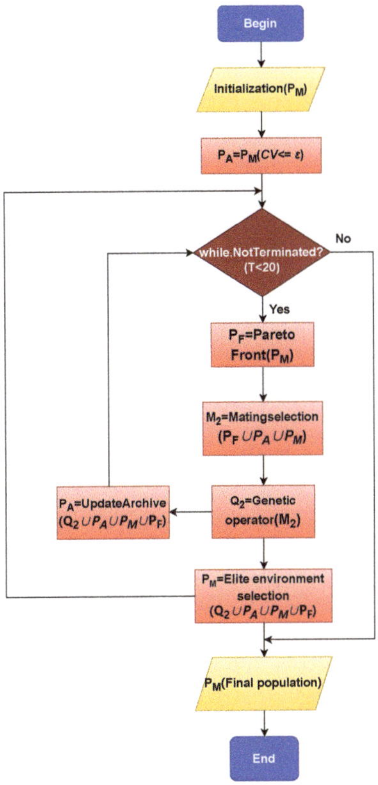

Figure 2. Flowchart of ACREA.

Algorithm 1 Framework of ACREA

Input: N (population size), T (max iterations)
Output: P (final population)

$P_M \leftarrow$ Initialize the population (N);
Calculate the CV values of solutions in P_M by Formula (3);
$P_A \leftarrow P_M(|CV| <= \omega^t)$
$t \leftarrow 0$
while $t < T$ **do**
  $P_F \leftarrow$ Obtain the P_F of P_M by non-dominated sorting;
  $P_1 \leftarrow P_M \cup P_F$
  $M_2 \leftarrow$ Perform the elite mating selection (P_M, P_A, N, *ratio*);
  $Q_2 \leftarrow$ Genetic operator (M_2);
  Archive $\leftarrow$ UpdatedArchive ($P_1 \cup Q_2$, P_A, N);
  $P_M \leftarrow$ Perform the elite environment selection ($P_1 \cup Q_2$, P_A);
  $t \leftarrow t + 1$
end while

3.2. Relaxed Constraint Learning Mechanism

The primary goal of using the constraint relaxation learning mechanism is to fully leverage the information from infeasible solutions to drive the population towards a complete CPF. The boundary values are adjusted adaptively based on the proportion of feasible solutions, as shown in Equation (5). As the proportion of feasible solutions increases, the boundaries begin to gradually relax, allowing for more feasible solutions to reduce the proportion of infeasibility and control the boundary's contraction capability, until the algorithm reaches its termination condition, at which point the constraint relaxation concludes. Figure 3 illustrates the entire constraint relaxation process. In Figure 3a, before constraint relaxation, infeasible solutions are ranked according to Equation (3) and poor solutions are removed. At this stage, many infeasible solutions are disregarded, significantly reducing the algorithm's performance. In Figure 3b, the constraints begin to relax. It is evident that as the boundaries expand, many infeasible solutions are considered. Solutions within the boundaries are diversity-ranked according to Equation (5), with lower-ranked solutions being eliminated. For example, although solution b is close to the front and has low constraint violation, it is ranked lower when infeasible solutions are included within the boundary and is thus removed, while solution e, ranked higher, is retained. In Figure 3c, as the constraint relaxation completes, the boundary values are scaled, removing solution h from the boundary. Solutions within the boundary are preserved based on non-dominated sorting and diversity ranking, retaining those with higher rankings. The mathematical model for constraint relaxation is as follows:

$$
\begin{aligned}
&\text{Minimize } L(x) = (f_1(x), \cdots, f_m(x), CV(x)) \\
&\qquad g(x) \leq \omega^t \\
&\text{Subject to } \omega^t = \left(\omega_1^t, \cdots, \omega_p^t\right), t = 0, \cdots, T \\
&\qquad x \in \Omega
\end{aligned}
\tag{4}
$$

t represents the current iteration number of the algorithm and T represents the maximum number of iterations. ω^t is a parameter threshold for relaxation, extending the constraint violation into the objective space. The motivation for the constraint relaxation mechanism is as follows: (1) To fully utilize information from infeasible solutions and encourage the population to traverse narrow infeasible regions, we appropriately relax the constraints, thereby enhancing the algorithm's search capability in the objective space. (2) During the evolution process, the algorithm obtains more information from infeasible solutions by appropriately relaxing the constraints, encouraging the population to approximate the CPF from both the feasible and infeasible sides. The mathematical formula for the value of ω^t is as follows:

$$
\omega^t = fr\left(1 - \frac{t}{T}\right)^{\frac{-\ln(fr)-4}{\ln(\lambda)}}
\tag{5}
$$

In the above formula, fr represents the proportion of feasible solutions, and λ indicates the rate of change set to 0.4. ω^t is adaptively adjusted based on the ratio of feasible solutions.

3.3. UpdatedArchive

Algorithm 2 describes the entire process of archive updating. When the number of solutions in the archive does not reach N, the solutions in the main population P are sorted in ascending order based on their CV values, and high-quality solutions are selected to supplement the archive. If the solution in the archive is greater than N, non-dominated sorting is applied on top of diversity sorting to remove redundant solutions. Diversity sorting is based on Equation (6), where each solution x is calculated and then sorted in descending order to remove redundant solutions. The main idea is to determine the quality of diversity by assessing whether the population solutions are evenly distributed. This promotes the convergence of the population towards the pareto front. The mathematical formula for diversity is as follows:

$$D(x) = \frac{1}{\sum_{i=1}^{k} d(x, \Omega_i) + 2} \tag{6}$$

$d(x, \Omega_i)$ represents the distance from the ith solution x to k neighboring solutions depending solely on k. i indicates the index of the solution [37]. $D(x)$ represents the crowding degree of solution x. The lower the crowding degree, the denser the solutions and the better the diversity; conversely, the higher the crowding degree, the worse the diversity.

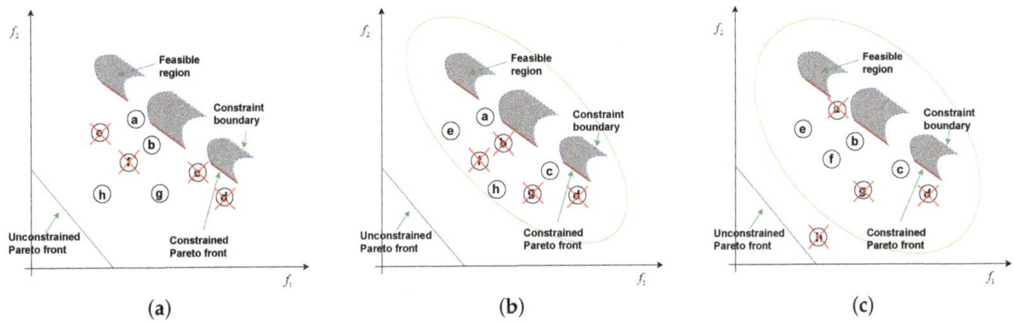

Figure 3. The entire process of relaxing constraint boundaries. (**a**) Unrelaxed constraint boundaries; (**b**) start of relaxing constraint boundaries; and (**c**) finish of relaxing constraint boundaries.

Algorithm 2 UpdatedArchive

Input: N (population size), U (combined population), P_A (Archive population)
Output: UpdatedArchive

```
if |P_A| ≤ N then
    Sort P in ascending order according to CV;
    P_A ← Select the first N solutions;
else
    P_A ← Perform the non-dominated sorting based on the diversity sorting (U);
end if
return UpdatedArchive
```

3.4. Elite Mating Pool Selection

Algorithm 3 describes the entire process of elite parent selection. First, the number of feasible solutions in P_M is calculated. If the number of feasible solutions is less than N or if the number of solutions in the P_A is less than N, two solutions are randomly selected from the combined population U, and their density is calculated using Equation (7). The solution with the lower density is selected. The density calculation formula is shown below:

$$D_i = \frac{1}{k} \sum_{j=1}^{k} d(i, j) \tag{7}$$

D_i represents the density of the ith solution. $d(i, j)$ represents the distance between the ith solution and the jth solution, and k represents the number of nearest neighbors.

Algorithm 3 The elite mating selection

Input: P_M (main population), P_A (Archive population), N (population size)
Output: M_1 (mating pool)

$U \leftarrow P_M \cup P_A$;
$N_f \leftarrow$ Calculate the number of feasible solutions in P_M;
if $N_f < N$ or $|P_A| < N$ **then**
    Randomly select two solutions from U;
    Calculate the density of the two solutions by Formula (7);
    $M_1 \leftarrow$ Select the solution with the smaller Density;
else
    if $rand < ratio$ **then**
        Randomly select two solutions (x_a and x_b) in P_A;
        Determine its dominance relationship by Formulas (9) and (10);
        if $x_a \prec x_b$ **then**
            $M_1 \leftarrow x_a$;
        else if $x_b \prec x_a$ **then**
            $M_1 \leftarrow x_a$;
        else
            $M_1 \leftarrow$ Select solutions with higher density;
        end if
    else
        Randomly select two solutions (x_a and x_b) in P_M;
        Determine its dominance relationship by Formulas (9) and (10);
        if $x_a \prec x_b$ **then**
            $M_1 \leftarrow x_a$;
        else if $x_b \prec x_a$ **then**
            $M_1 \leftarrow x_a$;
        else
            $M_1 \leftarrow$ Select solutions with higher density;
        end if
    end if
end if

$$\text{ratio} = \frac{1}{1 + \exp\left(-20\left(\frac{t}{T} - 0.5\right)\right)} \tag{8}$$

Conversely, two solutions are randomly selected from P_A and P_M based on the probability function ratio, and the solution with stronger dominance is chosen. Under stricter constraint dominance principles, the selected solutions exhibit strong convergence capability, facilitating P_M in obtaining a complete CPF. The constraint dominance formula is shown below:

$$r_{(x,y)} = \begin{cases} 1, & \text{if } y \prec_{\mathbf{CDP}} x \\ 0, & \text{otherwise} \end{cases} \tag{9}$$

$$R_x = \sum_{y \in C, y \neq x} r_{(x,y)} \tag{10}$$

If the two solutions do not mutually dominate each other, the solution with higher density is selected using Equation (7). At this point, the supplementary solutions have strong dominance, which improves the population's convergence speed toward the Pareto front (PF) and significantly enhances the convergence of the population. During the secondary selection, solutions with higher density are chosen to obtain a uniformly distributed set of solutions, thus maintaining the diversity of the population. The solutions selected under strict dominance principles and density support are of very high quality. This not only preserves the diversity of the population but also accelerates its convergence speed, indirectly maintaining a balance between diversity and convergence. This process continues until there are N remaining solutions in M_2.

3.5. Elite Environment Selection

Algorithm 4 describes the process of elite environment selection. First, the combined population is layered based on non-dominated sorting, categorizing feasible solutions into different fronts $(F_1, F_2, \cdots)$. If the number of feasible solutions in the combined population U exceeds N, layered sorting is performed for selection, as follows: if the number of feasible solutions in the first front exceeds N, non-dominated sorting based on reverse objectives and diversity sorting is applied to (F_1^*), and the top N solutions are selected. If the number of feasible solutions in the first front is less than N, the process moves to the next front (F_2^*) and continues with the same sorting method until P_M is filled to N solutions, and so on until (F_l^*) is reached, where (F_l^*) indicates that the number of feasible solutions only reaches N at layer l, thus ensuring P_M meets the requirement of N solutions. Conversely, when the number of feasible solutions in the combined population U is less than N, the infeasible solutions are sorted based on diversity and supplemented into the population P_M until it reaches N solutions.

Algorithm 4 Cascading sorting-based environment selection

Input: U (combined population), N (population size)
Output: P_M (main population)

```
1: {F_1, F_2, ···} ← Perform (m + 1) objective-based non-dominated sorting (U, N);
2: (F_1^* F_2^*, ···) ← Find the feasible solutions in each front (F_1, F_2, ···);
3: if |F_1^*| > N then
4:     P_M ← Perform the non-dominated sorting based on the reverse objective and diver-
       sity sorting (F_1^*);
5: else
6:     P_M ← Select N feasible solutions (F_1^*, F_2^*, ···);
7: end if
```

The cascading sorting used in elite environment selection ensures that the selected solutions not only possess strong dominance but also exhibit good diversity with the support of diversity metrics. This indirectly guarantees a balance between population diversity and convergence, preventing poor diversity from causing the population to become trapped in local optima.

4. Experiment Studies

This section discusses the experimental setup and algorithm comparison, concluding that ACREA significantly outperforms other competitors based on all the conclusions.

4.1. Experimental Setup

(1) Test problems: In this research work, we employ three sets of test instances: MW, LIRCMOP, and ZXH_CF, for comparative experiments. Among them, the decision space of MW is set to 15 for all instances. Except for MW4, MW8, and MW14, which are set to have 3 objectives, the rest are all set to have 2 objectives. The decision space of LIRCMOP is set to 30 for all instances. LIRCMOP13-14 instances are configured with 3 objectives, while LIRCMOP1-12 instances are configured with 2 objectives. ZXH_CF1-12 instances are configured with 3 objectives, and the decision space is set to 13. ZXH_CF13-16 instances are configured with 2 objectives, and the decision space is set to 12.

(2) Performance metrics: In this study, we employ the commonly used Inverted Generational Distance (IGD) [38] and Hypervolume (HV) [39] indicators to evaluate the diversity and convergence of algorithms. A smaller IGD value and a larger HV value indicate better overall performance of the algorithm. The settings for algorithm iterations are 20, evaluation counts are 100,000, and Wilcoxon's rank is set to 0.05. "NaN" in the

table indicates that no feasible solution is found. "+", "−", and "≈", respectively, denote superior to, inferior to, and comparable to competitors. All experimenters in this study are conducted on Platform PlatEMO 4.3 [40].

(3) Genetic operators: The SBX and PM for all experimental algorithms in this article are set to 1 and $1/D$, respectively. The distribution index is set to 20.

(4) Comparative algorithms: This paper compares with seven advanced algorithms, namely CMOEA/D, CTAEA, ToP, POCEA, CMOEMT [13], BiCo, and TiGE2. Both CMOEA/D and ToP adopt the decomposition approach. CMOEA/D decomposes the problem into weighted subproblems, while ToP decomposes the multi-objective into weighted single-objective. CTAEA applies an archive mechanism. BiCo employs a single-population archive framework. CMOEMT adopts a multi-population multi-stage approach. POCEA processes each problem with different weight vectors. TiGE2 employs a novel evaluation mechanism.

(5) Parameter settings for each algorithm: The population size of all algorithms in this paper is set to 100. The remaining settings are kept unchanged according to their respective papers to ensure fairness in experimental comparisons.

(6) Equipment requirements: In all experiments, the hardware used includes a processor model of i5-7300HQ (Intel, Santa Clara, CA, USA), with a system type based on a x64 processor and 8.00 GB of memory (RAM). On the software side, Windows 10 is used as the operating system, with MATLAB R2021a as the programming language. The toolbox utilized is the PlatEMO 4.6 toolbox in MATLAB.

4.2. Comparison Experiments with Seven Competitors

In this section, we assess ACREA's performance by contrasting ACREA against its seven competitors across the MW, LIRCMOP, and ZXH_CF test suites. In the MW test problem, many narrow infeasible regions are set, as shown in Figure 1. Many algorithms struggle to overcome this difficulty, resulting in incomplete frontier surfaces. In the LIRCMOP test suite, large infeasible regions are set to test whether the algorithms could traverse these regions and find the complete feasible area. Many algorithms, due to a lack of external search capability, end up in local optima. In ZXH_CF, many three-objective test problems are set to evaluate whether the algorithms can address the conflicts between multiple objectives. Many algorithms when handling this issue fail to maintain a balance between constraints and multiple objectives, thus reducing their performance. Next, we conduct a comprehensive analysis of the IGD and HV indicators separately.

(1) Comprehensive analysis of IGD indicators

As shown in Table 2, ToP did not find feasible solutions in the MW test suite for MW1 and MW10, primarily because it was unable to identify the true Pareto front in the face of narrow infeasible regions. To enhance ACREA's exploration capabilities, an adaptive constraint relaxation strategy was implemented to utilize more information from infeasible solutions, helping the population to traverse larger infeasible areas. This is a key reason why ACREA achieved optimal solutions in 10 test problems, while CMOEA/D only found optimal solutions in MW9 and MW12, indicating that ACREA excels far beyond its competitors in exploration and expansion. ACREA outperformed CMOEA/D, CTAEA, ToP, POCEA, CMOEMT, BiCo, and TiGE2 in 12, 12, 9, 13, 13, 13, and 13 test problems, respectively. CMOEA/D, CTAEA, ToP, POCEA, CMOEMT, BiCo, and TiGE2 performed similarly to ACREA in 0, 0, 3, 0, 0, 0, and 1 test problems. Overall, considering the MW test suite, ACREA significantly outperforms these seven competitors.

Table 2. The IGD results (mean and standard deviation) obtained by eight algorithms on the MW, LIRCMOP and ZXH_CF problems.

Problem	M	D	CMOEA/D	CTAEA	ToP	POCEA	CMOEMT	BiCo	TiGE2	ACREA
MW1	2	15	2.3584e-2 (6.07e-2) −	3.3830e-2 (3.48e-2) −	NaN (NaN)	1.3089e-2 (4.57e-3) −	9.0638e-2 (4.42e-2) −	2.0168e-1 (1.28e-1) −	5.2463e-2 (6.51e-2) −	2.0650e-3 (2.01e-3)
MW2	2	15	2.1518e-2 (7.13e-3) −	1.8133e-2 (7.89e-3) −	1.7940e-1 (1.48e-1) −	1.3531e-1 (1.04e-1) −	4.0501e-2 (2.85e-2) −	1.7818e-2 (7.95e-3) −	5.4455e-2 (3.51e-2) −	4.0575e-3 (1.55e-3)
MW3	2	15	5.6961e-3 (6.97e-4) −	1.2954e-2 (2.52e-3) −	2.2097e-1 (3.23e-1) −	2.7188e-2 (1.48e-2) −	1.6305e-2 (3.24e-3) −	2.1735e-2 (7.12e-3) −	5.1052e-2 (4.79e-2) −	5.2272e-3 (2.26e-4)
MW4	3	15	4.1786e-2 (1.00e-3) −	6.4495e-2 (2.06e-2) −	7.2571e-1 (0.00e+0) ≈	5.4908e-2 (3.34e-3) −	1.1079e-1 (2.35e-2) −	7.2513e-2 (1.34e-2) −	1.2132e-1 (6.19e-2) −	4.0860e-2 (2.78e-4)
MW5	2	15	1.9579e-3 (1.83e-3) −	1.4127e-2 (4.15e-3) −	7.5416e-1 (0.00e+0) ≈	7.6855e-2 (2.34e-2) −	7.7276e-2 (2.06e-2) −	1.1333e-3 (1.47e-3) −	4.7386e-2 (9.07e-3) −	3.6847e-4 (8.95e-5)
MW6	2	15	1.8220e-2 (1.07e-2) −	1.0959e-2 (6.47e-3) −	7.3029e-1 (3.51e-1) −	5.7904e-1 (3.67e-1) −	3.6539e-2 (1.27e-2) −	1.1876e-2 (9.02e-3) −	2.3935e-1 (3.09e-1) −	2.7746e-3 (3.06e-5)
MW7	2	15	2.7204e-2 (1.00e-1) −	6.7262e-3 (5.04e-4) −	5.7367e-2 (9.94e-2) −	5.2727e-2 (6.31e-2) −	1.5659e-2 (3.63e-3) −	4.7950e-3 (4.14e-4) −	3.1073e-2 (1.10e-2) −	4.3383e-3 (2.27e-4)
MW8	3	15	5.7801e-2 (1.92e-2) −	5.4905e-2 (3.09e-3) −	6.9878e-1 (4.11e-1) −	3.0482e-1 (2.45e-1) −	7.0693e-2 (2.33e-2) −	4.5375e-2 (1.80e-3) −	5.5415e-1 (2.77e-1) −	4.2826e-2 (5.43e-4)
MW9	2	15	1.1867e-2 (1.21e-2) +	8.7774e-3 (1.69e-3) +	8.5441e-1 (8.52e-2) −	1.0676e-1 (2.11e-1) −	9.5902e-2 (2.11e-1) −	5.6839e-3 (8.18e-4) +	9.8392e-2 (2.12e-1) −	6.1843e-2 (1.83e-2)
MW10	2	15	1.2514e-1 (1.73e-1) −	2.6026e-2 (1.65e-2) −	NaN (NaN)	2.9326e-1 (1.81e-1) −	8.3408e-2 (5.89e-2) −	1.1527e-1 (8.37e-2) −	7.7929e-2 (5.48e-2) −	6.0278e-3 (1.20e-2)
MW11	2	15	8.1605e-2 (2.11e-1) −	2.0545e-2 (7.72e-3) −	5.2819e-1 (2.69e-1) −	6.3878e-2 (7.87e-2) −	1.8706e-2 (4.97e-3) −	2.5423e-1 (3.30e-1) −	3.7307e-2 (8.00e-3) −	6.0104e-3 (1.33e-4)
MW12	2	15	5.2969e-3 (1.87e-3) +	6.1014e-2 (1.82e-1) +	8.3690e-1 (0.00e+0) ≈	4.7754e-2 (1.01e-1) +	2.6368e-2 (1.05e-2) +	3.8892e-1 (2.15e-1) −	1.2301e-1 (2.26e-1) ≈	6.4292e-2 (5.07e-2)
MW13	2	15	1.4945e-1 (3.06e-1) −	6.3400e-2 (3.47e-2) −	1.0845e+0 (7.97e-1) −	4.7870e-1 (3.54e-1) −	1.0459e-1 (3.46e-2) −	1.6096e-1 (8.07e-2) −	4.5309e-1 (1.69e-1) −	3.7435e-2 (4.95e-2)
MW14	3	15	2.1253e-1 (1.58e-3) −	4.9614e-1 (3.99e-1) −	8.5539e-1 (8.65e-1) −	5.8826e-1 (5.27e-1) −	7.1254e-1 (1.98e-1) −	8.8672e-1 (1.36e-1) −	1.8182e-1 (3.86e-2) −	9.6442e-2 (1.66e-3)
+/ − / ≈			2/12/0	2/12/0	0/9/3	1/13/0	1/13/0	1/13/0	0/13/1	
LIRCMOP1	2	30	2.6605e-1 (3.37e-2) −	3.0813e-1 (9.45e-2) −	3.2853e-1 (2.16e-2) −	1.7640e-1 (1.36e-1) ≈	3.3986e-1 (1.69e-2) −	2.1758e-1 (2.68e-2) −	2.0840e-1 (1.37e-2) −	1.1061e-1 (2.45e-2)
LIRCMOP2	2	30	2.4059e-1 (3.20e-2) −	2.4246e-1 (9.34e-2) −	2.8906e-1 (2.18e-2) −	1.5439e-1 (1.02e-1) ≈	2.7467e-1 (3.39e-2) −	1.8769e-1 (1.78e-2) −	1.9456e-1 (1.79e-2) −	9.2673e-2 (1.57e-2)
LIRCMOP3	2	30	2.9268e-1 (4.09e-2) −	3.4241e-1 (1.64e-1) −	3.4399e-1 (1.64e-2) −	2.0752e-1 (9.07e-2) −	2.9253e-1 (4.21e-2) −	2.2014e-1 (2.56e-2) −	2.1517e-1 (1.30e-2) −	1.3122e-1 (3.32e-2)
LIRCMOP4	2	30	2.7739e-1 (2.83e-2) −	2.9330e-1 (5.13e-2) −	3.2278e-1 (1.21e-2) −	2.3693e-1 (9.22e-2) −	2.8009e-1 (3.38e-2) −	2.0916e-1 (8.04e-3) −	2.1541e-1 (2.53e-2) −	1.4442e-1 (3.50e-2)
LIRCMOP5	2	30	1.3606e+0 (4.15e-1) −	1.2229e+0 (2.19e-1) −	1.1161e+0 (2.81e-1) +	1.2393e+0 (9.41e-1) ≈	1.3044e+0 (1.84e-1) −	1.2221e+0 (5.82e-3) −	9.5812e-1 (4.11e-1) ≈	1.2156e+0 (7.59e-3)
LIRCMOP6	2	30	1.3462e+0 (4.96e-4) −	1.4359e+0 (3.20e-1) −	1.3467e+0 (4.70e-4) −	1.0393e+0 (6.30e-1) ≈	1.3602e+0 (1.47e-2) −	1.3453e+0 (1.65e-4) ≈	9.6675e-1 (4.14e-1) ≈	1.3454e+0 (2.59e-4)
LIRCMOP7	2	30	1.2294e+0 (7.10e-1) −	8.2863e-1 (7.43e-1) −	1.3804e+0 (6.23e-1) −	1.2660e+0 (1.05e+0) −	1.0872e+0 (6.90e-1) −	5.2652e-1 (6.85e-1) ≈	3.2249e-1 (1.50e-1) +	4.8210e-1 (6.27e-1)
LIRCMOP8	2	30	1.5407e+0 (4.37e-1) −	1.3794e+0 (7.07e-1) +	1.5448e+0 (4.26e-1) −	1.1036e+0 (1.04e+0) ≈	1.3836e+0 (5.53e-1) +	1.0296e+0 (7.40e-1) +	5.1108e-1 (3.28e-1) +	1.3950e+0 (5.88e-1)
LIRCMOP9	2	30	8.6590e-1 (1.40e-1) −	8.1715e-1 (2.97e-1) −	5.9781e-1 (1.38e-1) ≈	9.0584e-1 (3.05e-1) −	1.0183e+0 (1.42e-1) −	9.6836e-1 (8.52e-2) −	7.2148e-1 (9.51e-2) −	5.2922e-1 (1.28e-1)
LIRCMOP10	2	30	8.0151e-1 (1.49e-1) −	7.2617e-1 (4.02e-1) ≈	4.2407e-1 (5.83e-2) +	8.4783e-1 (3.40e-1) ≈	1.0074e+0 (9.14e-2) −	9.5492e-1 (7.24e-2) −	8.5507e-1 (1.84e-1) −	6.5193e-1 (1.67e-1)
LIRCMOP11	2	30	8.8053e-1 (7.32e-2) −	6.2374e-1 (4.03e-1) ≈	4.7327e-1 (1.14e-1) +	7.8143e-1 (3.27e-1) −	9.3467e-1 (1.50e-1) −	7.0450e-1 (1.96e-1) −	7.9533e-1 (2.53e-1) −	5.6187e-1 (1.14e-1)
LIRCMOP12	2	30	6.8445e-1 (1.79e-1) −	6.5436e-1 (4.89e-1) ≈	3.1726e-1 (7.74e-2) ≈	7.1277e-1 (3.84e-1) −	8.7013e-1 (2.83e-1) −	6.3350e-1 (2.32e-1) −	4.5723e-1 (9.00e-2) −	3.4620e-1 (1.25e-1)
LIRCMOP13	3	30	1.3034e+0 (2.63e-4) +	7.2146e-1 (6.26e-1) ≈	1.3129e+0 (9.95e-2) +	7.9913e-1 (6.11e-1) ≈	2.7971e-1 (2.22e-2) +	1.3186e+0 (2.06e-3) −	1.2939e+0 (3.17e-1) +	1.3152e+0 (1.62e-3)
LIRCMOP14	3	30	1.2595e+0 (2.97e-4) +	1.1114e-1 (1.37e-3) +	1.3028e+0 (6.03e-3) −	9.6798e-1 (5.67e-1) ≈	2.4478e-1 (1.47e-2) +	1.2756e+0 (2.31e-3) −	1.3102e+0 (2.15e-1) −	1.2727e+0 (1.24e-3)
+/ − / ≈			2/12/0	2/8/4	4/8/2	0/6/8	3/11/0	1/11/2	3/9/2	

Table 2. *Cont.*

Problem	M	D	CMOEA/D	CTAEA	ToP	POCEA	CMOEMT	BiCo	TiGE2	ACREA
ZXH_CF1	3	13	4.4992e-2 (8.92e-4) +	4.8756e-2 (1.50e-3) −	9.7660e-2 (1.56e-2) −	5.2941e-2 (1.79e-2) −	5.2649e-2 (1.43e-3) −	4.6969e-2 (6.79e-4) ≈	1.2369e-1 (1.36e-2) −	4.7287e-2 (8.47e-4)
ZXH_CF2	3	13	1.3602e-1 (2.14e-1) −	9.6657e-2 (8.65e-2) −	3.1536e-1 (1.70e-1) −	1.5956e-1 (8.97e-2) −	6.4230e-2 (1.64e-3) −	7.0751e-2 (2.61e-2) −	2.6961e-1 (2.47e-1) −	5.8543e-2 (1.09e-3)
ZXH_CF3	3	13	7.4126e-2 (2.04e-3) −	7.5642e-2 (2.67e-3) −	2.2845e-1 (5.99e-2) −	1.8446e-1 (3.52e-2) −	6.7928e-2 (1.69e-3) −	6.1951e-2 (1.22e-3) +	1.2760e-1 (1.07e-2) −	6.3270e-2 (1.12e-3)
ZXH_CF4	3	13	1.3128e-1 (9.08e-2) −	1.1208e-1 (6.64e-2) −	1.2052e+0 (2.55e-1) −	7.1163e-1 (4.22e-1) −	1.1381e-1 (7.27e-2) −	1.4405e-1 (1.29e-1) ≈	3.0388e-1 (2.33e-1) −	7.7763e-2 (4.12e-2)
ZXH_CF5	3	13	8.3063e-2 (1.22e-1) −	5.7842e-2 (3.25e-2) −	1.1952e-1 (5.06e-2) −	8.5074e-2 (1.55e-2) −	4.5666e-2 (1.87e-2) −	6.0443e-2 (9.21e-2) −	1.9909e-1 (3.17e-1) −	3.2442e-2 (9.03e-4)
ZXH_CF6	3	13	5.1424e-2 (1.64e-3) −	3.6313e-2 (1.60e-3) −	5.6768e-2 (7.17e-3) −	7.0337e-2 (1.44e-2) −	3.5051e-2 (6.08e-4) −	3.1486e-2 (6.89e-4) ≈	5.9488e-2 (3.42e-3) −	3.1384e-2 (5.10e-4)
ZXH_CF7	3	13	1.1754e-1 (8.18e-2) ≈	9.3481e-2 (6.01e-2) ≈	5.5079e-1 (2.46e-1) −	6.2444e-1 (4.54e-1) −	7.5257e-2 (6.45e-2) ≈	1.2361e-1 (1.11e-1) ≈	2.2175e-1 (2.13e-1) −	9.6004e-2 (7.76e-2)
ZXH_CF8	3	13	6.3914e-2 (4.64e-3) −	5.6277e-2 (5.62e-3) −	2.4528e-1 (3.62e-1) −	1.3624e-1 (2.52e-2) −	4.0841e-2 (1.95e-3) −	3.2449e-2 (5.65e-4) +	7.3875e-2 (6.42e-3) −	3.3291e-2 (6.30e-4)
ZXH_CF9	3	13	9.8523e-2 (6.10e-2) −	6.5038e-2 (1.40e-2) −	5.1171e-1 (1.21e-1) −	3.8132e-1 (1.95e-1) −	3.0373e-2 (9.33e-4) −	2.6357e-2 (3.96e-4) +	1.0999e-1 (1.97e-2) −	2.8160e-2 (5.95e-3)
ZXH_CF10	3	13	2.2796e-1 (2.55e-1) ≈	1.2220e-1 (8.04e-2) ≈	1.1566e+0 (4.25e-1) −	1.1922e+0 (4.89e-1) −	9.2758e-2 (6.50e-2) ≈	1.0075e-1 (9.41e-2) ≈	1.6023e-1 (4.26e-2) −	1.0105e-1 (7.03e-2)
ZXH_CF11	3	13	1.1475e-1 (1.00e-1) −	3.5532e-2 (9.70e-4) −	5.1396e-1 (2.09e-1) −	6.9402e-2 (6.93e-3) −	3.0692e-2 (5.31e-4) −	2.8217e-2 (3.12e-4) −	1.8884e-1 (3.04e-2) −	2.7968e-2 (3.40e-4)
ZXH_CF12	3	13	2.2195e-1 (2.05e-1) −	7.5879e-2 (1.50e-1) −	4.8357e-1 (1.01e-1) −	1.1436e-1 (7.59e-2) −	2.9167e-2 (1.76e-3) −	5.4627e-2 (1.24e-1) −	2.4806e-1 (2.31e-1) −	2.3396e-2 (4.18e-4)
ZXH_CF13	2	12	8.9725e-2 (1.49e-1) ≈	7.4464e-2 (1.04e-1) ≈	9.5274e-1 (3.91e-1) −	7.8015e-1 (5.50e-1) −	9.4611e-2 (1.43e-1) ≈	6.8875e-2 (9.72e-2) ≈	1.2942e-1 (8.57e-2) ≈	1.3634e-1 (1.82e-1)
ZXH_CF14	2	12	7.9689e-3 (1.83e-2) −	2.8541e-3 (1.22e-4) −	1.4504e-1 (2.09e-1) −	1.6415e-2 (2.17e-3) −	3.3834e-3 (2.07e-4) −	2.3570e-3 (5.20e-5) +	3.5773e-2 (5.30e-3) −	2.4064e-3 (6.84e-5)
ZXH_CF15	2	12	9.8882e-2 (1.54e-1) −	5.6692e-3 (7.02e-4) −	1.8225e-1 (2.06e-1) −	3.5310e-2 (2.33e-2) −	2.0192e-2 (7.58e-2) −	3.1473e-2 (8.77e-2) −	7.1716e-2 (8.93e-2) −	2.8450e-3 (4.86e-5)
ZXH_CF16	2	12	7.4565e-2 (4.78e-2) −	1.4255e-2 (5.13e-3) −	2.7397e-2 (4.87e-2) −	1.5499e-2 (1.44e-3) −	2.6346e-3 (4.08e-5) +	2.6497e-3 (3.89e-5) ≈	2.9742e-2 (7.27e-3) −	2.6710e-3 (3.81e-5)
+/ − / ≈			1/12/3	0/13/3	0/16/0	0/16/0	1/12/3	4/5/7	0/15/1	

From Table 2, we can see the IGD metrics of the eight algorithms on the LIRCMOP test suite. With the support of strict dominance principles, the selected high-quality solutions are highly competitive, which contributes to ACREA's strong exploration and handling capabilities when facing irregular Pareto fronts. This is why CMOEA/D, CTAEA, ToP, POCEA, CMOEMT, BiCo, and TiGE2 perform worse than ACREA in 12, 8, 8, 6, 11, 11, and 9 test problems, respectively. Although slightly inferior to competitors in some test problems, overall, considering the 14 test problems, ACREA significantly outperforms other competing methods. POCEA only performs similarly to ACREA in 8 test problems and does not surpass ACREA in any test problem. The main reason for this is that the adaptive constraint relaxation expands the population's demand for solutions, while the strict dominance principle accelerates the population's convergence ability. The LIRCMOP test suite features numerous discontinuous feasible regions, posing significant challenges for algorithms. Many algorithms tend to overlook the balance between diversity and convergence, resulting in suboptimal performance. For example, CTAEA's dual-archive mechanism favors diversity, while POCEA's dynamic adaptive evolution strategy favors convergence. Although the algorithms improve performance in one aspect, their overall performance declines significantly. In contrast, ACREA enhances algorithm diversity through the design of an adaptive constraint relaxation strategy and implements a strict dominance principle to ensure rapid convergence to optimal solutions. Therefore, we can conclude that ACREA outperforms its competitors both theoretically and experimentally.

The ZXH_CF test suite places significant demands on the search capabilities of algorithms. During the search for the Pareto front, there are many small independent feasible regions, making it difficult for most algorithms to find a complete feasible domain, often leading them to become stuck in local optima. The representative ToP algorithm frequently fails to cross larger infeasible areas to find new feasible domains, resulting in the algorithm remaining in a local optimum and unable to achieve a complete CPF. In contrast, ACREA exhibits strong exploration capabilities, continuously updating its archive with diverse, high-ranking solutions, which helps the population obtain a complete CPF. This is a key reason why ACREA performs well on the 16 ZXH_CF test problems, achieving the best results in seven of them. CTAEA, ToP, POCEA, and TiGE2 did not achieve the best results in any of these 16 test problems. CMOEA/D only outperformed ACREA in the ZXH_CF1 test problem. ACREA significantly outperformed these seven competitors in 12, 13, 16, 16, 12, 5, and 15 test problems, respectively.

For example, the similar BiCO algorithm updates its archive based on the degree of constraint violation. Although it explores many infeasible solutions, the quality of these solutions is inconsistent, leading to a significant waste of algorithmic resources. This results in BiCO's inability to traverse infeasible areas on the ZXH_CF test problems, causing it to become stuck in local optima. In contrast, ACREA addresses this drawback by using diversity ranking as a criterion for solution selection, significantly enhancing the search capabilities of the population.

In summary, although ACREA did not perform well in some test problems, considering a total of 44 test problems, it significantly outperformed other competitors.

(2) Comprehensive analysis of HV indicators

From Table 3, we can see the HV metrics of the eight algorithms across the three benchmark test suites. The HV metric is mainly used to assess the diversity of the algorithms, measuring whether the solutions are evenly distributed along the constrained Pareto front. On the MW test suite, ACREA achieved the best results on 11 test problems, significantly outperforming its competitors. The primary reason for this is that the archive update process uses diversity metrics as a criterion for selecting solutions, greatly improving the quality of the selected solutions and thus enhancing the diversity of the population. Due to the ToP algorithm's lack of exploration capabilities, it is prone to becoming stuck in local optima when facing narrow Pareto fronts. For example, the reason ToP did not find feasible solutions in MW1 and MW10 is its poor exploration ability, which prevented it from finding the Pareto front. POCEA, CMOEMT, and BiCo achieved the best results in MW12,

MW12, and MW9, respectively, indicating that their strategies favor handling diversity. CMOEA/D and CTAEA each obtained two best results in MW9 and MW12. ACREA significantly outperformed CMOEA/D, CTAEA, ToP, POCEA, CMOEMT, BiCo, and TiGE2 on 11, 12, 9, 12, 12, 12, and 13 test problems, respectively. This indirectly demonstrates that ACREA's handling of diversity metrics in its archive is highly reliable.

Table 3. The HV results (mean and standard deviation) obtained by eight algorithms on the MW, LIRCMOP and ZXH_CF problems.

Problem	M	D	CMOEA/D	CTAEA	ToP	POCEA	CMOEMT	BiCo	TiGE2	ACREA
MW1	2	15	4.6948e-1 (5.16e-2) −	4.4028e-1 (5.14e-2) −	NaN (NaN)	4.6778e-1 (8.81e-3) −	3.7795e-1 (3.83e-2) −	2.7066e-1 (1.06e-1) −	4.3091e-1 (5.71e-2) −	4.8936e-1 (3.22e-3)
MW2	2	15	5.5149e-1 (1.16e-2) −	5.5749e-1 (1.36e-2) −	3.7181e-1 (1.54e-1) −	4.0848e-1 (1.04e-1) −	5.2371e-1 (3.92e-2) −	5.5816e-1 (1.19e-2) −	5.1177e-1 (3.26e-2) −	5.8179e-1 (2.57e-3)
MW3	2	15	5.4375e-1 (8.97e-4) ≈	5.3036e-1 (5.69e-3) −	3.8019e-1 (1.79e-1) −	5.1197e-1 (2.20e-2) −	5.2490e-1 (6.74e-3) −	5.1505e-1 (1.17e-2) −	5.0679e-1 (3.05e-2) −	5.4370e-1 (3.86e-4)
MW4	3	15	8.4106e-1 (8.60e-4) −	8.0781e-1 (3.59e-2) −	1.1720e-1 (0.00e+0) ≈	8.2053e-1 (4.97e-3) −	7.4032e-1 (3.39e-2) −	7.9419e-1 (1.67e-2) −	7.5360e-1 (5.62e-2) −	8.4173e-1 (3.40e-4)
MW5	2	15	3.2393e-1 (5.91e-4) −	3.1575e-1 (3.06e-3) −	5.6763e-2 (0.00e+0) ≈	2.5604e-1 (2.97e-2) −	2.3863e-1 (2.70e-2) −	3.2404e-1 (7.77e-4) −	2.9680e-1 (5.95e-3) −	3.2448e-1 (6.69e-5)
MW6	2	15	3.0532e-1 (1.52e-2) −	3.1273e-1 (9.65e-3) −	7.1210e-2 (5.91e-2) −	9.8677e-2 (9.92e-2) −	2.7929e-1 (1.85e-2) −	3.1451e-1 (1.31e-2) −	2.2186e-1 (7.25e-2) −	3.2851e-1 (1.46e-5)
MW7	2	15	4.0276e-1 (3.74e-2) −	4.0939e-1 (6.45e-4) −	3.7013e-1 (3.75e-2) −	3.7044e-1 (3.95e-2) −	3.9896e-1 (4.10e-3) −	4.1158e-1 (7.92e-4) ≈	3.9406e-1 (3.86e-3) −	4.1165e-1 (4.57e-4)
MW8	3	15	5.1728e-1 (4.40e-2) −	5.1979e-1 (1.35e-2) −	1.2738e-1 (1.54e-1) −	2.8547e-1 (1.49e-1) −	4.7820e-1 (4.53e-2) −	5.4199e-1 (1.07e-2) −	2.0847e-1 (1.47e-1) −	5.5239e-1 (9.55e-4)
MW9	2	15	3.8407e-1 (1.20e-2) +	3.9136e-1 (4.57e-3) +	0.0000e+0 (0.00e+0) −	3.1255e-1 (1.05e-1) ≈	3.2620e-1 (7.81e-2) ≈	3.9395e-1 (2.79e-3) +	3.2957e-1 (1.13e-1) −	3.3243e-1 (1.68e-2)
MW10	2	15	3.6891e-1 (8.88e-2) −	4.2774e-1 (1.64e-2) −	NaN (NaN)	2.6992e-1 (8.49e-2) −	3.8526e-1 (3.58e-2) −	3.6735e-1 (4.59e-2) −	3.8532e-1 (3.36e-2) −	4.5241e-1 (1.18e-2)
MW11	2	15	4.2815e-1 (5.34e-2) −	4.3958e-1 (3.89e-3) −	3.0696e-1 (5.99e-2) −	4.2041e-1 (2.57e-2) −	4.4071e-1 (1.88e-3) −	3.7685e-1 (7.73e-2) −	4.3233e-1 (3.57e-3) −	4.4796e-1 (1.44e-4)
MW12	2	15	6.0417e-1 (3.64e-3) +	5.5480e-1 (1.32e-1) +	0.0000e+0 (0.00e+0) ≈	5.6168e-1 (8.68e-2) +	5.7818e-1 (1.60e-2) +	2.7104e-1 (1.53e-1) −	4.9722e-1 (1.90e-1) ≈	5.4474e-1 (4.87e-2)
MW13	2	15	4.2945e-1 (5.41e-2) −	4.5178e-1 (1.60e-2) −	1.6784e-1 (1.39e-1) −	2.5860e-1 (1.24e-1) −	4.3310e-1 (1.60e-2) −	4.1121e-1 (2.83e-2) −	3.2082e-1 (5.20e-2) −	4.6158e-1 (2.83e-2)
MW14	3	15	4.4391e-1 (1.84e-3) −	2.8965e-1 (1.83e-1) −	2.4175e-1 (1.88e-1) −	2.9586e-1 (1.68e-1) −	2.2506e-1 (7.75e-2) −	1.2684e-1 (4.06e-2) −	4.3891e-1 (1.65e-2) −	4.7118e-1 (2.68e-3)
+/ − / ≈			2/11/1	2/12/0	0/9/3	1/12/1	1/12/1	1/12/1	0/13/1	
LIRCMOP1	2	30	1.2116e-1 (1.10e-2) −	1.1153e-1 (2.82e-2) −	1.0174e-1 (9.76e-3) −	1.5953e-1 (5.44e-2) ≈	1.0091e-1 (4.59e-3) −	1.3937e-1 (9.00e-3) −	1.4146e-1 (6.14e-3) −	1.7610e-1 (1.11e-2)
LIRCMOP2	2	30	2.3474e-1 (1.73e-2) −	2.4258e-1 (5.15e-2) −	2.1439e-1 (1.74e-2) −	2.8226e-1 (5.06e-2) ≈	2.1985e-1 (1.55e-2) −	2.5706e-1 (1.25e-2) −	2.6515e-1 (8.62e-3) −	3.0416e-1 (1.05e-2)
LIRCMOP3	2	30	1.0487e-1 (1.10e-2) −	9.9568e-2 (2.44e-2) −	9.3085e-2 (5.54e-3) −	1.3158e-1 (2.68e-2) −	1.0345e-1 (1.17e-2) −	1.2596e-1 (8.39e-3) −	1.2988e-1 (6.94e-3) −	1.5242e-1 (1.22e-2)
LIRCMOP4	2	30	1.9952e-1 (1.26e-2) −	1.9572e-1 (2.13e-2) −	1.7739e-1 (1.21e-2) −	2.1458e-1 (4.01e-2) −	1.9454e-1 (1.38e-2) −	2.2302e-1 (7.89e-3) −	2.2270e-1 (1.17e-2) −	2.5348e-1 (1.75e-2)
LIRCMOP5	2	30	0.0000e+0 (0.00e+0) ≈	7.1968e-3 (3.22e-2) ≈	2.0299e-2 (6.39e-2) ≈	7.2046e-2 (1.16e-1) +	0.0000e+0 (0.00e+0) ≈	0.0000e+0 (0.00e+0) ≈	4.3036e-2 (6.80e-2) +	0.0000e+0 (0.00e+0)
LIRCMOP6	2	30	0.0000e+0 (0.00e+0) ≈	0.0000e+0 (0.00e+0) ≈	0.0000e+0 (0.00e+0) ≈	4.5566e-2 (5.91e-2) +	0.0000e+0 (0.00e+0) ≈	0.0000e+0 (0.00e+0) ≈	3.8927e-2 (4.08e-2) +	0.0000e+0 (0.00e+0)
LIRCMOP7	2	30	7.0285e-2 (1.10e-1) −	1.3077e-1 (1.14e-1) ≈	4.8767e-2 (1.01e-1) −	9.2152e-2 (1.16e-1) −	8.6706e-2 (1.00e-1) −	1.8117e-1 (1.08e-1) ≈	1.9985e-1 (2.55e-2) +	1.8860e-1 (9.88e-2)
LIRCMOP8	2	30	2.1332e-2 (6.57e-2) ≈	5.8184e-2 (9.46e-2) ≈	1.9875e-2 (6.15e-2) ≈	1.1464e-1 (1.07e-1) ≈	4.2404e-2 (7.75e-2) ≈	9.9586e-2 (1.13e-1) ≈	1.6923e-1 (5.11e-2) +	4.4049e-2 (9.04e-2)
LIRCMOP9	2	30	1.6350e-1 (7.54e-2) −	1.9810e-1 (1.38e-1) −	2.8476e-1 (8.05e-2) −	1.8196e-1 (1.10e-1) −	1.1293e-1 (6.34e-2) −	1.3088e-1 (4.68e-2) −	2.3237e-1 (7.89e-2) −	3.6917e-1 (8.39e-2)
LIRCMOP10	2	30	1.5345e-1 (8.90e-2) −	2.8484e-1 (2.46e-1) ≈	4.7631e-1 (6.28e-2) +	1.8828e-1 (1.65e-1) ≈	7.3399e-2 (2.80e-2) −	7.8375e-2 (3.60e-2) −	1.4833e-1 (4.61e-2) −	2.5795e-1 (1.47e-1)
LIRCMOP11	2	30	1.9776e-1 (1.67e-2) −	3.7493e-1 (2.26e-1) ≈	3.7436e-1 (8.42e-2) +	2.6700e-1 (1.47e-1) ≈	1.7346e-1 (7.21e-2) −	2.7374e-1 (1.05e-1) −	2.1275e-1 (9.66e-2) −	3.0929e-1 (7.61e-2)
LIRCMOP12	2	30	3.4942e-1 (7.34e-2) −	3.3161e-1 (1.95e-1) ≈	4.6118e-1 (4.01e-2) ≈	3.3562e-1 (1.20e-1) −	2.2078e-1 (1.02e-1) −	3.4543e-1 (1.26e-1) −	3.8103e-1 (5.36e-2) −	4.6044e-1 (5.78e-2)
LIRCMOP13	3	30	4.3975e-4 (1.28e-5) +	2.7248e-1 (2.80e-1) ≈	5.3778e-3 (1.68e-2) ≈	2.3106e-1 (2.54e-1) ≈	3.6032e-1 (1.87e-2) +	1.0027e-4 (9.83e-5) ≈	3.5692e-2 (1.17e-1) +	1.7117e-4 (1.50e-4)
LIRCMOP14	3	30	9.8092e-4 (3.03e-5) +	5.4616e-1 (9.14e-4) +	2.5125e-4 (2.75e-4) −	1.5822e-1 (2.43e-1) ≈	4.0060e-1 (1.50e-2) +	4.3442e-4 (2.88e-4) −	1.5500e-2 (6.90e-2) +	6.3884e-4 (2.73e-4)
+/ − / ≈			2/9/3	1/5/8	2/7/5	2/5/7	2/9/3	0/9/5	6/8/0	
ZXH_CF1	3	13	8.3449e-1 (8.76e-4) +	8.3464e-1 (1.25e-3) +	7.6055e-1 (2.29e-2) −	8.0689e-1 (5.10e-2) −	8.2047e-1 (1.95e-3) −	8.3138e-1 (8.69e-4) +	7.5475e-1 (1.62e-2) −	8.3049e-1 (1.11e-3)
ZXH_CF2	3	13	4.7412e-1 (1.58e-1) −	4.9353e-1 (1.25e-1) −	2.3984e-1 (1.04e-1) −	4.0154e-1 (8.37e-2) −	5.2960e-1 (3.51e-3) −	5.2343e-1 (5.43e-2) ≈	3.9404e-1 (1.45e-1) −	5.4743e-1 (1.86e-3)
ZXH_CF3	3	13	5.0966e-1 (2.87e-3) −	5.1163e-1 (2.57e-3) ≈	2.5602e-1 (5.77e-2) −	4.2994e-1 (1.99e-2) −	4.9615e-1 (3.61e-3) −	5.1487e-1 (2.04e-3) +	4.4603e-1 (1.25e-2) −	5.1159e-1 (2.71e-3)
ZXH_CF4	3	13	3.2362e-1 (1.17e-1) −	3.4425e-1 (9.58e-2) −	0.0000e+0 (0.00e+0) −	5.8954e-2 (1.29e-1) −	3.2821e-1 (9.97e-2) −	3.0874e-1 (1.34e-1) ≈	1.7839e-1 (1.38e-1) −	3.7717e-1 (6.72e-2)
ZXH_CF5	3	13	2.7373e-1 (6.83e-2) −	2.7618e-1 (4.36e-2) −	1.9029e-1 (4.81e-2) −	2.4109e-1 (1.24e-2) −	2.8224e-1 (2.58e-2) −	2.7979e-1 (7.02e-2) −	2.0341e-1 (9.31e-2) −	3.0637e-1 (1.48e-3)
ZXH_CF6	3	13	2.1543e-1 (2.00e-3) −	2.2440e-1 (1.01e-3) ≈	1.9209e-1 (8.92e-3) −	1.8694e-1 (1.09e-2) −	2.1727e-1 (1.05e-3) −	2.2490e-1 (1.14e-3) ≈	2.0066e-1 (2.91e-3) −	2.2453e-1 (9.61e-4)
ZXH_CF7	3	13	2.4956e-1 (1.12e-1) ≈	2.6190e-1 (9.00e-2) ≈	2.8320e-2 (5.66e-2) −	7.0418e-2 (1.04e-1) −	2.9140e-1 (8.89e-2) ≈	2.4202e-1 (1.22e-1) ≈	1.7165e-1 (1.25e-1) −	2.6874e-1 (1.02e-1)
ZXH_CF8	3	13	2.2692e-1 (1.94e-3) −	2.1152e-1 (5.81e-3) −	1.0386e-1 (3.34e-2) −	1.2063e-1 (1.91e-2) −	2.2296e-1 (2.93e-3) −	2.3451e-1 (1.61e-3) +	2.1263e-1 (5.15e-3) −	2.3302e-1 (1.06e-3)
ZXH_CF9	3	13	2.5625e-1 (2.74e-2) −	2.3990e-1 (9.76e-3) −	8.0970e-2 (3.67e-2) −	1.1181e-1 (3.97e-2) −	2.6303e-1 (2.74e-3) −	2.7150e-1 (1.74e-3) ≈	2.4880e-1 (5.50e-3) −	2.6806e-1 (1.71e-2)
ZXH_CF10	3	13	2.4240e-1 (1.07e-1) ≈	1.8661e-1 (1.01e-1) ≈	1.2733e-2 (2.89e-2) −	3.5459e-3 (5.36e-3) −	2.1794e-1 (1.08e-1) ≈	2.2483e-1 (1.22e-1) ≈	2.1093e-1 (1.07e-1) ≈	2.0681e-1 (1.12e-1)
ZXH_CF11	3	13	3.9492e-1 (4.84e-2) ≈	3.8991e-1 (8.71e-3) −	1.9864e-1 (6.11e-2) −	3.5334e-1 (1.34e-2) −	4.1834e-1 (3.44e-3) −	4.2578e-1 (2.23e-3) ≈	2.8437e-1 (1.85e-2) −	4.2645e-1 (1.83e-3)
ZXH_CF12	3	13	6.1528e-1 (1.42e-1) −	6.7025e-1 (2.02e-1) −	3.0386e-1 (1.08e-1) −	5.8553e-1 (1.03e-1) −	7.4573e-1 (6.03e-3) −	7.1094e-1 (1.68e-1) −	4.5357e-1 (2.56e-1) −	7.5662e-1 (1.54e-3)
ZXH_CF13	2	12	2.4997e-1 (1.19e-1) ≈	2.4196e-1 (1.10e-1) ≈	4.6817e-3 (1.40e-2) −	2.7546e-2 (6.94e-2) −	2.3574e-1 (1.22e-1) ≈	2.4759e-1 (1.04e-1) ≈	1.8601e-1 (1.13e-1) ≈	2.0406e-1 (1.23e-1)
ZXH_CF14	2	12	5.3856e-1 (1.37e-2) −	5.4203e-1 (5.07e-4) −	3.8169e-1 (1.07e-1) −	5.1251e-1 (4.30e-3) −	5.4114e-1 (3.36e-4) −	5.4325e-1 (1.90e-4) ≈	4.9882e-1 (9.92e-3) −	5.4321e-1 (1.92e-4)
ZXH_CF15	2	12	6.1734e-1 (9.73e-2) −	6.6107e-1 (2.27e-4) −	4.4797e-1 (1.43e-1) −	6.2683e-1 (2.55e-2) −	6.4283e-1 (8.01e-2) −	6.2999e-1 (9.60e-2) ≈	5.9186e-1 (1.01e-1) −	6.6196e-1 (1.09e-4)
ZXH_CF16	2	12	7.6180e-1 (1.78e-2) −	7.6380e-1 (7.24e-3) −	7.6813e-1 (1.59e-2) −	7.6596e-1 (2.85e-3) −	7.7809e-1 (1.65e-4) −	7.7828e-1 (9.34e-5) ≈	7.5343e-1 (6.85e-3) −	7.7825e-1 (8.64e-5)
+/ − / ≈			1/11/4	1/10/5	0/16/0	0/16/0	0/13/3	3/2/11	0/14/2	

The LIRCMOP test suite includes many large infeasible regions to evaluate the algorithms' ability to traverse these areas. From the HV metrics of the LIRCMOP test suite, it is evident that most algorithms struggle to cross large infeasible regions in search of feasible solutions, significantly reducing their overall performance. For example, in the LIRCMOP6 test problem, there are extensive infeasible regions, and many algorithms, despite searching within the local space, fail to find suitable solutions, which greatly wastes algorithmic resources. To address this challenge, it is essential not only to enhance the algorithm's exploration capabilities but also to strictly select high-quality solutions. With this approach in mind, ACREA relaxes constraints to gather more information from infeasible solutions, thereby increasing its ability to explore further. At the same time, it adopts a strict density dominance principle to select high-quality solutions, ensuring that the population obtains a set of optimal solutions. These two aspects are the primary reasons why ACREA outperforms the seven competitors in 9, 5, 7, 5, 9, 9, and 8 test problems.

In the ZXH_CF test suite, ToP, POCEA, CMOEMT, and TiGE2 did not achieve the best results on any test problems, indirectly indicating that this type of algorithm has poor exploration capabilities and fails to obtain the full feasible region, resulting in suboptimal solutions. In contrast, CMOEA/D and CTAEA achieved the best results on the ZXH_CF1 test problem, demonstrating that their algorithms perform well in terms of diversity. Compared to these, ACREA achieved the best results on six test problems, indirectly proving the effectiveness of its diversity metrics. The traditional exploration strategies fall short of enabling the algorithm to obtain better solutions. Although ACREA did not achieve the best performance on some test problems, considering the 16 ZXH_CF test problems and the seven comparative algorithms, ACREA outperforms its competitors.

From the above analysis, it can be seen that across 44 different test problems, ACREA's overall performance far surpasses its competitors, fully demonstrating the superiority and competitiveness of ACREA.

4.3. *The Validation of Parameter λ in ACREA*

In this section, we validate parameter λ using an equidistant strategy and conduct comparative experiments on the LIRCMOP test suite with different settings of λ. From the IGD metric in Table 4, it can be seen that ACREA (λ = 0.4) outperforms ACREA (λ = 0, 0.2, 0.6, 0.8, and 1) on 2, 2, 1, 2, and 1 test problems, respectively. From the HV metric in Table 5, it can be seen that ACREA (λ = 0, 0.2, 0.6, 0.8, and 1) performs worse than ACREA (λ = 0.4) on 0, 2, 1, 1, and 1 test problems, respectively. Although ACREA (λ = 0) achieves the same HV metric as ACREA (λ = 0.4) on the LIRCMOP test suite, it performs worse on 2 test problems in the IGD metric compared to ACREA (λ = 0.4). In summary, the results obtained by ACREA (λ = 0.4) are the best. Therefore, setting λ to 0.4 is optimal.

Table 4. The IGD results (mean and standard deviation) of ACREA (λ = 0, 0.2, 0.4, 0.6, 0.8, and 1) on the LIRCMOP test suite.

Problem	M	D	ACREA (λ = 0)	ACREA (λ = 0.2)	ACREA (λ = 0.6)	ACREA (λ = 0.8)	ACREA (λ = 1)	ACREA (λ = 0.4)
LIRCMOP1	2	30	1.2506e-1 (2.76e-2) −	1.3145e-1 (2.37e-2) −	1.2833e-1 (2.41e-2) −	1.2704e-1 (1.84e-2) −	1.3136e-1 (2.45e-2) −	1.1061e-1 (2.45e-2)
LIRCMOP2	2	30	1.0014e-1 (1.61e-2) ≈	1.0500e-1 (1.78e-2) −	1.0071e-1 (1.33e-2) ≈	1.0073e-1 (1.52e-2) ≈	9.8759e-2 (1.58e-2) ≈	9.2673e-2 (1.57e-2)
LIRCMOP3	2	30	1.3429e-1 (2.43e-2) ≈	1.2848e-1 (2.64e-2) ≈	1.4182e-1 (2.19e-2) ≈	1.3866e-1 (3.19e-2) ≈	1.3094e-1 (2.85e-2) ≈	1.3122e-1 (3.32e-2)
LIRCMOP4	2	30	1.4046e-1 (2.89e-2) ≈	1.3183e-1 (3.07e-2) ≈	1.3722e-1 (3.18e-2) ≈	1.2986e-1 (2.58e-2) ≈	1.3986e-1 (2.75e-2) ≈	1.4442e-1 (3.50e-2)
LIRCMOP5	2	30	1.2206e+0 (7.48e-3) −	1.2201e+0 (8.57e-3) ≈	1.2177e+0 (8.54e-3) ≈	1.2174e+0 (8.17e-3) ≈	1.2149e+0 (1.21e-2) ≈	1.2156e+0 (7.59e-3)
LIRCMOP6	2	30	1.3455e+0 (2.18e-4) ≈	1.3455e+0 (1.81e-4) ≈	1.3454e+0 (2.55e-4) ≈	1.3454e+0 (1.66e-4) ≈	1.3455e+0 (2.85e-4) ≈	1.3454e+0 (2.59e-4)
LIRCMOP7	2	30	6.1919e-1 (7.17e-1) ≈	5.3444e-1 (6.81e-1) ≈	6.0558e-1 (7.23e-1) ≈	2.9229e-1 (4.77e-1) ≈	4.8099e-1 (6.21e-1) ≈	4.8210e-1 (6.27e-1)
LIRCMOP8	2	30	1.3332e+0 (6.20e-1) ≈	1.2236e+0 (6.58e-1) ≈	1.4625e+0 (5.35e-1) ≈	1.1913e+0 (6.87e-1) ≈	1.2455e+0 (6.84e-1) ≈	1.3950e+0 (5.88e-1)
LIRCMOP9	2	30	5.4482e-1 (1.18e-1) ≈	5.5301e-1 (1.14e-1) ≈	5.5117e-1 (1.40e-1) ≈	5.6146e-1 (1.35e-1) ≈	5.6448e-1 (1.24e-1) ≈	5.2922e-1 (1.28e-1)
LIRCMOP10	2	30	6.3475e-1 (1.81e-1) ≈	6.2310e-1 (1.85e-1) ≈	6.3372e-1 (1.96e-1) ≈	7.5640e-1 (1.65e-1) −	5.9253e-1 (2.02e-1) ≈	6.5193e-1 (1.67e-1)
LIRCMOP11	2	30	5.3027e-1 (1.21e-1) ≈	5.5273e-1 (1.63e-1) ≈	6.0785e-1 (1.37e-1) ≈	5.2048e-1 (1.32e-1) ≈	5.2028e-1 (1.12e-1) ≈	5.6187e-1 (1.14e-1)
LIRCMOP12	2	30	2.7881e-1 (8.14e-2) ≈	3.5553e-1 (1.46e-1) ≈	3.4480e-1 (1.16e-1) ≈	2.9271e-1 (8.93e-2) ≈	3.3023e-1 (9.60e-2) ≈	3.4620e-1 (1.25e-1)
LIRCMOP13	3	30	1.3157e+0 (1.59e-3) ≈	1.3161e+0 (1.53e-3) ≈	1.3162e+0 (2.06e-3) ≈	1.3153e+0 (1.69e-3) ≈	1.3156e+0 (1.90e-3) ≈	1.3152e+0 (1.62e-3)
LIRCMOP14	3	30	1.2723e+0 (1.84e-3) ≈	1.2725e+0 (2.16e-3) ≈	1.2727e+0 (1.21e-3) ≈	1.2723e+0 (1.70e-3) ≈	1.2722e+0 (1.63e-3) ≈	1.2727e+0 (1.24e-3)
+/ − / ≈			0/2/12	0/2/12	0/1/13	0/2/12	0/1/13	

4.4. *Performance Analysis*

From Table 6, we can see the Wilcoxon rank analysis between ACREA and the comparative algorithms. R^+, R^-, and p-value, respectively, represent superior to, inferior to, and similar to values. In IGD's R^-, CMOEMT reached the highest at 187.0, while in HV's R^-, CTAEA achieved 257.0. However, in comparison to the values of competitors in R^+, both for IGD and HV, they were all above 700, with the best reaching a peak value of 899.0. Therefore, overall, the performance of ACREA far surpasses that of its competitors. From Figure 4, we can see the PF of the 8 algorithms on MW4. ToP did not find the Pareto front, while TiGE2 and POCEA only found partial Pareto fronts. CTAEA, CMOEMT, and CMOEA/D have some missing solutions that are not on the Pareto front and are relatively sparse. Although all solutions of BiCo are on the Pareto front, they are not as uniformly distributed and dense as compared to ACREA.

Table 5. The HV results (mean and standard deviation) of ACREA (λ = 0, 0.2, 0.4, 0.6, 0.8, and 1) on the LIRCMOP test suite.

Problem	M	D	ACREA (λ = 0)	ACREA (λ = 0.2)	ACREA (λ = 0.6)	ACREA (λ = 0.8)	ACREA (λ = 1)	ACREA (λ = 0.4)
LIRCMOP1	2	30	1.7106e-1 (1.20e-2) ≈	1.6777e-1 (1.05e-2) −	1.6916e-1 (1.22e-2) −	1.7252e-1 (1.15e-2) ≈	1.6735e-1 (1.17e-2) −	1.7610e-1 (1.11e-2)
LIRCMOP2	2	30	3.0315e-1 (8.29e-3) ≈	3.0069e-1 (1.11e-2) ≈	3.0006e-1 (9.13e-3) ≈	3.0055e-1 (9.02e-3) ≈	3.0072e-1 (9.74e-3) ≈	3.0416e-1 (1.05e-2)
LIRCMOP3	2	30	1.5210e-1 (9.94e-3) ≈	1.5361e-1 (9.75e-3) ≈	1.5000e-1 (8.44e-3) ≈	1.4987e-1 (1.06e-2) ≈	1.5300e-1 (9.57e-3) ≈	1.5242e-1 (1.22e-2)
LIRCMOP4	2	30	2.5587e-1 (1.37e-2) ≈	2.5842e-1 (1.48e-2) ≈	2.5618e-1 (1.33e-2) ≈	2.5939e-1 (1.30e-2) ≈	2.5361e-1 (1.39e-2) ≈	2.5348e-1 (1.75e-2)
LIRCMOP5	2	30	0.0000e+0 (0.00e+0) ≈	0.0000e+0 (0.00e+0) ≈	0.0000e+0 (0.00e+0) ≈	0.0000e+0 (0.00e+0) ≈	0.0000e+0 (0.00e+0) ≈	0.0000e+0 (0.00e+0)
LIRCMOP6	2	30	0.0000e+0 (0.00e+0) ≈	0.0000e+0 (0.00e+0) ≈	0.0000e+0 (0.00e+0) ≈	0.0000e+0 (0.00e+0) ≈	0.0000e+0 (0.00e+0) ≈	0.0000e+0 (0.00e+0)
LIRCMOP7	2	30	1.6488e-1 (1.13e-1) ≈	1.7976e-1 (1.07e-1) ≈	1.6946e-1 (1.14e-1) ≈	2.1981e-1 (7.62e-2) ≈	1.8716e-1 (9.80e-2) ≈	1.8860e-1 (9.88e-2)
LIRCMOP8	2	30	5.1586e-2 (9.24e-2) ≈	7.0517e-2 (1.02e-1) ≈	3.3199e-2 (8.11e-2) ≈	7.5814e-2 (1.06e-1) ≈	6.6749e-2 (1.05e-1) ≈	4.4049e-2 (9.04e-2)
LIRCMOP9	2	30	3.5598e-1 (7.38e-2) ≈	3.5097e-1 (7.75e-2) ≈	3.6132e-1 (8.79e-2) ≈	3.4443e-1 (8.10e-2) ≈	3.3537e-1 (8.48e-2) ≈	3.6917e-1 (8.39e-2)
LIRCMOP10	2	30	2.7572e-1 (1.59e-1) ≈	2.8507e-1 (1.60e-1) ≈	2.8397e-1 (1.60e-1) ≈	1.7292e-1 (1.29e-1) −	3.1896e-1 (1.74e-1) ≈	2.5795e-1 (1.47e-1)
LIRCMOP11	2	30	3.3192e-1 (8.21e-2) ≈	3.2432e-1 (1.02e-1) ≈	2.9214e-1 (7.81e-2) ≈	3.3939e-1 (8.36e-2) ≈	3.4103e-1 (7.25e-2) ≈	3.0929e-1 (7.61e-2)
LIRCMOP12	2	30	4.8166e-1 (4.45e-2) ≈	4.5804e-1 (5.89e-2) ≈	4.5633e-1 (5.34e-2) ≈	4.7458e-1 (4.83e-2) ≈	4.6187e-1 (4.42e-2) ≈	4.6044e-1 (5.78e-2)
LIRCMOP13	3	30	1.7638e-4 (1.21e-4) ≈	5.3638e-5 (7.60e-5) −	1.1290e-4 (1.23e-4) ≈	1.2054e-4 (1.33e-4) ≈	1.0322e-4 (1.15e-4) ≈	1.7117e-4 (1.50e-4)
LIRCMOP14	3	30	6.8294e-4 (3.01e-4) ≈	5.3264e-4 (3.10e-4) ≈	5.8149e-4 (3.29e-4) ≈	4.6205e-4 (2.97e-4) ≈	6.6766e-4 (2.69e-4) ≈	6.3884e-4 (2.73e-4)
+/ − / ≈			0/0/14	0/2/12	0/1/13	0/1/13	0/1/13	

Table 6. Wilcoxon's rank sum test results based on mean IGD and HV values on the three test suite.

ACREA vs.	IGD			HV		
	R^+	R^-	p-Value	R^+	R^-	p-Value
CMOEAD	868.0	78.0	0.000002	843.5	146.5	0.000043
CTAEA	774.0	172.0	0.000272	733.0	257.0	0.004923
ToP	897.0	49.0	0	899.0	47.0	0
POCEA	853.0	137.0	0.000029	851.0	139.0	0.00003
CMOEMT	803.0	187.0	0.000318	783.0	163.0	0.000162
BiCo	827.0	163.0	0.000104	806.0	184.0	0.000278
TiGE2	829.0	161.0	0.000095	887.0	103.0	0.000005

As shown in Figure 5, the convergence plots comparing ACREA with five representative algorithms clearly demonstrate the results. In Figure 4a, ACREA's IGD metric remains at the lowest level as the evaluation count increases, indicating that lower IGD values reflect better algorithm performance. Conversely, in Figure 4b, ACREA's HV metric consistently stays at a leading standard as the evaluation count increases, with higher HV values representing better algorithm performance. Therefore, considering the convergence plots of both IGD and HV metrics, ACREA outperforms its competitors.

Analyzing from the perspective of time complexity, traditional CMOED algorithms such as CTAEA, ToP, POCEA, CMOEMT, BiCo, and TiGE2 have a time complexity of $O(N^2)$. However, ACREA also has a complexity of $O(N^2)$, but the experimental results of the seven competing algorithms are far inferior to those of ACREA. Additionally, the space complexity of eight CMOEAs is $O(N)$, indicating that the proposed ACREA algorithm not only significantly saves computational resources but also achieves ideal results.

In conclusion, ACREA achieved good performance in Wilcoxon rank-sum analysis, the Pareto front plot of MW4, time complexity, IGD convergence plots, and HV convergence plots, further demonstrating the superiority and competitiveness of ACREA.

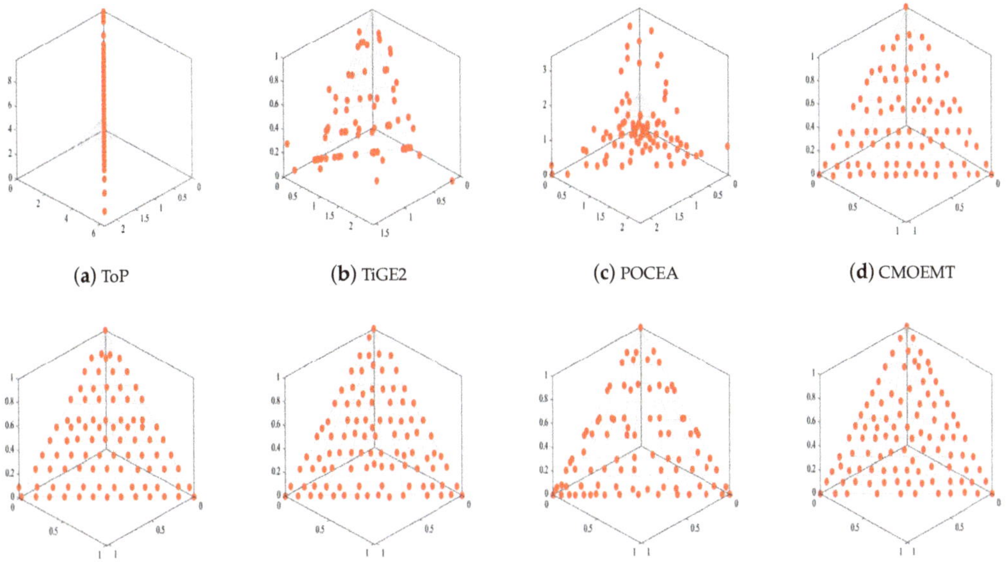

(**a**) ToP (**b**) TiGE2 (**c**) POCEA (**d**) CMOEMT

(**e**) CMOEAD (**f**) BiCo (**g**) CTAEA (**h**) ACREA

Figure 4. The Pareto front (PF) plot obtained in MW4 test problem.

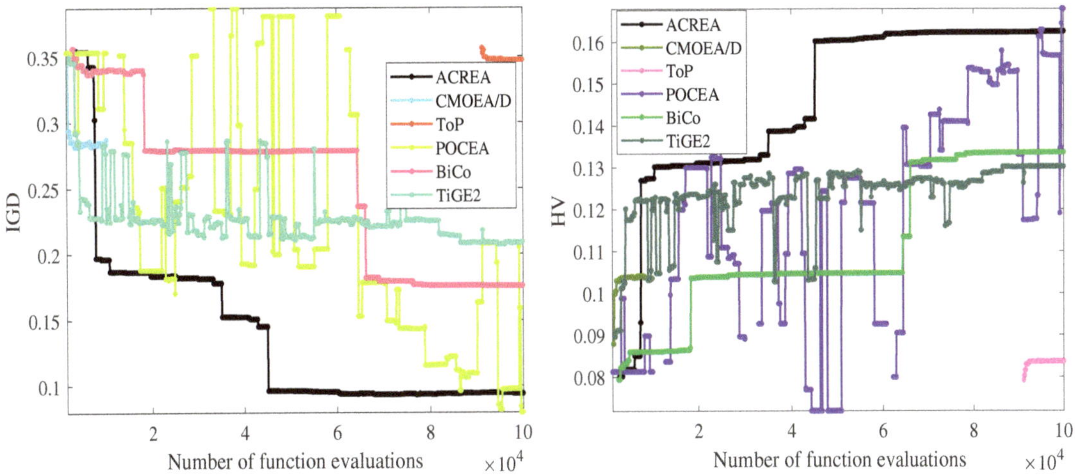

(**a**) HV convergence plot (**b**) IGD convergence plot

Figure 5. HV and IGD convergence plots.

4.5. Effectiveness of Core Components of ACREA

To further verify the effectiveness of ACREA, we conducted a comparative analysis of three variants and ACREA on the LIRCMOP test suite. The specific details are as follows:

(1) ACREA1: Remove the boundary constraint learning mechanism and the corresponding constraint handling technique.
(2) ACREA2: Remove the archive and replace it with the archive mechanism of CTSEA.

(3) ACREA3: Remove the elite selection mechanism of the parent generation and replace it with binary tournament selection.

As shown in Table 7, the IGD metrics of the three variants and ACREA on LIRCMOP can be observed. When the boundary constraint mechanism and the corresponding constraint handling technique were removed, the performance of ACREA1 significantly decreased, further illustrating the importance of the boundary constraint handling mechanism. ACREA2 deleted the archive and performed worse than ACREA on eight test problems, indicating that the archiving mechanism significantly enhances the overall performance of the algorithm. ACREA outperformed ACREA3 on nine test problems, with only one test problem performing worse than ACREA3, thus fully validating the effectiveness of parent elite selection. ACREA outperforms the other three variants on 9, 8, and 9 test problems, respectively. As shown in Table 8, the three variants and ACREA in terms of the HV indicator in LIRCMOP. ACREA far outperforms the other three variants, once again validating the effectiveness of constraint boundary learning, archiving mechanism, and parent elite selection.

In conclusion, the analysis of IGD and HV indicators on the LIRCMOP test suite for the three variants and ACREA further demonstrates the effectiveness of ACREA.

Table 7. The IGD results (mean and standard deviation) of ACREA and three variants of it on LIRCMOP test suite.

Problem	*M*	*D*	ACREA1	ACREA2	ACREA3	ACREA
LIRCMOP1	2	30	2.5126e-1 (2.15e-2) −	2.4680e-1 (2.84e-2) −	2.7802e-1 (1.98e-2) −	1.1061e-1 (2.45e-2)
LIRCMOP2	2	30	1.9515e-1 (2.33e-2) −	1.7677e-1 (2.83e-2) −	2.5457e-1 (1.37e-2) −	9.2673e-2 (1.57e-2)
LIRCMOP3	2	30	2.1620e-1 (2.07e-2) −	1.9357e-1 (3.34e-2) −	3.1490e-1 (2.78e-2) −	1.3122e-1 (3.32e-2)
LIRCMOP4	2	30	2.1652e-1 (2.94e-2) −	1.8669e-1 (3.59e-2) −	2.7240e-1 (3.12e-2) −	1.4442e-1 (3.50e-2)
LIRCMOP5	2	30	1.2196e+0 (1.56e-2) ≈	1.2150e+0 (1.10e-2) ≈	1.2212e+0 (6.86e-3) −	1.2156e+0 (7.59e-3)
LIRCMOP6	2	30	1.3455e+0 (2.14e-4) ≈	1.3459e+0 (1.81e-3) ≈	1.3453e+0 (2.20e-4) ≈	1.3454e+0 (2.59e-4)
LIRCMOP7	2	30	1.2365e+0 (6.98e-1) −	7.7288e-1 (7.62e-1) ≈	7.0061e-1 (7.43e-1) ≈	4.8210e-1 (6.27e-1)
LIRCMOP8	2	30	1.3400e+0 (6.17e-1) ≈	1.3612e+0 (5.74e-1) ≈	1.2565e+0 (6.67e-1) +	1.3950e+0 (5.88e-1)
LIRCMOP9	2	30	8.7315e-1 (1.69e-1) −	9.2451e-1 (1.55e-1) −	1.0128e+0 (1.14e-1) −	5.2922e-1 (1.28e-1)
LIRCMOP10	2	30	8.4546e-1 (1.17e-1) −	8.7443e-1 (1.20e-1) −	9.5300e-1 (4.36e-2) −	6.5193e-1 (1.67e-1)
LIRCMOP11	2	30	7.3926e-1 (6.95e-2) −	7.4791e-1 (3.37e-2) −	8.6312e-1 (1.10e-1) −	5.6187e-1 (1.14e-1)
LIRCMOP12	2	30	7.7156e-1 (1.63e-1) −	7.9126e-1 (1.90e-1) −	8.6827e-1 (1.57e-1) −	3.4620e-1 (1.25e-1)
LIRCMOP13	3	30	1.3163e+0 (1.60e-3) ≈	1.3158e+0 (1.58e-3) ≈	1.3161e+0 (1.71e-3) ≈	1.3152e+0 (1.62e-3)
LIRCMOP14	3	30	1.2722e+0 (2.26e-3) ≈	1.2722e+0 (2.05e-3) ≈	1.2727e+0 (1.54e-3) ≈	1.2727e+0 (1.24e-3)
+/ − / ≈			0/9/5	0/8/6	1/9/4	

Table 8. The HV results (mean and standard deviation) of ACREA and three variants of it on LIRCMOP test suite.

Problem	*M*	*D*	ACREA1	ACREA2	ACREA3	ACREA
LIRCMOP1	2	30	1.2767e-1 (7.91e-3) −	1.2828e-1 (1.05e-2) −	1.1882e-1 (7.47e-3) −	1.7610e-1 (1.11e-2)
LIRCMOP2	2	30	2.5666e-1 (1.26e-2) −	2.6234e-1 (1.43e-2) −	2.2984e-1 (1.05e-2) −	3.0416e-1 (1.05e-2)
LIRCMOP3	2	30	1.2614e-1 (6.15e-3) −	1.3252e-1 (9.64e-3) −	9.8497e-2 (9.30e-3) −	1.5242e-1 (1.22e-2)
LIRCMOP4	2	30	2.1996e-1 (1.30e-2) −	2.3401e-1 (1.46e-2) −	1.9949e-1 (1.45e-2) −	2.5348e-1 (1.75e-2)
LIRCMOP5	2	30	0.0000e+0 (0.00e+0) ≈	0.0000e+0 (0.00e+0) ≈	0.0000e+0 (0.00e+0) ≈	0.0000e+0 (0.00e+0)
LIRCMOP6	2	30	0.0000e+0 (0.00e+0) ≈	0.0000e+0 (0.00e+0) ≈	0.0000e+0 (0.00e+0) ≈	0.0000e+0 (0.00e+0)
LIRCMOP7	2	30	6.8526e-2 (1.08e-1) −	1.4132e-1 (1.19e-1) ≈	1.5239e-1 (1.17e-1) ≈	1.8860e-1 (9.88e-2)
LIRCMOP8	2	30	5.0263e-2 (9.32e-2) ≈	4.8626e-2 (8.75e-2) ≈	6.3603e-2 (1.00e-1) ≈	4.4049e-2 (9.04e-2)
LIRCMOP9	2	30	1.5668e-1 (8.21e-2) −	1.4404e-1 (7.43e-2) −	1.0725e-1 (4.18e-2) −	3.6917e-1 (8.39e-2)
LIRCMOP10	2	30	1.1153e-1 (9.55e-2) −	1.0460e-1 (8.90e-2) −	7.8915e-2 (2.41e-2) −	2.5795e-1 (1.47e-1)
LIRCMOP11	2	30	2.3909e-1 (5.14e-2) −	2.2859e-1 (8.44e-3) −	1.8798e-1 (3.38e-2) −	3.0929e-1 (7.61e-2)
LIRCMOP12	2	30	2.4835e-1 (8.25e-2) −	2.6859e-1 (8.56e-2) −	2.3595e-1 (8.59e-2) −	4.6044e-1 (5.78e-2)
LIRCMOP13	3	30	1.7262e-4 (1.28e-4) ≈	8.5829e-5 (1.06e-4) ≈	7.5357e-5 (9.57e-5) −	1.7117e-4 (1.50e-4)
LIRCMOP14	3	30	4.7869e-4 (3.23e-4) ≈	5.5208e-4 (3.20e-4) ≈	5.8565e-4 (3.09e-4) ≈	6.3884e-4 (2.73e-4)
+/ − / ≈			0/9/5	0/8/6	0/9/5	

4.6. Real Case Problem Testing for ACREA

In this subsection, extending the application of ACREA to real-world problems, we select nine of the most common real-world problems to contrast the eight algorithms in our experiments. For example, the water resource management problem (WRM) [41] and the speed reducer design problem (SRD) [42], which are currently of most interest, have a WRM setup that includes 5 objectives and 7 constraints, and a SRD that has 2 objectives and 11 constraints. As shown in Table 9, ACREA outperforms 7 seven competitors in 8, 9, 9, 9, 9, 9, 7 and 9 real-world problems, which is enough to prove that ACREA is highly scalable in real-world applications.

Table 9. The HV results (mean and standard deviation) of ACREA on the real-world case problem.

Problem	M	D	CMOEA/D	CTAEA	ToP	POCEA	CMOEMT	BiCo	TiGE2	ACREA
TBTD	2	3	1.0257e-1 (1.55e-2) −	8.8768e-1 (1.21e-2) −	9.0175e-1 (2.26e-4) −	2.3952e-1 (1.66e-1) −	8.9847e-1 (6.65e-4) −	8.9981e-1 (5.55e-4) −	8.9583e-1 (1.39e-3) −	9.0209e-1 (2.11e-4)
WBD	2	4	1.9462e-2 (3.54e-2) −	8.5106e-1 (1.25e-2) −	8.6267e-1 (2.21e-4) −	3.4838e-2 (1.43e-1) −	8.5661e-1 (1.41e-3) −	8.5894e-1 (2.43e-3) −	8.3175e-1 (6.68e-3) −	8.6324e-1 (3.94e-4)
DBD	2	4	4.2455e-1 (7.03e-3) −	4.3173e-1 (1.64e-3) −	4.3452e-1 (1.02e-4) −	4.2557e-1 (1.61e-3) −	4.3450e-1 (1.68e-4) −	4.3495e-1 (1.15e-4) −	4.2078e-1 (4.95e-3) −	4.3503e-1 (1.37e-4)
SRD	2	7	2.7649e-1 (8.02e-6) −	2.4217e-1 (3.89e-2) −	2.7702e-1 (3.56e-4) −	2.7421e-1 (1.21e-3) −	2.7642e-1 (1.06e-4) −	2.7725e-1 (1.32e-5) ≈	2.7086e-1 (1.37e-3) −	2.7725e-1 (1.14e-5)
FBPD	2	4	5.3073e-2 (4.29e-5) −	4.0882e-1 (4.77e-4) −	4.0929e-1 (1.30e-4) −	4.0634e-1 (1.24e-3) −	4.0952e-1 (1.22e-4) −	4.0981e-1 (6.37e-5) −	3.9604e-1 (3.92e-3) −	4.0988e-1 (8.30e-5)
TBPT	2	2	7.9374e-2 (4.89e-4) −	8.4173e-1 (4.34e-3) −	8.4736e-1 (1.20e-4) −	8.3907e-1 (3.51e-3) −	8.4206e-1 (1.85e-3) −	8.4750e-1 (5.14e-5) ≈	8.4108e-1 (2.75e-3) −	8.4749e-1 (5.95e-5)
WRM	5	3	5.8796e-2 (9.96e-5) −	9.4576e-2 (9.78e-4) −	8.6757e-2 (2.75e-3) −	5.7791e-2 (9.80e-3) −	9.0453e-2 (2.45e-3) −	9.6073e-2 (5.06e-4) −	9.5972e-2 (5.60e-4) −	9.6987e-2 (5.14e-4)
SI-BD	2	4	7.0147e-2 (8.75e-3) −	5.4770e-1 (7.78e-3) −	5.6025e-1 (3.26e-4) −	3.3342e-1 (1.53e-2) −	5.5558e-1 (1.30e-3) −	5.5677e-1 (1.06e-3) −	5.4944e-1 (2.79e-3) −	5.6107e-1 (1.90e-4)
GBD	3	7	8.8158e-2 (3.14e-5) ≈	8.6644e-2 (6.45e-4) −	8.7701e-2 (1.20e-4) −	6.5544e-2 (1.30e-2) −	8.7082e-2 (1.93e-4) −	8.7992e-2 (9.92e-5) −	8.5329e-2 (7.18e-4) −	8.8108e-2 (8.79e-5)
+/−/≈			0/8/1	0/9/0	0/9/0	0/9/0	0/9/0	0/7/2	0/9/0	

5. Conclusions

In this study, we cleverly designed a novel archiving mechanism to retain high-quality solutions, assisting the main population in approaching the CPF from both feasible and infeasible regions, in order to effectively address CMOPS. To further exploit information from infeasible solutions, a novel boundary relaxation constraint learning mechanism was established. The learning mechanism can adaptively relax the constraints according to the proportion of feasible solutions, enhance the search ability of the population, and promote the population to obtain a complete CPF. In terms of parent selection, strict constraint dominance principles and crowding distance definitions were established to drive competition between solutions. This approach helps select higher-quality solution sets, enabling the population to traverse large and narrow infeasible regions.

Comprehensive analysis of the experimental data shows that ACREA achieved 54.6% of the best values in the IGD metric across 44 benchmark test problems and 50% of the best values in the HV metric while obtaining seven best values among nine real-world problems. This once again verifies that ACREA not only outperforms its competitors but also demonstrates strong scalability in practical problems. Although ACREA achieved good results, there are still some areas for improvement. For example, the lack of interaction between the population and the archive not only leads to the mishandling of important information but also greatly reduces the speed of convergence to the Pareto front. Additionally, the threshold settings for parameters (λ) in real-world problems are not precise enough, hindering the algorithm from truly achieving optimality in practical applications. In future research, we will enhance the information transfer between the population and the archive and optimize the precision of the threshold, embedding these improvements into a large-scale model for evaluation.

Author Contributions: Conceptualization, J.C. and K.Z.; Methodology, J.C.; Software, J.C.; Validation, J.C. and Z.D.; Formal analysis, J.C.; Investigation, J.C.; Resources, J.D. and Z.D.; Data curation, J.C. and K.Z.; Writing—original draft, J.C., K.Z., H.Z., J.Y. and J.D.; Writing—review & editing, J.C., K.Z. and J.Y.; Visualization, J.C.; Supervision, J.D. and Z.D.; Project administration, Z.D.; Funding acquisition, Z.D. All authors have read and agreed to the published version of the manuscript.

Funding: This research received no external funding.

Data Availability Statement: Dataset available on request from the authors.

Conflicts of Interest: The authors declare no conflict of interest.

References

1. Prasanthi, A.; Shareef, H.; Errouissi, R.; Asna, M.; Wahyudie, A. Quantum chaotic butterfly optimization algorithm with ranking strategy for constrained optimization problems. *IEEE Access* **2021**, *9*, 114587–114608. [CrossRef]
2. Liu, J.; Wang, Y.; Fan, N.; Wei, S.; Tong, W. A convergence-diversity balanced fitness evaluation mechanism for decomposition-based many-objective optimization algorithm. *Integr. Comput.-Aided Eng.* **2019**, *26*, 159–184. [CrossRef]
3. Li, Y.; Sun, K.; Men, R.; Wang, F.; Li, D.; Han, Y.; Qu, Y. Study on the Optimization of Multi-Objective Water Resources Allocation in the Henan Yellow River Water Supply Zone. *Water* **2023**, *15*, 4009. [CrossRef]
4. Yang, R.; Zhou, Q.; Mo, Q.; Gan, L.; Hu, R. Using an Improved Artificial Hummingbird Algorithm for Vision-Guided Optimization And Grasping of Multi-Objective Robots. *J. Phys. Conf. Ser.* **2022**, *2365*, 012052. [CrossRef]
5. Wang, Y.; Sun, X.; Zhang, Y.; Gong, D.; Hu, H.; Zuo, M. Linear Regression-based Autonomous Intelligent Optimization for Constrained Multi-objective Problems. *IEEE Trans. Artif. Intell.* **2024**, *5*, 4620–4634. [CrossRef]
6. Pavankumar, Y.; Debnath, S.; Paul, S. Multi-objective pareto optimal unbalance voltage compensation in the microgrid. *Electr. Power Syst. Res.* **2023**, *217*, 109104. [CrossRef]
7. Li, Y.; Zhang, Y.; Hu, W. Adaptive multi-objective particle swarm optimization based on virtual Pareto front. *Inf. Sci.* **2023**, *625*, 206–236. [CrossRef]
8. Liang, J.; Chen, Z.; Wang, Y.; Ban, X.; Qiao, K.; Yu, K. A dual-population constrained multi-objective evolutionary algorithm with variable auxiliary population size. *Complex Intell. Syst.* **2023**, *9*, 5907–5922. [CrossRef]
9. Li, Y.; Zhao, Q.; Luo, K. Differential evolution improvement by adaptive ranking-based constraint handling technique. *Soft Comput.* **2023**, *27*, 11485–11504. [CrossRef]
10. Alofairi, A.A.; Mabrouk, E.; Elsemman, I.E. Constraint-based models for dominating protein interaction networks. *IET Syst. Biol.* **2021**, *15*, 148–162. [CrossRef]
11. Liu, M.; Yang, J.; Huang, Z. Research and Analysis of Vegetable Pricing Strategy Model Based on Single Objective Optimization Algorithm. *Inf. Syst. Econ.* **2023**, *4*, 116–126.
12. Vallerio, M.; Hufkens, J.; Van Impe, J.; Logist, F. An interactive decision-support system for multi-objective optimization of nonlinear dynamic processes with uncertainty. *Expert Syst. Appl.* **2015**, *42*, 7710–7731. [CrossRef]
13. Ming, F.; Gong, W.; Wang, L.; Gao, L. Constrained multi-objective optimization via multitasking and knowledge transfer. *IEEE Trans. Evol. Comput.* **2022**, *28*, 77–89. [CrossRef]
14. Li, K.; Chen, R.; Fu, G.; Yao, X. Two-archive evolutionary algorithm for constrained multiobjective optimization. *IEEE Trans. Evol. Comput.* **2018**, *23*, 303–315. [CrossRef]
15. Liu, Z.Z.; Wang, B.C.; Tang, K. Handling constrained multiobjective optimization problems via bidirectional coevolution. *IEEE Trans. Cybern.* **2021**, *52*, 10163–10176. [CrossRef]
16. Yang, K.; Zheng, J.; Zou, J.; Yu, F.; Yang, S. A dual-population evolutionary algorithm based on adaptive constraint strength for constrained multi-objective optimization. *Swarm Evol. Comput.* **2023**, *77*, 101247. [CrossRef]
17. Wang, Y.; Zuo, M.; Gong, D. Migration-based algorithm library enrichment for constrained multi-objective optimization and applications in algorithm selection. *Inf. Sci.* **2023**, *649*, 119593. [CrossRef]
18. Premkumar, M.; Kumar, C.; Dharma Raj, T.; Sundarsingh Jebaseelan, S.D.T.; Jangir, P.; Haes Alhelou, H. A reliable optimization framework using ensembled successive history adaptive differential evolutionary algorithm for optimal power flow problems. *IET Gener. Transm. Distrib.* **2023**, *17*, 1333–1357. [CrossRef]
19. He, Z.; Shao, H.; Cheng, J.; Zhao, X.; Yang, Y. Support tensor machine with dynamic penalty factors and its application to the fault diagnosis of rotating machinery with unbalanced data. *Mech. Syst. Signal Process.* **2020**, *141*, 106441. [CrossRef]
20. Tao, R.; Meng, Z.; Zhou, H. A self-adaptive strategy based firefly algorithm for constrained engineering design problems. *Appl. Soft Comput.* **2021**, *107*, 107417. [CrossRef]
21. Kale, I.R.; Kulkarni, A.J. Cohort intelligence with self-adaptive penalty function approach hybridized with colliding bodies optimization algorithm for discrete and mixed variable constrained problems. *Complex Intell. Syst.* **2021**, *7*, 1565–1596. [CrossRef]
22. Deb, K.; Pratap, A.; Agarwal, S.; Meyarivan, T. A fast and elitist multiobjective genetic algorithm: NSGA-II. *IEEE Trans. Evol. Comput.* **2002**, *6*, 182–197. [CrossRef]
23. Fan, Z.; Fang, Y.; Li, W.; Cai, X.; Wei, C.; Goodman, E. MOEA/D with angle-based constrained dominance principle for constrained multi-objective optimization problems. *Appl. Soft Comput.* **2019**, *74*, 621–633. [CrossRef]
24. Ma, Z.; Wang, Y.; Song, W. A new fitness function with two rankings for evolutionary constrained multiobjective optimization. *IEEE Trans. Syst. Man Cybern. Syst.* **2019**, *51*, 5005–5016. [CrossRef]
25. Takahama, T.; Sakai, S.; Iwane, N. Solving nonlinear constrained optimization problems by the ε constrained differential evolution. In Proceedings of the 2006 IEEE International Conference on Systems, Man and Cybernetics, Taipei, Taiwan, 8–11 October 2006; Volume 3, pp. 2322–2327.
26. Fan, Z.; Li, W.; Cai, X.; Huang, H.; Fang, Y.; You, Y.; Mo, J.; Wei, C.; Goodman, E. An improved epsilon constraint-handling method in MOEA/D for CMOPs with large infeasible regions. *Soft Comput.* **2019**, *23*, 12491–12510. [CrossRef]
27. Peng, C.; Liu, H.L.; Gu, F. An evolutionary algorithm with directed weights for constrained multi-objective optimization. *Appl. Soft Comput.* **2017**, *60*, 613–622. [CrossRef]
28. Younis, A.; Dong, Z. Adaptive surrogate assisted multi-objective optimization approach for highly nonlinear and complex engineering design problems. *Appl. Soft Comput.* **2024**, *150*, 111065. [CrossRef]

29. Liu, Z.Z.; Wang, Y. Handling constrained multiobjective optimization problems with constraints in both the decision and objective spaces. *IEEE Trans. Evol. Comput.* **2019**, *23*, 870–884. [CrossRef]
30. Jain, H.; Deb, K. An evolutionary many-objective optimization algorithm using reference-point based nondominated sorting approach, part II: Handling constraints and extending to an adaptive approach. *IEEE Trans. Evol. Comput.* **2013**, *18*, 602–622. [CrossRef]
31. He, C.; Cheng, R.; Tian, Y.; Zhang, X.; Tan, K.C.; Jin, Y. Paired offspring generation for constrained large-scale multiobjective optimization. *IEEE Trans. Evol. Comput.* **2020**, *25*, 448–462. [CrossRef]
32. Zhou, Y.; Zhu, M.; Wang, J.; Zhang, Z.; Xiang, Y.; Zhang, J. Tri-goal evolution framework for constrained many-objective optimization. *IEEE Trans. Syst. Man Cybern. Syst.* **2018**, *50*, 3086–3099. [CrossRef]
33. Ming, F.; Gong, W.; Zhen, H.; Li, S.; Wang, L.; Liao, Z. A simple two-stage evolutionary algorithm for constrained multi-objective optimization. *Knowl.-Based Syst.* **2021**, *228*, 107263. [CrossRef]
34. Li, Y.; Feng, X.; Yu, H. A constrained multiobjective evolutionary algorithm with the two-archive weak cooperation. *Inf. Sci.* **2022**, *615*, 415–430. [CrossRef]
35. Ma, H.; Wei, H.; Tian, Y.; Cheng, R.; Zhang, X. A multi-stage evolutionary algorithm for multi-objective optimization with complex constraints. *Inf. Sci.* **2021**, *560*, 68–91. [CrossRef]
36. Liu, Z.Z.; Qin, Y.; Song, W.; Zhang, J.; Li, K. Multiobjective-based constraint-handling technique for evolutionary constrained multiobjective optimization: A new perspective. *IEEE Trans. Evol. Comput.* **2022**, *27*, 1370–1384. [CrossRef]
37. Silverman, B.W. *Density Estimation for Statistics and Data Analysis*; Routledge: New York, NY, USA, 2018.
38. Liang, J.; Ban, X.; Yu, K.; Qu, B.; Qiao, K.; Yue, C.; Chen, K.; Tan, K.C. A survey on evolutionary constrained multiobjective optimization. *IEEE Trans. Evol. Comput.* **2022**, *27*, 201–221. [CrossRef]
39. Gu, Q.; Wang, Q.; Xiong, N.N.; Jiang, S.; Chen, L. Surrogate-assisted evolutionary algorithm for expensive constrained multi-objective discrete optimization problems. *Complex Intell. Syst.* **2022**, *8*, 2699–2718. [CrossRef]
40. Tian, Y.; Zhu, W.; Zhang, X.; Jin, Y. A practical tutorial on solving optimization problems via PlatEMO. *Neurocomputing* **2023**, *518*, 190–205. [CrossRef]
41. Garcia, J.A.; Alamanos, A. A multi-objective optimization framework for water resources allocation considering stakeholder input. *Environ. Sci. Proc.* **2023**, *25*, 32. [CrossRef]
42. Xu, X.; Chen, X.; Liu, Z.; Yang, J.; Xu, Y.; Zhang, Y.; Gao, Y. Multi-objective reliability-based design optimization for the reducer housing of electric vehicles. *Eng. Optim.* **2022**, *54*, 1324–1340. [CrossRef]

mathematics

MDPI

Article

Distributed Optimization Control for the System with Second-Order Dynamic

Yueqing Wang, Hao Zhang and Zhi Li *

School of Mechano-Engineering, Xidian University, Xi'an 710126, China
* Correspondence: zhli@xidian.edu.cn

Abstract: No matter whether with constraint or without constraint, most of the research about distributed optimization is studied for the kind of quadratic performance criteria that does not have an integrator; these optimization problems only concern the state value at the time of the final state, not the whole process of the system change. For this problem, this paper discusses second-order multi-agent systems with a discrete-time dynamic and a continuous-time dynamic, respectively, for distributed optimization control problems, and proposes sufficient conditions to ensure the quadratic performance criteria with an integrator is positive. Specifically, under sufficient conditions, we describe the multi-agent systems that are considered in this paper to be connected topology; all the agents can obtain the information from their neighbors. In addition, the structure of our controller only relies on the Laplace matrix of the system's topology, and the reaction coefficients in the controller are the parameters in the performance criteria. Finally, the analysis of convergence is given and verified by numerical examples and simulations.

Keywords: multi-agent; optimization control; distributed control

MSC: 93A16

1. Introduction

The problem with distributed optimization control is designing a suitable distributed controller to make the system finish its assignment while optimizing the performance criteria or objective function [1–8]. However, no matter whether with constraint or without constraint, most of this research about distributed optimization is studied for the kind of quadratic performance criteria that does not have an integrator; these optimization problems only concern the state value at the time of the final state, not the whole process of the system change. In particular, sometimes the optimal solution can only be calculated from a feasible set due to the constraints of the actual system, which makes the constrained optimization problem begin to be noticed. In addition, most of the research on distributed optimization, whether constrained or unconstrained, is aimed at the quadratic performance criteria without integration. In other words, these optimization problems are concerned only with the state values at the end of the state, not with the entire process of changing the system. This paper was launched in response to the above problems.

Specifically, for the distributed estimation problem without constraint, Tsitsiklis and colleagues [9] used the gradient of the local objective function and the weighted average of self-estimation and neighbor estimations, which is calculated by row stochastic matrix and Laplacian matrix, to approach the optimal estimation value. Harold and colleagues [10] considered the problem with random noise; this conclusion has been put into use in many engineering applications such as space allocation [11], power network optimization [12], and parameter estimation [13,14]. However, the local information sharing among the agents of the system must be guaranteed before this optimization strategy is available. This requirement brings a huge communication cost to the system, which leads to the creation of a "de-centration" optimization strategy. The problem of how to optimize the sum of multiple convex functions has been considered in [15], which proposed the "de-centration" optimization strategy first. Next, convex intersection calculation is discussed in [16], and the distributed convex intersection algorithm based on approximate projection is given to solve this kind of problem. Besides, the optimization with constraint sets is translated to the optimization without constraint through the penalty function [17]. Similar problems about optimization without constraint have been concluded as a generalized form in [18]. From this, lots of attention is put on optimization without constraint under the different surroundings. For example, the objective function that is strongly convex with the Lipschitz continuous gradient is studied in [19]; also, the gradient of the objective function on some specific points can be obtained. Another situation in the objective function is the convex and continuously quadratic differential, which is studied in [20]. However, sometimes, because of the constraint of real systems, the optimized solution can only be calculated from a feasible set; this makes the optimization problem with constraint begin to be noticed. To address this problem, the system with the same and different constraint sets for each local smooth objective function are analyzed, respectively, in [12] and [21]. Relatively, the differentiable prime–dual contained algorithm is proposed when the objective function is not smooth [22]. Otherwise, some constraint sets with special structures are studied, in [23,24]; authors proposed a distributed saddle point search algorithm based on the Lagrange function to deal with the constraint formed in a vector. Chang and colleagues [25] proposed the disturbance saddle point algorithm to overcome the strictly convex assumption further. However, all of those methods require that the information be globally shared. In addition, due to the system states and inputs being continuous-time, a general method that transfers the control algorithm used in the discrete-time system to a suitable form in the continuous-time system is present, [15,19] gives the error analysis while using a fix step algorithm in the continuous-time system and discrete-time system, respectively. Another method is quantizing the system states and inputs; the effect of which is analyzed in [26].

Nevertheless, most of the above research about distributed optimization control, no matter whether with constraint or without constraint was studied for the kind of quadratic performance criteria without an integrator. In other words, these optimization problems only concern the state value at the time of the final state, not the whole process of the system change. For the problem, Zhang and colleagues [27] researched the distributed optimization control of the first-order discrete-time system with the quadratic performance criteria with the integrator in fixed topology, as well as designed the distributed optimization consensus controller based on the results of the distributed consensus algorithm published in [28–32]. Also, since the agents considered have second-order dynamics, which have great differences from first-order dynamics, the distributed algorithms proposed in [33,34] are invalid here. In [34], state-dependent gradient gains were introduced into the distributed optimal algorithm to tackle this problem of first-order multi-agent networks; meanwhile, it demonstrated that the team objective function can be minimized asymptotically or in finite time. Inspired by [27,33,34], this paper goes on to discuss the distributed optimization control in second-order discrete-time systems and continuous-time systems with the quadratic performance criteria with an integrator under the fixed topology. Additionally, sufficient conditions to ensure the existence of a distributed optimization control system and the form of the controller are given in the form of analysis expression. The stability of the controller is proven and verified by simulations.

The paper is organized as follows: the preparation and the problem formulation are presented in Section 2. In Section 3, distributed optimization control problems in second-order discrete-time systems are described and analyzed. In Section 4, some simulation examples are provided to illustrate the distributed optimization control in second-order discrete-time systems and continuous-time systems with the quadratic performance criteria with an integrator under fixed topology. Conclusions are drawn in Section 5.

2. Problem Statement

In this part, we discuss the distributed optimization problem in second-order continuous-time systems and second-order discrete-time systems, respectively, in two sections.

2.1. Continuous-Time Dynamic

In this section, we discuss distributed optimization control problems in second-order continuous-time systems. This kind of problem can be described as follows.

2.1.1. System Describe

A dynamic system

$$\hat{x} = (A \otimes I_N)x + (B \otimes I_N)u \tag{1}$$

where $\hat{x}$ denotes the differential x, $A = \begin{bmatrix} 0 & 1 \\ 0 & 0 \end{bmatrix}$, and $B = \begin{bmatrix} 0 & 0 \\ 1 & 0 \end{bmatrix}$.

Performance index:

$$J = \frac{1}{2}\int_0^\infty [x^T Q x + u^T (I_n \otimes R)u]dt \tag{2}$$

We hope to design a distributed optimization control system, which can make the system states in Equation (1) achieve consensus; meanwhile, the quadratic performance criteria (2) are minimum. Before solving this problem, we give the following definitions and theorems.

Definition 1. *For the system in Equation* (1)*, we can construct a weight matrix Q as follows.*

$$\begin{aligned} Q &= -(K \otimes L)[(A \otimes I) - (BB^T K \otimes R^{-1}L] - (A^T K \otimes L) \\ R &= rI_N \end{aligned} \tag{3}$$

where A and B are described in Equation (1), K and L are as follows:

$$K = \begin{bmatrix} k_0 & k_1 \\ k_1 & k_2 \end{bmatrix}, \quad L = hI_N + L_0$$

where L_0 is the Laplace matrix of the system topology, and h is a self-coupling coefficient.

Theorem 1. *For the weight matrix Q, it is positive semi-definite if the following condition holds*

$$r^{-1}\mu_i \geq \max\left\{ \frac{2k_1}{{k_1}^2 + {k_2}^2}, \frac{{k_0}^2}{2k_1(k_0 k_2 - {k_1}^2)} \right\} \tag{4}$$

Meanwhile, $r^{-1}\mu_i$ satisfied the following Equation.

$$[2k_1 - ({k_1}^2 + {k_2}^2)r^{-1}\mu_i]^2 \geq 4[2k_3(k_0 k_2 - {k_1}^2)r^{-1}\mu_i - {k_0}^2] \tag{5}$$

Proof.

$$\begin{aligned} Q &= -\begin{bmatrix} k_0 L & k_1 L \\ k_1 L & k_2 L \end{bmatrix} \begin{bmatrix} 0 & I_N \\ -k_1 r^{-1} L & -k_2 r^{-1} L \end{bmatrix} - \begin{bmatrix} 0 & 0 \\ k_0 L & k_1 L \end{bmatrix} \\ &= \begin{bmatrix} {k_1}^2 r^{-1} L^2 & k_1 k_2 r^{-1} L^2 - k_0 L \\ k_1 k_2 r^{-1} L^2 - k_0 L & {k_2}^2 r^{-1} L^2 - 2k_1 L \end{bmatrix} \\ &= \begin{bmatrix} {k_1}^2 r^{-1} L & k_1 k_2 r^{-1} L - k_0 I \\ k_1 k_2 r^{-1} L - k_0 I & {k_2}^2 r^{-1} L - 2k_1 I \end{bmatrix} \cdot \begin{bmatrix} L & 0 \\ 0 & L \end{bmatrix} \\ &= M \times N \end{aligned}$$

Matrix N is positive semi-definite. Next, we calculate the eigenvalues of matrix M.

$$\det(\lambda I - M) = \det\begin{bmatrix} \lambda I_N - {k_1}^2 r^{-1} L & k_1 k_2 r^{-1} L - k_0 I_N \\ k_1 k_2 r^{-1} L - k_0 I_N & \lambda I_N - {k_2}^2 r^{-1} L + 2k_1 I_N \end{bmatrix}$$

$$= \det\Big\{ I_N \lambda^2 + [2k_1 I_N - ({k_1}^2 + {k_2}^2)]\lambda - 2{k_1}^3 r^{-1} L$$

$$-{k_0}^2 I_N + 2k_0 k_1 k_2 r^{-1} L \Big\}$$

$$= \prod_{i=1}^{N} \Big\{ \lambda^2 + [2k_1 - ({k_1}^2 + {k_2}^2) r^{-1} \mu_i]\lambda + [2k_1 (k_0 k_2$$

$$- {k_1}^2) r^{-1} \mu_i - {k_0}^2] \Big\}$$

Because matrix M is real symmetric, and

$$r^{-1}\mu_i \geq \max\left\{ \frac{2k_1}{{k_1}^2 + {k_2}^2}, \frac{{k_0}^2}{2k_1(k_0 k_2 - {k_1}^2)} \right\}$$

We can obtain

$$\begin{cases} r^{-1}\mu_i \geq \frac{2k_1}{{k_1}^2 + {k_2}^2} \\ r^{-1}\mu_i \geq \frac{{k_0}^2}{2k_1(k_0 k_2 - {k_1}^2)} \end{cases}$$

$$\Rightarrow \begin{cases} 2k_1 - ({k_1}^2 + {k_2}^2) r^{-1}\mu_i \leq 0 \\ 2k_1(k_0 k_2 - {k_1}^2) r^{-1}\mu_i - {k_0}^2 \geq 0 \end{cases}$$

It is obvious that matrix N is semi-definite, and matrix Q is positive semi-definite. □

2.1.2. Controller Design

Now, we give the design of the distributed optimization control system. For the multi-agent system described in Equation (1) with the quadratic performance criteria described in Equation (2), we have the following theorem.

Theorem 2. *For the system* (1)*, if the weight matrix Q and R in Equation* (2) *satisfies the condition as follows.*

$$\begin{cases} Q = -(K \otimes L)[(A \otimes I) - (BB^T K \otimes R^{-1} L] - (A^T K \otimes L) \\ R = rI \end{cases} \tag{6}$$

There must be an optimization distributed control that can be designed to minimize the quadratic performance criteria in Equation (2).

Proof. First, according to the continuous minimum principle, we can introduce the Lagrange multiplier.

$$\vec{\lambda}^T(t) = [\lambda_1(t), \cdots, \lambda_{2N}(t)]^T$$

Then, for the optimization problem described in Equations (1) and (2), we can structure the Hamiltonian function as follows:

$$H = \frac{1}{2}[x^T Q x + u^T (I_n \otimes R) u] + \lambda^T [(A \otimes I_N) x + (B \otimes I_N) u]$$

Next, when we take partials to the H, we can obtain

$$\begin{cases} \hat{\lambda} = -\frac{\partial H}{\partial x} = -Qx - \left(A^T \otimes I_N\right)\lambda \\ \frac{\partial H}{\partial x} = (I_N \otimes R)u + (B^T \otimes I_N)\lambda = 0 \\ \hat{x} = (A \otimes I_N)x + (B \otimes I_N)u \end{cases}$$

$$\begin{cases} \hat{\lambda} = -\frac{\partial H}{\partial x} = -Qx^* - \left(A^T \otimes I_N\right)\lambda \\ u^* = -\left(B^T \otimes R^{-1}\right)\lambda \\ \hat{x}^* = (A \otimes I_N)x^* + (B \otimes I_N)u^* \end{cases}$$

$$\begin{cases} \hat{\lambda} = -Qx^* - \left(A^T \otimes I_N\right)\lambda \\ \hat{x}^* = (A \otimes I_N)x^* - \left(BB^T \otimes R^{-1}\right)\lambda \end{cases} \tag{7}$$

where $u^*(t)$ is the optimization control system to be solved, and $x^*(t)$ is the optimization track.

Because the system (1) is linear, we can assume that

$$\lambda(t) = Vx * (t) \tag{8}$$

From Equation (7), we know that matrix V and Q satisfy the following Riccati Equation.

$$(A^T \otimes I_N)V + V(A \otimes I_N) - V(BB^T \otimes R^{-1})V = -Q \tag{9}$$

Insert Equation (6) into Equation (9); we obtain

$$\begin{aligned} V &= K \otimes L \\ \lambda(t) &= (K \otimes L)x * (t) \end{aligned}$$

We obtain the optimization control system.

$$u * (t) = -(B^T K \otimes R^{-1} L)x * (t)$$

The optimization track is $\hat{x}^*(t) = \left[(A \otimes I_N) - \left(BB^T K \otimes R^{-1} L\right)\right]x^*(t)$. □

2.1.3. Convergence Analysis

Now, we give the convergence analysis for the system under the effect of the optimization control system.

Let

$$P = [(A \otimes I_N) - (BB^T K \otimes R^{-1} L)]$$

We can calculate

$$\begin{aligned} \det(\lambda I - P) &= \det\begin{pmatrix} \lambda I_N & -I_N \\ k_1 r^{-1} L & \lambda I_N + 2k_2 r^{-1} I_N \end{pmatrix} \\ &= \det\left(\lambda^2 I_N + k_2 r^{-1} L\lambda + k_1 r^{-1} L\right) \\ &= \prod_{i=1}^{N} \left(\lambda^2 I_N + k_2 r^{-1}\mu_i\lambda + k_1 r^{-1}\mu_i\right) \\ &= 0 \end{aligned}$$

The eigenvalue is

$$\lambda = \frac{-k_2 r^{-1}\mu_i \pm \sqrt{k_2{}^2 r^{-1}\mu_i{}^2 - 4k_1 r^{-1}\mu_i}}{2}$$

It is easy to know that

$$\because k_1 > 0, \mu_i > 0$$
$$\therefore \text{Re}(\lambda) < 0$$

Thus, the system must be stable.

The distributed optimization control for the continuous-time system is finished hereto. In the next section, we discuss the condition of a discrete-time system.

3. Discrete-Time Dynamic

In this section, we discuss distributed optimization control problems in second-order discrete-time systems. This kind of problem can be described as follows.

3.1. System Describe

Dynamic System

$$x(k+1) = (I_N \otimes A)x(k) + (I_N \otimes B)u(k) \tag{10}$$

where $A = \begin{bmatrix} 1 & 1 \\ 0 & 1 \end{bmatrix}$ and $B = \begin{bmatrix} 0 & 0 \\ 1 & 0 \end{bmatrix}$.

Performance index:

$$J = \frac{1}{2}\sum_{k=0}^{\infty}\left[x^T(k)Qx(k) + u^T(k)(R \otimes I_n)u(k)\right] \tag{11}$$

where $R = rI_N$, r is constant.

Similar to section A, the following definitions and theorems are given first.

Definition 2. *For the system in Equation* (9), *we can construct a weight matrix Q as follows.*

$$Q = (L \otimes K)[(I_N \otimes A) - (R^{-1}L \otimes BB^TK)]^{-1} - (L \otimes A^TK) \tag{12}$$

where A and B are described in Equation (9); K is as follows:

$$K = \begin{bmatrix} k_1 & k_2 \\ k_3 & k_4 \end{bmatrix}, \quad L = hI_N + L_0$$

L0 is the Laplace matrix of the system, and h is a self-coupling coefficient.

Theorem 3. *For the matrix Q described in Equation* (10), *if the following condition holds, Q must be existent.*

$$r^{-1}\mu_i \neq \frac{1}{k_4 - k_3}$$

where μ_i is the eigenvalue of L.

Proof. Let $P = [(I_N \otimes A) - (R^{-1}L \otimes BB^TK)]$ and $\det(P) = 0$; we have

$$\begin{aligned} \det(P) &= \det\begin{vmatrix} I_N & I_N \\ -k_3r^{-1}L & I_N - k_4r^{-1}L \end{vmatrix} \\ &= \det[I_N - (k_4 - k_3)r^{-1}L] \\ &= \prod_{i=1}^{N}[1 - (k_4 - k_3)r^{-1}\mu_i] \\ &= 0 \\ r^{-1}\mu_i &= \tfrac{1}{k_4 - k_3} \end{aligned}$$

Because $r^{-1}\mu_i \neq \frac{1}{k_4-k_3}$, $\det(P) \neq 0$, the P^{-1} is existent, and Q is existent. □

Theorem 4. *For a block matrix*

$$M = \begin{bmatrix} A & B \\ C & D \end{bmatrix}$$

If it satisfies $AB = BA$; $CD = DC$ and $AD - BC$ is non-singular.
Then, we can obtain

$$M^{-1} = \begin{bmatrix} D & -B \\ -C & A \end{bmatrix} \times \begin{bmatrix} AD - BC & 0 \\ 0 & AD - BC \end{bmatrix}^{-1}$$

Proof.

$$\begin{aligned} M \cdot M^{-1} &= \begin{bmatrix} A & B \\ C & D \end{bmatrix} \times \begin{bmatrix} D & -B \\ -C & A \end{bmatrix} \times \begin{bmatrix} AD - BC & 0 \\ 0 & AD - BC \end{bmatrix}^{-1} \\ &= \begin{bmatrix} AD - BC & BA - AB \\ CD - DC & AD - BC \end{bmatrix} \times \begin{bmatrix} AD - BC & 0 \\ 0 & AD - BC \end{bmatrix}^{-1} \\ &= \begin{bmatrix} AD - BC & 0 \\ 0 & AD - BC \end{bmatrix} \times \begin{bmatrix} AD - BC & 0 \\ 0 & AD - BC \end{bmatrix}^{-1} \\ &= \begin{bmatrix} I & 0 \\ 0 & I \end{bmatrix} \end{aligned}$$

□

Theorem 5. *For the weight matrix Q described in Equation (12), it is positive semi-definite when the following condition holds*

$$\begin{cases} 2(k_4 - k_3) > k_3 \geq 1 \\ \frac{4k_3}{k_4{}^2} \leq r^{-1}\mu_i < \min\left\{\frac{4}{k_4}, \frac{4}{2k_4 - k_3}, \frac{1}{k_4 - k_3}\right\} \end{cases} \tag{13}$$

Meanwhile, k_2 satisfied the following in equations.

$$k_2 = k_1 + k_3 \leq \frac{k_3{}^2 r^{-1}\mu_i + k_4(k_4 - k_3)r^{-1}\mu_i - k_3}{1 - (k_4 - k_3)r^{-1}\mu_i} \tag{14}$$

$$[1 - (k_4 - k_3)r^{-1}\mu_i]k_2{}^2 - k_3[2 - k_3 r^{-1}\mu_i]k_2 + k_3{}^2[1 + k_4 r^{-1}\mu_i] \leq 0 \tag{15}$$

Proof. Before proofing Theorem 5, we need to give the existence proof of k_2. In other words, the k_2 satisfied in Equations (14) and (15) must exist.

First, we prove that the solution of k_2 satisfied in Equation (15) must be existent. Equation (14) is a quadratic in the equation in one unknown of k_2, calculating the Δ_1 of Equation (16).

$$\begin{aligned} \Delta_1 &= b^2 - 4ac \\ &= k_3{}^2[2 - k_3 r^{-1}\mu_i]^2 - 4k_3{}^2[1 - (k_4 - k_3)r^{-1}\mu_i][1 + k_4 r^{-1}\mu_i] \\ &= k_3{}^2(2k_4 - k_3)^2 r^{-2}\mu_i{}^2 \geq 0 \end{aligned} \tag{16}$$

Thus, the solution of k_2 satisfied in Equation (15) must be existent. Next, we need to illustrate that the intersection of Equations (14) and (15) is existent.

From Equation (15), we can calculate its axis of symmetry.

$$-\frac{b}{2a} = \frac{k_3(2 - k_3 r^{-1}\mu_i)}{2[1 - (k_4 - k_3)r^{-1}\mu_i]} \tag{17}$$

Let the right of Equation (14) minus the right of Equation (17)

$$\begin{aligned} &\frac{k_3{}^2r^{-1}\mu_i+k_4(k_4-k_3)r^{-1}\mu_i-k_3}{1-(k_4-k_3)r^{-1}\mu_i}-\frac{k_3(2-k_3r^{-1}\mu_i)}{2[1-(k_4-k_3)r^{-1}\mu_i]} \\ &=\frac{2k_4(k_4-k_3)r^{-1}\mu_i+3k_3{}^2r^{-1}\mu_i-4k_3}{2[1-(k_4-k_3)r^{-1}\mu_i]} \end{aligned} \tag{18}$$

From Condition (13), we know the denominator of Equation (18) is greater than zero. Meanwhile, the member is an increasing function $r^{-1}\mu_i$. We take the minimum value of $r^{-1}\mu_i$ into the member of Equation (18).

$$\begin{aligned} &2k_4(k_4-k_3)r^{-1}\mu_i+3k_3{}^2r^{-1}\mu_i-4k_3\Big|_{r^{-1}\mu_i=\frac{4k_3}{k_4{}^2}} \\ &=[2k_4(k_4-k_3)+3k_3{}^2]\tfrac{4k_3}{k_4{}^2}-4k_3 \\ &=\left\{[3k_3{}^2+2k_4(k_4-k_3)]-k_4{}^2\right\}\times\tfrac{4k_3}{k_4{}^2} \\ &=[2k_3{}^2+(k_4-k_3)^2]\times\tfrac{4k_3}{k_4{}^2}>0 \end{aligned} \tag{19}$$

Thus, the factors satisfied in Equations (14) and (15) must be existent. Now, we give the proof of the positive semidefinite of weight matrix Q.

$$\begin{aligned} Q\ &=(L\otimes K)[(I_N\otimes A)-(R^{-1}L\otimes BB^TK)]^{-1}-(L\otimes A^TK) \\ &=\{(L\otimes K)-(L\otimes A^TK)[(I_N\otimes A)-(R^{-1}L\otimes BB^TK)]\} \\ &\times[(I_N\otimes A)-(R^{-1}L\otimes BB^TK)]^{-1} \\ &=\{[L\otimes(K-A^TKA)]+(LR^{-1}L\otimes A^TKBB^TK)\} \\ &\times[(I_N\otimes A)-(R^{-1}L\otimes BB^TK)]^{-1} \\ &=\{[L\otimes(K-A^TKA)]+(LR^{-1}L\otimes A^TKBB^TK)\}\times P^{-1} \end{aligned}$$

From Theorem 2, we have

$$P^{-1}=\begin{bmatrix} I_N-k_4r^{-1}L & -I_N \\ k3r^{-1}L & I_N-k_4r^{-1}L \end{bmatrix}\times\begin{bmatrix} I_N-(k_4-k_3)r^{-1}L & 0 \\ 0 & I_N-(k_4-k_3)r^{-1}L \end{bmatrix}^{-1}$$

Thus

$$\begin{aligned} &Q=\begin{bmatrix} L & 0 \\ 0 & L \end{bmatrix} \\ &\begin{bmatrix} k_3{}^2r^{-1}L & -k_1I+k_2(k_4-k_3)r^{-1}L \\ -k_1I+k_2(k_4-k_3)r^{-1}L & -k_1I+(k_2+k_4)(k_4-k_3)r^{-1}L \end{bmatrix} \\ &\begin{bmatrix} I_N+(k_3-k_4)r^{-1}L & 0 \\ 0 & I_N+(k_3-k_4)r^{-1}L \end{bmatrix}^{-1} \end{aligned}$$

For convenience, we make the symbol definition as follows,

$$L'=\begin{bmatrix} L & 0 \\ 0 & L \end{bmatrix}$$

$$M=\begin{bmatrix} k_3{}^2r^{-1}L & -k_1I+k_2(k_4-k_3)r^{-1}L \\ -k_1I+k_2(k_4-k_3)r^{-1}L & -k_1I+(k_2+k_4)(k_4-k_3)r^{-1}L \end{bmatrix}$$

$$N=\begin{bmatrix} I_N+(k_3-k_4)r^{-1}L & 0 \\ 0 & I_N+(k_3-k_4)r^{-1}L \end{bmatrix}$$

Then, Q can be expressed as $Q = L'MN^{-1}$ and L' is positive semi-definite. Next, we solve the eigenvalues of matrix N.

$$\det(\lambda_n I_N - N) = \prod_{i=1}^{N}\left\{(\lambda_n - 1) + (k_4 - k_3)r^{-1}\mu_i\right\}^2 = 0$$
$$\lambda_n = 1 - (k_4 - k_3)r^{-1}\mu_i$$

Because $r^{-1}\mu_i < \frac{1}{k_4-k_3}$, all the eigenvalues of N are greater than zero, and matrix N is positive semi-definite. The eigenvalues of matrix M are solved in Equation (20), and the judgment of Equation (20) is shown in Equation (21)

$$\begin{aligned}
\det(\lambda I_N - M) &= \det\left\{\begin{bmatrix} \lambda I_N & 0 \\ 0 & \lambda I_N \end{bmatrix} - \begin{bmatrix} {k_3}^2 r^{-1}L & -k_1 I + k_2(k_4 - k_3)r^{-1}L \\ -k_1 I + k_2(k_4 - k_3)r^{-1}L & -k_1 I + (k_2 + k_4)(k_4 - k_3)r^{-1}L \end{bmatrix}\right\} \\
&= \det\left\{\lambda^2 I_N + [(k_2 + k_3)I_N - (k_2 + k_4)(k_4 - k_3)r^{-1}L - {k_3}^2 r^{-1}L]\lambda + {k_3}^2(k_2 + k_4)(k_4 - k_3)r^{-2}L^2\right. \\
&\quad \left. - (k_2 - k_3)^2 I_N - {k_3}^2(k_2 + k_3)r^{-1}L + 2k_2(k_4 - k_3)(k_2 - k_3)r^{-1}L - {k_2}^2(k_4 - k_3)^2 r^{-2}L^2\right\} \\
&= \prod_{i=1}^{N}\left\{\lambda^2 + [(k_2 + k_3) - (k_2 + k_4)(k_4 - k_3)r^{-1}\mu_i - {k_3}^2 r^{-1}\mu_i]\lambda + {k_3}^2(k_2 + k_4)(k_4 - k_3)r^{-2}{\mu_i}^2\right. \\
&\quad \left. - (k_2 - k_3)^2 I_N - {k_3}^2(k_2 + k_3)r^{-1}\mu_i + 2k_2(k_4 - k_3)(k_2 - k_3)r^{-1}\mu_i - {k_2}^2(k_4 - k_3)^2 r^{-2}{\mu_i}^2\right\}
\end{aligned} \tag{20}$$

$$\begin{aligned}
\Delta_2 = b^2 - 4ac &= [(k_2 + k_3) - (k_2 + k_4)(k_4 - k_3)r^{-1}\mu_i - {k_3}^2 r^{-1}\mu_i]^2 - 4[{k_3}^2(k_2 + k_4)(k_4 - k_3)r^{-2}{\mu_i}^2 \\
&\quad - (k_2 - k_3)^2 I_N - {k_3}^2(k_2 + k_3)r^{-1}\mu_i + 2k_2(k_4 - k_3)(k_2 - k_3)r^{-1}\mu_i - {k_2}^2(k_4 - k_3)^2 r^{-2}{\mu_i}^2] \\
&= [(k_2 + k_3) - (k_2 + k_4)(k_4 - k_3)r^{-1}\mu_i - {k_3}^2 r^{-1}\mu_i]^2 + 4[(k_2 - k_3) - k_2(k_4 - k_3)r^{-1}\mu_i]^2 \\
&\quad - 4[{k_3}^2(k_2 + k_4)(k_4 - k_3)r^{-2}{\mu_i}^2 - {k_3}^2(k_2 + k_3)r^{-1}\mu_i] \\
&= \left\{(k_2 + k_3) - [(k_2 + k_4)(k_4 - k_3)r^{-1}\mu_i - {k_3}^2]r^{-1}\mu_i\right\}^2 + 4[(k_2 - k_3) - k_2(k_4 - k_3)r^{-1}\mu_i]^2 \\
&\geq 0
\end{aligned} \tag{21}$$

Then, we judge the positive and negative coefficient of a quadratic Equation (20) (see Equations (22)–(24)).

$$a = 1 > 0 \tag{22}$$

$$\begin{aligned}
b &= [(k_2 + k_3) - (k_2 + k_4)(k_4 - k_3)r^{-1}\mu_i - {k_3}^2 r^{-1}\mu_i] \\
&= [1 - (k_4 - k_3)r^{-1}\mu_i]k_2 - [{k_3}^2 r^{-1}\mu_i \\
&\quad + k_4(k_4 - k_3)r^{-1}\mu_i - k_3] \\
&\because k_2 \leq \tfrac{{k_3}^2 r^{-1}\mu_i + k_4(k_4 - k_3)r^{-1}\mu_i - k_3}{1 - (k_4 - k_3)r^{-1}\mu_i} \\
&\therefore b \leq 0
\end{aligned} \tag{23}$$

$$\begin{aligned}
c &= \left\{{k_3}^2(k_2 + k_4)(k_4 - k_3)r^{-2}{\mu_i}^2 - (k_2 - k_3)^2 I_N - {k_3}^2(k_2 + k_3)r^{-1}\mu_i + \right. \\
&\quad \left. 2k_2(k_4 - k_3)(k_2 - k_3)r^{-1}\mu_i - {k_2}^2(k_4 - k_3)^2 r^{-2}{\mu_i}^2\right\} \\
&= -[(k_4 - k_3)r^{-1}\mu_i - 1]^2{k_2}^2 + [{k_3}^2(k_4 - k_3)r^{-2}{\mu_i}^2 - 2k_3(k_4 - k_3)r^{-1}\mu_i - {k_3}^2 r^{-1}\mu_i + 2k_3]k_2 \\
&\quad + [(k_4 - k_3){k_3}^2 k_4 r^{-2}{\mu_i}^2 - {k_3}^3 r^{-1}\mu_i - {k_3}^2] \\
&= -[1 - (k_4 - k_3)r^{-1}\mu_i]\left\{[1 - (k_4 - k_3)r^{-1}\mu_i]{k_2}^2 - k_3[2 - k_3 r^{-1}\mu_i]k_2 + {k_3}^2[1 + k_4 r^{-1}\mu_i]\right\} \\
&\because [1 - (k_4 - k_3)r^{-1}\mu_i]{k_2}^2 - k_3[2 - k_3 r^{-1}\mu_i]k_2 + {k_3}^2[1 + k_4 r^{-1}\mu_i] \leq 0 \\
&\quad r^{-1}\mu_i < \tfrac{1}{k_4 - k_3} \\
&\therefore c \geq 0
\end{aligned} \tag{24}$$

So, all the eigenvalues of M are greater than zero and matrix M is a positive semi-definite because matrix L', M, and N are all symmetric positive definite. Additionally, they are satisfied.

$$\begin{cases} L'M = ML' \\ (L'M)N^{-1} = N^{-1}(L'M) \end{cases}$$

Thus, Q is positive semi-definite. □

3.2. Controller Design

For the multi-agent systems described in Equation (10) with the quadratic performance criteria described in Equation (11), we have the following theorem.

Theorem 6. *For the system* (10)*, if the weight matrix Q and R in Equation* (11) *are designed as Equation* (12)*, there must be an optimization distributed control system that can be designed to minimize the performance index in Equation* (11) *and the distributed control system and optimization track are as follows.*

$$\begin{cases} u*(k) = -(R^{-1}L \otimes B^T K)x*(k) \\ x*(k+1) = [(I_N \otimes A) - (R^{-1}L \otimes BB^T K)]x*(k) \end{cases} \quad (25)$$

Proof. First, according to the discrete minimum principle, we can introduce the Lagrange multiplier $\overset{\rightarrow T}{\lambda}(k) = [\lambda_1(k), \cdots, \lambda_{2N}(k)]^T$.

Then, for the optimization problem described in Equations (10) and (11), we can structure the discrete-time Hamiltonian function as follows.

$$\begin{cases} H_k = \frac{1}{2}[x^T(k)Qx(k) + u^T(k)(R \otimes I_n)u(k)] \\ \qquad + \lambda^T(k+1)[-x(k+1) + (I_N \otimes A)x(k) + (I_N \otimes B)u(k)] \\ H_{k-1} = \frac{1}{2}[x^T(k-1)Qx(k-1) + u^T(k-1)(R \otimes I_n)u(k-1)] \\ \qquad + \lambda^T(k)[-x(k) + (I_N \otimes A)x(k-1) + (I_N \otimes B)u(k-1)] \end{cases}$$

Next, taking partials to the H_k and, we can obtain

$$\begin{cases} \frac{\partial H_k}{\partial x(k)} = Qx(k) + (I_N \otimes A^T)\lambda(k+1) \\ \frac{\partial H_{k-1}}{\partial x(k)} = -\lambda(k) \\ \frac{\partial H_k}{\partial u(k)} = (R \otimes I_n)u(k) + (I_N \otimes B^T)\lambda(k+1) \end{cases}$$
$$\Rightarrow \begin{cases} \lambda(k+1) = (I_N \otimes A^{-T})^{-1}(\lambda(k) - Qx*(k)) \\ u*(k) = -(R^{-1} \otimes I_n)(I_N \otimes B^T)\lambda(k+1) \\ x*(k+1) = (I_N \otimes A)x*(k) + (I_N \otimes B)u*(k) \end{cases} \quad (26)$$

where $u*(k)$ is the optimization control system to be solved, and $x*(k)$ is the optimization track.

Assume

$$\begin{cases} \lambda(k) = Wx(k) \\ \lambda(k+1) = Vx(k) \end{cases} \quad (27)$$

We substitute terminal Condition (27) into Equation (26), and we can obtain the following equations.

$$\begin{cases} W = (I_N \otimes A^T)[(I_N \otimes I_n) + W(I_N \otimes B)(R^{-1} \otimes I_n)(I_N \otimes B^T)]^{-1} \\ \times W(I_N \otimes A) + Q \\ V = (I_N \otimes A^T)^{-1}(W - Q) \end{cases} \quad (28)$$

The optimization control system $u*(k)$ and optimization track $x*(k)$ can be obtained by substituting the result of Equation (12) into Condition (26):

$$\begin{array}{l} V = L \otimes K \\ \lambda(k+1) = (L \otimes K)x*(k) \\ u*(k) = -(R^{-1}L \otimes B^T K)x*(k) \\ x*(k+1) = [(I_N \otimes A) - (R^{-1}L \otimes BB^T K)]x*(k) \end{array} \tag{29}$$

□

Remark 1. *According to Equation (29), we can see that the optimization track under the optimization control system is distributed.*

3.3. Convergence Analysis

Let $P = [(A \otimes I_N) - (BB^T K \otimes R^{-1}L)]$; we have

$$\begin{aligned} \det(\lambda I - P) &= \det\begin{pmatrix} \lambda I_N - I_N & -I_N \\ -k_3 r^{-1} L & \lambda I_N - I_N + k_4 r^{-1} L \end{pmatrix} \\ &= \det\left\{(\lambda I_N - I_N)^2 + k_4 r^{-1} L(\lambda I_N - I_N) + k_3 r^{-1} L\right\} \\ &= \prod_{i=1}^{N}\left\{(\lambda - 1)^2 + k_4 r^{-1}\mu_i(\lambda - 1) + k_3 r^{-1}\mu_i\right\} \quad = 0 \end{aligned}$$

The eigenvalue is

$$\lambda_{i1,2} = \frac{-k_4 r^{-1}\mu_i \pm \sqrt{{k_4}^2 r^{-2}{\mu_i}^2 - 4k_3 r^{-1}\mu_i}}{2} + 1$$

From

$$0 < \frac{4k_3}{{k_4}^2} \le r^{-1}\mu_i < \min\left\{\frac{4}{k_4}, \frac{4}{2k_4 - k_3}, \frac{1}{k_4 - k_3}\right\}$$

We can obtain

$$\begin{array}{l} {k_4}^2 r^{-2}{\mu_i}^2 > {k_4}^2 r^{-2}{\mu_i}^2 - 4k_3 r^{-1}\mu_i \ge 0 \\ \Rightarrow \frac{-k_4 r^{-1}\mu_i + \sqrt{{k_4}^2 r^{-2}{\mu_i}^2 - 4k_3 r^{-1}\mu_i}}{2} + 1 < 1 \end{array}$$

and

$$\begin{array}{l} r^{-1}\mu_i < \frac{4}{2k_4 - k_3} \\ -k_3 r^{-1}\mu_i < 4 - 2k_4 r^{-1}\mu_i \\ {k_4}^2 r^{-2}{\mu_i}^2 - 4k_3 r^{-1}\mu_i < 16 - 8k_4 r^{-1}\mu_i + {k_4}^2 r^{-2}{\mu_i}^2 \\ \sqrt{{k_4}^2 r^{-2}{\mu_i}^2 - 4k_3 r^{-1}\mu_i} < 4 - k_4 r^{-1}\mu_i \\ -1 < \frac{-k_4 r^{-1}\mu_i - \sqrt{{k_4}^2 r^{-2}{\mu_i}^2 - 4k_3 r^{-1}\mu_i}}{2} + 1 \end{array} \tag{30}$$

It is noticed that all the eigenvalues of matrix P are in the unit circle. Thus, the system under the distributed controller must be stable.

4. Simulation and Analysis

This section provides a simulation to verify the effectiveness optimization designed in this paper.

4.1. Continuous-Time System

We assume a multi-agent system including five agents, the self-coupling coefficient $h = 1$, and the adjacent matrix A' of the system is as Equation (1):

$$\hat{x} = (A \otimes I_N)x + (B \otimes I_N)u$$

where $A = \begin{bmatrix} 0 & 1 \\ 0 & 0 \end{bmatrix}, B = \begin{bmatrix} 0 & 0 \\ 1 & 0 \end{bmatrix}, A' = \begin{bmatrix} 0 & 1 & 1 & 0 & 0 \\ 1 & 0 & 0 & 1 & 1 \\ 1 & 0 & 0 & 0 & 0 \\ 0 & 1 & 0 & 0 & 1 \\ 0 & 1 & 0 & 1 & 0 \end{bmatrix}$, and $L = \begin{bmatrix} 3 & -1 & -1 & 0 & 0 \\ -1 & 4 & 0 & -1 & -1 \\ -1 & 0 & 2 & 0 & 0 \\ 0 & -1 & 0 & 3 & -1 \\ 0 & -1 & 0 & -1 & 3 \end{bmatrix}$.

The initial states of the system are as follows.

$$\begin{bmatrix} x_1 & x_2 & x_3 & x_4 & x_5 \end{bmatrix} = \begin{bmatrix} 18 & 21 & 15 & 70 & 10 \end{bmatrix}$$
$$\begin{bmatrix} v_1 & v_2 & v_3 & v_4 & v_5 \end{bmatrix} = \begin{bmatrix} 14 & 28 & -4 & 1 & 19 \end{bmatrix}$$

Performance index:

$$J = \frac{1}{2}\int_0^\infty [x^T Q x + u^T (I_n \otimes R)u]dt$$

where R is shown in Equation (31) and Q is shown in Equation (32)

$$R = \begin{bmatrix} 3 & 0 & 0 & 0 & 0 \\ 0 & 3 & 0 & 0 & 0 \\ 0 & 0 & 3 & 0 & 0 \\ 0 & 0 & 0 & 3 & 0 \\ 0 & 0 & 0 & 0 & 3 \end{bmatrix} \quad (31)$$

$$Q = \begin{bmatrix} 91.67 & 89.00 & -58.33 & -63.00 & -41.67 & -43.00 & 8.33 & 10.00 & 8.33 & 10.00 \\ 89.00 & 102.00 & -63.00 & -74.00 & -43.00 & -50.00 & 10.00 & 12.00 & 10.00 & 12.00 \\ -58.33 & -63.00 & 158.33 & 162.00 & 8.33 & 10.00 & -50.00 & -53.00 & -50.00 & -53.00 \\ -63.00 & -74.00 & 162.00 & 188.00 & 10.00 & 12.00 & -53.00 & -62.00 & -53.00 & -62.00 \\ -41.67 & -43.00 & 8.33 & 10.00 & 41.67 & 36.00 & 0 & 0 & 0 & 0 \\ -43.00 & -50.00 & 10.00 & 12.00 & 36.00 & 40.00 & 0 & 0 & 0 & 0 \\ 8.33 & 10.00 & -50.00 & -53.00 & 0 & 0 & 91.67 & 89.00 & -41.67 & -43.00 \\ 10.00 & 12.00 & -53.00 & -62.00 & 0 & 0 & 89.00 & 102.00 & -43.00 & -50.00 \\ 8.33 & 10.00 & -50.00 & -53.00 & 0 & 0 & -41.67 & -43.00 & 91.67 & 89.00 \\ 10.00 & 12.00 & -53.00 & -62.00 & 0 & 0 & -43.00 & -50.00 & 89.00 & 102.00 \end{bmatrix} \quad (32)$$

It is easy to verify if the optimization problem satisfies Conditions (1) and (2) and Equation (6). Thus, we can design the following optimization control system.

$$u * (t) = -(B^T K \otimes R^{-1} L)x * (t) \quad (33)$$

where

$$K = \begin{bmatrix} 7 & 5 \\ 5 & 6 \end{bmatrix} \quad (34)$$

The optimization trick is

$$\hat{x}^*(t) = \left[(A \otimes I_N) - \left(BB^T K \otimes R^{-1} L\right)\right]x^*(t) = Px^*(t) \quad (35)$$

The changes in system states under our optimization control system are shown in Figure 1.

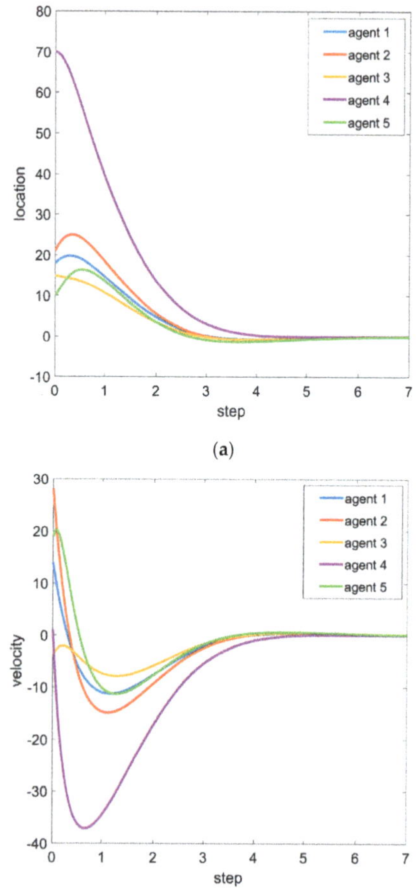

(**a**)

(**b**)

Figure 1. States of continuous-time system. (**a**) State of the agents' location, (**b**) state of the agents' velocity.

4.2. Discrete-Time Dynamic

Similar to the continuous-time system, we assume a multi-agent system including five agents, and the adjacent matrix A' of the system does not change, but its self-coupling coefficient $h = 0.1$, and the adjacent matrix A' of the system is as Equation (1):

$$\hat{x} = (A \otimes I_N)x + (B \otimes I_N)u$$

where $A = \begin{bmatrix} 1 & 1 \\ 0 & 1 \end{bmatrix}, B = \begin{bmatrix} 0 & 0 \\ 1 & 0 \end{bmatrix}$.

The initial states of the system are as follows.

$$\begin{aligned} \begin{bmatrix} x_1 & x_2 & x_3 & x_4 & x_5 \end{bmatrix} &= \begin{bmatrix} 18 & 21 & 15 & 70 & 10 \end{bmatrix} \\ \begin{bmatrix} v_1 & v_2 & v_3 & v_4 & v_5 \end{bmatrix} &= \begin{bmatrix} 14 & 28 & -4 & 1 & 10 \end{bmatrix} \end{aligned} \tag{36}$$

Performance index:

$$J = \frac{1}{2}\sum_{k=0}^{\infty}\left[x^T(k)Qx(k) + u^T(k)(R \otimes I_n)u(k)\right]$$

where Q is shown in Equation (37) and R is shown in Equation (38)

$$Q = \begin{bmatrix} 0.2844 & 0.4599 & -0.0181 & -0.1125 & -0.0172 & -0.1049 & 0.0004 & 0.0037 & 0.0004 & 0.0037 \\ 0.4599 & 12.5391 & -0.1125 & -1.2124 & -0.1049 & -1.1441 & 0.0037 & 0.0337 & 0.0037 & 0.0337 \\ -0.0181 & -0.1125 & 0.3029 & 0.5761 & 0.0004 & 0.0037 & -0.0176 & -0.1087 & -0.0176 & -0.1087 \\ -0.1125 & -1.2124 & 0.5761 & 13.7852 & 0.0037 & 0.0337 & -0.1087 & -1.1782 & -0.1087 & -1.1782 \\ -0.0172 & -0.1049 & 0.0004 & 0.0037 & 0.2668 & 0.3513 & -0.0000 & -0.0001 & -0.0000 & -0.0001 \\ -0.1049 & -1.1441 & 0.0037 & 0.0337 & 0.3513 & 11.3613 & -0.0001 & -0.0005 & -0.0001 & -0.0005 \\ 0.0004 & 0.0037 & -0.0176 & -0.1087 & -0.0000 & -0.0001 & 0.2844 & 0.4598 & -0.0172 & -0.1048 \\ 0.0037 & 0.0337 & -0.1087 & -1.1782 & -0.0001 & -0.0005 & 0.4598 & 12.5386 & -0.1048 & -1.1436 \\ 0.0004 & 0.0037 & -0.0176 & -0.1087 & -0.0000 & -0.0001 & -0.0172 & -0.1048 & 0.2844 & 0.4598 \\ 0.0037 & 0.0337 & -0.1087 & -1.1782 & -0.0001 & -0.0005 & -0.1048 & -1.1436 & 0.4598 & 12.5386 \end{bmatrix} \quad (37)$$

$$R = \begin{bmatrix} 100 & 0 & 0 & 0 & 0 \\ 0 & 100 & 0 & 0 & 0 \\ 0 & 0 & 100 & 0 & 0 \\ 0 & 0 & 0 & 100 & 0 \\ 0 & 0 & 0 & 0 & 100 \end{bmatrix} \quad (38)$$

It is easy to verify the optimization problem that satisfies Conditions (1) and (2) and Equation (6). Thus, we can design the following optimization control system.

$$u*(k) = -(R^{-1}L \otimes B^T K)x*(k) \quad (39)$$

where

$$K = \begin{bmatrix} 0.5 & 1.5 \\ 1.0 & 10.0 \end{bmatrix} \quad (40)$$

The optimization trick is

$$x*(k+1) = [(I_N \otimes A) - (R^{-1}L \otimes BB^T K)]x*(k) \quad (41)$$

The changes in system states under our optimization control system are shown in Figure 2; we can see that all the system states reached a consensus under the effect of the distributed optimization control system.

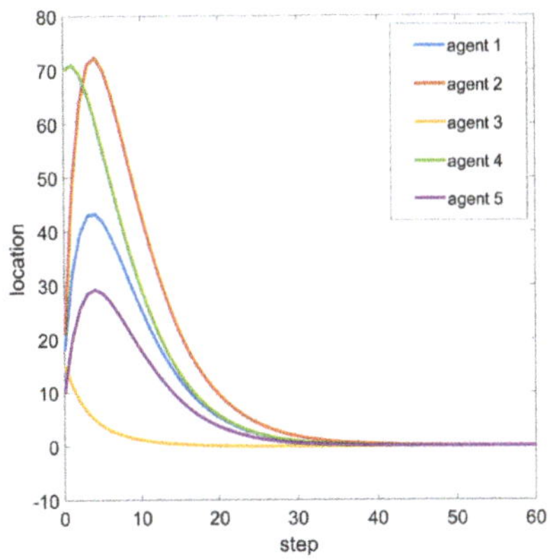

(a)

Figure 2. *Cont.*

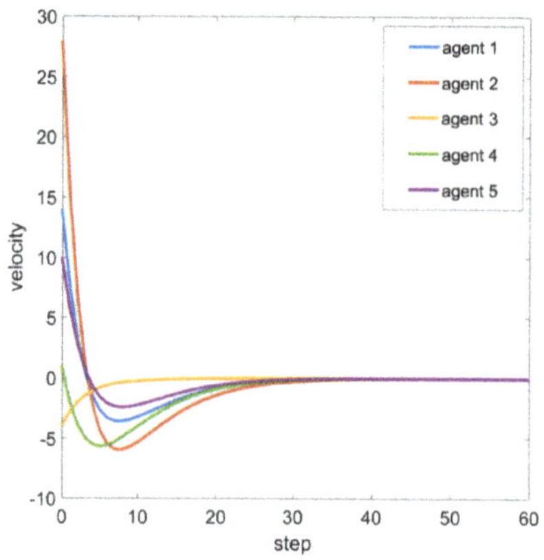

(**b**)

Figure 2. States of discrete-time system. (**a**) State of the agents' location, (**b**) state of the agents' velocity.

5. Conclusions

In this paper, we have solved the distributed optimization control for second-order multi-agent systems with a discrete-time dynamic and a continuous-time dynamic, when the objective function of the quadratic performance criteria with an integrator is positive. The sufficient conditions to ensure the quadratic performance criteria with an integrator are positive and the existence of a distributed optimization control system is given. So, this has potential applications in future automated transportation, smart cities, and smart power grids, as well as robots that will replace humans in hazardous workplaces and situations. However, this paper does not consider the problem of transmission delay, but in practice, several issues arise in implementing distributed methods due to the use of a communication network, such as quantization and link delays. These two aspects are currently of great interest as they are the bottleneck for the efficiency of the methods. Studies of the effects of quantization in distributed methods have been somewhat limited [35,36]. Very recently, a distributed algorithm that factors in link delays in communications has been proposed and investigated [37]. The transmission delay will cause each node and each neighbor node in the information interaction to be untimely. The transmission delay will cause each node and each neighbor node in the information interaction to be untimely. The failure to interact with real-time information can result in poor consistency performance. These questions are also the focus of follow-up research.

Author Contributions: Conceptualization, methodology, software, writing—original draft preparation, Y.W. and H.Z.; conceptualization, validation, formal analysis, investigation, writing—review and editing, supervision, project administration, funding acquisition, Z.L. All authors have read and agreed to the published version of the manuscript.

Funding: This research was funded by the National Natural Science Foundation of China, Grant/Award Number: 61673310.

Data Availability Statement: All the data generated or analyzed during this study are included in this article.

Conflicts of Interest: The authors declare no conflicts of interest.

References

1. Nedić, A.; Liu, J. Distributed optimization for control. *Annu. Rev. Control Robot. Auton. Syst.* **2018**, *1*, 77–103. [CrossRef]
2. Yang, T.; Yi, X.; Wu, J.; Yuan, Y.; Wu, D.; Meng, Z.; Hong, Y.; Wang, H.; Lin, Z.; Johansson, K.H. A survey of distributed optimization. *Annu. Rev. Control* **2019**, *47*, 278–305. [CrossRef]

3. Nedic, A. Distributed gradient methods for convex machine learning problems in networks: Distributed optimization. *IEEE Signal Process. Mag.* **2020**, *37*, 92–101. [CrossRef]
4. Zhu, M.; Martínez, S. Distributed Optimization-Based Control of Multi-Agent Networks in Complex Environments. Springer: Berlin/Heidelberg, Germany, 2015. [CrossRef]
5. Molzahn, D.K.; Dörfler, F.; Sandberg, H.; Low, S.H.; Chakrabarti, S.; Baldick, R.; Lavaei, J. A Survey of Distributed Optimization and Control Algorithms for Electric Power Systems. *IEEE Trans. Smart Grid* **2017**, *8*, 2941–2962. [CrossRef]
6. Ying, S.; Gesualdo, S.; Amir, D. Distributed Optimization Based on Gradient Tracking Revisited: Enhancing Convergence Rate via Surrogation. *SIAM J. Optim.* **2022**, *32*, 354–385. [CrossRef]
7. Lin, P.; Ren, W.; Yang, C.; Gui, W. Distributed Optimization with Nonconvex Velocity Constraints, Nonuniform Position Constraints, and Nonuniform Stepsizes. *IEEE Trans. Autom. Control* **2019**, *64*, 2575–2582. [CrossRef]
8. Sundararajan, A.; Van Scoy, B.; Lessard, L. Analysis and Design of First-Order Distributed Optimization Algorithms Over Time-Varying Graphs. *IEEE Trans. Control Netw. Syst.* **2020**, *7*, 1597–1608. [CrossRef]
9. Tsitsiklis, J.N.; Bertsekas, D.P.; Athans, M. Distributed asynchronous deterministic and stochastic gradient optimization algorithms. *IEEE Trans. Autom. Control* **1986**, *31*, 803–812. [CrossRef]
10. Kushner, H.J.; Yin, G. Asymptotic properties of distributed and communicating stochastic approximation algorithms. *SIAM J. Control Optim.* **1987**, *25*, 1266–1290. [CrossRef]
11. Martinez, S.; Cortes, J.; Bullo, F. Motion Coordination with Distributed Information. *IEEE Control Syst. Mag.* **2007**, *27*, 75–88. [CrossRef]
12. Yi, P.; Hong, Y.; Liu, F. Distributed gradient algorithm for constrained optimization with application to load sharing in power systems. *Syst. Control Lett.* **2015**, *83*, 45–52. [CrossRef]
13. Shi, W.; Ling, Q.; Yuan, K.; Wu, G.; Yin, W. On the Linear Convergence of the ADMM in Decentralized Consensus Optimization. *IEEE Trans. Signal Process.* **2014**, *62*, 1750–1761. [CrossRef]
14. Jakovetic, D.; Xavier, J.M.F.; Moura, J.M.F. Convergence Rates of Distributed Nesterov-Like Gradient Methods on Random Networks. *IEEE Trans. Signal Process.* **2014**, *62*, 868–882. [CrossRef]
15. Nedic, A.; Ozdaglar, A. Distributed sub-gradient methods for multi-agent optimization. *IEEE Trans. Autom. Control* **2009**, *54*, 48–61. [CrossRef]
16. Lou, Y.; Shi, G.; Johansson, K.H.; Hong, Y. Approximate projected consensus for convex intersection computation: Convergence analysis and critical error angle. *IEEE Trans. Autom. Control* **2014**, *59*, 1722–1736. [CrossRef]
17. Towfic, Z.J.; Sayed, A.H. Adaptive penalty-based distributed stochastic convex optimization. *IEEE Trans. Signal Process.* **2014**, *62*, 3924–3938. [CrossRef]
18. Zhang, Y.; Lou, Y.; Hong, Y.; Xie, L. Distributed projection-based algorithms for source localization in wireless sensor Networks. *IEEE Trans. Wirel. Commun.* **2015**, *14*, 3131–3142. [CrossRef]
19. Shi, W.; Ling, Q.; Wu, G.; Yin, W. EXTRA: An Exact First-Order Algorithm for Decentralized Consensus Optimization. *SIAM J. Optim.* **2015**, *25*, 944–966. [CrossRef]
20. Varagnolo, D.; Zanella, F.; Cenedese, A.; Pillonetto, G.; Schenato, L. Newton-Raphson Consensus for Distributed Convex Optimization. *IEEE Trans. Autom. Control* **2016**, *61*, 994–1009. [CrossRef]
21. Nedic, A.; Ozdaglar, A.; Parrilo, P. Constrained consensus and optimization in multi-agent networks. *IEEE Trans. Autom. Control* **2010**, *55*, 922–938. [CrossRef]
22. Liu, Q.; Wang, J. A Second-Order Multi-Agent Network for Bound-Constrained Distributed Optimization. *IEEE Trans. Autom. Control* **2015**, *60*, 3310–3315. [CrossRef]
23. Yuan, D.; Xu, S.; Zhao, H. Distributed Primal–Dual Subgradient Method for Multiagent Optimization via Consensus Algorithms. *IEEE Trans. Syst. Man Cybern. Part B (Cybern.)* **2011**, *41*, 1715–1724. [CrossRef] [PubMed]
24. Zhu, M.; Martinez, S. On Distributed Convex Optimization Under Inequality and Equality Constraints. *IEEE Trans. Autom. Control* **2012**, *57*, 151–164. [CrossRef]
25. Chang, T.-H.; Nedic, A.; Scaglione, A. Distributed Constrained Optimization by Consensus-Based Primal-Dual Perturbation Method. *IEEE Trans. Autom. Control* **2014**, *59*, 1524–1538. [CrossRef]
26. Yuan, D.; Xu, S.; Zhao, H.; Rong, L. Distributed dual averaging method for multi-agent optimization with quantized communication. *Syst. Control Lett.* **2012**, *61*, 1053–1061. [CrossRef]
27. Zhang, F.; Wang, W.; Zhang, H. Design and Analysis of Distributed Optimal Controller for Identical Multiagent Systems. *Asian J. Control* **2015**, *17*, 263–273. [CrossRef]
28. Olfati-Saber, R.; Murray, R.M. Consensus Problems in Networks of Agents with Switching Topology and Time-Delays. *IEEE Trans. Autom. Control* **2004**, *49*, 1520–1533. [CrossRef]
29. Olfati-Saber, R.; Fax, J.A.; Murray, R.M. Consensus and Cooperation in Networked Multi-Agent Systems. *Proc. IEEE* **2007**, *95*, 215–233. [CrossRef]
30. Yu, W.; Chen, G.; Cao, M. Some necessary and sufficient conditions for second-order consensus in multi-agent dynamical systems. *Automatica* **2010**, *46*, 1089–1095. [CrossRef]
31. Yu, W.; Chen, G.; Cao, M.; Kurths, J. Second-Order Consensus for Multiagent Systems with Directed Topologies and Nonlinear Dynamics. *IEEE Trans. Syst. Man Cybern. Part B (Cybern.)* **2010**, *40*, 881–891. [CrossRef]

32. Xie, D.; Wang, S. Consensus of second-order discrete-time multi-agent systems with fixed topology. *J. Math. Anal. Appl.* **2012**, *387*, 8–16. [CrossRef]
33. Lin, P.; Ren, W.; Yang, C.; Gui, W. Distributed Continuous-Time and Discrete-Time Optimization with Nonuniform Unbounded Convex Constraint Sets and Nonuniform Stepsizes. *IEEE Trans. Autom. Control* **2019**, *64*, 5148–5155. [CrossRef]
34. Lin, P.; Ren, W.; Farrell, J.A. Distributed Continuous-Time Optimization: Nonuniform Gradient Gains, Finite-Time Convergence, and Convex Constraint Set. *IEEE Trans. Autom. Control* **2017**, *62*, 2239–2253. [CrossRef]
35. Rabbat, M.; Nowak, R. Quantized incremental algorithms for distributed optimization. *IEEE J. Sel. Areas Commun.* **2005**, *23*, 798–808. [CrossRef]
36. Koloskova, A.; Stich, S.; Jaggi, M. Decentralized Stochastic Optimization and Gossip Algorithms with Compressed Communication. *arXiv* **2019**, arXiv:1902.00340. [CrossRef]
37. Wang, J.; Sahu, A.K.; Yang, Z.; Joshi, G.; Kar, S. MATCHA: Speeding Up Decentralized SGD via Matching Decomposition Sampling. In Proceedings of the 2019 Sixth Indian Control Conference (ICC), Hyderabad, India, 2019; pp. 299–300.

mathematics

Article

Coupled Alternating Neural Networks for Solving Multi-Population High-Dimensional Mean-Field Games

Guofang Wang [1,*], Jing Fang [1], Lulu Jiang [1], Wang Yao [2] and Ning Li [1]

1 Marine Human Factors Engineering Laboratory, China Institute of Marine Technology and Economy, Beijing 100081, China
2 Institute of Artificial Intelligence, Beihang University, Beijing 100191, China
* Correspondence: wangguofang@buaa.edu.cn

Abstract: Multi-population mean-field game is a critical subclass of mean-field games (MFGs). It is a theoretically feasible multi-agent model for simulating and analyzing the game between multiple heterogeneous populations of interacting massive agents. Due to the factors of game complexity, dimensionality disaster and disturbances should be taken into account simultaneously to solve the multi-population high-dimensional stochastic MFG problem, which is a great challenge. We present CA-Net, a coupled alternating neural network approach for tractably solving multi-population high-dimensional MFGs. First, we provide a universal modeling framework for large-scale heterogeneous multi-agent game systems, which is strictly expressed as a multi-population MFG problem. Next, we generalize the potential variational primal–dual structure that MFGs exhibit, then phrase the multi-population MFG problem as a convex–concave saddle-point problem. Last but not least, we design a generative adversarial network (GAN) with multiple generators and multiple discriminators—the solving network—which parameterizes the value functions and the density functions of multiple populations by two sets of neural networks, respectively. In multi-group quadcopter trajectory-planning numerical experiments, the convergence results of HJB residuals, control, and average speed show the effectiveness of the CA-Net algorithm, and the comparison with baseline methods—cluster game, HJB-NN, Lax–Friedrichs, ML, and APAC-Net—shows the progressiveness of our solution method.

Keywords: multi-population model; mean-field game (MFG); high-dimensional solution space; generative adversarial network

MSC: 91A16; 93-10; 49N80

1. Introduction

Mean-field games (MFGs) are a class of models that simulate and analyze large populations of interacting agents [1–3]. MFG theory can be used to solve the communication and calculation difficulties caused by large-scale multi-agent system (MAS) scenarios, i.e., the core is to transform the 1-vs-N game form into a 1-vs-1 game form. In other words, the communication and computational complexities are no longer related to the agent number. They are widely used in economics, finance, industrial engineering, epidemic modeling, data science, material dynamics [4–6], opinion evolution [7], crowd motion [8], and swarm robotics [9–12].

From the perspective of the implementation of MFG theory, we will find that although MFG theoretical research is relatively advanced and mature, its numerical-solution technology is far from reaching the needs of actual scenarios [13]. Many researchers have investigated the numerical solution of MFGs and have produced many excellent results. However, most of them are directed against a single population. Specifically, the simultaneous pioneering works of MFG theory are proposed by Lasry & Lions [1–3] and Huang, Malhame

& Caines [4–6], independently. After that, some literature has used rigorous analytical methods to study numerical algorithms in various situations, including continuous-state problems [14–20] and finite-state problems [21,22]. In the absence of explicit solutions, there have been too many fast solvers for the solution of MFGs in two and three dimensions [23–28], but they all need grid-based spatial discretization. Grid-based numerical solutions will be cursed by dimensionality. Specifically, their computational complexity increases exponentially with the spatial dimension [29], while the numerical-solution method based on neural networks will be more suitable for the high-dimensional HJB–FPK coupled equations [30]. In terms of the numerical methods for solving high-dimensional MFGs, ref. [13] perfectly avoids spatial grids of high-dimensional MFGs based on the machine-learning framework, but their work is limited to the deterministic setting ($\sigma = 0$). Furthermore, ref. [31] is the first document to solve high-dimensional MFGs under a stochastic setting ($\sigma > 0$), which utilizes the natural connection between MFGs and generative adversarial neural networks (GANs) [32]. Based on the original technical difficulties (large scale, high dimensional), the multi-population model increases the complexity of sequential games, including heterogeneous group communication and two-level game reasoning. This makes the numerical framework for solving single-population MFGs no longer applicable. To sum up, to meet the high requirements of more complex actual scene modeling, there is an urgent need to break through the numerical-solution technology of multi-population high-dimensional stochastic MFGs.

Multi-population mean-field games, as an important subclass of MFGs, naturally arise in most practical applications [33]. Since the original contribution of [5], many researchers have studied it using analytical methods, but the technical gap in the calculation of equilibrium solution is particularly prominent. Refs. [34,35] dealt with ergodic MFGs of multi-population under different boundary conditions, including the existence and uniqueness results of systems. Refs. [36,37] considered mean-field control problems with several populations, and the authors introduced these models for crowd motion (with local and non-local interactions, respectively). They have studied optimality conditions and provided numerical results. Ref. [38] studied the issue of urban settlements and residential choice using the MFG model to describe the interactions between two populations and provides some numerical simulations. Refs. [33,39] systematically studied the problems of mean-field games and mean-field-type control problems with multi-population by analyzing the interaction of two populations. It can be seen that the above authors have studied the theory and application of multi-population MFGs, but the equilibrium solution parts generally adopt analytical methods, and their numerical examples are limited to low dimensions (ordinarily one-dimensional or two-dimensional). The numerical-solution method of multi-population high-dimensional MFGs is still relatively blank.

Inspired by the above-mentioned cutting-edge works, in this paper, we are committed to solving the difficult problem of numerical solution for multi-population high-dimensional MFGs with stochasticity, which needs to take into account factors of game complexity, dimensionality disaster, and disturbances simultaneously.

Main Contribution

We present CA-Net, a coupled alternating neural network approach for tractably solving multi-population high-dimensional stochastic MFGs. To this end, we have made the following contributions.

(1) We provide a general framework for modeling large-scale heterogeneous multi-agent game systems, give a unified expression of multi-population MFGs under a two-layer game structure, and ensure the existence of equilibrium of such systems. Of course, it also theoretically solves the problems of information-sharing and dimensional explosion that are common in large-scale heterogeneous multi-agent complex game systems.

(2) We generalize the potential variational primal–dual structure that MFGs exhibit and phrase the multi-population MFG problem as a convex–concave saddle-point problem. In this way, we circumvent spatial grids or uniformly sampling in high dimensions (the

curse of dimensionality) and provide the cornerstone for the construction of the following solving network.

(3) Based on the saddle-point problem, we parameterize the value functions and the density functions of multiple populations by two sets of neural networks, respectively. Then, we design a generative adversarial network (GAN), a nonlinear coupled alternating neural network composed of multiple generators and multiple discriminators, i.e., the solving network, referred to as CA-Net.

(4) We simulate a classic task of heterogeneous MAS with numerical examples and verify and analyze the feasibility and effectiveness of the multi-population high-dimensional stochastic MFG model and CA-Net algorithm. In addition, the comparison with the baseline methods shows the advanced nature of our method.

2. System Model and Problem Formulation

2.1. Control Formulation of Multi-Population Model

We consider a multi-agent system (MAS) with N agents indexed by $i \in I = \{1, \dots, N\}$, who take part in the game are not all homogeneous, and can be subdivided into P agent populations indexed by $p(i) \in Q = \{1, \dots, P\}$, as illustrated in Figure 1. In addition, each continuum population p with small rational agents plays a non-cooperative differential game on a time horizon $[0, T]$. To model the set of P distinct and interconnected populations, we assume a graph $G = (Q, E)$ is given, where $Q = \{1, \dots, P\}$ is the set of vertices, one per each agent population, and $E \subseteq Q \times Q$ is the set of all weighted edges. More specifically, $\arg(p, q)$ belongs to E if the corresponding weight $v_{p,q} > 0$. A positive scalar weight $v_{p,q}$ means the relative influence that population p assigns to population q. For example, $v_{p,q}$ could be calculated as the ratio of the number of agents for population q to the total number of agents for all the neighbor populations. Although most results are easily extended to more general graphs, possibly directed, time-varying, for the sake of simplicity, we henceforward assume that $G = (Q, E)$ is a connected undirected graph. We denote the set of neighbors of p by $V(p) = \{q \in Q | (p, q) \in E\}$, and the cardinality of the set $V(p)$ by $|V(p)|$.

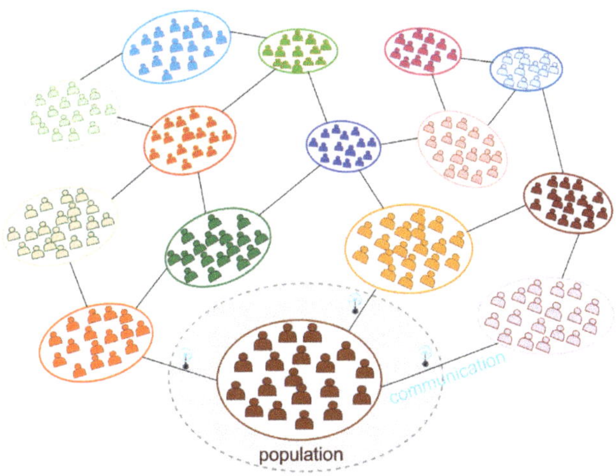

Figure 1. Illustration of a multi-population model with local interactions. Large-scale agents are divided into different populations (indicated by different colors) according to different characteristics to participate in the game. The communication between populations follows the communication topology diagram (the population is the vertex, and the communication is the black solid line). A representative continuum population (bottom shaded part) with small rational agents communicates with three neighboring populations to play a non-cooperative differential game on a time horizon.

In the same agent population, we argue that the agents share a common characteristic (e.g., type, function, angle range, or upper bound of velocity). Each agent $i \in I$ belongs to a population $p(i) \in Q$ and is characterized by a state $x^p(t) \in \mathbb{R}^n$ at time $t \in [0, T]$. More precisely, we consider that the state of the generic player i of population p is a stochastic process $\{x^p_{p\in Q}\}$ in $\mathbb{R}^{Pn}$ with the following forward McKean–Vlasov dynamics

$$dx^p = h^p(x^p, \rho^p, \rho^{-p}, u^p)dt + \sigma^p dw^p \tag{1}$$

where $u^p : [0, T] \to \mathcal{U}_p \subseteq \mathbb{R}^m$ is the control input (strategy), $\rho^p : \mathbb{R}^n \times [0, T] \to \mathcal{P}_2(\mathbb{R}^n)$ is the probability density function, $\rho^{-p} = (\rho^q)_{q\in V(p)} : \mathbb{R}^n \times [0, T] \to \mathcal{P}_2(\mathbb{R}^n)^{|V(p)|}$ describes the distribution vector of neighbor populations, $h^p : \mathbb{R}^n \times \mathcal{P}_2(\mathbb{R}^n)^{|V(p)|+1} \times \mathcal{U}_p \to \mathbb{R}^n$ is the nonlinear evolution function, $\sigma^p > 0$, w^p denotes an m-dimensional Wiener process (standard Brownian motion) comes from the environment, where each component w^p_k is independent of w^p_l for all $k \neq l$, $p = 1, \ldots, P$.

Then, for the generic player i of population p, $p = 1, \ldots, P$, we consider the following cost function

$$\begin{aligned} J_p(u^p, \rho^p, \rho^{-p}) = &\mathbb{E}\bigg[\int_0^T L_p(x^p(t), u^p(t)) \\ &+ F_p(x^p(t), \rho^p(x^p(t), t), \rho^{-p}(x^{-p}(t), t))dt \\ &+ G_p(x^p(T), \rho^p(x^p(T), T), \rho^{-p}(x^{-p}(T), T))\bigg] \end{aligned} \tag{2}$$

where $L_p : \mathbb{R}^n \times \mathcal{U}_p \to \mathbb{R}$ is a running cost incurred by an agent based solely on their actions, $F_p : \mathbb{R}^n \times \mathcal{P}_2(\mathbb{R}^n)^{|V(p)|+1} \to \mathbb{R}$ is a running cost incurred by an agent based on their interaction with the rest of the same population and the neighbor populations, and $G_p : \mathbb{R}^n \times \mathcal{P}_2(\mathbb{R}^n)^{|V(p)|+1} \to \mathbb{R}$ is a terminal cost incurred by an agent based on their final state and the final distribution of the whole related populations. The terms F and G are called mean-field terms because they encode the interaction of a single agent with the rest of the populations.

2.2. The Formulation of Multi-Population Mean-Field Game

Mean-field games (MFGs) are a class of problems that encode large populations of interacting agents into systems of coupled partial differential equations. As an important subclass of MFGs, the multi-population mean-field game not only has the advantages of MFG, e.g., it overcomes the difficulties of large-scale and information-sharing, but allows for the representation of some more realistic situations, such as large-scale multi-group instances of [36,38,40].

For every population $p = 1, \ldots, P$, each agent i of population $p(i)$ forecasts a distribution of the population $\{\rho^p(\cdot, t)\}_{t=0}^T$, and aims at minimizing their cost, which eventually reaches the Nash equilibrium where no agent can reduce individual cost by changing its control strategy unilaterally, i.e., for every $x^p \in \mathbb{R}^n$,

$$J_p(\hat{u^p}, \rho^p, \rho^{-p}) \leq J_p(u^p, \rho^p, \rho^{-p}), \quad \forall u^p : [0, T] \to \mathcal{U}_p \tag{3}$$

where $\hat{u^p}$ is the equilibrium strategy of an agent at state x^p. Here, we assume that agents are small, and their unilateral actions do not alter the density ρ^p. References [33,39], regarding multi-population MFGs, provides sufficient and necessary conditions for the solution to the coupled system of forward–backward stochastic partial differential equations (SPDEs), respectively.

Remark 1. *Under appropriate assumptions, the solution to the MFG provides an approximate Nash equilibrium for the corresponding game with a large but finite number of agents [33].*

From Equation (3), we show that each agent i of population $p(i)$ *solves an optimal control problem that has a value function*

$$\Phi_p(x^p, t) = \inf_{u^p} J_p(u^p, \rho^p, \rho^{-p}), \text{ subject to Equation (1)} \tag{4}$$

From the optimal control theory (for details, see reference [41], sections 2.2, 2.3, and 3.4.2 or reference [39], section 4.1), we show that Φ_p *solves the following HJB equation*

$$\begin{aligned} &-\partial_t \Phi_p(x^p, t) - \frac{\sigma^{p2}}{2}\Delta\Phi_p(x^p, t) + H_p(x^p, \rho^p, \rho^{-p}, \nabla\Phi_p(x^p, t)) \\ &= F_p(x^p, \rho^p(x^p, t), \rho^{-p}(x^{-p}, t)) \\ &\text{s.t. } \Phi_p(x^p, T) = G_p(x^p, \rho^p(x^p, T), \rho^{-p}(x^{-p}, T)) \end{aligned} \tag{5}$$

where the Hamiltonian, $H_p : \mathbb{R}^n \times \mathcal{P}_2(\mathbb{R}^n)^{|V(p)|+1} \times \mathbb{R}^n \to \mathbb{R}$, *is defined as*

$$H_p(x^p, \rho^p, \rho^{-p}, z^p) = \sup_{u^p}\{-L_p(x^p, u^p) - z^{p\top} h^p(x^p, \rho^p, \rho^{-p}, u^p)\} \tag{6}$$

Hence, we have

$$z^p = \nabla_{x^p}\Phi_p(x^p, t) \tag{7}$$

$$h^p(x^p, \rho^p, \rho^{-p}, \hat{u^p}) = -\nabla_{z^p} H_p(x^p, \rho^p, \rho^{-p}, \nabla\Phi_p(x^p, t)) \tag{8}$$

According to Ito's lemma (for details, see reference [41], sections 2.2 and 3.2.2), ρ^p *satisfies the forward equation of* x^p, *i.e., the following FPK equation*

$$\begin{aligned} &\partial_t \rho^p(x^p, t) - \frac{\sigma^{p2}}{2}\Delta\rho^p(x^p, t) \\ &- \operatorname{div}(\rho^p(x^p, t)\nabla_{z^p} H_p(x^p, \rho^p, \rho^{-p}, \nabla\Phi_p(x^p, t))) = 0 \\ &\text{s.t. } \rho^p(x^p, 0) = \rho_0^p(x^p) \end{aligned} \tag{9}$$

where $\rho_0^p \in \mathcal{P}_2(\mathbb{R}^n)$ *is the given population density at time* $t = 0$.

The above discussion provides an alternative to optimizing the strategy u^p *individually for each agent of the multi-population model. One can obtain the optimal strategy for all agents of multi-population simultaneously by solving the coupled SPDEs system given by the HJB (5) and the FPK (9). Following this macroscopic approach, our first step is to accurately establish a multi-population agent model and reduce the immense computational challenges and communication energy consumption caused by heterogeneous multi-agent systems .*

Remark 2. *Instead of including all agents' states in the value function [42–44], the MFGs' deterministic flows of probability density describe the population's current information. Utilizing the density distribution can benefit from two aspects: (1) the dimension of the density distribution is independent of the number of agents, so the dimension disaster is overcome theoretically, and (2) the density distribution can be obtained by locally solving the FPK equation so information-sharing between all agents is not necessary.*

Remark 3. *From an engineering angle, the proposed multi-population MFG model can provide an accurate and feasible scheme for the large-scale heterogeneous MAS because it breaks the dimensionality curse of the system theoretically and ensures the Nash equilibrium solution under limit conditions.*

To compute the optimal control policy of the large-scale heterogeneous MAS, the mean-field Equations (5) and (9) need to be solved in real time. However, the HJB and FPK are two high-dimensional nonlinear SPDEs that are also solved in different directions. Therefore, the analytical solution is nearly impossible to obtain. In this article, a novel

CA-Net algorithm induced from the idea of the generative adversarial network (GAN) is developed to find the solution of the coupled HJB–FPK equations in high dimensions.

3. GAN-Based Approach for High-Dimensional SPDEs of Multi-Population Problem

In this section, we formally propose a numerical-solution method for solving the multi-population high-dimensional mean-field game problem described in Section 2. First, we phrase the multi-population MFG problem as a saddle-point problem and parameterize the value functions and the density functions of multi-population in Section 3.1. Then, we use a coupled alternating neural network (CA-Net) to find the equilibrium solution in Section 3.2.

3.1. Variational Primal–Dual Formulation of Multi-Population Mean-Field Game

According to the natural connection between MFGs and GANs, we deduce the multi-population MFG formulation to a primal–dual convex–concave one, then can obtain a tailored coupled alternating network to find the equilibrium solution.

A multi-population MFG system consists of the two Equations (5) and (9), and is called potential if there exist functionals $\mathcal{F}_p, \mathcal{G}_p : \mathcal{P}_2(\mathbb{R}^n) \to \mathbb{R}$, $p = 1, \ldots, P$ such that

$$\delta_{\rho^p}\mathcal{F}_p = F_p(x^p, \rho^p, \rho^{-p}) \quad \text{and} \quad \delta_{\rho^p}\mathcal{G}_p = G_p(x^p, \rho^p, \rho^{-p})$$

where

$$\int_{\mathbb{R}^n} F_p(x^p, \rho^p)\mu(x^p)\mathrm{d}x^p = \lim_{h\to 0} \frac{\mathcal{F}_p(\rho^p + h\mu) - \mathcal{F}_p(\rho^p)}{h}, \forall \mu$$

$$\int_{\mathbb{R}^n} G_p(x^p, \rho^p)\mu(x^p)\mathrm{d}x^p = \lim_{h\to 0} \frac{\mathcal{G}_p(\rho^p + h\mu) - \mathcal{G}_p(\rho^p)}{h}, \forall \mu$$

That is, there exist functionals $\mathcal{F}, \mathcal{G}$ such that their variational derivatives with respect to ρ are the interaction and terminal costs F and G from (5) and (9). A key feature of potential MFG is that it can be equivalently expressed as a convex–concave saddle-point optimization problem. So, the multi-population MFG problem in (5) and (9) can be reformulated as a variational problem [3,24]. For the generic player i of population p, we obtain:

$$\begin{aligned}
&\inf_{\rho^p, u^p} \int_0^T \int_{\mathbb{R}^n} \rho^p(x^p, t) L_p(x^p(t), u^p(t))\mathrm{d}x^p \mathrm{d}t \\
&\quad + \int_0^T \mathcal{F}_p(x^p(t), \rho^p(x^p(t), t), \rho^{-p}(x^{-p}(t), t))\mathrm{d}t \\
&\quad + \mathcal{G}_p(x^p(T), \rho^p(x^p(T), T), \rho^{-p}(x^{-p}(T), T)) \\
&\text{s.t. } \partial_t \rho^p - \frac{\sigma^{p2}}{2}\Delta\rho^p + \nabla\cdot(\rho^p h^p) = 0, \quad \rho^p(x^p, 0) = \rho_0^p(x^p) \\
&\partial_t \rho^q - \frac{\sigma^{q2}}{2}\Delta\rho^q + \nabla\cdot(\rho^q h^q) = 0, \quad \rho^q(x^q, 0) = \rho_0^q(x^q) \\
&\rho^{-p} = (\rho^q)_{q\in V(p)}
\end{aligned} \tag{10}$$

Now, the running cost L_p could be regarded as the Lagrangian function corresponding to the Legendre transform of the Hamiltonian H_p (6), and $\mathcal{F}_p, \mathcal{G}_p$ are mean-field interaction terms corresponding to F_p, G_p in (2).

To obtain the Lagrangian dual problem of (10) [40,45], we start with introducing the value function $\Phi_p(x^p, t)$ as a Lagrange multiplier, then insert the constraint (FPK equations) into the objective (cost function) to obtain the following extended cost function:

$$\sup_{\Phi_p} \inf_{\rho^p,u^p} \int_0^T \int_{\mathbb{R}^n} \rho^p(x^p,t) L_p(x^p(t),u^p(t)) \mathrm{d}x^p \mathrm{d}t$$
$$+ \int_0^T \mathcal{F}_p(x^p(t),\rho^p(x^p(t),t),\rho^{-p}(x^{-p}(t),t)) \mathrm{d}t$$
$$+ \mathcal{G}_p(x^p(T),\rho^p(x^p(T),T),\rho^{-p}(x^{-p}(T),T))$$
$$- \int_0^T \int_\Omega \Phi_p(x^p,t) \Bigg(\partial_t \rho^p - \frac{\sigma^{p2}}{2}\Delta\rho^p \tag{11}$$
$$+ \nabla \cdot \left(\rho^p(x^p,t) h^p(x^p,\rho^p,\rho^{-p},u^p)\right)\Bigg) \mathrm{d}x^p \mathrm{d}t$$
$$- \sum_{q\in V(p)} \int_0^T \int_\Omega \Phi_q(x^q,t) \Bigg(\partial_t \rho^q - \frac{\sigma^{q2}}{2}\Delta\rho^q$$
$$+ \nabla \cdot \left(\rho^q(x^q,t) h^q(x^q,\rho^q,\rho^{-q},u^q)\right)\Bigg) \mathrm{d}x^q \mathrm{d}t$$

Following the approach of [24,46,47], we write the constraint $\partial_t\rho^p - \frac{\sigma^{p2}}{2}\Delta\rho^p + \nabla \cdot (\rho^p h^p) = 0$, $p = 1, \dots, P$ in weak form, i.e.,

$$\int_0^T \int_{\mathbb{R}^n} \rho^p \partial_t \Phi_p + \frac{\sigma^{p2}}{2}\Delta\Phi_p \rho^p + \nabla\Phi_p \cdot (\rho^p h^p) \mathrm{d}x^p \mathrm{d}t$$
$$+ \int_{\mathbb{R}^n} \Phi_p(x^p,0)\rho_0^p(x^p)\mathrm{d}x^p - \int_{\mathbb{R}^n} \Phi_p(x^p,T)\rho^p(x^p,T)\mathrm{d}x^p = 0 \tag{12}$$

Finally, utilizing (12) and integrating by parts, we can rewrite our problem as

$$\inf_{\rho^p} \sup_{\Phi_p} \int_0^T \int_{\mathbb{R}^n} \left(\partial_t\Phi_p + \frac{\sigma^{p2}}{2}\Delta\Phi_p - H_p(x^p,\nabla\Phi_p) \right) \rho^p(x^p,t) \mathrm{d}x^p \mathrm{d}t$$
$$+ \int_0^T \mathcal{F}_p(x^p(t),\rho^p(x^p(t),t),\rho^{-p}(x^{-p}(t),t)) \mathrm{d}t$$
$$+ \mathcal{G}_p(x^p(T),\rho^p(x^p(T),T),\rho^{-p}(x^{-p}(T),T))$$
$$+ \int_{\mathbb{R}^n} \Phi_p(x^p,0)\rho_0^p(x^p)\mathrm{d}x^p - \int_{\mathbb{R}^n} \Phi_p(x^p,T)\rho^p(x^p,T)\mathrm{d}x^p \tag{13}$$
$$+ \sum_{q\in V(p)} \Bigg\{ \int_0^T \int_{\mathbb{R}^n} \left(\partial_t\Phi_q + \frac{\sigma^{q2}}{2}\Delta\Phi_q + \nabla\Phi_q \cdot h^q \right) \rho^q(x^q,t) \mathrm{d}x^q \mathrm{d}t$$
$$+ \int_{\mathbb{R}^n} \Phi_q(x^q,0)\rho_0^q(x^q)\mathrm{d}x^q - \int_{\mathbb{R}^n} \Phi_q(x^q,T)\rho^q(x^q,T)\mathrm{d}x^q \Bigg\}$$

This formula can also be deduced in the context of HJB equations in probability measure spaces [25] or by integrating the HJB (5) and the FPK (9) equations for Φ_p and ρ^p, respectively [48].

In [48], it has been shown that all MFG systems coincide with an infinite-dimensional two-player general-sum game, and the potential MFGs are the ones that correspond to zero-sum games. In its elaboration, Player 1 represents the whole population and their strategy is the population's probability distribution. While Player 2 represents the generic agent, their strategy is the value function. The goal of Player 2 is to provide a strategy that yields the best response of a generic agent against the population. This elaboration is consistent with the intuition behind generative adversarial networks (GANs). By drawing from a natural connection between MFGs and GANs, ref. [31] presents APAC-Net, an alternating population and agent control neural network, which is the first model for solving high-dimensional MFGs of a single population in the stochastic case. We extended this methodology to multiple characteristic populations and solved the HJB–FPK coupled system (5)–(9) for a certain population p of the multi-population high-dimensional MFG.

Remark 4. *Under mild assumptions on $\mathcal{F}_p$ and $\mathcal{G}_p$, each spatial integral is really an expectation from ρ^p, $p = 1, \dots, P$. The formulation (13) is the cornerstone of our approach.*

3.2. CA-Net

Recall that from Riemann integral to Lebesgue integral, the former focuses on grid points of the definition domain, while the latter focuses on values of the function. The following proposed CA-Net does not discretize the domain and solve for the function values on grid points but avoids these problems by parameterizing the function and solving for the function itself. This is also the fundamental reason CA-Net can overcome the dimensional disaster of high-dimensional MFG equations. Another important point is that although the idea is inspired by GANs, the training process of single-population MFG solving networks is analog to that of GANs (a single generator and discriminator). A multi-population MFG solving network is a nonlinear coupled alternating neural network formed by multiple generators and multiple discriminators. We show the structure and training process of our CA-Net in the diagram Figure 2.

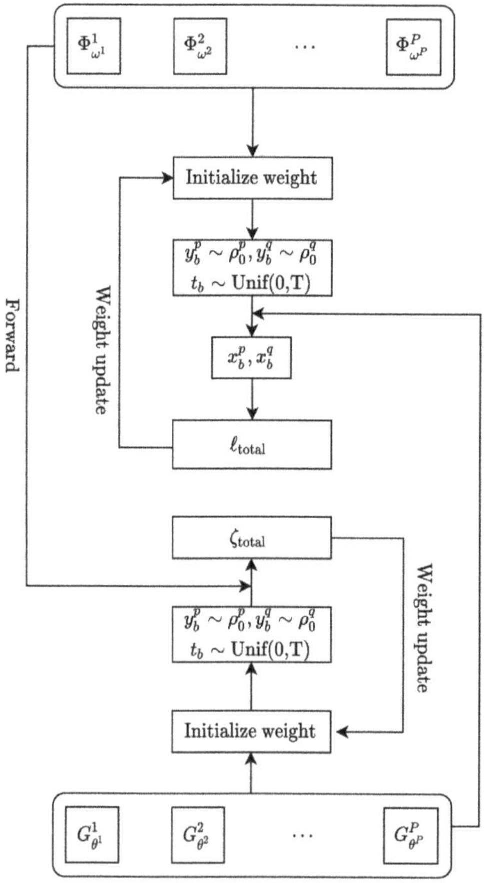

Figure 2. Visualization of the structure and training process of CA-Net. CA-Net is composed of multiple generators (bottom) and multiple discriminators (top). Its training process is divided into

two coupled alternating training parts. To initialize the weights of $\Phi^p_{\omega^p}$ and $\mathcal{G}^p_{\theta^p}$, $p = 1,\ldots,P$ randomly, the first step is to train the value function network $\Phi^p_{\omega^p}$, batch a random sample point y^p_b, y^q_b, t_b, $b = 1,\ldots,B$, obtain x^p_b, x^q_b forward through the density function network $\mathcal{G}^p_{\theta^p}$. The weight ω^p of $\Phi^p_{\omega^p}$ is updated by the gradient descent algorithm to minimize loss function ℓ_{total}. The second step is to train the density function network $\mathcal{G}^p_{\theta^p}$, batch a random sample points y^p_b, y^q_b, t_b, $b = 1,\ldots,B$, and update the weight θ^p of $\mathcal{G}^p_{\theta^p}$ through the value function network $\Phi^p_{\omega^p}$ and the gradient descent algorithm to minimize loss function ζ_{total}. Then, loop the two parts to achieve the optimal result.

We initialize P pairs of neural networks $N^p_{\omega^p}(x^p,t)$ and $N^p_{\theta^p}(y^p,t)$, $p = 1,\ldots,P$. We then let

$$\begin{aligned} \Phi^p_{\omega^p}(x^p,t) &= (1-t)N^p_{\omega^p}(x^p,t) + tG_p(x^p) \\ \mathcal{G}^p_{\theta^p}(y^p,t) &= (1-t)y^p + tN^p_{\theta^p}(y^p,t) \end{aligned} \tag{14}$$

where $y^p \sim \rho^p_0$ are samples drawn from the initial distribution, and $\mathcal{G}^p_{\theta^p}$ produces samples from ρ^p_0 at $t = 0$. When we set $\rho^p(\cdot,t) = \mathcal{G}^p_{\theta^p}(\cdot,t)_{\#\rho^p_0}$, it is the push-forward of ρ^p_0. In this setting, we train $\mathcal{G}^p_{\theta^p}(\cdot,t)$ to produce samples from $\rho^p(\cdot,t)$. We note that $\Phi^p_{\omega^p}$ and $\mathcal{G}^p_{\theta^p}$ automatically satisfy the terminal and initial condition, respectively.

Our approach for training neural networks includes parallel alternately training P pairs of $\mathcal{G}^p_{\theta^p}$ (the density distribution of population p) and $\Phi^p_{\omega^p}$ (the value function for the generic agent of population p). Intuitively, in order to obtain the equilibrium of multi-population MFG, we are training coupled alternating neural networks (CA-Net) about multi-group distributions and agent controls. Specifically, we train $\Phi^p_{\omega^p}$ by first sampling a batch $\left\{y^p_b\right\}^B_{b=1}$ from the given initial density ρ^p_0, and $\{t_b\}^B_{b=1}$ uniformly from $[0,1]$, i.e., we are sampling from $\rho^p_0 \times \text{Unif}([0,1])$. Next, we compute the push-forward states $x^p_b = \mathcal{G}^p_{\theta^p}\left(y^p_b, t_b\right)$ for $b = 1,\ldots,B$. It should be emphasized that we construct the loss functions of CA-Net according to the variational primal–dual formulation (13) of multi-population MFG. Therefore, here is the main loss item for training the discriminator,

$$\begin{aligned} \text{loss}_{\Phi^p} =& \frac{1}{B}\sum_{b=1}^{B} \Phi^p_{\omega^p}\left(x^p_b, 0\right) + \frac{1}{B}\sum_{b=1}^{B}\{\partial_t \Phi^p_{\omega^p}\left(x^p_b, t_b\right) \\ &+ \frac{\sigma^{p2}}{2}\Delta\Phi^p_{\omega^p}\left(x^p_b, t_b\right) - H_p\left(\nabla_{x^p}\Phi^p_{\omega^p}\left(x^p_b, t_b\right)\right)\} \end{aligned} \tag{15}$$

Of course, we need to consider adding a dual penalty term from neighbors to correct for the density update of other populations (tending to obey the FPK equations).

$$\begin{aligned} \text{penalty}_{\text{neighbors}} =& \eta \sum_{q\in V(p)} \{\frac{1}{B}\sum_{b=1}^{B}[\partial_t \Phi^q_{\omega^q}\left(x^q_b, t_b\right) + \frac{\sigma^{q2}}{2}\Delta\Phi^q_{\omega^q}\left(x^q_b, t_b\right) \\ &+ \nabla_{x^q}\Phi^q_{\omega^q}\left(x^q_b, t_b\right) \cdot h^q\left(x^q_b, x^p_b, t_b\right)]\} \end{aligned} \tag{16}$$

And we can optionally add a regularization term to penalize deviations from the HJB equations [13,49].

$$\begin{aligned} \text{penalty}_{\text{HJB}} =& \lambda\frac{1}{B}\sum_{b=1}^{B} \|\partial_t \Phi^p_{\omega^p}\left(x^p_b, t_b\right) + \frac{\sigma^{p2}}{2}\Delta\Phi^p_{\omega^p}\left(x^p_b, t_b\right) \\ &- H_p\left(\nabla_{x^p}\Phi^p_{\omega^p}\left(x^p_b, t_b\right)\right) + F_p\left(x^p_b, x^q_b, t_b\right)\| \end{aligned} \tag{17}$$

This extra regularization term has also been found effective in, e.g., Wasserstein GANs [50]. Finally, we backpropagate loss ℓ_{total} to the weights of $\Phi^p_{\omega^p}$. To train the generator, we again sample $\left\{y_b^p\right\}_{b=1}^{B}$ and $\{t_b\}_{b=1}^{B}$ as before, and compute

$$\begin{aligned}\text{loss}_{\mathcal{G}^p} =& \frac{1}{B}\sum_{b=1}^{B}\{\partial_t\Phi^p_{\omega^p}\left(\mathcal{G}^p_{\theta^p}\left(y_b^p\right),t_b\right)+\frac{\sigma^{p2}}{2}\Delta\Phi^p_{\omega^p}\left(\mathcal{G}^p_{\theta^p}\left(y_b^p\right),t_b\right)\\ &-H_p\left(\nabla_{x^p}\Phi^p_{\omega^p}\left(\mathcal{G}^p_{\theta^p}\left(y_b^p\right),t_b\right)\right)+F_p\left(\mathcal{G}^p_{\theta^p}\left(y_b^p\right),\mathcal{G}^q_{\theta^q}\left(y_b^q\right),t_b\right)\}\end{aligned} \tag{18}$$

Finally, we backpropagate loss ζ_{total} to the weights of $\mathcal{G}^p_{\theta^p}$. Please refer to Algorithm 1 for detailed operation flow.

Algorithm 1: CA-Net

Require: σ^p diffusion parameter, G_p terminal cost, H_p Hamiltonian, F_p interaction term, $p = 1, \ldots, P$.
Require: Initialize neural networks $N^p_{\omega^p}$ and $N^p_{\theta^p}$, batch size B.
Require: Set $\Phi^p_{\omega^p}$ and $\mathcal{G}^p_{\theta^p}$ as in (14).
while *not converged* **do**
  train $\Phi^p_{\omega^p}$:
  Sample batch $\left\{\left(y_b^p,t_b\right)\right\}_{b=1}^{B}$, $\left\{\left(y_b^q,t_b\right)\right\}_{b=1}^{B}$, $q \in V(p)$ where $y_b^p \sim \rho_0^p$, $y_b^q \sim \rho_0^q$ and $t_b \sim \text{Unif}(0,T)$.
  $x_b^p \leftarrow \mathcal{G}^p_{\theta^p}\left(y_b^p,t_b\right)$, $x_b^q \leftarrow \mathcal{G}^q_{\theta^q}\left(y_b^q,t_b\right)$ for $b = 1,\ldots,B$.
  $\ell_0^p \leftarrow \frac{1}{B}\sum_{b=1}^{B}\Phi^p_{\omega^p}\left(x_b^p,0\right)$
  $\ell_t^p \leftarrow \frac{1}{B}\sum_{b=1}^{B}\{\partial_t\Phi^p_{\omega^p}\left(x_b^p,t_b\right)+\frac{\sigma^{p2}}{2}\Delta\Phi^p_{\omega^p}\left(x_b^p,t_b\right)-H_p\left(\nabla_{x^p}\Phi^p_{\omega^p}\left(x_b^p,t_b\right)\right)\}$
  $\ell^p_{\text{neighbors}} \leftarrow \eta\sum_{q\in V(p)}\frac{1}{B}\sum_{b=1}^{B}\{\partial_t\Phi^q_{\omega^q}\left(x_b^q,t_b\right)+\frac{\sigma^{q2}}{2}\Delta\Phi^q_{\omega^q}\left(x_b^q,t_b\right)+\nabla_{x^q}\Phi^q_{\omega^q}\left(x_b^q,t_b\right)\cdot h^q\left(x_b^q,x_b^p,t_b\right)\}$
  $\ell^p_{\text{HJB}} \leftarrow \lambda\frac{1}{B}\sum_{b=1}^{B}\|\partial_t\Phi^p_{\omega^p}\left(x_b^p,t_b\right)+\frac{\sigma^{p2}}{2}\Delta\Phi^p_{\omega^p}\left(x_b^p,t_b\right)-H_p\left(\nabla_{x^p}\Phi^p_{\omega^p}\left(x_b^p,t_b\right)\right)+F_p\left(x_b^p,x_b^q,t_b\right)\|$
  $\ell^p_{\text{total}} \leftarrow \ell_0^p+\ell_t^p+\ell^p_{\text{neighbors}}+\ell^p_{\text{HJB}}$
  Backpropagate total loss $\ell_{\text{total}} = \sum_p \ell^p_{\text{total}}$ to $\omega = (\omega^p)_{p=1,\ldots,P}$ weights.

  train $\mathcal{G}^p_{\theta^p}$:
  Sample batch $\left\{\left(y_b^p,t_b\right)\right\}_{b=1}^{B}$, $\left\{\left(y_b^q,t_b\right)\right\}_{b=1}^{B}$, $q \in V(p)$ where $y_b^p \sim \rho_0^p$, $y_b^q \sim \rho_0^q$ and $t_b \sim \text{Unif}(0,T)$.
  $\zeta_t^p \leftarrow \frac{1}{B}\sum_{b=1}^{B}\{\partial_t\Phi^p_{\omega^p}\left(\mathcal{G}^p_{\theta^p}\left(y_b^p,t_b\right),t_b\right)+\frac{\sigma^{p2}}{2}\Delta\Phi^p_{\omega^p}\left(\mathcal{G}^p_{\theta^p}\left(y_b^p,t_b\right),t_b\right)-H_p\left(\nabla_{x^p}\Phi^p_{\omega^p}\left(\mathcal{G}^p_{\theta^p}\left(y_b^p,t_b\right),t_b\right)\right)+F_p\left(\mathcal{G}^p_{\theta^p}\left(y_b^p,t_b\right),\mathcal{G}^q_{\theta^q}\left(y_b^q,t_b\right),t_b\right)\}$
  Backpropagate total loss $\zeta_{\text{total}} = \sum_p \zeta_t^p$ to $\theta = (\theta^p)_{p=1,\ldots,P}$ weights.
end

4. Numerical Experiments

In this section, we demonstrate the potential of the proposed CA-Net on large-scale heterogeneous MAS control problems. First, we show the feasibility of using multi-population MFG to model large-scale heterogeneous MAS and the convergence of using CA-Net to solve the corresponding problems in high-dimensional space in Section 4.1. Second, we also illustrate the behaviors of the multi-population MFG solutions for different values of stochastic characteristic σ in Section 4.2. Third, we further reveal the relationship between algorithm parameters and costs in Section 4.3. Last, to demonstrate the competitiveness of our approach, we compare the CA-Net algorithm's performance against baseline methods in Section 4.4.

4.1. Multi-Group Quadcopters Trajectory-Planning Example

This experiment is inspired by [31,42,51], we examine a realistic scenario where the dynamics are that of a quadcopter, which is an aerial vehicle with four rotary wings and utilizes its four rotors to propel itself across space from an initial state to target state. The designed test environment is a 3-D real flight space and has a total of a thousand drones, which are divided into five populations with different velocity ranges to perform tasks—flying from their initial distribution to the common terminal distribution. Here, graph $G = (Q, E)$ is considered to be a global communication between groups. The dynamics of the generic quadrotor craft i of population p, $p = 1, \ldots, P$ are given as

$$\begin{cases} \ddot{x}_p = \frac{u_p}{m_p}(\sin(\phi_p)\sin(\psi_p) + \cos(\phi_p)\cos(\psi_p)\sin(\theta_p)) \\ \ddot{y}_p = \frac{u_p}{m_p}(-\cos(\psi_p)\sin(\phi_p) + \cos(\phi_p)\sin(\theta_p)\sin(\psi_p)) \\ \ddot{z}_p = \frac{u_p}{m_p}\cos(\theta_p)\cos(\phi_p) - g \\ \ddot{\psi}_p = \tilde{\tau}_{\psi_p} \\ \ddot{\theta}_p = \tilde{\tau}_{\theta_p} \\ \ddot{\phi}_p = \tilde{\tau}_{\phi_p} \end{cases} \tag{19}$$

where x_p, y_p, and z_p are the usual Euclidean spatial coordinates of the quadcopter, and ϕ_p, θ_p and ψ_p are the angular coordinates of roll, pitch, and yaw, respectively. The constant m_p is the quadcopter's mass, and g is the gravitation acceleration constant on Earth. The variables $u_p, \tilde{\tau}_{\psi_p}, \tilde{\tau}_{\theta_p}, \tilde{\tau}_{\phi_p}$ are the controls representing thrust, and angular acceleration, respectively [52]. To fit a control framework, the above second-order system is turned into a first-order system:

$$\begin{cases} \dot{x}_p = v_{x_p} \\ \dot{y}_p = v_{y_p} \\ \dot{z}_p = v_{z_p} \\ \dot{\psi}_p = v_{\psi_p} \\ \dot{\theta}_p = v_{\theta_p} \\ \dot{\phi}_p = v_{\phi_p} \\ \dot{v}_{x_p} = \frac{u_p}{m_p}(\sin(\phi_p)\sin(\psi_p) + \cos(\phi_p)\cos(\psi_p)\sin(\theta_p)) \\ \dot{v}_{y_p} = \frac{u_p}{m_p}(-\cos(\psi_p)\sin(\phi_p) + \cos(\phi_p)\sin(\theta_p)\sin(\psi_p)) \\ \dot{v}_{z_p} = \frac{u_p}{m_p}(\cos(\theta_p)\cos(\phi_p)) - g \\ \dot{v}_{\psi_p} = \tilde{\tau}_{\psi_p} \\ \dot{v}_{\theta_p} = \tilde{\tau}_{\theta_p} \\ \dot{v}_{\phi_p} = \tilde{\tau}_{\phi_p} \end{cases} \tag{20}$$

which we will compactly denote as $\dot{\mathbf{x}^p} = \mathbf{h}^p(\mathbf{x}^p, \mathbf{u}^p)$, where $\mathbf{h}^p$ is a 12-dimensional vector function in the right-hand side of (20), $\mathbf{x}^p = [x_p, y_p, z_p, \psi_p, \theta_p, \phi_p, v_{x_p}, v_{y_p}, v_{z_p}, v_{\psi_p}, v_{\theta_p}, v_{\phi_p}]^\top \in \mathbb{R}^{12}$ is the state with velocities $\mathbf{v}^p = [v_{x_p}, v_{y_p}, v_{z_p}, v_{\psi_p}, v_{\theta_p}, v_{\phi_p}]^\top \in \mathbb{R}^6$, and $\mathbf{u}^p = [u_p, \tilde{\tau}_{\psi_p}, \tilde{\tau}_{\theta_p}, \tilde{\tau}_{\phi_p}]^\top \in \mathbb{R}^4$ is the control. As can be seen, (20) is a 12-dimensional system that is highly coupled, nonlinear and high-dimensional. In the stochastic case, we add a noise term to the dynamics: $\mathrm{d}\mathbf{x}^p = \mathbf{h}^p(\mathbf{x}^p, \mathbf{u}^p)\mathrm{d}t + \sigma^p \mathrm{d}\mathbf{W}_t^p$, where $\mathbf{W}$ denotes a Wiener process (standard Brownian motion). The interpretation here is that we are modeling the situation when the quadcopter suffers from noisy measurements.

For the Lagrangian cost function, we consider

$$\begin{aligned} L_p(\mathbf{u}^p) &= \frac{1}{2}\|\mathbf{u}^p(t)\|_2^2 \\ &= \frac{1}{2}\left(u_p^2(t) + \tilde{\tau}_{\psi_p}^2(t) + \tilde{\tau}_{\theta_p}^2(t) + \tilde{\tau}_{\phi_p}^2(t)\right) \end{aligned} \tag{21}$$

We consider the Hamiltonian in (6) where $\mathbf{z^p} = [z_1^p, z_2^p, \ldots, z_{12}^p]^\top \in \mathbb{R}^{12}$. Noting the optimality conditions of (6) for the quadcopter problem are obtained by

$$\begin{aligned} &-\nabla_{\mathbf{u}^p} L_p(\mathbf{u}^p) - \mathbf{z^p}^\top \nabla_{\mathbf{u}^p} \mathbf{h}^p = \mathbf{0} \\ \Rightarrow -&\begin{bmatrix} u_p \\ \tilde{\tau}_{\psi_p} \\ \tilde{\tau}_{\theta_p} \\ \tilde{\tau}_{\phi_p} \end{bmatrix} - \begin{bmatrix} z_7^p \\ z_8^p \\ z_9^p \\ z_{10}^p \\ z_{11}^p \\ z_{12}^p \end{bmatrix}^\top \begin{bmatrix} h_7/m_p & 0 & 0 & 0 \\ h_8/m_p & 0 & 0 & 0 \\ h_9/m_p & 0 & 0 & 0 \\ 0 & 1 & 0 & 0 \\ 0 & 0 & 1 & 0 \\ 0 & 0 & 0 & 1 \end{bmatrix} = \mathbf{0} \\ \Rightarrow -&\begin{bmatrix} u_p \\ \tilde{\tau}_{\psi_p} \\ \tilde{\tau}_{\theta_p} \\ \tilde{\tau}_{\phi_p} \end{bmatrix} - \begin{bmatrix} \frac{1}{m_p}\left(z_7^p h_7 + z_8^p h_8 + z_9^p h_9\right) \\ z_{10}^p \\ z_{11}^p \\ z_{12}^p \end{bmatrix} = \mathbf{0} \end{aligned} \tag{22}$$

We can derive an expression for the controls as

$$\begin{aligned} u_p &= -\frac{1}{m_p}\left(z_7^p h_7 + z_8^p h_8 + z_9^p h_9\right), \\ \tilde{\tau}_{\psi_p} &= -z_{10}^p, \tilde{\tau}_{\theta_p} = -z_{11}^p, \tilde{\tau}_{\phi_p} = -z_{12}^p \end{aligned} \tag{23}$$

We therefore can compute the Hamiltonian

$$\begin{aligned} H_p(t, \mathbf{x}^p, \mathbf{z^p}) &= -L_p(\mathbf{u}^p) - \begin{bmatrix} v_{x_p} v_{y_p} v_{z_p} \end{bmatrix} \begin{bmatrix} z_1^p \\ z_2^p \\ z_3^p \end{bmatrix} \\ &- \begin{bmatrix} v_{\psi_p} v_{\theta_p} v_{\phi_p} \end{bmatrix} \begin{bmatrix} z_4^p \\ z_5^p \\ z_6^p \end{bmatrix} + \frac{1}{m_p^2}\left(z_7^p h_7 + z_8^p h_8 + z_9^p h_9\right)^2 \\ &+ z_9^p g + \left({z_{10}^p}^2 + {z_{11}^p}^2 + {z_{12}^p}^2\right) \end{aligned} \tag{24}$$

Finally, using (7) and (23), we compute the controls $\mathbf{u}^p$ using the CA-Net with

$$\begin{aligned} u_p &= -\frac{1}{m_p}\left(h_7 \frac{\partial \Phi_p}{\partial v_{x_p}} + h_8 \frac{\partial \Phi_p}{\partial v_{y_p}} + h_9 \frac{\partial \Phi_p}{\partial v_{z_p}}\right), \\ \tilde{\tau}_{\psi_p} &= -\frac{\partial \Phi_p}{\partial v_{\psi_p}}, \tilde{\tau}_{\theta_p} = -\frac{\partial \Phi_p}{\partial v_{\theta_p}}, \tilde{\tau}_{\phi_p} = -\frac{\partial \Phi_p}{\partial v_{\phi_p}} \end{aligned} \tag{25}$$

We assume that the initial density of the five populations is Gaussian distributions ρ_0^p, $p = 1, 2, 3, 4, 5$. In addition, their centers in the spatial coordinates (x, y, z) are located in $(-1, -5, -8)$, $(4\cos(\frac{2\pi}{5}) - 5, 4\sin(\frac{2\pi}{5}) - 5, -6)$, $(4\cos(\frac{4\pi}{5}) - 5, 4\sin(\frac{4\pi}{5}) - 5, -6)$, $(4\cos(\frac{6\pi}{5}) - 5, 4\sin(\frac{6\pi}{5}) - 5, -4)$ and $(4\cos(\frac{8\pi}{5}) - 5, 4\sin(\frac{8\pi}{5}) - 5, -2)$ with same standard deviation 0.5, respectively. Note that we set all other initial coordinates to zero (i.e., initial angular position, initial velocity, and initial angular velocity are all set to zero). We set the terminal cost to be a simple norm difference between the agent's current position and the terminal distribution center position $(8,8,8)$, and we also want the agents to have zero velocity at the terminal point, i.e.

$$\begin{aligned} &\mathcal{G}_p(\rho^p(\cdot,T),\rho^{-p}(\cdot,T)) = \\ &\int_{\mathbb{R}^n} \|(x_p,y_p,z_p,\psi_p,\ldots,v_{\phi_p}) - (8,8,8,0,\ldots,0)\|_2 \rho^p(\mathbf{x}^p,T)\mathrm{d}\mathbf{x}^p \\ &+ \sum_{q\in V(p)} \int_{\mathbb{R}^n} \|(x_q,y_q,z_q,\psi_q,\ldots,v_{\phi_q}) - (8,8,8,0,\ldots,0)\|_2 \rho^q(\mathbf{x}^q,T)\mathrm{d}\mathbf{x}^q \end{aligned} \tag{26}$$

In our experiments, we set the final time to be $T = 4$.

We choose the interaction term to penalize congestion (a.k.a. interactive running cost) in our experiments, where the congestion is in the spatial positions, to encourage agents to spread out (and thus make mid-air collisions less likely). The first and second terms of the right formula of (27) are intra-group and inter-group congestion terms, respectively:

$$\begin{aligned} &\mathcal{F}_p(\rho^p(x_p,y_p,z_p),\rho^{-p}(x_{-p},y_{-p},z_{-p})) = \\ &\gamma_{\mathrm{cong}} \frac{1}{(2\pi)^{\frac{3}{2}}} \int_{\mathbb{R}^n}\int_{\mathbb{R}^n} e^{\left(-\frac{1}{2}\|(x_p,y_p,z_p)-(\hat{x_p},\hat{y_p},\hat{z_p})\|_2^2\right)} \mathrm{d}\rho^p(x_p,y_p,z_p)\mathrm{d}\rho^p(\hat{x_p},\hat{y_p},\hat{z_p}) + \beta_{\mathrm{cong}} \\ &\times \frac{1}{(2\pi)^{\frac{3}{2}}} \sum_{q\in V(p)} \int_{\mathbb{R}^n}\int_{\mathbb{R}^n} e^{\left(-\frac{1}{2}\|(x_p,y_p,z_p)-(x_q,y_q,z_q)\|_2^2\right)} \mathrm{d}\rho^p(x_p,y_p,z_p)\mathrm{d}\rho^q(x_q,y_q,z_q) \end{aligned} \tag{27}$$

where, in our experiments, we put intra-group congestion coefficient $\gamma_{\mathrm{cong}} = 20$, and inter-group congestion coefficient $\beta_{\mathrm{cong}} = 1 \times 10^4$.

In all experiments, our neural networks have three hidden layers, with 100 hidden units per layer, which is a lightweight network for solving PDEs. We use a residual neural network (ResNet) for both networks, with a skip connection weight of 0.5. For $\Phi^p_{\omega^p}$, we use the Tanh activation function, and for $G^p_{\theta^p}$, we use the ReLU activation function. For training, we use ADAM with $\beta = (0.5, 0.9)$, learning rate 4×10^{-4} for $\Phi^p_{\omega^p}$, learning rate 1×10^{-4} for $G^p_{\theta^p}$, weight decay of 1×10^{-4} for both networks, batch size 250, $\lambda = 1$ (the HJB penalty parameter), and $\eta = 2.5 \times 10^{-3}$ (the neighbors penalty parameter) in Algorithm 1. The algorithm runs on a computer with a 2.5 GHz dual-core Intel Core i7 processor and 16 GB 2133 MHz LPDDR3 memory. In the following figures, time is represented by color. Specifically, blue denotes the starting time, red denotes the final time, and the intermediate colors denote intermediate times. As in standard machine-learning methods, all the plots in Section 4 are generated using validation data, i.e., data not used in training, to gauge the generalizability of CA-Net.

Figure 3 shows the trajectories of $N = 1000$ quadcopters under the multi-population MFG method. Through the observation and analysis of the obtained trajectories corresponding to eight groups of parameters, we can see that with noise σ, the agents add an envelope of uncertainty, so we do see that the agents are not as streamlined as in the noiseless cases, and not moving as close to the terminal point of $(8,8,8)$ at terminal time. This is the comparison of subgraphs (e–h) with (a–d), respectively. Furthermore, in the presence of intra-group congestion coefficient γ_{cong}, the agents of intra-group spread out more as expected. This is the comparison of subgraphs between (a–h). In addition, in the presence of inter-group congestion coefficient β_{cong}, the clusters are more diffuse, and their terminal distributions do not fully gather to the expected terminal point of $(8,8,8)$. This is the comparison of subgraphs between (a–h). We also plot the HJB residual errors in Figure 4, i.e., ℓ^p_{HJB} in Algorithm 1, which shows the convergence of CA-Net. Without an efficient strategy control, the HJB residuals under different cases are relatively high. HJB residuals drop fast after we apply a series of controls. After around 4×10^4 iterations, the error curves tend to be stable and close to zero when we obtain an optimal control for quadcopters. Moreover, it is obvious that the CA-Net algorithm converges faster without noise, and the red curve (no A, no B, with

C)—without noise, without intra-group congestion, but with inter-group congestion—converges the fastest.

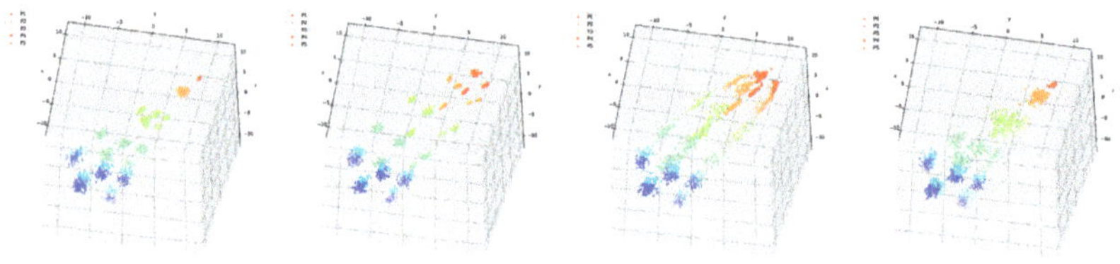

(**a**) no A, no B, no C (**b**) no A, no B, with C (**c**) no A, with B, with C (**d**) no A, with B, no C

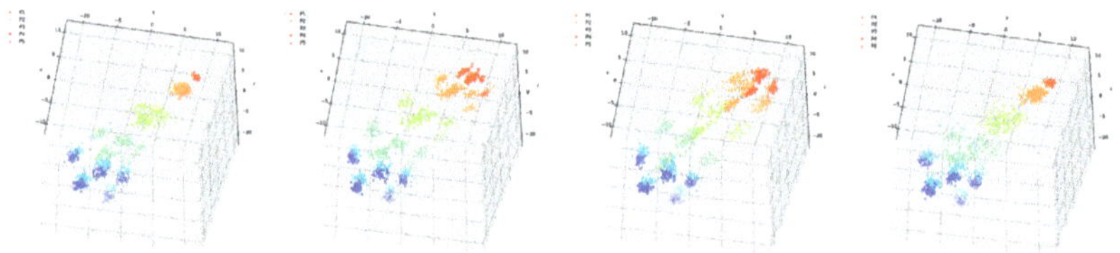

(**e**) with A, no B, no C (**f**) with A, no B, with C (**g**) with A, with B, with C (**h**) with A, with B, no C

Figure 3. Illustration of multi-group quadcopter trajectory-planning problem. The initial density (bottom left) and target density (top right) are Gaussians at the bottom and top, respectively, of these subplots' domains. The five groups of agents start from the initial distribution, aiming to move towards the target distribution while avoiding intra-group and inter-group congestion. The colors in each subplot represent time, thus presenting the trajectories of the agents over time. Under different parameter configurations, the trajectories of the agents are different. A stands for noise $\sigma = 1 \times 10^{-2}$, B for intra-group congestion coefficient $\gamma_{\text{cong}} = 20$ and C for inter-group congestion coefficient $\beta_{\text{cong}} = 1 \times 10^4$. Comparing sub-pictures (**a**–**h**), it can be seen that with σ, the agents add an envelope of uncertainty; with γ_{cong}, the agents of intra-group spread out more as expected; with β_{cong}, the clusters are more diffuse.

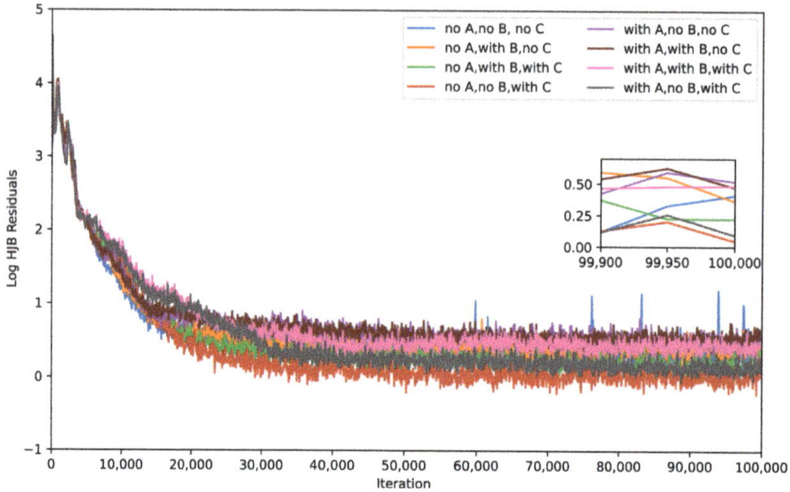

Figure 4. Log HJB residual errors comparison with eight cases in Figure 3. The horizontal axis is the number of iterations, and the vertical axis is ℓ_{HJB} in Algorithm 1.

4.2. Effect of Stochasticity Parameter σ

We investigate the effect of the stochasticity parameter σ on the behavior of the HJB residual errors and the multi-population MFG solutions.

In Figure 5, we show the convergence behavior of the HJB residual errors of quadcopters with different stochasticity parameters. The HJB residual error decreases more and more slowly with the increase of noise σ. This means that the smaller σ, the faster the CA-Net algorithm converges.

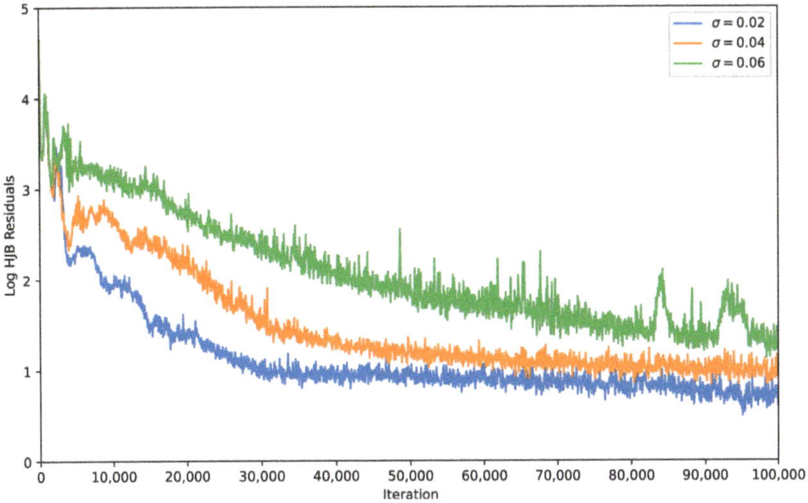

Figure 5. Comparison of log HJB residual errors with stochasticity parameter $\sigma = 0.02$, 0.04 and 0.06.

In Figure 6, we show the controls for multi-group quadcopter trajectory planning using $\sigma = 0.02, 0.04$, and 0.06. As σ increases, the control curves of the agent fluctuates more.

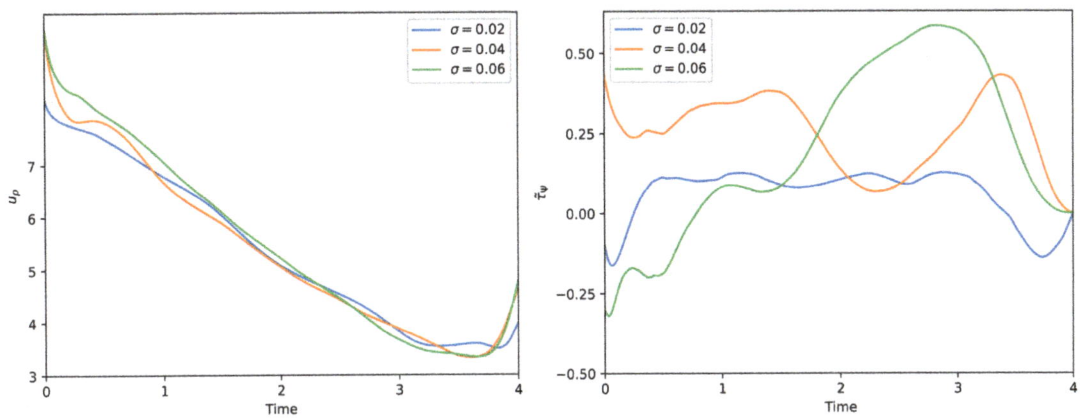

Figure 6. *Cont.*

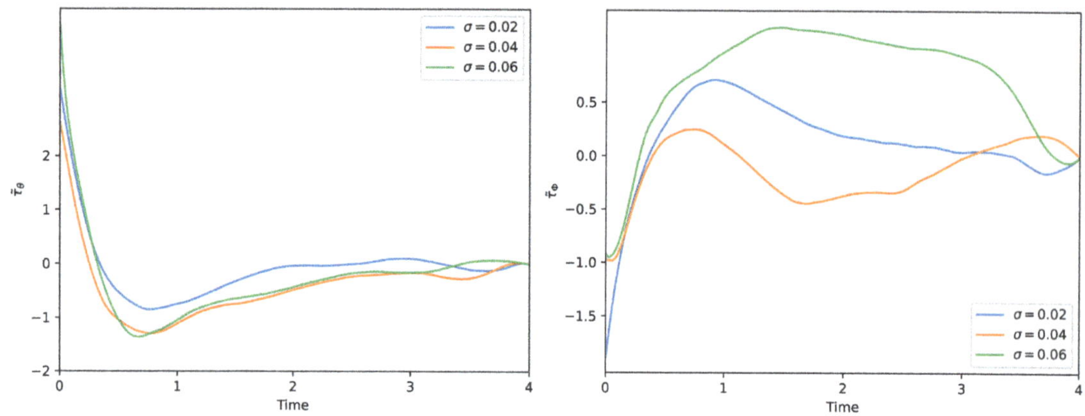

Figure 6. Comparison of controls with different stochasticity parameters. The horizontal axis is time and the vertical axis is u_p (**Top Left**), $\tilde{\tau}_{\psi_p}$ (**Top Right**), $\tilde{\tau}_{\theta_p}$ (**Bottom Left**), $\tilde{\tau}_{\phi_p}$ (**Bottom Right**), respectively.

In Figure 7, we show the optimal velocity of quadcopters obtained by Algorithm 1. The initial average speed of drones is zero, and it increases first and then decreases gradually when they approach the target distribution to minimize their loss functions. Moreover, before approaching the peak, when σ is larger, the quadcopter tends to choose a faster speed. After the strategic speed change, at the terminal time $T = 4$, the smaller σ is, the closer the quadcopter terminal speed is to zero.

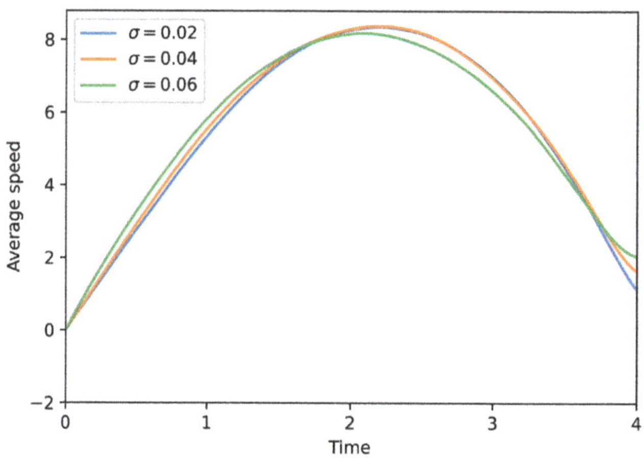

Figure 7. Comparison of average speed with different stochasticity parameters.

4.3. Comparison with Costs

To further reveal the role of some important parameters in the design of the CA-Net algorithm. We show the transport $\mathcal{L}_p$, intra-running $\mathcal{F}_p{}^{\text{intra}}$, inter-running $\mathcal{F}_p{}^{\text{inter}}$, terminal $\mathcal{G}_p$, and objective J_p costs in Table 1 under the change in parameters.

From Table 1, first, we compare the influence of the σ parameter and fix other parameters. From the first line to the third line, it can be seen that the larger stochasticity σ, the greater the transport cost $\mathcal{L}_p$, the smaller the intra-group collision cost ${\mathcal{F}_p}^{\text{intra}}$, and the greater the total cost J_p. Comparing lines 6 and 10, 7 and 11, 8 and 12, and 9 and 13, we can see that if σ exists, the total cost J_p is relatively large. Second, comparing the influence of parameter η, it can be seen from the fourth and fifth lines that if the neighbor dual penalty item exists, the smaller the transport cost $\mathcal{L}_p$, the greater the intra-group ${\mathcal{F}_p}^{\text{intra}}$ and inter-group ${\mathcal{F}_p}^{\text{inter}}$ cost, the constant terminal cost $\mathcal{G}_p$, and the smaller the total cost J_p. Third, compare the influence of the parameter λ. It can be seen from lines 13 and 14 that if the HJB penalty item exists, the smaller the transport cost $\mathcal{L}_p$, the smaller the total cost J_p. Fourth, compare the influence of the parameter γ_{cong}. It can be seen from lines 6 and 8 or lines 10 and 12 that if the intra-group congestion coefficient γ_{cong} exists, the intra-group collision cost ${\mathcal{F}_p}^{\text{intra}}$ will be relatively small. Fifth, compare the impact of parameter β_{cong}. It can be seen from lines 6 and 7 or lines 10 and 11 that if the inter-group congestion coefficient β_{cong} exists, the inter-group collision cost ${\mathcal{F}_p}^{\text{inter}}$ is relatively small. Sixth, compare the influence of the network parameter width, i.e., the network width of each layer. By observing lines 13 and 15, we can see that smaller networks can also achieve convergence, and the total cost J_p is small. As shown in Figure 8, for networks with the same depth, the training convergence speed is faster if each layer is appropriately widened. The larger networks have good robustness and better generalization in complex cases. Finally, comparing the parameter time steps, i.e., lines 13 and 16, the time steps are reduced from 600 to 300, and the total cost fluctuates by nearly 1%, which means that our network is convergent and stable.

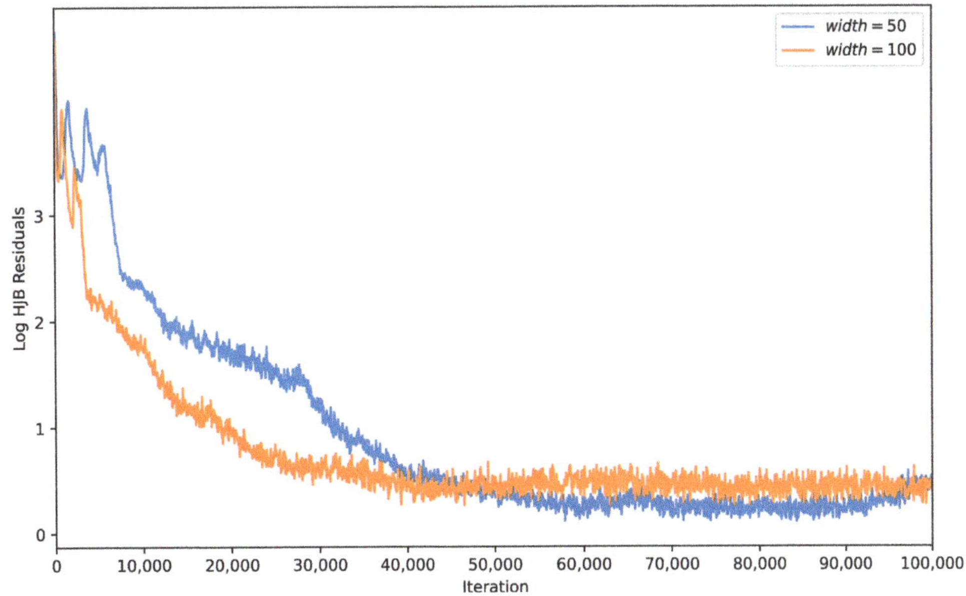

Figure 8. Comparison of log HJB residual errors under different network widths.

Table 1. Comparison with Costs.

Number	Width	Time Steps	σ	η	λ	γ_{cong}	β_{cong}	$\mathcal{L}_p$	${\mathcal{F}_p}^{\text{intra}}$	${\mathcal{F}_p}^{\text{inter}}$	$\mathcal{G}_p$	J_p
1	100	600	0.02	2.5×10^{-3}	1	20	1×10^5	16.8	2.33×10^{-2}	5.03×10^{-2}	14.5	31.4
2	100	600	0.04	2.5×10^{-3}	1	20	1×10^5	17.9	1.85×10^{-2}	5.54×10^{-2}	14.9	32.9
3	100	600	0.06	2.5×10^{-3}	1	20	1×10^5	19.9	1.26×10^{-2}	3.15×10^{-2}	14.7	34.7
4	100	600	0.01	0	1	20	1×10^5	16.4	2.33×10^{-2}	4.30×10^{-2}	14.6	31.1
5	100	600	0.01	1×10^{-2}	1	20	1×10^5	15.2	2.86×10^{-2}	5.22×10^{-2}	14.6	29.8
6	100	600	0	2.5×10^{-3}	1	0	0	15.6	4.73×10^{-2}	1.41×10^{-1}	14.1	29.8
7	100	600	0	2.5×10^{-3}	1	0	1×10^5	15.7	4.71×10^{-2}	6.85×10^{-2}	14.5	30.3
8	100	600	0	2.5×10^{-3}	1	20	0	16.5	3.11×10^{-2}	5.64×10^{-2}	14.1	30.7
9	100	600	0	2.5×10^{-3}	1	20	1×10^5	15.5	2.86×10^{-2}	6.08×10^{-2}	14.7	30.3
10	100	600	0.01	2.5×10^{-3}	1	0	0	15.9	3.76×10^{-2}	9.28×10^{-2}	14	30.1
11	100	600	0.01	2.5×10^{-3}	1	0	1×10^5	16.1	3.30×10^{-2}	5.83×10^{-2}	14.9	31.1
12	100	600	0.01	2.5×10^{-3}	1	20	0	16.6	2.49×10^{-2}	5.40×10^{-2}	14.2	30.8
13	100	600	0.01	2.5×10^{-3}	1	20	1×10^5	16.5	2.43×10^{-2}	6.27×10^{-2}	14.7	31.3
14	100	600	0.01	2.5×10^{-3}	0	20	1×10^5	16.8	2.76×10^{-2}	5.89×10^{-2}	14.6	31.5
15	50	600	0.01	2.5×10^{-3}	1	20	1×10^5	15.3	2.27×10^{-2}	6.45×10^{-2}	15.1	30.4
16	100	300	0.01	2.5×10^{-3}	1	20	1×10^5	16.3	2.57×10^{-2}	5.97×10^{-2}	14.5	30.9

All values were approximated using the validation points; σ, stochasticity; η, neighbor penalty coefficient; λ, HJB penalty coefficient; γ_{cong}, intra-group congestion coefficient; β_{cong}, inter-group congestion coefficient; $\mathcal{L}_p$, transport costs; ${\mathcal{F}_p}^{\text{intra}}$, intra-running costs; ${\mathcal{F}_p}^{\text{inter}}$, inter-running costs; $\mathcal{G}_p$, terminal costs; J_p, objective costs.

4.4. Comparison with Baselines

As the last part of the numerical experiment, we verify the superiority of our method by comparing it to some typical baseline methods, including cluster game [53], HJB-NN [42], Lax–Friedrichs [40], ML [13], and APAC-Net [31]. For more details of these baseline methods, please refer to the related documents [13,31,40,42,53], etc. We give the performance comparison of the above algorithms in Table 2.

Table 2. Comparison with baseline methods.

Method	Communication	Computation	Scale (N)	Dimension (n)	Population (P)	Stochasticity (σ)
Cluster game [53]	$\mathcal{O}(N)$	$\mathcal{O}(n!)$	Small	Low	Multiple	No
HJB-NN [42]	$\mathcal{O}(N)$	$\mathcal{O}(n)$	Large	High	Single	No
Lax–Friedrichs [40]	$\mathcal{O}(1)$	$\mathcal{O}(n!)$	Large	Low	Multiple	Yes
ML [13]	$\mathcal{O}(1)$	$\mathcal{O}(n)$	Large	High	Single	No
APAC-Net [31]	$\mathcal{O}(1)$	$\mathcal{O}(n)$	Large	High	Single	Yes
CA-Net	$\mathcal{O}(1)$	$\mathcal{O}(n)$	Large	High	Multiple	Yes

$\mathcal{O}()$, infinitesimal of the same order; $n!$, the factorial of n.

For cluster game [53], it is a game model for small-scale multi-group agent control problems that communicates through a given point-to-point communication topology. The equilibrium calculation adopts an analytical solution based on grid calculation. The solution space is generally low-dimensional, and special interference is usually not considered. HJB-NN [42] is a neural network approach for solving high-dimensional optimal control problems. This method can be used for large-scale group modeling. In addition, the information interaction between agents is point-to-point communication, which means that the communication cost is relatively high. Reference [40] describes a multi-population social network MFG problem, which is solved analytically using the adjoint method. Its corresponding algorithm uses a numerical scheme called the Lax–Friedrichs scheme [41] belonging to the finite-difference method. Therefore, the numerical solution is cursed by dimension and is only suitable for low-dimensional solution space. Reference [13] provides a machine-learning framework for solving high-dimensional MFG and mean-field control problems. However, it is limited to solving the single-group deterministic MFGs. APAC-Net [31] is an alternating population and agent control neural network for solving high-dimensional stochastic MFGs. It is indeed suitable for large-scale homogeneous agent systems. Our proposed CA-Net is a nonlinear coupled alternating neural network tailored for multi-population high-dimensional stochastic MFGs, which can be induced by optimal control problems of large-scale multi-agent heterogeneous systems. To sum up, we can see the superiority of the CA-Net algorithm in all-around performance from Table 2.

5. Conclusions

We formally propose a numerical-solution scheme for the multi-population high-dimensional stochastic MFG system. The execution algorithm here is CA-Net, a nonlinear coupled alternating neural network. To this end, the proposed modeling framework strictly represents the large-scale heterogeneous multi-agent game system as a multi-population MFG model. Our algorithm avoids the use of spatial grids by parameterizing the value functions and the density functions of multiple populations by two sets of neural networks, respectively. We design multiple generators and multiple discriminators GAN, where density functions act as generative networks and value functions act as discriminative networks. Unlike other GANs, CA-Net incorporates the structure of multi-population MFGs, which absolves the network from learning an entire multi-population MFG solution from the ground up, provides numerical solutions for the multi-population MFG, and improves the solution efficiency. Consequently, our method is geared toward multi-population high-dimensional instances of MFGs that are beyond reach with existing solution methods. CA-Net, therefore, sets the stage for solving realistic multi-population high-dimensional MFGs arising in, e.g., crowd motion, swarm robotics, and epidemic modeling. To verify the feasibility of the multi-population MFG model, we provide a practical numerical simulation case, multi-group quadcopter trajectory planning. The convergence results regarding HJB residual error, control, and average speed show the effectiveness of the CA-Net algorithm. To reveal the role of multi-dimensional parameters in the design of the CA-Net, we show the costs of transport, intra-running, inter-running, terminal, and objective under the change in these parameters. Finally, the comparison with baseline methods—cluster game, HJB-NN, Lax–Friedrichs, ML, and APAC-Net—makes clear the advanced nature of our solution method. In the future, we will consider the application and adaptation of the CA-Net method in more complex scenarios of heterogeneous multi-agent systems, such as complex communication conditions (time-varying, partial rejection) and obstacles (static, dynamic).

Author Contributions: Conceptualization, G.W. and W.Y.; methodology, G.W.; software, G.W. and J.F.; validation, G.W. and L.J.; formal analysis, N.L.; investigation, G.W.; resources, G.W.; data curation, G.W.; writing—original draft preparation, G.W.; writing—review and editing, J.F., L.J. and W.Y.; visualization, G.W.; supervision, L.J.; project administration, N.L.; funding acquisition, N.L. All authors have read and agreed to the published version of the manuscript.

Funding: This research was funded by the Equipment Advanced Research Project Foundation of China, grant number 50912020105, the Naval Weaponry Advance Research Project Foundation of China, grant number 3020904040301 and the Science and Technology Innovation 2030-Key Project grant number 2020AAA0108200.

Data Availability Statement: Data are contained within the article.

Conflicts of Interest: The authors declare no conflicts of interest. The funders had no role in the design of the study, in the collection, analyses, or interpretation of data, in the writing of the manuscript, or in the decision to publish the results.

Notations

The following notations are used in this manuscript:

N	The total number of intelligent agents
$I = \{1, \ldots, N\}$	Intelligent agent set of heterogeneous multi-agent system
P	Total number of intelligent agent populations
$Q = \{1, \ldots, P\}$	Population set of heterogeneous multi-agent system
$G = (Q, E)$	Communication topology graph in heterogeneous multi-agent system
$E \subseteq Q \times Q$	The set of all weighted edges in $G = (Q, E)$

$\arg(p,q)$	The connection edge between populations p and q
$v_{p,q}$	The weight of the edge $\arg(p,q)$
$V(p) = \{q \in Q \mid (p,q) \in E\}$	The set of neighbors of population p
$\lvert V(p) \rvert$	The cardinality of the set $V(p)$
$t \in [0,T]$	time
$x^p(t) \in \mathbb{R}^n$	The state of agent i at time t which belongs to a population $p(i)$
h	The nonlinear evolution function
u	The control input (strategy)
ρ	The probability density function
σ	Noise coefficient/diffusion parameter/stochasticity parameter
w	An m-dimensional Wiener process (standard Brownian motion)
J	Cost function
L	A running cost incurred by an agent based solely on its actions
F	A running cost incurred by an agent based on its interaction with the rest of the same population and the neighbor populations
G	A terminal cost incurred by an agent based on its final state and the final distribution of the whole related populations
Φ	Value function
H	Hamiltonian
$\mathcal{F}$	The potential function of F
$\mathcal{G}$	The potential function of G
$G^p_{\theta^p}$	The density distribution of population p, we train $G^p_{\theta^p}(\cdot,t)$ to produce samples from $\rho^p(\cdot,t)$
$\Phi^p_{\omega^p}$	The value function for the generic agent of population p

References

1. Lasry, J.M.; Lions, P.L. Jeux à champ moyen. I. Le cas stationnaire. *Comptes Rendus Math.* **2006**, *343*, 619–625. [CrossRef]
2. Lasry, J.M.; Lions, P.L. Jeux à champ moyen. II. Horizon fini et contrôle optimal. *Comptes Rendus Math.* **2006**, *343*, 679–684. [CrossRef]
3. Lasry, J.M.; Lions, P.L. Mean field games. *Jpn. J. Math.* **2007**, *2*, 229–260. [CrossRef]
4. Huang, M.Y.; Caines, P.E.; Malhamé, R.P. Individual and mass behaviour in large population stochastic wireless power control problems: centralized and nash equilibrium solutions. In Proceedings of the IEEE Conference on Decision and Control, Maui , HI, USA, 9–12 December 2003; pp. 98–103.
5. Huang, M.Y.; Malhamé, R.P.; Caines, P.E. Large population stochastic dynamic games: Closed-loop McKean-Vlasov systems and the Nash certainty equivalence principle. *Commun. Inf. Syst.* **2006**, *6*, 221–251.
6. Huang, M.Y.; Caines, P.E.; Malhamé, R.P. Large-population cost-coupled LQG problems with nonuniform agents: Individual-mass behavior and decentralized ϵ-Nash equilibria. *IEEE Trans. Autom. Control* **2007**, *52*, 1560–1571. [CrossRef]
7. Ren, L.; Jin, Y.; Niu, Z.; Yao, W.; Zhang, X. Hierarchical cooperation in LQ multi-population mean field game with its application to opinion evolution. *IEEE Trans. Netw. Sci. Eng.* **2024**, *11*, 5008–5022. [CrossRef]
8. Liu, J.; Yao, W.; Zhang, X.; Pégard, C. An MFG online path planning algorithm based on upper and lower structure. In *Intelligent Robotics and Applications*; Springer Nature: Singapore, 2023; pp. 355–366.
9. Wang, G.; Li, Z.; Yao, W.; Xia, S. A multi-population mean-field game approach for large-scale agents cooperative attack-defense evolution in high-dimensional environments. *Mathematics* **2022**, *10*, 4075. [CrossRef]
10. Wang, G.; Yao, W.; Zhang, X.; Li, Z. A mean-field game control for large-scale swarm formation flight in dense environments. *Sensors* **2022**, *22*, 5437. [CrossRef] [PubMed]
11. Ren, L.; Jin, Y.; Niu, Z.; Wang, G.; Yao, W.; Zhang, X. Optimal strategies for large-scale pursuers against one evader: A mean field game-based hierarchical control approach. *Syst. Control. Lett.* **2024**, *183*, 105697. [CrossRef]
12. Niu, Z.; Yao, W.; Jin, Y.; Huang, S.; Zhang, X.; Qian, L. Integrated task assignment and trajectory planning for a massive number of agents based on bilayer-coupled mean field games. *IEEE Trans. Autom. Sci. Eng.* **2024**, 1–20. [CrossRef]
13. Ruthotto, L.; Osher, S.J.; Li, W.; Nurbekyan, L.; Fung, S.W. A machine learning framework for solving high-dimensional mean field game and mean field control problems. *Proc. Natl. Acad. Sci. USA* **2020**, *117*, 9183–9193. [CrossRef] [PubMed]
14. Achdou, Y.; Camilli, F.; Capuzzo-Dolcetta, I. Mean field games: Numerical methods for the planning problem. *SIAM J. Control Optim.* **2012**, *50*, 77–109. [CrossRef]
15. Guéant, O. Mean field games equations with quadratic Hamiltonian: A specific approach. *Math. Models Methods Appl. Sci.* **2012**, *22*, 1250022.
16. Camilli, F.; Festa, A.; Schieborn, D. An approximation scheme for a Hamilton–Jacobi equation defined on a network. *Appl. Numer. Math.* **2013**, *73*, 33–47. [CrossRef]
17. Carlini, E.; Silva, F.J. A fully discrete semi-Lagrangian scheme for a first order mean field game problem. *SIAM J. Numer. Anal.* **2014**, *52*, 45–67. [CrossRef]

18. Cacace, S.; Camilli, F. Ergodic problems for Hamilton-Jacobi equations: Yet another but efficient numerical method. *arXiv* **2016**, arXiv:1601.07107.
19. Almulla, N.; Ferreira, R.; Gomes, D. Two numerical approaches to stationary mean-field games. *Dyn. Games Appl.* **2017**, *7*, 657–682.
20. Cardaliaguet, P.; Hadikhanloo, S. Learning in mean field games: The fictitious play. *ESAIM Control Optim. Calc. Var.* **2017**, *23*, 569–591. [CrossRef]
21. Gomes, D.; Velho, R.M.; Wolfram, M.T. Dual two-state mean-field games. In Proceedings of the 53rd IEEE Conference on Decision and Control, Los Angeles, CA, USA, 15–17 December 2014.
22. Gomes, D.; Velho, R.M.; Wolfram, M.T. Socio-economic applications of finite state mean field games. *Philos. Trans. R. Soc. Lond. Ser. A Math. Phys. Eng. Sci.* **2014**, *372*, 20130405. [CrossRef]
23. Achdou, Y.; Capuzzo-Dolcetta, I. Mean field games: Numerical methods. *SIAM J. Numer. Anal.* **2010**, *48*, 1136–1162. [CrossRef]
24. Benamou, J.D.; Carlier, G.; Santambrogio, F. Variational mean field games. In *Active Particles*; Springer International Publishing: Berlin/Heidelberg, Germany, 2017; pp. 141–171.
25. Chow, Y.T.; Li, W.; Osher, S.; Yin, W. Algorithm for hamilton–jacobi equations in density space via a generalized hopf formula. *J. Sci. Comput.* **2019**, *80*, 1195–1239. [CrossRef]
26. Chow, Y.T.; Darbon, J.; Osher, S.; Yin, W. Algorithm for overcoming the curse of dimensionality for time-dependent non-convex hamilton-jacobi equations arising from optimal control and differential games problems. *J. Sci. Comput.* **2017**, *73*, 617–643. [CrossRef]
27. Chow, Y.T.; Darbon, J.; Osher, S.; Yin, W. Algorithm for overcoming the curse of dimensionality for certain non-convex hamilton–jacobi equations, projections and differential games. *Ann. Math. Sci. Appl.* **2018**, *3*, 369–403. [CrossRef]
28. Jacobs, M.; Léger, F.; Li, W.; Osher, S. Solving large-scale optimization problems with a convergence rate independent of grid size. SIAM Journal on Numerical Analysis. *SIAM J. Numer. Anal.* **2019**, *57*, 1100–1123. [CrossRef]
29. Bellman, R. *Dynamic Programming*; Princeton University Press: Princeton, NJ, USA, 1957.
30. Han, J.; Arnulf, J.; Weinan, E. Solving high-dimensional partial differential equations using deep learning. *Proc. Natl. Acad. Sci. USA* **2018**, *115*, 8505–8510. [CrossRef] [PubMed]
31. Lin, A.T.; Fung, S.W.; Li, W.; Nurbekyan, L.; Osher, S.J. Alternating the population and control neural networks to solve high-dimensional stochastic mean-field games. *Proc. Natl. Acad. Sci. USA* **2021**, *118*, 0027–8424. [CrossRef]
32. Goodfellow, I.; Pouget-Abadie, J.; Mirza, M.; Xu, B.; Warde-Farley, D.; Ozair, S.; Courville, A.; Bengio, Y. Generative adversarial nets. In *Advances in Neural Information Processing Systems*; MIT Press: Cambridge, MA, USA, 2014 ; pp. 2672–2680.
33. Fujii, M. Probabilistic Approach to Mean Field Games and Mean Field Type Control Problems with Multiple Populations. *arXiv* **2020**, arXiv:1911.11501v3. [CrossRef]
34. Feleqi, E. The derivation of ergodic mean field game equations for several population of players. *Dyn. Games Appl.* **2013**, *3*, 523–536. [CrossRef]
35. Cirant, M. Multi-population mean field games system with Neumann boundary conditions. *J. Math. Pures Appl.* **2015**, *103*, 1294–1315. [CrossRef]
36. Lachapelle, A.; Wolfram, M. On a mean field game approach modeling congestion and aversion in pedestrian crowds. *Transp. Res. Part B* **2011**, *45*, 1572–1589. [CrossRef]
37. Aurell, A.; Djehiche, B. Mean-field type modeling of nonlocal crowd aversion in pedestrian crowd dynamics. *SIAM J. Contrl Optim.* **2018**, *56*, 434–455. [CrossRef]
38. Achdou, Y.; Bardi, M.; Cirant, M. Mean field games models of segregation. *Math. Model. Methods Appl. Sci.* **2017**, *27*, 75–113. [CrossRef]
39. Bensoussan, A.; Tao, H.; Laurière, M. Mean field control and mean field game models with several populations. *Minimax Theory Its Applilications* **2018**, *3*, 173–209.
40. Banez, R. A.; Gao, H.; Li, L.; Yang, C.; Han, Z.; Poor, H.V. Belief and opinion evolution in social networks based on a multi-population mean field game approach. In Proceedings of the ICC 2020—2020 IEEE International Conference on Communications (ICC), Los Angeles, CA, USA, 15–17 December 2014; IEEE: Piscataway, NJ, USA, 2020.
41. Schulte, J.M. Adjoint Methods for Hamilton-Jacobi-Bellman Equations. Ph.D. Thesis, University of Munster: Munster, Germany, 2010.
42. Onken, D.; Nurbekyan, L.; Li, X.; Fung, S.W.; Osher, S.; Ruthotto, L. A Neural Network Approach for High-Dimensional Optimal Control. *arXiv* **2021**, arXiv:2104.03270v1.
43. Wang, Y.W.; Lei, Y.; Bian, T.; Guan, Z.H. Distributed control of nonlinear multiagent systems with unknown and nonidentical control directions via event-triggered communication. *IEEE Trans. Cybern.* **2020**, *50*, 1820–1832. [CrossRef] [PubMed]
44. Olfati-Saber, R.; Fax, J.A.; Murray, R.M. Consensus and cooperation in networked multi-agent systems. *Proc. IEEE* **2007**, *95*, 215–233. [CrossRef]
45. Gao, H.; Lee, W.; Li, W.; Han, Z.; Osher, S.; Poor, H.V. Energy-efficient velocity control for massive numbers of rotary-wing UAVs: A mean field game approach. In Proceedings of the GLOBECOM 2020—2020 IEEE Global Communications Conference, Taipei, Taiwan, 7–11 December 2020; IEEE: Piscataway, NJ, USA, 2020.
46. Cardaliaguet, P.; Graber, P.J. Mean field games systems of first order. *ESAIM Control Optim. Calc. Var.* **2015**, *21*, 690–722. [CrossRef]

47. Cardaliaguet, P.; Graber, P.J.; Porretta, A.; Tonon, D. Second order mean field games with degenerate diffusion and local coupling. *Nonlinear Differ. Equ. Appl. NoDEA* **2015**, *22*, 1287–1317. [CrossRef]
48. Cirant, M.; Nurbekyan, L. The variational structure and time-periodic solutions for mean-field games systems. *Minimax Theory Appl.* **2018**, *3*, 227–260.
49. Onken, D.; Fung, S.W.; Li, X.; Ruthotto, L. OT-Flow: Fast and accurate continuous normalizing flows via optimal transport. *arXiv* **2020**, arXiv: 2006.00104. [CrossRef]
50. Guéant, O.; Lasry, J.M.; Lions, P.L. Mean field games and applications. In *Paris-Princeton Lectures on Mathematical Finance 2010*; Springer: Berlin/Heidelberg, Germany, 2011; pp. 205–266.
51. Lin, A.T.; Chow, Y.T.; Osher, S.J. A splitting method for overcoming the curse of dimensionality in Hamilton–Jacobi equations arising from nonlinear optimal control and differential games with applications to trajectory generation. *Commun. Math.* **2018**, *16*, 1933–1973. [CrossRef]
52. Carrillo, L.R.G.; López, A.E.D.; Lozano, R.; Pégard, C. Modeling the quad-rotor mini-rotorcraft. In *Quad Rotorcraft Control*; Springer: Berlin/Heidelberg, Germany, 2013; pp. 23–34.
53. Ye, M.; Hu, G.; Lozano, R.; Lewis, F.L.; Xie, L. A unified strategy for solution seeking in graphical n-coalition noncooperative games. *IEEE Trans. Autom. Control* **2019**, *64*, 4645–4652. [CrossRef]

mathematics

MDPI

Article

Cooperative Control Approach for Library Group Therapy with Constraint Conditions

Lingyu Yang [1], Jiahao Xu [2,*] and Wenguang Zhang [3]

[1] Library of Xiaoxiang Campus, Central South University, Changsha 410083, China
[2] School of Automation, Central South University, Changsha 410083, China
[3] School of Control and Computer Engineering, North China Electric Power University, Beijing 102206, China
* Correspondence: xujiahaocsu@csu.edu.cn

Abstract: In this paper, group therapy behavior is studied from the viewpoint of cooperative control. To describe the range of emotional changes in each participant, nonconvex constraint sets are employed, which can be used to quantitatively represent the differences among all the participants. Then, a cooperative control model is proposed to describe the interaction between participants. Based on this model, emotion analysis is performed, and it is shown that all participants finally reach an emotion consensus regardless of facilitators being involved. In particular, when facilitators are absent, the final states of all participants cannot be controlled, while when facilitators are involved, the final states of all participants can be driven to a desired state of mental health. Numerical simulation examples are given to illustrate the theoretical conclusions.

Keywords: distributed cooperative algorithm; library group therapy behavior; nonlinear constraints

MSC: 93C95

1. Introduction

As an important branch of mental health problems, group therapy has received more and more attention from researchers in the education system [1–10]. For example, in [2], the self-growth process in the graduate school of counseling was studied through a group art therapy class. In [6], a single-session approach was studied for creative art university students for group therapy. In [7,8], group cohesion and group alliance were studied to improve mental health recovery. All of these works have greatly promoted the development of group therapy. However, research [1–10] has focused on the impact of some group therapy behaviors on the mental health of participants and has not considered the process of emotional changes.

In this study, we were interested in group therapy and investigated the emotional changes in participants from the viewpoint of cooperative control. Cooperative control was first studied in [11–13]. Existing studies focus on applying cooperative control theory to subject services and embedded services [14–16], including collaborative filtering algorithms for library data mining [17], models for collaborative learning spaces in Korean university libraries [18], and analysis of abnormal collaborative behaviors in smart libraries [19], aiming to optimize group collaboration dynamics. While less attention has been paid to solving group dynamics by using cooperative control theory. The objective of cooperative control is to propose algorithms to drive all agents to complete a task in a cooperative manner. Group therapy is essentially a kind of group control of behavior. To better understand the role of group therapy, in this paper, we first use nonconvex constraint sets to describe the range of emotional changes for each participant, which can be used to quantitatively represent the differences among all the participants. Then, we propose a cooperative control model to describe the interaction between participants. Based on this model, emotion analysis is performed, and it is shown that all participants finally reach an emotional consensus regardless of facilitators being involved. In particular, when facilitators are absent, the final states of all participants cannot be controlled, while, when facilitators are involved, the final states of all participants can be driven to a desired state of mental health.

2. Main Results

2.1. Graph Theory

Let $\mathcal{G} = (\mathcal{V}, \mathcal{E}, \mathcal{A})$ denote a group therapy space, where $\mathcal{V} = \{1, 2, \ldots, n\}$ denotes the set of participants, $\mathcal{E} \subseteq \mathcal{V} \times \mathcal{V}$ denotes the set of edges, and $\mathcal{A}$ denotes the weighted adjacency matrix. Define $a_{ij} > 0$, if $(i, j) \in \mathcal{E}$; otherwise, $a_{ij} = 0$. Let the neighbor set of i be defined as $\mathcal{N}_i = \{j \in \mathcal{V} \mid (j, i) \in \mathcal{E}\}$ and π_i be the number of neighbors in $\mathcal{N}_i$.

2.2. Problem Formulation

The objective of this paper is to try to understand the process of emotional changes during group therapy in a quantitative way so as to promote the effects of group therapy, which is different from most of the existing works, which focused on the behaviors and phenomena that might appear.

Consider a group of participants, where each participant is assumed to have the following dynamics:

$$x_i(k+1) = x_i(k) + \sum_{j \in \mathcal{N}_i} S_{U_{ij}}[a_{ij}(x_j(k) - x_i(k))] \tag{1}$$

where $x_i(k) \in \mathbb{R}$ denotes the ith participant's emotion state at time k, and

$$S_{U_{ij}}(x) = \begin{cases} \frac{x}{\|x\|} \sup\limits_{0 \le \beta \le \|x\|} \left\{\beta : \frac{\alpha\beta x}{\|x\|} \in U_{ij}, 0 < \alpha < \beta\right\}, \\ \text{if } x \neq 0, \\ 0, \text{if } x = 0. \end{cases}$$

In (1), the term $a_{ij}(x_j(k) - x_i(k))$ denotes the weighted emotion interaction between participants; the term $a_{ij}(x_j(k) - x_i(k))$ denotes the weighted effect of $x_j(k)$ on $x_i(k)$. As the emotion interaction might widely differ between different participants, the operator $S_{U_{ij}}(\cdot)$, which was first proposed in [20] and successfully studied in [21], is introduced to describe the different interaction parts of $a_{ij}(x_j(k) - x_i(k))$. When $s = 0$, $S_{U_{ij}}(s) = 0$ means that participants are highly similar; they are more likely to understand both themselves and others. When $s \neq 0$, the whole term $\sum_{j \in \mathcal{N}_i} S_{U_{ij}}[a_{ij}(x_j(k) - x_i(k))]$ denotes the sum of the emotional interaction between participants.

It should be noted that the specific form of $S_{U_{ij}}(\cdot)$ is not given here because, in the following theorems, it is shown that all participants reach a consensus state no matter what form $S_{U_{ij}}(\cdot)$ takes.

Group identification according to the psychological conditions of participants should be performed before we start our analyses. Some projects on group emotion identification and classification have made headway. For example, based on the six basic emotions of human beings, the participants of the "Libraries of emotions" project redistributed their collected resources and developed an open-source methodology for presenting the role of reading therapy and emotion in reading. With this method, this project helped readers connect their emotional experience during reading with their experiences in real life, which had a positive impact on their mental health [22]. The "Dan Dan growth" of "Dan Dan happy reading" activities, carried out by Fudan University Library, are other examples. The applicants' psychological disorders, mental needs, reading habits, and other information were identified using a questionnaire survey. Then, based on this questionnaire, selected applicants who were appropriate for the current topic participated in a group therapy activity. In this program, Fudan University Library invited internal and external psychologists, who guided participants to read together and carried out various face-to-face group activities.

In the following, we analyze the group therapy behaviors between participants based on the system dynamics in (1). First, we present some necessary assumptions.

Assumption 1. *Suppose that* $\sum_{j=1}^{n} a_{ij} < \eta$ *for some constant* $0 < \eta < 1$.

Assumption 2 ([20])**.** *Suppose that each* $U_{ij} \subseteq \mathbb{R}^r$, $i = 1, 2, \ldots, n$ *is nonempty and closed.*

$$\sup_{x \in U_{ij}} \|S_{U_{ij}}(x)\| = \overline{\sigma}_i > 0$$
$$\inf_{x \notin U_{ij}} \|S_{U_{ij}}(x)\| = \underline{\sigma}_i > 0$$

for all i.

Assumption 2 means that the distance from any point outside U_{ij} to the origin is lower-bounded by a positive constant. That is, the participants can interact from all directions, and, no matter what happens, the emotional states of all participants are upper-bounded.

Under this assumption, we have the following theorem:

Theorem 1. *Suppose that the communication graph is connected. Under Assumption 1, the emotional state of all participants reaches a consensus as time evolves. That is,* $\lim_{t \to +\infty} (x_i(k) - x_j(k)) = 0$ *for all* i, j.

Proof. Let

$$e_{ij}(k) = \frac{S_{U_{ij}}[a_{ij}(x_i(k) - x_j(k))]}{x_i(k) - x_j(k)}.$$

When $a_{ij}(x_i(k) - x_j(k)) = 0$, we define $e_{ij}(k) = 1$. When $a_{ij}(x_i(k) - x_j(k)) \neq 0$ and $s_{U_{ij}}[a_{ij}(x_i(k) - x_j(k))] = a_{ij}(x_i(k) - x_j(k))$, we have $e_{ij}(k) = 1$. When $a_{ij}(x_i(k) - x_j(k)) \neq 0$ and $S_{U_{ij}}[a_{ij}(x_i(k) - x_j(k))] \neq a_{ij}(x_i(k) - x_j(k))$, from the definition of operator $S_{U_{ij}}(\cdot)$, we have

$$0 < \frac{\underline{\sigma}_i}{\|x_i(k) - x_j(k)\|} \leq e_{ij}(k) < 1.$$

Using $e_{ij}(k)$, (1) is equivalent to

$$x_i(k+1) = x_i(k) + \sum_{j \in \mathcal{N}_i} e_{ij}(k) a_{ij}(x_j(k) - x_i(k)). \tag{2}$$

Writing (2) in matrix form, we have

$$x(k+1) = \Psi(k) x(k), \tag{3}$$

where $x(k) = [x_1(k), \cdots, x_n(k)]^T$, $[\Psi(k)]_{ii} = 1 - \sum_{j \in \mathcal{N}_i} e_{ij}(k) a_{ij}$ is the iith entry of $\Psi(k)$; if $j \in \mathcal{N}_i$, $[\Psi(k)]_{ij} = e_{ij}(k) a_{ij}$ is the ijth entry of $\Psi(k)$; if $j \notin \mathcal{N}_i$, $[\Psi(k)]_{ij} = 0$. It can be easily checked that each row sum of $\Psi(k)$ is 1, and each entry is non-negative. Hence, $\Psi(k)$ is a stochastic matrix.

Now, we prove that each nonzero entry of $\Psi(k)$ is lower-bounded by a positive constant. First, consider the quantity $\max_{i\in\mathcal{I}} x_i(k)$, where $\mathcal{I} = \{1, 2, \ldots, n\}$.

Since $\Psi(k)$ is a stochastic matrix, each $x_i(k+1)$ is a convex combination of all $x_i(k)$, and hence

$$x_i(k+1) \leq \max_{i\in\mathcal{I}} x_i(k).$$

That is,

$$\max_{i\in\mathcal{I}} x_i(k+1) \leq \max_{i\in\mathcal{I}} x_i(k).$$

With a similar approach, it can be proved that

$$\min_{i\in\mathcal{I}} x_i(k+1) \geq \min_{i\in\mathcal{I}} x_i(k).$$

Therefore,

$$\begin{aligned} & |x_i(k+1) - x_j(k+1)| \\ \leq \; & \max_{i\in\mathcal{I}} x_i(k) - \min_{i\in\mathcal{I}} x_i(k) \\ \leq \; & \max_{i\in\mathcal{I}} x_i(0) - \min_{i\in\mathcal{I}} x_i(0). \end{aligned}$$

As a result,

$$e_{ij}(k) \geq \frac{\underline{\sigma}_i}{\max_{i\in\mathcal{I}} x_i(0) - \min_{i\in\mathcal{I}} x_i(0)}$$

for each $j \in N_i$. Moreover, under Assumption 1,

$$1 - \sum_{j\in N_i} e_{ij} a_{ij} > 1 - \eta.$$

Therefore, $[\Psi(k)]_{ii}$ is nonzero for all i, and each nonzero entry of $\Psi(k)$ is lower-bounded by a positive constant.

Next, we prove the consensus convergence of the system. Consider a matrix sequence, $\Lambda(0), \Lambda(1), \ldots$, where $\Lambda(m) = \Psi((m+1)n-1)\Psi((m+1)n-2)\ldots\Psi((m+1)n-n)$. Note that the communication graph is connected under Assumption 2. Since $[\Psi(k)]_{ii}$ is nonzero for all i, and each nonzero entry of $\Psi(k)$ is lower-bounded by a positive constant, it follows from graph theory that each entry of $\Lambda(m)$ is nonzero and lower-bounded by a constant, denoted by c. Note that $x((m+1)n) = \Lambda(m)x(mn)$. It follows that

$$\begin{aligned} & x_i((m+1)n) = \sum_{j=1}^{n} [\Lambda(m)]_{ij} x_j(mn) \\ & \sum_{j=1, j\neq i_0}^{n} [\Lambda(m)]_{ij} x_j(mn) + [\Lambda(m)]_{ii_0} x_{i_0}(mn) \\ & \leq (1 - [\Lambda(m)]_{ii_0}) \max_{j=1, j\neq i_0} x_j(mn) \\ & \quad + [\Lambda(m)]_{ii_0} x_{i_0}(mn) \\ & \leq (1-c) \max_{j\in\mathcal{I}} x_j(mn) + c \min_{j\in\mathcal{I}} x_j(mn) \end{aligned} \tag{4}$$

for all i, where $x_{i_0}(mn) = \min_{j\in\mathcal{I}} x_j(mn)$.

Similarly, it can be obtained that $x_i((m+1)n) \geq (1-c)\min_{j\in\mathcal{I}} x_j(mn) + c \max_{j\in\mathcal{I}} x_j(mn)$ for all x. Then,

$$\begin{aligned} & \max_{i\in\mathcal{I}} x_i((m+1)n) - \min_{i\in\mathcal{I}} x_i((m+1)n) \\ & \leq (1-2c)(\max_{\mathcal{I}} x_i(mn) - \min_{i\in\mathcal{I}} x_i(mn)). \end{aligned} \tag{5}$$

This means that $\lim_{m\to+\infty}(\max_{i\in\mathcal{I}} x_i((m+1)n) - \min_{i\in\mathcal{I}} x_i((m+1)n)) = 0$ for all i, j. From the definition of the limitation, there must exist a constant $T_0 > 0$ for any $\epsilon > 0$ such that

$$\max_{i\in\mathcal{I}} x_i((m+1)n) - \min_{i\in\mathcal{I}} x_i((m+1)n) < \epsilon.$$

From (2), we have

$$\begin{aligned}&|x_i((m+1)n+1) - x_j((m+1)n+1)|\\ &\leq n|x_i(((m+1)n) - x_j(((m+1)n)|\\ &< n\epsilon.\end{aligned}$$

This means that $\lim_{m\to+\infty}(\max_{i\in\mathcal{I}} x_i((m+1)n+1) - \min_{i\in\mathcal{I}} x_i((m+1)n+1)) = 0$ for all i,j. By analogy, it can be proven that $\lim_{t\to+\infty}(x_i(k) - x_j(k)) = 0$ for all i,j. This completes the proof. □

Theorem 1 means that all participants can reach a consensus emotional mental health state, indicating that mutual interaction might result in the same emotional state. This is consistent with the idea of the Swiss psychologist Jean Piaget: the formation of cognition is a process of the gradual assimilation and adaptation of psychology [23].

Mutual interactions among participants are spontaneous, and they might have professional limitations. In order to avoid being affected by each other's negative emotions, the psychological intervention and guidance of facilitators should play an oriented role in group therapy. On the one hand, under the constraints of the rules and regulations of the facilitators, participants transform spontaneous conflict into cohesion with others. On the other hand, the rational distribution of facilitator resources can match the library collection of resources with the needs of participants more effectively. At the same time, it can strengthen the cooperation between a university library and the other departments of a university, in particular for the departments of psychological counseling and psychological education, to establish a sound long-term mechanism together to solve the professional limitation problem with participants.

In Theorem 1, the case where there are no facilitators or constraint conditions is studied. In the following, we study the case where there are facilitators, where each participant is assumed to have the following dynamics:

$$\begin{aligned}x_i(k+1) =& x_i(k) + \sum_{j\in\mathcal{N}_i} S_{U_{ij}}[a_{ij}(x_j(k) - x_i(k))]\\ &+ a_{i0}(k)(x_0 - x_i(k))\end{aligned} \tag{6}$$

for all $i \in \mathcal{I}$, where x_0 is the desired emotional state given by the facilitator, and $a_{i0}(k) \neq 0$ if the ith participant can receive the information from the facilitator, and $a_{i0}(k) = 0$ otherwise.

Assumption 3. *Suppose that $\sum_{j=1}^{n} a_{ij} + a_{i0}(k) < \eta$ for some constant $0 < \eta < 1$ and all k, and $a_{i0}(k) \neq 0$ for some i and all k.*

Under this assumption, we have the following theorem:

Theorem 2. *Suppose that the communication graph is connected. Under Assumption 3, the behaviors of all participants reach the desired state x_0 as time evolves. That is, $\lim_{t\to+\infty}(x_i(k) - x_0) = 0$ for all i.*

Proof. Let $\tilde{x}_i(k) = x_i(k) - x_0$. Then, system (6) can be written as

$$\begin{aligned}\tilde{x}_i(k+1) =& (1 - a_{i0}(k))\tilde{x}_i(k)\\ &+ \sum_{j\in\mathcal{N}_i} e_{ij}(k)a_{ij}(\tilde{x}_j(k) - \tilde{x}_i(k)).\end{aligned} \tag{7}$$

Writing (7) in matrix form, we have

$$\tilde{x}(k+1) = \tilde{\Psi}(k)\tilde{x}(k). \quad (8)$$

where $\tilde{x}(k) = [\tilde{x}_1(k), \cdots, \tilde{x}_n(k)]^T$, $[\tilde{\Psi}(k)]_{ii} = 1 - \sum_{j\in\mathcal{N}_i} e_{ij}(k)a_{ij} - a_{i0}(k)$ is the iith entry of $\tilde{\Psi}(k)$, $[\tilde{\Psi}(k)]_{ij} = e_{ij}(k)a_{ij}$ is the ijth entry of $\Psi(k)$ if $j \in \mathcal{N}_i$, and $[\tilde{\Psi}(k)]_{ij} = 0$ if $j \notin \mathcal{N}_i$.

Consider a matrix sequence $\tilde{\Lambda}(0), \tilde{\Lambda}(1), \cdots$, where $\tilde{\Lambda}(m) = \tilde{\Psi}((m+1)n-1)\tilde{\Psi}((m+1)n-2)\cdots\tilde{\Psi}((m+1)n-n)$. When

$$a_{i0}(k) \neq 0, 0 < \sum_{j=1}^{n}[\tilde{\Psi}]_{ij} < 1.$$

Under Assumption 3, it follows from graph theory that each row sum of $\tilde{\Lambda}(m)$ is no larger than a positive constant, denoted as $0 \leq \gamma_c < 1$. From Gasgolin's theorem, all of the norms of the eigenvalues of $\tilde{\Psi}$ are no larger than $0 \leq \gamma_c < 1$. From control theory, it follows that $\lim_{m\to+\infty} \tilde{x}_i((m+1)n) = 0$ for all i. Similar to the proof of Theorem 1, we have $\lim_{k\to+\infty} \tilde{x}_i(k) = 0$ for all i. That is, $\lim_{t\to+\infty}(x_i(k) - x_0) = 0$ for all i. This completes the proof. □

Theorem 2 shows that all participants can be driven to a desired emotional mental health state under the guidance of facilitators. In future studies, we will consider treating indicators such as the evaluation of participants' psychotherapy effects as optimization functions for each agent in [24] to achieve the optimal psychotherapy effect.

3. Simulations

Consider a group of 8 participants. Figure 1 shows the communication graph between participants, where each nonzero a_{ij} is $a_{ij} = 0.3$, and the sampling time of simulation is chosen as 0.1 s. Each constraint set U_{ij} was adopted as $U_{ij} = \{s \mid \|s\| \leq 1\}$, and the desired state was $(20, 20)$. The initial emotion states for the participants were $(0,2)$, $(0,1)$, $(5,0)$, $(8,4)$, $(8,0)$, $(12,3)$, $(11,0)$ and $(10,4)$.

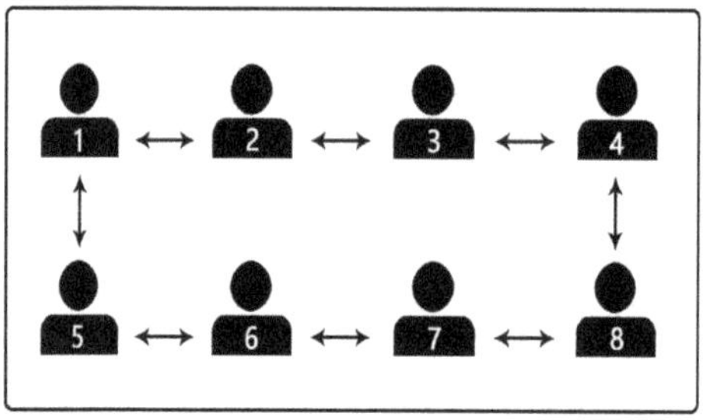

Figure 1. A group of 8 participants without a facilitator.

First, we consider the case where there is no facilitator to guide the participants. Figures 2 and 3 show the simulation results. It is clear that the participants cannot reach the desired state $(20, 20)$. Note that, in this case as discussed in the proof of Theorem 1, system (1) is equivalent to (2) which is a time-varying linear system; hence the final common emotion state is strongly related to the initial states. In this case, all participants update their emotional state based on the states of their neighbors. The final consensus state is generally a function of the initial states of all participants, converging to a weighted average or another combination of these initial conditions. Without external guidance from facilitators, the intrinsic dynamics drive the system toward a state that reflects these starting values.

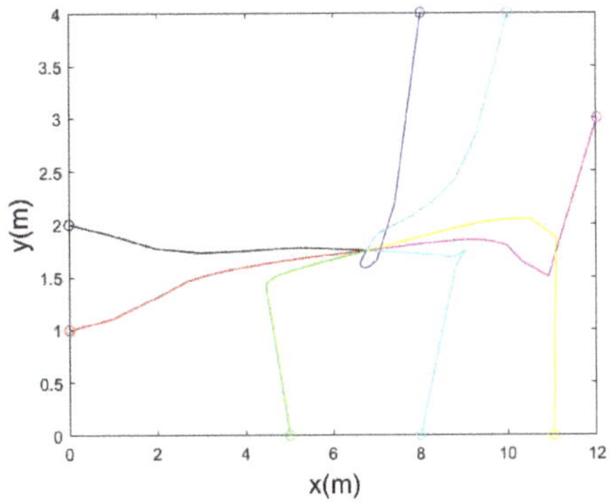

Figure 2. The participants without facilitator cannot reach the desired state.

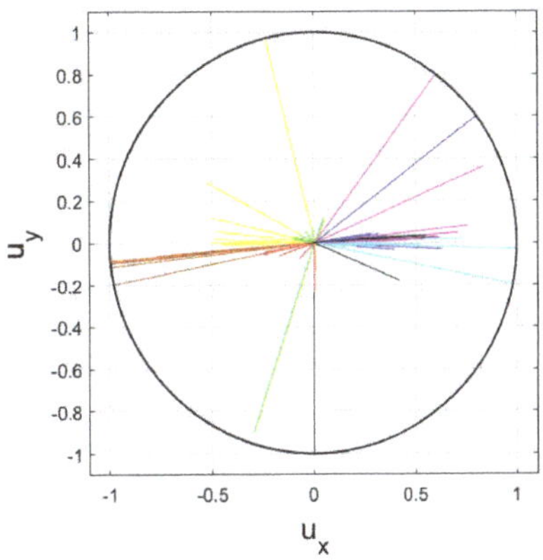

Figure 3. The weighted emotion interaction $u_x/u_y = a_{ij}[x_j(k) - x_i(k)]$ between all participants i, j without a facilitator.

Now, we consider the case where there is a facilitator to guide participants 3 and 4, and the communication graph is shown in Figure 4. Figures 5 and 6 show the simulation results. It is clear that the final common state has no relationship with the initial emotional states of the participants, and, under the guidance of a facilitator, all participants reach the desired state $(20, 20)$ with $a_{i0}(k) = 0.3$ for all i, k.

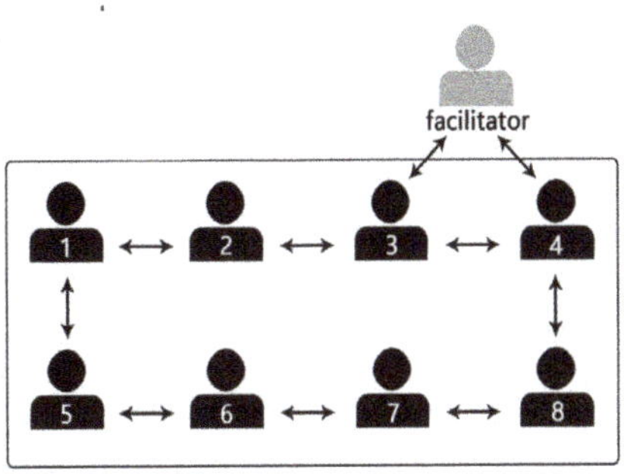

Figure 4. There is a facilitator to guide participants 3 and 4.

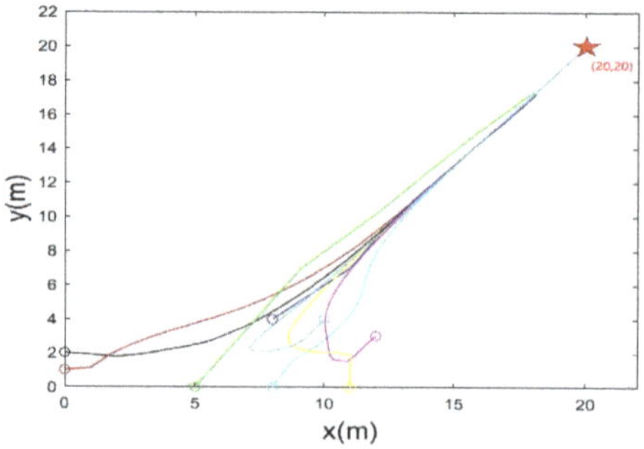

Figure 5. All participants reach the desired state with a facilitator.

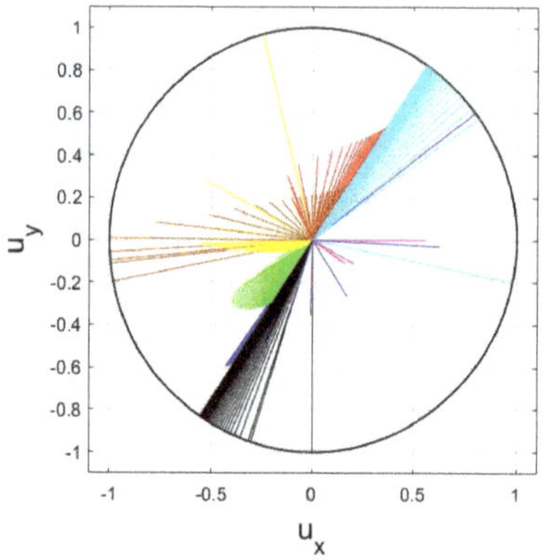

Figure 6. The weighted emotional interaction $u_x/u_y = a_{ij}[x_j(k) - x_i(k)]$ between all participants i, j with a facilitator.

4. Conclusions

In this paper, group therapy behavior was studied from the viewpoint of cooperative control. To describe the range of emotional changes for each participant, nonconvex constraint set was employed, which was used to quantitatively represent the differences among all the participants. Then a cooperative control model was constructed to describe the interactions between participants. Based on this model, it was shown that all participants finally reached an emotional consensus regardless of facilitators being involved. In particular, when facilitators were absent, the final states of all participants could not be controlled, while, when facilitators were involved, the final emotion states of all participants could be driven to a desired emotional mental health state.

Author Contributions: Conceptualization, L.Y.; methodology, L.Y.; software, L.Y.; validation, L.Y. and J.X.; formal analysis, W.Z.; investigation, L.Y.; resources, J.X. and W.Z.; data curation, L.Y. and W.Z.; writing—original draft, L.Y.; writing—review and editing, J.X.; visualization, L.Y.; supervision, J.X. and W.Z.; project administration, W.Z.; funding acquisition, W.Z. All authors have read and agreed to the published version of this manuscript.

Funding: This research received no external funding.

Data Availability Statement: The original contributions presented in the study are included in the article, further inquiries can be directed to the corresponding author.

Conflicts of Interest: The authors declare no conflicts of interest.

References

1. Jiří, K.; Miroslav, C.; Libuše, L. Czech Arts Therapies in Educational Institutions. *Educ. Sci.* **2019**, *9*, 82. [CrossRef]
2. Chae, Y. A Study on the Self-growth Process of the Graduate School of Counseling through the Group Art Therapy Class. *Korea Open Access J.* **2019**, *9*, 1–21.
3. Shir, H.; Dafna, R.; Sharon, S.; Racheli, R. Perceptions of Art Therapy in Adolescent Clients Treated within the School System. *Front. Psychol.* **2020**, *11*, 518304.
4. Theresa, V.L.; Andrea, C.; Scott, M.P.; Gregg, D.S.; Megan, B. Mindfulness based art therapy study protocol to determine efficacy in reducing college stress and anxiety. *BMC Psychol.* **2021**, *9*, 134.
5. Tal, S.; Hod, O.; Felicity, A.B.; David, G.; Girija, K. Editorial: The State of the Art in Creative Arts Therapies. *Front. Psychol.* **2020**, *11*, 68.
6. Elizabeth, W. Novel Solutions to Student Problems: A Phenomenological Exploration of a Single Session Approach to Art Therapy with Creative Arts University Students. *Front. Psychol.* **2021**, *11*, 600214.
7. Jennifer, L.B.; McFerran, K.S. Musical recovery: The role of group singing in regaining healthy relationships with music to promote mental health recovery. *Nord. J. Music. Ther.* **2018**, *27*, 235–251.
8. Marziali, E.; Munroe-Blum, H.; McCleary, L. The contribution of group cohesion and group alliance to the outcome of group psychotherapy. *Int. J. Group Psychother.* **1997**, *47*, 475–497. [CrossRef]
9. Burlingame, G.M.; McClendon, D.T.; Alonso, J. Cohesion in group therapy. *Psychotherapy* **2011**, *48*, 34–42. [CrossRef]
10. Wang, J. Investigation and Analysis on the Status Quo of Reading Therapy Practice in Chinese University Libraries. *J. Natl. Libr. China* **2021**, *30*, 75–82.
11. Degroot, M.H. Reaching a consensus. *J. Am. Stat. Assoc.* **1974**, *69*, 118–121. [CrossRef]
12. Reynolds, C.W. Flocks, herds and schools: A distributed behavioral model. *ACM SIGGRAPH Comput. Graph.* **1987**, *21*, 25–34. [CrossRef]
13. Vicsek T.; Czirok A.; Jacob E.B. Novel type of phase transaction in a system of self-driven particles. *Phys. Rev. Lett.* **1995**, *75*, 1226–1229. [CrossRef] [PubMed]
14. Xie, S. Collaborative Information Behavior between Subject Libraries and Researchers Based on Embedded Scientific Research Service. *Inf. Stud. Theory Appl.* **2017**, *40*, 88–92.
15. Song, X.; Li, L.; Wei, Y. Research on Data Curation Embedded Librarianship Model in the Research Context in College and University Libraries. *Res. Libr. Sci.* **2020**, *3*, 54–60.
16. Zhang, Y.; Wang, H.; Li, G.; Du, X.; Wang, Q. E-Reserves Service of University Library Embedded in Digital Campus from the Perspective of "Information Collaboration". *J. Acad. Libr.* **2022**, *40*, 27–35.
17. Liu, Y. Data Mining of University Library Management Based on Improved Collaborative Filtering Association Rules Algorithm. *Wirel. Pers. Commun.* **2018**, *102*, 3781–3790. [CrossRef]
18. Jung, Y.; Ju, L.E. A Study on the Development of Creative and Cooperative Learning Spaces for University Libraries in Korea. *J. Korean Libr. Inf. Sci. Soc.* **2020**, *51*, 201–225.
19. Bai, S. Analysis and Reflections on Abnormal Collaborative Information Behavior in Smart Libraries. *Inf. Stud. Theory Appl.* **2022**, *45*, 146–151+145.
20. Lin, P.; Ren, W.; Gao, H. Distributed velocity-constrained consensus of discrete-time multi-agent systems with nonconvex constraints, switching topologies, and delays. *IEEE Trans. Autom. Control* **2017**, *62*, 5788–5794. [CrossRef]
21. Lin, P.; Tian, Y.; Gui, G.; Yang, C. Cooperative control for multiple train systems: Self-adjusting zones, collision avoidance and constraints. *Automatica* **2022**, *144*, 110470. [CrossRef]
22. Libraries of Emotions. "Libraries of Emotions" Project Website. 2022. Available online: http://librariesofemotions.eu/ (accessed on 6 September 2022).
23. Wang, M. Experiment and Trend of "Interactive Reading Therapy": A Case of the Reading Promotion Work of Shandong University of Technology Library. *Libr. Work. Coll. Univ.* **2017**, *37*, 23–26.
24. Lin, P.; Xu, J.; Ren, W.; Yang, C.; Gui, W. Angle-based analysis approach for distributed constrained optimization. *IEEE Trans. Autom. Control* **2021**, *66*, 5569–5576. [CrossRef]

MDPI AG
Grosspeteranlage 5
4052 Basel
Switzerland
Tel.: +41 61 683 77 34

Mathematics Editorial Office
E-mail: mathematics@mdpi.com
www.mdpi.com/journal/mathematics

www.ingramcontent.com/pod-product-compliance
Lightning Source LLC
Chambersburg PA
CBHW061843210926
51850CB00006B/956